HACKERS
Updated
TOEFL
READING

학습을 위한
추가 혜택

단어암기 MP3

iBT 리딩
실전모의고사

이용방법 해커스인강(HackersIngang.com) 접속 ▶
상단 메뉴 [토플 → MP3/자료 → 무료 MP3/자료] 클릭 ▶ 본 교재 선택하여 이용하기

MP3/자료 바로 가기 ▶

토플 보카 외우기

이용방법 고우해커스(goHackers.com) 접속 ▶
상단 메뉴 [TOEFL → 토플보카외우기] 클릭하여 이용하기

토플 스피킹/라이팅 첨삭 게시판

이용방법 고우해커스(goHackers.com) 접속 ▶
상단 메뉴 [TOEFL → 스피킹게시판/라이팅게시판] 클릭하여 이용하기

토플 공부전략 강의

이용방법 고우해커스(goHackers.com) 접속 ▶
상단 메뉴 [TOEFL → 토플공부전략] 클릭하여 이용하기

토플 자료 및 유학 정보

이용방법 고우해커스(goHackers.com)에 접속하여 다양한 토플 자료 및 유학 정보 이용하기

고우해커스 바로 가기 ▶

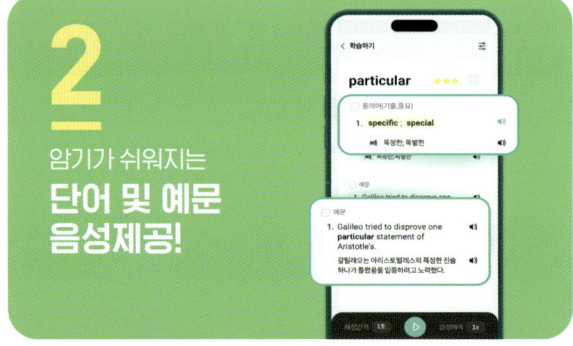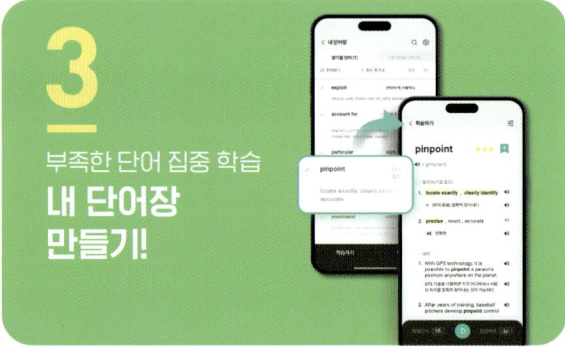

2026년 1월 21일 시행

Updated TOEFL

심층 분석, 이렇게 바뀐다

시대의 변화에 따라 영어 사용 환경이 달라진 것을 반영하여, 2026년 1월 21일 TOEFL 시험이 대대적으로 바뀐다.

『Hackers Updated TOEFL』은 수험자들이 **Updated TOEFL** 시험에도 철저히 대비할 수 있도록, 시험 변경사항과 새로운 문제 유형을 철저히 분석하여 가장 효과적인 핵심 전략과 출제 경향을 완벽 반영한 실전문제를 수록하고 있다.

Updated TOEFL, 얼마나 알고 계신가요?

	YES	NO
Q1. 시험 소요시간이 줄어들었다.	☐	☐
Q2. 리딩/리스닝 영역에서는 전반부 채점 결과에 따라 후반부 구성과 난이도가 달라진다.	☐	☐
Q3. 스피킹 영역이 시험의 마지막 순서다.	☐	☐

*정답은 모두 YES! 자세한 시험 변경사항은 이어지는 페이지에서 확인할 수 있습니다.

Updated TOEFL, 이렇게 바뀐다!

영역	문제 유형	문항 수 Module1	문항 수 Module2 Lower	문항 수 Module2 Upper	예상 시간	점수
Reading 총 35문항 *더미 문제가 출제될 경우, 최대 48문항	TASK 1 Complete the Words 단어의 철자 완성하기	10문항	10문항	10문항	18~27분	1~6점
	TASK 2 Read in Daily Life 일상 지문 읽고 문제 풀기	5문항	5문항	0문항		
	TASK 3 Read an Academic Passage 학술 지문 읽고 문제 풀기	5문항	0문항	5문항		
Listening 총 35문항 *더미 문제가 출제될 경우, 최대 45문항	TASK 1 Listen and Choose a Response 문장 듣고 이어질 응답 고르기	8문항	7문항	3문항	18~27분	1~6점
	TASK 2 Listen to a Conversation 대화 듣고 문제 풀기	4문항	4문항	4문항		
	TASK 3 Listen to an Announcement 공지 듣고 문제 풀기	4문항	4문항	0문항		
	TASK 4 Listen to an Academic Talk 강의 듣고 문제 풀기	4문항	0문항	8문항		
Writing 총 12문항	TASK 1 Build a Sentence 단어 배열하여 문장 완성하기	10문항			23분	1~6점
	TASK 2 Write an Email 이메일 쓰기	1문항				
	TASK 3 Write for an Academic Discussion 학술 토론 의견 쓰기	1문항				
Speaking 총 11문항	TASK 1 Listen and Repeat 문장 듣고 따라 말하기	7문항			8분	1~6점
	TASK 2 Take an Interview 인터뷰 질문에 답변하기	4문항				
				Total	1시간 30분 내외	1~6점

시험 응시 72시간 이내 성적 발표

일상 지문이 추가되고, 단계별 적응형 구조가 도입된다.
- 단어 완성하기 유형과 일상 지문 읽기 유형이 추가되고, 학술 지문의 길이 감소
- Module 1의 결과에 따라 Module 2의 난이도와 구성이 달라지는 단계별 적응형 구조(multistage adaptive testing) 도입
- Module 1에 채점되지 않는 더미 문제 출제 가능 (Reading/Listening 영역 중 한 영역에서 출제)

 일상 대화와 교내 공지가 추가되고, 단계별 적응형 구조가 도입된다.
- 짧은 일상 대화와 교내 공지 유형이 추가되고, 강의 지문의 길이 감소
- Module 1의 결과에 따라 Module 2의 난이도와 구성이 달라지는 단계별 적응형 구조(multistage adaptive testing) 도입
- Module 1에 채점되지 않는 더미 문제 출제 가능 (Reading/Listening 영역 중 한 영역에서 출제)

 문장 완성 유형과 이메일 쓰기 유형이 추가된다.
- 문장 완성 유형과 이메일 쓰기 유형 추가
- 기존의 토론 글쓰기 유형은 그대로 유지
- 시험의 마지막 영역에서 세 번째 영역으로 순서 변경

 문제 유형이 모두 바뀌고, 준비 시간이 없어진다.
- 따라 말하기 유형과 인터뷰 유형 추가
- 모든 유형에서 별도의 답변 준비 시간 없이 바로 답변 시작
- 시험의 세 번째 영역에서 마지막 영역으로 순서 변경

 시험 소요 시간과 성적 발표 기간이 줄고, 점수 체계가 바뀐다.
- 시험 전체 소요 시간과 성적 발표 기간 감소
- 성적 체계가 0~120점 체계에서 1~6점 체계로 변경되고, 전체 점수 계산 방식이 영역별 합계에서 평균으로 변경

Updated TOEFL, 이렇게 대비하라!

■ READING

TASK 1	**Complete the Words** 단어의 철자 완성하기 (1지문 10문항)	
	• 학술 지문에서 앞부분 절반의 철자만 제시되는 단어 10개의 뒷부분을 채워 완성하는 유형이다.	
	• 다양한 학술 분야 주제의 지문이 70~100단어 분량으로 출제된다.	
TASK 2	**Read in Daily Life** 일상 지문 읽고 문제 풀기 (1지문 2~3문항)	
	• 이메일, 문자메시지, 광고, 공지, 기사, SNS 포스팅, 양식 등 다양한 형태의 지문이 출제된다.	
	• 지문 길이는 15~100단어 분량으로 짧은 편이며, 일상적인 주제와 소재를 다룬다.	
TASK 3	**Read an Academic Passage** 학술 지문 읽고 문제 풀기 (1지문 5문항)	
	• 기존의 리딩 유형과 가장 유사하지만, 지문의 길이가 175~200단어로 감소했다.	
	• 전공 심화 수준의 까다로운 내용은 출제되지 않으며, 문화적 편향 없는 보편적인 주제와 소재가 출제된다.	

영역 심층 분석

1. 학술 지문의 비중이 줄고, 기본적인 어휘력과 일상생활에서 접하는 다양한 글을 읽고 이해하는 능력이 중요해진다.
2. 단계별 적응형 구조(multistage adaptive testing)가 도입된다.
   - 두 단계(Module)로 구성되며, Module 1의 결과에 따라 Module 2의 난이도와 구성이 조정된다.
   - Module 2에서 낮은 난이도의 구성이 나오면 리딩 영역 만점(6점)을 받는 것은 불가능하다.
3. 문항 당 풀이 시간은 줄어든다.
   - 전체 문항 수는 20문항에서 35~48문항으로 증가하고, 소요 시간은 약 35분에서 18~27분으로 감소했다.

핵심 대비 전략

TASK 1 풀이 시간을 단축하기 위해 어휘력을 키우고, 단어의 앞부분 철자만 보고 뒤에 이어질 철자를 채우는 연습을 한다.
- 평소에 영어로 된 글을 자주 읽으면서 다양한 단어에 익숙해진다. 특히, 단어의 정확한 철자까지 알아 둔다.
- 앞부분의 철자만 주어지고 뒷부분은 빈칸으로 주어지는 TASK 1 문제 형태에 익숙해지도록 많은 문제를 풀어 본다.

TASK 2 정답의 근거를 빠르게 찾을 수 있도록, 다양한 일상 지문의 형태와 흐름을 익힌다.
- 이메일, 메시지 대화문, 공지, 각종 양식 등, 다양한 일상 지문의 형태와 일반적인 흐름을 익힌다.

TASK 3 다양한 배경지식을 쌓고, 빠르고 정확한 독해를 통해 정답의 근거를 찾는 연습을 한다.
- 지문의 길이가 줄어도, TASK 3의 학술 지문은 여전히 난이도가 높기 때문에 빠르고 정확한 독해가 관건이다.
- 다양한 배경지식을 쌓으면 친숙하지 않은 주제의 지문을 보더라도 쉽고 빠르게 지문의 내용을 이해할 수 있다.

LISTENING

TASK 1	**Listen and Choose a Response** 문장 듣고 이어질 응답 고르기 · 7~8단어로 이루어진 한 문장을 듣고 이어질 응답을 고르는 유형이다. · 일상적인 대화 상황이 출제되며, 종종 구어체도 나온다. · 문항 당 풀이 시간은 최대 20초이다.
TASK 2	**Listen to a Conversation** 대화 듣고 문제 풀기 (1지문 2문항) · 식사, 쇼핑, 약속 등 일상적인 주제에 관한 두 사람 사이의 대화가 출제된다. · 대화 길이는 약 23초, 문항 당 풀이 시간은 최대 20초이다.
TASK 3	**Listen to an Announcement** 공지 듣고 문제 풀기 (1지문 2문항) · 대학 캠퍼스 내에서 행사, 강의, 시설 등에 대해 안내하는 공지가 출제된다. · 공지 길이는 약 21초, 문항 당 풀이 시간은 최대 20초이다.
TASK 4	**Listen to an Academic Talk** 강의 듣고 문제 풀기 (1지문 4문항) · 기존의 리스닝 강의 유형과 유사하지만, 지문의 길이가 약 1분 20초로 감소했다. · 전공 심화 수준의 까다로운 내용은 출제되지 않으며, 문화적 편향 없는 보편적인 주제와 소재가 출제된다. · 문항 당 풀이 시간은 최대 30초이다.

영역 심층 분석

1. 학술적인 내용뿐 아니라, 일상적인 주제에 대한 짧은 대화나 공지를 듣고 화자의 의도를 이해하는 능력도 평가한다.
2. 북미, 영국, 호주, 뉴질랜드 발음이 골고루 출제된다.
3. 단계별 적응형 구조(multistage adaptive testing)가 도입된다.
   · 두 단계(Module)로 구성되며, Module 1의 결과에 따라 Module 2의 난이도와 구성이 조정된다.
   · Module 2에서 낮은 난이도의 구성이 나오면 리스닝 영역 만점(6점)을 받는 것은 불가능하다.

핵심 대비 전략

TASK 1 질문을 확실하게 듣는 연습을 하고, 자주 출제되는 오답 패턴에 대비한다.
· 짧고 빠르게 지나가는 질문 문장을 놓치지 않고 들을 수 있도록 집중력을 강화한다.
· 자주 출제되는 오답 패턴을 확실히 익히고, 자주 틀리는 문제에 대해 자신이 오답을 선택한 이유를 꼼꼼하게 분석한다.

TASK 2&3 정확한 근거를 갖고 정답을 고를 수 있도록, 지문의 흐름과 내용을 정확히 파악하여 듣는 연습을 한다.
· 대화와 공지의 앞부분을 놓치지 않고 듣는 연습을 통해 주제를 확실히 파악할 수 있도록 한다.
· 일상 대화에서 자주 출제되는 구어체 표현에 익숙해진다.
· 공지의 빈출 주제와 일반적인 흐름, 자주 나오는 표현을 익힌다.

TASK 4 다양한 배경지식을 쌓고, 강의의 핵심 내용을 정리하며 듣는 연습을 한다.
· 지문의 길이가 줄어도, TASK 4의 강의는 여전히 난이도가 높기 때문에 핵심 내용을 놓치지 않고 정확히 듣는 것이 중요하다.
· 다양한 배경지식을 쌓으면 친숙하지 않은 주제의 강의를 듣더라도 내용을 정확히 파악할 수 있다.
· 평소에 문제를 풀 때 집중해서 들으며 주요 내용을 노트테이킹하는 연습을 한다.

Updated TOEFL, 이렇게 대비하라!

■ WRITING

TASK 1	**Build a Sentence** 단어 배열하여 문장 완성하기 • 완전한 형태로 주어지는 한 문장을 보고, 보기 단어를 배열하여 이어질 응답 문장을 완성하는 유형이다. • 문법적으로 정확하면서도 문맥에 맞는 자연스러운 응답이 될 수 있는 문장을 완성해야 한다. • 10문항이 출제되고, TASK 전체 제한 시간은 약 5분 50초이다.
TASK 2	**Write an Email** 이메일 쓰기 • 학교나 일상에서 일어날 법한 상황과 이메일을 쓰는 목적이 주어지고, 그에 맞춰 이메일을 작성하는 유형이다. • 일반적인 이메일의 구조에 맞게 작성해야 하며, 초대, 추천, 문제점 전달, 해결책 제안 등의 다양한 의사소통 목적에 맞는 형식과 표현을 적절히 활용해야 한다. • 7분 동안 최대한 길게 작성하도록 요구되는데, 110~130 단어 분량이 적절하다.
TASK 3	**Write for an Academic Discussion** 학술 토론 의견 쓰기 • 기존 토플에서 그대로 유지되는 유일한 유형이다. • 교수가 토론 주제를 간단히 설명하며 던진 질문과, 다른 학생 두 명의 의견을 읽고, 자신의 의견을 작성하는 유형이다. • 10분 동안 최소 100단어 이상 작성해야 한다.

영역 심층 분석

1. **기본적인 문법 규칙에 따라 문장을 쓰는 능력을 평가한다.**
   • 전달하고자 하는 의미를 제대로 전달하기 위해 지켜야 할 문법 규칙들을 잘 알고 있는지를 평가한다.
2. **온라인 의사소통 형식에 적절한 글을 쓰는 역량이 중요하다.**
   • 글을 쓰는 목적, 상대방과의 관계 등에 따라 적절한 문장 구조와 표현을 구사할 수 있어야 한다.

핵심 대비 전략

TASK 1 기본적인 영어 어순과 문법 규칙을 지키며 문장을 쓰는 연습을 한다.
• 수 일치, 시제 일치, 대명사와 접속사의 쓰임 등 기본적인 문법 규칙을 익혀 둔다.

TASK 2 이메일의 기본 구조를 익히고, 일상적인 의사소통 목적에 따라 자주 쓰는 표현을 익힌다.
• 인사말, 목적, 세부사항, 맺음말로 이어지는 이메일의 기본 구조를 지켜 답안을 작성하는 연습을 한다.
• 문의, 부탁, 항의, 감사 등 다양한 의사소통 목적 별로 자주 쓰이는 표현을 익혀 둔다.
• 평소에 많은 문제를 풀어 보며, 1~2분 동안 아웃라인을 잡고, 4~5분 동안 실제 답안을 쓰는 연습을 한다.

TASK 3 평소에 다양한 주제에 대해 브레인스토밍해 보고, 논리적인 답안을 쓰는 연습을 한다.
• 자신의 주장에 대해 논리적으로 타당한 이유와 근거를 생각해내는 연습을 한다.
• 다양한 주제에 대해 나올 수 있는 질문들과 답안에 활용할 수 있는 아이디어를 정리해 둔다.
• 평소에 2~3분 동안 답변 내용을 구상하고, 7분 동안 답안을 작성하는 연습을 한다.

SPEAKING

TASK 1	**Listen and Repeat** 문장 듣고 따라 말하기
	• 음성으로만 들려주는 문장 7개를 한 개씩 듣고 그대로 따라 말하는 유형이다.
	• 일상 및 학교에서 접할 수 있는 시설, 행사, 절차 등에 대해 사람들에게 안내하는 상황이 제시되고, 배경이 되는 장소를 묘사한 그림이 제시된다.
	• 각 문장은 한 번씩만 들려주고, 3초의 간격 후에 8~12초의 답변 시간이 주어진다.

TASK 2	**Take an Interview** 인터뷰 질문에 답변하기
	• 특정 주제에 대한 인터뷰 질문 4개에 답변하는 유형이다.
	• 교육, 사회, 과학기술, 여가 등 다양한 주제로 인터뷰가 진행된다.
	• 인터뷰 질문은 음성으로만 들려주고, 준비 시간 없이 바로 답변해야 한다.
	• 한 질문에 대한 답변 시간은 45초가 주어진다.

영역 심층 분석

1. 실생활에서의 의사소통 방식을 반영하여, 즉각적으로 적절한 말을 하는 능력을 평가한다.
   - 상대방의 말을 정확히 듣고 기억하여 그대로 전달할 수 있어야 한다.
   - 상대방의 질문에 대해 즉각적으로 자신의 의견을 타당한 이유나 근거와 함께 말할 수 있어야 한다.
2. 북미, 영국, 호주, 뉴질랜드 발음이 골고루 출제된다.

핵심 대비 전략

TASK 1 문장을 들으면서 정확히 기억하고 그대로 따라 말하는 연습을 한다.
- 쉐도잉 연습을 통해 들리는 문장을 그대로 따라 말할 수 있도록 한다.
- 다양한 안내 상황 별로 자주 출제되는 표현을 익힌다.

TASK 2 질문을 듣는 동시에 답변 내용을 생각하고 바로 말할 수 있도록 충분히 연습한다.
- 기본적인 답변 구조를 익히고 그에 맞춰 말하는 연습을 충분히 해 둔다.
- 다양한 인터뷰 주제에 대해 나올 수 있는 질문들과 답변에 활용할 수 있는 아이디어를 정리해 둔다.

해커스 토플이 제공하는
토플 정복을 위한
특별한 혜택!

01
토플 적중 예상특강
(HackersIngang.com)

해커스어학원 선생님들의 이번 달 토플 적중 예상특강 제공

02
온라인 실전모의고사
(HackersIngang.com)

출제 경향을 완벽 반영한 온라인 모의고사로 실전 완벽 대비

03
단어암기 MP3
(HackersIngang.com)

단어암기 MP3로 언제, 어디서든 효과적인 단어 학습 가능

04
토플 스피킹/라이팅 첨삭 게시판
(goHackers.com)

무제한 1:1 첨삭을 통한 확실한 실력 향상

05
토플 쉐도잉 & 말하기 연습 프로그램
(goHackers.com)

쉐도잉 & 말하기 반복 훈련으로 빠른 실력 향상

06
토플 자료 및 유학 정보
(goHackers.com)

성공적인 토플 학습방법부터 유학 정보와 다양한 무료 학습자료까지 풍부한 정보 제공

HACKERS
Updated
TOEFL
READING

PREFACE

『Hackers Updated TOEFL Reading』을 내면서

해커스 토플은 단순한 시험 대비를 넘어, 여러분의 실질적인 영어 실력 향상에 도움이 되고자 하는 작은 진심으로 출발했습니다. 해커스 토플 전 시리즈가 오랜 세월 **베스트셀러를 넘어 스테디셀러로 자리**할 수 있었던 이유는, 늘 **처음과 같은 마음**으로 더 좋은 책을 만들기 위해 고민하고, 최신 경향을 반영하기 위해 끊임없이 노력하기 때문입니다.

이번 『Hackers Updated TOEFL』 시리즈 또한 해커스의 전문성과 축적된 노하우를 바탕으로, 변화된 시험의 모든 유형을 면밀히 분석하고 정교한 문제 해결 전략을 담아 **실전 대비의 완결판**으로 완성하였습니다.

Updated TOEFL 경향을 반영한 방대한 양의 실전 문제를 수록하였으며, 실전과 동일한 난이도와 구성의 실전모의고사를 온라인으로 제공하여 보다 철저히 실전에 대비할 수 있도록 하였습니다. 이 교재의 학습 과정을 충실히 따라간다면 누구나 실전에 철저히 대비할 수 있으며, 궁극적으로 **고득점 달성**으로 이어질 것이라 확신합니다.

『Hackers Updated TOEFL Reading』이 여러분의 토플 목표 점수 달성에 확실한 해결책이 될 뿐 아니라, 실질적인 영어 실력의 향상과 함께 더 큰 꿈을 향해 나아가는 길에서 **든든한 동반자**가 되기를 소망합니다.

David Cho
& 해커스어학연구소

Hackers Updated TOEFL READING

CONTENTS

『해커스 토플 리딩』이 특별한 이유!	6
TOEFL iBT 소개	10
TOEFL iBT READING 소개	12
TOEFL iBT READING 화면 구성	14
성향별 맞춤 공부 방법	16
해커스 학습플랜	18
DIAGNOSTIC TEST	21

TASK 1 Complete the Words

Introduction … 30

Section I. Blank Types
1. Intuitive Blanks … 34
2. Contextual Blanks … 44

Section II. Passage Topics
1. Humanities … 56
2. Arts … 60
3. Social Science … 64
4. Physical Science … 68
5. Life Science … 72

TASK 2 Read in Daily Life

Introduction … 78

Section I. Question Types
1. Main Topic/Purpose Questions … 82
2. Detail Questions … 92
3. Fact/Negative Fact Questions … 102
4. Vocabulary Questions … 112
5. Inference Questions … 122
6. Intention Questions … 132

Section II. Passage Types
1. Email … 144
2. Text-Message Chain … 152
3. Notice … 160
4. Advertisement … 168
5. Social Media Post … 176
6. News Article … 184
7. Form … 192

TASK 3 Read an Academic Passage

Introduction 202

Section I. Question Types

1. Main Topic Questions 206
2. Detail Questions 218
3. Fact/Negative Fact Questions 230
4. Vocabulary Questions 242
5. Rhetorical Purpose Questions 254
6. Inference Questions 266
7. Insertion Questions 278

Section II. Passage Topics

1. Humanities 292
2. Arts 304
3. Social Science 316
4. Physical Science 328
5. Life Science 340

ACTUAL TEST 1 356
ACTUAL TEST 2 366
TASK별 실전 필수 어휘 [부록] 379
정답·해석·정답단서 [책 속의 책] 401

실전모의고사(온라인) 2회분
해커스인강(HackersIngang.com) 접속 → [MP3/자료] 클릭 → [무료 MP3/자료] 클릭하여 이용

『해커스 토플 리딩』이 특별한 이유!

 ## Updated TOEFL 출제 경향 완벽 반영!

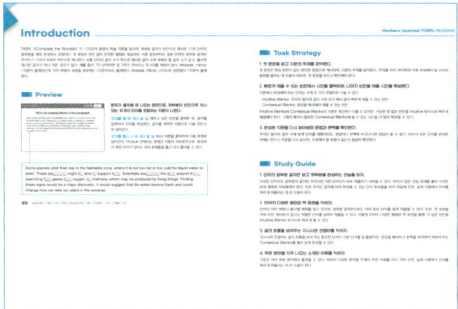

Task Introduction
Updated TOEFL Reading의 각 Task 별 특징, 시험 진행 방식을 확인하고, 실전에서 고득점을 달성하기 위한 전략과 학습 방법을 확인할 수 있다.

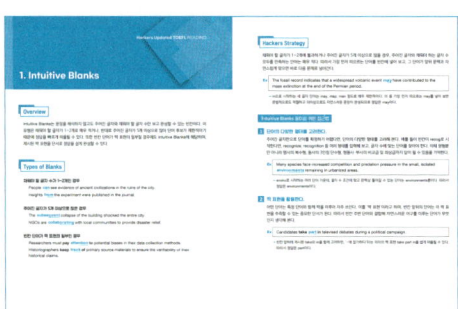

Hackers Strategy
모든 문제 유형에 대해 문제 풀이에 실질적인 도움이 되는 핵심 전략과 자주 나오는 정답 및 오답 패턴을 학습할 수 있다.

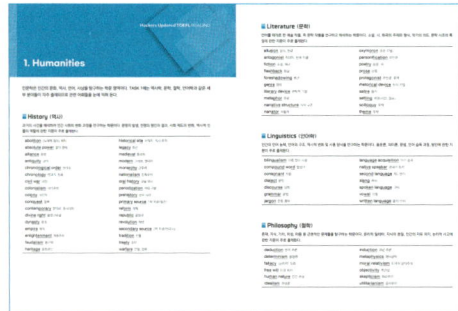

Background Knowledge & Expressions
지문 유형별로 꼭 알아야 할 배경지식과 빈출 표현을 효과적으로 습득할 수 있다.

02 풍부한 문제 풀이로 실전에 철저하게 대비!

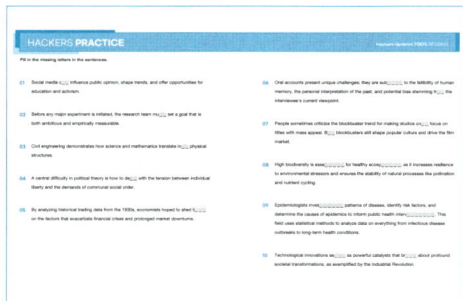

Hackers Practice
유형별 전략을 문제에 적용하는 연습을 통해 실전 토플에 필요한 탄탄한 실력을 다질 수 있다.

Hackers Test
출제 경향을 완벽 반영한 실전 문제들을 집중적으로 풀어봄으로써 실전 감각을 키울 수 있다.

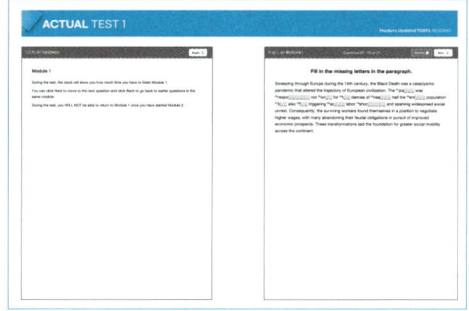

Actual Test
실제 시험의 구성과 난이도를 그대로 반영한 ACTUAL TEST 2회분을 풀어보며 자신의 실력을 최종 점검할 수 있다.

『해커스 토플 리딩』이 특별한 이유!

03 체계적이고 탄탄한 단계별 학습 구성!

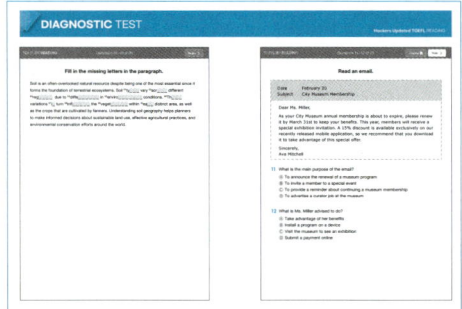

Diagnostic Test

Updated TOEFL Reading 시험의 전반적인 유형 및 난이도 등을 이해하고, 현재 자신의 실력을 진단하여 더욱 효과적인 학습을 계획할 수 있다.

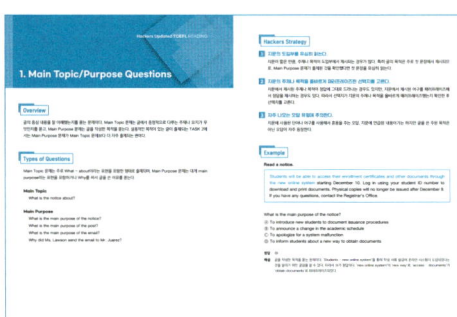

문제 유형별 학습

각 Task의 문제 유형을 하나씩 학습하며 각 유형별로 최적화된 전략을 확실히 자신의 것으로 만들 수 있다.

지문 주제별 학습

각 Task의 빈출 지문 주제를 확인하고 꼭 알아야 할 표현 및 배경지식을 학습할 수 있다.

Hackers Updated TOEFL READING

04 다양한 부가학습자료로 확실한 복습!

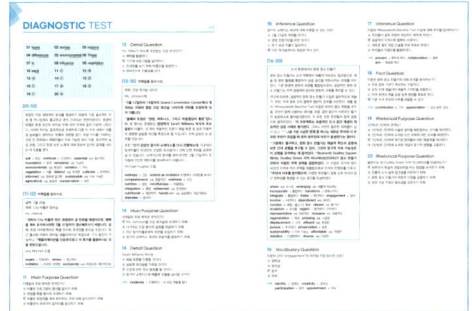

정답·해석·정답단서 [책속의 책]

교재에 수록된 모든 지문과 문제의 정확한 해석, 정답의 단서를 제공한다. 이를 통해 학습자가 지문을 보다 쉽게 이해하고 정답과 오답의 근거를 스스로 파악할 수 있다.

TASK별 실전 필수 어휘 [부록]

각 Task의 핵심 어휘를 정리한 부록과 온라인으로 제공하는 단어암기 MP3로, 이동할 때나 자투리 시간에 효율적으로 단어를 암기할 수 있다.

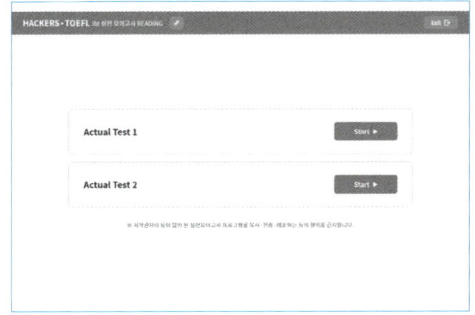

온라인 실전모의고사 [온라인]

온라인 실전모의고사 2회분을 풀어보며 실전에서 흔들림 없이 실력을 발휘할 수 있다.

TOEFL iBT 소개

■ TOEFL iBT란?

TOEFL(Test of English as a Foreign Language) iBT(Internet-based test)는 미국의 비영리기관인 ETS(Educational Testing Service)에서 주관하는 국제 공인 영어 시험으로, 영어가 모국어가 아닌 수험자의 영어 실력을 읽기·듣기·쓰기·말하기 네 영역으로 나누어 평가한다. 2026년 1월 21일부터 바뀌는 Updated TOEFL 시험은 Reading, Listening, Writing, Speaking 영역의 순서로 진행된다. Reading과 Listening 영역은 각 응시자의 Module 1 채점 결과에 따라 Module 2의 난이도와 구성이 달라지는 단계별 적응형 구조(multistage adaptive testing)로 진행된다.

■ TOEFL iBT 시험 구성

영역	TASK		문항 수	시험 시간	점수
Reading	TASK 1	Complete the Words	35~48문항 · Module 1: 20~33문항 · Module 2: 15문항	약 18~27분	1~6점
	TASK 2	Read in Daily Life (1지문 2~3문항)			
	TASK 3	Read an Academic Passage (1지문 5문항)			
Listening	TASK 1	Listen and Choose a Response	35~45문항 · Module 1: 20~30문항 · Module 2: 15문항	약 18~27분	1~6점
	TASK 2	Listen to a Conversation (1지문 2문항)			
	TASK 3	Listen to an Announcement (1지문 2문항)			
	TASK 4	Listen to an Academic Talk (1지문 4문항)			
Writing	TASK 1	Build a Sentence	12문항	약 23분	1~6점
	TASK 2	Write an Email			
	TASK 3	Write for an Academic Discussion			
Speaking	TASK 1	Listen and Repeat (1세트 7문항)	11문항	약 8분	1~6점
	TASK 2	Take an Interview (1세트 4문항)			
				약 2시간	1~6점

· Reading 또는 Listening 중 한 영역의 Module 1에서 더미 문제가 출제된다.
· Reading과 Listening 영역의 Module 1에서는 모든 TASK가 출제되지만, Module 2에서는 난이도에 따라 일부 TASK만 출제된다.

■ TOEFL iBT 점수 체계

2026년 1월 21일 시행되는 Updated TOEFL은 세계적으로 널리 쓰이는 외국어 능력 공통 기준인 CEFR(Common European Framework of Reference for Languages) 6단계와 직관적으로 연계되는 1~6점 구간 점수제(banded scoring scale)를 도입한다. 각 영역 점수와 총점은 0.5점 단위로 올라가는 1~6점 점수대로 표시되고, 총점은 4개 영역 점수의 평균값을 가장 가까운 0.5 단위로 반올림하여 산출한다. (예: 4개 영역 점수 평균이 5.25이면, 총점은 5.5로 표기)

* Updated TOEFL 시행 2년 동안은 기존의 0~120점 점수대도 함께 표기된다.

TOEFL 점수와 CEFR Level 환산표

TOEFL 점수	1.0	1.5	2.0	2.5	3.0	3.5	4.0	4.5	5.0	5.5	6.0
CEFR Level	A1		A2		B1		B2		C1		C2

■ TOEFL iBT 접수 및 성적 확인

실시일	· ETS Test Center 시험: 일주일에 약 2~3일 실시 · 홈에디션 시험: 일주일에 약 4~5일 실시
시험 장소	· ETS Test Center에서 치르거나, 집에서 홈에디션 시험으로 응시 가능
접수 방법	· ETS 토플 웹사이트 또는 전화상으로 접수
시험 당일 준비물	· 공인된 신분증 원본 반드시 지참 (자세한 신분증 규정은 ETS 토플 웹사이트에서 확인 가능) · 홈에디션 시험에 응시할 경우, 사전에 ETS 토플 웹사이트에서 필요한 프로그램 설치 및 준비물 확인하여 지참
성적 및 리포팅	· 시험 응시 후 바로 Reading/Listening 영역 비공식 점수 확인 가능 · 시험 응시일로부터 72시간 후에 온라인으로 성적 확인 가능 · 시험 접수 시, 자동으로 성적 리포팅 받을 기관 선택 가능 · MyBest Scores 제도 시행 (최근 2년간의 시험 성적 중 영역별 최고 점수 합산하여 유효 성적으로 인정)

TOEFL iBT READING 소개

TOEFL iBT READING 영역은 영어를 사용하는 국가의 대학 또는 일상 생활에서 접할 수 있는 다양한 글을 읽고 이해하는 능력을 평가한다. 문제에 답하기 위해 해당 지문에 관한 특별한 지식이 필요하지는 않으며 문제를 푸는 데 필요한 모든 정보는 지문에서 찾을 수 있다.

■ TOEFL iBT READING 구성

TOEFL iBT READING 영역은 두 개의 Module로 구성되며, Module 1의 결과에 따라 Module 2의 구성과 난이도가 달라지는 단계별 적응형 구조(multistage adaptive testing)로 진행된다. Module 1에서는 세 가지 TASK가 모두 출제되지만, Module 2에서는 난이도에 따라 출제되는 TASK가 달라진다. 또한, Module 1에서는 더미 문제가 출제될 수 있다.

Module 1	
TASK 1 Complete the Words	10~20문항 (1~2지문)
TASK 2 Read in Daily Life	5~8문항 (2~3지문)
TASK 3 Read an Academic Passage	5~10문항 (1~2지문)
	총 20~33문항

Module 1의 결과에 따라 Module 2의 구성과 난이도가 달라진다.

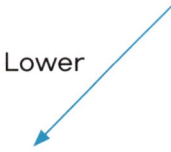 Lower  Upper

Module 2: Lower	
TASK 1 Complete the Words	10문항 (1지문)
TASK 2 Read in Daily Life	5문항 (2지문)
TASK 3 Read an Academic Passage	0문항
	총 15문항

Module 2: Upper	
TASK 1 Complete the Words	10문항 (1지문)
TASK 2 Read in Daily Life	0문항
TASK 3 Read an Academic Passage	5문항 (1지문)
	총 15문항

Hackers Updated TOEFL READING

■ TOEFL iBT READING TASK 별 특징

TASK 1 Complete the Words (1지문 10문항)
학술 지문에서 앞부분 절반의 철자만 제시된 단어 10개의 뒷부분 빈칸을 채워 단어를 완성하는 유형이다. 지문의 길이는 70~100단어 정도이며, 첫 문장은 빈칸이 없이 완전한 문장으로 제시된다. 빈칸을 마우스로 클릭한 뒤 철자를 입력하면 다음 빈칸으로 넘어가며, 문제 내에서의 이동이 자유롭다.

TASK 2 Read in Daily Life (1지문 2~3문항)
이메일, 문자 메시지, 광고 등 일상 생활에서 흔히 접할 수 있는 지문을 읽고 지문 내용과 관련된 문제의 답을 고르는 유형이다. 지문의 길이는 15~150단어 정도이며, 지문의 길이에 따라 한 지문에서 2문항 또는 3문항이 출제된다.

TASK 3 Read an Academic Passage (1지문 5문항)
학술 주제 지문을 읽고 지문 내용과 관련된 문제의 답을 고르는 유형이다. 인문학, 예술, 사회과학, 물리과학, 자연과학 등 다양한 학문 분야의 주제를 다루며, 영어권 고등학교 또는 대학교 교과서에 등장하는 수준으로 출제된다. 지문의 길이는 175~200단어 정도이며, 한 지문에 5문항이 출제된다.

TOEFL iBT READING 화면 구성

1. Reading Direction 화면

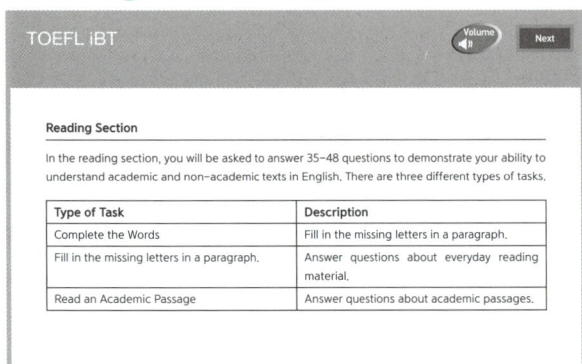

리딩 시험에 대한 전반적인 설명이 주어지는 화면이다. 총 35-48문항이 출제되고, 크게 3가지 TASK로 구성된다는 설명이 나온다.

2. Module 시작 화면

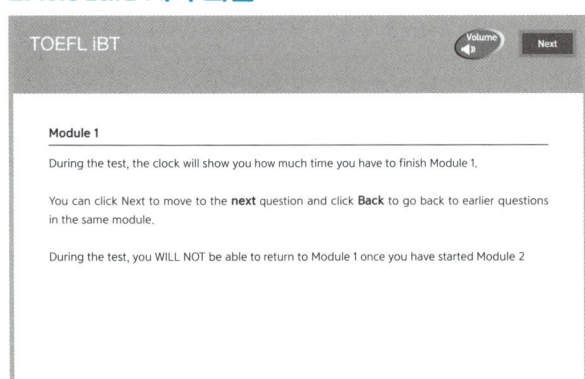

Module 진행 방식에 대한 설명이 주어지는 화면이다. 화면에서 Module 제한 시간이 표시되며, 같은 Module 안에서는 Next 버튼과 Back 버튼을 사용하여 문제 간 이동이 가능하다는 설명이 나온다.

3. TASK 1 지문과 문제 화면

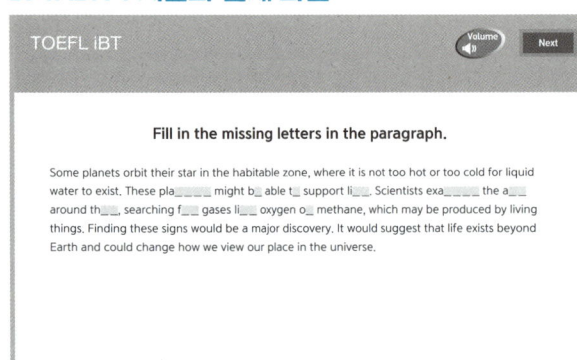

뒷부분 절반이 빈칸으로 제시되는 단어 10개가 포함된 지문이 제시된다. 채우고 싶은 빈칸을 클릭한 후, 철자를 입력하면 다음 빈칸으로 자동으로 넘어간다. Next 버튼을 클릭하여 다음 문제로 넘어갈 수 있다.

4. TASK 2~3 지문과 문제 화면

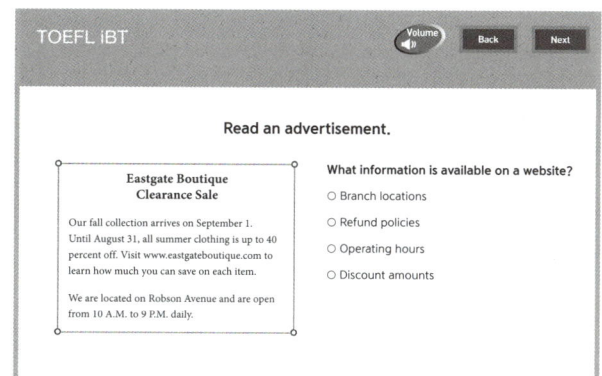

화면 왼쪽에 지문이 제시되고, 오른쪽에 문제가 한 개씩 제시된다. 보기 앞에 있는 칸을 클릭하여 답을 표시한다. Next 버튼을 클릭하여 다음 문제로 넘어가거나, Back 버튼을 클릭하여 이전 문제로 돌아갈 수 있다.

5. Module 종료 화면

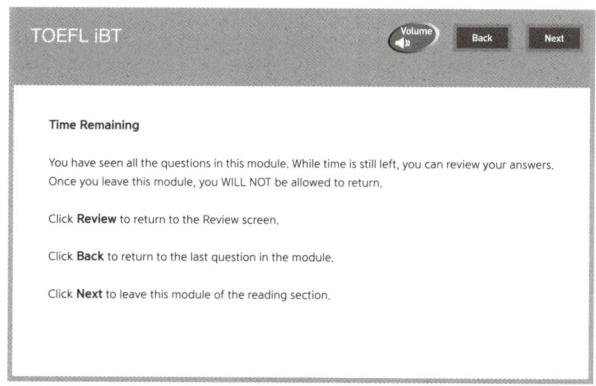

Module을 종료하면 나오는 화면이다. Back 버튼을 누르면 자신의 정답을 다시 점검할 수 있다. Next 버튼을 클릭하면 다음 Module이나 다음 영역으로 넘어간다.

성향별 맞춤 공부 방법

* 해커스 학습플랜은 p.18~19에 수록되어 있습니다.

 개별학습 혼자서 공부할 때 가장 집중이 잘 된다!

1. 나만의 학습플랜을 세운다!
 p.21의 DIAGNOSTIC TEST를 통하여 자신의 현재 실력을 확인하고, 해커스 학습플랜을 참고하여 본인에게 맞는 학습 계획을 세운다.

2. 매일매일 정해진 학습 분량을 공부한다!
 학습플랜에 따라 매일의 정해진 분량을 반드시 마치도록 하고, 만약 그러지 못했을 경우에는 계속 진도를 나가되 일주일이 지나기 전에 해당 주의 학습 분량을 모두 끝낸다.

3. 문제를 미리 보지 않고 풀며 오답 분석을 한다.
 문제를 풀 때에는 항상 문제를 미리 보지 않고 푸는 것을 원칙으로 하며, 문제를 다 푼 후에는 스크립트와 본인이 들은 내용을 비교하며 확인하고 정답과 오답을 분석한다.
  * 고우해커스(goHackers.com)의 [해커스 Books > 토플 리스닝 Q&A]에서 궁금한 사항을 질문할 수 있습니다.

 스터디학습 다른 사람과 함께 공부할 때 더 열심히 한다!

1. 개별 예습으로 스터디를 준비한다!
 본문 내용을 예습하고 문제를 미리 풀어 본다.

2. 토론 학습으로 완벽하게 이해한다!
 미리 예습해 온 문제를 함께 토론하면서 답을 수렴해 나간다. 서로의 답을 공개하고 왜 그것을 답으로 선택하게 되었는지 토론한 후, 책의 정답을 확인한다.

3. 개별 복습으로 마무리한다!
 스터디가 끝난 후, 해커스인강(HackersIngang.com)에서 무료로 다운로드 받을 수 있는 단어암기 MP3를 활용하여 단어를 학습하고, 스터디했던 내용을 개별 복습한다.

Hackers Updated TOEFL READING

▶ 인강학습 원하는 시간, 원하는 장소에서 강의를 듣고 싶다!

1. 나만의 학습플랜을 세운다!
해커스인강(HackersIngang.com)에서 『샘플강의보기』를 통해 강의 구성을 미리 파악하고, 『스터디플랜』에 따라 자신의 학습 계획을 세운다.

2. 이해될 때까지 반복해서 듣는다!
학습플랜에 따라 오늘 공부해야 할 강의를 집중해서 듣고, 잘 이해가 되지 않는 부분은 완전히 이해될 때까지 반복해서 시청한다.

3. 『선생님께 질문하기』를 적극 활용한다!
강의를 듣다가 모르는 부분이 있거나 질문할 것이 생기면 『선생님께 질문하기』를 이용하여 확실히 이해하도록 한다.

학원학습 선생님의 강의를 직접 들을 때 가장 효과적이다!

1. 100% 출석을 목표로 한다!
자신의 스케줄에 맞는 수업을 등록하고, 개강일부터 종강일까지 100% 출석을 목표로 빠짐없이 수업에 참여한다.

2. 예습과 복습을 철저히 한다!
수업 전에 미리 그날 배울 내용을 훑어본다. 수업이 끝난 후에는 자신이 취약한 부분을 확인하고 복습한다.

3. 적극적으로 질문한다!
수업 시간에 잘 이해되지 않은 부분은 쉬는 시간이나 해커스어학원(Hackers.ac)의 『반별게시판』을 이용해 선생님께 질문함으로써 확실히 짚고 넘어간다.

해커스 학습플랜

p.21의 DIAGNOSTIC TEST를 풀어 본 후, 그 결과에 따라 본인의 실력에 적합한 학습플랜에 맞게 공부한다.

- 맞은 개수 0~5개 : 40일 동안 학습한다. (20일 완성 학습플랜의 1일 분량을 이틀에 나누어 학습)
- 맞은 개수 6~11개 : 30일 완성 학습플랜에 따라 학습한다.
- 맞은 개수 12~17개 : 20일 완성 학습플랜에 따라 학습한다.
- 맞은 개수 18~20개 : 10일 동안 학습한다. (20일 완성 학습플랜의 2일 분량을 하루에 학습)

■ 20일 완성 학습플랜

DAY 1	DAY 2	DAY 3	DAY 4	DAY 5
□ DIAGNOSTIC TEST □ 어휘 DAY 01	□ T1 Sec.I-1 □ T1 Sec.I-2 □ 어휘 DAY 02	□ T1 Sec.II-1 □ T1 Sec.II-2 □ 어휘 DAY 03	□ T1 Sec.II-3 □ T1 Sec.II-4 □ 어휘 DAY 04	□ T1 Sec.II-5 □ T2 Sec.I-1 □ 어휘 DAY 05

DAY 6	DAY 7	DAY 8	DAY 9	DAY 10
□ T2 Sec.I-2 □ T2 Sec.I-3 □ 어휘 DAY 06	□ T2 Sec.I-4 □ T2 Sec.I-5 □ 어휘 DAY 07	□ T2 Sec.I-6 □ T2 Sec.II-1 □ 어휘 DAY 08	□ T2 Sec.II-2 □ T2 Sec.II-3 □ 어휘 DAY 09	□ T2 Sec.II-4 □ T2 Sec.II-5 □ 어휘 DAY 10

DAY 11	DAY 12	DAY 13	DAY 14	DAY 15
□ T2 Sec.II-6 □ T2 Sec.II-7 □ 어휘 DAY 11	□ T3 Sec.I-1 □ T3 Sec.I-2 □ 어휘 DAY 12	□ T3 Sec.I-3 □ T3 Sec.I-4 □ 어휘 DAY 13	□ T3 Sec.I-5 □ T3 Sec.I-6 □ 어휘 DAY 14	□ T3 Sec.I-7 □ T3 Sec.II-1 □ 어휘 DAY 15

DAY 16	DAY 17	DAY 18	DAY 19	DAY 20
□ T3 Sec.II-2 □ T3 Sec.II-3 □ 어휘 DAY 16	□ T3 Sec.II-4 □ T3 Sec.II-5 □ 어휘 DAY 17	□ Actual Test 1 □ 어휘 DAY 18	□ Actual Test 2 □ 어휘 DAY 19	□ 온라인 모의고사 1 □ 온라인 모의고사 2 □ 어휘 DAY 20

T: TASK   Sec: Section   어휘: TASK별 실전 필수 어휘[부록]
매일 학습이 완료된 부분에 체크(v) 표시한다.

Hackers Updated TOEFL READING

■ 30일 완성 학습플랜

DAY 1	DAY 2	DAY 3	DAY 4	DAY 5
☐ DIAGNOSTIC TEST ☐ 어휘 DAY 01	☐ T1 Sec.I-1 ☐ T1 Sec.I-2 ☐ 어휘 DAY 02	☐ T1 Sec.II-1 ☐ T1 Sec.II-2 ☐ 어휘 DAY 03	☐ T1 Sec.II-3 ☐ T1 Sec.II-4 ☐ 어휘 DAY 04	☐ T1 Sec.II-5 ☐ T2 Sec.I-1 ☐ 어휘 DAY 05

DAY 6	DAY 7	DAY 8	DAY 9	DAY 10
☐ T2 Sec.I-2 ☐ T2 Sec.I-3 ☐ 어휘 DAY 06	☐ T2 Sec.I-4 ☐ T2 Sec.I-5 ☐ 어휘 DAY 07	☐ T2 Sec.I-6 ☐ T2 Sec.II-1 ☐ 어휘 DAY 08	☐ T2 Sec.II-2 ☐ 어휘 DAY 09	☐ T2 Sec.II-3 ☐ 어휘 DAY 10

DAY 11	DAY 12	DAY 13	DAY 14	DAY 15
☐ T2 Sec.II-4 ☐ 어휘 DAY 11	☐ T2 Sec.II-5 ☐ 어휘 DAY 12	☐ T2 Sec.II-6 ☐ 어휘 DAY 13	☐ T2 Sec.II-7 ☐ 어휘 DAY 14	☐ T3 Sec.I-1 ☐ 어휘 DAY 15

DAY 16	DAY 17	DAY 18	DAY 19	DAY 20
☐ T3 Sec.I-2 ☐ 어휘 DAY 16	☐ T3 Sec.I-3 ☐ 어휘 DAY 17	☐ T3 Sec.I-4 ☐ 어휘 DAY 18	☐ T3 Sec.I-5 ☐ 어휘 DAY 19	☐ T3 Sec.I-6 ☐ 어휘 DAY 20

DAY 21	DAY 22	DAY 23	DAY 24	DAY 25
☐ T3 Sec.I-7 ☐ 어휘 DAY 01-02 복습	☐ T3 Sec.II-1 ☐ 어휘 DAY 03-04 복습	☐ T3 Sec.II-2 ☐ 어휘 DAY 05-06 복습	☐ T3 Sec.II-3 ☐ 어휘 DAY 07-08 복습	☐ T3 Sec.II-4 ☐ 어휘 DAY 09-10 복습

DAY 26	DAY 27	DAY 28	DAY 29	DAY 30
☐ T3 Sec.II-5 ☐ 어휘 DAY 11-12 복습	☐ Actual Test 1 ☐ 어휘 DAY 13-14 복습	☐ Actual Test 2 ☐ 어휘 DAY 15-16 복습	☐ 온라인 모의고사 1 ☐ 어휘 DAY 17-18 복습	☐ 온라인 모의고사 2 ☐ 어휘 DAY 19-20 복습

T: TASK   Sec: Section   어휘: TASK별 실전 필수 어휘[부록]
매일 학습이 완료된 부분에 체크(v) 표시한다.

무료 토플자료·유학정보 제공
goHackers.com

DIAGNOSTIC TEST

Hackers
Updated TOEFL
READING

실제 TOEFL 리딩 시험과 유사한 DIAGNOSTIC TEST를 통해 본인의 실력을 평가해 봅니다.
그리고 본인에게 맞는 학습방법(p.18)을 확인한 후, 본 교재를 효율적으로 학습합니다.

DIAGNOSTIC TEST

TOEFL iBT READING Questions 01~10 of 20 Begin >

Fill in the missing letters in the paragraph.

Soil is an often-overlooked natural resource despite being one of the most essential since it forms the foundation of terrestrial ecosystems. Soil [01]ty____ vary [02]acr____ different [03]reg____ due to [04]diffe_____ in [05]enviro_____ conditions. [06]Th____ variations [07]i_ turn [08]infl_____ the [09]veget_____ within [10]ea__ distinct area, as well as the crops that are cultivated by farmers. Understanding soil geography helps planners to make informed decisions about sustainable land use, effective agricultural practices, and environmental conservation efforts around the world.

Read an email.

Date: February 20
Subject: City Museum Membership

Dear Ms. Miller,

As your City Museum annual membership is about to expire, please renew it by March 31 to keep your benefits. This year, members will receive a special exhibition invitation. A 15% discount is available exclusively on our recently released mobile application, so we recommend that you download it to take advantage of this special offer.

Sincerely,
Ava Mitchell

11 What is the main purpose of the email?

Ⓐ To announce the renewal of a museum program
Ⓑ To invite a member to a special event
Ⓒ To provide a reminder about continuing a museum membership
Ⓓ To advertise a curator job at the museum

12 What is Ms. Miller advised to do?

Ⓐ Take advantage of her benefits
Ⓑ Install a program on a device
Ⓒ Visit the museum to see an exhibition
Ⓓ Submit payment online

Read an email.

Subject: Wellness Workshop Series

Dear Ms. Johnson,

We're pleased to extend an invitation to our Comprehensive Wellness Workshop Series, taking place from March 12 to 14 at the Grand Convention Center.

This year's focus is "Nutrition, Fitness, and Mindfulness Integration." The event will feature a keynote address from esteemed nutritionist Dr. Sarah Williams, alongside four dynamic expert panel discussions and interactive, hands-on sessions. A full schedule will be shared shortly.

We're also bringing back the popular Participant Showcase, where attendees can share their own healthy recipes or personal fitness routines. If you'd like to be a part of the showcase, please send a brief proposal to the organizing team by February 25.

Warm regards,
Michael Hughes

13 What is the main purpose of the email?

   Ⓐ To invite Ms. Johnson to a wellness workshop
   Ⓑ To provide a schedule of upcoming wellness events
   Ⓒ To collect feedback from past participants
   Ⓓ To announce the winners of the Participant Showcase sessions

14 Dr. Sarah Williams will

   Ⓐ moderate panel discussions
   Ⓑ teach hands-on workshops
   Ⓒ deliver the main presentation on wellness
   Ⓓ judge the Participant Showcase submissions

15 What can be inferred about the Participant Showcase sessions?

   Ⓐ They will be held on February 25.
   Ⓑ They are exclusively for nutrition experts.
   Ⓒ They require payment of an additional fee.
   Ⓓ They have been offered in previous workshops.

Cultural Placemaking in Urban Environments

Cultural placemaking, an emerging approach in urban planning, refers to the practice of incorporating arts and cultural activities to transform public spaces. By integrating cultural expressions into existing environments, successful cultural placemaking can foster community engagement and cultural exchange.

Research indicates that a successful cultural placemaking initiative typically involves collaborative partnerships between artists, residents, and local governments. For example, Milwaukee's Beerline Trail project transformed an abandoned railway corridor into a vibrant public space with sculptures, community tables, lighting, and performance areas—all co-designed with residents. The project is regarded as a representative success story of inclusive urban space regeneration. However, significant challenges remain. One of the most pressing concerns is the displacement of original residents, which often occurs when new investments and more affluent populations enter the area.

Nevertheless, cultural placemaking can pursue a balance between artistic innovation and community preservation. Its long-term sustainability depends on maintaining that balance. In Boston's Dudley Square, the Dudley Street Neighborhood Initiative (DSNI) combined placemaking and affordable housing strategies. By creating inexpensive homes in a formerly neglected area, the initiative stabilized the neighborhood and helped prevent displacement while also creating spaces where diverse populations could develop shared ownership and collective identity.

16 The word "engagement" in the passage is closest in meaning to

  Ⓐ identity
  Ⓑ creativity
  Ⓒ participation
  Ⓓ appointment

17 What does the passage suggest about Milwaukee's Beerline Trail project?

  Ⓐ It prevented residents from intervening in the design process.
  Ⓑ It is an example of successful community collaboration.
  Ⓒ It primarily aimed to construct a new railway corridor.
  Ⓓ It only utilized the work of residents.

18 What does the passage indicate about cultural placemaking?

  Ⓐ It is an initiative primarily directed by government agencies.
  Ⓑ It features artistic contributions solely from local artists.
  Ⓒ It aims to improve the artistic appreciation of the local population.
  Ⓓ It can cause the displacement of the area's original residents.

19 What is the relationship between paragraphs 2 and 3?

  Ⓐ Paragraph 3 provides evidence supporting the idea described in paragraph 2.
  Ⓑ Paragraph 3 extends the discussion of challenges introduced in paragraph 2.
  Ⓒ Paragraph 3 proposes a solution to the problems presented in paragraph 2.
  Ⓓ Paragraph 3 examines the long-term effects of the concept introduced in paragraph 2.

20 Why does the author mention the Dudley Street Neighborhood Initiative?

  Ⓐ To illustrate how the inclusion of original residents can be ensured
  Ⓑ To criticize traditional approaches to urban design
  Ⓒ To demonstrate the financial benefits of cultural placemaking
  Ⓓ To highlight the importance of government funding

Answers p.402

*채점 후, p.18을 보고 본인의 맞은 개수에 해당하는 학습방법을 참고하세요.

무료 토플자료·유학정보 제공
goHackers.com

Hackers Updated TOEFL READING

TASK 1

Complete the Words

Introduction

Section I. Blank Types
1. Intuitive Blanks
2. Contextual Blanks

Section II. Passage Topics
1. Humanities
2. Arts
3. Social Science
4. Physical Science
5. Life Science

Introduction

TASK 1(Complete the Words)은 70~100단어 분량의 학술 지문을 읽으며, 뒷부분 글자가 빈칸으로 제시된 10개 단어의 뒷부분을 채워 완성하는 유형이다. 첫 문장은 빈칸 없이 온전한 형태로 제공되며, 이후 문장부터는 일부 단어의 앞부분 글자만 주어지고 나머지 부분은 빈칸으로 제시된다. 보통 단어의 글자 수가 짝수면 제시된 글자 수와 채워야 할 글자 수가 같고, 홀수면 제시된 글자가 하나 적은 경우가 많다. 예를 들어 7자 단어라면 앞 3자가 주어지고 뒤 4자를 채워야 한다. Module 1에서는 1지문이 출제되는데, 더미 문항이 포함될 경우에는 2지문까지도 출제된다. Module 2에서는 난이도와 상관없이 1지문씩 출제된다.

■ Preview

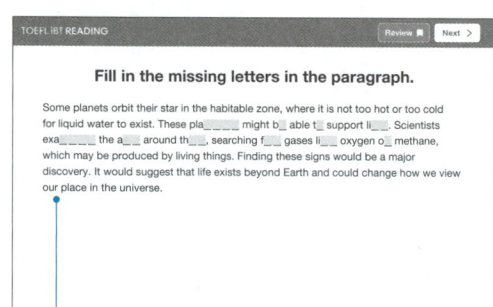

문제가 출제될 때 나오는 화면으로, 뒷부분이 빈칸으로 제시되는 10개의 단어를 포함하는 지문이 나온다.

문제를 풀 때 해야 할 일: 채우고 싶은 빈칸을 클릭한 뒤, 글자를 입력하여 단어를 완성한다. 글자를 채우면 자동으로 다음 빈칸으로 넘어간다.

문제를 풀고 난 후 해야 할 일: Next 버튼을 클릭하여 다음 문제로 넘어간다. Module 안에서는 문제간 이동이 자유로우므로, 완성하지 못한 단어가 있어도 뒤의 문제들을 풀고 다시 돌아올 수 있다.

> Some planets orbit their star in the habitable zone, where it is not too hot or too cold for liquid water to exist. These pla_____ might b_ able t_ support li___. Scientists exa_____ the a__ around th___, searching f___ gases li___ oxygen o_ methane, which may be produced by living things. Finding these signs would be a major discovery. It would suggest that life exists beyond Earth and could change how we view our place in the universe.

정답   planets / be / to / life / examine / air / them / for / like / or

Task Strategy

1. 첫 문장을 읽고 지문의 주제를 파악한다.

첫 문장은 항상 빈칸이 없는 완전한 문장으로 제시되며, 지문의 주제를 알려준다. 주제를 미리 파악하면 이후 완성해야 할 단어의 범위를 좁히는 데 도움이 되므로, 첫 문장을 반드시 확인해야 한다.

2. 빠르게 채울 수 있는 빈칸에서 시간을 절약하여, 나머지 빈칸을 채울 시간을 확보한다.

지문에서 완성해야 하는 단어는 크게 두 가지 유형으로 나눌 수 있다.
· Intuitive Blanks: 주어진 철자와 글자 수만 보고 해석 없이 빠르게 채울 수 있는 빈칸
· Contextual Blanks: 문장을 해석해야 채울 수 있는 빈칸

Intuitive Blanks와 Contextual Blanks의 기준은 개인마다 다를 수 있지만, 가능한 한 많은 빈칸을 Intuitive 방식으로 빠르게 해결해야 한다. 그래야 해석이 필요한 Contextual Blanks에 쓸 수 있는 시간을 더 많이 확보할 수 있다.

3. 완성된 지문을 다시 읽어보며 문법과 문맥을 확인한다.

주어진 철자와 글자 수에 맞게 단어를 채웠더라도, 문법이나 문맥에 어긋난다면 정답이 될 수 없다. 따라서 모든 단어를 완성한 뒤에는 반드시 지문을 다시 읽으며, 수정해야 할 부분이 없는지 꼼꼼히 확인한다.

Study Guide

1. 단어의 앞부분 글자만 보고 뒷부분을 완성하는 연습을 하자.

익숙한 단어라도 앞부분의 글자만 주어지면 어떤 단어인지 바로 떠올리기 어려울 수 있다. 따라서 많은 연습 문제를 풀며 이러한 문제 형태에 익숙해져야 한다. 또한 주어진 글자에 따라 완성될 수 있는 단어 후보들을 미리 학습해 두면, 실제 시험에서 단어를 빠르게 떠올리는 데 큰 도움이 된다.

2. 단어의 다양한 형태와 짝 표현을 익히자.

단어의 어미 변화나 품사별 형태를 알고 있으면, 앞부분 글자만으로도 여러 후보 단어를 쉽게 떠올릴 수 있다. 또한, 짝 표현을 익혀 두면, 해석하지 않고도 적절한 단어를 곧바로 떠올릴 수 있다. 이렇게 단어의 다양한 형태와 짝 표현을 통해, 더 많은 빈칸을 Intuitive Blanks 방식으로 빠르게 풀 수 있다.

3. 글의 흐름을 보여주는 지시사와 연결어를 익히자.

지시사와 연결어는 글의 흐름을 보여 주는 중요한 단서다. 이런 단서를 잘 활용하면, 문장을 해석하고 문맥을 파악하여 채워야 하는 Contextual Blanks를 훨씬 쉽게 완성할 수 있다.

4. 학문 분야별 자주 나오는 소재와 어휘를 익히자.

지문은 여러 학문 분야에서 출제될 수 있다. 따라서 다양한 분야별 주제와 관련 어휘를 미리 익혀 두면, 실제 시험에서 단어를 빠르게 떠올리는 데 큰 도움이 된다.

무료 토플자료·유학정보 제공
goHackers.com

Section I
Blank Types

Section I에서는 TASK 1의 빈칸 유형을 해석하지 않아도 채울 수 있는 Intuitive Blanks와 해석이 필요한 Contextual Blanks로 구분하여 각 유형의 특징과 풀이 전략을 소개하고 있다. 또한 풍부한 연습 문제와 실전 문제를 통해 각 빈칸 유형을 효과적으로 공략할 수 있도록 하였다.

TASK 1의 Blank Types에는 다음의 2가지가 있다.

1. Intuitive Blanks
2. Contextual Blanks

1. Intuitive Blanks

Overview

Intuitive Blanks는 문장을 해석하지 않고도 주어진 글자와 채워야 할 글자 수만 보고 완성할 수 있는 빈칸이다. 이 유형은 채워야 할 글자가 1~2개로 매우 적거나, 반대로 주어진 글자가 5개 이상으로 많아 단어 후보가 제한적이기 때문에 정답을 빠르게 떠올릴 수 있다. 또한 빈칸 단어가 짝 표현의 일부일 경우에도 Intuitive Blanks에 해당하며, 제시된 짝 표현을 단서로 정답을 쉽게 완성할 수 있다.

Types of Blanks

채워야 할 글자 수가 1~2개인 경우

People **can** see evidence of ancient civilizations in the ruins of the city.

Insights **from** the experiment were published in the journal.

주어진 글자가 5개 이상으로 많은 경우

The **subsequent** collapse of the building shocked the entire city.

NGOs are **collaborating** with local communities to provide disaster relief.

빈칸 단어가 짝 표현의 일부인 경우

Researchers must **pay attention to** potential biases in their data collection methods.

Historiographers **keep track of** primary source materials to ensure the verifiability of their historical claims.

Hackers Strategy

채워야 할 글자가 1~2개에 불과하거나 주어진 글자가 5개 이상으로 많을 경우, 주어진 글자와 채워야 하는 글자 수 모두를 만족하는 단어는 매우 적다. 따라서 가장 먼저 떠오르는 단어를 빈칸에 넣어 보고, 그 단어가 앞뒤 문맥과 자연스럽게 맞으면 바로 다음 문제로 넘어간다.

> **Ex** The fossil record indicates that a widespread volcanic event **may** have contributed to the mass extinction at the end of the Permian period.

→ m으로 시작하는 세 글자 단어는 may, map, man 정도로 매우 제한적이다. 이 중 가장 먼저 떠오르는 may를 넣어 보면 문법적으로도 적절하고 의미상으로도 자연스러운 문장이 완성되므로 정답은 may이다.

Intuitive Blanks 풀이를 위한 접근법

1 단어의 다양한 형태를 고려한다.

주어진 글자만으로 단어를 확정하기 어렵다면, 단어의 다양한 형태를 고려해 본다. 예를 들어 빈칸이 recog로 시작한다면, recognize, recognition 등 여러 형태를 입력해 보고, 글자 수에 맞는 단어를 찾아야 한다. 이때 원형뿐만 아니라 명사의 복수형, 동사의 3인칭 단수형, 형용사·부사의 비교급 및 최상급까지 답이 될 수 있음을 기억한다.

> **Ex** Many species face increased competition and predation pressure in the small, isolated **environments** remaining in urbanized areas.

→ enviro로 시작하는 여러 단어 가운데, 글자 수 조건에 맞고 문맥상 들어갈 수 있는 단어는 environments뿐이다. 따라서 정답은 environments이다.

2 짝 표현을 활용한다.

어떤 단어는 특정 단어와 함께 짝을 이루어 자주 쓰인다. 이를 '짝 표현'이라고 하며, 빈칸 앞뒤의 단어는 이 짝 표현을 추측할 수 있는 중요한 단서가 된다. 따라서 빈칸 주변 단어와 결합해 자연스러운 어구를 이루는 단어가 무엇인지 생각해 본다.

> **Ex** Candidates **take part** in televised debates during a political campaign.

→ 빈칸 앞뒤에 제시된 take와 in을 함께 고려하면, '~에 참가하다'라는 의미의 짝 표현 take part in을 쉽게 떠올릴 수 있다. 따라서 정답은 part이다.

Intuitive Blanks 풀이를 돕는 주요 단서

1 채워야 할 글자가 1~2개인 단어

단어가 실제 문제에서 제시되는 형태에 익숙해지면, 실전에서 단어를 쉽게 떠올릴 수 있다.

1글자	a_	an, at, as	o_	of, on, or
	b_	be, by	s_	so
	d_	do	t_	to
	h_	he	u_	up, us
	i_	it, is, in, if	w_	we
	n_	no		
2글자	a_ _	are, and, any, ago	m_ _	may
	b_ _	but	n_ _	not, nor
	c_ _	can	o_ _	one, out, off, our, own
	d_ _	did	p_ _	per
	f_ _	few, for, far	s_ _	she
	h_ _	has, had, how, his, her, him	t_ _	the, too, two
	g_ _	get, got	w_ _	who, why, was
	i_ _	its	y_ _	you, yet
	be_	best, been	ne_	need, near
	bo_	both	on_	only, once, onto, ones
	do_	does, done, down	ov_	over
	ea_	each	so_	some, soon
	fr_ _	from	th_ _	that, this, they, them, than, then, thus
	ha_ _	have	up_ _	upon
	in_ _	into	wh_ _	what, when, whom
	ma_ _	many	wi_ _	will, with
	mo_ _	more, most		
	mu_ _	must, much		

2 품사별 주요 어미

품사별 주요 어미를 미리 익혀 두면, 주어진 철자와 글자 수 조건에 맞는 단어를 떠올리는 데 도움이 된다.

명사 어미	-ion	-ment	-ness	-ity	-ance / -ence
	-ism	-ist	-er / -or	-dom	-hood
형용사 어미	-al	-ic	-ive	-ous	-able / -ible
	-ish	-y	-ate	-ent / -ant	-less
	-ful				
동사 어미	-ate	-fy	-en	-ize	
부사 어미	-ly	-ward	-wise	-fold	

3 짝 표현

함께 쓰이는 짝 표현을 많이 익혀 두면, 빈칸 앞뒤 단어를 단서로 삼아 빈칸을 빠르게 채울 수 있다.

bear in mind 명심하다, 염두에 두다	look forward to ~을 고대하다
break a record 기록을 깨다	look into 조사하다
bring about 야기하다, 초래하다	lose control 통제력을 잃다
call off 취소하다	make a decision 결정을 내리다
chain reaction 연쇄 반응	out of the blue 갑자기, 불쑥
come to an end 끝나다, 종결되다	pay attention to 주의를 기울이다
come to terms with ~을 받아들이다, 타협하다	play a role 역할을 맡다
come true 실현되다	point of view 관점
come up with ~을 생각해 내다	put off 연기하다, 미루다
common interest 공동의 이익	put up with ~을 참다, 견디다
deal with ~을 다루다	raise a question 질문을 제기하다
depend on ~에 의존하다	reach a conclusion 결론에 도달하다
draw a line 선을 긋다, 한계를 정하다	rely on ~에 의존하다
fall into a category 범주에 속하다	result in ~을 초래하다
get along with ~와 잘 지내다	run out of ~을 다 써버리다
get over 극복하다	save time 시간을 절약하다
give a chance 기회를 주다	set a goal 목표를 정하다
give rise to ~을 낳다, 야기하다	shed light on ~을 명확히 설명하다, 밝히다
go the extra mile 특별히 더 노력하다	strike a balance 균형을 맞추다
have a say 발언권/결정권이 있다	suffer from ~을 겪다, 고통받다
in the long run 결국에는, 장기적으로는	take a risk 위험을 무릅쓰다
keep an eye on ~을 계속 지켜보다, 감시하다	take care of ~을 돌보다
keep track of ~을 기록하다, 추적하다	take over ~을 인계받다, 장악하다
last resort 최후의 수단	turn down 거절하다
lead to ~을 초래하다	yield results 결과를 산출하다

HACKERS PRACTICE

Fill in the missing letters in the sentences.

01 Social media c___ influence public opinion, shape trends, and offer opportunities for education and activism.

02 Before any major experiment is initiated, the research team mu___ set a goal that is both ambitious and empirically measurable.

03 Civil engineering demonstrates how science and mathematics translate in___ physical structures.

04 A central difficulty in political theory is how to de___ with the tension between individual liberty and the demands of communal social order.

05 By analyzing historical trading data from the 1930s, economists hoped to shed li___ on the factors that exacerbate financial crises and prolonged market downturns.

06 Oral accounts present unique challenges; they are sub_____ to the fallibility of human memory, the personal interpretation of the past, and potential bias stemming fr___ the interviewee's current viewpoint.

07 People sometimes criticize the blockbuster trend for making studios on___ focus on titles with mass appeal. B___ blockbusters still shape popular culture and drive the film market.

08 High biodiversity is esse_____ for healthy ecosy_____, as it increases resilience to environmental stressors and ensures the stability of natural processes like pollination and nutrient cycling.

09 Epidemiologists inves_____ patterns of disease, identify risk factors, and determine the causes of epidemics to inform public health interv_____. This field uses statistical methods to analyze data on everything from infectious disease outbreaks to long-term health conditions.

10 Technological innovations se____ as powerful catalysts that br____ about profound societal transformations, as exemplified by the Industrial Revolution.

HACKERS PRACTICE

11 The infamous trolley problem is a thought experiment in ethics designed to test and chal_____ moral intuitions. The basic scen_____ involves deciding whe_____ to pull a lever to divert a runaway trolley from a track where it will kill five people to a track where it will kill only one.

12 Harmony involves simultaneously combining the notes to form chords and the relationships between them. Unl____ melody, wh____ is a linear succe_____ of tones, harmony focuses on the vertical aspect of music.

13 Erosion is the geolo_____ process by which soil and rock material are worn aw___ and transported by natural forces, such as wind, water, or ice. Over millennia, moving water and glaciation can exert powerful effects on the landscape, carving valleys and transporting enor_____ sediment loads.

14 Global efforts are now foc_____ on developing strategies to mitigate emissions of greenhouse ga____, as the current trajectory continues to po___ a significant threat to future planetary stability.

15 Effective leade_____ requires the ability to ma___ a decision under conditions of uncertainty, even if it means leaders must occasionally take a ri___ with unproven strategies.

16 Wh__ a company faces a public relations crisis, the communication team must deliver the right message to prevent a loss of investor confi_____. Allowing speculation to circulate can trigger a negative ch____ reaction in the media, rapidly eroding the company's reput_____.

17 While some critics believe the author's inten_____ should guide our unders_____ of a text, others argue th___, once published, liter_____ takes on a life of its own.

18 Bamboo is crucial f___ environmental conser_____; its strong ro____ help prevent soil erosion. It can also absorb pollutants from the soil, making it easier for ot____ plants to grow near bamboo.

19 The concept of the social contract is a founda_____ idea in political philo_____, postulating that individuals volun_____ surrender some of their freedoms and submit to the auth_____ of a ruler or government in exchange for protection of their remaining rights and the maintenance of social order.

20 Opportunity cost is not the monetary price of a good, but rat____ the value of the next best alternative that must be forgone as a res____ of making a deci_____. Every choice, whether by an individual, a firm, or a government, involves a trade-off, and opportunity cost repre_____ the true sacrifice being made.

Answers p.404

HACKERS TEST

Fill in the missing letters in the paragraph.

[01~10]

The hippocampus is a small, curved region deep within the temporal lobe of the brain. It ⁰¹pl____ a ⁰²ro___ in ⁰³t___ creation ⁰⁴o_ new ⁰⁵memo_____ and the ⁰⁶organi_____ of ⁰⁷exper_____. It ⁰⁸bec_____ active ⁰⁹dur____ tasks ¹⁰th__ involve learning information or recalling specific events. Damage to this area can weaken one's ability to remember events after an injury. Treating post-injury patients and others suffering from memory-related disorders, therefore, requires more research into and understanding of the hippocampus.

[11~20]

Black holes are regions in space where gravity is so strong that not even light can escape. Because ¹¹o_ this ¹²charact_____, it ¹³i_ not ¹⁴poss_____ to ¹⁵s___ them ¹⁶wi__ our ¹⁷ey___. Astronomers ¹⁸ins_____ figure ¹⁹o___ their ²⁰loca_____ by observing their effects on nearby stars and gas. The effects that black holes have on their surroundings help astronomers discover new facts about the universe, such as how galaxies are formed. This is what makes the study of black holes an important area of research in astronomy.

[21~30]

One major challenge that rapidly growing cities face is traffic congestion. The [21]incr_____ reliance [22]o__ personal [23]vehi_____ gradually [24]ma____ the [25]str_____ crowded, [26]resu_____ in [27]del____ and [28]acci_____. Simply [29]buil_____ more [30]ro____ may not reduce traffic congestion, as it can cause even more people to choose to drive. A better solution would be to improve public transit systems; they transport a significantly greater number of people using less road space. Efficient transit networks not only reduce congestion but also improve the overall quality of urban life.

[31~40]

Dunes are landforms created by the deposition of sand, typically found in deserts and coastal areas. They [31]fo___ when [32]wi___ energy [33]i_ high [34]eno____ to [35]tran_____ sand [36]part_____, which [37]accum_____ around [38]obst_____. Their [39]sh____ is [40]deter_____ by factors like wind direction, wind speed, and sand availability. Crescent-shaped dunes form when there is a steady wind from one direction and a limited supply of sand. In contrast, star dunes, characterized by multiple arms radiating from a central point, form in locations with multi-directional winds and an abundant supply of sand.

Answers p.405

2. Contextual Blanks

Overview

Contextual Blanks는 문장을 해석해 빈칸에 들어갈 의미를 먼저 파악해야 하는 빈칸이다. 주어진 글자와 글자 수만 으로는 답을 찾기 어렵기 때문에, 문맥을 해석해 의미를 확인한 뒤 그 조건에 맞는 단어를 선택해야 한다.

Types of Blanks

직접적인 단서가 없고 문맥 해석이 필요한 경우

Foreshadowing is used by authors to subtly **prepare** the reader for significant events that will unfold later in the narrative.

빈칸 주변에 지시사·대명사가 있는 경우

Ancient astronomers meticulously mapped the movements of the planets and stars, and **these celestial** observations formed the foundation of early calendar systems.

빈칸 주변에 연결어가 있는 경우

The conventional view posits that the Neolithic shift led to a universal increase in life expectancy due to a more stable food supply. **However**, early agricultural societies experienced a higher incidence of **disease**.

빈칸에 들어갈 수 있는 단어 후보가 두 개 이상인 경우

Median income is a key indicator for evaluating the economic status of the **population** of citizens.

(단어 후보가 population과 popularity)

Hackers Strategy

문장을 해석해 문맥상 빈칸에 필요한 의미를 파악한 뒤, 그 의미에 맞는 단어 중에서 주어진 글자와 빈칸 개수를 만족하는 단어를 선택해 빈칸을 채운다.

> **Ex** Photosynthesis allows plants to produce energy from sunlight, which is essential for their **growth**.

→ '광합성은 식물이 햇빛으로부터 에너지를 생성하게 해 주며, 이는 식물의 ___에 필수적이다'라는 의미이다. 광합성은 식물의 '성장'에 꼭 필요한 과정이므로, 빈칸에는 growth가 들어가야 한다.

Contextual Blanks 풀이를 위한 접근법

1 지시사나 대명사가 가리키는 대상이 무엇인지 확인한다.

this, that, these 같은 지시사나 대명사가 빈칸 앞에 있으면, 앞 문장을 확인해 무엇을 가리키는지 파악함으로써 빈칸에 들어갈 단어를 파악할 수 있다.

> **Ex** The heart pumps blood through the body's circulatory system. **This organ** delivers oxygen and nutrients to every cell.

→ 빈칸 앞의 This가 앞 문장의 The heart를 가리키므로, 빈칸에는 이를 나타내는 단어 organ이 들어가야 한다.

2 연결어를 통해 앞뒤 문장의 관계를 파악한다.

so, however, such as 같은 연결어는 앞뒤 문장의 관계(원인·결과, 대조, 예시 등)를 드러낸다. 따라서 빈칸 주변에 있는 연결어의 의미를 파악하면, 빈칸에 들어갈 단어의 후보를 좁힐 수 있다.

> **Ex** The company failed to invest in new technology, **so profits** dropped significantly.

→ so는 인과를 나타내므로, 빈칸에는 앞의 failed to invest라는 원인으로 인한 결과가 와야 한다. 따라서 빈칸에는 profits가 들어가야 한다.

3 조건을 충족하는 단어가 여럿 있다면, 해석을 통해 맞는 단어를 완성한다.

주어진 글자와 글자 수 조건을 충족하면서 품사까지 같은 단어가 여러 개일 수 있다. 이 경우에는 각 단어를 넣어 문장을 해석해 보고, 문맥에 가장 잘 어울리는 단어를 선택해야 한다.

> **Ex** Areas with dense ground **vegetation** are less likely to experience rapid soil erosion.

→ veget로 시작하는 단어 중 vegetation과 vegetables가 모두 빈칸에 들어갈 수 있다. 그러나 뒤의 soil erosion과 자연스럽게 어울리는 것은 '식물 전반'을 뜻하는 vegetation이다.

> **TIP**
> 정답이 지문의 다른 부분에 그대로 반복되거나, 어미만 바꾸어 다시 등장하는 경우가 있다. 따라서 주어진 글자와 같은 글자로 시작하는 단어가 지문에 있는지 확인하는 것도 도움이 된다.
>
> **Ex** Individuals often **deceive** others to gain a strategic advantage. While a conscious act, **deception** can be a subtle form of manipulation designed to mislead for personal gain.
>
> → 빈칸에 주어진 dec로 시작하는 단어 deception이 두 번째 문장에 있다. deception을 단서로, 같은 어근을 가진 deceive를 빈칸에 넣으면 문맥이 자연스러운 것을 확인할 수 있다.

Contextual Blanks 풀이를 돕는 주요 단서

1 연결어

Contextual Blanks를 풀 때는 문맥을 드러내는 연결어에 주목하는 것이 중요하다. 연결어는 앞뒤 문장의 관계를 보여주므로, 이를 활용하면 빈칸에 들어갈 단어의 후보를 좁힐 수 있다.

대조	while, however, but, on the other hand와 같은 대조 연결어는 앞뒤 문장의 내용이 서로 반대되거나 대비됨을 보여준다. **Ex** Some regions produce abundant crops, **while** others face **famine**. → while 앞에서 produce abundant crops(풍부한 농작물을 생산하다)를 언급했으므로, 빈칸에는 그와 반대되는 의미의 famine(기근)이 들어가야 한다.
예시	such as, for example, for instance와 같은 예시 연결어는 앞의 상위 개념과 구체적인 하위 예시를 연결한다. **Ex** Various social **platforms**, **such as** blogs and forums, can expand audience reach. → such as 뒤에 blogs and forums(블로그와 포럼)라는 예시가 나오므로, 빈칸에는 이를 포함하는 상위 개념인 platforms(플랫폼)가 들어가야 한다.
부연 설명	meaning, which is/are, known as와 같은 부연 설명 연결어는 앞의 내용을 다시 풀어 쓰거나 이전에 언급된 개념을 정의 및 설명한다. **Ex** Many of the foods are **organic**, **meaning** that they are grown without synthetic chemicals. → meaning that 뒤의 설명이 grown without synthetic chemicals(합성 화학물질 없이 재배됨)이므로, 빈칸에는 이를 가리키는 표현인 organic(유기농인)이 들어가야 한다.
인과	so, as a result, therefore, thus, consequently와 같은 인과 연결어는 앞의 원인과 뒤의 결과를 이어준다. **Ex** Deforestation continued across large areas of the region, **so** land **degradation** became severe. → so 뒤에는 앞에서 언급한 Deforestation(삼림 파괴)의 결과가 와야 한다. 따라서 빈칸에는 land degradation(토지 황폐화)과 같이 삼림 파괴가 초래하는 결과가 들어가야 한다.
나열	also, in addition, moreover, furthermore, and와 같은 나열 연결어는 앞 문장의 내용에 대한 추가적인 정보를 제시한다. **Ex** Mechanical engineers design innovative machinery. They **also create** detailed technical specifications. → also 뒤에는 앞에서 언급한 design innovative machinery(혁신적인 기계를 설계한다)와 같은 범주의 활동이 와야 한다. 따라서 빈칸에는 기술 사양서를 작성한다는 의미를 완성하는 create(작성하다)가 들어가야 한다.

2 혼동하기 쉬운 단어의 의미 차이

앞부분 철자, 글자 수, 품사가 모두 같고 의미가 유사한 단어의 경우, 단어의 뉘앙스 차이를 생각하며 문맥을 확인해 알맞은 단어를 선택해야 한다.

collection 수집품, 소장품   VS   **collective** 집단, 공동체
물건을 가리킬 때 사용한다.   사람이 모인 집단을 가리킬 때 사용한다.

We need to find ways to promote the well-being of the (**collection**, **collective**). 우리는 집단의 복지를 증진할 방법을 찾아야 한다.

---

economies 경기, 경제   VS   **economics** 경제학
경제 활동·상황을 가리킬 때 사용한다.   학문 분야를 가리킬 때 사용한다.

Advances in behavioral (**economies**, **economics**) have helped explain why people sometimes make irrational financial decisions. 행동 경제학의 발전은 사람들이 때때로 비이성적인 금융 결정을 내리는 이유를 설명하는 데 도움이 되어 왔다.

---

vegetation 식물, 초목   VS   **vegetables** 채소들
전체 식물의 집합을 가리킬 때 사용한다.   식용 식물을 가리킬 때 사용한다.

The canopy of the rainforest prevents light from reaching the lower layers of (**vegetation**, **vegetables**) on the forest floor. 열대우림의 캐노피(상층부)는 빛이 숲 바닥의 더 낮은 식물층에 도달하지 못하게 한다.

---

governance 지배, 통치 방식   VS   **government** 정부, 정권
방식·제도를 가리킬 때 사용한다.   기관을 가리킬 때 사용한다.

The concept of corporate (**governance**, **government**) focuses on how companies are directed and controlled. 기업 지배 구조(corporate governance)라는 개념은 회사가 어떻게 운영되고 통제되는지에 초점을 맞춘다.

---

narration 해설, 내레이션   VS   **narrative** 이야기, 서술 구조
이야기하는 행위·방식을 가리킬 때 사용한다.   이야기의 내용·구조를 가리킬 때 사용한다.

The novel's (**narration**, **narrative**) is told from the perspective of a child. 그 소설의 이야기는 아이의 시점에서 전개된다.

---

mechanical 기계적인, 기계의   VS   **mechanized** 기계화된
특성을 가리킬 때 사용한다.   변화된 상태를 가리킬 때 사용한다.

Fatigue testing is crucial for predicting the stress limit at which a component is likely to experience (**mechanical**, **mechanized**) failure. 피로 시험은 부품이 기계적 고장을 겪을 가능성이 있는 응력의 한계를 예측하는 데 중요하다.

HACKERS PRACTICE

Fill in the missing letters in the sentences.

01 To pre_____ the concentration of authority and protect liberty, many modern democracies adopt the doctrine of the separation of powers.

02 An important task for any historian is distinguishing between pri_____ sources and secondary sources, as this distinction determines the reliability and directness of evidence.

03 Kant urges us to exa_____ our actions not based on their consequences, but on the universal principle—the Categorical Imperative—that guides them.

04 Following the introduction of the steam engine, textile production became increasingly mecha_____.

05 Deductive reasoning starts from general laws, but inductive reasoning starts with specific observ_____.

06 Situating observ_____ at high altitudes is essential for minimizing atmospheric interference and capturing clear astronomical data. Higher sites ben_____ from thinner air, reduced light pollution, and lower humidity, all of which contribute to superior viewing conditions.

07 Before the advent of widespread digitization, scholars who were not flu_____ in Old Norse struggled to acc_____ the original source material for Viking-age studies, relying solely on translated and often filtered secondary accounts.

08 Human wants and needs are virtually limitless, yet the resources available to satisfy those des_____—time, land, labor, and capital—are fin_____.

09 The arts involve var_____ creative media. For instance, literature, music, and painting use different techniques to exp_____ ideas.

10 Providing con_____ is important for historians. This means that they construct mea_____ by clearly delineating the settings and surrounding events.

HACKERS PRACTICE

11 Newton's First Law of Motion sta____ that an object at rest remains at rest, and an object in motion remains in motion with the same sp____ and in the same dire_____, unless acted upon by an unbalanced external force.

12 Culture is typically div_____ into two main categories: nonmaterial culture, which incl_____ ideas and attitudes, and material culture, which cons_____ of tangible artifacts like tools and architecture.

13 The Doppler effect describes the cha____ in frequency or wavelength of a wave in rela_____ to an observer who is moving relative to the wave source. For example, when a celestial object moves tow____ Earth, its light waves are compressed; when it moves away, the waves are stretched.

14 Modern research relies on dist_____ methods that compl_____ one another. For instance, quantitative research identifies broad statistical patterns but lacks depth, while qualitative research offers rich det_____ but struggles with generalizability.

15 Sustainable design seeks to minimize the negative environmental imp____ of buildings by efficiently using resources, creating hea_____ environments, and reducing energy consumption. This approach considers the building's ent____ lifecycle, from the sourcing of materials to construction, operation, and eventual demolition or reuse.

16 The law of sup____ and dem____ is the bedrock prin_____ of market economics, describing the inter_____ between the availability of a resource and the desire for that resource.

17 Motivation is the process that starts, directs, and sustains someone's beha_____ toward goals. It can be driven by internal satisf_____ or fueled by external incen_____ like rewards or pra____.

18 Language is not a fi____ system but a constantly evolving one. New words eme____, old forms disappear, and meanings shift over time. Linguists ana_____ these changes to understand both cogn_____ processes and social dynamics.

19 Mod____ telescopes, both on Earth and in space, allow scientists to observe dis_____ galaxies, nebulae, and exoplanets orbiting other stars. The discovery of these exoplanets has intensified the search for extraterrestrial life, rai_____ questions about whether Earth is uni____.

20 The concept of the *longue durée* (long term) emphasizes the profound influence of slow-moving, structural fac_____—such as geography, cli_____ patterns, or demographics—that shape civilizations over generations. This period of sub____, gra_____ transformation is considered by many scholars to be more fundamental to human history than the spectacular, instantaneous events that capture headlines.

Answers p.406

HACKERS TEST

Fill in the missing letters in the paragraph.

[01~10]

The Streisand Effect is a phenomenon that reveals the paradox of censorship. It [01]desc_____ situations [02]wh____ people [03]att_____ to [04]cen____ or [05]rem____ certain [06]infor_____, instead [07]cau_____ it [08]t_ spread [09]ev__ more [10]wid____ than it would have. It is named after Barbra Streisand, who took legal action to have aerial photographs of her Malibu home taken down from a website. Her action ironically drew huge public attention to the photos, and the photos were viewed more than 400,000 times. This illustrates the psychological concept of reactance, where the suppression of freedom impels individuals to restore that freedom.

[11~20]

Human rights are the basic freedoms that everyone is entitled to, regardless of nationality, gender, or background. They [11]fos____ equality [12]am____ various [13]gro____ and [14]pro____ essential [15]prote_____ from [16]ab____ and [17]discrim_____ against [18]vulne_____ people. [19]Ev____ government [20]str_____ to ensure that these rights are upheld. International treaties and local laws are in place to protect them. Citizens can also advocate for these rights when they are violated. By understanding them, people can recognize injustices and work toward a fairer society, which benefits everyone.

[21~30]

Urbanization draws people from rural areas into expanding cities across the globe. This ²¹mas_____ shift, ²²dri____ by more ²³car____ opportunities ²⁴a___ a ²⁵bet____ quality ²⁶o_ life, ²⁷cre_____ vibrant ²⁸cen_____ of ²⁹innov_____. Cities ³⁰n___ serve as the primary engines of economic activity, fostering technological advancement and social progress. However, this rapid growth also presents challenges, including sustainability issues and social inequality, which require thoughtful planning and solutions.

[31~40]

The application of pesticides in modern agriculture has significantly boosted crop yields and improved food security. However, ³¹th___ widespread ³²prac_____ has ³³rai____ considerable ³⁴con_____ regarding ³⁵to____ residues ³⁶o_ fresh ³⁷pro_____. These ³⁸subst_____ can ³⁹ha___ long-term ⁴⁰chr_____ effects. Consequently, regulatory bodies worldwide are balancing the need for effective pest control with the imperative of protecting public health. They have implemented stringent monitoring, testing harvested goods to detect and measure any residual harmful chemicals. They also enforce strict residue limits, which define the maximum allowable levels for pesticides in support of sustainable agricultural practices.

Answers p.408

무료 토플자료·유학정보 제공
goHackers.com

Section II
Passage Topics

Section II에서는 TASK 1에 자주 출제되는 주제들을 중심으로 각 세부 단원을 구성하였다. TASK 1에는 다양한 학문 분야들이 출제되는데, 크게 인문학, 예술, 사회과학, 물리과학, 생명과학으로 나누어 볼 수 있다.

TASK 1의 Passage Topics에는 다음의 5가지가 있다.

1. Humanities
2. Arts
3. Social Science
4. Physical Science
5. Life Science

1. Humanities

인문학은 인간의 문화, 역사, 언어, 사상을 탐구하는 학문 영역이다. TASK 1에는 역사학, 문학, 철학, 언어학과 같은 세부 분야들이 자주 출제되므로 관련 어휘들을 눈에 익혀 둔다.

■ History (역사)

과거의 사건을 해석하여 인간 사회의 변화 과정을 연구하는 학문이다. 문명의 발생, 전쟁의 원인과 결과, 사회 제도의 변화, 역사적 인물의 역할에 관한 지문이 주로 출제된다.

abolition (노예제 등의) 폐지	historical site 사적지, 역사 유적
absolute power 절대 권력	legacy 유산
alliance 동맹	medieval 중세의
antiquity 고대	modern 근대의, 현대의
chronological order 연대순	monarchy 군주제
chronology 연대기, 연표	nationalism 민족주의
civil war 내전	oral history 구술 역사
colonialism 식민주의	periodization 시대 구분
colony 식민지	prehistory 선사 시대
conquest 정복	primary source 1차 자료(원전)
contemporary 현대의, 동시대의	reform 개혁
divine right 왕권신수설	republic 공화국
dynasty 왕조	revolution 혁명
empire 제국	secondary source 2차 자료(연구서)
enlightenment 계몽주의	tradition 전통
feudalism 봉건제	treaty 조약
heritage 문화유산	warfare 전쟁, 전투

■ Literature (문학)

언어를 매개로 한 예술 작품, 즉 문학 작품을 연구하고 해석하는 학문이다. 소설, 시, 희곡의 주제와 형식, 작가의 의도, 문학 사조의 특징에 관한 지문이 주로 출제된다.

allusion 암시, 언급	oxymoron 모순 어법
antagonist 적대자, 반동 인물	personification 의인화
fiction 소설, 허구	poetry 운문, 시
flashback 회상	prose 산문
foreshadowing 복선	protagonist 주인공, 주역
genre 장르	rhetorical device 수사 기법
literary device 문학적 기법	satire 풍자
metaphor 은유	setting 배경(시간, 장소)
narrative structure 서사 구조	soliloquy 독백
narrator 서술자	theme 주제

■ Linguistics (언어학)

인간의 언어 능력, 언어의 구조, 역사적 변화 및 사용 양식을 연구하는 학문이다. 음운론, 의미론, 문법, 언어 습득 과정, 방언에 관한 지문이 주로 출제된다.

bilingualism 이중 언어 사용	language acquisition 언어 습득
compound word 합성어	native speaker 모국어 화자
consonant 자음	second language 제2 언어
dialect 방언	slang 속어
discourse 담화	spoken language 구어
grammar 문법	vowel 모음
jargon 전문 용어	written language 문자 언어

■ Philosophy (철학)

존재, 지식, 가치, 이성, 마음 등 근본적인 문제들을 탐구하는 학문이다. 윤리적 딜레마, 지식의 본질, 인간의 자유 의지, 논리적 사고에 관한 지문이 주로 출제된다.

deduction 연역 추론	induction 귀납 추론
determinism 결정론	metaphysics 형이상학
fallacy (논리적) 오류	moral relativism 도덕적 상대주의
free will 자유 의지	objectivity 객관성
human nature 인간 본성	skepticism 회의주의
idealism 관념론	utilitarianism 공리주의

HACKERS TEST

Fill in the missing letters in the paragraph.

[01~10]

The Renaissance was a period in European history from the fourteenth to the seventeenth centuries. This ⁰¹e___ is ⁰²charac_____ by ⁰³ren_____ interest ⁰⁴i_ classical ⁰⁵cul_____. It ⁰⁶sta_____ a ⁰⁷flour_____ in ⁰⁸a___ and ⁰⁹sci_____. Artists ¹⁰li___ Leonardo da Vinci and Michelangelo created masterpieces that celebrated human potential, while the rise in rationality challenged traditional beliefs. The Renaissance led to major shifts in thought and society, paving the way for the Age of Exploration and the Scientific Revolution. The intense focus on humanism and empirical inquiry marked the Renaissance as the dawn of modernity.

[11~20]

One of the world's earliest writing systems was developed by the ancient Egyptians around 3000 BC using pictures called hieroglyphs. Hieroglyph ¹¹sym_____ can ¹²repr_____ both ¹³conc_____ and ¹⁴sou_____. The ¹⁵im____ that ¹⁶rese_____ an ¹⁷e___ has the ¹⁸mea_____ of ¹⁹lis____ and ²⁰corre_____ to the consonants *j, d,* and *n*. These multiple layers of significance made it extremely difficult for modern linguists to understand hieroglyphs. The script remained a mystery until 1822, when researchers finally deciphered it by studying an artifact called the Rosetta Stone, which included the exact same text in both hieroglyphs and Greek letters.

[21~30]

Language acquisition involves the process through which humans develop the ability to understand and produce language. Children [21]aro____ the [22]wo____ follow [23]sim_____ developmental [24]sta____, regardless [25]o_ what [26]spec_____ language [27]th___ are [28]lear_____. They [29]fi____ babble, [30]prog_____ to single words, and eventually construct complex sentences. Research suggests that humans possess an innate capacity for language, a trait that distinguishes us from other species. This innate capacity suggests a biological predisposition—often referred to as "universal grammar"—that guides the acquisition process.

[31~40]

Folklore is a collection of traditional stories, customs, and beliefs shared by groups of people. It [31]i_ passed [32]fr___ one [33]gener_____ to [34]ano_____ through [35]spo____ words. [36]Th____ stories [37]te____ moral [38]les_____, help [39]exp_____ natural [40]phen_____, and give people a sense of cultural identity. Many folktales use imaginary characters, magical objects, or talking animals to make the stories entertaining. This tradition contributes to bringing communities together and keeping shared values alive.

Answers p.409

2. Arts

예술은 인간의 감정과 사상을 시각, 청각, 공연 매체로 창조적으로 표현하는 활동을 다루는 영역이다. TASK 1에는 미술, 영화, 음악, 건축과 같은 주제가 자주 출제되므로 이와 관련된 어휘들을 눈에 익혀 둔다.

■ Fine Arts (미술)

인간의 미적 감각을 형상화시키는 창조 활동과 그 결과물인 작품을 다루는 분야이다. 회화, 조각, 디자인의 특징, 시대별 양식의 변화, 예술가의 창작 의도에 관한 지문이 주로 출제된다.

abstract art 추상 미술	perspective 원근법
aesthetics 미학	pigment 안료
avant-garde 아방가르드, 전위 예술	portrait 초상화
canvas 캔버스	saturation 채도
curator 큐레이터	sculpture 조각
gallery 화랑, 미술관	still life 정물화
landscape 풍경화	vanishing point 소실점
mural 벽화	watercolor 수채화

■ Film (영화)

움직이는 이미지와 소리를 통해 이야기를 전달하는 예술이다. 촬영 기법, 편집 기술, 영화 사조, 감독의 연출 스타일, 영화의 사회적 영향에 관한 지문이 주로 출제된다.

blockbuster 블록버스터	documentary 다큐멘터리
box office 흥행 수입, 매표소	film festival 영화제
camera angle 카메라 앵글	soundtrack 사운드트랙
cinematography 촬영술, 영화 촬영	special effects 특수 효과
director 감독	visual effects 시각 효과

■ Music (음악)

소리를 소재로 하여 박자·선율·화성·음색 등을 일정한 법칙과 형식으로 조합하여 사상과 감정을 표현하는 예술이다. 음계와 화성에 관한 지문이 주로 출제된다.

chamber music 실내악	melody 멜로디, 선율
chord 화음	orchestra 오케스트라, 관현악단
composer 작곡가	performer 연주자
concerto 협주곡	rhythm 리듬, 율동
conductor 지휘자	symphony 교향곡
harmony 화성, 화음	time signature 박자표

■ Architecture (건축)

인간의 생활을 보조하기 위해 여러 가지 용도의 구축물을 세우는 공간 예술이다. 건축의 역사, 시대별 다양한 건축 양식에 관한 지문이 주로 출제된다.

arch 아치	insulation 단열
balcony 발코니	monument 기념비, 기념물
ceiling 천장	skyscraper 고층 건물, 마천루
column 기둥	terrace 테라스
concrete 콘크리트	urban planning 도시 계획
demolition 철거	ventilation 환기

HACKERS TEST

Fill in the missing letters in the paragraph.

[01~10]

Jazz is a highly influential music style recognized for its profound history and distinctive character. This [01]uni____ genre [02]w___ born [03]fr___ the [04]crea_____ fusion [05]o__ diverse [06]tradi_____—a [07]powe_____ expression [08]b__ artists [09]ba____ on [10]th____ cultural backgrounds. The work of these musicians resulted in music that was both deeply rooted in various ethnic heritages and entirely fresh, quickly attracting a global following. Widely performed and enjoyed today, this expressive genre has subsequently shaped and influenced countless other musical styles, including R&B, funk, and progressive rock.

[11~20]

Cubism, as exemplified by the influential works of Pablo Picasso and Georges Braque, is often hailed as one of the most significant modern art movements. Its [11]subj_____ were [12]bro____ and [13]rearr_____ in an [14]abst_____ form [15]th___ simultaneously [16]empha_____ multiple [17]perspe_____. Critics [18]ar____ that [19]th____ techniques [20]capt_____ the atmosphere of the early 20th century, including industrialization and the tensions that led up to World War I. Thus, Cubism is considered an ideal representation of the period.

[21~30]

Theater, in its diverse forms, has been a central part of human culture across the globe. Unlike [21]fi___, which [22]c___ be [23]reco_____ and [24]proj_____, theater [25]rel____ on [26]t___ immediate, [27]liv____ connection [28]bet_____ the [29]act_____ and [30]audi_____ in a shared space. This interaction allows for an energy and spontaneity that cannot be replicated, making each performance a singular, unrepeatable event. Theater's reliance on physical presence also means that lighting, set design, and sound are experienced organically, directly influencing the audience's emotional and intellectual engagement.

[31~40]

Brutalism emerged in the mid-twentieth century, prioritizing practical design over decorative elements. Brutalist [31]struc_____ are [32]so_____ and [33]impo_____ because [34]th___ use [35]bo___ shapes [36]a____ raw, [37]exp_____ materials [38]su___ as [39]conc_____. Brutalist [40]archit_____ sought to develop buildings that highlight simple forms to promote social goals like openness and collective benefit, especially in public institutions. While opinions on Brutalism vary, it remains an influential movement that challenged traditional notions of beauty and design in modern architecture.

Answers p.409

3. Social Science

사회과학은 개인과 집단의 행동이나 사회 제도의 구조와 변화를 과학적으로 연구하는 학문 영역이다. TASK 1에는 경제학, 인류학, 심리학, 사회학과 같은 세부 분야들이 자주 출제되므로 관련 어휘들을 눈에 익혀 둔다.

■ Economics (경제학)

자원의 희소성 속에서 인간의 선택과 그에 따른 사회적 결과를 연구하는 학문이다. 수요와 공급의 법칙, 시장의 원리, 인플레이션, 경제 정책, 국제 무역에 관한 지문이 주로 출제된다.

adverse selection 역선택	interest rate 이자율, 금리
bankruptcy 파산	labor market 노동 시장
bond market 채권 시장	marginal cost 한계비용
budget deficit 재정 적자	marginal utility 한계 효용
commodity 상품, 원자재	market failure 시장 실패
comparative advantage 비교 우위	monetary policy 통화 정책
consumption 소비	monopoly 독점
deflation 디플레이션, 물가 하락	opportunity cost 기회비용
demand 수요	poverty line 빈곤선
exchange rate 환율	recession 경기 침체
expenditure 지출, 경비	revenue 수익
fiscal policy 재정 정책	speculation 투기
free trade 자유 무역	stock market 주식 시장
gross domestic product 국내총생산	sunk cost 매몰 비용
gross national income 국민총소득	supply 공급
human capital 인적 자본	tariff 관세
income inequality 소득 불평등	taxation 과세
inflation 인플레이션, 물가 상승	unemployment rate 실업률

■ Archaeology (인류학)

인간이 남긴 유적이나 유물의 시기와 특징을 밝혀 과거의 문화, 역사 및 생활방식을 연구하는 학문이다. 선사시대의 각 시대 특징이나 고고학의 연구 방법에 관한 지문이 주로 출제된다.

agriculture 농경	pottery 토기
artifact 인공물, 유물	prehistory 선사 시대
ceramics 도기, 토기	radiocarbon dating 방사성 탄소 연대 측정법
pastoralism 목축	trade route 무역로

■ Psychology (심리학)

인간 혹은 동물의 행동과 정신 활동을 연구하는 학문이다. 심리 작용, 성격 발달, 정신 건강에 관한 지문이 주로 출제된다.

anxiety disorder 불안 장애	introversion 내향성
attachment theory 애착 이론	mood disorder 기분 장애
behavior pattern 행동 패턴	motivation 동기
bystander effect 방관자 효과	obedience 복종
cognition 인지	perception 지각
cognitive dissonance 인지 부조화	personality test 성격 검사
confirmation bias 확증 편향	psychotherapy 심리 치료
conformity 동조	punishment 벌
consciousness 의식	rationalization 합리화
defense mechanism 방어 기제	repression 억압
depression 우울증	self-esteem 자존감
disposition 기질, 성향	sensation 감각
egocentrism 자기 중심성	stereotype 고정관념
emotional stability 정서적 안정성	temperament 기질
extroversion 외향성	theory of mind 마음 이론 (타인의 마음 이해)

■ Sociology (사회학)

인간의 사회 구조, 관계 및 문화, 사회적 행동을 연구하는 학문이다. 사회 계층, 가족 형태의 변화, 사회 문제, 일탈 행동에 관한 지문이 주로 출제된다.

alienation 소외	governance 통치 구조
ascribed status 귀속 지위	hierarchy 위계질서
assimilation 동화	minority group 소수 집단
civil society 시민 사회	peer group 또래 집단
collective behavior 집합 행동	social mobility 사회 이동성
counterculture 반문화	social norm 사회 규범
cultural capital 문화적 자본	social status 사회적 지위
discrimination 차별	socialization 사회화
gender role 성 역할	socioeconomic status 사회 경제적 지위

HACKERS TEST

Fill in the missing letters in the paragraph.

[01~10]

Social norms represent shared understandings about acceptable conduct within communities. They ⁰¹gu___ the ⁰²beha_____ of ⁰³mem____ of ⁰⁴soci_____ and ⁰⁵main____ order ⁰⁶wit___ a ⁰⁷gr___. For ⁰⁸inst_____, it ⁰⁹i_ a ¹⁰com____ expectation in many places to stand in line at a bus stop, which guarantees fairness among waiting passengers. Norms shape how people interact and make choices every day. By following social norms, people feel more connected, forming stronger social bonds with others.

[11~20]

Cognitive dissonance refers to a state of mental discomfort that occurs when a person's values conflict with new information. People ¹¹inher_____ seek ¹²alig_____ of ¹³th____ thoughts ¹⁴a___ actions. ¹⁵Discr_____ between ¹⁶wh___ one ¹⁷beli_____ and ¹⁸h___ one ¹⁹beh_____ brings ²⁰ab____ mental distress. To mitigate this unease, individuals may justify their behavior or deny information that challenges their views. The magnitude of this dissonance is greatest when the conflicting elements are central to one's self-concept and values. This psychological process affects many aspects of daily life, from personal decisions to how people interpret new information.

[21~30]

The Bronze Age marked a pivotal era in human history, characterized by the extensive adoption of bronze in crafting superior tools, weaponry, and decorative items. This [21]innov_____ yielded [22]stro_____ implements, [23]wh____ not [24]on___ advanced [25]agric_____ and [26]constr_____ but [27]al___ transformed [28]war_____. Consequently, [29]com_____ social [30]sys_____ began to develop, establishing specialized roles within communities that enhanced the efficient organization of both labor and essential resources. The Bronze Age served as a crucial bridge between the earlier Neolithic period and the subsequent rise of advanced early civilizations, laying the groundwork for major cultural and technological progress.

[31~40]

Economics examines how individuals and societies make decisions in the face of limited resources. To [31]incr_____ profitability, [32]comp_____ must [33]ass____ marginal [34]co___, the [35]exp_____ of [36]prod_____ an [37]addit_____ unit [38]o__ output. [39]Simi_____, a [40]gover_____ must weigh the utility of allocating a significant portion of its annual budget to one major public sector initiative rather than another. These calculated decisions mirror how economic agents allocate resources and affect both market behavior and indicators such as gross domestic product. Economic models use quantitative data and behavioral insights to forecast market trends and evaluate policy effectiveness.

Answers p.410

4. Physical Science

물리과학은 자연계의 기본 법칙과 물질의 성질을 탐구하는 학문 영역이다. TASK 1에는 천문학, 화학, 물리학, 지질학, 기상학과 같은 세부 분야들이 자주 출제되므로 관련 어휘들을 눈에 익혀 둔다.

■ Astronomy (천문학)

지구 대기권 밖의 천체 및 그와 관련된 현상을 관측하고 연구하는 학문이다. 행성, 항성, 은하의 생성 및 진화, 우주의 구조와 역사에 관한 지문이 주로 출제된다.

asteroid 소행성	light year 광년
astronomical unit 천문단위	lunar eclipse 월식
big bang theory 빅뱅 이론	meteorite 운석
celestial body 천체	nebula 성운
constellation 별자리, 성좌	observatory 천문대
dark matter 암흑 물질	revolution 공전
equator 적도	rotation 자전
exoplanet 외계 행성	solar system 태양계
extraterrestrial 외계의	supernova 초신성
giant star 거성(직경과 질량이 현저히 큰 별)	terrestrial planet 지구형 행성

■ Chemistry (화학)

물질의 성질, 구조 및 변화 과정을 연구하는 학문이다. 원자와 분자의 결합, 화학 반응, 유기 화합물, 물질의 상태 변화에 관한 지문이 주로 출제된다.

acid 산	element 원소
atom 원자	fatty acid 지방산
base 염기	freezing point 어는점
boiling point 끓는점	melting point 녹는점
carbohydrate 탄수화물	molecule 분자
catalyst 촉매	oxidation 산화
compound 화합물	solution 용액
distillation 증류	solvent 용매

■ Physics (물리학)

물질과 에너지, 그리고 그들 사이의 상호작용에 내재된 근본적인 법칙을 연구하는 학문이다. 운동, 힘, 열역학, 전자기학, 양자 역학에 관한 지문이 주로 출제된다.

acceleration 가속도	nuclear reaction 핵반응
amplitude 진폭	oscillation 진동
convection 대류	potential energy 위치 에너지
electric charge 전하	pressure 압력
frequency 진동수, 주파수	radioactivity 방사능
friction 마찰	reflection 반사
gravity 중력	refraction 굴절
inertia 관성	resistance 저항
kinetic energy 운동 에너지	temperature 온도
magnetic field 자기장	voltage 전압
momentum 운동량	wave length 파장

■ Geology (지질학)

지구의 구조, 구성 물질, 역사 및 그 변화 과정을 연구하는 학문이다. 암석의 생성, 광물 자원, 판 구조론, 지진, 화산 활동에 관한 지문이 주로 출제된다.

continental crust 대륙 지각	mineral 광물
continental drift 대륙 이동	plate boundary 판 경계
deposition 퇴적	plate tectonics 판 구조론
erosion 침식	seismic wave 지진파
fault line 단층선	tectonic plate 지각판, 판 구조
glacier 빙하	weathering 풍화

■ Meteorology (기상학)

대기 현상과 기후를 연구하여 날씨의 변화와 원인을 분석하는 학문이다. 구름의 형성, 강수 현상, 태풍, 지구 기후 시스템에 관한 지문이 주로 출제된다.

air pressure 기압	hail 우박
blizzard 눈보라	humidity 습도
climatology 기후학	jet stream 제트 기류
condensation 응결	precipitation 강수
evaporation 증발	weather front 전선(성질이 다른 공기가 만나는 경계)

HACKERS TEST

Fill in the missing letters in the paragraph.

[01~10]

Unlike a simple hot spring that flows continuously, a geyser is defined by its intermittent and forceful eruptions. It [01]requ_____ a [02]parti_____ geological [03]config_____: a [04]he___ source, [05]abun_____ water, [06]a___ a [07]tig_____ constricted [08]under_____ plumbing system [09]th___ allows [10]pres_____ to build. This setup traps superheated water until it can no longer be contained and bursts forth in a signature column of water and steam that reflects the volatile conditions below the surface. The sheer power released during an eruption makes geysers among Earth's most dynamic hydrothermal features.

[11~20]

The residue remaining after nuclear fuel has been utilized is known as nuclear waste. This [11]mate_____ is [12]gene_____ primarily [13]i_ the [14]cou_____ of [15]prod_____ electrical [16]po____, which [17]invo_____ nuclear [18]reac_____ that [19]em____ tremendous [20]amo_____ of energy. Given that this waste can retain its perilous nature for millennia, an important task for global societies is developing safe, long-term disposal strategies to shield both human populations and natural habitats from enduring damage. Common methods include placing the highly radioactive matter deep beneath the Earth's surface in purpose-built geological repositories.

[21~30]

Hail is a type of precipitation consisting of solid ice spheres, called hailstones, that fall from thunderstorm clouds. They ²¹fo___ when ²²str____ updraft ²³wi____ carry ²⁴wa____ droplets ²⁵hi___ into ²⁶extr_____ cold ²⁷reg_____ of ²⁸clo____. Hailstones ²⁹fre____ and ³⁰gr___ in size as they collide with and collect supercooled water until they become too heavy for the updrafts to support. They can vary in size, ranging from small pea-sized pellets to stones as large as golf balls or even larger, posing a major threat to crops and property.

[31~40]

A neutron star is a stellar remnant that marks the final stage in the life cycle of a massive star. When ³¹gi____ stars ³²hea_____ than ³³t___ Sun ³⁴exh_____ their ³⁵fu___, their ³⁶co___ implodes. ³⁷Wh___ remains ³⁸i_ a ³⁹sph____ so ⁴⁰den_____ packed that its gravity crushes protons and electrons together, forming a mass composed almost entirely of neutrons. These stars are only about 12 miles (20 km) in diameter, yet they contain more mass than the Sun. This means just a teaspoon of a neutron star would weigh billions of tons.

5. Life Science

생명과학은 생명체의 구조, 기능, 진화를 연구하는 학문 영역이다. TASK 1에는 생물학, 환경과학, 생태학, 생리학, 고생물학과 같은 세부 분야들이 출제되므로 관련 어휘들을 눈에 익혀 둔다.

■ Biology (생물학)

생물의 구조, 특성, 분류를 연구하는 학문이다. 생물의 적응, 에너지 전환(광합성 등), 생식, 분류와 계통에 관한 지문이 출제된다.

appendage 사지, 부속기관	infection 감염
cellular 세포의	metamorphosis 변태 (곤충이 성체로 변하는 과정)
chromosome 염색체	microorganism 미생물
convergent evolution 수렴 진화	mutation 돌연변이
embryo 배아	natural selection 자연 선택
enzyme 효소	nucleus 핵
evolution 진화	organism 생물
fertilization 수정, 수분	pathogen 병원체
gene expression 유전자 발현	photosynthesis 광합성
genetic engineering 유전 공학	pollination 수분
genetic modification 유전자 변형	regeneration 재생
heredity 유전	stem cell 줄기세포

■ Environmental Science (환경과학)

생물과 환경 사이의 상호작용 및 인간 활동이 환경에 미치는 영향을 연구하는 학문이다. 기후 변화, 환경, 오염, 생태계 보전, 지속 가능한 개발에 관한 지문이 주로 출제된다.

acid rain 산성비	greenhouse gas 온실가스
atmosphere 대기	hazardous waste 유해 폐기물
carbon cycle 탄소 순환	natural resource 천연자원
carbon footprint 탄소 발자국	ozone layer 오존층
climate change 기후 변화	pollution 오염
deforestation 삼림 벌채	renewable energy 재생 에너지
ecological footprint 생태 발자국	sustainability 지속 가능성

Ecology (생태학)

생물과 환경 사이의 상호작용을 연구하는 학문이다. 생물 다양성, 외래종 유입, 멸종, 공생 관계에 관한 지문이 주로 출제된다.

apex predator 최상위 포식자	homing instinct 귀소본능, 회귀본능
biodiversity 생물 다양성	indicator species 지표종
camouflage 위장	invasive species 침입종, 외래종
carnivore 육식 동물	keystone species 핵심종
decomposer 분해자	mimicry 의태
ecological niche 생태적 지위	mutualism 상리 공생
ecosystem 생태계	nocturnal animal 야행성 동물
endemic species 고유종	omnivore 잡식 동물
food web 먹이 그물	parasitism 기생
greenhouse effect 온실 효과	predator 포식자
habitat 서식지	scavenging 청소 (다른 동물이 사냥한 고기 먹기)
herbivore 초식 동물	species diversity 종 다양성

Physiology (생리학)

생명체의 기능과 작용을 연구하는 학문이다. 호흡, 순환, 신경 전달, 항상성 등 생리적 과정에 관한 지문이 주로 출제된다.

absorption 흡수	immunity 면역
antibody 항체	inflammation 염증
cardiovascular system 심혈관계	metabolism 신진대사
circadian 일주기 (생체 리듬)	nervous system 신경계
circulatory 순환의	neuron 뉴런, 신경세포
digestive 소화의	receptor 수용체
homeostasis 항상성	respiration 호흡
hormonal balance 호르몬 균형	respiratory system 호흡계
immune system 면역계	skeletal 골격의

Paleontology (고생물학)

지구상에 살았던 생명체의 흔적인 화석을 연구하는 학문이다. 생물의 진화와 멸종 과정에 관한 지문이 주로 출제된다.

fossil 화석	preserved remains 보존된 유해
mass extinction 대량 멸종	trace fossil 흔적 화석

HACKERS TEST

Fill in the missing letters in the paragraph.

[01~10]

Bacteria are microscopic single-celled organisms that exist in virtually every environment on Earth. These [01]sim____ microorganisms [02]la__ complex [03]struc_____ found [04]i_ more [05]adva_____ cells. [06]Th__ reproduce [07]rap_____, which [08]all____ them [09]t_ adapt [10]qui_____ to changing conditions. Some species cause diseases such as pneumonia and tuberculosis, while others are beneficial, helping with digestion or producing antibiotics. With over 30,000 species identified, they represent one of the three major domains of life.

[11~20]

Genes are the fundamental biological units of heredity that carry information determining an organism's traits. Scientists [11]al____ them [12]thr_____ a [13]pro_____ known [14]a_ genetic [15]modifi_____. Sophisticated [16]techn_____ make [17]poss_____ the [18]introd_____ of [19]desi_____ traits [20]in__ various organisms, ranging from plants and animals to bacteria. This enables researchers to develop solutions for major challenges in fields such as agriculture and medicine. However, as genetic modification becomes more widespread, it continues to spark debate about its impact on society and the environment.

[21~30]

Owls are nocturnal birds found in diverse habitats around the world. They ²¹hu_ _ primarily ²²a_ night, ²³us_ _ _ _ their ²⁴excep_ _ _ _ _ _ _ sensory ²⁵abil_ _ _ _ _ _ to ²⁶loc_ _ _ _ a ²⁷tar_ _ _ _. Many ²⁸o_ these ²⁹pred_ _ _ _ _ _ fly ³⁰sile_ _ _ _ _, reducing the chance that the animals being hunted notice them. Their large, forward-facing eyes, along with the fact that they can rotate their heads up to 270 degrees, characterize this unique bird. Their characteristics and mysterious nighttime habits have inspired countless myths and legends in many cultures.

[31~40]

When facing danger, a person's body swiftly initiates several physiological shifts known as the fight-or-flight response. This ³¹mech_ _ _ _ _ _ starts ³²wi_ _ a ³³dist_ _ _ _ _ signal ³⁴aler_ _ _ _ _ the ³⁵ner_ _ _ _ _ system, ³⁶wh_ _ _ _ promptly ³⁷secr_ _ _ _ _ the ³⁸chem_ _ _ _ _ adrenaline ³⁹in_ _ _ the ⁴⁰blood_ _ _ _ _ _ _ _. Circulating throughout the body, adrenaline triggers an expansion of lung capacity and an acceleration of the heart rate. The resulting surge of oxygen delivers a burst of energy that enhances readiness and thereby increases the individual's ability to either successfully address the threat or flee from it.

Answers p.412

무료 토플자료·유학정보 제공
goHackers.com

**Hackers
Updated TOEFL
READING**

TASK 2

Read in Daily Life

Introduction

Section I. Question Types

1. Main Topic/Purpose Questions
2. Detail Questions
3. Fact/Negative Fact Questions
4. Vocabulary Questions
5. Inference Questions
6. Intention Questions

Section II. Passage Types

1. Email
2. Text-Message Chain
3. Notice
4. Advertisement
5. Social Media Post
6. News Article
7. Forms

Introduction

TASK 2(Read in Daily Life)는 일상에서 접할 수 있는 다양한 형태의 글을 읽고 문제를 푸는 유형이다. 이메일, 메시지 대화문, 광고, 기사, SNS 게시글, 각종 양식 등 다양한 형태의 지문이 출제되며, 주제 또한 안내, 공지, 홍보처럼 일상과 밀접하고 친숙한 주제가 출제된다. 지문은 15~150단어 분량이며, 지문의 길이에 따라 2개 또는 3개의 문제가 출제된다. Module 1에서는 2문제짜리 지문과 3문제짜리 지문이 각각 1개씩 출제되는데, 더미 문항이 포함될 경우 각각 2지문까지 더 출제되어 최대 4지문이 출제될 수 있다. Upper Module 2에서는 이 유형이 출제되지 않으며, Lower Module 2에서만 각각 1개씩, 총 2개의 지문이 출제된다.

▋ Preview

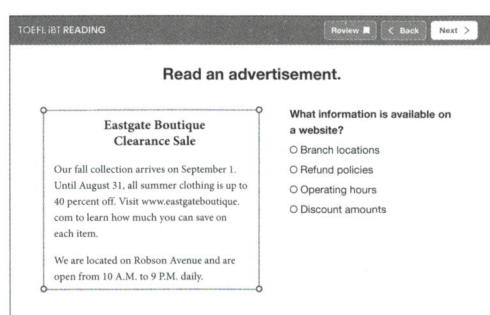

문제가 출제될 때 나오는 화면으로, 상단에는 지문 유형을 알려주는 디렉션 문장이 나온다. 그 아래로 왼쪽에는 지문, 오른쪽에는 문제와 선택지가 나온다.

문제를 풀 때 해야 할 일: 지문과 문제, 보기를 읽은 후 보기 앞에 있는 칸을 클릭하여 답을 표시한다.

문제를 풀고 난 후 해야 할 일: Next 버튼을 클릭하여 다음 문제로 넘어간다. Module 안에서는 문제간 이동이 자유로우므로, 헷갈리는 문제가 있다면 넘어갔다가 뒤의 문제들을 풀고 다시 돌아올 수 있다.

Task Strategy

1. 지문의 형식에 따라 주의 깊게 살펴봐야 할 부분을 확인한다.

지문의 형식에 따라 주의 깊게 봐야 할 부분에는 차이가 있다. 이메일이나 공고는 글의 목적이 드러나는 도입부를 잘 봐야 하고, 메시지 대화문은 대화의 흐름을 파악할 필요가 있으며, 양식 지문은 날짜, 가격 등 수치적 정보를 꼼꼼히 확인할 필요가 있다.

2. 문제에서 묻는 포인트가 어디에 언급되는지 찾는다.

Main Topic 문제나 Main Purpose 문제가 있다면, 지문의 첫 문장을 유심히 읽는다. 또 When으로 시작하는 문제가 있다면, 지문에서 시점을 가리키는 단어(날짜, 시간 등)에 유의하며 지문을 읽는다.

3. 지문의 내용을 올바르게 패러프레이즈한 선택지를 고른다.

정답은 지문에 사용된 표현을 그대로 제시할 수도 있지만, 유의어를 사용하거나 문장 구조를 바꾸는 방식으로 패러프레이즈해서 제시하기도 한다. 따라서 선택지가 지문의 내용을 올바르게 패러프레이즈했는지 확인한 후 선택지를 고른다.

Study Guide

1. 문제 유형별로 알맞은 풀이 전략을 익히자.

문제 유형별로 풀이 전략을 익혀 두면 실전 시험에서 문제 풀이를 하는 것이 쉬워진다. 예를 들어, Detail 문제의 경우 질문에서 의문사와 핵심 어구를 확인하고 지문에서 그와 관련된 정답의 단서를 빠르게 찾는 연습을 통해 시간을 단축할 수 있다.

2. 지문 형식별 구조와 흐름에 익숙해지자.

출제될 수 있는 지문의 형식이 매우 다양하며, 지문 형식별로 글의 구조와 흐름이 다를 수 있다. 예를 들어, 한 사람이 뚜렷한 목적을 가지고 쓰는 글인 이메일에 비해, 여러 사람이 대화에 참여하는 메시지 대화문의 흐름이 파악하기 더 어려울 수 있다. 따라서 지문 형식에 따른 구조와 흐름을 익혀 두는 것이 좋다.

무료 토플자료·유학정보 제공
goHackers.com

**Hackers
Updated TOEFL
READING**

Section I
Question Types

Section I에서는 TASK 2에 출제되는 문제 유형을 6가지로 구분하여 각 유형의 특징과 질문 형태, 실제 문제 풀이에 적용 가능한 전략들을 소개하고 있다. 또한 풍부한 연습 문제와 실전 문제를 통해 각 문제 유형을 효과적으로 공략할 수 있도록 하였다.

TASK 2의 Question Types에는 다음의 6가지가 있다.

1. Main Topic/Purpose Questions
2. Detail Questions
3. Fact/Negative Fact Questions
4. Vocabulary Questions
5. Inference Questions
6. Intention Questions

1. Main Topic/Purpose Questions

Overview

글의 중심 내용을 잘 이해했는지를 묻는 문제이다. Main Topic 문제는 글에서 중점적으로 다루는 주제나 요지가 무엇인지를 묻고, Main Purpose 문제는 글을 작성한 목적을 묻는다. 실용적인 목적이 있는 글이 출제되는 TASK 2에서는 Main Purpose 문제가 Main Topic 문제보다 더 자주 출제되는 편이다.

Types of Questions

Main Topic 문제는 주로 What ~ about이라는 표현을 포함한 형태로 출제되며, Main Purpose 문제는 대개 main purpose라는 표현을 포함하거나 Why를 써서 글을 쓴 이유를 묻는다.

Main Topic

   What is the notice about?

Main Purpose

   What is the main purpose of the notice?
   What is the main purpose of the post?
   What is the main purpose of the email?
   Why did Ms. Lawson send the email to Mr. Juarez?

Hackers Strategy

1 지문의 도입부를 유심히 읽는다.

지문이 짧은 만큼, 주제나 목적이 도입부에서 제시되는 경우가 많다. 특히 글의 목적은 주로 첫 문장에서 제시되므로, Main Purpose 문제가 출제된 것을 확인했다면 첫 문장을 유심히 읽는다.

2 지문의 주제나 목적을 올바르게 패러프레이즈한 선택지를 고른다.

지문에서 제시된 주제나 목적이 정답에 그대로 드러나는 경우도 있지만, 지문에서 제시된 어구를 패러프레이즈해서 정답을 제시하는 경우도 있다. 따라서 선택지가 지문의 주제나 목적을 올바르게 패러프레이즈했는지 확인한 후 선택지를 고른다.

3 자주 나오는 오답 유형에 주의한다.

지문에 사용된 단어나 어구를 사용해서 혼동을 주는 오답, 지문에 언급된 내용이기는 하지만 글을 쓴 주된 목적은 아닌 오답이 자주 등장한다.

Example

Read a notice.

> Students will be able to access their enrollment certificates and other documents through the new online system starting December 10. Log in using your student ID number to download and print documents. Physical copies will no longer be issued after December 9. If you have any questions, contact the Registrar's Office.

What is the main purpose of the notice?

Ⓐ To introduce new students to document issuance procedures
Ⓑ To announce a change in the academic schedule
Ⓒ To apologize for a system malfunction
Ⓓ To inform students about a new way to obtain documents

정답 Ⓓ

해설 글을 작성한 목적을 묻는 문제이다. 'Students ~ new online system'을 통해 학생 서류 발급에 온라인 시스템이 도입되었다는 것을 알리기 위한 글임을 알 수 있다. 따라서 Ⓓ가 정답이다. 'new online system'이 'new way'로, 'access ~ documents'가 'obtain documents'로 패러프레이즈되었다.

HACKERS PRACTICE

01 Read an email.

> Subject: RE: Painting Workshop
>
> Dear Ms. Simons,
> Your seat for the still life painting workshop on May 27th has been confirmed. All you need to bring is an apron. We'll have all the other supplies—paints, brushes, and a canvas—ready for you when you arrive.
>
> Best regards,
> Francisco Mondi

What is the main purpose of the email?

Ⓐ To specify payment details
Ⓑ To confirm a registration
Ⓒ To outline registration benefits
Ⓓ To introduce a new instructor

02 Read an advertisement.

> **MOVE IN READY**
>
> This four-bedroom, two-bath house is now available in the Kingswood Subdivision. The house was recently renovated and features a modern kitchen with new appliances, a spacious open floor plan, and a spa-style master bathroom. The property was also professionally landscaped and has a beautiful backyard with a large swimming pool and hot tub.
>
> The new owner will enjoy easy access to the city's best schools, retail outlets, and public transportation as well as all of the Kingswood Subdivision's amenities, including a private lake, community center, and sports complex. Priced at only $275,000, this is a great opportunity for a family looking to upgrade their home and lifestyle. For more information, call Margaret Benes at 555-0872.

What is the main purpose of the advertisement?

Ⓐ To advertise a newly opened subdivision
Ⓑ To announce a price cut on a property
Ⓒ To introduce a house for sale
Ⓓ To highlight some renovations

03 Read a notice.

Dear Valued Customers,

Our rooftop garden will be closed for seasonal maintenance from May 25 to June 1. We will be working daily to perform safety checks and plant new flowers to ensure the garden remains a safe and pleasant space for everyone. We look forward to welcoming you back on June 2!

What is the main purpose of the notice?

Ⓐ To inform visitors of the temporary facility closure
Ⓑ To invite visitors to the renewed rooftop garden
Ⓒ To announce a schedule to staff members
Ⓓ To advertise a re-opening event

04 Read an email.

Subject: Request to Reschedule Tennis Lesson

Dear Mr. Lin,

I am writing to reschedule my tennis lesson, which is currently booked for this Wednesday, May 6, at 5:00 P.M. Unfortunately, a work commitment has come up, so I will not be able to make it at the scheduled time.

I would like to know if it would be possible to move my lesson to this Friday, May 8, at 10:00 A.M. If that time is not available, I am also free any time after 4:00 P.M. on Friday. I would also appreciate it if you could suggest an alternative instructor in case you are not available on Friday.

Thank you for your understanding.

Kind regards,
Laura Mondale

Why is Ms. Mondale contacting Mr. Lin?

Ⓐ To cancel her membership
Ⓑ To change her lesson date
Ⓒ To sign up for a tennis lesson
Ⓓ To book a tennis court

Answers p.414

HACKERS TEST

[01-02] Read an email.

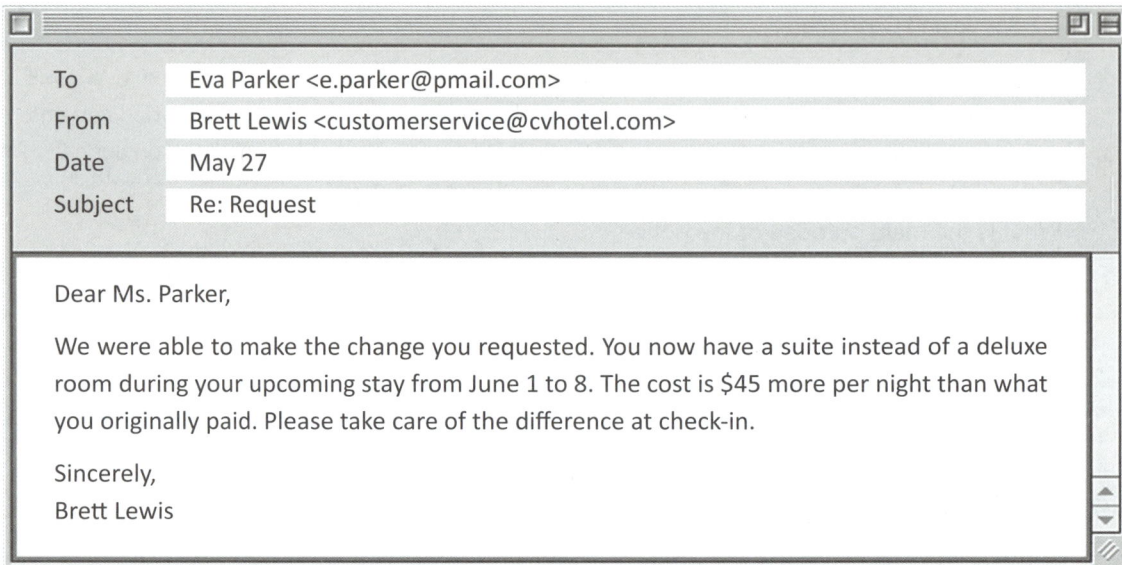

To: Eva Parker <e.parker@pmail.com>
From: Brett Lewis <customerservice@cvhotel.com>
Date: May 27
Subject: Re: Request

Dear Ms. Parker,

We were able to make the change you requested. You now have a suite instead of a deluxe room during your upcoming stay from June 1 to 8. The cost is $45 more per night than what you originally paid. Please take care of the difference at check-in.

Sincerely,
Brett Lewis

01 What is the main purpose of the email?

Ⓐ To explain a seasonal promotion
Ⓑ To determine a room preference
Ⓒ To confirm a reservation change
Ⓓ To address a customer complaint

02 What does Mr. Lewis ask Ms. Parker to do?

Ⓐ Call a front desk clerk
Ⓑ Provide a copy of a receipt
Ⓒ Specify the length of stay
Ⓓ Pay an outstanding balance

[03-04] Read a notice.

Dear residents,

Window cleaning will take place on the exterior of Building B from 10:00 A.M. to 1:00 P.M. on April 6. Please keep windows closed during this time for safety and a thorough cleaning. Also, please move any personal items, such as plants or decorations, from the windowsills.

03 What is the main purpose of the notice?

Ⓐ To ask residents for help with a cleaning project
Ⓑ To inform residents about a temporary change in building policy
Ⓒ To announce scheduled window cleaning to residents
Ⓓ To provide details on new installations within the facility

04 Why does the notice mention personal items?

Ⓐ To provide instruction on what to remove from the windowsills
Ⓑ To inform residents that those items are not allowed in the building
Ⓒ To explain that the crew is not responsible for damages
Ⓓ To specify the designated areas for temporarily storing possessions

HACKERS TEST

[05-06] Read a poster.

BELLE AND THE BEASTS
Live in concert at
Red Rock Arena

Enjoy the punk band playing hits from its new album

Date:
Saturday, August 11
Doors open at 6:00 P.M.
Performance begins at 7:00 P.M.

Tickets:
$45 at the door
$35 in advance online
www.redrockarena.com/tickets

---

05 What is the main purpose of the poster?

Ⓐ To promote a musical performance
Ⓑ To announce a new album
Ⓒ To advertise a local band
Ⓓ To provide some contact information

06 How can one get a discount?

Ⓐ By visiting an arena
Ⓑ By showing up early
Ⓒ By using a website
Ⓓ By joining a fan club

[07-09] Read a social media post.

Adam Lancaster

I love exploring cities on a bicycle. There's something special about feeling the wind on my face while discovering hidden spots. Last summer, I spent a week cycling around Amsterdam, and it was amazing. I found small cafés, beautiful parks, and quiet canals that I never would have noticed otherwise.

If my experience has inspired you, here are some practical tips to consider before you plan your own city bike tour. You'll need to figure out how to make your ride smooth and enjoyable. I'd recommend renting a bike locally rather than bringing your own, as many rental shops offer daily or weekly options. Using bike-specific apps can help you avoid busy roads and make the most of your time. You should also keep safety in mind. Make sure to follow local traffic rules and bike lane signs, and wear a helmet and reflective gear.

LIKE **COMMENT**

07 What is the main purpose of the post?

Ⓐ To describe the author's cycling preferences in detail
Ⓑ To share practical bike-touring tips
Ⓒ To explain the history of cycling in European cities
Ⓓ To compare different bike rental services

08 Why does the post mention Amsterdam?

Ⓐ To list the city's most favored spots
Ⓑ To provide an example of a great city cycling experience
Ⓒ To introduce an ideal city bike tour destination
Ⓓ To show that Amsterdam has the best bike lanes in Europe

09 What can be inferred about bike-specific apps?

Ⓐ They are mainly used for booking bikes in advance.
Ⓑ They list cafés and parks that are accessible to cyclists.
Ⓒ They provide real-time road information.
Ⓓ They are necessary for making bike rental payments.

HACKERS TEST

[10-12] Read a news article.

> Riverdale—International chip maker Trimark Semiconductors held the grand opening for its newest factory yesterday. Located in the Riverdale Industrial Zone, the new facility will produce microchips for smartphones, computers, and other electronic devices.
>
> Trimark's president, Carl Grove, was on hand for the opening of the company's new 12,000 square meter factory and said it was only the beginning of the company's investments in Riverdale. "The factory is only the first part of a complex we have planned for the area. Eventually, we plan to move our entire operations to the area, including our international headquarters."
>
> Riverdale mayor Karen Beatty thanked the company and its representatives for their commitment to Riverdale. She highlighted the economic impact of the decision of the business, especially the direct creation of more than 4,000 jobs. In recognition of his company's actions, Mayor Beatty awarded Mr. Grove a special civic honor.

10 What is the news article about?

Ⓐ A smartphone release
Ⓑ A manufacturing facility
Ⓒ A construction project
Ⓓ A city-sponsored event

11 Who is Carl Grove?

Ⓐ A city official
Ⓑ A factory worker
Ⓒ A corporate investor
Ⓓ A business executive

12 What can be inferred about the company from the news article?

Ⓐ It has closed other factories.
Ⓑ It was founded in Riverdale.
Ⓒ It will do more local hiring in the future.
Ⓓ It is receiving incentives from the city.

[13-15] Read a social media post.

 Chloe Winchester

I've finally secured a new apartment in Birchwood! Finding a place here was no easy task—apartments get snapped up almost instantly, so I had to move quickly when this opportunity arose. It's a cozy, bright one-bedroom on the fifth floor of a quiet building. I chose this apartment because it's conveniently located just steps from the Oak Avenue bus stop.

Moving in has been exciting, though it's been a bit nerve-wracking adjusting to a new neighborhood. I've been exploring the nearby streets and checking out local shops. One of the highlights so far is a charming café right across the street, perfect for breakfast. I also noticed a few fitness centers nearby. I'm now looking for reliable laundry services because I don't want to worry about doing laundry daily.

This new chapter feels full of possibilities. I can't wait to see all that Birchwood has to offer!

LIKE   **COMMENT**

13 What is the main purpose of the post?

Ⓐ To describe the amenities of an apartment building
Ⓑ To provide a detailed analysis of the local housing market
Ⓒ To ask for recommendations for local shops
Ⓓ To announce a successful apartment search

14 Why did Ms. Winchester choose this apartment?

Ⓐ Its public transit access is convenient.
Ⓑ Its rent was significantly lower than other nearby units.
Ⓒ It is bright and cozy.
Ⓓ It is situated in a quiet setting.

15 What is Ms. Winchester currently looking for?

Ⓐ Information on the local bus route
Ⓑ A café with a breakfast menu
Ⓒ A dependable laundry service
Ⓓ A well-equipped gym

Answers p.415

2. Detail Questions

Overview

지문을 통해 알 수 있는 다양한 세부 사실을 묻는 문제 유형이다. TASK 2에서 가장 많은 비중을 차지하는 문제 유형으로, 지문에 나오는 다양한 세부 정보를 빠르게 찾아내는 능력이 필요하다.

Types of Questions

세부적으로 묻고자 하는 내용에 따라 의문사 What, How, Why, When, Where, Who가 쓰인다. 지문에 언급되지 않은 것을 고르는 문제가 출제되기도 하는데, 이때는 NOT 또는 EXCEPT라는 표현이 쓰인다.

Detail

What will be covered in the training session?

How can a customer request a refund for a damaged item?

What will students NOT experience?

All team members must attend the workshop to

Hackers Strategy

1 문제의 키워드에 관한 내용을 지문에서 확인한다.

문제의 키워드가 언급된 곳을 찾은 후, 그 키워드 앞뒤 내용을 확인한다. 또한, 문제에 제시된 의문사와 관련 있는 정보가 언급되는 곳을 주의 깊게 본다. 예를 들어 How 문제는 방법에 관한 설명을, When 문제는 날짜나 시간이 언급되는 부분을 확인한다.

2 지문의 내용을 올바르게 패러프레이즈한 선택지를 고른다.

지문의 내용이 정답에 그대로 드러나는 경우도 있지만, 패러프레이즈되어 있는 경우도 있다는 점에 유의한다. 따라서 선택지가 지문의 내용을 올바르게 패러프레이즈했는지 확인한 후 선택지를 고른다.

3 자주 나오는 오답 유형에 주의한다.

지문에 언급된 단어를 그대로 사용하여 혼동을 주는 오답, 지문에 아예 언급되지 않은 내용을 제시하는 오답이 자주 출제된다. When 문제는 지문에 언급된 다른 날짜/시각이 오답으로 제시되기도 한다. 반대로 이러한 선택지가 NOT/EXCEPT 문제에서는 정답이 된다.

Example

Read a notice.

> An inspection of the entire office building's electrical system is scheduled for Wednesday, June 11, between 9:00 A.M. and 6:00 P.M. During this time, the building's power will be shut down. All employees will be required to work remotely on that day.

When will the electrical system inspection begin?

Ⓐ June 11, 9:00 A.M.
Ⓑ June 11, 6:00 P.M.
Ⓒ June 12, 9:00 A.M.
Ⓓ June 12, 6:00 P.M.

정답 Ⓐ

해설 전기 시스템 점검이 언제 시작하는지 묻는 문제이다. 'An inspection ~ June 11, between 9:00 A.M. and 6:00 P.M.'을 통해 전기 시스템 점검이 6월 11일 오전 9시에 시작함을 알 수 있다. 따라서 Ⓐ가 정답이다.

HACKERS PRACTICE

01   Read an email.

> Subject: Exclusive Invitation
>
> Dear Ms. Gray,
>
> I would like to invite you to an exclusive preview of our new sculpture exhibit. The event will be held on Monday, April 8th, at 6:00 P.M. We kindly request that you RSVP by 5:30 P.M. on April 6th. We would be honored if you could share your insights as a critic.
>
> Oliver Chan
> Director, Winslow Artspace

When is the exhibit preview scheduled?

Ⓐ April 6th at 5:30 P.M.
Ⓑ April 6th at 6:00 P.M.
Ⓒ April 8th at 5:30 P.M.
Ⓓ April 8th at 6:00 P.M.

02   Read a text-message chain.

> **Mary Crockett (10:00 A.M.)**   Good morning, everyone. I just wanted to let you all know that I've hired a new receptionist for our salon. She will start on Monday.
>
> **Hiro Yamamoto (10:05 A.M.)**   That's great news. It's been really hard without one for the last two weeks.
>
> **Cindy Sullivan (10:10 A.M.)**   Yes. Having to answer the phone and greet customers while also trying to do our client's hair has been quite stressful.
>
> **Meghan Tran (10:15 A.M.)**   I agree. Maybe we should have a little welcoming party before we open on Monday.
>
> **Mary Crockett (10:20 A.M.)**   That's a great idea. Let's come in 30 minutes before opening. I'll get some pastries from the bakery next door.
>
> **Meghan Tran (10:21 A.M.)**   Perfect. I'll be there. I'll pick up some coffee too.

Why will everyone show up early at the salon on Monday?

Ⓐ To begin work early
Ⓑ To make some pastries
Ⓒ To greet a new staff member
Ⓓ To meet the needs of customers

03 Read an email.

Subject: Schedule Change - Flight RN 218

Dear Mr. Martel,

Your flight, RN 218, has been rescheduled to depart at 7:45 A.M., 50 minutes earlier than originally scheduled. Please review the new itinerary in your account. If the new time does not work for you, you may switch to another flight or request a refund within 24 hours on our website.

Best regards,
Clara Wilson
Customer Service Representative, Kairos Airlines

How can Mr. Martel request a refund?

Ⓐ By emailing customer relations
Ⓑ By visiting the airline website
Ⓒ By calling the airport ticket desk
Ⓓ By waiting for an automatic reimbursement

04 Read a social media post.

Calling all book lovers! This Thursday, come to The Inkpot Café for an evening with local authors. I'll be guiding the event and hosting a short Q&A with each writer to get everyone involved.

We're especially excited to have author Marissa Keane, who will be giving a special presentation on the writing process for her critically acclaimed novel, *Echoes of the Gilded Age*. She will share personal insights into her creative journey, from the initial spark of an idea to the final edits.

The doors open at 6:00 P.M., and the event will run from 6:30 P.M. until 8:00 P.M. Just a heads-up: seating is first come, first served, and we'll have standing room available once the chairs are full. Also, we'll be live-streaming the whole thing with captions. The link will be posted here at 5:30 P.M.

Marissa Keane will

Ⓐ read a passage from her novel
Ⓑ guide the event and Q&A
Ⓒ talk about her writing process
Ⓓ sign copies of her book

Answers p.417

HACKERS TEST

[01-02] Read a sign.

Attention All Customers

From May 10 to 14, Wallace Department Store will be closed. A new fire alarm and sprinkler system will be set up in our building during this period. To make up for the inconvenience, we are offering all customers a $10 digital gift certificate. Just download our mobile app to access it.

01 According to the sign, what will happen in May?

Ⓐ A redecorating project will be started.
Ⓑ Safety equipment will be installed.
Ⓒ A building inspection will be conducted.
Ⓓ Emergency procedures will be tested.

02 How can customers receive a gift certificate?

Ⓐ By accessing a website
Ⓑ By downloading a form
Ⓒ By speaking with an employee
Ⓓ By installing an application

[03-04] Read an advertisement.

> Piano for Sale. Rarely used Stonebrook & Sons grand piano in excellent condition. Perfect for both beginners and advanced players. $3,900, including delivery, in-home setup, and professional tuning. Visit Vintage Tone Emporium or call 555-2841 for more information.

03 The price of the piano does NOT include

   Ⓐ Delivery costs
   Ⓑ Placement in the home
   Ⓒ An extended warranty
   Ⓓ Sound adjustments

04 What can be inferred about the piano from the advertisement?

   Ⓐ It is currently in storage.
   Ⓑ It is being sold by a business.
   Ⓒ It was owned by a professional.
   Ⓓ It can be delivered the same day.

HACKERS TEST

[05-06] Read a receipt.

Nelson Office Furniture

Customer: Brad Wilcox **Order:** 93809
Date: July 7 **Store #:** 009

Item	Quantity	Price
Lyman Desk	4	$350.00
Neo Chair	4	$125.00
A $25 delivery fee is charged on orders under $500.	Shipping	N/A
	Tax	$45.00
	Total	$520.00

Visit www.nelsonoffice.com to leave feedback and to create a Nelson Loyalty Club membership.

05 What is suggested about Nelson Office Furniture?

  Ⓐ It offers discounts on online orders.
  Ⓑ It sent out a shipment on July 7.
  Ⓒ It introduced a new product line.
  Ⓓ It operates multiple branches.

06 Why was Mr. Wilcox not charged for delivery?

  Ⓐ He became a loyalty club member.
  Ⓑ He posted a review of an item.
  Ⓒ He picked up an order from a store.
  Ⓓ He made the minimum purchase.

[07-09] Read an email.

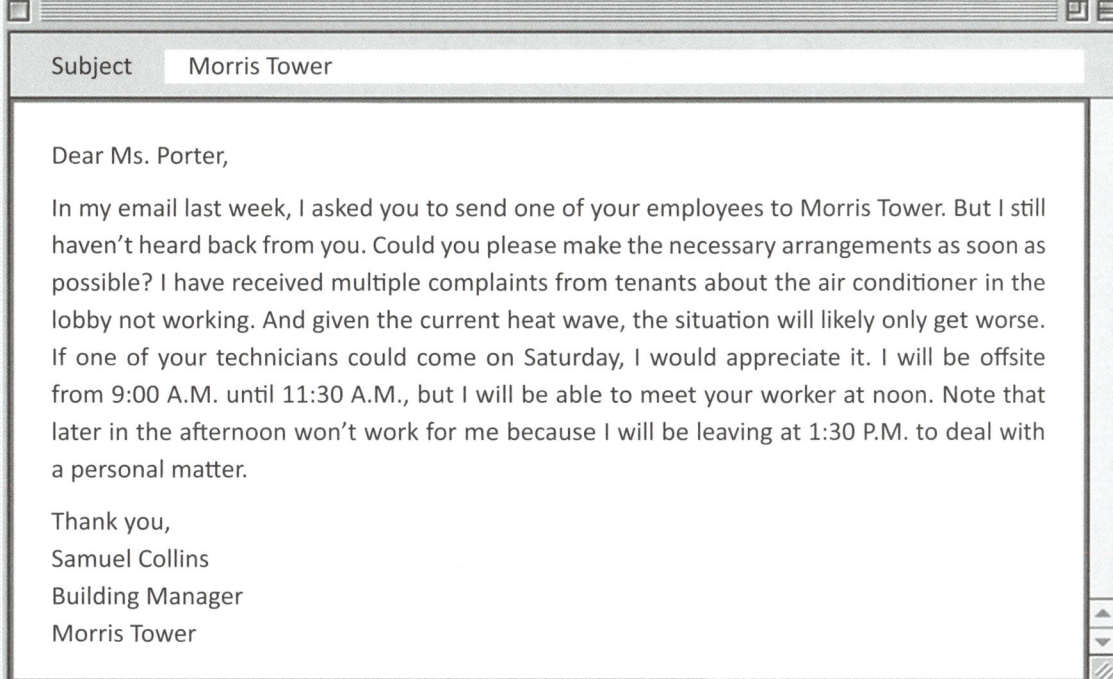

Subject: Morris Tower

Dear Ms. Porter,

In my email last week, I asked you to send one of your employees to Morris Tower. But I still haven't heard back from you. Could you please make the necessary arrangements as soon as possible? I have received multiple complaints from tenants about the air conditioner in the lobby not working. And given the current heat wave, the situation will likely only get worse. If one of your technicians could come on Saturday, I would appreciate it. I will be offsite from 9:00 A.M. until 11:30 A.M., but I will be able to meet your worker at noon. Note that later in the afternoon won't work for me because I will be leaving at 1:30 P.M. to deal with a personal matter.

Thank you,
Samuel Collins
Building Manager
Morris Tower

07 Why did Mr. Collins send the email to Ms. Porter?

Ⓐ To provide a status report
Ⓑ To follow up on a request
Ⓒ To change an appointment
Ⓓ To apologize for a delay

08 What have tenants complained about?

Ⓐ A maintenance project was canceled.
Ⓑ A building needs to be cleaned.
Ⓒ An appliance is malfunctioning.
Ⓓ An entranceway has been blocked.

09 What time does Mr. Collins want to meet on Saturday?

Ⓐ At 9:00 A.M.
Ⓑ At 11:30 A.M.
Ⓒ At 12:00 P.M.
Ⓓ At 1:30 P.M.

HACKERS TEST

[10-12] Read an advertisement.

Summer Special

Located in the heart of the Titan Mountains, Pine Ridge Lodge offers a lot more than just the world-class skiing it is known for. Summer visitors can enjoy hiking, fishing, white-water rafting and more!

To make summer trips even better, all rooms booked by April 30 for a stay between June and September will be discounted by up to 50 percent, depending on the trip duration.*

Length of stay	Discount
1-2 nights	15%
3-4 nights	25%
5-6 nights	35%
7+ nights	50%

To make a reservation, call the lodge's reservation hotline directly at 801-555-7453 or visit www.pine-ridge.com. To make special arrangements for large groups, or to book a private event at the property, reach out to our Director of Sales, Evan Singleton at EvanS@pine-ridge.com.

*Subject to availability. Discounts not valid over the Independence Day holiday weekend.

10 What can be inferred about Pine Ridge Lodge?

Ⓐ It is only open in summer months.
Ⓑ It has seen a drop in revenue.
Ⓒ It is located near a waterway.
Ⓓ It primarily caters to international guests.

11 What discount will guests who stay for two weeks receive?

Ⓐ 15%
Ⓑ 25%
Ⓒ 35%
Ⓓ 50%

12 How can a venue for a private function be arranged?

Ⓐ By calling a phone number
Ⓑ By visiting the property in person
Ⓒ By going to a website
Ⓓ By contacting the sales director

[13-15] Read a form.

Global Digital Banking Summit Registration

The registration desk will open at 8:00 A.M. daily. Please present your email confirmation to collect your badge. Access to the keynote speech and main sessions is included with your registration. Private workshops require separate pre-registration. The conference runs daily from 9:00 A.M. to 5:30 P.M., with networking opportunities available throughout the day.

Participant ID #: 2409	**Attendee:** Samantha Hargrove
Organization: Zenith Investment Group	**Dates of Attendance:** April 14 – April 16

---

13 What is this form used for?

  Ⓐ Applying for a keynote speaker role
  Ⓑ Requesting a network device
  Ⓒ Signing up for a sponsorship program
  Ⓓ Registering for a conference

14 What should participants bring to the registration desk?

  Ⓐ Business card
  Ⓑ Photo ID card
  Ⓒ Passport
  Ⓓ Email confirmation

15 What activity requires separate registration?

  Ⓐ Keynote speech
  Ⓑ Main sessions
  Ⓒ Private workshops
  Ⓓ Networking opportunities

3. Fact/Negative Fact Questions

Overview

선택지로 주어진 문장의 내용이 지문의 내용과 일치하는지를 판단할 것을 요구하는 문제이다. Fact 문제는 지문의 내용과 일치하는 선택지를, Negative Fact는 지문의 내용과 동떨어진 선택지를 고르는 문제이다.

Types of Questions

주로 'indicated about ~', 'true about ~'과 같은 형태로 문제가 제시된다. about의 목적어가 문제의 키워드이므로, 지문에서 이 키워드가 언급되는 곳, 그리고 그 키워드와 관련된 내용을 유심히 봐야 한다.

Fact

What is indicated about the company's security policy?
What does the email indicate about shipping fees?

Negative Fact

According to the passage, all of the following are true about the construction project EXCEPT:

Hackers Strategy

1 지문을 빠르게 훑어보고, 문제에서 묻는 키워드가 어디에 있는지 파악한다.

문제의 'about' 뒤에 나오는 키워드가 지문의 어디에 언급되는지 확인하고, 키워드에 관한 내용을 더 자세히 읽는다.

2 지문의 내용을 올바르게 패러프레이즈한 선택지를 고른다.

지문의 내용이 정답에 그대로 드러나는 경우도 있지만, 패러프레이즈되어 있는 경우도 있다는 점에 유의한다. 따라서 선택지가 지문의 내용을 올바르게 패러프레이즈했는지 확인한 후 선택지를 고른다.

3 자주 나오는 오답 유형에 주의한다.

지문에 아예 언급되지 않은 내용이나 지문의 내용과 반대되는 내용을 제시하는 오답이 자주 출제된다. 또한, 고난도 오답으로는 지문에 언급된 내용이기는 하지만 문제에서 묻는 내용과는 상관없는 오답, 지문에 언급된 단어를 사용하여 혼동을 주는 오답이 등장한다. 반대로 이러한 선택지가 Negative Fact 문제에서는 정답이 된다.

Example

Read a notice.

> Subject: Exam Timetable Update
>
> Dear Students,
>
> The school exam schedule has been updated. All final exams will be held from June 3 to June 10, starting at 9 A.M. each day in Building B. Please check the course portal for your specific subjects and seating arrangements. If you have exam conflicts, email the academic office immediately. Should there be any updates regarding exam locations or dates, we will inform you by email. We work to maintain a fair and organized examination process. Thank you for your cooperation.

What is indicated about seating arrangements?

Ⓐ They might be updated before the exams.
Ⓑ They differ for each exam.
Ⓒ They can be found on the course portal.
Ⓓ They are selected by students.

정답 Ⓒ

해설 좌석 배치에 관한 내용을 묻는 문제이다. 'Please check ~ seating arrangements'를 통해 좌석 배치는 강의 포털(course portal)에서 확인할 수 있음을 알 수 있다. 따라서 Ⓒ가 정답이다.

HACKERS PRACTICE

01 Read a notice.

> A new shuttle bus service will begin on August 25. The bus will operate between Downsview Station and City Hall from 7:00 A.M. to 7:00 P.M., running every 30 minutes. Please note that the service is available on weekdays only. No reservation is required, and there is no charge for using the service.

What does the notice indicate about the shuttle bus service?

Ⓐ It requires a reservation in advance.
Ⓑ It can be used at no cost.
Ⓒ It operates only on weekends.
Ⓓ It is available once an hour.

02 Read an advertisement.

> We are launching a new era in prepared meal solutions with Green Plate, our entry into the plant-based food industry. With our expertise in the food sector, each Green Plate meal is designed with exceptional taste and balanced nutrition. Subscribe by March 24 to get 35 percent off your first two-week trial kit.

What does the advertisement indicate about Green Plate meals?

Ⓐ They are primarily made up of plant.
Ⓑ They must be cooked by consumers.
Ⓒ They are available at major supermarkets.
Ⓓ They are shipped at no cost to customers.

03 Read a notice.

> Dear Customers,
>
> A system upgrade is scheduled, and our online banking services will be unavailable from 9:00 P.M. to 11:00 P.M. on Saturday, March 27. We recommend that customers complete any urgent online transactions before this period. ATM services will not be affected.

What is indicated about the online banking services on the night of March 27?

Ⓐ They will display warning messages.
Ⓑ They will be available only to corporate clients.
Ⓒ They will not accept deposits.
Ⓓ They will be unavailable.

04 Read a news article.

> Elmhurst—The city of Elmhurst is preparing for its upcoming elections. On November 5, residents will go to the ballot boxes to elect a new mayor to replace Sandra Moretti who is retiring after three terms in office.
>
> The race has become heated with more than a dozen candidates vying for office. Currently in the lead is local businessperson David Smith. Recent polls show that Mr. Smith has a five-point lead over his closest rival, city council president Annie Tobin. However, the race will likely result in a run-off election between the two due to electoral rules that require the winning candidate to win at least 50 percent of the total vote. Should a second election be required, it will take place on December 10.

All of the following are true about the election EXCEPT:

Ⓐ It will be held in November.
Ⓑ It is for a city office.
Ⓒ It has two dozen candidates.
Ⓓ It requires a winner to get more than half of the votes.

Answers p.420

HACKERS TEST

[01-02] Read an email.

| Subject: | Maintenance inspection |

Dear Residents,

This is a reminder that the annual maintenance inspection will take place on November 11. Building staff must visit each apartment to look for issues that need to be addressed. Please provide them access to your unit. Thank you for your cooperation.

Stan Leighton
Building Superintendent

01 What is the main purpose of the email?

Ⓐ To announce a change to the inspection schedule
Ⓑ To ask residents to report maintenance issues in their units
Ⓒ To notify staff members about a building maintenance inspection
Ⓓ To remind residents to allow building staff to access their units

02 What does the email indicate about the inspection?

Ⓐ It is voluntary.
Ⓑ It will take 11 days.
Ⓒ It is for safety issues.
Ⓓ It happens every year.

[03-04] Read a news article.

The Dallas Tigers, a popular local baseball team, is getting ready for its season opener on March 15. Coach Brian Radcliffe, who led the Houston Hurricanes to the league championship last season, is thrilled to have signed a contract with his new team. "I am confident we will perform well this year, especially with the last-minute addition of star pitcher Davis Wilkins," he said during a recent interview. "All of the players are training hard, and there is a high level of confidence in the locker room," he added.

To show appreciation to its fans, the team will be handing out free baseball caps to the first 100 people to arrive at the game on March 15. If you want one of these, make sure to show up at the stadium at least an hour before the game begins.

03 What can be inferred about Mr. Radcliffe?

Ⓐ He has not coached a team before.
Ⓑ He used to play baseball in Dallas.
Ⓒ He left the Houston Hurricanes recently.
Ⓓ He has not signed a contract yet.

04 What is indicated about the Dallas Tigers?

Ⓐ It won a league championship.
Ⓑ It recruited a new player.
Ⓒ It upgraded a locker room.
Ⓓ It postponed a training session.

HACKERS TEST

[05-06] Read an advertisement.

Take Your Safety in Your Own Hands

Sign up for private self-defense classes with former army instructor and security expert Matthew Bates.

- More than 30 years of military and commercial teaching experience
- $40 for each 90-minute class
- Classes tailored to individual needs and abilities

Call 555-2327 for more information.

---

05 What is this advertisement promoting?

    Ⓐ Military service
    Ⓑ Security systems
    Ⓒ Group fitness classes
    Ⓓ Protective skills training

06 All of the following are true about Matthew Bates EXCEPT

    Ⓐ He was in the army.
    Ⓑ He charges $40 per hour.
    Ⓒ He customizes his services for each customer.
    Ⓓ He has more than three decades of experience.

[07-09] Read an email.

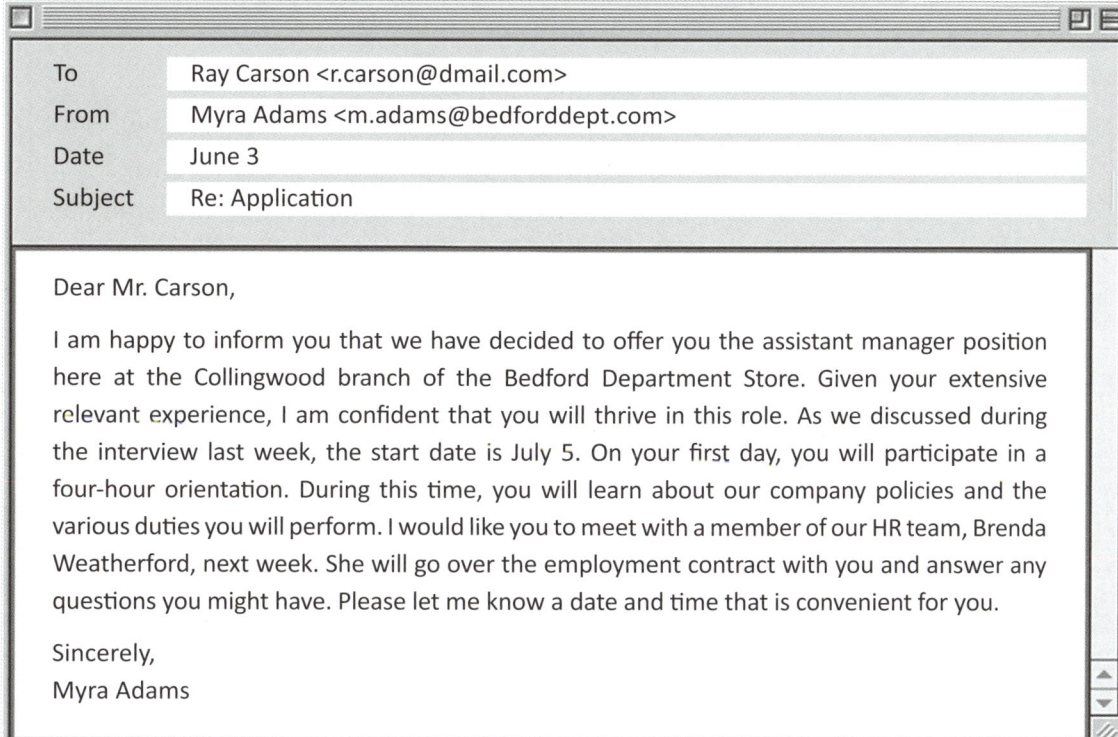

To: Ray Carson <r.carson@dmail.com>
From: Myra Adams <m.adams@bedforddept.com>
Date: June 3
Subject: Re: Application

Dear Mr. Carson,

I am happy to inform you that we have decided to offer you the assistant manager position here at the Collingwood branch of the Bedford Department Store. Given your extensive relevant experience, I am confident that you will thrive in this role. As we discussed during the interview last week, the start date is July 5. On your first day, you will participate in a four-hour orientation. During this time, you will learn about our company policies and the various duties you will perform. I would like you to meet with a member of our HR team, Brenda Weatherford, next week. She will go over the employment contract with you and answer any questions you might have. Please let me know a date and time that is convenient for you.

Sincerely,
Myra Adams

07 What can be inferred about Mr. Carson?

Ⓐ He transferred to another branch.
Ⓑ He requested a start date be changed.
Ⓒ He submitted an application in June.
Ⓓ He worked at a retail outlet before.

08 What will happen on July 5?

Ⓐ A company policy will be updated.
Ⓑ A job interview will be conducted.
Ⓒ A training session will be held.
Ⓓ A team leader will be announced.

09 What does the email indicate about Ms. Weatherford?

Ⓐ She is a member of the management team.
Ⓑ She will discuss a legal agreement with Mr. Carson.
Ⓒ She is the facilitator of the orientation.
Ⓓ She will be Mr. Carson's direct supervisor.

HACKERS TEST

[10-12] Read a social media post.

City of Riverside @RiversideCity | April 21

The big day is quickly approaching. Only 14 days until the 52nd Riverside Fun Run! Are you ready?

The annual race is open to everyone who wishes to participate, whether they want to run, walk, or roll. Participants can choose the 5K or 10K course or the full marathon. Separate winners will be awarded trophies for each race and all who take part will receive a participation certificate, water bottle, and a t-shirt.

But you don't have to race to have fun. We will also have live music, a local vendor show case, and a special play area for children.

Events start at City Hall at 8 A.M. on May 5.
Registration is open until April 30.
Registration fee: $25

All proceeds raised from the event will support city programs providing food for children, seniors, and families in need.

10 What is the main purpose of the post?

  Ⓐ To announce a schedule change
  Ⓑ To promote an upcoming event
  Ⓒ To encourage people to try running
  Ⓓ To raise money for charity

11 What is indicated about the Riverside Fun Run?

  Ⓐ It is being held for the first time.
  Ⓑ It offers only one fixed course distance.
  Ⓒ It is accompanied by side events.
  Ⓓ It includes a special race for children.

12 When will the races be held?

  Ⓐ April 21
  Ⓑ April 30
  Ⓒ May 5
  Ⓓ May 10

[13-15] Read a text-message chain.

Mitch Henderson (2:30 P.M.)
The client presentation for the Melville Industries contract is set for Friday. Could you please update me on your progress?

Rachel Norton (2:33 P.M.)
I've finished the financial projections section. The cost analysis shows that implementing our automation system could cut their operating expenses by 5 percent in the first year alone.

Brandon West (2:36 P.M.)
The technical specifications are complete. I've included detailed timelines for each phase of the installation, including the robotic units and sensor network components.

Catherine Walsh (2:40 P.M.)
I'm drafting the risk assessment report. I've identified a possible safety compliance issue with the automated conveyor systems, so I'm planning to revisit the technical documents.

Brandon West (2:43 P.M.)
Let me know what you need, Catherine. I can send over the latest data.

Mitch Henderson (2:45 P.M.)
Great. To ensure everything is aligned, let's schedule a full rehearsal on Thursday at 3:00 P.M.

13 What is the main purpose of the text chain?

  Ⓐ To gain insight into preparations for a client presentation
  Ⓑ To discuss budget adjustments for a current project
  Ⓒ To review quarterly performance targets with team members
  Ⓓ To schedule regular team meetings for project management

14 At 2:40 P.M., what does Ms. Walsh imply when she writes "I'm planning to revisit the technical documents"?

  Ⓐ She believes the technical specifications are incorrect.
  Ⓑ She needs to check on some equipment in person.
  Ⓒ She intends to delay the risk assessment until Friday.
  Ⓓ She needs to re-examine the technical specifications.

15 All of the following statements are true about the automation system EXCEPT:

  Ⓐ It requires a multi-stage installation.
  Ⓑ It is projected to result in lower operational spending.
  Ⓒ It has previously been cited for safety issues.
  Ⓓ It incorporates mechanized equipment.

Answers p.421

4. Vocabulary Questions

Overview

지문에 주어진 어휘와 의미가 가장 가까운 어휘를 묻는 문제이다. 정답 어휘는 주어진 어휘의 동의어일 수도 있고, 완벽한 동의어는 아니지만 문맥상 의미가 유사한 어휘일 수도 있다.

Types of Questions

Vocabulary 문제는 주로 다음의 형태로 제시된다. 문제에서 묻는 어휘는 지문 내에 음영으로 표시된다.

Vocabulary

The word "proceed" in the passage is closest in meaning to

The phrase "make sure" in the first paragraph is closest in meaning to

Hackers Strategy

1 단어의 사전적 의미를 바탕으로 정답을 고른다.

많은 Vocabulary 문제는 단어의 사전적 의미와 동의어를 알고 있다면 바로 풀 수 있다. 따라서 주어진 단어의 앞뒤 문맥을 확인하기 전에, 선택지 중 주어진 단어의 사전적 동의어가 있는지 확인하고, 정답을 고른다.

2 사전적 의미를 통해 정답을 고를 수 없다면, 자연스러운 문맥을 만드는 선택지를 고른다.

선택지 중 주어진 단어와 완벽한 동의어가 없는 경우, 주어진 단어와 같은 의미로 쓰일 수 있는 단어가 여러 개인 경우, 또는 단어의 의미를 몰라서 정답을 고를 수 없는 경우에는 주어진 단어 자리에 넣었을 때 앞뒤 내용과 가장 자연스러운 문맥을 만드는 선택지를 정답으로 고른다.

Example

Read a news article.

> The cost of generating electricity from renewable methods has plummeted over the last decade, fundamentally changing market dynamics. Technological improvements, driven by intense research and development, have made solar panels and wind turbines far more efficient and significantly cheaper to produce and install. This makes green energy an increasingly compelling and often cheaper alternative to traditional, carbon-intensive power sources for consumers, businesses, and entire utility grids worldwide. The market momentum is now decisively in favor of renewables.

The word "plummeted" in the passage is closest in meaning to

Ⓐ struggled
Ⓑ decreased
Ⓒ hesitated
Ⓓ weakened

정답 Ⓑ

해설 plummeted(급락했다)의 동의어인 decreased(감소했다)를 지문에 넣으면 재생 가능한 방식으로 전기를 생산하는 비용이 줄어들었다는 의미가 되어 문맥상 자연스럽다. 따라서 Ⓑ가 정답이다.

HACKERS PRACTICE

01 Read an email.

> Subject: Mobile Payment Partnership
>
> Dear Mr. Reilly,
>
> Thank you for meeting me yesterday. I was very happy to hear that your company is open to a partnership to develop a new mobile payment application together. I think this will be a lucrative project for both of our companies.
>
> Sincerely,
> Sumin Na

The word "lucrative" in the last sentence is closest in meaning to

Ⓐ cooperative
Ⓑ profitable
Ⓒ arduous
Ⓓ risky

02 Read an email.

> Subject: Accommodations
>
> Dear Sir or Madam,
>
> I would like to get more information about the availability of rooms at your hotel in downtown Montreal.
>
> I work nearby at the headquarters of Monterra Industries. We are hosting some international clients for a meeting and will need to secure accommodations for them from October 6 to October 14. There will be six guests, but two are a couple, so we will need five rooms. We would prefer that they be suites if possible.
>
> Please check your availability for this period and if you have vacancies, let me know what types of rooms they are and what the price would be for all of them, including the cost of your airport shuttle service. I hope to hear from you soon.
>
> Jim Taylor

The word "vacancies" in the third paragraph is closest in meaning to

Ⓐ facilities
Ⓑ halls
Ⓒ openings
Ⓓ reservations

03 Read an email.

> Subject: Order confirmation
>
> Dear Mr. Osborne,
>
> Thank you for choosing OfficeMate for your office equipment needs. We have received your order and, as per your request, will expedite the shipment of the new XJ-2200 printer. You should receive it no later than tomorrow evening.
>
> Katy Griffin, Customer Service Representative

The word "expedite" in the second sentence is closest in meaning to

Ⓐ guarantee
Ⓑ process
Ⓒ review
Ⓓ hasten

04 Read a social media post.

> I just returned from Marrakesh Café and it may be my new favorite restaurant in town. It's unlike anything you'll find elsewhere.
>
> From the moment I walked in, the cozy ambiance and friendly staff made me feel welcome. It was more like visiting a friend's house than going to a restaurant.
>
> Having been to Morocco once before, I knew I wanted to order my favorite dish I had in Casablanca—lamb tagine. Unfortunately, it was already sold out for the day. The waiter gave me some other suggestions that all sounded great. I ended up ordering a stuffed chicken dish called *ferakh maamer*. It was so good that I was actually happy that my first choice wasn't available.
>
> If you're interested in trying something new and delicious, stop by Marrakesh Café! It's open from 11 A.M. to 11 P.M. daily, except for Tuesdays.

The word "ambiance" in the second paragraph is closest in meaning to

Ⓐ location
Ⓑ furniture
Ⓒ decoration
Ⓓ atmosphere

Answers p.424

HACKERS TEST

[01-02] Read an email.

Subject:	Meeting Time Change

Dear Staff,

This afternoon's meeting will be postponed until tomorrow morning due to the number of people out of the office. Please meet in the conference room at 10 A.M. and don't forget to bring your project updates so we can go over them. Thanks.

Max Lipscott, Team Manager

01 What is the main purpose of the email?

   Ⓐ To announce an absence
   Ⓑ To remind of requirements
   Ⓒ To inform of a schedule change
   Ⓓ To inquire about attendance

02 The phrase "go over" in the passage is closest in meaning to

   Ⓐ discuss
   Ⓑ complete
   Ⓒ avoid
   Ⓓ delay

[03-04] Read a notice.

Attention FitPlus Members:

Please be advised that the indoor running track will be closed from May 1 to June 11 for refurbishment. During this time, members are encouraged to use the outdoor running track or other facilities at the gym.

03 The word "refurbishment" in the passage is closest in meaning to

Ⓐ restoration
Ⓑ sanitation
Ⓒ renovation
Ⓓ expansion

04 What can be inferred about FitPlus?

Ⓐ It has multiple running areas.
Ⓑ It will cancel all running classes.
Ⓒ Its members will receive a discount.
Ⓓ Its classes will be held outdoors.

HACKERS TEST

[05-06] Read a poster.

■■■ TECH CAREER DAY ■■■

Are you looking for a job in the technology sector? Then come to the Tech Career Day!

Hundreds of technology companies will be there seeking prospective candidates for jobs in hardware development, programming, AI, and more!

Date: Saturday, July 10
Location: Abramson Center, 442 Northwood Street

05 The word "prospective" in the passage is closest in meaning to

  Ⓐ qualified
  Ⓑ potential
  Ⓒ reputable
  Ⓓ experienced

06 What does the poster suggest about the Tech Career Day?

  Ⓐ It will be held over several days.
  Ⓑ It will provide opportunities to meet numerous employers.
  Ⓒ It includes a lecture on programming.
  Ⓓ It is an annual event.

[07-09] Read a news article.

Potterton, March 28—The city of Potterton is preparing for its annual Tulip Festival, which begins on April 13 this year. The weeklong event celebrates the blooming of nearly 600,000 of the vibrant flowers across the city.

In addition to the garden tours, spring market, and Main Street Tulip Parade featuring vehicles and floats decorated with the flowers, visitors can look forward to a fair for the first time. A variety of amusement park rides and games will be set up at Holmes Park this year. There will also be live music and fireworks displays each night.

City officials hope the expanded options will break past attendance records, possibly even topping one million attendees. According to Mayor Davies, this would make the festival Potterton's biggest tourist draw and bring more than $100 million in revenue to the local economy.

07 What is this article mainly about?

Ⓐ Highlights of this year's Tulip Festival
Ⓑ Potterton's famous tourist draws
Ⓒ The ecology of tulip flowers
Ⓓ The history of Potterton's tourism policy

08 The word "vibrant" in the first paragraph is closest in meaning to

Ⓐ hardy
Ⓑ native
Ⓒ colorful
Ⓓ dramatic

09 What will visitors NOT experience?

Ⓐ Riding an amusement park ride
Ⓑ Visiting gardens
Ⓒ Learning how to grow tulips
Ⓓ Enjoying nightly performances

HACKERS TEST

[10-12] Read an email.

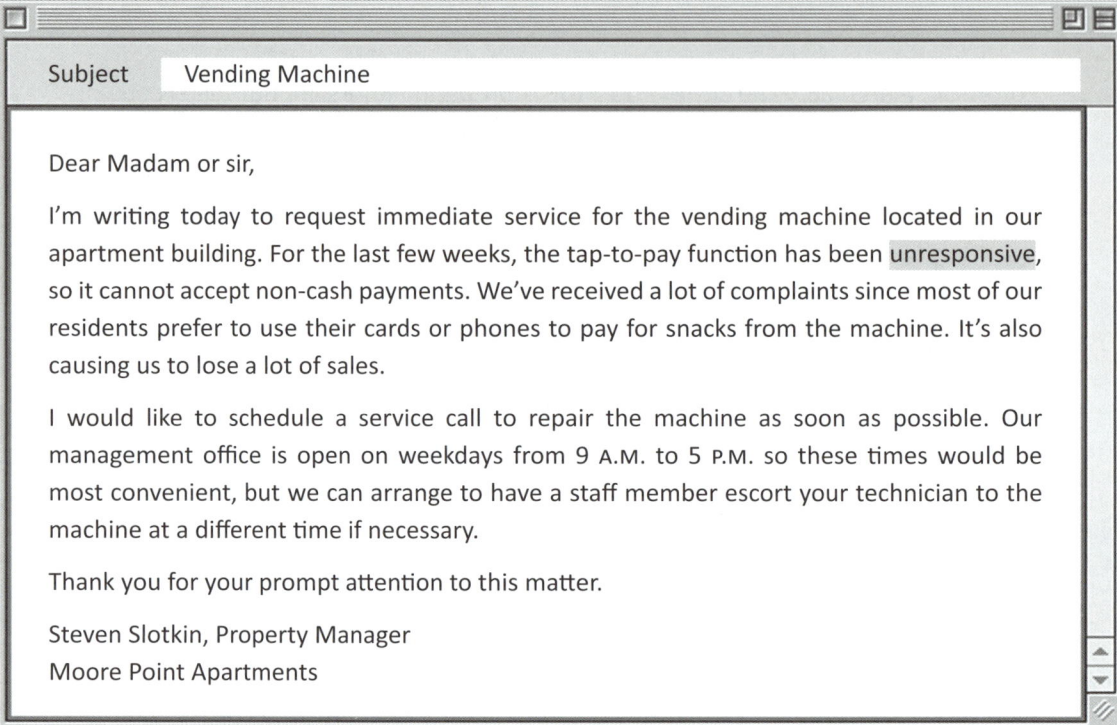

Subject: Vending Machine

Dear Madam or sir,

I'm writing today to request immediate service for the vending machine located in our apartment building. For the last few weeks, the tap-to-pay function has been unresponsive, so it cannot accept non-cash payments. We've received a lot of complaints since most of our residents prefer to use their cards or phones to pay for snacks from the machine. It's also causing us to lose a lot of sales.

I would like to schedule a service call to repair the machine as soon as possible. Our management office is open on weekdays from 9 A.M. to 5 P.M. so these times would be most convenient, but we can arrange to have a staff member escort your technician to the machine at a different time if necessary.

Thank you for your prompt attention to this matter.

Steven Slotkin, Property Manager
Moore Point Apartments

10 What is the main purpose of the email?

Ⓐ To request a cash payment
Ⓑ To highlight a credit card option
Ⓒ To ask for an urgent repair service
Ⓓ To explain the location of a machine

11 The word "unresponsive" in the first paragraph is closest in meaning to

Ⓐ silent
Ⓑ dormant
Ⓒ disconnected
Ⓓ nonfunctional

12 What kind of business does Mr. Slotkin work for?

Ⓐ A credit card company
Ⓑ A housing provider
Ⓒ A machine shop
Ⓓ A snack maker

[13-15] Read a notice.

Attention Residents of Hudson Tower

Multiple tenants have submitted formal complaints about their difficulties in finding parking spots. To address this issue, we will be implementing the following changes to the building's parking policies:

- Effective July 3, each unit will be assigned a single parking space at no charge. Please visit the administration office by this date to secure your space. One additional space per unit may be reserved for a $65 monthly fee. Note that the number of additional spaces is limited, and these will be allocated on a first-come, first-served basis.

- The top floor of our parking facility (30 spaces in total) will be designated as the visitor-only parking area. Vehicles parked here must display a temporary parking pass, which will be issued by the security guard at the entrance to our building's grounds.

We appreciate your understanding in this matter.

---

13 The word "submitted" in the first paragraph is closest in meaning to

Ⓐ appealed
Ⓑ enforced
Ⓒ presented
Ⓓ generated

14 What are tenants required to do by July 3?

Ⓐ Make a request for a reserved spot
Ⓑ Pay a fee at an administration office
Ⓒ Give a visitor's name to a security guard
Ⓓ Confirm availability of an additional space

15 What can be concluded about the parking facility's top floor?

Ⓐ It will be reserved for building employees.
Ⓑ It is currently used for storing equipment.
Ⓒ It is being renovated to optimize its capacity.
Ⓓ It will be off-limits to residents' vehicles.

5. Inference Questions

Overview

Inference 문제는 지문에 주어진 정보를 근거로, 지문에 명확히 드러나지 않은 내용을 추론할 것을 요구하는 문제이다. 짧은 지문과 긴 지문 중, 대개 긴 지문에서 출제되는 유형이다.

Types of Questions

Inference 문제는 보통 What can be inferred로 시작하지만, suggest 동사가 쓰인 문제 중에도 추론이 필요한 문제가 출제될 수 있다.

Inference

What can be inferred about the seminar participants?

What is suggested about Mr. Malek's travel plans?

Hackers Strategy

1 문제에서 묻는 키워드를 지문에서 찾는다.

문제에서 묻는 키워드, 즉 "What can be inferred about _____?"에서 about의 목적어 부분이 지문의 어디에 제시되었는지 찾는다. 문제에서 묻는 키워드가 지문 전반의 주제에 해당하여 정답의 단서를 찾는 데 도움이 되지 못하는 문제도 있을 수 있다. 이때는 각 선택지의 키워드가 지문의 어디에 언급되어 있는지를 확인한다.

2 앞뒤에 주어진 정보와 문맥을 바탕으로, 올바르게 추론한 선택지를 고른다.

보통은 특정 문장을 근거로 추론할 수 있지만, 간혹 두 문장 이상을 확인해야 추론할 수 있는 문제가 출제될 수도 있다. 따라서 키워드 앞뒤의 내용도 확인하며 선택지의 내용을 추론할 수 있는지 확인한다.

3 자주 나오는 오답 유형에 주의한다.

지문의 내용과 반대되는 내용을 제시하는 오답, 지문에 아예 언급되지 않은 내용을 제시하는 오답이 자주 출제된다. 또한, 고난도 오답으로는 지문에 언급된 내용이기는 하지만 문제에서 묻는 내용과는 상관없는 오답, 지문의 내용과 일부만 일치하는 오답이 등장한다.

Example

Read a notice.

> The university gym will begin a major upgrade project on September 5 and is expected to finish by October 25. This project aims to install new equipment, expand the weight room, and add a dedicated group fitness studio. The gym undergoes small-scale maintenance and updates every winter break. However, this larger-scale upgrade was planned after a recent survey of campus fitness needs.
>
> During this time, all gym facilities will be closed. Scheduled classes and team practices will be held at alternate locations, and affected participants will receive separate notifications. Regular updates regarding progress will be communicated through the university website.

What can be inferred about the gym facility?

Ⓐ It undergoes routine improvements every year.
Ⓑ It will be significantly larger after the work.
Ⓒ It will be the only gym available after the upgrade.
Ⓓ It is not used for classes.

정답 Ⓐ

해설 체육관 시설에 대해 추론할 수 있는 것을 묻는 문제이다. 'The gym undergoes ~ every winter break'를 통해 매년 겨울방학마다 소규모 유지보수 및 개선이 진행됨을 알 수 있고, 이를 통해 매년 개선이 이루어짐을 추론할 수 있다. 따라서 Ⓐ가 정답이다.

HACKERS PRACTICE

01 Read a notice.

Attention Customers

Due to limited supply, the recently released PlayBox video game console will be limited to one per customer. We appreciate your understanding as we work to ensure more customers have the opportunity to purchase the system.

What can be inferred about the PlayBox video game console?

Ⓐ It replaces an earlier model.
Ⓑ It is in high demand.
Ⓒ It must be reserved in advance.
Ⓓ It can only be played by one person.

02 Read an email.

To: meganwoods@hmail.com
From: careers@globaltechsolutions.com
Subject: Interview Invitation

Dear Ms. Woods,

Thank you for your interest in the marketing specialist position at GlobalTech Solutions. We were impressed by your background in digital marketing and would like to invite you to an interview to discuss your application further. We are actively seeking a talented individual to fill the vacancy as we expand our digital presence, and your profile aligns well with our needs.

We would like to schedule an interview for Thursday, February 22, at 3:00 P.M. The interview will be held at our office located in the Apex Building, 500 Venture Plaza. During the interview, we will explore your qualifications, past experience, and understanding of the role. We will also discuss the compensation as well as the anticipated start date.

Please confirm your availability. If you are unable to attend in person, we can arrange for a video interview instead. We look forward to hearing from you soon.

Best regards,
Cassian Walker

What can be inferred about the marketing specialist position at GlobalTech Solutions?

Ⓐ It requires extensive travel.
Ⓑ It is currently vacant.
Ⓒ It offers flexible working hours.
Ⓓ It is a managerial position.

03 Read a notice.

> **RECALL WARNING**
>
> Due to potential contamination, all Lindendale Farms sausages manufactured on December 10 are being recalled. Customers are warned not to consume these products under any circumstances. Please return sausages with this manufacturing date to the place of purchase for a new package whether they have been opened or not.

What can be inferred about Lindendale Farms sausages?

Ⓐ They cannot be returned if they have been opened.
Ⓑ They should be destroyed by the purchaser.
Ⓒ They are sold at only one store.
Ⓓ They can be consumed if made on a different day.

04 Read a social media post.

> **Erin McCarthy**
>
> Last week, I joined the city's Sunday walking tour program. It was a way to experience familiar streets in a new light. We wandered through historic neighborhoods, where the old architecture told stories of past generations. Colorful wall paintings added bursts of creativity and character to otherwise ordinary streets. We even visited an outdoor gallery with intriguing works from emerging artists.
>
> This tour offered a combination of physical activity, exploration, and social connection—all without leaving the city limits. Walking nearly eight kilometers, I felt both energized and reflective. The guide shared fascinating insights about the city's history, and finishing with a group lunch added a warm, communal touch.
>
> The route changes every week, so there's always something new to discover. If you're looking for a way to uncover hidden corners of the city you thought you knew, give it a try! You can easily sign up for the event online through the city's website.

What is suggested about the city's walking tour?

Ⓐ It is offered during the evening hours.
Ⓑ Its participants must bring their own refreshments.
Ⓒ It is held every week.
Ⓓ Its guides are certified in history.

Answers p.427

HACKERS TEST

[01-02] Read a news article.

> Baytown—Jefferson Avenue will be closed between 9 A.M. and 6 P.M. on Saturday, July 10 due to the Founder's Day Parade. Drivers should make plans for alternative routes. Those planning to attend the event are encouraged to use the subway system.

01 What are drivers advised to do?

  Ⓐ Leave early in the morning
  Ⓑ Park near the parade route
  Ⓒ Avoid the closed street
  Ⓓ Take the subway instead

02 What can be inferred about the Founder's Day Parade?

  Ⓐ It is expected to be attended by many people.
  Ⓑ It takes place all over Baytown.
  Ⓒ Its route is expected to vary.
  Ⓓ Its location is accessible from a subway station.

[03-04] Read an invoice.

INVOICE:

Premier Solutions
482 S. Washington St.
555-2123

Invoice#: 0148-249150
Date: February 4
Bill to: Peak Energy Consultants

Service	Rate	Amount
Network Install	$250/hr	$2,500
System Training (group)	$200/hr	$600
Total Due:		$3,100

Terms: Payment due within 30 days. Late accounts will be assessed a 10 percent fee.

Thank you for choosing
Premier Solutions

03 What type of service did Peak Energy Consultants purchase?

Ⓐ Network installation
Ⓑ Individual training
Ⓒ Payment processing
Ⓓ Energy consulting

04 What can be inferred about Premier Solutions?

Ⓐ It offers group discounts.
Ⓑ It specializes in energy-efficient systems.
Ⓒ It is an IT company.
Ⓓ It accepts various payments.

HACKERS TEST

[05-06] Read a notice.

To: All Employees
Subject: Leave Requests
Date: August 15

Effective September 1, the minimum required notice for a leave request will be increased from two weeks to three. The goal is to minimize disruptions to projects. Please speak with our team member, Jared Andrews, if you have any questions. Our office is in Room 403. Thank you.

Violet Parson
Human Resources Manager

---

05 What is the main purpose of the notice?

Ⓐ To extend a project deadline
Ⓑ To introduce a department goal
Ⓒ To request a status update
Ⓓ To announce a policy change

06 What can be inferred about Mr. Andrews?

Ⓐ He moved into a new office recently.
Ⓑ He belongs to the human resources team.
Ⓒ He is Ms. Parson's immediate supervisor.
Ⓓ He was assigned to a different position.

[07-09] Read a news article.

Museum Showcases Cajun Culture and History

August 28—The Beaumont Heritage Foundation has opened its new Museum of Cajun Culture, a facility focused on the history of the region's Acadian people. The new museum features displays of rare documents, photographs, and artifacts that trace the group from its expulsion from East Coast Canada to the modern day.

Housed in a fully restored traditional home on a homestead established in 1765, the museum offers visitors a first-hand view of what life was like for the early settlers. Staff dressed in period costumes also conduct demonstrations to show how difficult it would have been to tame the wild landscape in which they found themselves.

The Foundation hopes the museum will attract visitors interested in the region's unique history and ignite cultural pride in local residents. It is open from Tuesday to Sunday from 10 A.M. to 6 P.M. and will offer special events on local and national holidays.

07 What is the main topic of the article?

Ⓐ The history of the region
Ⓑ A unique local culture
Ⓒ Some recently discovered artifacts
Ⓓ A newly opened museum

08 What can be inferred about early settlers from the article?

Ⓐ They came from multiple regions.
Ⓑ They found the area easy to live in.
Ⓒ They mixed with other local cultures.
Ⓓ They arrived in the eighteenth century.

09 The word "ignite" in the final paragraph is closest in meaning to

Ⓐ prepare
Ⓑ define
Ⓒ awaken
Ⓓ verify

HACKERS TEST

[10-12] Read a web page.

10 What is the main purpose of the page?

   Ⓐ To discuss a foreign cuisine
   Ⓑ To review the city's dining scene
   Ⓒ To give a recipe for an Asian dish
   Ⓓ To recommend a newly opened restaurant

11 What can be inferred about the dishes tried?

   Ⓐ They were cheaper than those of other places.
   Ⓑ They were served in small quantities.
   Ⓒ They all contained some kind of lamb.
   Ⓓ They were recommended by the staff.

12 What was provided at no cost?

   Ⓐ A decorative tile
   Ⓑ A sweet treat
   Ⓒ A guide to Uzbek food
   Ⓓ A traditional plate

[13-15] Read a news article.

During a recent press conference, Mayor Roberts announced that approval for a 500-unit apartment complex on the property next to Anderson Park has been granted by city council. The developer will begin building the structure on March 28. Mayor Roberts claimed that the project will attract new residents and businesses to the city. "I'm very proud to have been able to launch this development before the end of my term and my retirement from politics," she explained.

Despite her excitement, many residents of the Mulberry Heights neighborhood have expressed opposition to the project, arguing that it will lead to increased traffic congestion and other problems. In response, the city government has posted a survey on its website and is asking everyone living in Mulberry Heights to fill it out. Once their feedback is reviewed, policies to address concerns will be considered.

13 What is the main topic of the article?

Ⓐ The opening of a recreation facility
Ⓑ The construction of a housing complex
Ⓒ The revision of a government policy
Ⓓ The results of a property inspection

14 What can be inferred about Mayor Roberts?

Ⓐ She owns land next to Anderson Park.
Ⓑ She does not plan to run for reelection.
Ⓒ She intends to leave Mulberry Heights next year.
Ⓓ She does not have city council's support.

15 Residents of the Mulberry Heights neighborhood have been asked to

Ⓐ read feedback on a website
Ⓑ participate in a meeting
Ⓒ complete a questionnaire
Ⓓ review a business proposal

Answers p.428

6. Intention Questions

Overview

지문의 특정 어구나 문장 또는 특정 정보가 지문의 문맥과 상황 속에서 어떤 의도나 의미를 나타내는지 묻는 문제이다. 메시지 대화문이나 이메일 지문에서 특히 자주 출제되며, 문제에서 묻는 문장은 구어체 표현을 사용할 수도 있다.

Types of Questions

Intention 문제는 4가지 세부 유형으로 분류할 수 있다.

Phrase Meaning

What does the phrase 'project rollout' most likely mean in this context?

Sentence Meaning

At 2:20 P.M., what does Mr. Humphreys most likely mean when he writes, "You might want to double-check the figures"?

Purpose

Why does the message mention an attached file?

Attitude

What does Carla's mention of "being willing to take on extra work" suggest about her attitude?

Hackers Strategy

1 문제에서 언급한 어구나 문장을 찾아, 그 표면적 의미를 확인한다.

어구나 문장의 의미를 우선 확인한 후, 선택지 중 표면적 의미와 크게 어긋나는 것부터 우선 소거한다.

2 어구나 문장의 앞뒤의 문맥을 통해 그 의미를 추론한다.

표면적 의미가 같다고 해도, 앞뒤의 문맥에 따라 실제로 나타내는 의미는 다를 수 있다. 따라서 앞뒤 문장의 내용 및 의미 관계를 확인하여 실제 의미를 추론한다.

3 자주 나오는 오답 유형에 주의한다.

지문의 내용과 관련이 있는 키워드를 사용해서 혼동을 주는 오답, 상황에 따라서는 정답이 될 수 있지만 지문에서 제시된 상황과 문맥에서는 답이 될 수 없는 오답이 자주 출제된다.

Example

Read a notice.

> Please be advised that the parking lot behind the West Building will be closed on Saturday, August 16th, due to routine maintenance. All vehicles must be removed by 8:00 P.M. on Friday. The lot will reopen at 6:00 A.M. on Sunday. During this time, employees and visitors should use the East parking lot. Thank you for your cooperation.

Why does the notice mention the East parking lot?

Ⓐ To provide directions for maintenance staff
Ⓑ To notify about a special event
Ⓒ To explain a change in parking fees
Ⓓ To suggest an alternative parking lot

정답　Ⓓ

해설　동쪽 주차장을 언급한 이유를 묻는 문제이다. 'the parking lot ~ will be closed'를 통해 서쪽 빌딩의 주차장이 폐쇄될 것이라고 했고, 'During this time ~ the East parking lot'을 통해 그 기간에는 동쪽 주차장을 이용하라는 내용임을 알 수 있다. 따라서 Ⓓ가 정답이다.

HACKERS PRACTICE

01 Read an email.

> Subject: Catering confirmation
>
> Dear Ms. Leigh,
>
> We are confirming your catering order for Thursday's workshop. To ensure all dietary restrictions are met with accuracy and quality, please send any updates by 5:00 P.M. today. Our kitchen requires the final confirmation this evening. We appreciate your prompt response.
>
> Derek Halloway

What does Mr. Halloway's mention of requiring "the final confirmation this evening" suggest about his attitude?

Ⓐ He worries that Ms. Leigh will forget to provide updates.
Ⓑ He is concerned that the requested meal quality cannot be achieved.
Ⓒ He wants to stress the final deadline.
Ⓓ He is willing to accept changes well past the specified deadline.

02 Read a text-message chain.

> **Madison Bennett (1:00 P.M.)** Hello, team. Just a reminder that the Data Literacy Training session is next Tuesday. Please make sure all preparation tasks are completed by Monday morning.
>
> **Liam King (1:05 P.M.)** OK, Madison. I'm finalizing the "Bias and Ethical Considerations in Data" part, and I will upload it today.
>
> **Riley Hayes (1:10 P.M.)** I'll finish preparing the "Interactive Data Storytelling" case studies and share them with everyone by Monday morning.
>
> **Noah Cardew (1:15 P.M.)** I have an off-site meeting on Friday, but I will complete integrating the basic data analysis techniques slides over the weekend.
>
> **Madison Bennett (1:20 P.M.)** Thank you all for being so proactive! Your hard work will give us time to review everything before the training.

At 1:20 P.M., what does Ms. Bennett most likely mean when she writes, "Thank you all for being so proactive"?

Ⓐ She is urging the team to complete their tasks more quickly.
Ⓑ She is commending the team's plans to finish before the deadline.
Ⓒ She is thanking the team for sending messages promptly.
Ⓓ She appreciates the team's willingness to attend optional social gatherings.

03 Read a news article.

GIA Express Set to Open

Greenville—The City Transportation Director has announced that the new airport rail line will open on Monday, June 1. The service will connect Greenville International Airport (GIA) to the city's central transportation hub from which travelers can connect to the main subway system or to the nationwide rail and bus networks.

The GIA Express will offer only non-stop service and complete the 40-mile trip in just under 15 minutes. Trains will depart in either direction every 20 minutes from 5:00 A.M. to 11:00 P.M. Tickets will be $10 per person each way or $18 for a round trip. $2 discounts on all fares will be offered to children under 10 years of age, senior citizens, and the disabled.

What does the term 'transportation hub' most likely mean in this context?

Ⓐ A location where people can reserve transportation
Ⓑ A location where international transportation services are offered
Ⓒ A location where transportation executives work
Ⓓ A location where different transportation options meet

04 Read a news article.

Nexus Data Solutions, the local financial technology powerhouse, announced a technological alliance with Frankfurt-based Pinnacle Consulting yesterday. This strategic move will see Nexus Data bolster its cyber-risk and compliance capabilities by integrating a specialist team focused on pioneering digital security standards for the financial sector. To prepare for this strategic integration, Nexus Data's primary development facility in One North is set for a major upgrade.

Nexus Data Solutions cemented its global reputation by consistently outperforming competitors in three successive global security audits for major central banks. However, few realize that the company's very first project was a pro-bono initiative—developing a secure data management platform for local non-profits—a legacy it continues to honor through its small independent grant foundation in Mumbai.

Why does the article mention a grant foundation?

Ⓐ To acknowledge the firm's commitment to pro-bono work
Ⓑ To explain the rationale behind its technological alliance with Pinnacle Consulting
Ⓒ To forecast the company's future revenue growth in the financial sector
Ⓓ To describe the major physical upgrade of the One North facility

Answers p.430

HACKERS TEST

[01-02] Read a notice.

Lost and Found Procedure

If you misplace a personal item, please go to the security office immediately to file a report. You must fill out the official form and provide a detailed description. This step is necessary to initiate a fast search and secure its return.

01 Why does the notice mention the security office?

Ⓐ To explain the office's daily working hours
Ⓑ To state the cost of filing a report
Ⓒ To provide contact information
Ⓓ To inform readers where to file a report

02 What should people do to initiate a fast search?

Ⓐ Fill out an official form
Ⓑ File a police report
Ⓒ Call the manager
Ⓓ Check the lost and found list online

[03-04] Read an email.

| Subject: | Invoice Review |

Dear PrintMaster Inc. Billing Team,

I received an invoice for 50 units of the "ProPrint" printers. The invoice lists the shipping fee as $125, whereas the quoted amount was $50. Please double-check the entire invoice for any other potential errors and issue a revised one. I will process payment after receiving the corrected invoice.

Sincerely,

Emma Carrow
Acme Technologies

03 The word "quoted" in the passage is closest in meaning to

Ⓐ estimated
Ⓑ excessive
Ⓒ finalized
Ⓓ overdue

04 What does Ms. Carrow's mention of processing "payment after receiving the corrected invoice" suggest about her attitude?

Ⓐ She is pointing out that the shipping address was incorrectly entered.
Ⓑ She is expressing dissatisfaction with the quoted amount.
Ⓒ She is showing that additional errors may be included in the invoice.
Ⓓ She is suggesting that a shipping discount was not applied.

HACKERS TEST

[05-06] Read a sign.

FALL BOOK FAIR

Discover your next favorite read at Regency Books's Fall Book Fair!

Great deals available on all books (both new and used), gift packages, and stationery in stock.

Dates: Friday, October 3 - Sunday, October 5

Location: 1724-E Second Avenue

Come browse our inventory, you never know what you'll find!

05 What will NOT be included in the event?

  Ⓐ Used books
  Ⓑ Gift sets
  Ⓒ Items for writing
  Ⓓ E-reader devices

06 What does the phrase "great deals" most likely mean in this context?

  Ⓐ Low prices
  Ⓑ Large numbers
  Ⓒ Exclusive offers
  Ⓓ Good resolutions

[07-09] Read a text-message chain.

Melissa Watson (9:40 A.M.) Hello, team. Please note that the presentation on the mobile payment system update proposal is next Friday. Are we totally set with the final slides and demo?

Ben Klein (9:45 A.M.) The technical integration slides are finished, and the new checkout flow demo runs smoothly. Files are on the shared drive.

Lisa Payne (9:50 A.M.) The improvements to the user experience are clearly highlighted. I'll also focus on the improved user feedback with the new interface.

Melissa Watson (9:55 A.M.) Thank you, Ben and Lisa. Vanessa, what about the security part?

Vanessa Reed (9:57 A.M.) I'll emphasize the security upgrades, which will dramatically reduce transaction errors. I'll also handle any questions about future user growth.

Melissa Watson (10:01 A.M.) Perfect. That should impress the executive team. See you at the conference room at 3 P.M. for the prep session.

07 At 10:01 A.M., what does Melissa Watson most likely mean when she writes, "That should impress the executive team"?

Ⓐ She thinks that the executive team should be concerned about the security issues.
Ⓑ She is concerned that the presentation slides are incomplete.
Ⓒ She is indicating that the team should add more data on user satisfaction.
Ⓓ She believes the content will be very well received.

08 What can be inferred about the mobile payment system?

Ⓐ It is currently prone to payment errors.
Ⓑ It requires special hardware devices to process payments.
Ⓒ Its interface is a major source of user dissatisfaction.
Ⓓ Its design is based on a competitor's platform.

09 What will NOT be updated in the mobile payment system?

Ⓐ Checkout process
Ⓑ User interface
Ⓒ Refund management system
Ⓓ Security system

HACKERS TEST

[10-12] Read a notice.

To promote safe drone flying, the city government designated Elmford Park for recreational drone use. Flying is permitted daily from 9:00 A.M. to sunset, and only drones weighing less than 55 pounds are permitted.

Please operate only inside the boundary markers. For safety, keep your device under 120 meters in altitude, maintain visual line of sight at all times, and never fly over people. In addition, to preserve situational awareness, avoid using headsets that block surrounding sounds or your field of view. Also, please yield to others so everyone can share the area comfortably.

Check cityofelmford.gov/parks for a full list of rules and regulations regarding the park and drone usage.

10 What is the main purpose of the notice?

Ⓐ To advertise workshops on professional drone photography
Ⓑ To inform residents about new citywide drone regulations
Ⓒ To provide rules for recreational drone use in a park
Ⓓ To announce an upcoming drone festival

11 What is NOT a requirement for drone operators at Elmford Park?

Ⓐ Staying within the marked boundary
Ⓑ Operating only during the designated hours
Ⓒ Allowing others to use the area
Ⓓ Registering as a drone operator

12 What does the phrase "maintain visual line of sight" most likely mean in this context?

Ⓐ Allow others to watch the drone while it is flying
Ⓑ Keep the drone within eyesight at all times
Ⓒ Use binoculars to extend viewing distance
Ⓓ Keep the drone out of sight from other park visitors

[13-15] Read a text-message chain.

Jessica Martinez (3:15 P.M.) The regional marketing conference is next month. Let's get a quick update on everyone's progress.

Robert Chang (3:18 P.M.) I've prepared the opening session on market trends. The slides include our third quarter analysis and industry forecasts.

Amanda Foster (3:22 P.M.) My session on customer engagement strategies is ready. I'll need the conference room set up with the interactive display by 2:00 P.M.

Emilio Santos (3:25 P.M.) The networking lunch has been arranged. Catering for 150 attendees is confirmed, and the venue layout is set.

Jessica Martinez (3:28 P.M.) Excellent progress, everyone. Emilio, have you received confirmation from the keynote speaker yet?

Emilio Santos (3:30 P.M.) I'm still waiting on Dr. Newsom's personal schedule. Her assistant said she'll confirm by tomorrow morning.

Jessica Martinez (3:33 P.M.) We should have a backup plan ready. Last year's conference taught us a lesson.

13 What is Mr. Santos's responsibility?

Ⓐ Setting up interactive displays for sessions
Ⓑ Handling the keynote speaker's travel arrangements
Ⓒ Organizing the networking lunch
Ⓓ Confirming conference room bookings

14 At 3:33 P.M., what does Ms. Martinez imply when she writes, "Last year's conference taught us a lesson"?

Ⓐ They faced difficulties requiring alternative arrangements.
Ⓑ They managed all conference logistics smoothly.
Ⓒ They received positive feedback from participants.
Ⓓ They learned useful presentation techniques from other speakers.

15 What can be inferred about the conference?

Ⓐ It will have 150 attendees.
Ⓑ It is an online webinar.
Ⓒ Its venue has been changed.
Ⓓ Its keynote speaker has canceled her attendance.

Answers p.431

무료 토플자료·유학정보 제공
goHackers.com

… Hackers
Updated TOEFL
READING

Section II
Passage Types

Section II에서는 TASK 2에 자주 등장하는 지문 형태를 중심으로 각 세부 단원을 구성하였다. TASK 2에는 일상 생활에서 접할 수 있는 다양한 글이 출제되는데, 크게 이메일, 문자 메시지, 공지, 광고, 소셜 미디어 게시물, 뉴스 기사, 각종 양식으로 나눌 수 있다.

TASK 2의 Passage Types에는 다음의 7가지가 있다.

1. Email
2. Text-Message Chain
3. Notice
4. Advertisement
5. Social Media Post
6. News Article
7. Form

1. Email

Overview

이메일은 일상 생활, 직장, 학교 등에서 흔히 접할 수 있는 상황을 다룬다. 보통 도입부에서 글의 목적을, 본론에서 세부 사항을 설명한다. 첫인사 앞에 제목이 있을 수도 있다. 이메일의 제목이 단서가 되는 문제도 있으므로, 제목도 확인하는 것이 좋다.

Topics

예약 확인   예약 내역, 수업 등록 내역 등을 확인하는 이메일
공지   행사 개최, 점검 일정 등을 공지하는 이메일
홍보   제품 출시, 개업 등을 홍보하는 이메일
요청   직원 간에 업무상 필요한 사항을 요청하는 이메일

Types of Questions

Main Topic/   이메일을 보낸 목적을 묻는 문제가 출제된다.
Main Purpose   What is the main purpose of the email?
                     Why did Ms. Price send the email to Mr. Morales?

Detail   이메일에 언급된 날짜나 요청 사항을 묻는 문제가 자주 출제된다.
                     When is the date of the product launch?
                     What is Mr. Moore asked to do for Thursday's meeting?

Inference   이메일에 언급된 사람이나 특정 사항에 관해 추론하는 문제가 자주 출제된다.
                     What can be inferred about Ms. Cooper?
                     What can be inferred about the technical demonstration?

Example

Read an email.

To: danielspencer@sqmail.com
From: susanbaxter@sqmail.com
Date: August 11
Subject: Department Meeting

Dear Mr. Spencer,

[1]I am writing to notify you about the upcoming department meeting scheduled for Monday, August 25, at 2:00 P.M. in Conference Room B of the main office.

The meeting will address finalizing budget allocations for the second half of the year and review updates to project timelines.

[2]Please bring a copy of your latest budget report and be prepared to discuss progress on current initiatives.

If you have specific topics to include in the agenda, please email them to me by Friday, August 22. For questions or concerns, contact me at 555-1147.

Best regards,
Susan Baxter

- 목적
- 세부 사항
- 요청 사항
- 끝인사

1. What is the main purpose of the email?

Ⓐ To explain the details of a meeting
Ⓑ To announce a new office policy
Ⓒ To request feedback on a report
Ⓓ To confirm a budget decision

2. What should Mr. Spencer bring?

Ⓐ An annual review
Ⓑ A new business proposal
Ⓒ A recent fiscal overview
Ⓓ A progress report

정답 1. Ⓐ   2. Ⓒ

해설 1. 글을 작성한 목적을 묻는 문제이다. 'I am writing ~ department meeting'을 통해 부서 회의에 관해 알리기 위한 글임을 알 수 있다. 따라서 Ⓐ가 정답이다.

2. Mr. Spencer가 지참해야 하는 것을 묻는 문제이다. 'Please bring ~ budget report'를 통해 예산 보고서를 가지고 가야 함을 알 수 있다. 따라서 Ⓒ가 정답이다.

HACKERS TEST

[01-02] Read an email.

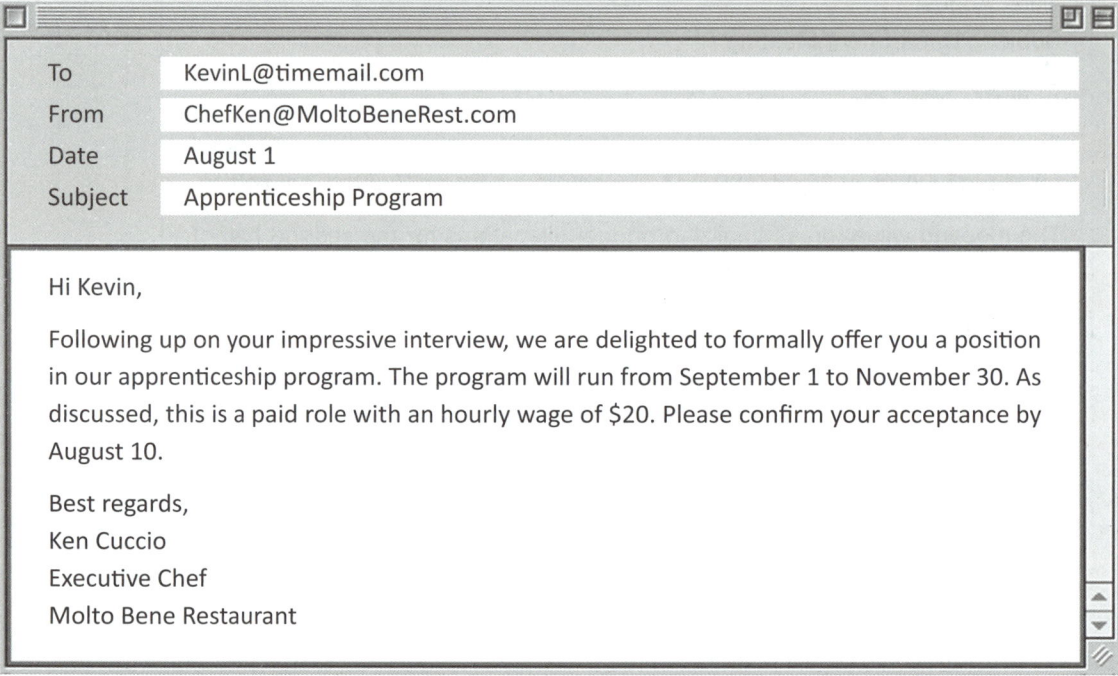

To	KevinL@timemail.com
From	ChefKen@MoltoBeneRest.com
Date	August 1
Subject	Apprenticeship Program

Hi Kevin,

Following up on your impressive interview, we are delighted to formally offer you a position in our apprenticeship program. The program will run from September 1 to November 30. As discussed, this is a paid role with an hourly wage of $20. Please confirm your acceptance by August 10.

Best regards,
Ken Cuccio
Executive Chef
Molto Bene Restaurant

01 What is the main purpose of the email?

Ⓐ To offer a job to a candidate
Ⓑ To discuss the employment period
Ⓒ To arrange a follow-up interview
Ⓓ To provide a list of required supplies

02 When is the first day of the program?

Ⓐ August 1
Ⓑ August 10
Ⓒ September 1
Ⓓ November 30

[03-04] Read an email.

Subject:	Rescheduling of Your Dance Class

Dear Mr. Clark,

The October 26 5:00 P.M. dance class you registered for has been rescheduled due to a sudden conflict with the instructor's personal schedule. The session will now be held on October 28 at 6:00 P.M. If this new time does not work for you, your registration fee will be fully refunded.

Best regards,
Sophie Allen

03 Why was the dance class rescheduled?

Ⓐ The dance studio needed urgent repairs.
Ⓑ The instructor had an unexpected schedule change.
Ⓒ The original class was canceled due to low enrollment.
Ⓓ The dance studio had a scheduling conflict with another event.

04 When is the revised date and time for the dance class?

Ⓐ October 26 at 5:00 P.M.
Ⓑ October 26 at 6:00 P.M.
Ⓒ October 28 at 5:00 P.M.
Ⓓ October 28 at 6:00 P.M.

HACKERS TEST

[05-06] Read an email.

TO	Service@ForthAir.com
FROM	ABKant@mailape.com
DATE	August 9
SUBJECT	Baggage compensation

To whom it may concern,

I still haven't received my checked baggage from my flight on August 7. Luckily, I had a few changes of clothes in my carry-on, but I'm running out of them. I need to know whether I can get compensation by tomorrow.

Thank you,

Abigail Kant

05 When was Ms. Kant's flight?

Ⓐ August 7
Ⓑ August 8
Ⓒ August 9
Ⓓ August 10

06 What can be inferred about Ms. Kant?

Ⓐ She is a regular customer.
Ⓑ She had multiple bags.
Ⓒ She received payment already.
Ⓓ She bought expensive clothing.

[07-09] Read an email.

Subject:	ATM Service Request

Dear SmartATM Service Group Support Team,

This is an urgent service request for our lobby ATM (Unit #4721) at the Turner Plaza Branch. Since approximately 9:15 A.M. today, the unit has been failing all withdrawal attempts, displaying the error: "Unable to process transaction – contact support" although it is fully stocked with cash. Other functions like balance inquiries are still working normally.

This malfunction is significantly disrupting service during our peak morning hours. To manage the disruption, we are currently redirecting customers to our nearby locations.

We require the dispatch of a technician to diagnose and repair this issue. Please confirm their estimated time of arrival.

Contact me directly at 1-555-3321-7890 for coordination upon dispatch. Thank you for your prompt attention.

Best regards,

Emily Carter
Branch Operations Manager
Continental Bridge Bank

07 What is the main purpose of the email?

Ⓐ To demand prompt service due to a system error
Ⓑ To outline a strategy for handling customer service
Ⓒ To ask for advice on repairing a malfunctioning machine
Ⓓ To schedule a routine maintenance check

08 What did the Turner Plaza Branch do before sending the email?

Ⓐ It contacted the support line to log the error code.
Ⓑ It guided customers to alternative bank locations.
Ⓒ It received confirmation of the technician's estimated arrival time.
Ⓓ It conducted a thorough review of the ATM unit.

09 What can be inferred about the lobby ATM?

Ⓐ The component involved in dispensing cash has failed.
Ⓑ It is currently out of service because of a network outage.
Ⓒ It has run out of cash and cannot dispense money.
Ⓓ It will be completely replaced by a technician today.

HACKERS TEST

[10-12] Read an email.

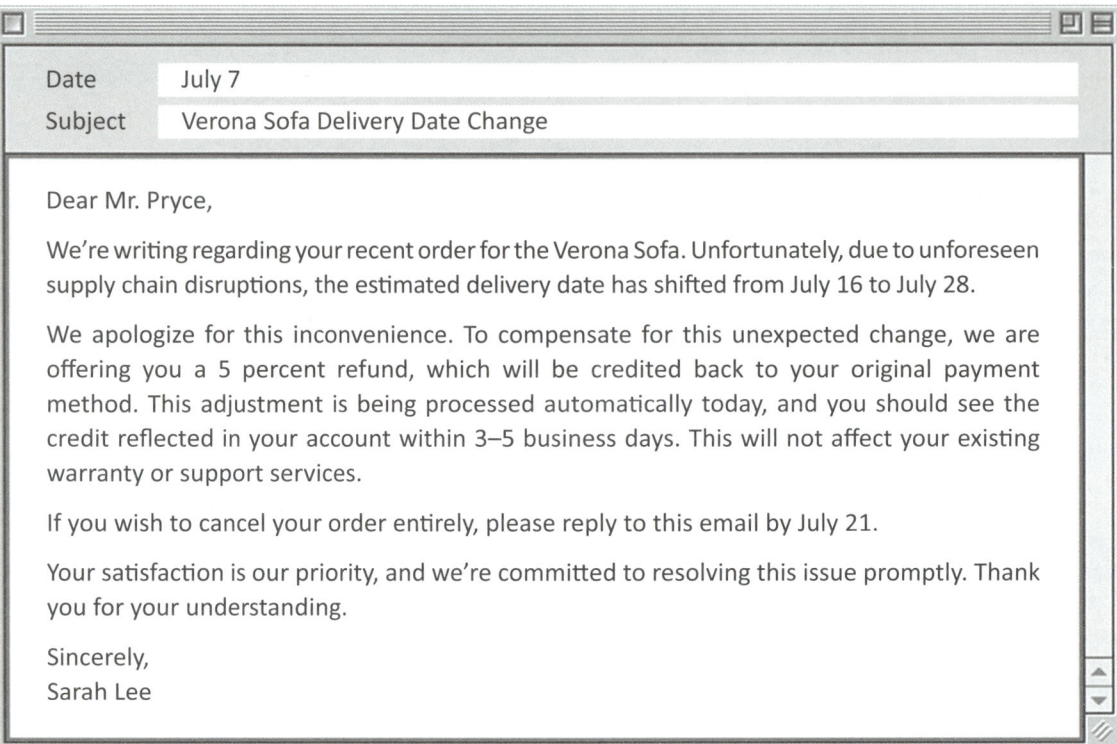

10 What does the company offer to do?

Ⓐ Change the delivery company
Ⓑ Extend the product warranty
Ⓒ Give a discount on a future purchase
Ⓓ Provide monetary compensation

11 What was the original delivery date?

Ⓐ July 7
Ⓑ July 16
Ⓒ July 21
Ⓓ July 28

12 What should Mr. Pryce do in order to cancel his order?

Ⓐ Send an email
Ⓑ Call a salesperson
Ⓒ Visit a store
Ⓓ Fill out an online form

[13-15] Read an email.

| Subject: | Scheduled Air Conditioning Service (September 19th) |

Dear Ms. Jackson,

This is to confirm the scheduled air conditioning maintenance service for your unit on September 19th. Technicians from CoolPro Air Conditioning are expected to arrive between 9:00 A.M. and 11:00 A.M. They will call you approximately 30 minutes before arrival.

To assist the technicians, please clear at least three feet around the air conditioning units and ensure valuable items are secured in advance. For safety, they will turn off the power before starting. The service includes drainage system testing and, if necessary, air filter replacement.

If this time is inconvenient, please notify us by 5:00 P.M. on September 12th via email or phone so we can reschedule. After the service, a notice tag or service summary will be left detailing the work completed.

Regards,

Leo Koval
East Corner Apartments

13 What is the main purpose of the email?

Ⓐ To confirm an air conditioning service appointment
Ⓑ To explain how to replace an air filter
Ⓒ To request payment for the air conditioning service
Ⓓ To provide safety guidelines regarding air conditioners

14 Which is Ms. Jackson NOT required to do?

Ⓐ Put away personal belongings beforehand
Ⓑ Vacate the apartment during the service
Ⓒ Clear space around the air conditioner
Ⓓ Contact the office if the appointment is unsuitable

15 What is the earliest time that the technicians may contact Ms. Jackson?

Ⓐ September 19th, 8:30 A.M.
Ⓑ September 19th, 9:00 A.M.
Ⓒ September 19th, 10:30 A.M.
Ⓓ September 19th, 11:00 A.M.

2. Text-Message Chain

Overview

메시지 대화문은 문자 메시지나 온라인 채팅을 통해 여러 사람 간에 이루어지는 대화를 다룬다. 두 사람 간의 대화보다는 여러 사람이 동시에 나누는 대화가 주로 출제된다. 또한, 지문의 특성상 구어적인 표현이 사용될 수 있다.

Topics

회사 생활   업무 진행 상황 확인, 회의 준비 등 회사에서 직원들 사이에 이루어지는 대화
학교 생활   조별 과제 준비 등 학교에서 학생들 사이에 이루어지는 대화

Types of Questions

Detail 대화자가 해야 할 일, 대화에서 언급되는 세부 사항을 주로 묻는다.
What is Victor's responsibility?
What project is being discussed?

Inference 대화자 또는 대화문에 언급된 사람이나 특정 사항에 관해 추론할 수 있는 것을 주로 묻는다.
What can be concluded about Jennifer's schedule?

Intention 대화문에서 특정 어구가 어떤 의도로 쓰였는지를 묻는다.
At 8:45 A.M., what does Ms. Brown imply when she writes, "The warning signs were there all along"?
What does the phrase 'team coordination meeting' most likely mean in this context?

Example

Read a text-message chain.

> **Nina Park (9:00 A.M.)**
> Good morning, team! Reminder: All investor presentation slides and demo videos for Friday's meeting must be finalized by Thursday.
>
> **Mohammed Aziz (9:05 A.M.)**
> [1]I'll finish the slide design and send it out for initial feedback by Wednesday.
>
> **Marco Enriquez (9:09 A.M.)**
> I'll gather updated user feedback from last month's beta test and highlight key points for the demo video.
>
> **Nina Park (9:12 A.M.)**
> Great. We also need to double-check the compatibility for the devices in advance. Remember what happened with the webinar last month.
>
> **Marco Enriquez (9:15 A.M.)**
> [2]Yes, the webinar last month had some glitches. I'll conduct a thorough compatibility check on all devices by Wednesday.
>
> **Nina Park (9:20 A.M.)**
> Great job, team! I'm confident we'll deliver a flawless presentation together.

• 연락한 목적

• 세부 사항

• 끝맺음

1. What is Mr. Aziz's responsibility?

Ⓐ Collecting user feedback
Ⓑ Finalizing a slide design
Ⓒ Sending feedback for presentation slides
Ⓓ Presenting a demo video

2. At 9:12 A.M., what does Ms. Park most likely mean when she writes, "Remember what happened with the webinar last month"?

Ⓐ She wants to make sure technical issues do not occur again.
Ⓑ She is suggesting to reschedule the upcoming meeting.
Ⓒ She believes last month's webinar was unnecessary.
Ⓓ She wants to skip the device compatibility check this time.

정답   1. Ⓑ   2. Ⓐ

해설   1. Mr. Aziz가 맡은 일이 무엇인지 묻는 문제이다. 'I'll finish the slide design'을 통해 Mr. Aziz가 슬라이드 디자인을 완성할 것임을 알 수 있다. 따라서 Ⓑ가 정답이다.

   2. Ms. Park이 한 말의 의미를 묻는 문제이다. Ms. Park이 '장비 호환성을 사전에 다시 한번 확인해야 한다'고 했고, Mr. Enriquez가 '지난달 웨비나 때 약간의 기술적 문제가 있었다'고 했다. 이를 통해 Ms. Park이 한 말의 의미는 '장비 호환성 문제가 다시 발생하지 않도록 확실히 하기를 원함'임을 알 수 있다. 따라서 Ⓐ가 정답이다.

HACKERS TEST

[01-02] Read a text-message chain.

Sam Howe   10:14 A.M.
Hi, team. I wanted to remind everyone that the deadline for our financial reports has changed. Since Monday is now a holiday, we need to have everything completed by Friday.

Grace Malone   10:16 A.M.
Thanks for reminding us. I'm almost finished compiling all of the data. I'll send it to Jacob this afternoon. Hopefully, he will be able to create the graphs needed for the report and the presentation materials by Wednesday.

Jacob Cho   10:17 A.M.
That shouldn't be a problem. It will only take me a few hours to do them.

Tanner Gonzalez   10:21 A.M.
That's perfect. Send them to me as soon as they're done and I'll get everything edited and print things out.

Sam Howe   10:25 A.M.
Thanks, everyone. It looks we've got everything handled and we'll finish on time.

---

01 At 10:17 A.M., what does Jacob Cho mean when he writes, "That shouldn't be a problem"?

   Ⓐ He agrees with Ms. Malone's statement.
   Ⓑ He has already accomplished a task.
   Ⓒ He is willing to work overtime.
   Ⓓ He can finish by Wednesday.

02 What can be inferred about Tanner Gonzalez?

   Ⓐ He is the newest team member.
   Ⓑ He will correct the materials.
   Ⓒ He needs some additional time.
   Ⓓ He is presenting the material.

[03-04] Read a text-message chain.

Marc Bishop [1:11 P.M.]
Our department head is unable to attend our budget presentation on Monday. He's meeting with a client in Chicago and won't be back until Tuesday. Maybe we should push back our presentation until the day after he returns.

Danielle Newman [1:13 P.M.]
OK. Let's reserve the main conference room from 2 to 4 P.M. on that day.

Liu Zhou [1:15 P.M.]
I just checked the reservation schedule. The marketing team has a workshop planned. We'll have to do the presentation in the morning instead. We could start at 10 A.M.

Marc Bishop [1:16 P.M.]
That works. And since we have a few more days to prepare, we should consider how to improve our presentation.

Danielle Newman [1:18 P.M.]
Why don't I go through all of the data in the charts to make sure everything is accurate?

Liu Zhou [1:20 P.M.]
Great. While you do that, I'm going to see if any improvements can be made to the handouts.

03 Why does Mr. Bishop suggest postponing a presentation?

Ⓐ He plans to take a business trip.
Ⓑ He needs to meet with a client.
Ⓒ He wants a manager to attend.
Ⓓ He intends to revise a budget.

04 At 1:15 P.M., what does Ms. Zhou imply when she writes, "The marketing team has a workshop planned"?

Ⓐ A group project has been canceled.
Ⓑ A weekly schedule was updated.
Ⓒ A training session will be useful.
Ⓓ A meeting space is unavailable.

HACKERS TEST

[05-06] Read an instant message chain.

Genet Tesfaye [6:00 P.M.]   Thank you for contacting Saffron Table. How may I assist you today?

Aarav Sharma [6:01 P.M.]   I'd like to make a reservation for 7:00 P.M. this Friday.

Genet Tesfaye [6:02 P.M.]   I apologize, but we are fully booked for this Friday evening. However, we currently have availability for Thursday at 8:00 P.M. That also happens to be our Wine & Appetizer Special night, which offers a 5 percent discount on all appetizers and select wines.

Aarav Sharma [6:03 P.M.]   In that case, I'll go with Thursday at 8:00 P.M.

Genet Tesfaye [6:05 P.M.]   How many guests will be attending?

Aarav Sharma [6:07 P.M.]   A table for 2, please.

Genet Tesfaye [6:09 P.M.]   Thank you. Your table for 2 at 8:00 P.M. on Thursday is now confirmed. The discount will be applied automatically to eligible items.

Aarav Sharma [6:10 P.M.]   Sounds good.

---

05 What does Ms. Tesfaye's mention of the "Wine & Appetizer Special night" suggest about her attitude?

    Ⓐ She thinks a discount might appeal to the customer.
    Ⓑ She is trying to encourage the customer to order more food and drinks.
    Ⓒ She is encouraging the customer to visit on the weekend.
    Ⓓ She wants to emphasize the popularity of the restaurant on Thursday.

06 What does the phrase 'eligible items' most likely mean in this context?

    Ⓐ All food and drink items available that evening
    Ⓑ The most expensive items on the menu
    Ⓒ Appetizers and wines that qualify for the special offer
    Ⓓ Main courses served on Thursdays

[07-09] Read a text-message chain.

> **Dana Scott** [2:00 P.M.]
> Afternoon, team. The client reviewed our packaging draft for their GlowHerb line and requested two more options that better highlight the product's benefits and natural ingredients.
>
> **Natalie Jones** [2:05 P.M.]
> I'll edit the current labeling to make it more visible with an emphasis on the "organic" and "vegan" ingredients.
>
> **Paul Dunaway** [2:10 P.M.]
> I'll come up with a new design concept and send drafts by Friday. Should I emphasize the "soothing" and "hydrating" benefits?
>
> **Dana Scott** [2:15 P.M.]
> Yes, highlight those benefits. Also, the client wanted to feature the texture and natural appearance of the product to visually represent those benefits.
>
> **Paul Dunaway** [2:20 P.M.]
> To do that, I'll need more high-resolution images of the product. Should I reach out to the client directly to ask for them?
>
> **Dana Scott** [2:25 P.M.]
> I'll take the lead on reaching out for those.

07 What does Natalie Jones indicate?

Ⓐ She believes the current design already sufficiently features the key ingredients.
Ⓑ She will begin by consulting with the client about the new labeling options.
Ⓒ She will revise the packaging to better highlight the product components.
Ⓓ She is responsible for designing new packaging concepts.

08 At 2:25 P.M., what does Dana Scott most likely mean when she writes, "I'll take the lead on reaching out for those"?

Ⓐ She will wait for the client to contact her with the images.
Ⓑ She is worried that Paul will forget to ask for the images.
Ⓒ She will be the one to contact the client to request the images.
Ⓓ She will focus on the design concept before requesting the images.

09 The client wants the packaging design to highlight all of the following aspects of their product EXCEPT

Ⓐ Therapeutic effects
Ⓑ Price
Ⓒ Physical texture
Ⓓ Components

HACKERS TEST

[10-12] Read a text-message chain.

Lena Thompson [8:45 A.M.]
For our Innovation Showcase next week, several guests from partner companies will be coming.

Maya Patel [8:46 A.M.]
Are there special parking arrangements for visitors?

Lena Thompson [8:47 A.M.]
The spots in the east parking lot will be reserved for guests only. Signage will be in place, and our security team will assist.

Julio Rivera [8:50 A.M.]
I have a client, Sophia Baumgartner, who will be arriving from London. Where should I tell her to go when she arrives?

Lena Thompson [8:52 A.M.]
Tell her to go to the front desk to check in. One of our staff will escort her to reserved seating.

Joshua O'Connor [8:55 A.M.]
Will we need to wear special badges tomorrow?

Lena Thompson [8:57 A.M.]
No, but please use the west entrance for all staff and bring your security card at all times.

10 Which of the following is true about the Innovation Showcase?

Ⓐ It will feature presentations from guests.
Ⓑ It will be attended by many non-employees.
Ⓒ It will require all staff to wear special badges.
Ⓓ It will take place in London.

11 What does the phrase 'parking arrangements' most likely mean in this context?

Ⓐ The act of parking one's car in a designated spot
Ⓑ The written rules and fines for parking on company property
Ⓒ The construction and maintenance of a parking lot
Ⓓ The details or plans for organizing parking spaces

12 What can be inferred about Sophia Baumgartner?

Ⓐ She will have to wait for the general staff to park their cars first.
Ⓑ She will be escorted by Mr. Rivera.
Ⓒ She will be seated in a reserved area upon arrival.
Ⓓ She will check in at the east parking lot.

[13-15] Read a text-message chain.

James Holloway [1:00 P.M.]
Due to an unexpected client issue, our ATAC Tech Summit delegation must be reduced from five to three. The remaining delegates are Alex, Maria, and myself.

Alex Wright [1:03 P.M.]
That significantly impacts our goals. The other two members were focusing on the two high-priority vendor meetings, and Maria and I were preparing for the presentation on AI.

James Holloway [1:05 P.M.]
Securing those deals is now our top priority. I want you to work on that, Alex. Let's meet via videoconference at 3 P.M. to finalize the revised task list.

Maria Perez [1:07 P.M.]
Understood. In the meantime, should I contact the airline and hotel to see whether the two team members' non-refundable costs can be converted into credits for future use?

James Holloway [1:08 P.M.]
Good catch. Let me know what you can salvage before the 3 P.M. meeting.

13 What can be inferred about Alex Wright?

Ⓐ He will remain at the office.
Ⓑ He will prepare a report on company finances.
Ⓒ He will attend a vendor meeting.
Ⓓ He will travel for a client meeting next week.

14 What will Maria Perez do before a videoconference?

Ⓐ Contact service providers to minimize financial losses
Ⓑ Manage the unexpected client crisis
Ⓒ Choose the three delegates
Ⓓ Prepare for a presentation

15 At 1:08 P.M., what does James Holloway most likely mean when he writes, "Good catch"?

Ⓐ He agrees that Alex made an error.
Ⓑ He is complimenting Maria for identifying a task that was overlooked.
Ⓒ He is reminding Maria to contact the high-priority vendors.
Ⓓ He is acknowledging Maria for reserving the meeting room in advance.

Answers p.437

3. Notice

Overview

공지는 많은 사람들에게 알려야 할 사항을 다루는 글로, 크게 사내 공지와 일반 공지로 나눌 수 있다. 사내 공지는 회의 일정, 회사 시설 점검 등에 관해 다루고, 일반 공지는 이용 규칙, 행사 안내 등 일상 생활에서 접할 수 있는 다양한 내용을 다룬다.

Topics

사내 공지   회의 일정 변경, 사무실 전기 점검, 휴무 신청 방법 변경 등을 알리는 글
일반 공지   도서관 이용 규칙, 학술 세미나, 지역 축제 등을 알리는 글

Types of Questions

Main Topic/ Main Purpose
공지의 주제나 목적을 묻는 문제가 출제된다.
What is the notice about?
What is the main purpose of the notice?

Detail
공지에 언급된 일정, 요청 사항이나 세부 사항 등을 묻는 문제가 주로 출제된다.
Where will the meeting take place?
What will visitors NOT experience?

Fact/ Negative Fact
공지에 언급된 사람, 사물 등에 대해 일치하거나 일치하지 않는 것을 묻는 문제가 출제된다.
What does the notice indicate about Ms. Murray?
What is indicated about electronic devices?

Example

Read a notice.

Dear Residents,

[1]Please be advised that regular pest control will be conducted on October 28, from 10:00 A.M to 12:00 P.M.

For your safety, please [2A]vacate your apartment during the service. In addition, please [2C]store all food items in sealed containers and [2D]ensure all windows are closed and locked.

• 목적

• 세부 사항

1. What is the main purpose of the notice?

Ⓐ To explain a change in building management
Ⓑ To announce scheduled pest control
Ⓒ To inform of a building's exterior cleaning
Ⓓ To notify of some elevator maintenance

2. What are residents NOT required to do?

Ⓐ Leave their home temporarily
Ⓑ Clean the apartment in advance
Ⓒ Keep food items in airtight containers
Ⓓ Shut all windows in the building

정답 1. Ⓑ   2. Ⓑ

해설 1. 공지를 작성한 목적을 묻는 문제이다. 'Please be advised ~ will be conducted'를 통해 정기 해충 방제 실시를 알리기 위한 글임을 알 수 있다. 따라서 Ⓑ가 정답이다.

2. 입주민들이 요구받지 않은 것을 묻는 문제이다. 'vacate your apartment'를 통해 Ⓐ가, 'store all food ~ sealed containers'를 통해 Ⓒ가, 'ensure all windows ~ locked'를 통해 Ⓓ가 언급되었음을 알 수 있다. 따라서 Ⓑ가 정답이다.

HACKERS TEST

[01-02] Read a notice.

Due to construction on Sunset Avenue, the employee shuttle will temporarily bypass this road from January 28 to February 2. Instead, it will use Maple Avenue, one block west. Staff are advised to board at the temporary stops along the alternative route. We apologize for any inconvenience.

01 What is the main purpose of the notice?

Ⓐ To announce the introduction of a new bus service
Ⓑ To explain a construction plan on a road
Ⓒ To inform staff of the temporary route change
Ⓓ To warn about traffic congestion on a road

02 What are the staff advised to do?

Ⓐ Delay travel until the construction ends
Ⓑ Use bus stops one block west
Ⓒ Find alternative transportation
Ⓓ Check the construction schedule

[03-04] Read a sign.

TRES CHIC BOUTIQUE
GRAND OPENING!

Celebrate our grand opening this Saturday!

Save 10–20 percent on accessories, 25 percent on clothing items, and 30 percent on perfumes.

Doors open at 9 A.M. and the first 100 customers will receive a free tote bag!

Store Hours:
Monday-Friday: 10 A.M. – 9 P.M.
Saturday-Sunday: 9 A.M. – 10 P.M.

03 How can customers receive a free tote bag?

Ⓐ By making a minimum purchase
Ⓑ By buying select perfumes
Ⓒ By going to the store early
Ⓓ By contacting a store

04 What discount is available on shirts?

Ⓐ 10 percent
Ⓑ 20 percent
Ⓒ 25 percent
Ⓓ 30 percent

HACKERS TEST

[05-06] Read a poster.

CITY FITNESS MOVING

We're moving to a larger location to better serve our members.

New Location: San Pedro Shopping Center, 133 East Elm Drive
Opening Day: Monday, October 1

Memberships will automatically transfer to the new location.

If you have questions or concerns, please call 555-8210

05 What will change after the move?

Ⓐ The cost of membership
Ⓑ The facility's size
Ⓒ The opening times
Ⓓ The facility staff

06 What can be inferred about members?

Ⓐ They do not have to reregister.
Ⓑ They should respond by October 1.
Ⓒ They can choose from multiple locations.
Ⓓ They must call a number.

[07-09] Read a notice.

Short-Term Rentals Registration

All hosts must register their short-term rentals by Friday, November 1st. Failure to register will result in a penalty of up to $500 per day for noncompliant properties, starting November 2nd. Additionally, hosts are required to display the city registration number on all accommodation advertisements.

You can register your short-term rentals either online or in person. A $75 fee is due upon submission.

Online Registration: Visit brookdale.gov/short_term_rentals. The required documents include a photo ID, your latest property tax bill, a parking plan, and a floor plan.

In-Person Registration: Register at City Hall, Room 204, on weekdays from 9:00 A.M. to 5:00 P.M. Please bring the same documents as for online registration.

Online applications are processed within 3 to 5 business days once all required documents and payment are received. In-person applications may take up to 7 business days as staff must enter records manually.

07 What is the main purpose of the notice?

Ⓐ To announce an increase in taxes for short-term rentals
Ⓑ To explain parking regulations for accommodations
Ⓒ To provide guidance on a required procedure
Ⓓ To promote recommended accommodations

08 What can be concluded about online registration?

Ⓐ It requires fewer documents than in-person registration.
Ⓑ It does not require manual record entry by staff.
Ⓒ It allows more time to submit after the November 1st deadline.
Ⓓ It is free of charge for all applicants.

09 Which of the following is NOT required of hosts?

Ⓐ Property tax bill
Ⓑ Floor plan
Ⓒ Proof of insurance
Ⓓ Photo ID

HACKERS TEST

[10-12] Read a notice.

Notice for Visitors to the Intensive Care Unit (ICU)

Please follow these guidelines. Your cooperation is vital for patient recovery and safety.

1. **Visiting Hours:** Visiting hours are strictly observed. They are 11:00 A.M. to 12:00 P.M. and 6:00 P.M. to 7:00 P.M.
2. **Infection Control:** If you have any symptoms of illness (cold, flu, fever, cough), please do not enter the ICU.
3. **Hand Hygiene:** Before entering and upon leaving the ICU, you must thoroughly sanitize your hands. Use the provided antiseptic gel.
4. **Personal Items:** For patient safety and infection control, only minimal personal items are permitted. Outside food and drinks are strictly prohibited. Please leave all large coats and bags (e.g., backpacks, shopping bags) outside the unit.
5. **Noise:** Please speak softly and keep conversations brief in the hallways and patient rooms. Silence or turn off all mobile phones to prevent disturbance.

---

10 What is the main purpose of the notice?

    Ⓐ To advertise the facilities at the ICU
    Ⓑ To provide guidelines to ensure patient safety and recovery
    Ⓒ To promote volunteer opportunities in the ICU
    Ⓓ To explain how to use the medical equipment

11 Why does the notice mention an antiseptic gel?

    Ⓐ To give an example of a drug used on critical patients
    Ⓑ To specify an item prohibited in the intensive care unit
    Ⓒ To ask visitors to bring their own hand sanitizer
    Ⓓ To instruct visitors on how to clean their hands

12 What can the visitors bring to the Intensive Care Unit?

    Ⓐ A backpack
    Ⓑ A cup of coffee
    Ⓒ A mobile phone
    Ⓓ A large coat

[13-15] Read a notice.

Dear Residents,

Management would like to remind everyone about the complex's rules regarding the charging of personal electric vehicles, including electric bicycles and electric scooters, following recent safety concerns about fire hazards. Charging of these electric vehicles is prohibited in individual residences, balconies, common areas, or stairwells.

Personal electric vehicles must only be charged at the designated charging stations, which are equipped with fire-safety equipment and proper ventilation. The stations are located in the outdoor parking lot (near the main management office) and near the main gate. More locations will be added in the near future.

Any resident found charging a personal mobility device in an unauthorized area will first receive a written warning. Repeated noncompliance will lead to further disciplinary action as outlined in the lease agreement. Please note that we recently refused to renew a resident's lease because of this issue.

We appreciate your cooperation for the well-being of all residents.

13 What is the main purpose of the notice?

Ⓐ To remind residents of a regulation
Ⓑ To announce the opening of new charging stations
Ⓒ To explain how to use fire-safety equipment
Ⓓ To inform residents about lease renewal procedures

14 What could happen if someone repeatedly charges an electric vehicle in an unauthorized area?

Ⓐ They might be fined.
Ⓑ They might receive a written warning.
Ⓒ Their device might be confiscated.
Ⓓ Their lease might not be renewed.

15 What can be inferred about the management office?

Ⓐ It plans to build more charging stations soon.
Ⓑ It has heard complaints about electric vehicle charging.
Ⓒ It is located near the main gate.
Ⓓ It was recently damaged in a fire.

Answers p.440

4. Advertisement

Overview

광고는 상품, 서비스 등 홍보하고자 하는 여러 가지 것들을 광고하는 글로서, 크게 일반 광고와 구인 광고로 나눌 수 있다. 광고는 온전한 문장으로 구성될 수도 있지만, 간결함을 위해 어구 단위로 구성되거나 주어가 생략될 수도 있다. 이때는 축약된 정보의 의미를 빠르게 이해하는 것이 중요하다.

Topics

일반 광고	행사, 공연, 강의, 회사의 제품 및 서비스 등을 홍보하는 광고
구인 광고	회사 및 기관에서 직원들을 모집하는 광고

Types of Questions

Main Topic/ Main Purpose	광고되고 있는 것이 무엇인지 묻는 문제가 출제된다. What does the advertisement promote?
Detail	광고되는 상품, 서비스에 대한 세부 사항을 묻는 문제가 주로 출제된다. What is the final date for program enrollment? What are the benefits of an early registration?

Example

Read an advertisement.

Horizon Haven Resort

We are thrilled to announce the grand reopening of Horizon Haven Resort on June 15th. We invite you to discover a sanctuary of wellness and serenity.

Nestled along the pristine beaches, our resort offers a tranquil environment with lush tropical gardens and ocean views. The newly upgraded suites include [1]a fully equipped kitchen, a spacious bathroom, and a private terrace.

Other features include:
- On-site spa offering massages, facials, and wellness treatments
- Organic dining options with locally sourced ingredients
- Fitness center and outdoor pool access
- Utilities and resort fees fully covered in booking price
- Fresh linens, bathrobes, and wellness kits provided
- High-speed Wi-Fi available throughout the resort

Secure your wellness escape today! [2]Confirm your booking by May 5th to receive a 15 percent discount. To reserve your dates, visit http://www.horizonhavenresort.com/reservation

1. What can be inferred about Horizon Haven Resort?

Ⓐ It provides a special area for internet access.
Ⓑ It offers private training sessions.
Ⓒ It allows guests to cook food in their rooms.
Ⓓ It requires an additional charge for some utilities.

2. By when should an individual reserve a date in order to get a discount?

Ⓐ May 5th
Ⓑ May 15th
Ⓒ June 5th
Ⓓ June 15th

정답 1. Ⓒ   2. Ⓐ

해설 1. Horizon Haven 리조트에 관해 추론할 수 있는 것을 묻는 문제이다. 'a fully equipped kitchen'을 통해 객실 내에 주방이 있음을 알 수 있고, 이를 통해 투숙객들이 객실에서 음식을 조리할 수 있음을 추론할 수 있다. 따라서 Ⓒ가 정답이다.

2. 할인을 받기 위해 언제까지 예약해야 하는지 묻는 문제이다. 'Confirm your booking ~ discount'를 통해 15 퍼센트 할인을 받기 위해서는 5월 5일까지 예약을 확정해야 함을 알 수 있다. 따라서 Ⓐ가 정답이다.

HACKERS TEST

[01-02] Read an advertisement.

This week, swing by the Campus Bookstore for the Spring Semester Sale! Save 30 percent on all used textbooks and 20 percent on new books and computer software. You can also get up to half off on all school-branded apparel. Purchase more than $100 and get a free coffee mug!

01 The phrase "swing by" in the passage is closest in meaning to

Ⓐ visit
Ⓑ contact
Ⓒ explore
Ⓓ follow

02 What items are being given away with qualifying purchases?

Ⓐ Used textbooks
Ⓑ School-branded clothing
Ⓒ Computer software
Ⓓ Coffee cups

[03-04] Read an advertisement.

Language Exchange

Do you want to practice speaking another language? Then come to the Language Exchange Night at the Central Brew Café every Friday at 7 P.M. People from around the world participate and share their native languages with others. $5 entry fee includes coffee, tea, and finger foods all evening.

03 What is indicated about the event?

Ⓐ It takes place once a week.
Ⓑ It has been held for many years.
Ⓒ It changes venues regularly.
Ⓓ It features fun foreign language games.

04 What is NOT covered by the $5 fee?

Ⓐ Entry to the event
Ⓑ Complimentary beverages
Ⓒ Free snacks
Ⓓ A practice book

HACKERS TEST

[05-06] Read an advertisement.

New Fitness Classes

The community center will offer free fitness classes for all residents. Classes on offer will range from yoga and Pilates to dance and strength training. Each class will last one hour. Space is limited, so register in person at the center's front desk as early as possible.

05 What is this advertisement promoting?

Ⓐ Wellness programs at a community center
Ⓑ Free equipment rentals for residents
Ⓒ Local sports tournaments and competitions
Ⓓ Nutrition workshops and meal planning

06 How can residents sign up?

Ⓐ By attending the first class
Ⓑ By visiting the center's front desk
Ⓒ By calling the community center
Ⓓ By accessing the center's website

[07-09] Read an advertisement.

Learn the World

Do you dream of taking a long trip to another country? The Semester Abroad program can make your dreams come true without interrupting your current studies. This exciting program allows students to immerse themselves in the local culture while studying for a semester at a partner university in one of more than 50 countries, including Japan, Italy, and Australia. Participants earn full academic credit for all courses they take and have the opportunity to learn outside the classroom on cultural excursions.

Program fees, which cover tuition, meals, health insurance, and a homestay, are affordable and some students may even qualify for grants and other financial aid packages that cover the entire cost. To learn more about the program, attend the orientation session being held in Fletcher Hall on Monday, June 13 at 10 A.M. It may be the first step on an incredible journey!

07 What is a benefit of the program?

Ⓐ It takes place between semesters.
Ⓑ It allows travel to multiple countries.
Ⓒ It provides academic credit for studies.
Ⓓ It is conducted entirely out of classrooms.

08 What is NOT included in the cost of the program?

Ⓐ Course costs
Ⓑ Health insurance
Ⓒ Food and lodging
Ⓓ Travel expenses

09 What can be inferred about the program?

Ⓐ It takes place only during one semester a year.
Ⓑ It is free for some participants.
Ⓒ It requires students to speak a foreign language.
Ⓓ It begins on June 13.

HACKERS TEST

[10-12] Read an advertisement.

Managerial Excellence Workshop

In today's dynamic business environment, effective management is the key to organizational success. Elevate your leadership skills and drive better results by enrolling in the managerial excellence workshop.

The workshop will be held at Innovation Valley Center on Tuesday, January 15th, from 9 A.M. to 5 P.M. and is designed for supervisors and managers across various departments, including operations, finance, human resources, and sales.

It is a crucial opportunity to gain insights into modern leadership strategies, conflict resolution, performance coaching, and effective delegation, directly from industry-leading consultants. Whether you need to master setting clear goals or provide constructive feedback, our expert facilitators will teach you how.

This year, for the first time, the workshop will also include a specialized module on digital transformation and remote team management to help you navigate the future of work. You don't want to miss this vital professional development opportunity.

10 What can be inferred about the workshop?

Ⓐ It will primarily focus on finance and sales.
Ⓑ It has been held before.
Ⓒ Its attendees are required to bring a detailed professional portfolio.
Ⓓ Its primary goal is to help managers find a new job.

11 Why does the advertisement mention a specialized module?

Ⓐ To emphasize the need for technical IT training
Ⓑ To inform attendees of a prerequisite skill
Ⓒ To offer an added benefit of the workshop
Ⓓ To explain a required change in the company's operating structure

12 What will the attendees learn?

Ⓐ How to supervise employees working outside the office
Ⓑ How to implement an efficient performance review system
Ⓒ How to facilitate communication among team members
Ⓓ How to receive an official certificate for digital transformation

[13-15] Read an advertisement.

Cozy Corner

Cozy Corner is hiring enthusiastic full-time and part-time staff.

The role involves all aspects of the dining experience, including taking orders, serving, preparing drinks, processing payments, and cleaning.

Requirements & Compensation:
- Ability to stand for long periods
- Prior experience helpful but not required (we welcome trainees!)
- Flexible availability, including nights and weekends
- Competitive starting wage of $15.00/hour plus tips

All new hires must submit the necessary food safety certification within 30 days of the hiring date.

To apply: Visit the diner with your résumé between 2 P.M. and 4 P.M., Monday to Friday.

---

13 What is this advertisement promoting?

Ⓐ A job opening at a local diner
Ⓑ A training session on customer service skills
Ⓒ A short-term course on food safety
Ⓓ A new menu at a restaurant

14 What can be inferred about Cozy Corner?

Ⓐ It does not operate between 2 P.M. and 4 P.M.
Ⓑ It only hires experienced staff.
Ⓒ Its most popular items are drinks.
Ⓓ Its employees may work only on nights and weekends.

15 Why does the advertisement mention food safety certification?

Ⓐ To specify a job requirement
Ⓑ To inform that training is available
Ⓒ To suggest a compensation package
Ⓓ To give instructions on how to apply

Answers p.442

5. Social Media Post

Overview

소셜 미디어 게시물은 많은 독자를 대상으로 온라인 플랫폼에 올리는 글이다. 주로 행사에 대해 알리는 글, 개인의 경험을 공유하는 글이 출제된다.

Topics

홍보	지역 행사, 점포 개업 등에 관해 홍보하는 게시물
경험 공유	식당 후기, 전시회 후기 등 개인의 경험에 관해 공유하는 게시물

Types of Questions

Main Topic/ Main Purpose	게시물의 주제나 목적을 묻는 문제가 출제된다. What is the post mainly about? What is the main purpose of the post?
Detail	게시물에 언급된 사람이나 행사에 대한 세부 사항을 묻는 문제가 출제된다. Why must attendees reserve a spot before Friday? Why does the shelter require foster families to have a securely fenced yard?

Example

Read a social media post.

Marie Sanders

Book lovers, get ready! [1]The community book fair is just around the corner, and it's going to be bigger and better than ever. Visit the local community center this Saturday to celebrate the simple joy of reading.

We have something for every reader. Browse dozens of tables with everything from beloved classics and bestselling graphic novels to the latest picture books for kids. You can also [2A]explore your favorite genres at our lively themed sections like mystery, memoirs, and science fiction.

Beyond the books, enjoy a variety of interactive activities. We have storytelling circles, [2D]a fun bookmark-making station, and [2B]a silent auction for unique collectibles. Friendly volunteers will be on hand to help you find exactly what you're looking for.

All proceeds support our library's literacy programs. Bring your friends and share your favorite recommendations. We can't wait to see you there!

• 홍보하는 것

• 세부 사항

1. What is the main purpose of the post?

Ⓐ To compare various literary genres
Ⓑ To recruit volunteers for a book fair
Ⓒ To highlight literacy issues in the community
Ⓓ To promote a community book fair

2. What will visitors NOT experience?

Ⓐ Exploring themed sections
Ⓑ Bidding in an auction
Ⓒ Attending a book signing
Ⓓ Making bookmarks

정답 1. Ⓓ   2. Ⓒ

해설 1. 글을 작성한 목적을 묻는 문제이다. 'Visit ~ reading'을 통해 지역 도서 박람회를 홍보하기 위한 글임을 알 수 있다. 따라서 Ⓓ가 정답이다.

2. 방문객들이 경험하지 않을 것을 묻는 문제이다. 'explore ~ themed sections'를 통해 Ⓐ가, 'a silent auction ~ collectibles'를 통해 Ⓑ가, 'a fun bookmark-making station'을 통해 Ⓓ가 지문의 내용과 일치함을 알 수 있다. 따라서 Ⓒ가 정답이다.

[01-02] Read a social media post.

01 What is the main purpose of the post?

Ⓐ To promote a cycling club
Ⓑ To advertise an upcoming trip
Ⓒ To give bicycle safety advice
Ⓓ To describe a bike ride

02 What is suggested about Tyler Banks?

Ⓐ He got a new bike.
Ⓑ He lives in Plymouth.
Ⓒ He recently joined a group.
Ⓓ He took pictures of the scenery.

[03-04] Read a social media post.

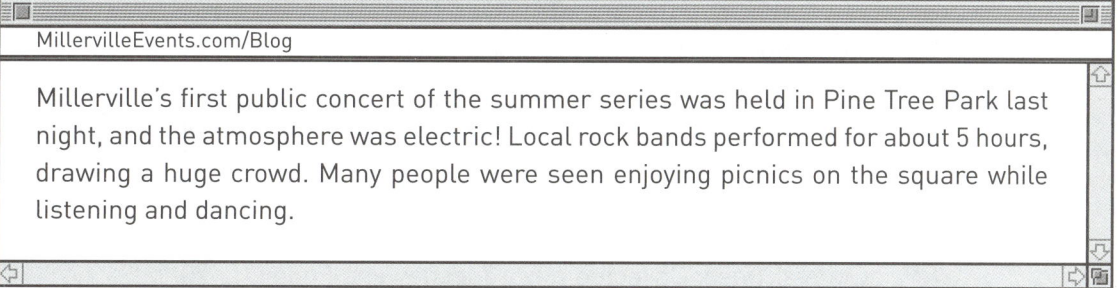

MillervilleEvents.com/Blog

Millerville's first public concert of the summer series was held in Pine Tree Park last night, and the atmosphere was electric! Local rock bands performed for about 5 hours, drawing a huge crowd. Many people were seen enjoying picnics on the square while listening and dancing.

03 Where did the performance take place?

   Ⓐ At a concert hall
   Ⓑ At a park
   Ⓒ At a rock club
   Ⓓ At a stadium

04 What can be inferred about the concert?

   Ⓐ It will be followed by more.
   Ⓑ It included multiple music genres.
   Ⓒ It attracted bands from different areas.
   Ⓓ It featured a professional dance routine.

HACKERS TEST

[05-06] Read a social media post.

City of Temple @TempleOfficial | Thursday, May 1

Quick heads-up, Temple residents! We've updated our waste collection schedule to help keep our city clean and green!

The New Schedule:
General Trash: Collected every Tuesday and Friday
Food Scraps: Collected on Thursdays only
Recycling: Collected on Wednesdays only

Color Code Reminder (Let's get this right!):
Black Bins: General Trash
Green Bins: Compost & Food Scraps (That includes leftovers!)
Blue Bins: Recycling (Including food boxes and drink cans)

Thanks for pitching in and keeping our neighborhoods tidy!

#TempleCares #WasteCollection #CityUpdate

05 When will food boxes be collected?

   Ⓐ On Tuesdays
   Ⓑ On Wednesdays
   Ⓒ On Thursdays
   Ⓓ On Fridays

06 What should residents do with leftover food?

   Ⓐ Put it in a green bin
   Ⓑ Add it to the general waste
   Ⓒ Throw it out daily
   Ⓓ Wrap it in a black bag

[07-09] Read a social media post.

BIG ANNOUNCEMENT

First off, we would like to thank you all for the support you've shown at our Bao Wow pop-up events. The reception to our fusion buns has been so positive that we've decided to take a big step—we're getting a food truck!

Starting next month, Bao Wow will have a location at the Second Street Food Truck Park (2824 Second Street across from the City Pier). We'll be serving all of your favorite buns from our pop-up events, including the bestselling Korean chicken buns and the Mexican street corn buns, as well as adding several exciting new options and weekly specials.

To celebrate the grand opening, we're going to offer all of our social media followers a 20 percent discount for the first two weeks. All you have to do is show that you follow us to get the discount.

See you next month!!!

LIKE   **COMMENT**

07 What can be inferred about Bao Wow?

Ⓐ It does not have a permanent location.
Ⓑ It currently provides food for receptions.
Ⓒ It received positive reviews from critics.
Ⓓ It serves traditional Chinese food.

08 What is located at 2824 Second Street?

Ⓐ A city pier
Ⓑ A new restaurant
Ⓒ A pop-up location
Ⓓ A food truck complex

09 What do guests have to do to receive a discount?

Ⓐ Purchase more than $20 in food
Ⓑ Prove that they follow an account
Ⓒ Make a social media post
Ⓓ Present a discount coupon

HACKERS TEST

[10-12] Read a web page.

10 Why did Ms. Waters visit Gleeman's Bistro?

(A) To attend a retirement party
(B) To meet with a customer
(C) To celebrate a promotion
(D) To take part in a family event

11 What are diners charged extra for?

(A) A delivery service
(B) A parking space
(C) A private room
(D) A special dish

12 Ms. Waters was NOT satisfied with

(A) the size of a facility
(B) the skill of the staff
(C) the quality of the food
(D) the cost of a meal

[13-15] Read a social media post.

The annual Willow Creek Neighborhood Science Fair was an absolute success, showcasing the thriving spirit of scientific inquiry locally. The Community Center was filled with infectious energy as young minds from Willow Creek and the surrounding area shared the projects they had poured their efforts into.

The event featured an incredibly diverse projects, from dynamic solar system models to sharp, well-researched experiments on sustainable local farming. Another standout project was a smart recycling sorting device designed to address local waste management issues. The creativity and ingenuity on display made the judging—carried out by local engineers and scientists—quite challenging.

Beyond the competition, the fair was a wonderful community event. Parents and neighbors came together to cheer on the participants. This day demonstrated the huge potential within Willow Creek. A massive well done to all participants!

LIKE   **COMMENT**

13 What is the main purpose of the post?

Ⓐ To introduce the winning projects of a science fair
Ⓑ To describe the success of a science fair
Ⓒ To share an experience as a judge at a science fair
Ⓓ To criticize the organization of a science fair

14 What can be inferred about the science fair?

Ⓐ It involved only students from Willow Creek.
Ⓑ It accompanied a community event.
Ⓒ It was open to young participants.
Ⓓ It was judged by local educators.

15 Which of the following was NOT exhibited at the science fair?

Ⓐ Dynamic solar system models
Ⓑ Experiments on sustainable local farming
Ⓒ Smart recycling sorting device
Ⓓ Student-created robots

6. News Article

Overview

기사는 신문, 온라인 뉴스에서 볼 수 있는 보도문이다. 지역 사회의 동향, 시사 이슈 등 새로운 소식을 알리는 내용으로 출제된다.

Topics

지역 사회 동향   지역 행사, 가게 개점 등 지역 사회에 관한 소식을 알리는 기사
시사 이슈   비즈니스, 환경 등 시사 이슈를 설명하는 기사

Types of Questions

Main Topic/ Main Purpose   기사의 주제나 목적을 묻는 문제가 출제된다.
What is the article mainly about?
What is the main purpose of the article?

Detail   기사에 언급된 사람이나 제품, 규정 등에 대한 세부 사항을 묻는 문제가 출제된다.
What specific organism was the focus of Dr. Rostova's research?
What new regulation will take effect beginning next month?

Example

Read a news article.

Artists in Their Autumn Years Find a New Purpose on Canvas

A new exhibition at the Amherst Mills Art Center, "Lifelong Studio," is proving that it's never too late to embrace artistic creativity. ¹This exhibition highlights seniors who have found a new purpose through art after retirement.

Among the featured artists is 78-year-old Beverly Kendrick, who began painting for the first time in her golden years. Kendrick shared that painting has helped her find new vitality. Her oil painting, ²"Twilight Reflections," captures a vibrant cityscape and is a highlight of the exhibition.

The art center's spokesperson noted that the exhibit was designed to showcase how seniors remain an active and vital part of the community, continuously learning new skills and contributing to culture.

The exhibition runs through the end of next month.

1. What is the main purpose of the article?

Ⓐ To advertise a painting class for seniors
Ⓑ To announce an art exhibition featuring senior artists
Ⓒ To encourage retired people to take up oil painting
Ⓓ To critique the works of art featured in an exhibition

2. What does "Twilight Reflections" depict?

Ⓐ A quiet, rural landscape at sunset
Ⓑ A self-portrait of the artist
Ⓒ A lively urban scene
Ⓓ An artist's studio

정답 1. Ⓑ 2. Ⓒ

해설 1. 글을 작성한 목적을 묻는 문제이다. 'This exhibition ~ after retirement'를 통해 고령 작가들의 작품을 다루는 미술 전시회를 알리기 위한 글임을 알 수 있다. 따라서 Ⓑ가 정답이다.

2. "Twilight Reflections"가 무엇을 묘사하는지 묻는 문제이다. '"Twilight Reflections" ~ a vibrant cityscape'를 통해 활기찬 도시 풍경을 묘사함을 알 수 있다. 따라서 Ⓒ가 정답이다.

HACKERS TEST

[01-02] Read a news article.

City Pool One-Day Closure

Meadville—The city swimming pool will be closed for maintenance on July 10. The closure will allow for the installation of a new water filtration system. The pool will resume its usual afternoon operating hours on July 11, and all swimming lessons will continue as scheduled.

01 Why is the pool being temporarily closed?

  Ⓐ To accommodate swimming lessons
  Ⓑ To check on some systems
  Ⓒ To clean the pool's water
  Ⓓ To install new equipment

02 What can be inferred about the pool?

  Ⓐ It is closed every morning.
  Ⓑ It is experiencing staffing problems.
  Ⓒ It is hiring new maintenance workers.
  Ⓓ It is adding more times for lessons.

[03-04] Read a news article.

> Quantum Innovations, a local tech company, donated $10,000 to Harrington High School to upgrade its outdated science laboratories and establish a new, fully-funded after-school robotics club. The contribution aims to inspire student interest and enhance the overall quality of local education and future job skills.

03 What is the main purpose of the article?

Ⓐ To ask for further donations for a local school
Ⓑ To detail the science curriculum of a local school
Ⓒ To report on a company's financial contribution to a local school
Ⓓ To criticize the outdated facilities at a local school

04 What area did Quantum Innovations' donation fund?

Ⓐ Establishing job-training classes
Ⓑ Modernizing science facilities
Ⓒ Hiring science teachers
Ⓓ Purchasing new textbooks

HACKERS TEST

[05-06] Read a news article.

> The City of Eastwick is introducing a new brand identity. The new logo features a multi-colored design, a stark contrast to the old one. The website has been updated, and official documents and signs are to follow. Official merchandise featuring the new brand will also be released.

05 What can be inferred about the old logo?

- Ⓐ It did not have multiple colors.
- Ⓑ It was designed by a local company.
- Ⓒ It was intended for printed use only.
- Ⓓ It was not liked by residents.

06 The new logo is currently found on

- Ⓐ public street signs
- Ⓑ official merchandise
- Ⓒ the official online page
- Ⓓ government-issued documents

[07-09] Read a news article.

The National Weather Service has issued a winter storm warning for all communities in the northwestern area of the state. People living in this region should be aware that heavy snow, icy roads, and high winds are expected, and take the necessary precautions. The weather is expected to begin deteriorating on December 2, and the storm will last two or three days. During this period, state road crews will work extra shifts to ensure that all major roads remain clear of snow and ice, but there is concern that the large amount of snow expected may make this impossible. Therefore, residents are asked to drive only when absolutely necessary. In light of this situation, the education department has already made the decision to shut down numerous schools temporarily. These are listed on its website, which will be updated as necessary.

07 What is the main purpose of the article?

Ⓐ To welcome visitors to a community
Ⓑ To explain the cancellation of an event
Ⓒ To warn residents of unsafe conditions
Ⓓ To correct an earlier weather forecast

08 The article suggests that state road crews will be

Ⓐ assigned to other regions temporarily
Ⓑ unable to perform an assigned task
Ⓒ prepared to work with other departments
Ⓓ helping drivers who are stranded

09 What can be found online?

Ⓐ An update on project costs
Ⓑ A map of alternative routes
Ⓒ A report on school policies
Ⓓ A list of closed schools

HACKERS TEST

[10-12] Read a news article.

Library Announces Changes

Franklinton—In order to better serve the community, the Franklinton Public Library has announced a major expansion of its hours of operation. Beginning next week, the library will be open from 8 A.M. to 10 P.M. on weekdays and 10 A.M. to 8 P.M. on weekends. Library staff hope that by closing its doors two hours later every day, it will be able to better accommodate students who need study spaces, professionals involved in research, and those who use the library's other services, such as its free Internet and video-viewing room.

In addition, the library will implement other changes to answer the demands of their patrons. These include adding more private study areas and group meeting rooms, as well as offering evening workshops on research techniques, database usage, and basic digital literacy. Officials hope these changes will serve the community better and offer more opportunities for lifelong learning.

10 What can be inferred about the library before the changes?

Ⓐ It had a smaller location.
Ⓑ It closed at 8 P.M. on weekdays.
Ⓒ It had fewer staff members.
Ⓓ It did not offer free Internet service.

11 The word "patrons" in the passage is closest in meaning to

Ⓐ visitors
Ⓑ employees
Ⓒ observers
Ⓓ volunteers

12 What new change will the library implement?

Ⓐ Extending the hours of operation further
Ⓑ Offering training sessions on digital and research skills
Ⓒ Launching a support program for local researchers
Ⓓ Adding new multimedia facilities

[13-15] Read a news article.

The Sedona Transportation Department is testing a new bike-sharing program, hoping to improve commuting in the city.

In the initial phases of the pilot program, 200 bicycles will be available at 20 docking stations located throughout the downtown area. To borrow a bike, users simply log on to the service's mobile application. When finished, the bike can be returned to any of the stations. The cost of each ride will depend on the time and distance traveled, but the program's director estimates the average cost per trip to be less than $3, making it an economical option for people in all income levels.

City officials expect the program to reduce traffic congestion, as fewer cars will be needed. If successful, they say that the program will be expanded to other areas of the city and dedicated bike lanes will be added to all city streets.

13 What is this article mainly about?

  Ⓐ How a city managed traffic congestion
  Ⓑ The growing popularity of bike-sharing programs
  Ⓒ A sharp rise in demand for bike lanes
  Ⓓ A new transportation initiative in a city

14 What can be inferred about the new program?

  Ⓐ It will target low-income earners.
  Ⓑ It will require private donations.
  Ⓒ It may cost more than expected.
  Ⓓ It may lead to new infrastructure.

15 What does the term "pilot program" most likely mean in this context?

  Ⓐ A small-scale test of a new project
  Ⓑ A program for professional cyclists
  Ⓒ A city-wide transportation plan
  Ⓓ A marketing campaign for the new service

Answers p.447

7. Form

Overview

양식은 일정한 틀을 갖춘 문서로, 크게 양식, 영수증, 송장, 일정표, 메뉴판으로 나눌 수 있다. 간결함을 위해 동사가 생략될 수 있으므로, 의미를 정확하게 파악하는 것이 중요하다. 또한 금액, 시간 등의 수치 정보를 헷갈리지 않고 정확하게 파악할 필요가 있다.

Topics

양식	업무 경비 정산 신청서, 고객 만족도 조사
영수증, 송장	사무용품 구매 내역, 가구 주문 내역
일정표	행사 일정표, 회의 일정표, 운동 경기 일정표
메뉴판	식사 메뉴, 음료 메뉴

Types of Question

Main Topic/ Main Purpose
양식의 목적이 무엇인지 묻는 문제가 주로 출제된다.
What is this form used for?

Detail
양식에 언급된 규정이나 혜택 등에 대한 세부 사항을 묻는 문제가 주로 출제된다.
How can a user formally dispute an unexpected charge?
What is the discount percentage afforded to Gold Tier members?

Example

Read a form.

Class Satisfaction Survey

Thank you for taking a class at Rhythm Street Dance Academy! Your feedback helps us improve our classes and provide the best possible experience. Please take a moment to fill out this survey. [1]Upon completion, you will receive a 10 percent discount on your next class.

Student Name: Kathy Chen
Course Name: Hip-Hop Foundations
Instructor Name: Ethan Brooks

	Poor	Fair	Good	Excellent
Quality of Instruction				X
Class Choreography				X
Music Selection			X	
Facility		X		

Comment:

The instructor had amazing energy and really made the class fun! The choreography was challenging but manageable. The studio space was clean and spacious, perfect for practicing. However, [2]the ventilation in the practice room could be better. It felt a bit stuffy during the class after a lot of activity. I'm excited to continue my dance journey here!

1. What will Ms. Chen receive after completing the survey?

   Ⓐ A discount on studio rentals
   Ⓑ A free class voucher
   Ⓒ A free guest pass for a friend
   Ⓓ A discount on the tuition fee

2. What is Ms. Chen's complaint?

   Ⓐ The instructor is unfriendly.
   Ⓑ The choreography is too difficult.
   Ⓒ The practice room is poorly ventilated.
   Ⓓ The studio space is too small and cramped.

정답 1. Ⓓ 2. Ⓒ

해설 1. Ms. Chen이 설문지를 작성한 후 무엇을 받을지를 묻는 문제이다. 'Upon completion, ~ next class'를 통해 설문조사 작성을 완료하면 다음 수업에 할인을 받을 수 있음을 알 수 있다. 따라서 Ⓓ가 정답이다.

2. Ms. Chen의 불만이 무엇인지 묻는 문제이다. 'the ventilation ~ better'를 통해 Ms. Chen이 연습실의 환기에 대해 불만이 있음을 알 수 있다. 따라서 Ⓒ가 정답이다.

HACKERS TEST

[01-02] Read a receipt.

Brentwood Department Store

Serving Chicago for almost two decades!

Date: August 18 **Branch:** 10th Street

LAPTOP BAG	$20.00
BATTERY CHARGER	$5.00
TUMBLER	$12.00
BICYCLE LOCK	$18.00
ALL ELECTRONICS ARE 10 PERCENT OFF.	TAX $6.00
	TOTAL $61.00

We are open until 10 P.M. in July and August. Our closing time returns to 9 P.M. in September.

---

01 Which item was discounted?

   Ⓐ Laptop Bag
   Ⓑ Battery Charger
   Ⓒ Tumbler
   Ⓓ Bicycle Lock

02 What can be inferred about the Brentwood Department Store?

   Ⓐ It has opened branches in multiple cities.
   Ⓑ It extends its operating hours in the summer.
   Ⓒ It will hold a promotional event in September.
   Ⓓ It has been in operation for over 20 years.

[03-04] Read a menu.

Salsa on Wheels
The most popular food truck in San Diego!

Lunch Specials	
Chicken Burrito	$8.00
Fish Taco	$7.00
Beef Quesadilla	$10.00

Our seafood dishes include whatever is freshest at the market each day. Leave a review on our website to get a digital coupon for a complimentary soda.

03 What is suggested about the fish taco?

Ⓐ It is only offered at lunch time.
Ⓑ Its availability is limited on weekdays.
Ⓒ Its ingredients change regularly.
Ⓓ It is the most popular menu item.

04 How can customers get a free beverage?

Ⓐ By placing an advance order
Ⓑ By posting an online review
Ⓒ By purchasing a lunch special
Ⓓ By downloading an application

HACKERS TEST

[05-06] Read a receipt.

ElectroMarket

1741 Talbot Avenue

Tel: (701) 555-8000

Date: April 10
Cashier: P. Blanda

- USB charging cable $25.00
  -50% clearance discount.. -$12.50
- ePhone Max (black)........... $499.00

Subtotal:	$511.50
Sales Tax (8%):	$40.92
Total:	$552.42

Payment Method: Cash

Please save this receipt for warranty or returns. All sales final on sale items.

---

05 How much was paid in cash?

Ⓐ $40.92
Ⓑ $499.00
Ⓒ $511.50
Ⓓ $552.42

06 What can be inferred about the USB charging cable?

Ⓐ It was available in only one color.
Ⓑ It is for use with a mobile phone only.
Ⓒ It cannot be returned.
Ⓓ It was previously used.

[07-09] Read an invoice.

Fresh Farms
Wholesale Produce Supplier

Date: May 13
Ship To: Belmont Diner
　　　　　1402 Station St.,
　　　　　Seattle WA, 98039

Invoice #: 948958
Bill To: Casey Robbins
Account #: 938475
555-0394

Item	Quantity	Price
Romaine Lettuce	10 kilograms	$40.00
White Potatoes	50 kilograms	$35.00
Green Onions	20 kilograms	$25.00
	Tax	$15.00
	Delivery	N/A
	Total	$115.00

Notes: Shipping fees are waived for orders of $100 or more. Otherwise, a $15 delivery fee is applied. Clients with business accounts are required to make full payment within 21 days of receipt of goods. Failure to do so will result in a late-payment penalty fee.

Please confirm the quality of the goods immediately upon arrival. If any items are spoiled, take a picture and send it to service@freshfarms.com. The value of the spoiled items will then be credited to your account.

07 What is suggested about Ms. Robbins?

Ⓐ She is a new client of Fresh Farms.
Ⓑ She is the owner of a restaurant.
Ⓒ She is required to pay a penalty fee.
Ⓓ She is eligible to receive a discount.

08 What must customers do to avoid a delivery fee?

Ⓐ Sign up for a special promotion
Ⓑ Create a business account
Ⓒ Make an advanced payment
Ⓓ Place a minimum order

09 Why would a customer send an image to Fresh Farms?

Ⓐ To indicate a product preference
Ⓑ To request a partial refund
Ⓒ To confirm arrival of a shipment
Ⓓ To demand replacement of an item

HACKERS TEST

[10-12] Read a schedule.

The Bradley Institute's Human Resources and Development Conference will be held on September 3.

It is expected to attract more than twice the number of participants as in previous years. The scheduled speakers are as follows:

Time	Speaker	Presentation Title
9:00 A.M. – 10:00 A.M.	Tina Ellis	Effective Screening Methods to Identify Talented Applicants
10:30 A.M. – 11:30 A.M.	Bill Cooke	How to Equip Experienced Employees with New Skills
LUNCH		
1:30 P.M. – 2:30 P.M.	Sara Yang	Compensation: The Relationship Between Salary and Benefits
3:00 P.M. – 4:00 P.M.	Matt Gomez	The Role of Employee Feedback in Shaping Company Policies

To sign up for the conference, visit www.bradleyinstitute.com. Note that there is a $25 registration fee. However, we offer a special price of $20 per person for groups of 15 or more. Call our events coordinator Dale Peterson at 555-0938 if this applies to you.

10 What can be inferred about the Bradley Institute?

Ⓐ It postponed an event until September 3.
Ⓑ It specializes in corporate training programs.
Ⓒ It has organized conferences previously.
Ⓓ It offers consulting services to companies.

11 When will the presentation about training begin?

Ⓐ At 9:00 A.M.
Ⓑ At 10:30 A.M.
Ⓒ At 1:30 P.M.
Ⓓ At 3:00 P.M.

12 Why would a participant contact Mr. Peterson?

Ⓐ By confirm a registration date
Ⓑ To request a discounted rate
Ⓒ To arrange a group session
Ⓓ To discuss an event topic

[13-15] Read a form.

Metro Sportswear - Application Form

Position Applied for: Sales Representative
Preferred Location: Any store in Fresno
Date of Availability: May 25
Hours: Full-time ☐ Part-time ■

Personal Information

Name: Neal Owen	E-mail: n.owen@ymail.com
Address: 15 Elm St., Fresno, California 93611	Phone Number: 555-0093

Education:

Coast High School	High School Diploma
Cheswick College	Enrolled (third-year business major)

Employment History

Vera Office Supply	Cashier (1 year, 2 months)
Core Sportswear	Sales Representative (8 months)

Notes: I am looking for a part-time summer job. However, I should mention that I have agreed to volunteer at an academic conference organized by my school, so I will need to take the first week of August off. I hope this won't be a problem. Thank you for considering my application, and feel free to contact me if you have any questions.

---

13 What is indicated about Metro Sportswear?

Ⓐ It is only hiring part-time staff.
Ⓑ It recently relocated to Fresno.
Ⓒ It operates multiple branches in Fresno.
Ⓓ It is planning to open a new store.

14 All of the following statements are true about Mr. Owen EXCEPT:

Ⓐ He is a former student of Coast High School.
Ⓑ He is in his third year of study at college.
Ⓒ He has worked for Metro Sportswear before.
Ⓓ He has over a year's experience as a cashier.

15 Why will Mr. Owen be required to take leave in August?

Ⓐ To join a study-abroad program
Ⓑ To assist with a university event
Ⓒ to volunteer at a local charity
Ⓓ To take an academic course

Answers p.450

무료 토플자료·유학정보 제공
goHackers.com

Hackers Updated TOEFL READING

TASK 3

Read an Academic Passage

Introduction

Section I. Question Types
1. Main Topic Questions
2. Detail Questions
3. Fact/Negative Fact Questions
4. Vocabulary Questions
5. Rhetorical Purpose Questions
6. Inference Questions
7. Insertion Questions

Section II. Passage Topics
1. Humanities
2. Arts
3. Social Science
4. Physical Science
5. Life Science

Introduction

TASK 3(Read an Academic Passage)는 학술적 주제에 관한 글을 읽고 문제를 푸는 유형이다. 지문의 주제는 인문학, 예술, 사회과학, 물리과학, 자연과학 등의 다양한 학문 분야에서 선정된다. 지문의 길이는 175~200단어 분량이고, 난이도는 영어권 고등학교 또는 대학교 교과서에서 등장하는 수준이다. 1지문에 5개의 문제가 출제된다. Module 1에서는 1지문이 출제되는데, 더미 문항이 포함될 경우에는 2지문까지도 출제된다. Lower Module 2에는 이 유형이 출제되지 않으며, Upper Module 2에서만 1지문이 출제된다.

■ Preview

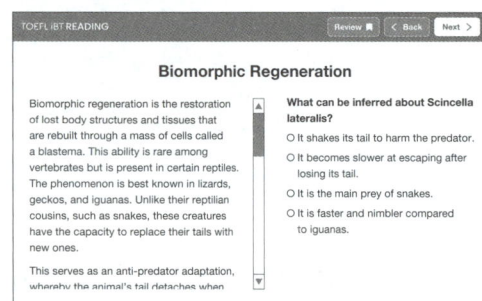

문제가 출제될 때 나오는 화면으로, 상단에는 지문의 제목이 나온다. 그 아래로 왼쪽에는 지문, 오른쪽에는 문제와 선택지가 나온다.

문제를 풀 때 해야 할 일: 지문과 문제, 보기를 읽은 후 보기 앞에 있는 칸을 클릭하여 답을 표시한다.

문제를 풀고 난 후 해야 할 일: Next 버튼을 클릭하여 다음 문제로 넘어간다. Module 안에서는 문제간 이동이 자유로우므로, 헷갈리는 문제가 있다면 넘어갔다가 뒤의 문제들을 풀고 다시 돌아올 수 있다.

■ Task Strategy

1. 제목을 통해 지문 전체의 주제를 파악하고 내용을 예상한다.
Academic Passage의 제목은 지문에서 다루는 핵심 개념 및 주제를 드러낸다. 따라서 제목을 통해 지문이 어떤 내용을 다룰 것인지를 예상할 수 있다.

2. 각 문제에서 다루는 키워드가 지문의 어떤 부분에 등장하는지 확인한다.
TASK 2에 비해 지문이 길기 때문에 각 키워드가 어디에 언급되는지 빠르게 파악하는 것이 중요하다.

3. 각 단락의 주제와 단락 간의 관계를 파악한다.
각 단락의 요점이 무엇이고 어떤 기능을 하는지를 파악하면서 지문을 읽는다면 지문을 더 빠르게 이해할 수 있다. 특히 단락의 기능 및 단락 간의 관계를 묻는 Rhetorical Purpose 문제를 더 효율적으로 풀 수 있다.

■ Study Guide

1. 문제 유형별로 알맞은 풀이 전략을 익히자.
문제 유형별로 풀이 전략을 익혀 두면 실전 시험에서 문제 풀이를 하는 것이 쉬워진다. 예를 들어, Detail 문제의 경우 질문에서 의문사와 핵심 어구를 확인하고 지문에서 그와 관련된 정답의 단서를 빠르게 찾는 연습을 통해 시간을 단축할 수 있다.

2. 학술 용어와 기초 배경 지식을 알아두자.
TASK 3의 지문은 전공 심화 수준의 어려운 내용을 다루지는 않지만, 낯선 분야의 지문이 나오면 빠르게 내용을 이해하기 어려울 수 있다. 평소에 TOEFL에 자주 출제되는 학문 분야의 용어와 기본적인 배경 지식을 알아두면 지문의 내용을 이해하기 더욱 수월해진다.

무료 토플자료·유학정보 제공
goHackers.com

**Hackers
Updated TOEFL
READING**

Section I
Question Types

Section I에서는 TASK 3에 출제되는 문제 유형을 7가지로 구분하여 각 유형의 특징과 질문 형태, 실제 문제 풀이에 적용 가능한 전략들을 소개하고 있다. 또한 풍부한 연습 문제와 실전 문제를 통해 각 문제 유형을 충분히 습득하고 공략할 수 있도록 하였다.

TASK 3의 Question Types에는 다음의 7가지가 있다.

1. Main Topic Questions
2. Detail Questions
3. Fact/Negative Fact Questions
4. Vocabulary Questions
5. Rhetorical Purpose Questions
6. Inference Questions
7. Insertion Questions

1. Main Topic Questions

Overview

지문의 주제나 중심 생각이 무엇인지 묻는 문제 유형이다. Main Topic 문제의 출제 비율은 낮은 편이지만, 실제로 출제될 경우 추론을 필요로 하는 형태로 까다롭게 출제될 수도 있다. 따라서 지문의 주제와 중심 생각을 올바르게 풀어서 쓴 선택지를 고를 수 있어야 한다.

Types of Questions

질문에 mainly about이나 main idea가 포함된다.

Main Topic
  What is the passage mainly about?
  Which of the following best states the main idea of the passage?

Hackers Strategy

1 지문의 제목과 첫 단락을 특히 주의 깊게 읽는다.
   제목은 지문에서 다루는 학술 개념을 직접적으로 드러내며, 첫 단락은 그 학술 개념에 대한 정의와 요점을 제시한다. 따라서 제목과 첫 단락을 통해 지문의 주제 및 중심 생각을 파악할 수 있다.

2 지문의 주제나 요지를 올바르게 패러프레이즈한 선택지를 고른다.
   Main Topic 유형의 정답은 지문에서 사용한 표현을 그대로 사용하기보다는, 지문의 주제나 중심 생각을 패러프레이즈해서 제시하는 것이 일반적이다. 따라서, 지문의 주제나 중심 생각을 올바르게 패러프레이즈했는지 확인한 후 선택지를 고른다.

3 자주 나오는 오답 유형에 주의한다.
   지문의 일부 내용만을 다루는 오답, 지문의 내용과 반대되는 오답, 지문에 언급된 단어를 사용하여 혼동을 주는 오답이 자주 등장한다. 특히 지문의 일부 내용만을 다루는 오답은 헷갈리기 쉬우므로 주의한다.

Example

The Value of Forgetting

Forgetting has often been undervalued compared to the high regard given to memory. However, forgetting helps the brain focus on new tasks and prevents cognitive overload, whereas retaining unnecessary past details could slow reasoning and impair decision-making.

Neuroscience now views forgetting as an active regulatory process rather than passive decay. Research from the Frankland Lab focused on the birth of new neurons, a process called hippocampal neurogenesis. In mouse studies, researchers found an inverse relationship between the rate of neurogenesis and memory persistence. When they genetically or environmentally increased the birth of new neurons, the animals demonstrated a measurable loss of older memories.

This suggests that new cells remodel memory circuits to clear out old information, allowing the brain to prioritize and store newer, more useful knowledge. This same mechanism is a leading hypothesis for explaining infantile amnesia, as the high rate of neurogenesis in early development may prevent the long-term consolidation of memories.

Far from being a flaw, this loss of information can enhance mental efficiency by making space for more useful knowledge. By clearing away irrelevant details, the brain can adapt quickly to new environments and prioritize what truly matters in the present.

Which of the following best states the main idea of the passage?

Ⓐ The brain accidentally forgets due to weak memory.
Ⓑ Forgetting unnecessary information enables better decisions and adaptability.
Ⓒ Effective decision-making hinges on recalling.
Ⓓ Suppression of memory always leads to loss of important knowledge.

정답　Ⓑ

해설　지문의 중심 생각을 묻는 문제이다. 지문의 제목 'The Value of Forgetting', 첫 번째 단락 후반부의 'However ~ cognitive overload', 그리고 세 번째 단락 후반부의 'By clearing away ~ in the present'를 통해 불필요한 정보를 잊는 것이 더 나은 결정과 적응을 가능하게 한다는 지문의 중심 생각을 확인할 수 있다. 따라서 Ⓑ가 정답이다.

HACKERS PRACTICE

01

Food deserts are areas where people have poor access to fresh, affordable food. They are often found in minority communities. Unfair housing policies and home loan lending practices historically pushed low-income groups into districts that lacked the investment needed to support retail businesses like grocery stores. Instead of building in these areas, developers followed the available capital and opened supermarkets in the suburbs.

Many residents of inner-city neighborhoods do not own cars, and public transit is slow and requires multiple transfers, making grocery trips to the suburbs overly time-consuming. As a result, people turn to fast-food chains and convenience stores clustered along busy roads, offering convenient but unhealthy food. This leads to diets with fewer fresh items and higher rates of diet-related disease.

What is the passage mainly about?

Ⓐ The role of fast-food chains in shaping diets
Ⓑ Policies for improving public transportation in cities
Ⓒ The impact of housing policies on access to fresh food
Ⓓ Community investment projects and neighborhood cohesion

02

Cargo cults are religious movements that originated in Melanesia amid the disruption of traditional societies. These communities experienced colonization, which stripped them of traditional authority and introduced vastly different material goods. Then, during World War II, when the islands became strategic military bases, these communities witnessed foreign military personnel arriving with vast quantities of food, weapons, and other "cargo." The people interpreted what they saw through the framework of local beliefs about the importance of ritual, and sought ways to share in the material abundance by imitating the behavior of the outsiders.

The most cited example is the John Frum movement on the island of Tanna in Vanuatu. Followers of the movement hold ceremonies, raise flags, and sometimes build symbolic airstrips or wooden radios to welcome expected deliveries. Today, while the original belief in an imminent, literal delivery of massive cargo has waned, the performance of the associated rituals persists, serving as a powerful symbol of enduring communal identity.

What is the passage mainly about?

Ⓐ Logistical systems that supplied armed forces during World War II
Ⓑ Ritual movements born as responses to disruption and inequality
Ⓒ Religious conversions in Melanesia driven by missionaries
Ⓓ Traditional leadership structures and social order in island societies

03

Body modification involves making permanent changes to the body. In cultures around the world, people mark, pierce, and shape their bodies as a form of expression. For example, in Polynesia, dense tattoo patterns reveal one's family ties and rank in society, and among the Maori, social identity is similarly conveyed through their facial designs that represent ancestry. Modifications can also signify a special life stage being reached. In parts of West Africa, scarification marks entry into adulthood. Among Inuit communities, women's facial tattooing historically signaled maturity and readiness for marriage. Likewise, in South Asia, ear and nose piercings are linked to marital status, publicly acknowledging the person's role within the family.

Which of the following best states the main idea of the passage?

Ⓐ Body modification is a negative and dangerous practice that has been criticized across cultures.
Ⓑ Body modification is a universal human practice that conveys identity and social meaning.
Ⓒ Body modification is a modern urban trend with little historical significance.
Ⓓ Body modification is a refined cosmetic technique focused on enhancing personal appearance.

04

The Zeigarnik effect suggests that people remember unfinished or interrupted tasks more easily than completed ones. Psychologist Bluma Zeigarnik decided to study this after hearing about waiters who had better recall of unpaid orders than settled ones. When Zeigarnik conducted her experiments, she found that people were, in fact, twice as likely to remember interrupted tasks as completed ones.

This finding supported the idea that unfinished activities create cognitive tension, making them more salient in memory. Students can take advantage of this effect. By taking breaks during their study session, they maintain cognitive tension, which helps improve their memory of the material being studied.

Which of the following best states the main idea of the passage?

Ⓐ Interruptions generally hinder memory and motivation.
Ⓑ Unfinished tasks can have cognitive and motivational effects.
Ⓒ Enjoyment of a certain task is the main factor influencing recall.
Ⓓ Finishing tasks is always more rewarding than leaving them unfinished.

Answers p.453

[01-05]

Horizontal Gene Transfer

Horizontal gene transfer is the process by which genetic material moves between different organisms outside the parent-offspring relationship. This rapid exchange is accomplished in bacteria through three primary methods: direct physical contact (conjugation), transfer by viruses (transduction), and absorption of genetic fragments from the environment (transformation). This process allows genetic traits, such as those conferring antibiotic resistance, to spread quickly and widely among different species.

This phenomenon is not just limited to bacteria. For example, some plants have acquired resistance genes from neighboring species, helping them survive environmental peril. Among animals, certain aphid (a type of small insect) species have gained the ability to produce red pigments after obtaining related genes from fungi. These examples show that horizontal gene transfer can happen across very different types of organisms.

The significance of horizontal gene transfer is substantial. It speeds up evolution and adaptation, letting organisms gain useful traits without waiting for many generations. Because of this, scientists see horizontal gene transfer as a force that continuously reshapes life on Earth.

01 What is this passage mainly about?

　Ⓐ A biological theory regarding gene loss in evolution
　Ⓑ An uncommon genetic mutation among organisms
　Ⓒ An important method of genetic material delivery
　Ⓓ An unexpected pattern of genetic inheritance

02 The word "peril" in the second paragraph is closest in meaning to

　Ⓐ drawback
　Ⓑ durability
　Ⓒ threat
　Ⓓ obstacle

03 Why does the author mention viruses?

　Ⓐ To describe why some organisms cannot acquire new traits
　Ⓑ To suggest that viruses only play a minor role in genetic evolution
　Ⓒ To specify a mechanism by which genetic material is shared
　Ⓓ To highlight the limitations of horizontal gene transfer

04 How did certain aphids acquire the ability to produce red pigments?

　Ⓐ Through mutations in their own genes
　Ⓑ Through selective breeding by researchers
　Ⓒ By absorbing pigments from their red-colored food
　Ⓓ By acquiring genes from a different type of organism

05 What does the passage indicate about the effect of horizontal gene transfer on evolutionary speed?

　Ⓐ It speeds up transmission to the offspring.
　Ⓑ It delays adaptation in most organisms.
　Ⓒ It allows beneficial traits to spread rapidly.
　Ⓓ It only accelerates changes in microscopic species.

HACKERS TEST

[06-10]

Cardiac Cycle

The cardiac cycle refers to the repeating sequence by which the heart pumps blood throughout the body. The process begins with atrial contraction, during which the thin-walled right and left atria push blood into the thicker ventricles. This is followed by ventricular contraction, when the right and left ventricles force blood into the arteries connected to other parts of the body. Afterward, all four chambers relax during the filling phase.

A These phases are coordinated by electrical impulses, ensuring that the heart beats normally. **B** This electrical activation does not happen uniformly across the entire heart, causing the chambers to begin contraction fractions of a second apart during each stage of the cardiac cycle. **C** While these delays are a normal part of the process, other disruptions can lead to health problems. **D**

The cardiac cycle is highly adaptive. In response to physical activity or stress, the cycle becomes faster, reducing the relative length of the relaxation phase but still maintaining effective blood flow. In contrast, the cycle slows down during sleep. The heart also adjusts the force of contraction to match the body's changing oxygen demands, such as when a person exercises or experiences strong emotions.

06 What is the passage mainly about?

　Ⓐ The warning signs of an abnormal heartbeat
　Ⓑ The complex process of each heartbeat
　Ⓒ The method for monitoring cardiac cycles
　Ⓓ The physical structure of cardiac muscles

07 The word "sequence" in the passage is closest in meaning to

　Ⓐ rotation
　Ⓑ division
　Ⓒ progression
　Ⓓ segment

08 What happens during the ventricular contraction phase?

　Ⓐ The flow of blood within the heart is reversed.
　Ⓑ Blood pressure in the body drops to its lowest point.
　Ⓒ Blood is delivered to other parts of the body.
　Ⓓ Only the heart's left side is actively contracted.

09 Why does the author mention that the cardiac cycle slows down during sleep?

　Ⓐ To show how the heart adapts to changing needs
　Ⓑ To indicate that oversleeping can strain the heart
　Ⓒ To argue that rest is more important than exercise
　Ⓓ To suggest the time when the heart is most vulnerable

10 There are four locations [■] in the passage that indicate where the following sentence could be added.

For instance, timing irregularities can contribute to symptoms like fatigue or dizziness.

Where would the sentence best fit? Select a location [■] where the sentence could be added to the passage.

HACKERS TEST

[11-15]

The Tragedy of the Commons

The tragedy of the commons is an economic and social concept that explains how individuals, acting rationally according to their self-interest, can ultimately deplete or ruin shared resources. A commonly cited example is the use of communal pastures. Each herder gains by adding more animals, but if all herders do this, the pasture becomes overgrazed and eventually useless to everyone.

Another example is overfishing in the oceans. Since no single authority can enforce strict catch limits in international waters, fishing fleets are motivated to catch as many fish as possible before others do the same. While each actor benefits in the short term, the cumulative effects lead to declining fish populations, threatening the ecosystem and the livelihoods of everyone involved. Similar situations occur with water usage in shared river basins and logging in unregulated forests.

To prevent resource depletion, communities and governments can implement strategies that limit the usage of shared resources, including resource quotas and monitoring systems. There can also be economic incentives, such as shared profits from sustainable harvesting and compensation systems that reward communities for maintaining resource conservation practices. Without some form of cooperation or oversight, resources vital for long-term sustainability may be used up or destroyed.

11 Which of the following best states the main idea of the passage?

Ⓐ Collective resources can be preserved through technological advancement.
Ⓑ Overuse of common property is mostly caused by ineffective distribution systems.
Ⓒ Economic growth is primarily driven by competition over shared resources.
Ⓓ Unregulated use of communal assets can lead to their eventual loss.

12 The word "deplete" in the first paragraph is closest in meaning to

Ⓐ exhaust
Ⓑ supervise
Ⓒ protect
Ⓓ transfer

13 Why does the author mention communal pastures?

Ⓐ To argue that communal land ownership is often inefficient
Ⓑ To emphasize economic inequality among farmers in shared lands
Ⓒ To show how the example of overfishing is different from other examples
Ⓓ To provide a simple illustration of a concept presented earlier in the passage

14 Click on the sentence in paragraph 2 that identifies specific circumstances contributing to the loss of a shared resource.

Ⓐ Another example is overfishing in the oceans.
Ⓑ Since no single authority can enforce strict catch limits in international waters, fishing fleets are motivated to catch as many fish as possible before others do the same.
Ⓒ While each actor benefits in the short term, the cumulative effects lead to declining fish populations, threatening the ecosystem and the livelihoods of everyone involved.
Ⓓ Similar situations occur with water usage in shared river basins and logging in unregulated forests.

15 All of the following are mentioned as possible measures for sustainable resource management EXCEPT

Ⓐ Monitoring systems
Ⓑ Quotas for resources
Ⓒ State ownership of natural resources
Ⓓ Compensation for conservation

HACKERS TEST

[16-20]

The Strange Situation Experiment

The Strange Situation Experiment, conducted by psychologist Mary Ainsworth in the 1970s, determined the attachment behavior of infants toward their caregivers. In this experiment, a mother brought her infant into a room with toys. After a short period, the mother left the child alone or with a stranger, and then later returned. Researchers carefully observed the baby's reactions during separation and reunion.

Based on these observations, different attachment types were identified. Some infants were visibly upset when the mother left and were quickly comforted upon her return; these were classified as securely attached. Others showed anxiety and avoidance or were hard to console once their mothers returned. A few infants showed mixed reactions when their mother came back, wanting comfort but also resisting it.

This experiment was groundbreaking because it provided specific labels for different child-caregiver bonds. Later research confirmed that attachment styles early in life influence later development. The insights from this experiment have helped shape social policy, early education approaches, and understanding of parent-child relationships, underlining the importance of healthy early bonds for emotional well-being.

16 What is the passage mainly about?

   Ⓐ The results of a psychological study about language development
   Ⓑ An experiment that categorized different infant attachment styles
   Ⓒ A study of methods to comfort young children after separation
   Ⓓ The influence of nurturing styles on child-caregiver relationships

17 The word "console" in the passage is closest in meaning to

   Ⓐ distract
   Ⓑ praise
   Ⓒ support
   Ⓓ soothe

18 Which of the following is NOT mentioned as a response infants showed in the experiment?

   Ⓐ Being quickly comforted when the mother came back
   Ⓑ Playing alone without noticing the caregiver's absence
   Ⓒ Showing anxious behaviors after the caregiver returned
   Ⓓ Seeking and resisting comfort at the same time

19 What is suggested about early attachment?

   Ⓐ It has a major effect on later development.
   Ⓑ It is strengthened through early education.
   Ⓒ It is unrelated to adult relationships.
   Ⓓ It remains unchanged until a child matures.

20 What is the relationship between paragraphs 2 and 3?

   Ⓐ Paragraph 3 provides examples of attachment styles identified in paragraph 2.
   Ⓑ Paragraph 3 discusses the limitations of the experiment outlined in paragraph 2.
   Ⓒ Paragraph 3 introduces the broader impacts of the findings mentioned in paragraph 2.
   Ⓓ Paragraph 3 offers solutions for the attachment issues discussed in paragraph 2.

Answers p.454

2. Detail Questions

Overview

'무엇을', '어떻게', '왜'와 같은 세부 사항에 관해 묻는 문제이다. 지문에 나오는 다양한 세부 사항을 빠르게 찾아내는 능력이 필요하다.

Types of Questions

주로 What, How, Why 등의 의문사가 문제에 포함된다. 선택지 중에서 지문에 언급되지 않은 것을 고르는 문제가 출제될 경우, NOT 또는 EXCEPT가 문제에 포함된다.

Detail

What is one physiological response to chronic stress discussed in the passage?

How do circadian rhythms regulate hormone production in mammals?

Which of the following is NOT mentioned as a limitation of renewable energy technologies?

All of the following are essential functions of the cell membrane EXCEPT

Hackers Strategy

1 문제의 핵심 어구에 관한 내용을 지문에서 확인한다.

문제의 핵심 어구가 언급된 곳을 찾은 후 앞뒤의 내용을 확인한다. 또한, 문제에 제시된 의문사에 따라 특정 정보가 언급되는 곳을 주의 깊게 본다. 예를 들어 How라면 방법이, Why라면 이유가 언급되는 부분을 집중적으로 본다.

2 지문의 내용을 올바르게 패러프레이즈한 선택지를 고른다.

지문에 제시된 세부 사항이 정답에 그대로 드러나는 경우도 있지만, 패러프레이즈되어 있는 경우도 있다.

3 자주 나오는 오답 유형에 주의한다.

지문에 언급된 단어를 그대로 사용하여 혼동을 주는 오답, 지문에 언급되기는 했지만 문제의 키워드와는 관련이 없는 오답, 지문의 내용과 반대되는 오답이 자주 출제된다. 반대로 이러한 선택지가 NOT/EXCEPT 문제에서는 정답이 된다.

Example

Human Migration

Human migration has shaped societies across the globe for thousands of years. Throughout history, various forces—such as wars, famines, economic conditions, and political changes—have prompted waves of people to relocate, shaping the cultural landscapes of entire continents. The story of human migration is a testament to human adaptability and the constant search for opportunity and security.

Early migrations occurred as nomadic groups moved in search of food and favorable climates, spreading human populations across distant regions. The Silk Road facilitated movement between East and West, allowing not only goods but also languages, religions, and ideas to travel vast distances. In the nineteenth and twentieth centuries, industrialization and urban growth prompted millions to seek new lives in rapidly expanding cities. Migration continues today, driven by factors such as globalization and environmental changes.

While migration can foster cultural exchange and diversity, it also presents challenges, such as adaptation and integration, for both migrants and host communities. Modern societies rely on effective policies to manage population movement, safeguard rights, and promote social cohesion. Understanding the causes and effects of migration is essential for addressing contemporary issues related to displacement and identity.

What change did industrialization bring during the nineteenth and twentieth centuries?

Ⓐ Decline in the quality of urban life
Ⓑ Shift of population to urban areas
Ⓒ Increase in employment opportunities
Ⓓ Exchange of languages and religions

정답 Ⓑ

해설 19세기와 20세기 동안 산업화가 어떤 변화를 불러왔는지 묻는 문제이다. 'nineteenth ~ expanding cities'를 통해 19세기와 20세기 산업화가 인구의 도시 지역으로의 이동을 일으켰음을 알 수 있다. 따라서 Ⓑ가 정답이다.

HACKERS PRACTICE

01

Anthropomorphism is the attribution of human qualities to non-human entities. It is rooted in our evolutionary history and helps us make sense of the world, but we must be cautious when applying it to other species. Drawing conclusions about the behavior of non-human animals feels natural because we are animals too. Like them, we seek food and warmth and care for our young. However, non-human animals have evolved under different conditions, and assuming they have feelings or motives identical to ours can lead to misunderstanding or even harm.

For instance, visitors at a zoo might worry that a tiger living alone in its enclosure is lonely, because that is how they themselves would feel in such a situation. In reality, tigers are territorial, and introducing another tiger into the enclosure would cause stress to the animal.

Researchers who study animals must be wary of anthropomorphism, as it can bias their work. Chimpanzees, for example, often display what looks like a smile when they are distressed. If this expression is misinterpreted through a human lens, it could be mistaken for happiness instead.

What is a common misunderstanding about non-human animals?

Ⓐ They take care of their young.
Ⓑ They prefer solitary lives.
Ⓒ They prioritize emotional needs over physical ones.
Ⓓ They experience the same emotions as humans.

02

Magnetic Resonance Imaging (MRI) is a non-invasive medical method used to create images of the inside of the body. During an MRI, the patient is placed within a strong magnetic field, which causes many of the hydrogen atoms in the body to temporarily align in a specific direction. Hydrogen atoms are ideal targets for scanning because the human body consists mainly of water and fat, which are rich in hydrogen.

The MRI machine emits short pulses of radio waves. These waves disrupt the protons at the center of the hydrogen atoms, forcing them out of their aligned state. When the radio waves stop, the protons return to their original position. During this process, they emit faint signals. The scanner captures these signals, which computers convert into detailed cross-sectional images.

What happens when the radio waves in an MRI scan stop?

Ⓐ Protons disappear from the magnetic field.
Ⓑ The magnetic field starts to generate current.
Ⓒ Protons revert to their prior, aligned state.
Ⓓ The scanner produces cross-sectional images.

03

Presolar grains are tiny, solid particles ejected by dying stars over 4.6 billion years ago, before the Sun formed. They are older than anything on Earth.

Scientists first suspected the grains' existence in the 1960s while studying the composition of ancient meteorites. They discovered elements whose high quantities did not match models of the solar system. Their suspicions were later confirmed in the 1980s when laboratory technology had sufficiently advanced. Researchers got a further boost in the 2010s when samples with high concentrations were obtained from nearby asteroids. Because asteroids float in space, they are less exposed to chemical processes that impact grain preservation.

Scientists have now cataloged thousands of grains and organized them into the Presolar Grain Database. Most of these are carbon-based materials such as diamonds, graphite, and more. They not only provide direct evidence of early stars but also reveal clues about the evolution of our solar system.

What have scientists learned about presolar grains?

Ⓐ They can be artificially recreated in a lab.
Ⓑ They mainly consist of carbon compounds.
Ⓒ They have properties with practical applications.
Ⓓ They are more common than other solar particles.

04

Third culture kids (TCKs) are children who spend a significant part of their formative years in a culture different from that of their parents. The reason is often an international relocation related to their parents' jobs. TCKs grow up balancing the values and customs of their parents' culture (the first culture) with those of the host country (the second culture) to create a unique third culture.

Growing up as a TCK offers several advantages. These children typically develop strong cross-cultural communication skills, global awareness, and flexibility in unfamiliar environments. They tend to be open-minded, making it easier to build friendships across diverse communities.

However, the TCK experience also has its challenges. It can disrupt social networks and leave these children feeling rootless and unsure of their cultural identity. Some TCKs might feel permanently unsettled and find it hard to define where they are from.

Which of the following is NOT mentioned as a challenge faced by TCKs in the passage?

Ⓐ Losing social connections
Ⓑ Struggling to determine their sense of cultural belonging
Ⓒ Having difficulty with communication
Ⓓ Experiencing a lingering sense of instability

Answers p.457

HACKERS TEST

[01-05]

Lactose Intolerance

Lactose intolerance is a condition in which adults have difficulty digesting lactose, the main sugar in milk. The reason for this issue is that, for most mammals after the juvenile stage, the body produces much less of an enzyme called lactase, which breaks down lactose in the digestive system. When there is not enough lactase, lactose passes into the colon undigested, where it interacts with bacteria and leads to symptoms such as bloating and diarrhea. While found throughout the world, lactose intolerance is prominent among East Asians, Africans, and Indigenous populations in the Americas and Australia.

If lactose intolerance is the norm, how did some people gain the ability to digest lactose into adulthood? It is the result of evolutionary history and cultural dietary practices. Over many generations, certain groups, especially people of Northern European descent, developed a genetic adaptation allowing them to continue lactase production in response to their longstanding consumption of dairy products. Interestingly, Mongolian herders exhibit very few symptoms of lactose intolerance despite lacking the genetic mutation for lactase persistence. This phenomenon is attributed to their consumption of a diet rich in fermented dairy products, which facilitate lactose digestion by supplying probiotic microbes.

01 The word "adaptation" in the passage is closest in meaning to

Ⓐ disease
Ⓑ change
Ⓒ composition
Ⓓ reaction

02 What happens when there is not enough lactase?

Ⓐ Lactose is absorbed in the stomach more easily.
Ⓑ Lactose is converted into protein by gut bacteria.
Ⓒ Lactose passes into the colon without being digested.
Ⓓ Lactose interacts with stomach acid to cause bloating.

03 According to the passage, people of Northern European descent

Ⓐ are more likely to suffer from bloating than diarrhea due to lactose
Ⓑ normally continue to produce lactase as adults
Ⓒ usually develop severe lactose intolerance symptoms
Ⓓ tend to lose the ability to digest lactose after childhood

04 Why does the author mention Mongolian herders?

Ⓐ To introduce the historical origins of dairy consumption in Central Asia
Ⓑ To argue that lactose intolerance is primarily determined by genetics across populations
Ⓒ To highlight an exception where diet enables lactose digestion despite genetic limits
Ⓓ To suggest that Asian populations generally avoid dairy products

05 What does the passage suggest about lactose intolerance?

Ⓐ It can lead to serious health consequences.
Ⓑ It is caused by a failure in the colon's function.
Ⓒ Its geographic distribution is extensive.
Ⓓ Its primary cause is the consumption of fermented products.

HACKERS TEST

[06-10]

Psychological Projection

Psychological projection is a protective response through which individuals attribute their own undesirable thoughts or feelings to others. Projection allows a person to protect their self-image by avoiding inner conflicts and shifting unwanted emotions outward. In psychological theory, this process is seen as an unconscious strategy, not a deliberate action.

Suppose an employee is experiencing intense anxiety about their job performance. Instead of acknowledging their own personal insecurity and seeking help, the employee insists that it is the colleagues who feel anxious and then judges them critically. This pattern of assigning anxiety to others instead of recognizing it internally is common. And it may persist until the employee receives feedback or gains insight into their behavior. Without intervention, such a projection can escalate workplace tensions and affect team dynamics.

Projection can delay personal growth. By externalizing internal conflict, people may be less likely to resolve their own emotional issues, which can lead to communication difficulties and tense relationships with others. Awareness and recognition of projection are considered central to therapeutic approaches, helping individuals develop healthier coping strategies and improve social interactions.

06 The word "attribute" in the passage is closest in meaning to

Ⓐ question
Ⓑ ascribe
Ⓒ reject
Ⓓ express

07 Why might a person use projection?

Ⓐ To control their environment
Ⓑ To prevent confrontation with others
Ⓒ To gain approval from colleagues
Ⓓ To avoid facing inner conflicts

08 Why does the author mention the employee who insists colleagues are anxious?

Ⓐ To show that clear communication can resolve misunderstandings
Ⓑ To critique contemporary dynamics in workplaces
Ⓒ To explain how projection operates in everyday situations
Ⓓ To suggest that anxiety is common in professional settings

09 What does the passage suggest about therapeutic approaches to projection?

Ⓐ They focus on increasing awareness of projection.
Ⓑ They encourage people to project only difficult emotions.
Ⓒ They help people project their emotions in a controlled setting.
Ⓓ They prioritize analyzing others' feelings over self-reflection.

10 What is one possible consequence of using projection?

Ⓐ It may prevent people from resolving their own emotional problems.
Ⓑ It can cause people to become overly critical of their own behavior.
Ⓒ It leads people to aggressively attack the character of others.
Ⓓ It may reduce the individual's ability to empathize with others.

HACKERS TEST

[11-15]

Radiocarbon Dating

Radiocarbon dating is a technique used to determine the age of objects that include substances once part of a living organism. It is based on measuring the amount of a special type of carbon, called carbon-14, found in organic materials such as wood, bone, or charcoal. Carbon-14 is created in the atmosphere and absorbed by living things throughout their life. When the organism dies, it stops absorbing carbon-14, and the carbon-14 inside starts to decrease.

Scientists can estimate how long it has been since the organism died by measuring the residual carbon-14. This method makes it possible to determine the age of items that are up to 50,000 years old. Archaeologists use radiocarbon dating to study human history and learn about past environments. It has helped to identify the age of prehistoric tools, fossils, cave art, and ancient buildings.

Radiocarbon dating is not always accurate because the results are affected by previous variations in atmospheric concentrations of carbon-14. To account for this, scientists collect tree-ring and marine reservoir data to track changes over extended periods of time. This information is then used to calibrate findings from radiocarbon dating.

11. The word "residual" in the passage is closest in meaning to

    Ⓐ lacking
    Ⓑ remaining
    Ⓒ diminishing
    Ⓓ growing

12. What does the passage indicate about radiocarbon dating?

    Ⓐ It cannot be used to date natural objects.
    Ⓑ Its findings do not require calibration.
    Ⓒ It cannot determine the age of inorganic objects.
    Ⓓ Its accuracy depends on the age of the object.

13. How does carbon-14 respond once an organism dies?

    Ⓐ It gradually accumulates over time.
    Ⓑ It remains constant without change.
    Ⓒ It diminishes gradually.
    Ⓓ It transforms into oxygen.

14. What is the relationship between paragraphs 2 and 3?

    Ⓐ Paragraph 3 provides an alternative explanation for the phenomenon described in paragraph 2.
    Ⓑ Paragraph 3 introduces a flaw in the technique detailed in paragraph 2 and provides the solution.
    Ⓒ Paragraph 3 elaborates on the scientific uses of radiocarbon dating discussed in paragraph 2.
    Ⓓ Paragraph 3 provides additional scientific background to the explanations given in paragraph 2.

15. What can be inferred about the tree-ring and marine reservoir data used by scientists?

    Ⓐ It suggests that calibration techniques need to be improved.
    Ⓑ It enables an alternative way of calculating an object's age.
    Ⓒ It directly contradicts the findings from radiocarbon dating.
    Ⓓ It indicates previous variations of atmospheric carbon-14.

HACKERS TEST

[16-20]

Yeast Fermentation

Yeast fermentation is the metabolic process by which yeast cells convert sugars into energy. This reaction typically occurs in environments with little or no oxygen. Fermentation begins when enzymes produced by yeast break down glucose or other simple sugars. As the sugar is broken down inside the yeast, intermediate compounds are released that then change into ethanol and carbon dioxide.

The process is essential in making bread, beer, and wine. In bread making, carbon dioxide causes the dough to rise, creating a light texture. In alcoholic beverage production, fermentation is controlled to obtain the desired ethanol content. Yeast fermentation also plays a key role in the production of biofuels and pharmaceuticals.

The speed and efficiency of fermentation depend on the yeast strain. Different yeast strains possess unique metabolic characteristics that influence how rapidly and completely they convert sugars into ethanol and carbon dioxide. For example, baker's yeast ferments sugars quickly and is commonly used for baking, while ale yeast achieves a more complete sugar conversion and is, therefore, optimal for beer brewing. Some yeast strains can tolerate higher alcohol concentrations, making them suitable for producing wine and spirits.

16 How does yeast begin the fermentation process?

Ⓐ It transforms into ethanol and carbon dioxide.
Ⓑ It absorbs nutrients from the sugar solution.
Ⓒ It produces enzymes that break down sugars.
Ⓓ It combines carbon dioxide with alcohol.

17 The word "intermediate" in the passage is closest in meaning to

Ⓐ elaborate
Ⓑ momentary
Ⓒ in-between
Ⓓ mandatory

18 What causes bread dough to rise during yeast fermentation?

Ⓐ The production of ethanol
Ⓑ The absorption of water
Ⓒ The release of carbon dioxide
Ⓓ The absence of oxygen

19 Why does the author mention "baker's yeast" and "ale yeast"?

Ⓐ To describe the history of fermentation in different cultures
Ⓑ To provide examples of yeast strains used for different purposes
Ⓒ To suggest that baker's yeast is generally more suitable for fermentation
Ⓓ To show that fermentation cannot occur without modern technology

20 What is one industrial application of yeast fermentation mentioned in the passage?

Ⓐ The development of food preservatives
Ⓑ The extraction of carbon dioxide
Ⓒ The production of medicine
Ⓓ The refinement of crude oil

Answers p.459

3. Fact/Negative Fact Questions

Overview

선택지로 주어진 문장의 내용과 지문의 내용이 일치하는지를 묻는 문제이다. Fact 문제는 지문의 내용과 일치하는 선택지를, Negative Fact는 지문의 내용과 일치하지 않는 선택지를 고르는 문제이다.

Types of Questions

주로 'indicated about ~', 'true about ~'과 같은 형태로 문제가 제시된다. about 뒤에는 지문에서 언급한 세부 개념이 올 수도 있지만, 지문 전체의 주제가 올 수도 있다.

Fact
　What is indicated in the passage about ancient trade networks?
　What is suggested in the passage about Gothic architecture?

Negative Fact
　All of the following are true about the human circulatory system EXCEPT:

Hackers Strategy

1　문제와 선택지의 핵심 어구와 관련된 내용을 지문에서 확인한다.
문제의 핵심 어구가 세부 개념이라면, 그 개념이 언급된 문장을 찾아 내용을 확인한다. 문제의 핵심 어구가 지문 전체의 주제라면, 각 선택지의 핵심 어구가 언급된 문장을 찾아 내용을 확인한다.

2　지문의 내용을 올바르게 패러프레이즈한 선택지를 고른다.
지문의 내용이 정답에 그대로 드러나는 경우도 있지만, 패러프레이즈되어 있는 경우도 있다는 점에 유의한다.

3　자주 나오는 오답 유형에 주의한다.
지문에 아예 언급되지 않은 내용이나 지문의 내용과 반대되는 내용을 제시하는 오답이 자주 출제된다. 또한, 고난도 오답으로는 지문에 언급된 단어를 사용하여 혼동을 주는 오답, 지문의 내용과 일부만 일치하는 오답이 등장한다. 반대로 이러한 선택지가 Negative Fact 문제에서는 정답이 된다.

Example

Acoustic Camouflage

Acoustic camouflage is an adaptive strategy employed by various animal species to avoid detection by predators or prey through the manipulation of sound. Some moths, for example, possess specialized wing scales that scatter or absorb sound waves used by predators for detection, making them less detectable. Owls possess specialized feathers that enable silent flight, preventing prey from hearing their approach.

In addition to anatomical adaptations, behavioral strategies play a crucial role. Certain insects, such as katydids, exploit background environmental noise to mask their own calls, blending into the acoustic environment and reducing the risk of predation. Similarly, frogs may synchronize their calls to create overlapping noise, making it difficult for predators to isolate an individual call. Bats, on the other hand, may modulate the timing or frequency of their calls to avoid interference or to reduce detectability by prey.

Research indicates that many acoustic camouflage mechanisms have evolved in response to specific listening technologies used by predators, such as echolocation. This evolutionary arms race highlights the importance of sound in predator-prey interactions. Scientists continue to study these interactions to better understand how animals exploit acoustic properties for survival, revealing intricate adaptations tied to sensory ecology.

What does the passage indicate about frogs?

Ⓐ They coordinate their calls to obscure individual sounds.
Ⓑ They exploit background environmental noise to mask their calls.
Ⓒ They mainly use anatomical adaptations.
Ⓓ They modulate the timing of their echolocation calls.

정답   Ⓐ

해설   지문에서 개구리에 관해 명시하는 내용을 묻는 문제이다. 'frogs may synchronize ~ individual call'을 통해 개구리들이 울음을 조정하여 각각의 소리를 듣기 힘들게 함을 알 수 있다. 따라서 Ⓐ가 정답이다.

HACKERS PRACTICE

01

The Gaia hypothesis argues that Earth and its life forms collectively function as a self-regulating system that sustains habitability. Chemist James Lovelock introduced the idea in the 1970s while examining how life might alter the chemical composition of planetary atmospheres.

According to this hypothesis, Earth's biological and physical systems operate like organs in a body to keep the planet stable. For instance, ocean plankton release certain compounds that boost cloud formation, which cools the planet to livable temperatures. Also, plants absorb carbon dioxide and release oxygen, helping modulate atmospheric composition to support life.

There are "weak" and "strong" versions of the hypothesis. The weak version suggests that biological and physical processes passively influence environmental conditions on Earth. The strong version, however, claims that life intentionally maintains Earth's stability.

What does the passage indicate about ocean plankton?

Ⓐ They release greenhouse gases and warm the atmosphere.
Ⓑ They absorb oxygen and release carbon dioxide.
Ⓒ They stimulate the production of clouds, leading to a cooler global climate.
Ⓓ They prevent water evaporation to balance low rainfall.

02

Gentrification is the process by which affluent individuals move into lower-income urban neighborhoods, leading to significant changes in the local environment and community. This influx typically results in new businesses, renovated buildings, and increased property values. While the transformation may improve infrastructure and provide new amenities, it also tends to drive up living costs and alter the social fabric of the area.

For example, New York City's Williamsburg has experienced waves of gentrification. This area became trendy as artists and young professionals settled there, followed by the arrival of upscale shops. However, long-time residents often found themselves facing higher rent and property taxes, making it difficult to remain in their homes. Businesses with long-term ties to the neighborhood were sometimes replaced by establishments that catered to newer, wealthier customers.

What is indicated about New York City's Williamsburg?

Ⓐ Its residents include young individuals with professional careers.
Ⓑ Its local businesses opposed the neighborhood's transformation.
Ⓒ It had many upscale shops before its redevelopment.
Ⓓ It has become less attractive to new businesses and investors.

03

Stendhal syndrome is a condition characterized by intense psychological and physical symptoms when individuals are exposed to exceptional works of art or overwhelming beauty. The syndrome was named after the nineteenth-century French author Stendhal, who described experiencing such symptoms while viewing Renaissance masterpieces in Florence.

Several cases have been reported, especially among tourists visiting art-rich locations such as Florence's Uffizi Gallery. Symptoms can include rapid heartbeat, dizziness, confusion, fainting, and panic in response to powerful artistic or architectural displays. Some visitors have also experienced strong feelings of existential anxiety and even hallucinations.

All of the following are mentioned about Stendhal syndrome EXCEPT:

Ⓐ It can cause rapid heartbeat and dizziness.
Ⓑ It affects tourists visiting locations that are rich in art.
Ⓒ It occurs most frequently among professional artists.
Ⓓ It can induce hallucinations in response to artistic displays.

04

Gallstones are solid deposits that form in the gallbladder, which is a small organ beneath the liver and stores digestive fluid called bile. They form when substances in bile, such as cholesterol, become concentrated and crystallize. They can range from tiny particles to stones the size of golf balls. When gallstones block the bile ducts, this obstruction results in extreme pain. They affect millions of people worldwide, with certain populations being more susceptible than others.

Untreated stones can cause cholangitis, a serious bile duct infection, or migrate to block the pancreas and trigger acute pancreatitis. When gallbladder inflammation progresses to tissue death, emergency surgery becomes unavoidable. However, these life-threatening complications are largely preventable through lifestyle modifications that address the root causes of stone formation.

All of the following are true about gallstones EXCEPT:

Ⓐ They form when bile substances become concentrated.
Ⓑ They may trigger acute pancreatitis.
Ⓒ They require immediate surgical intervention.
Ⓓ They are more prevalent among some groups of individuals.

Answers p.462

HACKERS TEST

[01-05]

Phantom Pain

Phantom pain is a phenomenon in which individuals feel sensations, often pain, in a part of the body that is no longer present, typically after amputation. This type of pain is not caused by external injury and can vary from mild tingling to intense discomfort. For example, a person who has lost a leg may experience stinging, burning, or pressure where the leg used to be.

The most widely accepted explanation is that the brain and nervous system are responsible for phantom pain. After an amputation, the nerves that once carried signals from the missing limb to the brain are still active. These nerves may send unexpected signals, which the brain interprets as coming from the absent body part. Also, the areas of the brain that once processed information from the lost limb remain active and can respond to stimuli from nearby body regions.

Phantom pain can last for a short period after surgery or persist for months or years. Treatments focus on managing symptoms with pain relief methods, physical therapy, and mirror therapy, which uses visual feedback to retrain the brain's response to pain signals. Phantom pain reveals the complexity of how the nervous system and brain generate perception.

01 What is a reason that the brain perceives sensations in a missing limb?

Ⓐ The amputation creates nerve gaps that cause electrical misfiring.
Ⓑ Active nerves send unexpected signals to the brain.
Ⓒ Damaged nerve endings regenerate incorrectly and send wrong messages.
Ⓓ Muscle contractions trigger false nerve signals.

02 Why does the author mention stinging, burning, and pressure?

Ⓐ To explain the medical treatment options for phantom pain
Ⓑ To give an example of how doctors diagnose phantom pain
Ⓒ To illustrate sensations that people may feel as phantom pain
Ⓓ To argue that phantom pain is less severe than other pain types

03 The word "responsible" in the passage is closest in meaning to

Ⓐ negligent
Ⓑ auxiliary
Ⓒ accountable
Ⓓ susceptible

04 All of the following are true about phantom pain EXCEPT:

Ⓐ It can endure for months or years after the limb's removal.
Ⓑ It may be eased by therapies that adjust the brain's reaction.
Ⓒ It requires surgical removal of the remaining nerve tissue.
Ⓓ It results from the combined activity of the brain and the nervous system.

05 Which of the following best describes the purpose of the third paragraph?

Ⓐ Paragraph 3 compares phantom pain with other types of neurological pain.
Ⓑ Paragraph 3 discusses the possible treatment options for phantom pain.
Ⓒ Paragraph 3 summarizes the causes of phantom pain mentioned earlier.
Ⓓ Paragraph 3 suggests that phantom pain is psychological.

HACKERS TEST

[06-10]

Mere Exposure Effect

First identified by psychologist Robert Zajonc, the mere exposure effect shows that the more frequently people encounter something, the more they tend to like it, even with minimal interaction or awareness. This process operates unconsciously and can influence attitudes toward people, products, or even ideas.

For example, hearing a new song may result in indifference or even dislike. However, after several plays, it usually becomes more appealing. Similarly, the products in advertisements that are repeatedly shown are often perceived more positively, even if viewers pay little direct attention to the promotions themselves.

The effect is also evident in social situations. People tend to prefer the coworkers or neighbors they see regularly, even if their interactions are superficial. Within teams and clubs, repeated exposure increases perceived trustworthiness and willingness to cooperate, which strengthens group coordination and leads to the development of shared norms.

Despite its strengths, the effect has limits. It mostly affects neutral or mildly positive stimuli. And even when the stimuli are positive, overexposure can eventually provoke negative reactions. Being aware of this effect can help individuals reflect on whether their current interests stem from mere familiarity. If so, they may choose to explore pursuits they genuinely enjoy.

06 The word "superficial" in the passage is closest in meaning to

Ⓐ polite
Ⓑ casual
Ⓒ serious
Ⓓ permanent

07 Why does the author mention "a new song"?

Ⓐ To illustrate how familiarity can gradually increase appeal
Ⓑ To highlight how repetition can sometimes cause boredom
Ⓒ To show how songs are effective tools in advertisements
Ⓓ To emphasize the role of conscious choice in music preference

08 All of the following are true about the mere exposure effect EXCEPT:

Ⓐ It can also be applied to ideas.
Ⓑ It is typically beyond the scope of a person's conscious control.
Ⓒ It occurs when audience engagement is high.
Ⓓ It explains why people may prefer those they see regularly.

09 In which of the following situations is the mere exposure effect most clearly observed?

Ⓐ When people encounter something they initially detest
Ⓑ When a TV commercial is deliberately designed to be memorable
Ⓒ When coworkers seldom interact beyond greetings
Ⓓ When the stimulus is neither strongly attractive nor repulsive

10 What is the relationship between paragraphs 3 and 4?

Ⓐ Paragraph 4 introduces limitations not mentioned in paragraph 3.
Ⓑ Paragraph 4 adds to the examples presented in paragraph 3.
Ⓒ Paragraph 4 criticizes the examples discussed in paragraph 3.
Ⓓ Paragraph 4 provides cases that contradict the information in paragraph 3.

HACKERS TEST

[11-15]

Totemism

Totemism is a system of belief and social organization in which natural objects, animals, or plants (totems) are regarded as spiritually significant and symbolically linked to human groups. In many societies, a community might treat a certain animal as sacred, refraining from hunting it, and use its image in rituals. Such practices strengthen the community's shared values and provide moral lessons about respect for nature and social responsibility.

A totem represents a collective identity, such as a clan or lineage, and establishes a sense of belonging and cooperation among its members. These symbols serve as markers of kinship, defining obligations within the community and guiding rules about marriage. For example, a clan might prohibit marriage between members who share the same totem, as they are considered siblings.

■A Totemism encompasses a broad array of social and cultural practices. ■B In this broader frame, scholars debate whether totemism should be understood primarily as a social system or a way of interpreting the environment. ■C Despite these disagreements, most agree that it illustrates how humans assign symbolic meaning to the natural world in order to structure social life. ■D In this sense, totemism highlights the deep connections between culture, belief, and ecology.

11 The word "obligations" in the passage is closest in meaning to

   Ⓐ decorations
   Ⓑ duties
   Ⓒ inputs
   Ⓓ celebrations

12 What can be inferred about totemism's role?

   Ⓐ It ensures that every individual adopts identical ritual practices.
   Ⓑ It primarily functions as a way to influence neighboring communities.
   Ⓒ It integrates natural symbols into systems of social organization.
   Ⓓ It serves as direct evidence of early scientific reasoning.

13 Why does the author mention a sacred animal?

   Ⓐ To show how religious practices replaced political institutions in early cultures
   Ⓑ To argue that animals were more important than plants in traditional societies
   Ⓒ To suggest that totemism primarily developed as a form of animal worship
   Ⓓ To illustrate how natural symbols can serve as a basis for community identity

14 All of the following are true about totems EXCEPT:

   Ⓐ They provide moral lessons.
   Ⓑ They explain natural phenomena.
   Ⓒ They guide community rules.
   Ⓓ They strengthen group solidarity.

15 There are four locations [■] in the passage that indicate where the following sentence could be added.

   Even opposing theories acknowledge that totems translate physical landscapes into social rules.

   Where would the sentence best fit? Select a location [■] where the sentence could be added to the passage.

HACKERS TEST

[16-20]

Hypnagogic Hallucinations

Hypnagogic hallucinations are vivid sensory experiences that occur during the moments just before falling asleep. These perceptions can involve visual, auditory, or tactile sensations that feel strikingly real. Unlike ordinary dreams, hypnagogic hallucinations blend elements of the waking environment with the mind's own creations, producing hybrid experiences that bridge consciousness and sleep. This phenomenon offers a fascinating glimpse into the brain's transition from wakefulness to sleep. Hypnagogic hallucinations are especially common in those with sleep disorders such as narcolepsy.

Researchers have confirmed several roles of hypnagogic hallucinations. They appear linked to the brain's process of disengaging from external reality while preparing for rest. Some scientists suggest these hallucinations help the brain sort or integrate impressions accumulated during the day.

Research suggests that hypnagogic hallucinations may stem from unstable interactions between neural systems that regulate wakefulness and those that initiate sleep. Neuroimaging studies indicate that certain brain regions remain partially active during these transitional states, while others begin to decrease their activity as sleep sets in. However, the precise neurochemical processes driving hypnagogic hallucinations are still not fully understood and remain an ongoing area of investigation.

16 How do hypnagogic hallucinations differ from ordinary dreams?

    Ⓐ They occur mainly during the deepest stages of sleep.
    Ⓑ They are more likely to cause sleep paralysis.
    Ⓒ They have a higher chance of being recalled upon waking.
    Ⓓ They happen while the mind is still partially aware of the real world.

17 All of the following are true about hypnagogic hallucinations EXCEPT:

    Ⓐ They can take the form of sights, sounds, or physical feelings.
    Ⓑ They contribute to the brain's effort to organize daily experiences.
    Ⓒ They reflect a disengagement from internal thought.
    Ⓓ They involve some brain regions decreasing their level of activity.

18 Why does the author mention narcolepsy?

    Ⓐ To suggest that narcolepsy is the primary cause of hypnagogic hallucinations
    Ⓑ To point out the link between hypnagogic hallucinations and sleep disorders
    Ⓒ To demonstrate that narcolepsy patients have a heightened response to external stimuli
    Ⓓ To argue that hypnagogic hallucinations are mostly harmless experiences

19 The word "integrate" in the second paragraph is closest in meaning to

    Ⓐ combine
    Ⓑ isolate
    Ⓒ erase
    Ⓓ identify

20 What does the passage indicate about neural systems?

    Ⓐ They allow people to be creative.
    Ⓑ They stimulate the release of neurochemicals.
    Ⓒ They stay fully active during sleep transitions.
    Ⓓ They govern the body's cycle of rest and alertness.

Answers p.463

4. Vocabulary Questions

Overview

지문에 주어진 어휘와 의미가 가장 가까운 어휘를 묻는 문제이다. 정답 어휘는 주어진 어휘의 동의어일 수도 있고, 사전적 동의어는 아니지만 문맥상 의미가 통하는 어휘일 수도 있다.

Types of Questions

Vocabulary 문제는 주로 다음의 형태로 제시된다. 문제에서 묻는 어휘는 지문 내에 음영으로 표시된다.

Vocabulary

The word "significantly" in the passage is closest in meaning to

The word "alleviate" in the first paragraph is closest in meaning to

Hackers Strategy

1 단어의 사전적 의미를 바탕으로 정답을 고른다.

많은 Vocabulary 문제는 단어의 사전적 의미와 동의어를 알고 있다면 바로 풀 수 있다. 따라서 주어진 단어의 앞뒤 문맥을 확인하기 전에, 선택지 중 주어진 단어의 사전적 동의어가 있는지 확인하고, 정답을 고른다.

2 사전적 의미를 통해 정답을 고를 수 없다면, 자연스러운 문맥을 만드는 선택지를 고른다.

선택지 중 주어진 단어와 완벽한 동의어가 없는 경우, 주어진 단어와 같은 의미로 쓰일 수 있는 단어가 여러 개인 경우, 또는 단어의 의미를 몰라서 정답을 고를 수 없는 경우에는 주어진 단어 자리에 넣었을 때 앞뒤 내용과 가장 자연스러운 문맥을 만드는 선택지를 정답으로 고른다.

Example

Printing Press

The invention of the printing press played a pivotal role in shaping modern civilization. Before its creation, books were copied by hand, a laborious process that limited the spread of knowledge to a small, privileged class. In the mid-fifteenth century, Johannes Gutenberg introduced movable type printing in Europe, revolutionizing access to information. This technology made it possible to produce books quickly, efficiently, and in large quantities.

As the technology developed, early printing workshops began to appear across Europe, spreading the new method of book production. Artisans and merchants saw opportunities in the rapid duplication of religious texts, scientific treatises, and literature. The demand for printed materials grew quickly, leading to the establishment of printing centers in cities such as Venice, Paris, and London. This dissemination created a network of printers and publishers, accelerating the flow of information throughout the continent.

The spread of the printing press led to significant social and cultural changes. Wider book distribution promoted literacy among broader segments of society. Ideas and scientific discoveries circulated rapidly, initiating major movements such as the Renaissance and the Reformation. The printing press also facilitated the standardization of languages and texts, reducing inconsistencies caused by manual copying. Newspapers and pamphlets became common, fostering the development of public opinion and political engagement.

The word "initiating" in the passage is closest in meaning to

Ⓐ causing
Ⓑ sustaining
Ⓒ highlighting
Ⓓ hindering

정답 Ⓐ

해설 지문의 initiating(시작하다)과 의미상 가장 유사한 단어를 묻는 문제이다. initiating을 포함하고 있는 문장 'Ideas ~ the Reformation'을 통해 사상과 과학적 발견이 빠르게 보급됨으로써 르네상스나 종교 개혁과 같은 운동이 일어났다는 뜻으로 사용되었음을 알 수 있다. 따라서 Ⓐ가 정답이다.

HACKERS PRACTICE

01

> Launched in 1965, Amsterdam's White Bicycle Plan was the first public bike-sharing system in Europe. This project made several white bicycles available for use by the public at no charge. The scheme was short-lived due to theft and vandalism, but it inspired similar projects.
>
> Cities like Copenhagen and Paris implemented their own bike-sharing systems. Copenhagen's Bycyklen introduced improved bike designs and designated stations for pick-up and drop-off. Paris launched its large-scale Vélib' system, using automated stations across the city. Each city took steps to prevent theft and vandalism. Copenhagen used custom parts incompatible with other bicycles to ensure components were not stolen, while Paris employed GPS to keep track of the bikes.

The word "inspired" in the first paragraph is closest in meaning to

Ⓐ developed
Ⓑ influenced
Ⓒ abandoned
Ⓓ interrupted

02

> Researchers have presented theories to explain the psychological basis of different types of humor. One is the incongruity theory, which suggests that people find things funny when there is a disparity between expectations and reality. For example, a punch line that unexpectedly disrupts a familiar story structure leads to laughter because it surprises the listener.
>
> Another is the relief theory. It states that humor allows for the release of psychological tension. Jokes about stressful situations, such as work or exams, often serve to reduce anxiety among listeners. Laughter acts as an emotional release, making challenging events more manageable for individuals and groups.
>
> The superiority theory offers a different explanation. According to this theory, people experience humor when they feel a sense of superiority over others. For instance, slapstick comedy—where one character repeatedly fails or makes mistakes—evokes laughter because the audience feels superior to the person on stage or screen.

The word "disparity" in the passage is closest in meaning to

Ⓐ difficulty
Ⓑ comparison
Ⓒ difference
Ⓓ reason

03

Japanese woodblock prints are known as *ukiyo-e*, meaning "pictures of the transient world." The term *ukiyo* (meaning "transient world") was first used to describe the Buddhist concept of life's transience but later came to represent the pleasure-focused lifestyle of urban Japan from the seventeenth to the nineteenth centuries. The *ukiyo-e* prints include scenes from everyday life, nature, and entertainment.

The creation of these prints required collaboration. Artists designed the images, carvers prepared the wooden blocks, and printers applied ink to paper in precise layers. The use of vivid colors, strong outlines, and nuanced details, such as slight variations in paper texture, distinguished these prints. They were widely produced and affordable, making art accessible to newly emerging middle-class people.

The word "nuanced" in the passage is closest in meaning to

Ⓐ apparent
Ⓑ repetitive
Ⓒ subtle
Ⓓ intricate

04

Oncoviruses are viruses that can cause cancer in humans or animals. Many of these viruses work by inserting their genetic material into host cells, which can disrupt normal cell regulation and potentially lead to unhampered cell growth and tumor formation. Common examples of oncoviruses include human papillomavirus (HPV), which is linked to cervical and other types of cancer, and hepatitis B and C viruses, which are associated with liver cancer.

Not everyone infected with an oncovirus will develop cancer. The cancer risk depends on additional factors, such as the individual's genetic background, immune system status, and environmental influences. For example, about 90 percent of young and healthy individuals infected with HPV naturally clear the virus through their immune system within two years without developing any symptoms. Advances such as HPV vaccination have also proven successful in reducing infection rates and lowering cancer risk.

The word "unhampered" in the passage is closest in meaning to

Ⓐ unfinished
Ⓑ inconsistent
Ⓒ unrestrained
Ⓓ invisible

Answers p.466

[01-05]

Efficient-market Hypothesis

The efficient-market hypothesis (EMH) posits that asset prices in financial markets reflect available information so efficiently that achieving returns above the average market return, known as excess returns, becomes impossible. It was developed by American economist Eugene Fama, who received the 2013 Nobel Prize in Economics for his work.

It was traditionally believed that investors mainly profited from arbitrage, which exploits temporary price differences for the same asset between markets or gaps in people's information. However, Fama observed that markets incorporated relevant price information so quickly that they eliminated opportunities for arbitrage. He also found that short-term asset prices were impossible to predict and essentially followed a "random walk," a statistical term for the arbitrary fluctuations a data series takes over time.

EMH implied that no investor could consistently outperform the market by employing active investment strategies like market timing—the strategy of trying to predict future market price movements. Rather, EMH suggested that better results could be obtained by tracking overall market performance through an index fund, which is a type of fund designed to match the performance of a specific market index, such as the S&P 500, by holding all the stocks in that index.

01 The word "reflect" in the first paragraph is closest in meaning to

Ⓐ mirror
Ⓑ display
Ⓒ affect
Ⓓ contain

02 Which of the following best states the main idea of the passage?

Ⓐ Only well-informed investors can achieve excess returns.
Ⓑ It is impossible to consistently earn excess returns based on information.
Ⓒ Statistical analysis of stock data yields positive results.
Ⓓ No market satisfies Fama's definition of efficiency.

03 All of the following are true about Eugene Fama EXCEPT:

Ⓐ He was awarded the Nobel Prize in Economics in 2013 for his research.
Ⓑ He developed the popular investment vehicle known as the index fund.
Ⓒ He found that short-term price movements are unpredictable.
Ⓓ He demonstrated that fast information processing eliminated arbitrage opportunities.

04 Why does the author mention arbitrage?

Ⓐ To show how profits were understood before the efficient-market hypothesis
Ⓑ To explain the mechanism by which an efficient market operates
Ⓒ To argue that arbitrage is the only way for active investors to succeed
Ⓓ To illustrate how to exploit information gaps to achieve excess returns

05 What investment strategy is supported by the efficient-market hypothesis?

Ⓐ Studying short-term price fluctuations
Ⓑ Exploiting temporary price differences
Ⓒ Trying to predict future price movements
Ⓓ Tracking the performance of a specific market index

HACKERS TEST

[06-10]

Spotted Hyena Clans

Spotted hyena clans exemplify matriarchal social structures in which females outrank males. In these groups, the dominant female, or matriarch, determines the movement of the group and has priority access to food.

A key feature of the spotted hyena society is the inheritance of rank. Female cubs gradually inherit their mother's social status and surpass adult males in dominance. For example, young females of high social status have been frequently observed asserting control over feeding sites, with adult males deferring to them by eating last and avoiding challenging females to maintain clan harmony.

The matriarchal hierarchy of hyena clans significantly impacts group dynamics and survival strategies. Researchers have noted that related females form powerful alliances within the clan, supporting one another during conflicts or when defending territory from outsiders. Their leadership also ensures that food is distributed efficiently, reducing competition and supporting the survival of all clan members. At the same time, high-ranking females and their young gain priority access to carcasses and kills. This food availability promotes higher reproductive success, shorter interbirth intervals, and greater juvenile survival, reinforcing lineage dominance and supporting the clan's social stability.

06 What can be inferred about female cubs of high social status in hyena clans?

Ⓐ They assert authority over adult males.
Ⓑ They rarely join alliances within the clan.
Ⓒ They usually have a lower status than males.
Ⓓ They leave the clan when they grow older.

07 How is rank determined in spotted hyena clans?

Ⓐ Older hyenas automatically gain a higher rank.
Ⓑ Males inherit social status from their fathers.
Ⓒ Female cubs inherit their mother's status.
Ⓓ Each member is ranked by their physical strength.

08 The word "deferring" in the second paragraph is closest in meaning to

Ⓐ clinging
Ⓑ opposing
Ⓒ yielding
Ⓓ advising

09 Why does the author mention that high-ranking females tend to have higher reproductive success?

Ⓐ To show how reproductive patterns reflect ecological adaptation mechanisms
Ⓑ To explain how hierarchical social structure benefits the clan's survival
Ⓒ To demonstrate that reduced competition correlates with matriarchal leadership
Ⓓ To highlight that gender does not affect hyena social rank

10 What is the relationship between paragraphs 2 and 3?

Ⓐ Paragraph 3 provides problems that result from the social status described in paragraph 2.
Ⓑ Paragraph 3 expands upon the information about clan cooperation mentioned in paragraph 2.
Ⓒ Paragraph 3 presents exceptions to the social dynamics described in paragraph 2.
Ⓓ Paragraph 3 introduces a broader impact of the social structure explained in paragraph 2.

HACKERS TEST

[11-15]

Atmospheric Rivers

Atmospheric rivers are long, narrow bands of concentrated moisture that travel through the atmosphere, often spanning hundreds to thousands of kilometers. When these streams make landfall, they can release vast amounts of rain, mainly along coastal regions. The heavy rainfall associated with atmospheric rivers accounts for a large portion of the annual precipitation in places like California.

Atmospheric rivers function as both essential water suppliers and destructive forces, depending on their severity and regional conditions. These moisture-laden systems provide crucial precipitation for agricultural regions and help replenish reservoirs during dry seasons. However, when atmospheric rivers get stronger, they unleash devastating floods that damage infrastructure, displace communities, and cause billions in economic losses. The same phenomenon that delivers life-sustaining water can transform into life-threatening disasters.

Climate change amplifies these risks by increasing air and ocean temperatures, which strengthens the formation of atmospheric rivers by enabling them to carry significantly more moisture. Scientists predict more extreme precipitation events as these enhanced systems reach land. With atmospheric rivers becoming increasingly unpredictable and destructive, comprehensive monitoring and adaptive management strategies are essential for balancing water security with flood protection.

11 Why does the author mention California?

Ⓐ To give an example of a location affected by recent changes in the global climate
Ⓑ To highlight a region that receives much of its rainfall from atmospheric rivers
Ⓒ To show a place where atmospheric rivers caused flooding and property damage
Ⓓ To illustrate a region where water management is particularly important

12 The word "adaptive" in the passage is closest in meaning to

Ⓐ flexible
Ⓑ rigid
Ⓒ defensive
Ⓓ conventional

13 How can atmospheric rivers pose risks?

Ⓐ By transporting pollutants across long distances
Ⓑ By enabling warmer air temperatures to reduce atmospheric pressure
Ⓒ By carrying moisture that disrupts the ocean temperature balance
Ⓓ By triggering severe flooding in coastal areas

14 Why are atmospheric rivers predicted to be more intense in the future?

Ⓐ They will travel longer distances across oceans.
Ⓑ They will be strengthened by rising ocean temperatures.
Ⓒ They will create stronger wind patterns due to changes in atmospheric pressure.
Ⓓ They will become less detectable to the current monitoring systems.

15 Which of the following best describes the purpose of the third paragraph?

Ⓐ Paragraph 3 analyzes how monitoring systems can predict atmospheric river formation.
Ⓑ Paragraph 3 introduces solutions to mitigate the negative effects of atmospheric rivers.
Ⓒ Paragraph 3 explains the mechanisms by which climate change enhances atmospheric river risks.
Ⓓ Paragraph 3 contrasts the beneficial and harmful aspects of atmospheric rivers.

HACKERS TEST

[16-20]

Hotelling's Law

Hotelling's law is a competition theory proposed by economist Harold Hotelling in 1929. This principle explains why competing businesses, which otherwise offer the same products at comparable prices, tend to cluster together rather than spread out to different locations. By positioning themselves near the center of consumer demand, they seek to capture the largest possible market share.

Consider the concentration of coffee shops in a city. According to Hotelling's law, each competitor aims to position itself optimally to attract customers approaching from different parts of the area. If one coffee shop moves closer to the center of foot traffic, its competitor will follow suit to avoid losing market share, resulting in the clustering phenomenon we observe in urban business districts, where major chains and local coffee shops are located within blocks of each other.

Hotelling's law illustrates the adverse effects of individual profit maximization. While the socially optimal solution would have businesses spread out geographically to minimize consumer travel costs and expand service location options, competitive dynamics drive firms toward convergence, which ultimately reduces overall social welfare.

16 The word "adverse" in the passage is closest in meaning to

Ⓐ harmful
Ⓑ helpful
Ⓒ regular
Ⓓ primary

17 What is one factor that drives businesses to cluster near competitors?

Ⓐ The desire to reduce operational costs
Ⓑ The need to minimize consumer travel distances
Ⓒ The effort to capture maximum market share
Ⓓ The requirement to differentiate their services

18 What is the purpose of the second paragraph?

Ⓐ It illustrates the theoretical principle with a concrete example of clustering.
Ⓑ It compares different business models used by competing coffee shops.
Ⓒ It presents statistical evidence about coffee shop locations across the city.
Ⓓ It proves that stores clustering together makes it easier for customers to access them.

19 What can be inferred about individual profit maximization?

Ⓐ It can conflict with what benefits consumers most.
Ⓑ It maximizes the total combined revenue of all competitors.
Ⓒ It ensures equal distribution of customers among competitors.
Ⓓ It tends to lead to optimal social outcomes.

20 How does the convergence of businesses affect the consumers' shopping experience?

Ⓐ It makes it harder to find products that consumers need.
Ⓑ It reduces the variety of products available at different locations.
Ⓒ It allows consumers to visit multiple competing businesses on one trip.
Ⓓ It limits the convenience of accessing services in different areas.

Answers p.467

5. Rhetorical Purpose Questions

Overview

지문에 특정 정보가 언급된 목적을 묻는 문제이다. 특정 단어/어구, 문장, 단락이 지문 전개에서 어떤 기능(설명, 예시, 강조, 비교 등)을 하는지를 파악해야 한다.

Types of Questions

Rhetorical Purpose 문제는 크게 세 가지 세부 유형으로 분류할 수 있다.

Purpose
   Why does the author mention Plato's allegory of the cave?
   Which of the following best describes the purpose of the third paragraph?

Paragraph Relationship
   What is the relationship between paragraphs 2 and 3?

Sentence Identification
   Click on the sentence in paragraph 3 that establishes a direct causal link between early childhood language exposure and later cognitive development scores.

Hackers Strategy

1 문제에서 묻는 부분 앞뒤의 전개 방식과 일치하는 선택지를 고른다.

자주 출제되는 전개 방식과 각 방식에 해당하는 동사는 다음과 같다.
설명/서술: describe, discuss, elaborate, explain, suggest
예시: give/provide example, illustrate
강조: emphasize, highlight, underscore

2 선택지의 내용과 문제에서 묻는 부분 앞뒤의 내용이 일치하는지 확인한다.

전개 방식이 일치한다고 해도 선택지의 내용이 지문과 다르다면 오답이다. 따라서 선택지의 내용과 문제에서 묻는 부분 앞뒤의 내용이 일치하는지 확인한 후 정답을 확정한다.

Example

Gut-Brain Interaction

One emerging field in neuroscience focuses on gut-brain interactions, examining how the gut nervous system communicates with the central nervous system. This bidirectional communication occurs through neural, hormonal, and immune pathways, and has been shown to influence mood, cognition, and stress responses. Recent research suggests that the gut microbiota may play a central role in shaping neural activity by producing metabolites and neurotransmitter-like molecules that can cross into circulation and affect brain function.

A particularly intriguing discovery is the relationship between gut health and mental health conditions. Alterations in microbial composition have been linked to disorders such as depression and anxiety, suggesting that manipulating the microbiome through diet, probiotics, or targeted therapies could modulate brain activity. Animal studies have suggested that transferring gut bacteria from stressed or anxious individuals can lead to comparable behavioral patterns in the recipient, raising the possibility of a causal relationship.

Future research aims to map the precise mechanisms by which the gut influences specific brain circuits and behaviors. Advances in neuroimaging and molecular profiling are expected to reveal new therapeutic strategies that integrate nutrition, microbiology, and neuroscience. This integrative perspective may redefine our understanding of the brain as a system deeply interconnected with the body.

Why does the author mention depression and anxiety?

Ⓐ To describe the hormonal changes caused by stress
Ⓑ To propose a link between immune pathways and the brain
Ⓒ To give examples of conditions associated with changes in gut microbiota
Ⓓ To highlight the effectiveness of probiotics in treating mental health disorders

정답 Ⓒ

해설 글쓴이가 우울증과 불안을 언급하는 이유를 묻는 문제이다. depression and anxiety를 포함하고 있는 문장 'Alterations ~ brain activity'에서 미생물 소성의 변화가 우울증, 불안 등의 질병과 연관되어 있다는 내용을 언급하므로, 우울증과 불안을 언급한 것은 장내 미생물군의 변화와 관련된 질환의 예시를 제시하기 위함임을 알 수 있다. 따라서 Ⓒ가 정답이다.

HACKERS PRACTICE

01

Diaspora communities refer to groups of people who have migrated from their country of origin and settled in new locations, forming distinct cultural groups abroad. These communities are typically created in response to economic necessity and environmental pressure in their homelands. Transportation and communication networks then facilitate sustained growth by enabling the displaced population to form connections with communities abroad and build a transnational network.

Diaspora communities can create economic and professional networks to support members in their new environments. For instance, Jewish diaspora communities maintain the International Association of Jewish Free Loans. Organizations under this network offer interest-free loans to Jewish people around the world, helping old and new immigrants establish small businesses and purchase homes.

Why does the author mention the International Association of Jewish Free Loans?

Ⓐ To suggest that diaspora communities rely on financial aid for adaptation
Ⓑ To show that the Jews were the first to provide financial assistance to diaspora groups
Ⓒ To illustrate how diaspora communities create support networks for their members
Ⓓ To indicate that diaspora networks are limited to housing and small business support

02

In 1951, social psychologist Solomon Asch conducted a series of experiments on conformity and group psychology, demonstrating how a person could be influenced by pressure to conform to a group.

For the experiments, Asch recruited groups of students for simple tests of visual perception, which consisted of identifying two lines of matching length. However, only one participant in each group was a true test subject. The rest were actors whom Asch instructed to occasionally pick the wrong answer on purpose, thus forcing the subjects to choose between the evidently correct answer and an incorrect one that nonetheless conformed to the group's opinion.

Without the pressure to conform, subjects chose incorrectly less than 1 percent of the time. However, under the experimental conditions, that number rose to 36 percent. When asked to explain their decisions, most said they wanted to avoid the group's disapproval, while a smaller number said the group's influence had caused them to genuinely doubt their beliefs.

What is the relationship between paragraphs 2 and 3?

Ⓐ Paragraph 3 presents the results of the experiment described in paragraph 2.
Ⓑ Paragraph 3 questions the validity of the experiment explained in paragraph 2.
Ⓒ Paragraph 3 offers alternative explanations for the behaviors discussed in paragraph 2.
Ⓓ Paragraph 3 introduces a new experiment unrelated to the one mentioned in paragraph 2.

03

Deep-sea brine pools are unique environments located in isolated areas of the ocean floor at great depths. These pools contain water with extremely high concentrations of salt, which makes them much denser than the surrounding seawater. This difference in density creates a distinct boundary, resulting in what some describe as underwater lakes. They have extremely low to nonexistent levels of oxygen and are highly toxic to many forms of marine life.

Despite these inhospitable conditions, certain microorganisms, such as halophilic bacteria and archaea, can thrive in brine pools. These organisms have adapted to survive in water with high salt and low oxygen levels, and their metabolic processes can reveal important information about the limits of life. Scientists study these microorganisms to better understand how life can exist in extreme environments.

What can be concluded about paragraph 2?

Ⓐ It explains why microorganisms in an unusual environment are studied.
Ⓑ It offers an example of a biotechnology application in marine research.
Ⓒ It describes how brine pools contribute to global biogeochemical cycles.
Ⓓ It highlights the role of deep-sea brine pools in regulating ocean temperature.

04

Native to eastern Australia, the platypus is one of the most unusual animals in the world. It is classified as a mammal because of its ability to produce milk and its furry body. But it also possesses a duck-like bill and webbed feet. Especially rare among mammals, it lays eggs and uses electroreception to detect movements of prey underwater. Male platypuses even produce venom from spurs on their hind legs, which they use to deter predators.

The existence of the platypus challenged our understanding of animal classification. When the first platypus specimen was sent from Australia to Britain in the late eighteenth century, scientists thought it was a hoax. They believed someone had sewn together parts of different animals. This skepticism persisted for several decades until more specimens were studied and dissected, confirming its authenticity.

Select the sentence in paragraph 2 that illustrates how difficult it was to validate the discovery of the platypus.

Ⓐ The existence of the platypus challenged our understanding of animal classification.
Ⓑ When the first platypus specimen was sent from Australia to Britain in the late eighteenth century, scientists thought it was a hoax.
Ⓒ They believed someone had sewn together parts of different animals.
Ⓓ This skepticism persisted for several decades until more specimens were studied and dissected, confirming its authenticity.

Answers p.471

HACKERS TEST

[01-05]

Central Park

Covering over 800 acres in the heart of Manhattan, Central Park in New York City is one of the most iconic urban parks in the United States. Conceived during the mid-nineteenth century, the park was created as a response to rapid urbanization and industrial growth, which left city residents with little access to natural spaces. Frederick Law Olmsted, who co-designed the park with Calvert Vaux, saw parks as integral in creating healthier and more democratic cities.

Olmsted and Vaux employed a naturalistic style, incorporating meadows, woodlands, and bodies of water to evoke the countryside within the city. They also planned winding paths, scenic viewpoints, and diverse plantings that offered both beauty and function. This balance of utility and aesthetics marked a significant development in American landscape architecture.

For urban dwellers of all backgrounds, the park provided relief from the pressures of industrial city life. Its green spaces demonstrated how thoughtful planning could improve public health and enhance community well-being. Today, Central Park remains a case study for urban park planners and a lasting symbol of how landscape design can shape urban life through both aesthetics and social benefits.

01 What was the historical context in which Central Park was built?

Ⓐ A period when industrial development and urban growth accelerated
Ⓑ An era of suburban expansion with abundant access to natural areas
Ⓒ A time when New York City was losing population and farmland was plentiful
Ⓓ A phase dominated by postwar reconstruction and modern city planning

02 The word "integral" in the first paragraph is closest in meaning to

Ⓐ adequate
Ⓑ typical
Ⓒ essential
Ⓓ functional

03 Why does the author mention Frederick Law Olmsted's view of parks?

Ⓐ To demonstrate that Olmsted was the originator of the naturalistic landscape style
Ⓑ To provide the underlying philosophical reason for the park's design
Ⓒ To highlight that Olmsted focused only on aesthetic beauty
Ⓓ To show the importance of democratic processes in city planning

04 Which of the following best describes the purpose of paragraph 2?

Ⓐ Paragraph 2 details the social benefits derived from Central Park.
Ⓑ Paragraph 2 compares Central Park with other urban parks.
Ⓒ Paragraph 2 outlines the goals behind the establishment of Central Park.
Ⓓ Paragraph 2 describes the specific design features of Central Park.

05 What can be inferred about modern urban parks?

Ⓐ They are frequently located on city outskirts to maximize land availability.
Ⓑ They are often designed with lessons learned from Central Park.
Ⓒ They are primarily intended to replicate Central Park in design and purpose.
Ⓓ They are mainly valued for their aesthetic appeal rather than social benefits.

HACKERS TEST

[06-10]

Invasive Plants

Invasive plants are plants that spread outside their native range. When these plants possess traits such as aggressive growth, high reproductive rates, and resistance to local pests, they can outcompete indigenous vegetation for sunlight, water, and nutrients. Invasive species can be found in many ecosystems, from wetlands and forests to urban areas. Their presence may reduce biodiversity, alter soil composition, and disrupt water cycles.

These plants impact both natural and managed ecosystems. Natural areas may lose native plant populations, which negatively affects the insects and animals that rely on them. Agricultural lands often suffer from diminished crop yields, as invasive plants are difficult to control. Some species can also increase the risk of flooding. For example, Japanese knotweed overruns stream banks and makes it easy for water to overflow, while purple loosestrife forms dense clusters in wetlands.

Invasive plants often spread as a result of human activity, such as the unintentional transportation of seeds in cargo. Ornamental plants in gardens may also establish new populations in nearby areas. Animals and wind further aid the spread of invasive plants by dispersing seeds over large distances. Additionally, changes in land use, such as deforestation, can create environments that favor invasive species.

06 The word "unintentional" in the passage is closest in meaning to

Ⓐ deliberate
Ⓑ accidental
Ⓒ necessary
Ⓓ frequent

07 What is the impact invasive plants have on agricultural lands?

Ⓐ Faster soil erosion
Ⓑ Lower crop yields
Ⓒ Disruption of pollination
Ⓓ Transmission of plant diseases

08 Why does the author mention Japanese knotweed and purple loosestrife?

Ⓐ To highlight that invasive species reduce populations of local wildlife
Ⓑ To introduce unusual invasive plants that are economically valuable
Ⓒ To show how certain invasive species increase the risk of water-related hazards
Ⓓ To suggest that some invasive plants may actually be of benefit to farmers

09 Which of the following is NOT mentioned as a cause of the spread of invasive plants in the passage?

Ⓐ Human activity
Ⓑ Seasonal flooding
Ⓒ Dispersal by animals
Ⓓ Modification of landscapes

10 What is the relationship between paragraphs 2 and 3?

Ⓐ Paragraph 3 describes possible causes for the problems discussed in paragraph 2.
Ⓑ Paragraph 3 gives examples of native plants affected by the issues described in paragraph 2.
Ⓒ Paragraph 3 introduces another negative impact of invasive plants not mentioned in paragraph 2.
Ⓓ Paragraph 3 provides the economic benefits of invasive plants in contrast to paragraph 2.

HACKERS TEST

[11-15]

Habitus

Habitus is a concept developed by French sociologist Pierre Bourdieu. It refers to the deeply embedded habits, skills, and ways of perceiving the world that individuals develop through their cultural and social experiences. Habitus shapes unconscious actions, patterns of thought, and preferences in daily life and explains why people from similar backgrounds often display comparable behaviors.

A familiar example of habitus can be seen in classroom etiquette. Children who grow up in families emphasizing punctuality, quiet listening, and respect for authority often retain these <mark>dispositions</mark> until they graduate. Such students instinctively understand classroom expectations and adapt accordingly. On the other hand, children who were not exposed to these norms early in life may struggle to fit in despite wanting to, and this demonstrates how habitus operates below conscious awareness.

Habitus continues to influence behaviors in adulthood. For instance, professionals today who were raised in families working in the corporate world may feel more comfortable in formal business settings, understand unwritten rules of networking, and select business attire that suits the context. This invisible framework created by habitus guides choices and reactions throughout life, reflecting how social position and life experiences shape both individual identity and collective cultural practices.

11. The word "dispositions" in the passage is closest in meaning to

    Ⓐ instructions
    Ⓑ appearances
    Ⓒ tendencies
    Ⓓ resources

12. What is the passage mainly about?

    Ⓐ The importance of employment history in developing habitus
    Ⓑ The influence of habitus on individual and group behavior
    Ⓒ The impact of habitus on the classroom etiquette of students
    Ⓓ The role of formal public education in shaping habitus

13. What can be inferred about people with similar habitus?

    Ⓐ They may develop nearly identical personal interests.
    Ⓑ They will achieve the same level of academic success.
    Ⓒ They tend to display comparable behaviors in the same contexts.
    Ⓓ They could eventually reach equal status in their communities.

14. Click on the sentence in paragraph 2 that demonstrates how habitus shapes behavior independently of a person's intentional actions.

    Ⓐ A familiar example of habitus can be seen in classroom etiquette.
    Ⓑ Children who grow up in families emphasizing punctuality, quiet listening, and respect for authority often retain these dispositions until they graduate.
    Ⓒ Such students instinctively understand classroom expectations and adapt accordingly.
    Ⓓ On the other hand, children who were not exposed to these norms early in life may struggle to fit in despite wanting to, and this demonstrates how habitus operates below conscious awareness.

15. What can be concluded about paragraph 3?

    Ⓐ It illustrates that the effects of habitus extend beyond adolescence.
    Ⓑ It shows that adults are less affected by habitus than children.
    Ⓒ It offers a critique of Bourdieu's theory based on modern workplaces.
    Ⓓ It explains how professional families foster ambitions in their children.

HACKERS TEST

[16-20]

Lucy the Hominid

In 1974, a team of anthropologists discovered fossilized remains of a hominid (early human) in Ethiopia. The skeleton, later named "Lucy," comprised 47 bone fragments (about 40 percent of the total). Estimated to be a small adult female, she stood just over a meter tall and weighed around 29 kilograms. Her anatomy—long arms, and curved finger and toe bones—suggested she retained adaptations for climbing trees.

Before Lucy's discovery, scientists debated whether bipedalism (upright walking) or brain development came first. Early fossils were often found with few bones below the skulls, making it hard to establish a timeline of upright walking. The pelvis and leg fragments from Lucy's skeleton provided clear evidence of an early hominid that walked upright yet had a small brain, confirming that bipedalism evolved before large brain development.

Lucy's discovery also provided instrumental evidence for the anthropological understanding of human dispersal patterns by dating a bipedal hominid to 3.2 million years ago in East Africa. By placing the critical stages of early hominid evolution on the African continent, Lucy's discovery solidified Africa's role as the "cradle of humanity," reinforcing the importance of East Africa as the point of origin for fundamental human traits.

16 What can be inferred about Lucy?

Ⓐ Her skeleton was more intact than previously discovered hominid skeletons.
Ⓑ Her brain was small compared to later hominids.
Ⓒ She was not fully grown when she became fossilized.
Ⓓ She was unable to climb trees.

17 Why does the author mention pelvis and leg fragments?

Ⓐ To explain why Lucy's skeleton was found in fragments
Ⓑ To highlight the evidence that identified the sequence of hominid evolution
Ⓒ To compare the sizes of Lucy's bone fragments
Ⓓ To show that the pelvis and legs were important anatomical structures for early humans

18 Which of the following is NOT mentioned as an effect of Lucy's discovery?

Ⓐ Supporting Africa as humanity's evolutionary birthplace
Ⓑ Reshaping anthropological views about hominid evolution
Ⓒ Proving that the large brain came before upright walking
Ⓓ Establishing the dating of bipedalism

19 The word "instrumental" in the passage is closest in meaning to

Ⓐ theoretical
Ⓑ complex
Ⓒ crucial
Ⓓ convincing

20 What is the relationship between paragraphs 2 and 3?

Ⓐ Paragraph 3 contrasts Lucy's discovery with other fossil finds mentioned in paragraph 2.
Ⓑ Paragraph 3 presents an additional implication of the evidence established in paragraph 2.
Ⓒ Paragraph 3 introduces an alternative theory not discussed in paragraph 2.
Ⓓ Paragraph 3 gives a chronological account of the excavation process that began in paragraph 2.

Answers p.472

6. Inference Questions

Overview

지문에 주어진 정보를 근거로, 지문에 직접적으로 언급되지 않은 내용을 추론할 것을 요구하는 문제이다.

Types of Questions

Inference 문제는 보통 다음과 같이 What can be inferred about으로 시작한다. 간혹, suggest 동사가 쓰인 문제 중에도 추론이 필요한 문제가 있을 수 있다.

Inference

What can be inferred about Mars exploration missions?
What does the author suggest about the limitations of classical physics?

Hackers Strategy

1 문제에서 묻는 핵심 어구를 지문에서 찾는다.

지문을 빠르게 훑어보며, 문제에서 묻는 핵심 어구, 즉 문제에서 about의 목적어 부분이 지문의 어디에 제시되었는지 찾는다. 문제에서 묻는 핵심 어구가 지문 전반의 주제에 해당하여 정답의 단서를 찾는 데 도움이 되지 못하는 문제도 있을 수 있다. 이때는 각 선택지의 핵심 어구가 지문의 어디에 언급되어 있는지를 확인한다.

2 앞뒤에 주어진 정보와 문맥을 바탕으로, 올바르게 추론한 선택지를 고른다.

간혹 두 문장 이상, 또는 단락 단위 내용을 확인해야 추론할 수 있는 문제가 출제될 수도 있다. 따라서 핵심 어구가 언급된 곳 앞뒤의 내용도 확인하며 선택지의 내용을 추론할 수 있는지 확인한다.

3 자주 나오는 오답 유형에 주의한다.

지문의 내용과 반대되는 내용을 제시하는 오답, 지문에 아예 언급되지 않은 내용을 제시하는 오답이 자주 출제된다. 또한, 고난도 오답으로는 지문에 언급된 내용이기는 하지만 문제의 핵심 어구와는 상관없는 오답, 지문의 내용과 일부만 일치하는 오답이 등장한다.

Example

Genetic Diversity

Genetic diversity is the total number of variations within the genetic makeup of a species. This diversity allows populations to respond to environmental changes, such as new diseases or climate shifts. For example, within a species, some individuals may carry genes that make them resistant to certain illnesses, while others might be sensitive. This means that if a disease affects a population, not all individuals will be affected in the same way, allowing some to survive and reproduce.

Genetic diversity is crucial for agriculture. Plant breeders rely on selective breeding to develop crops with desirable traits like high yield. This often results in genetic uniformity, which renders the entire crop highly vulnerable to new diseases. For instance, the 1970 Southern corn leaf blight epidemic in the U.S. destroyed over half the maize crop because most commercial maize shared a susceptible genetic foundation.

To prevent such losses, scientists actively utilize the broad genetic diversity stored in gene banks. These facilities house seeds from thousands of plant varieties, including wild relatives. Researchers study this diversity to identify resistance genes and introduce them into commercial crops through breeding, thereby creating a crucial genetic defense against future threats.

What can be inferred about species with high genetic diversity?

Ⓐ They naturally produce higher crop yields.
Ⓑ They survive because diseases affect only some of them.
Ⓒ They exhibit varied breeding and mating patterns.
Ⓓ They are more vulnerable to environmental changes.

정답 Ⓑ

해설 유전적 다양성이 높은 종에 대해 추론할 수 있는 것을 묻는 문제이다. 'This means ~ survive and reproduce'를 통해 유전적 다양성이 높은 종은 질병이 덮칠 때 일부 개체가 생존하고 번식한다는 점을 알 수 있다. 이를 통해 유전적 다양성이 높은 종은 질병이 그 종의 일부만을 공격하기 때문에 종이 생존한다는 점을 추론할 수 있다. 따라서 Ⓑ가 정답이다.

HACKERS PRACTICE

01

Until around three million years ago, the apex marine predator was an eighteen-meter-long shark called *Carcharocles megalodon*. The demise of this species has been attributed to a number of factors. The initial catalyst was the cooling of the world's oceans, as megalodon was adapted to coastal tropical waters. For much of the period in which this species existed, the planet had vast swaths of warm, shallow water that supported a variety of marine life—the perfect hunting grounds for megalodon. However, the movement of the planet's landmasses began to alter the oceans, resulting in a general cooling trend and a corresponding reduction in suitable habitats for megalodon.

While megalodon may have eventually adapted to the new conditions, it also faced other challenges. Most importantly, its primary prey, baleen whales and other medium-sized whales, also began to decline in number due to global cooling. Of the twenty species known to exist, fourteen disappeared during this period. At the same time, new predators arose, such as the ancestor of the modern orca, that aggressively hunted the marine species megalodon relied on for nourishment.

What can be inferred about baleen whales?

Ⓐ They migrated in search of a new prey.
Ⓑ They outcompeted other types of whales.
Ⓒ They split into several distinct species.
Ⓓ They failed to adapt to climate change.

02

A zero-knowledge proof (ZKP) is a concept in cryptography that allows someone to prove that they know a fact without revealing any of the information about the fact itself. This idea transformed the way personal data is managed and protected in digital systems, from electronic voting to cryptocurrencies.

Zero-knowledge means that the verifier learns nothing except that the statement is true. Consider a scenario with Alice and Bob, where Alice claims she knows the combination to a locked safe, but Bob does not. To prove her claim, Bob asks Alice to open the safe without revealing the combination. Alice opens the safe, shows Bob that it is unlocked, and then closes it again. Bob is convinced she indeed knows the combination—without learning what that is himself.

What can be inferred about zero-knowledge proofs?

Ⓐ They were originally developed for electronic voting.
Ⓑ They require revealing partial information to operate.
Ⓒ They are limited to certain types of factual statements.
Ⓓ They have applications beyond just proving knowledge.

03

Telomeres are protective DNA-protein structures located at chromosome ends that function as molecular clocks for cellular aging. These structures shorten with each cell division, limiting the number of times a cell can replicate. When telomeres become too short, cells switch on damage signals and either enter a resting state or self-destruct. Recent research reveals that telomere length is strongly affected by external factors. Chronic stress, poor diet, and sedentary lifestyles significantly accelerate shortening.

The enzyme telomerase maintains the length of telomeres by adding DNA. Because telomerase maintains the proliferative capacity of stem cells, it holds potential for therapies targeting age-related diseases caused by tissue degeneration. At the same time, cancer cells can exploit telomerase to support their indefinite replication, leading to tumor formation. Therefore, current trials of telomerase activators, which offer promising insights into healthy aging and longevity interventions, have to be closely monitored and evaluated for cancer risk.

What can be inferred about telomeres?

Ⓐ Their length varies depending on lifestyle factors.
Ⓑ Their number of possible divisions depends on the cell type.
Ⓒ They can signal cells to continue replicating under stress.
Ⓓ They help slow the natural aging process.

04

Parasocial relationships are one-sided emotional bonds that people form with media figures, including fictional characters. These relationships often begin when individuals repeatedly watch, listen to, or read about a figure. Over time, they develop a strong sense of connection and even believe they know the figure, despite having no direct interactions.

Such relationships can have several drawbacks. They can lead to isolation or unrealistic expectations about real-world connections. In extreme cases, people may become overly absorbed in stories about the figures they admire, neglecting their real-life social relationships.

However, there are also possible positive effects. Parasocial bonds can provide comfort, reduce loneliness, and boost self-esteem. This is especially true for people who lack support from close friends and family members. Also, people may look to their favorite figures as role models, find inspiration in their stories, or use them as a safe way to explore social situations.

What can be inferred about people who lack support from friends and family members?

Ⓐ They are less likely to form parasocial relationships.
Ⓑ They may find parasocial relationships dangerous.
Ⓒ They tend to avoid one-way relationships.
Ⓓ They may experience the positive effects of parasocial bonds.

Answers p.475

HACKERS TEST

[01-05]

Pareidolia

Pareidolia is a phenomenon where the brain quickly perceives recognizable shapes, especially faces, in random patterns or objects. Research suggests that pareidolia occurs when the brain's pattern recognition systems become hyperactive, causing neural pathways to misinterpret ambiguous visual stimuli as meaningful objects. This cognitive shortcut leads the brain to "fill in" missing information based on stored memories and expectations.

A famous case of pareidolia called "the face on Mars" occurred in 1976, when NASA's Viking probe sent back a photo of the Martian surface. The image appeared to show a large human-like face, leading to widespread public speculation about life on Mars. Later, higher-definition pictures taken under different lighting revealed it to be a mesa, a type of rock formation also common on Earth. Nevertheless, the incident attracted global attention and fueled discussions of the possible existence of extraterrestrial intelligence.

From an evolutionary perspective, pareidolia likely developed as a survival advantage. Our ancestors who were highly sensitive to detecting faces could better identify social allies and potential predators. This hypersensitive face-detection system created beneficial "false positives," where occasionally seeing non-existent faces was preferable to missing real ones.

01 Why does pareidolia occur?

Ⓐ People actively search for patterns in their environment.
Ⓑ The brain tends to quickly identify familiar shapes.
Ⓒ Excess stored memories distort ambiguous visual input.
Ⓓ The brain cannot process random patterns.

02 Why does the author mention "shortcut"?

Ⓐ To explain why pareidolia only occurs in certain individuals
Ⓑ To describe the mental mechanism behind pareidolia
Ⓒ To suggest that pareidolia is a learned response
Ⓓ To demonstrate the connection between expectations and memory

03 The word "ambiguous" in the passage is closest in meaning to

Ⓐ specific
Ⓑ incorrect
Ⓒ unclear
Ⓓ authentic

04 What did higher-definition pictures reveal about "the face on Mars"?

Ⓐ It was a shadow from atmospheric conditions.
Ⓑ It was a geological feature also found on Earth.
Ⓒ It was a sand formation that was shaped by the wind.
Ⓓ It was a pattern formed by volcanic lava flows.

05 What can be inferred about pareidolia?

Ⓐ It became less important as humans developed advanced technology.
Ⓑ It emerged as a byproduct of increased brain size.
Ⓒ It was primarily useful for artistic and creative purposes.
Ⓓ It helped detect threats and allies.

HACKERS TEST

[06-10]

The Chinese Room

The Chinese room thought experiment, created by philosopher John Searle, is designed to question whether computers can truly understand language or if they just process symbols mechanically. In this scenario, a person who does not speak Chinese sits in a room. This person receives questions written in Chinese and uses an instruction manual to choose the correct Chinese symbols as answers. To outsiders, the responses seem fluent, yet the person does not understand the language. Searle argues that the person is merely manipulating symbols based on rules, not meaning.

This argument has generated several responses. Some philosophers claim that although the individual does not understand Chinese, the whole system—the room, the person, the instructions—constitutes a mind that does understand the language. Others suggest that the whole system would need to be able to interact with the outside world to develop genuine understanding. Another response proposes that if the system replicated the exact biological processes of a human brain, a true understanding of Chinese would emerge.

The Chinese room thought experiment highlights a core debate in artificial intelligence (AI): whether computational processes alone can create genuine understanding or consciousness. AI systems produce fluent responses without possessing conscious awareness. As technology advances, distinguishing between genuine understanding and sophisticated symbol manipulation becomes important.

06 What is the role of the instruction manual in the Chinese room thought experiment?

Ⓐ It teaches the person to speak Chinese fluently.
Ⓑ It provides rules for selecting symbols as answers.
Ⓒ It helps the person translate questions into Chinese.
Ⓓ It corrects the errors in the person's responses.

07 The passage mentions all of the following responses to Searle's argument EXCEPT:

Ⓐ Understanding arises not from a single part but from the whole system.
Ⓑ Real-world interaction could lead to understanding.
Ⓒ Replicating the brain's biological processes could achieve understanding.
Ⓓ Understanding can emerge from the collaboration of multiple systems.

08 The word "constitutes" in the second paragraph is closest in meaning to

Ⓐ forms
Ⓑ represents
Ⓒ considers
Ⓓ explains

09 What can be inferred about Searle's view on computers and understanding?

Ⓐ He believes computational processes alone are sufficient for true understanding.
Ⓑ He argues that all computational systems are capable of deep understanding.
Ⓒ He doubts that computers genuinely understand things beyond automatic rules.
Ⓓ He rejects the use of simple rule-based systems in artificial intelligence.

10 Why does the author mention artificial intelligence?

Ⓐ To demonstrate widespread interest in computational understanding
Ⓑ To suggest the relevance of the Chinese room thought experiment in ongoing discussions
Ⓒ To emphasize how the Chinese room thought experiment influenced modern AI
Ⓓ To introduce contemporary technology used for language processing

HACKERS TEST

[11-15]

The History of Passenger Jets

The history of passenger jets reflects the story of progress and advancement. Before the jet age, commercial air travel relied on slow propeller planes. In 1952, the De Havilland Comet became the first commercial jet to enter service, promising shorter flight times and greater comfort.

However, the initial excitement around the Comet quickly gave way to serious safety concerns. Within just a few years, several catastrophic accidents occurred with the Comet. Repeated cabin pressurization and flawed window design led to metal fatigue, causing ruptures during flight. These incidents severely undermined public trust in jet airliners.

A Lessons from the Comet paved the way for more reliable jets. **B** One of them, the Boeing 707, entered service in 1958, and though it was smaller than modern jets, it was widely adopted by airlines. **C** In 1970, the Boeing 747, the first wide-body passenger jet, entered service. **D** The arrival of wide-body jets transformed not only the airline industry but also global connectivity, making international tourism and trade much easier.

Today, passenger jets continue to evolve. New materials such as carbon fiber composites have made jet structures lighter and stronger, while quieter but more powerful engines have improved passenger comfort. These innovations will shape the future of global transportation.

11 What was one major issue that affected the De Havilland Comet jets?

Ⓐ Engine failure due to flawed design
Ⓑ Structural weaknesses in aircraft wings
Ⓒ Metal fatigue caused by repeated pressurization
Ⓓ Malfunctions of electronic navigation instruments

12 The word "undermined" in the passage is closest in meaning to

Ⓐ delayed
Ⓑ weakened
Ⓒ overlooked
Ⓓ justified

13 What can be inferred about the Boeing 747?

Ⓐ It focused primarily on domestic routes.
Ⓑ It used carbon fiber composites in its construction.
Ⓒ It was not as well-received as earlier models.
Ⓓ It was larger than its predecessors.

14 Why does the author mention carbon fiber composites?

Ⓐ To suggest how material innovations improve passenger comfort
Ⓑ To explain why modern jets are costlier compared to older models
Ⓒ To specify an innovation that has made planes lighter and stronger
Ⓓ To emphasize the environmental sustainability of aircraft construction

15 There are four locations [■] in the passage that indicate where the following sentence could be added.

This success firmly established the safety and profitability of jet travel, setting the stage for subsequent generations of large commercial aircraft.

Where would the sentence best fit? Select a location [■] where the sentence could be added to the passage.

[16-20]

Pigouvian Taxes

Pigouvian taxes offer a practical solution when business activities create unintended costs for others in society. For instance, factories consider the cost of manufacturing their goods but are not required to account for the health and environmental burdens they place on the public through the release of harmful pollutants. These indirect impacts—called externalities—are not reflected in the production costs and instead are borne by the public.

A Pigouvian tax addresses such problems by making businesses or individuals financially responsible for the broader costs they generate. Setting the tax equal to the estimated damage ensures that market efficiency is maintained while also encouraging producers and consumers to abandon harmful practices for the greater good. This mechanism is widely used by governments to tax manufacturers that produce carbon emissions or individuals who opt for a plastic bag at a store.

Externalities can also emerge from positive cases such as vaccination, which indirectly benefits everyone in the community by reducing disease spread and lowering individual healthcare needs. For socially beneficial products like vaccines, Pigouvian subsidies that make these goods more affordable and thus accessible align private interests with social welfare.

16 What is the main function of a Pigouvian tax?

Ⓐ Stabilizing markets by reducing uncertainty in production costs
Ⓑ Increasing the government budget for positive externalities such as vaccination
Ⓒ Holding those generating social costs accountable for their impact
Ⓓ Providing financial incentives for firms to expand their operations

17 The word "practical" in the passage is closest in meaning to

Ⓐ ideal
Ⓑ realistic
Ⓒ fair
Ⓓ critical

18 What can be inferred about production costs?

Ⓐ They often include environmental costs.
Ⓑ They do not fully reflect the real cost to society.
Ⓒ They are set by government decisions.
Ⓓ They are higher than necessary for consumers.

19 Vaccination is considered to have an externality because

Ⓐ it eliminates the need for governments to invest in public healthcare
Ⓑ it ensures that vaccine producers receive sufficient profit from the market
Ⓒ it lowers medical costs for those who choose to get vaccinated
Ⓓ it benefits the entire community beyond the vaccinated individuals

20 What is the relationship between paragraphs 2 and 3?

Ⓐ Paragraph 3 focuses on public health risks while paragraph 2 emphasizes environmental costs.
Ⓑ Paragraph 3 illustrates positive externalities while paragraph 2 focuses on negative externalities.
Ⓒ Paragraph 3 points out a flaw about Pigouvian policy while paragraph 2 describes its application.
Ⓓ Paragraph 3 introduces broader social benefits while paragraph 2 deals with individuals.

Answers p.476

7. Insertion Questions

Overview

주어진 문장을 삽입하기에 가장 적절한 위치를 묻는 유형이다. 지문 전체의 흐름을 정확하게 이해하고 문장과 문장 사이의 흐름을 파악하여 주어진 문장이 들어가기에 가장 적절한 위치를 선택해야 한다.

Types of Questions

문장을 삽입할 위치는 지문에 [■] 로 표시되어 있다.

Insertion

There are four locations [■] in the passage that indicate where the following sentence could be added.

This contrast highlights the complexity of social structures in early civilizations.

Where would the sentence best fit? Select a location [■] where the sentence could be added to the passage.

Hackers Strategy

1 주어진 문장을 읽고, 문장이 어떤 기능을 하는지 확인한다.

주어진 문장은 뒤에 나올 정보들을 아우르는 도입 문장일 수도 있고, 앞에 나온 정보에 대한 세부 정보일 수도 있다. 또는 새로운 정보를 소개하지는 않지만 독자들에게 질문을 던짐으로써 글의 흥미를 유지하는 역할을 하는 문장일 수도 있다.

2 주어진 문장이 들어가기에 적절한 곳을 찾는다.

문장의 기능을 알고 나면, 단락에서 어떤 부분에 들어가야 할지 짐작할 수 있다.

3 실제로 문장에 넣은 상태로 지문을 한 번 더 읽어본다.

기능과 목적은 앞뒤 문장과 맞는다고 해도 내용상 앞뒤 문맥과 맞지 않을 수도 있으므로, 주어진 문장을 실제로 지문에 넣어서 지문을 한 번 더 읽어본다.

Example

Literature's Impact on the Individual

Literature exerts a profound influence on individuals, shaping their thoughts, feelings, and worldviews in enduring ways. When people read novels, poems, or essays, they encounter characters and scenarios that may reflect their own experiences or introduce entirely new perspectives. Through engaging with intricate narratives, readers develop empathy by understanding the motives and emotions of others, even those quite different from themselves. Regular reading enhances emotional intelligence, enabling individuals to connect with others more effectively in everyday life.

Literature also serves as a powerful tool for personal reflection. Readers may identify their own struggles within the stories they read, which can offer comfort or insight during challenging moments. The process of interpreting literary elements encourages critical thinking, prompting readers to reconsider their beliefs and views. **A** Many people report that literature has helped them confront grief, overcome prejudice, or find new ambition. **B**

Furthermore, literature can prompt readers to reflect on society and collective responsibility. **C** For example, in Albert Camus's *The Plague*, the citizens' efforts to cope with a devastating epidemic illustrate cooperation and solidarity. **D** This encourages readers to consider how individuals contribute to communities and to examine their own roles in fostering social cohesion and ethical action.

There are four locations [■] in the passage that indicate where the following sentence could be added.

Such experiences demonstrate literature's capacity to facilitate growth on a practical level.

Where would the sentence best fit? Select a location [■] where the sentence could be added to the passage.

정답 Ⓑ

해설 주어진 문장 'Such experiences ~ practical level'을 삽입하기에 가장 적절한 위치를 묻는 문제이다. 주어진 문장은 '이러한 경험은 문학이 실질적인 차원에서 성장을 가능하게 하는 힘을 지녔음을 보여준다'라는 내용이고, Ⓑ 앞 문장 'literature ~ ambition'에서 문학이 슬픔을 극복하고, 편견을 없애며, 새로운 야망을 찾도록 돕는다는 내용을 언급하므로, 주어진 문장은 Ⓑ에 들어가는 것이 적절함을 알 수 있다. 따라서 Ⓑ가 정답이다.

HACKERS PRACTICE

01

The increase in carbon dioxide (CO_2) emissions since the early twentieth century is the primary driver of global warming. One of the most effective tools available to reverse this trend is the planet's forests, which collectively capture almost sixteen billion tons of CO_2 from the atmosphere each year.

This remarkable feat is achieved through photosynthesis, the process by which trees produce a substance necessary for their survival. **A** They absorb CO_2 from the atmosphere and then use sunlight and water to convert it into glucose, a type of sugar that provides energy. **B** Any glucose that is not immediately utilized is stored in the trunk of the tree as wood. **C** Although some CO_2 is released when a tree synthesizes glucose, the amount is significantly less than what is accumulated. **D**

There are four locations [■] in the passage that indicate where the following sentence could be added.

It will remain there for almost the entire life of the tree, which for some species can be hundreds of years.

Where would the sentence best fit? Select a location [■] where the sentence could be added to the passage.

02

The ancient Romans were master builders, constructing aqueducts, stadiums, military fortifications, and more. One of their most important construction materials was a type of concrete that has proven to be much more resistant to damage than its modern counterpart. The reason for this has long been a mystery.

The secret behind the toughness of Roman concrete was finally discovered nearly 2,000 years later. **A** A team of researchers determined that the key is the small pieces of lime. **B** When water enters a piece of Roman concrete through a crack, it comes into contact with the lime. **C** This causes a chemical reaction that produces a substance called calcium carbonate. **D** It quickly expands and then hardens, filling in the crack and preventing further damage. In effect, Roman concrete is self-repairing, which accounts for its amazing longevity.

There are four locations [■] in the passage that indicate where the following sentence could be added.

Most experts previously assumed such fragments were included by chance, but they are present in all Roman concrete.

Where would the sentence best fit? Select a location [■] where the sentence could be added to the passage.

03

A common assumption is that an individual in peril is more likely to receive aid if there are many people around. However, due to the bystander effect, this is not always the case. This phenomenon occurs when the presence of more than one witness to an emergency decreases the likelihood of assistance being provided to the victim. It was first studied by psychologists Bibb Latané and John Darley.

Latané and Darley identified two primary causes of this behavior. First, the greater the number of bystanders, the less personal responsibility each individual feels to intervene. **A** Everyone assumes someone else will help. **B** The other factor is that a person in an unfamiliar situation will observe others to determine the appropriate response. **C** Therefore, when nobody takes immediate action during an emergency, the bystanders interpret not getting involved as the correct reaction. **D** What Latané and Darley determined is that the bystander effect is not the result of callousness but rather an unfortunate outcome of group dynamics.

There are four locations [■] in the passage that indicate where the following sentence could be added.

In other words, the inaction of each individual serves as a social cue that others respond to.

Where would the sentence best fit? Select a location [■] where the sentence could be added to the passage.

04

Synesthesia is a neurological condition where stimulation of one sensory or cognitive pathway leads to automatic experiences in a second, unrelated pathway. As a result, sensory boundaries become blended, so certain types of input trigger sensations in other senses. **A** The exact cause of synesthesia is still not fully understood, but it is generally believed to have a genetic component and may be linked to increased connectivity between regions of the brain that process different senses. **B** However, these findings vary across studies and synesthetic types. **C** Researchers are continuing to investigate the specific neural mechanisms involved to gain a more sophisticated understanding of how sensory processing occurs in the human brain. **D**

There are four locations [■] in the passage that indicate where the following sentence could be added.

Neuroimaging studies of synesthetic individuals have revealed stronger functional and structural links between these typically separate brain regions.

Where would the sentence best fit? Select a location [■] where the sentence could be added to the passage.

Answers p.479

HACKERS TEST

[01-05]

Cone Snails

Cone snails are found mostly in the reefs and sandy coastal areas of tropical waters. Their shells display vibrant colors and unique patterns, making them highly sought after by collectors. Cone snails move slowly and use a tube-like organ called a siphon to detect prey such as small fish, marine worms, and other mollusks on the ocean floor.

One of the most remarkable features of cone snails is their venom. To catch prey, they deploy a specialized harpoon-like tooth that injects a mix of potent toxins known as conotoxins. These toxins quickly immobilize prey by interfering with the victim's nerve signals. For humans, the sting of certain species can be life-threatening, and there is no specific antivenom. Even if a person does not die from a cone snail sting, the venom can cause rapid and severe symptoms.

A Nonetheless, these snails are beneficial. **B** They consume small marine animals before they become too great in number for an ecosystem to support. **C** Scientists are also researching conotoxins to develop new painkillers and treatments for nervous system disorders, due to the ability of these substances to block targeted nerve channels. **D**

01 The word "potent" in the second paragraph is closest in meaning to

Ⓐ active
Ⓑ natural
Ⓒ powerful
Ⓓ ordinary

02 Why does the author mention the colors and patterns of cone snail shells?

Ⓐ To show the difficulty of identifying different species in the wild
Ⓑ To explain why cone snails are popular among collectors
Ⓒ To provide an example of visual traits that attract prey
Ⓓ To present a common characteristic of venomous animals

03 What do cone snails use their harpoon-like tooth for?

Ⓐ Burrowing into sand to hide from predators
Ⓑ Capturing prey by injecting toxins
Ⓒ Breaking down the shells of other mollusks
Ⓓ Attaching themselves to rocks and coral

04 What can be inferred about marine worms?

Ⓐ They can survive on the tropical ocean floor.
Ⓑ They do not have nerve signals.
Ⓒ They are immune to conotoxin.
Ⓓ They are eaten by small fish.

05 There are four locations [■] in the passage that indicate where the following sentence could be added.

This helps prevent overpopulation of certain invertebrates, maintaining ecological equilibrium in coral reefs.

Where would the sentence best fit? Select a location [■] where the sentence could be added to the passage.

HACKERS TEST

[06-10]

Cryptomnesia

Cryptomnesia is a psychological phenomenon in which a person believes they have generated an original idea, memory, or creative work, when in fact they are unconsciously recalling something they previously encountered. This term was coined by Swiss psychologist Theodore Flournoy during his research on automatic writing—producing words without conscious thought—where he observed subjects producing "new" material that was actually derived from forgotten sources.

Researchers suggest that cryptomnesia often arises from failures in source monitoring. Source monitoring refers to the mental process that allows people to distinguish between remembered and newly formed ideas. When this system breaks down, past material may resurface as if it were original. Such lapses underscore the instability of memory and its broad influence on how individuals think, create, and judge the originality of their own ideas.

Cryptomnesia cannot be identified with certainty, since no one method reliably distinguishes unconscious reuse from deliberate plagiarism. **A** Behavioral source-monitoring studies, drafts and timestamps, or computational similarity tools each provide partial insights. **B** However, researchers emphasize the value of cross-checking multiple clues. **C** In this way, they help raise justified suspicion of possible plagiarism. **D**

06 The word "coined" in the passage is closest in meaning to

- Ⓐ invented
- Ⓑ adopted
- Ⓒ popularized
- Ⓓ translated

07 What can be inferred about Theodore Flournoy's research?

- Ⓐ It indicated that the subjects intentionally copied ideas from previously encountered material.
- Ⓑ It suggested that automatic writing consistently produces completely new content.
- Ⓒ It showed that subjects presented previous material they thought was original.
- Ⓓ It concluded that unconscious memory processes work identically in all individuals.

08 What is the purpose of the second paragraph?

- Ⓐ It links cryptomnesia to a failure of the mental process of distinguishing between original ideas and memories.
- Ⓑ It provides historical examples and anecdotes of people experiencing cryptomnesia to illustrate the phenomenon.
- Ⓒ It argues that all creative work is ultimately influenced by prior memories and past experiences.
- Ⓓ It discusses methods and strategies that researchers use to detect instances of unconscious plagiarism in practical settings.

09 Why is it difficult to identify cryptomnesia?

- Ⓐ An honest memory lapse and a deliberate act of copying are hard to distinguish.
- Ⓑ The sources of the forgotten memories are almost impossible to trace.
- Ⓒ Judgments about originality are inherently subjective and cannot be informed by objective clues.
- Ⓓ The phenomenon was discovered only recently and therefore lacks sufficient academic research.

10 There are four locations [■] in the passage that indicate where the following sentence could be added.

Although no single clue can prove intent, their convergence can reasonably inform judgments.

Where would the sentence best fit? Select a location [■] where the sentence could be added to the passage.

HACKERS TEST

[11-15]

Sleep Spindles

Sleep spindles are brief bursts of brain activity lasting between half a second and two seconds that occur during sleep. They typically emerge every three to six seconds during non-rapid eye movement (NREM) sleep. The generation of sleep spindles involves interactions between the thalamus, which relays sensory signals, and the cerebral cortex, the brain's outer layer responsible for higher cognitive functions.

Research has verified that sleep spindles are vital for helping the brain consolidate new memories. In studies involving both children and adults, a direct relationship between spindle frequency and the ability to retain new facts or procedures after sleep has been found. Perhaps equally importantly, spindles appear to shield sleepers from being roused by noises or disruptions.

Further studies indicate that sleep spindles may also be related to other mental and physical conditions. **A** One area of inquiry is their importance for emotional regulation. **B** Beyond this, it seems increasingly likely that changes in the sleep patterns, more specifically, a decline in frequency and amplitude, are indicative of certain diseases. **C** Spindle activity disruptions have even been identified as biomarkers of not only cognitive decline and Alzheimer's disease, but also neurological conditions like Parkinson's disease. **D**

11 What can be inferred about sleep spindles?

Ⓐ They require coordination between multiple brain regions.
Ⓑ They could be influenced by lifestyle or physiological conditions.
Ⓒ They depend mainly on external environmental factors.
Ⓓ They may reflect interactions between neurons.

12 What is one established function of sleep spindles?

Ⓐ They help treat neurological conditions.
Ⓑ They coordinate the release of growth hormones.
Ⓒ They alleviate many types of sleep disorders.
Ⓓ They help process new memories.

13 What is the purpose of the third paragraph?

Ⓐ It describes how sleep spindles support brain function and sleep quality.
Ⓑ It compares sleep spindles with other types of brainwave patterns.
Ⓒ It introduces the clinical significance of sleep spindles.
Ⓓ It explains the methods used to measure sleep spindle frequency.

14 The word "roused" in the second paragraph is closest in meaning to

Ⓐ changed
Ⓑ woken
Ⓒ confused
Ⓓ disturbed

15 There are four locations [■] in the passage that indicate where the following sentence could be added.

Studies have shown that spindle rates increase in response to anxiety, suggesting that sleep spindles help process negative feelings.

Where would the sentence best fit? Select a location [■] where the sentence could be added to the passage.

HACKERS TEST

[16-20]

Phototropism

Phototropism is the movement or growth of plants in response to light. This phenomenon is most clearly observed when plants bend toward the sun, maximizing their ability to absorb sunlight for photosynthesis. Young bean plants, for instance, bend their leaves toward light. The underlying mechanisms are plant hormones such as auxin, which are redistributed within the plant, causing cells on the shaded side to elongate and direct growth toward the light.

A Phototropism plays an essential role in the survival of plants. **B** By orienting leaves and stems toward the sun, plants boost their photosynthetic efficiency, which results in increased energy production and growth. **C** In some cases, roots display negative phototropism, growing away from direct sunlight and deeper into the soil. **D** Their growth in this direction allows them to find water and nutrients needed for survival.

Ongoing studies seek to understand how different plant species regulate phototropism in diverse conditions. Insights gained from this research may lead to advances in agricultural technology, such as optimizing crop layouts and breeding new varieties with improved light-use efficiency. Learning more about auxin redistribution may allow scientists to engineer plants that maximize photosynthetic potential even in areas with limited sunlight exposure.

16 The word "elongate" in the passage is closest in meaning to

   Ⓐ multiply
   Ⓑ divide
   Ⓒ lengthen
   Ⓓ strengthen

17 According to the passage, all of the following are associated with phototropism EXCEPT

   Ⓐ Increased energy production
   Ⓑ Optimized crop layouts
   Ⓒ Maximized sunlight absorption
   Ⓓ Redistribution of plant hormones

18 Why does the author mention "new varieties"?

   Ⓐ To describe how the crop planting process is planned in traditional farming
   Ⓑ To suggest that crop layouts affect root phototropism
   Ⓒ To provide an example of a potential outcome of an area of study
   Ⓓ To indicate the role of phototropism in environmental conservation

19 What can be inferred about the agricultural applications of phototropism research?

   Ⓐ It could ensure successful cultivation in regions with low light.
   Ⓑ It could potentially decrease the rate of soil erosion.
   Ⓒ It might result in improved disease resistance in crops.
   Ⓓ It might allow farmers to grow crops without sunlight.

20 There are four locations [■] in the passage that indicate where the following sentence could be added.

   This adaptation also allows seedlings to capture light more quickly, especially in competitive or crowded environments.

   Where would the sentence best fit? Select a location [■] where the sentence could be added to the passage.

무료 토플자료·유학정보 제공
goHackers.com

Section II
Passage Topics

Hackers
Updated TOEFL
READING

Section II에서는 TASK 3에 자주 출제되는 주제들을 중심으로 각 세부 단원을 구성하였다. TASK 3에는 실제 대학 강의에서 다루는 다양한 학문 분야들이 출제되는데, 크게 인문학, 예술, 사회과학, 물리과학, 생명과학으로 나누어 볼 수 있다.

TASK 3의 Passage Topics에는 다음의 5가지가 있다.

1. Humanities
2. Arts
3. Social Science
4. Physical Science
5. Life Science

1. Humanities

TASK 3의 인문학 지문에서는 역사, 언어학, 문학과 관련된 주제가 출제된다. 인류 역사의 시대별 특징과 변화, 문자 체계와 언어에 관한 분석, 문학 작품의 분석 및 비평, 그리고 다양한 문예 사조와 관련된 개념들을 주로 다룬다.

History (역사)

주요 시대별 특징과 변화에 관한 지문이 주로 출제된다.

1. European History (유럽사)

Ancient Greece (고대 그리스)	기원전 2천 년경 에게해에서 발전한 문명으로, 지중해 문화에 큰 영향을 미쳤다. 기원전 8세기 무렵, 상업과 농업의 발전, 정착 생활 안정, 신전과 집회 중심의 사회 구조 확립 등을 기반으로 다양한 도시 국가(polis)가 등장해 독립적으로 운영되었다. 가장 대표적인 도시 국가로는 시민 참여 중심의 민주정(democracy)과 철학·예술의 발전으로 고전기(Classical) 문화를 이끌었던 아테네(Athens)와, 엄격한 군사 훈련과 중장보병(hoplites)으로 대표되는 스파르타(Sparta)가 있다.
Roman Empire (로마 제국)	이탈리아반도의 도시 로마를 중심으로 지중해 연안과 유럽, 중동, 북아프리카를 통합한 광대한 고대 문명이다. 기원전 1세기~기원후 2세기에 걸쳐 군사적 정복과 도로·항만 등 기반 시설 확충을 통해 영토를 확장했으며, 경제, 법제, 행정 체계를 정비하며 전성기를 누렸다. 하지만 3세기 이후 내·외부적 위기로 통치가 약화되었고, 4세기 동로마제국과 서로마제국으로 나뉘었다. 서로마제국은 476년 게르만족의 침입으로 멸망한 반면, 동로마제국은 1453년 콘스탄티노폴리스 함락까지 존속했다. 로마 제국은 법률, 건축, 군사, 언어, 행정 등 다양한 영역에서 후대 유럽 문명과 근대 국가 체계의 기반을 형성하는 깊은 영향을 미쳤다.
Vikings (바이킹)	8세기에서 11세기 사이 북유럽을 중심으로 활동한 해양 민족으로, 탐험, 정복, 교역을 통해 유럽 전역에 영향력을 미쳤다. 뛰어난 장거리 항해 능력과 해상 전술을 바탕으로 영국, 아일랜드, 프랑스 등지에 침략과 정착을 시도하며 교역과 문화적 교류를 동시에 진행했다. 바이킹 사회는 각 부족과 지역 지도자를 중심으로 조직되었으며, 민회를 통해 법과 분쟁 해결을 논의하는 집단적 의사결정 구조를 갖추었다. 바이킹은 항해 시 태양 위치를 추정하기 위해 '태양석(sunstone)'과 같은 도구를 사용했을 가능성이 제기되며, 이러한 기록은 그들이 단순한 약탈자뿐만 아니라 전략적이고 체계적인 항해 기술을 갖추었을 가능성을 보여준다.

Feudalism (봉건제)	로마 제국 멸망 이후 서유럽에서 형성된 정치·사회·경제 체제로, 영주(lord)와 봉신(vassal) 사이의 토지(봉토, fief) 분배와 군사·경제적 의무 교환을 통해 유지되었다. 이 구조에서 농민(peasant)과 농노(serf)는 토지를 경작하며 경제적 기반을 담당했는데, 특히 농노는 영주에게 법적·경제적으로 예속되었다는 점에서 농민과 차이가 있었다. 초기에는 지역 영주 권력이 강하고 자급적 농업 중심이었으나, 인구 증가, 기술 발전, 자유농민 확대, 시장 성장으로 점차 화폐 경제가 활성화되었다. 이후 도시 성장과 중앙 집권적 국가의 등장으로 점차 약화되었지만, 중세 유럽 사회의 정치·경제·사회 구조를 이해하는 핵심 개념으로 남아있다.
Guild (길드)	중세 유럽 도시에서 상인과 수공업자들이 조직한 협회로, 특정 직종이나 업종을 중심으로 결성되어 도시 경제에 큰 영향력을 행사했다. 상인 길드는 상품의 거래를 규율하고 가격·품질·교역 범위를 통제했으며, 수공업 길드는 도제-직인-장인으로 이어지는 직업 훈련 체계를 마련하고 생산 기준과 품질을 관리했다. 독일 북부와 발트해 연안 도시들은 길드와 연계하여 한자 동맹(Hanseatic League)을 구성했고, 13세기부터 북유럽의 장거리 무역을 주도하며 상업 네트워크를 확장했다. 한자 동맹은 도시 간 협력을 통해 안전한 교역망을 보장하고 곡물·모피·소금 등 주요 상품의 유통을 통제하며 지역 경제를 연결하는 핵심적 역할을 수행했다.
Renaissance (르네상스)	14세기 이탈리아에서 시작된 문화·예술 운동으로, 중세의 종교 중심 사고에서 벗어나 인간 중심적 사고(humanism)를 강조했다. 회화, 조각, 건축 등 예술 분야에서 고전 그리스·로마 문화를 재발견하고 발전시켰으며, 레오나르도 다빈치, 미켈란젤로, 라파엘로 등 대표적 예술가들이 활약했다. 과학 분야에서는 르네상스 시기 후반 니콜라우스 코페르니쿠스의 지동설 발표와 같은 새로운 과학적 탐구가 시작되었으며, 문학에서는 페트라르카의 인문주의적 서신과 시가 인간 경험과 감정을 중시하는 표현을 발전시키는 등 새로운 탐구와 표현이 활발히 이루어졌다.
Italian City States (이탈리아 도시 국가)	르네상스 시기, 이탈리아반도의 도시 국가들은 상업, 금융, 예술·문화의 중심지로 번영하였다. 피렌체는 13세기부터 양모 산업을 기반으로 번영했는데, 피렌체의 유력 가문이었던 메디치 가문은 주로 은행업과 금융 활동을 통해 축적한 부로 예술과 학문을 후원해 르네상스 문화 발전에 크게 기여했다. 베네치아는 아드리아해 연안의 해상 무역 중심지로, 상업 및 금융 네트워크와 선박·항로를 통해 동방 무역을 주도하였다. 밀라노는 스포르차 가문의 지배 아래 군사적 방어 체제와 함께 상업, 금속 가공과 무기·비단 산업을 중심으로 경제를 발전시켰다. 이 도시 국가들은 독립적 정치 체계를 유지하면서 경제력과 문화적 영향력으로 이탈리아와 유럽 전역에 중요한 역할을 수행했다.
Printing Press (인쇄술)	15세기 중반 독일의 요하네스 구텐베르크가 금속활자와 기계식 인쇄기를 결합해 대량 인쇄를 실현했다. 이 기술 혁신은 책과 문서의 대량 생산을 가능하게 했으며, 이로 인해 지식과 정보가 빠르게 확산되어 교육과 학문의 보급이 촉진되었다. 나아가 인쇄술은 언어의 표준화, 문화적 정체성 형성, 인쇄물을 통한 공론장 형성 등 근대 사회 변화의 기반을 마련한 핵심적인 기술이다. 마르틴 루터의 종교개혁(Reformation) 같은 사회·종교 운동에도 걸징직 영향을 미쳤다.
Industrial Revolution (산업혁명)	18세기 후반 영국에서 시작되어 19세기 유럽과 북미로 확산된 경제·사회적 대변혁이다. 증기기관, 방적기 및 방직기 등의 발명으로 생산력이 급격히 향상되었고, 석탄, 철, 기계 산업이 경제 성장을 이끌었다. 하지만 긍정적 변화와 함께, 아동 노동, 장시간·저임금 노동, 열악한 근로 조건 등 심각한 사회적 문제도 야기되었다.
Industrialization and Urbanization (산업화와 도시화)	19세기 산업화는 도시화(urbanization)를 촉진하여 많은 농촌 주민이 도시로 이주했다. 이는 공장 노동과 임금 상승의 기회를 제공했지만, 동시에 열악한 주거와 위생 문제로 콜레라, 결핵 같은 질병이 확산되는 결과를 낳았다. 이 시기 도시는 교통·통신·상업이 발전하면서 중산층이 부상했고, 중산층은 교육 확충과 공중 보건 개혁 등을 주도하며 근대 사회의 토대를 구축하는 데 중요한 역할을 했다.

2. American History (미국사)

Colonial America (아메리카 식민지)	1607년, 영국인들은 버지니아에 제임스타운을 세워 북미 최초의 영구적 식민지를 구축했다. 초기에는 농업과 담배 재배가 경제 기반이었으며, 원주민과의 교류와 충돌이 공존했다. 이후 영국 정부는 총독과 의회 체제를 통해 정치·경제를 조직하고 식민지 사회를 관리하며 통치를 본격화했다.
American Revolution (미국 독립 전쟁)	18세기 중반, 북미 식민지 주민들은 영국 본토의 세금 정책과 무역 규제에 불만을 품고 갈등을 겪었다. 특히 1773년 보스턴 차 사건은 차에 부과된 세금에 반발한 식민지인들의 상징적 저항이었으며, 이는 영국 정부의 강경 대응을 촉발했다. 이러한 갈등은 1776년 독립선언으로 이어져 식민지들이 정식 독립을 선언했다. 이후 1783년까지 이어진 미국 독립전쟁에서 프랑스, 스페인 등 외국의 지원을 받아 영국과의 무력 충돌 끝에 최종적으로 독립을 쟁취하며 미국이 탄생했다.
American Agriculture (미국의 농업)	미국 초기 북부 뉴잉글랜드 지역에서는 비교적 작은 토지에서 자급적 농업을 했으며 가족 단위 노동이 중심이었다. 이와 대조적으로 남부에서는 대규모 플랜테이션 농업이 발달하여 담배, 면화 등을 생산했다. 1793년 조면기(Cotton gin, 목화씨 분리기)의 발명으로 면화 생산이 급증하면서 노예 노동에 대한 의존도가 크게 증가했다. 이러한 지역별 농업 구조의 차이는 남북 간의 경제적, 사회적 갈등을 심화시켰으며, 이는 결국 남북전쟁(Civil War)으로 이어졌다.
Reconstruction (재건 시기)	남북전쟁 이후 1865년부터 1877년까지 이어진 시기로, 연방에서 이탈했던 남부 연합을 재통합하고 노예 해방 이후 아프리카계 미국인의 시민권과 사회적 지위를 회복하려는 노력이 핵심이었다. 동시에 이 시기에는 철도, 도로 등 교통 기반 시설 확장이 활발히 진행되어 경제와 산업 기반 재건을 지원했다. 특히 철도망의 확장은 농산물과 산업 자원의 운송을 용이하게 하고 남부와 북부를 연결하는 경제적 통합을 가능하게 했다.
American Industrialization (미국의 산업화)	미국의 산업화는 19세기 후반 철강, 석유, 철도 등 중공업을 중심으로 급속히 진행되며 경제 구조가 변화했다. 전화, 전등, 자동차 등 다양한 발명품이 산업 발전을 촉진했으며, 석유와 전기는 필수적인 에너지원으로 자리 잡았다. 앤드루 카네기(철강), 존 D. 록펠러(석유), 코닐리어스 밴더빌트(철도) 등의 기업가가 이 발전에 기여했다. 이 과정에서 장시간 노동, 낮은 임금, 열악한 작업 환경이 문제로 나타났으며, 노동자 권익 시위가 1886년 시카고 헤이마켓 사건과 같은 폭력 사태로 번지는 등 사회적 갈등이 심화되었다. 미국 북동부와 중서부의 일부 전통적 제조업 지역은 20세기 후반 산업 쇠퇴로 경제적 어려움을 겪었으며, 이를 '러스트 벨트(Rust Belt)'라고 부른다.
American Urbanization (미국의 도시화)	미국의 도시화는 산업혁명과 철도, 항만, 제조업 발달을 배경으로 19세기 후반부터 급속히 진행되었다. 동부 해안에는 뉴욕, 보스턴, 필라델피아, 워싱턴 D.C. 등이 연결되어 거대도시권(megalopolis)을 형성하며 경제, 금융, 문화 중심지로 발전했다. 동시에 중서부와 서부에서도 철도와 산업 확장으로 새로운 도시들이 성장했고, 20세기 이후 자동차와 교외 개발로 인해 도시 팽창(urban sprawl)이 나타나 도심 집중과 교외 거주 패턴이 혼재하는 구조가 형성되었다.
Great Depression (대공황)	1929년부터 약 10년간 지속된 경제 불황이다. 1929년 '검은 목요일(Black Thursday)' 증권시장 붕괴로 촉발되었으며, 은행 파산, 통화수축, 금본위제 고수 등이 복합적으로 작용하며 심화되었다. 사회적으로는 실업, 빈곤, 식량 부족이 심화되었고 많은 이민자와 농민들이 삶의 터전을 잃었다. 프랭클린 D. 루스벨트 대통령의 뉴딜 정책(공공사업, 복지 확대, 통화정책 조정)이 회복에 중요한 역할을 했으며, 제2차 세계대전 이전의 군수 산업 성장 역시 회복을 가속했다.

Linguistics (언어학)

문자 체계와 언어에 관한 지문이 주로 출제된다.

Hieroglyphics (상형문자)	고대 이집트에서 사용된 그림 문자로, 사물과 개념을 상징적으로 표현하여 의사소통과 기록에 활용되었다. 상형문자는 그림이나 기호를 이용해 단어, 소리, 의미를 동시에 표현할 수 있으며, 문맥과 위치에 따라 여러 가지 뜻으로 해석될 수 있다. 기원전 196년에 제작된 돌판인 로제타석(Rosetta Stone)에는 상형문자, 이집트 민중문자(demotic), 그리스어 세 가지로 동일한 내용이 기록되어 있다. 이는 19세기 초 장 프랑수아 샹폴리옹(Jean-François Champollion)이 상형문자를 해독하는 데 결정적 단서를 제공하였다.
Indo-European Language Family (인도유럽어족)	유럽과 남아시아를 중심으로 광범위하게 분포하는 언어 집단으로, 영어, 독일어, 프랑스어, 스페인어, 러시아어, 힌디어, 페르시아어 등이 포함된다. 이 언어들은 공통 조상어인 원인도유럽어(Proto-Indo-European)에서 갈라져 발전했으며, 문법적 특징과 어휘상의 유사성을 통해 계통학적 연구가 이루어졌다. 인도유럽어족은 언어학뿐 아니라 역사와 인류학 연구에서도 고대 민족 이동과 문화 교류를 이해하는 중요한 단서를 제공한다.

Literature (문학)

구체적인 문학 작품이나 작가에 관한 지문이 주로 출제된다.

The Iliad and the Odyssey (일리아드와 오디세이)	고대 그리스의 서사시로, 호메로스(Homer)가 집필한 것으로 전해진다. 일리아드는 트로이 전쟁(Trojan War) 동안 그리스 연합군과 트로이군 간의 갈등과 영웅들의 운명을 중심으로 전개되며, 전쟁과 명예, 인간의 운명을 탐구한다. 오디세이는 트로이 전쟁 후 영웅 오디세우스(Odysseus)가 고향 이타카(Ithaca)로 돌아오는 여정을 그리며 모험, 신화적 존재, 인간 지혜와 인내를 강조한다. 두 작품 모두 고대 그리스 문화와 신화, 가치관을 이해하는 중요한 자료로 평가된다.
William Shakespeare (셰익스피어)	영국 문학사를 빛낸 극작가(dramatist)이자 시인(poet)으로, 인간에 대한 통찰력(insight), 시적 상상력(poetic imagination), 언어 구사 능력(command of language)이 매우 뛰어나다는 평가를 받는다. 현재 전해지는 작품은 희곡(play) 38편, 소네트(sonnet) 154편, 장시(narrative poem) 2편이며, 제목만 전해지는 것도 있다. 그의 대표 희극(comedy)으로는 <한여름 밤의 꿈 A Midsummer Night's Dream>, <말괄량이 길들이기 The Taming of the Shrew>, <십이야 Twelfth Night>, <베니스의 상인 The Merchant of Venice> 등이 있고, 비극(tragedy)으로는 <로미오와 줄리엣 Romeo and Juliet>, <리어 왕 King Lear>, <맥베스 Macbeth>, <햄릿 Hamlet>, <오셀로 Othello> 등이 있다.

HACKERS TEST

[01-05]

Urban Sanitation Reforms

Urban sanitation dates back thousands of years; the Romans built aqueducts to bring in fresh water and drains to remove wastewater. However, by the Middle Ages, many European towns relied on pits and open gutters to store waste. As European cities grew overcrowded from industrialization in the nineteenth century, waste flowed into rivers and turned water sources foul and fueled epidemics.

A turning point came in London in 1854. Physician John Snow mapped cholera cases and traced the outbreak to a pump. He persuaded officials to remove the pump handle to restrict water access until the contamination could be addressed. This step reduced further exposure. Snow's evidence-based method in identifying the contamination source utilized careful observation and conclusive proof, and it changed public health discourse.

A Around the same time, engineer Joseph Bazalgette designed modern sewers but had not yet implemented his plans. **B** During the Great Stink of 1858, warm weather made the River Thames reek. **C** This accelerated the funding and construction of Bazalgette's sewer system. **D** The system reduced the threat of disease, contributed to cleaner city air, and inspired similar reforms in other cities. Modern sanitation rests on these reforms, linking science, policy, and engineering.

01 What is suggested in the passage about John Snow?

Ⓐ He built London's modern sewers to carry waste downstream.
Ⓑ He reduced disease cases by persuading officials to remove the pump handle.
Ⓒ He introduced a citywide policy requiring households to boil water before daily use.
Ⓓ He developed a vaccine that gradually stopped the cholera outbreak.

02 Why does the author mention pits and open gutters?

Ⓐ To show the influence of Roman aqueducts on medieval European cities
Ⓑ To contrast modern waste storage with earlier methods of disposal
Ⓒ To mention the archaeological methods used to excavate medieval European towns
Ⓓ To imply the historical context that caused the sanitation problems in nineteenth-century European cities

03 The word "conclusive" in the passage is closest in meaning to

Ⓐ decisive
Ⓑ tentative
Ⓒ ambiguous
Ⓓ statistical

04 What event accelerated funding and construction of Bazalgette's sewer system?

Ⓐ A drought that dried up the River Thames for weeks
Ⓑ A flood that caused widespread sewage overflow into the streets
Ⓒ An outbreak of a disease linked to contaminated water
Ⓓ A crisis involving a foul smell from the River Thames

05 There are four locations [■] in the passage that indicate where the following sentence could be added.

Even the members of Parliament soaked curtains in bleach and hung them to mask the stench, and growing press criticism and public petitions pushed the legislature to act.

Where would the sentence best fit? Select a location [■] where the sentence could be added to the passage.

HACKERS TEST

[06-10]

The Roaring Twenties

The Roaring Twenties refers to the decade following World War I, from 1920 to 1929, in the United States. This period was characterized by rapid economic expansion, rising urban incomes, and the broad diffusion of consumer goods.

The decade played a central role in the creation of a consumer economy based on mass production, advertising, and credit. Factories increased production, allowing goods such as automobiles, household appliances, and radios to become widely available. The growth of installment credit encouraged mass consumption, and low interest rates fueled construction, home purchases, and investment. The widespread availability of affordable automobiles and installment plans directly facilitated the growth of suburbs, as workers could now easily commute and afford homes outside the urban centers.

However, it also brought about major vulnerabilities: rising household and corporate debt, inadequate financial safeguards, and widespread speculation. Consumer prices for many goods declined, but farmers faced falling crop values and mounting debt, leaving many rural families behind. Immigration restrictions and weakened labor unions reshaped the workforce. The prohibition of alcohol impacted tax revenue, while limited government oversight created weaknesses in banks and financial markets. In addition, social divisions increased as income and regional inequalities widened and racial violence intensified.

06 The word "diffusion" in the first paragraph is closest in meaning to

Ⓐ concentration
Ⓑ segregation
Ⓒ distribution
Ⓓ formation

07 Click on the sentence in paragraph 2 that identifies a specific condition that resulted in the widespread availability of consumer goods.

Ⓐ The decade played a central role in the creation of a consumer economy based on mass production, advertising, and credit.
Ⓑ Factories increased production, allowing goods such as automobiles, household appliances, and radios to become widely available.
Ⓒ The growth of installment credit encouraged mass consumption, and low interest rates fueled construction, home purchases, and investment.
Ⓓ The widespread availability of affordable automobiles and installment plans directly facilitated the growth of suburbs, as workers could now easily commute and afford homes outside the urban centers.

08 What can be inferred about farmers in rural America during the 1920s?

Ⓐ They benefited the most from the decline in consumer prices.
Ⓑ They did not experience the same level of prosperity as people in cities.
Ⓒ They did not have access to credit to pay for supplies and equipment.
Ⓓ They were able to protect themselves through labor union activity.

09 Why does the author mention the prohibition of alcohol?

Ⓐ To highlight how it boosted industrial productivity and efficiency
Ⓑ To emphasize the dangers of excessive alcohol consumption
Ⓒ To show how moral reform movements shaped American values
Ⓓ To illustrate how policies influenced economic conditions

10 The passage mentions all of the following as weaknesses of the 1920s American economy EXCEPT

Ⓐ High corporate and consumer debt levels
Ⓑ Widening disparities in income
Ⓒ Frequent strikes by powerful labor unions
Ⓓ Inadequate market oversight

HACKERS TEST

[11-15]

The U.S. Library of Congress

The Library of Congress is the largest library in the world and the unofficial national library of the United States. Several key moments contributed to its creation.

America's early leaders were classically educated readers who believed books and knowledge were crucial to maintaining a democracy. So, when Washington, D.C. became the nation's capital in 1790, the groundwork was laid for the establishment of a library. It was officially founded in 1800. Its initial collection was housed in a chamber within the newly built Capitol Building.

Unfortunately, the Capitol building was attacked during the War of 1812 between the United States and the British Empire. Thomas Jefferson, one of the early leaders, subsequently offered to sell the government his personal collection of over 6,000 books. This decision inspired the Library to adopt its own mission to become a universal repository of books. Furthermore, in 1870, it became the home of the U.S. Copyright Office, which allowed it to continuously grow its collection of published material.

As the twentieth century dawned, the Library of Congress became a national institution for all Americans, making its resources accessible to all citizens.

11 The word "subsequently" in the passage is closest in meaning to

   Ⓐ beforehand
   Ⓑ instantly
   Ⓒ meanwhile
   Ⓓ afterward

12 What is indicated about the Library of Congress?

   Ⓐ It has the role of a national library but is not formally recognized as one.
   Ⓑ It has played a key role in improving the literacy of Americans.
   Ⓒ It is a major contributor to the cultural identity of the United States.
   Ⓓ It is where new books in America are published.

13 Why did America's early leaders want to establish a library?

   Ⓐ They had no place to store their book collections.
   Ⓑ They wanted to promote a spirit of democracy.
   Ⓒ They hoped to educate the American public.
   Ⓓ They needed to preserve the nation's historical records.

14 Why does the author mention the War of 1812?

   Ⓐ To describe a major event in early U.S. history
   Ⓑ To show how the British suppressed information
   Ⓒ To highlight a turning point in the Library's development
   Ⓓ To illustrate the Library's importance to America's founding

15 What is suggested about the Library of Congress in the twentieth century?

   Ⓐ It was opened to the public.
   Ⓑ It was moved to its current location.
   Ⓒ It was destroyed again in another war.
   Ⓓ It was visited by foreign heads of state.

HACKERS TEST

[16-20]

The Death of the Author

Literary theorist Roland Barthes wrote that "the birth of the reader must come at the cost of the death of the author." By this, he argued that meaning arises from the interpretive activity of readers and appealing to the author's intent to establish a single, correct reading is a mistake. This concept of "the Death of the Author" shifted authority over meaning from the writer to the reader.

For instance, a biographical note claiming the writer intended to convey a political message does not limit the text to that single meaning. Or imagine a novel whose narrator sounds like its writer. Even if the two overlap, the critical task is forming meaning by analyzing how the text constructs voice and perspective, not to assume the narrator is the author and then reduce interpretation to the intake of biographical information.

A This idea democratizes criticism by inviting multiple analytical readings rather than adhering to an author's declared aim. **B** However, it is by no means a perfect theory. **C** Critics argue that ignoring authors can erase marginalized voices or obscure power relations. **D** Still, it remains an important argument for interpretive freedom: meaning is made in the encounter between text and readers.

16 Which of the following best states the main idea of the passage?

Ⓐ Critics have little control over how readers perceive literary works.
Ⓑ A text's meaning comes from interpretation rather than intentions.
Ⓒ Authors should always clarify the intended meaning of their texts.
Ⓓ Narrators are the primary source of meaning in a story.

17 The word "adhering" in the passage is closest in meaning to

Ⓐ inducing
Ⓑ following
Ⓒ presenting
Ⓓ questioning

18 Why does the author mention a novel whose narrator sounds like its writer?

Ⓐ To stress that readers should analyze the meaning of the text independently
Ⓑ To suggest that novels are unreliable when the narrator mirrors the author
Ⓒ To illustrate that biographical context should take precedence over textual analysis
Ⓓ To argue that interpreting the text requires knowing the author's life story

19 What can be inferred about Roland Barthes?

Ⓐ He believed that readers are more important than authors in writing literary works.
Ⓑ He argued that literature should not be a vehicle for political commentary.
Ⓒ He highlighted the importance of multiple interpretations of a text.
Ⓓ He identified the limitations of an independent text-based analysis.

20 There are four locations [■] in the passage that indicate where the following sentence could be added.

Scholars also point out that the absence of a fixed meaning can lead to a kind of interpretive chaos, undermining the possibility of objective literary study.

Where would the sentence best fit? Select a location [■] where the sentence could be added to the passage.

Answers p.483

2. Arts

TASK 3에 출제되는 예술 관련 지문은 주로 회화, 건축, 영화, 사진, 연극과 관련된 주제를 다룬다. 각 분야의 역사, 주요 기법 및 기술과 관련된 내용이 주로 출제된다.

■ Painting (회화)

시대별 회화 기법의 발전과 미술 사조에 관한 지문이 주로 출제된다.

Cave Art (동굴 벽화)	동굴에서 발견된 선사시대 그림들로 동물, 인간 형상, 추상 기호를 표현한 예술이다. 연구자들은 이러한 미술이 사냥 의례(hunting rituals), 후대 교육, 종교적 의미(religious significance) 등 다양한 목적으로 제작되었다고 본다. 뼈·돌·나무 도구와 천연 안료를 애용하여 정교한 기법을 사용한 것과 접근이 어려운 위치에 작품을 제작한 것은 선사시대 인간의 상징적 사고(symbolic thinking)와 문화적 발전을 보여주는 중요한 증거가 된다. 라스코 동굴(Lascaux Cave), 알타미라 동굴(Altamira Cave) 등이 벽화로 잘 알려져 있다.
Fresco and Tempera (프레스코와 템페라)	프레스코(fresco)는 '신선한'을 뜻하는 이탈리아어에서 이름이 유래했으며, 젖은 석회반죽(wet plaster) 위에 안료를 칠하여 벽화를 완성하는 기법이다. 안료가 석회와 화학적으로 결합하여 색상이 오래 지속되며, 벽과 하나로 통합되는 특징이 있다. 르네상스 시기에는 교회와 궁전의 장엄한 장식에 널리 사용되었으며, 미켈란젤로(Michelangelo)의 시스티나 예배당(Sistine Chapel) 천장화가 대표적이다. 템페라(tempera)는 건조한 바탕 위에 안료를 달걀이나 수지 등과 혼합하여 칠하는 방식으로, 색상이 선명하고 세밀한 묘사가 가능하지만 내구성은 프레스코보다 낮다.
Perspective (원근법)	평면 위에 3차원 공간의 깊이와 거리를 표현하는 기법이다. 대표적인 것이 선 원근법(linear perspective)으로, 이 기법은 평면에 3차원 공간의 깊이를 표현하기 위해 수평선상의 소실점(vanishing point)을 기준으로 평행선들이 모이도록 했다. 15세기 초 이탈리아 건축가 필리포 브루넬레스키에 의해 체계화되었으며, 레온 바티스타 알베르티가 1435년 <회화론(De pictura)>에서 이론적으로 정립·체계화했다. 이후 레오나르도 다 빈치(Leonardo da Vinci)와 같은 화가들에 의해 널리 활용되었다.

Chiaroscuro and Sfumato (키아로스쿠로와 스푸마토)	키아로스쿠로는 빛과 어둠의 대비를 이용해 형태의 입체감과 공간감을 만들어 내는 기법으로, 은은한 명암 표현에서부터 극단적 명암 대비(tenebrism)에 이르기까지 폭넓게 사용된다. 이탈리아어로 chiaro는 '밝은', scuro는 '어두운'이라는 뜻이다. 르네상스에서는 주로 인물과 사물의 입체적 표현에 사용되었고, 16세기 카라바조(Caravaggio)와 같은 화가들은 극적·감정적 표현을 강화하는 방식으로 발전시켜 미술 전반에 큰 영향을 미쳤다. 스푸마토는 레오나르도 다 빈치가 발전시킨 기법으로, 경계를 연기처럼 흐리게 처리해 형태를 부드럽게 연결하는 기술이다. 그는 <모나리자(Mona Lisa)>와 <암굴의 성모(The Virgin of the Rocks)>에서 미세한 톤을 통해 깊이와 신비감을 구현하였다. 이 기법은 명암의 대비를 활용하는 키아로스쿠로와는 구별되며, 작품에 신비롭고 환상적인 분위기를 더하는 데 중요한 역할을 하였다.	
Oil Painting (유화)	안료를 기름에 혼합하여 캔버스나 목판에 칠하는 기법이다. 느리게 건조되는 특성 덕분에 색의 혼합(blending)과 레이어링(layering)이 가능하여 사실적 질감과 깊이 있는 색감을 구현할 수 있다. 15세기 중반 이탈리아 북부와 플랑드르 지역에서 발전했으며, 플랑드르의 얀 판 에이크(Jan van Eyck)는 유화를 활용해 세밀한 디테일과 투명한 느낌을 구현함으로써 사실주의적 표현을 정착시켰다. 유화는 풍경, 초상, 종교화 등 다양한 장르에서 활용되며 르네상스 미술의 색감과 표현력을 한층 높이는 역할을 하였다.	
Dutch Paintings (네덜란드 회화)	17세기 네덜란드 황금시대(Golden Age)에 번성한 미술 양식으로, 정물화(still life), 풍경화(landscape), 초상화(portrait) 등 일상적 소재를 세밀하고 사실적으로 묘사했다. 렘브란트(Rembrandt)는 빛과 그림자를 활용한 극적인 인물 표현으로 유명하며, 베르메르(Vermeer)는 가정 내 장면과 빛의 섬세한 표현으로 독특한 분위기를 창출하였다. 네덜란드 회화는 상업적 부유층과 도시 시민의 후원 속에서 발전하였으며, 세밀한 관찰과 사실주의(realism)적 접근이 미술사에 큰 영향을 미쳤다.	
Paint Tube (튜브 물감)	19세기 중반에 개발되어 회화의 제작 방식을 크게 바꾼 발명품이다. 이전에는 화가들이 안료를 아마인유 등 건성유와 혼합해 직접 유화 물감을 제조해 사용했지만, 튜브의 등장은 휴대와 보관을 용이하게 만들고 작업 중 물감의 산화와 건조를 늦출 수 있게 했다. 이로 인해 야외에서 직접 풍경을 관찰하며 그림을 그리는 인상파(impressionism) 화가들처럼 즉흥적이고 생생한 색감 표현이 가능해졌다. 또한 튜브 물감은 다양한 색상을 자유롭게 혼합하고 겹쳐 칠하는 레이어링 기법과 질감(texture)을 살리는 표현을 용이하게 하여, 회화 기술과 표현 범위를 크게 확장하였다.	
Art Market (미술 시장)	미술품 거래는 점차 제도화되고 상업적 성격이 강화되어왔다. 17세기 네덜란드에서는 화가와 수집가, 상인 간의 비교적 개방된 거래가 이루어졌으며, 18세기에는 경매시장이 본격화되었다. 19세기에는 상업 갤러리가 정착했으며, 런던, 파리, 뉴욕 등 대도시 중심으로 공인 중개인(dealer)과 경매사가 활발히 활동하며 가격 형성과 수요를 조정했다. 20세기에 들어서는 국제적 경매와 아트 페어(art fair), 갤러리 네트워크가 확장되어 미술품 거래가 국제화되었으며, 작품의 투자 가치와 수집 가치가 중요한 요소로 자리 잡았다.	

■ Architecture (건축)

고대 및 중세 문명의 주요 공학과 건축 기술에 관한 지문이 주로 출제된다.

Aqueducts (수도교)	먼 수원에서 도시와 농업지대로 물을 운반하도록 설계된 수로 체계이다. 로마 제국은 광범한 수도교망을 구축해 도시에 물을 공급했고, 중력과 정밀한 경사로 물이 지속적으로 흐르도록 했다. 이러한 수도교는 음용수를 제공했고, 분수와 공중목욕탕에 물을 공급하여 도시 생활과 위생을 크게 향상시켰으며, 일부는 농업 관개에도 활용되었다. 오늘날까지 남아있는 대표적 수도교 유적으로는 프랑스의 퐁 뒤 가르(Pont du Gard)가 있다.
Gothic Architecture (고딕 건축)	12세기 프랑스에서 시작되어 16세기까지 유럽 전역으로 확산된 건축 양식이다. 높은 첨탑, 뾰족한 아치(pointed arch), 벽과 외부 부벽을 아치형 부재로 연결해 하중을 측면으로 전달하는 외부 버팀 구조인 플라잉 버트레스(flying buttress), 그리고 스테인드 글라스(stained glass) 창문 등이 특징이며, 특히 스테인드 글라스는 교회와 성당에서 신의 위대함과 빛을 상징적으로 표현하는 데 활용되었다. 이러한 구조적 혁신은 건물의 벽을 얇게 하고 천장을 높이며, 넓은 내부 공간을 확보할 수 있게 하여 예배 공간과 채광을 극대화하였다. 고딕 건축은 또한 조각과 장식, 장미창(rose window) 등 시각적 요소를 통해 신앙적 메시지를 전달했으며, 샤르트르 대성당, 노트르담 대성당, 쾰른 대성당 등이 대표적 사례로 꼽힌다. 이 양식은 중세 유럽의 종교적·사회적 가치와 기술적 성취를 동시에 보여주는 중요한 건축 유산이다.
Irrigation (관개)	농업용 물을 인공적으로 공급하고 분배하도록 설계된 수로 체계이다. 고대 문명에서는 강과 저수지에서 농지로 물을 운반해 작물 생장을 지원했으며, 토양 비옥도와 수확량을 안정적으로 유지했다. 이러한 관개 시설을 만드는 것은 사회적·경제적 조직과 대규모 노동력을 필요로 했다. 메소포타미아의 티그리스·유프라테스 강 유역에서 발달한 운하·제방 중심의 관개 체계와 나일강 삼각주의 수로망이 대표적 사례로 알려져 있다.

■ Film (영화)

영화 기술이나 영화의 역사에 관한 지문이 주로 출제된다.

Silent Films and Sound Films (무성 영화와 유성 영화)	무성 영화(silent film)는 1890년대 후반부터 1920년대까지 영화의 초기 형태로, 대사 없이 영상과 자막, 음악으로 이야기를 전달하였다. 1927년 워너 브라더스의 <재즈 싱어(The Jazz Singer)>는 일부 대사와 노래에 동기화된 음향을 포함하여 최초로 상업적 성공을 거둔 영화로, 이를 계기로 유성 영화(sound films) 시대가 본격적으로 시작되었다. 이후 몇 년에 걸쳐 동시 녹음·동시 재생 기술이 영화 산업 전반에 확산되었다. 이로써 영화 산업은 이야기 전달 방식과 제작 기술 모두에서 새로운 전환점을 맞이하였다.
History of Film (영화의 역사)	1895년 뤼미에르 형제가 카메라와 영사기를 결합한 시네마토그래프(cinematograph)를 발명해 최초로 대중 상영을 하며 영화의 출발을 알렸다. 에디슨은 키네토그래프(kinetograph)와 개인 감상용 키네토스코프(kinetoscope)라는 접안 장치로 구성된 발명품을 개발해 음향 도입과 컬러 영화의 기반을 마련했다. 이어 멜리에스는 시나리오와 특수효과를 도입해 표현주의 영화의 창시자로 불리며, 그의 대표작 <달나라 여행>은 최초의 공상과학 영화로 알려져 있다.

■ Photography (사진)

사진술의 발달과 사진의 사조에 관한 지문이 주로 출제된다.

Pictorialism (픽토리얼리즘)	19세기 후반부터 20세기 초반까지 유행한 사진 미술 운동으로, 앨프리드 스티글리츠(Alfred Stieglitz), 에드워드 스타이컨(Edward Steichen) 등의 사진가들에 의해 주도되었다. 이들은 사진을 단순한 기록 수단이 아닌 예술적 표현 수단으로 승격시키려 했다. 촬영 기법과 인화 과정에서 소프트 포커스(soft focus), 렌즈 조작, 사진 조작 등을 활용해 회화적(painterly) 효과를 강조했으며, 감정과 분위기, 구성의 미적 요소를 중시하였다.

■ Theater (연극)

연극의 역사나 연극의 기법에 관한 지문이 주로 출제된다.

The History of Theater (연극의 역사)	연극은 고대 그리스 아테네에서 포도주와 풍요, 극 예술을 관장하는 신 디오니소스(Dionysus)를 기리던 행사 디오니소스 제전(Dionysia)에서 유래했다. 이 시기 연극은 극의 배경과 해설을 제공하는 코러스(chorus)와 가면(mask)을 활용했으며, 비극(tragedy)과 희극(comedy)이 발전하여 운명, 정의, 인간의 고통, 사회 풍자 등의 주제를 다루었다. 이후 고대 로마에서는 그리스 극의 전통을 이어받으면서도 정교한 무대 디자인 등을 활용해 극의 의미와 맥락을 더욱 풍부하게 표현하였다. 중세 유럽에서는 신비극(mystery play), 도덕극(morality play), 민속극(folk play)이 활발히 공연되며 공연 문화가 종교적 맥락 속에서 새로운 형식으로 지속·발전하였다. 르네상스 이후 전문 극단(professional troupe)과 희곡 문학이 발달하며 근대 연극으로 이어졌다. 셰익스피어(William Shakespeare)는 영국에서 비극과 희극을 결합하고 인간 심리를 깊이 탐구하며 연극 문학을 발전시켰다. 현대 연극은 다양한 장르와 매체를 혼합하여 사회적·문화적 메시지를 전달하는 예술로 자리 잡았다.
Theatron (그리스 극장)	그리스 극장(theatron)은 부채꼴(fan-shaped) 모양으로 객석(auditorium)이 무대 중심을 기준으로 약 230도에 걸쳐 배치되었다. 이는 광장(agora)에서 한 사람을 둘러싸듯 모이는 형태에서 유래하며, 최대 15,000~18,000명을 수용했음에도 음향 전달이 뛰어나, 작은 소리도 멀리까지 잘 들렸다. 극장은 산 정상부에 신전과 함께 배치되어 관객이 마을 경관을 배경 삼아 배우를 보게 하였고, 연극은 삶을 성찰하고 가치를 찾는 문화 행위가 되었다. 대표적인 예로 디오니소스(Dionysos) 극장과 에피다우로스(Epidaurus) 극장이 있다.

HACKERS TEST

[01-05]

Ephemeral Art

Ephemeral art refers to artworks intended to last only for a short time. Unlike pieces preserved in galleries and sold for value, ephemeral works are designed to weather, melt, fade, or be dismantled. Ephemeral art varies in its medium, message, and method of destruction.

A prominent example is the sand mandala. Painstakingly assembled over hours by Tibetan Buddhist monks, it forms a colorful and intricate design, only to be swept away with brooms as if it never existed. This practice signifies the impermanence of life and places value on the ritual of creating rather than the finished product. Ephemeral art is displayed in natural settings as well. Ice sculptures that melt throughout the day make climate and heat visible forces. Arrangements of fallen leaves or rock towers in rivers exist only as long as nature allows.

Performance art, in essence, is a type of ephemeral art. Even when repeated, performances are never identical, as the artist is never in the same mindset. When performed outdoors or in unconventional spaces, performance art disrupts the routines of passersby and encourages them to appreciate artistic expression outside of a gallery or museum. It reminds viewers that art can emerge—and disappear—from anywhere.

01 The word "dismantled" in the passage is closest in meaning to

Ⓐ constructed
Ⓑ separated
Ⓒ remembered
Ⓓ displayed

02 According to the passage, why do Tibetan monks destroy their sand mandalas?

Ⓐ To show that perfection can never be achieved
Ⓑ To represent the temporary nature of life
Ⓒ To recognize the importance of nature
Ⓓ To downplay the value of ritualistic practices

03 What is suggested about ephemeral art in nature?

Ⓐ It persists only as long as the environment permits it to.
Ⓑ It can leave a long-lasting impression on viewers' minds.
Ⓒ It is typically destroyed as soon as it is finished.
Ⓓ It reflects the recurring patterns of nature.

04 Why does the author mention ice sculptures?

Ⓐ To suggest that ice sculptors are highly skilled artists
Ⓑ To illustrate how art can turn natural forces into visible phenomena
Ⓒ To highlight the inherent randomness of ephemeral art
Ⓓ To explain how a work of ephemeral art can be preserved

05 What is one effect of outdoor performance art?

Ⓐ It encourages viewers to appreciate art in an unconventional way.
Ⓑ It reveals the artist's mindset in real-world contexts.
Ⓒ It proves that art can be appreciated and sold for value at the same time.
Ⓓ It draws attention to art's role in social engagement.

HACKERS TEST

[06-10]

The Fourth Wall

The fourth wall is an imaginary, invisible barrier that separates the performers on stage from the audience. In a standard theater setup, three physical walls frame the performance, while the fourth side, facing the spectators, is open. This convention establishes that the audience is merely observing events in a self-contained reality, where the characters are unaware they are being watched. Accepting the fourth wall is vital for maintaining the theatrical illusion, as it requires the audience to temporarily set aside their realistic doubts and become immersed in the story. This allows the audience to become emotionally invested in the narrative.

Breaking the fourth wall is the deliberate disruption of this barrier. It occurs when a character directly acknowledges the audience's presence, speaks to them, or references the constructed nature of the work. While ancient drama included similar techniques like the soliloquy, this device gained new prominence in modern theater, notably with Bertolt Brecht's epic theater. Brecht used it as an alienation effect to prevent passive absorption in the story. Instead, he prompted the audience to critically reflect on the play's social or political themes. This technique thus serves to explicitly remind the spectators that they are witnessing a performance.

06 What is the passage mainly about?

Ⓐ The evolution of theater and stage design
Ⓑ How the fourth wall limits creativity
Ⓒ A conceptual boundary in a theater
Ⓓ Why audiences are disturbed by the fourth wall

07 What is one benefit of establishing the fourth wall?

Ⓐ It makes performances more authentic and believable.
Ⓑ It lets the audience forget their daily lives and surroundings.
Ⓒ It helps actors concentrate on their own performance.
Ⓓ It prevents the audience from being excessively immersed.

08 Why does the author mention soliloquy?

Ⓐ To mention a technique used in modern plays
Ⓑ To show how an ancient technique has been revived
Ⓒ To argue that it is a better technique than the fourth wall
Ⓓ To provide a historical parallel to the modern technique

09 What was Brecht able to achieve by breaking the fourth wall?

Ⓐ Critical consideration of sociopolitical subjects
Ⓑ Passive absorption in the dramatic story
Ⓒ A complete focus on the play's main characters
Ⓓ A deeper understanding of theater history

10 The word "explicitly" in the passage is closest in meaning to

Ⓐ definitely
Ⓑ carefully
Ⓒ partially
Ⓓ vaguely

HACKERS TEST

[11-15]

The Harlem Renaissance

The Harlem Renaissance was a cultural awakening that flourished during the 1920s, centered in Harlem, New York. Fueled by the Great Migration of African Americans from the rural South to northern cities, this era witnessed an extraordinary outpouring of art, literature, and music that challenged racial stereotypes and asserted a bold new Black identity.

This creative movement was shaped by pioneering figures across different fields. In literature, poets such as Langston Hughes infused their verse with the rhythms of jazz and blues, capturing the authentic voices of everyday African Americans, while Zora Neale Hurston celebrated Black folk traditions and female autonomy in her novels. Musically, the defining soundtrack of the era was jazz, driven by the improvisational brilliance of artists like Duke Ellington and Louis Armstrong. In the visual arts, painters such as Aaron Douglas developed a distinctly Afrocentric modernism, portraying narratives of struggle, resilience, and pride.

By forging a strong collective identity and affirming Black humanity, the Harlem Renaissance inspired a deep sense of cultural pride and self-respect within the Black community. It also provided an intellectual and spiritual foundation—a narrative of resilience and creative genius—that empowered activists to challenge systemic injustice and permanently reshape American culture.

11 What was one factor that contributed to the Harlem Renaissance?

   Ⓐ A change in popular cultural tastes
   Ⓑ A demographic shift toward northern urban centers
   Ⓒ Support from publishers and patrons
   Ⓓ The rise of new artistic forms

12 Which of the following is NOT a genre mentioned as influenced by the Harlem Renaissance?

   Ⓐ Music
   Ⓑ Theater
   Ⓒ Literature
   Ⓓ Painting

13 Why does the author mention Zora Neale Hurston?

   Ⓐ To show how Harlem influenced the Black community
   Ⓑ To highlight how literature reflected social realities
   Ⓒ To suggest that literature was less influential than music or the visual arts
   Ⓓ To emphasize that the Harlem Renaissance was limited to entertainment

14 The word "forging" in the passage is closest in meaning to

   Ⓐ creating
   Ⓑ adapting
   Ⓒ changing
   Ⓓ resisting

15 What can be inferred about the Harlem Renaissance?

   Ⓐ It was primarily based on improvisational art.
   Ⓑ It established Harlem as the center of African American culture.
   Ⓒ It helped activists confront racial inequality.
   Ⓓ It sparked organized campaigns for equal rights.

HACKERS TEST

[16-20]

The Seikilos Epitaph

Dating back to the first or second century CE, the Seikilos epitaph is one of the oldest surviving complete musical compositions in history. The piece of music was discovered on a marble column in 1883 in an ancient Greek city, and its inscription provides clues about its origin and purpose.

Scholars believe the epitaph was created to honor the death of a loved one. **A** The lyrics of the epitaph convey a broader philosophical message about the nature of life. **B** Rather than mourning loss, the words encourage the listener to live joyfully and be mindful of time. **C** It serves as both a personal memorial and a universal meditation on human existence. **D**

The Seikilos epitaph can be heard today. Modern researchers were able to reconstruct the melody by deciphering the composition's ancient Greek notation system, which uses letters placed over the text to indicate pitch. Scholars also inferred the rhythm of the piece by analyzing the poetic meter of the text. Once the music and lyrics were combined, the resulting song was straightforward, with clear, recurring rhythmic patterns well suited for singing and simple instrumental accompaniment.

16 The word "inscription" in the passage is closest in meaning to

Ⓐ ornament
Ⓑ prediction
Ⓒ writing
Ⓓ symbol

17 What philosophical message do the lyrics of the Seikilos epitaph convey?

Ⓐ Mourning is necessary for healing and overcoming pain.
Ⓑ Life should be enjoyed and time should be valued.
Ⓒ Seek wisdom through study and contemplation.
Ⓓ Prepare for the afterlife by giving up earthly pleasures.

18 Which of the following best describes the purpose of the second paragraph?

Ⓐ It examines the thematic and emotional message of the composition.
Ⓑ It outlines the methodological approaches used in ancient music research.
Ⓒ It compares ancient Greek poetry with contemporary literary forms.
Ⓓ It introduces alternative theories about the epitaph's original function.

19 What can be inferred about ancient Greek musical notation?

Ⓐ It was mainly used to record detailed instrumental music.
Ⓑ It conveys exact rhythmic patterns for each musical phrase.
Ⓒ It employs symbols that modern scholars can interpret.
Ⓓ It has also been featured in works of poetry.

20 There are four locations [■] in the passage that indicate where the following sentence could be added.

This dual function helps explain its lasting resonance with people today.

Where would the sentence best fit? Select a location [■] where the sentence could be added to the passage.

Answers p.486

3. Social Science

TASK 3의 사회과학 지문에서는 주로 인류학, 심리학, 경제학, 사회학과 같은 세부 분야가 출제된다. 인류의 특징이나 초기 문명, 인간의 심리 및 행동의 이론적 배경, 다양한 경제 이론과 경제 현상, 인간 상호작용의 방식과 규범 등에 대한 내용이 주요 주제이다.

■ Anthropology (인류학)

인류의 특징과 인류의 다양한 문명에 관한 지문이 주로 출제된다.

1. Features of Humans (인류의 특징)

Agriculture (농업)	약 1만 년 전 신석기 시대에 인류가 채집·사냥 중심의 생활에서 벗어나 농업과 목축을 시작하며 안정적 식량 확보와 정착 생활을 이루었으며, 이를 농업 혁명(Agricultural Revolution)이라 부른다. 작물의 재배화 및 가축화(domestication)를 통해 유용한 특성을 가진 개체가 유지·증식되었고, 같은 밭에서 해마다 같은 작물을 심지 않고 작물을 바꿔 재배하는 윤작(crop rotation)은 토양의 양분 고갈을 막고 생산성을 유지하는 데 도움이 되었다. 이러한 변화는 정착 생활과 인구 증가, 사회 조직 발전의 기반이 되었다.
Cultural Adaptation (문화적 적응)	인간 집단이 생태적 제약과 사회적 기회에 맞춰 기술, 제도, 관습, 신념을 조정하는 과정이다. 이러한 적응은 음식 확보, 주거 형태, 의복, 의례, 사회 구조와 같은 다양한 생활 양식에 반영된다. 예를 들어 사막 유목민은 이동식 거처, 가축 관리, 물 저장과 운송 기술로 기후와 자원 변동에 대응하고, 열대우림의 농경민은 이동 경작, 혼작과 다층적 농원, 토양 관리로 강우와 토양 특성에 적응한다.
Domestication (재배화, 가축화)	인간이 유용한 동식물을 선택적으로 길러 생물의 성질과 형태를 변화시키는 과정으로, 정착 생활과 농업 발전, 식량 안정성 확보에 핵심적 역할을 했다. 작물의 경우 선택적 번식(selective breeding)으로 생산성과 내성을 높였고, 가축은 고기, 모피, 노동력 등 목적에 맞게 기르고 번식시켰다. 소와 말은 운반과 노동, 식량 자원으로 길러졌으며, 농경 이전부터 늑대가 가축화되어 길러지게 된 개는 사냥, 보호, 동반자 역할을 수행했다.

2. Early Civilizations (초기 문명)

Ancient Egypt (고대 이집트)	나일강(Nile) 유역에서 형성된 초기 문명이다. 나일강은 매년 여름에 범람했으며, 상류에서 운반된 영양분이 풍부한 토사가 하류 평야에 퇴적되어 농경지 토양을 비옥하게 만들었다. 이 덕분에 곡물 재배가 안정적으로 이루어져 식량 생산과 인구 증가가 가능했고, 이를 바탕으로 강력한 왕권과 조직화된 사회 구조가 형성되었다. 사회문화 외에도 의학 등의 분야 역시 발전했다, 고대 이집트 의학은 신체를 나일강과 같은 수로에 비유하여, 질병을 '막힘'으로 이해하고 이를 해소하기 위한 다양한 치료법을 개발했다. 이집트 의사들은 절개와 봉합, 골절의 정복 및 고정, 상처 세척과 꿀·포도주 등 천연 물질을 활용한 감염 억제와 통증 완화 등의 처치를 수행했다. 또한 약리학 분야에서도 오늘날 아스피린의 원료인 버드나무 껍질을 사용하여 통증을 완화하는 등 현대 의학에서 사용되는 일부 치료법의 전신을 고안했다.
Bering Land Bridge (베링 육교)	빙하기 동안 해수면이 낮아져 시베리아와 알래스카 사이에 위치한 오늘날의 베링 해협(Bering Strait)에 형성된 육지 통로이다. 대략 2만~1만 년 전, 인류는 이 육교를 통해 아시아에서 북아메리카로 이동했으며, 이 과정에서 사냥과 채집에 적응한 초기 인류 집단이 북아메리카 대륙에 정착하였다. 이러한 이동은 북미 원주민 사회의 기원과 초기 문화 형성에 중요한 역할을 했다.
Easter Island (이스터섬)	태평양 동남부에 있는 고립된 섬으로, 라파누이(Rapa Nui)라고도 불린다. 서기 1200년경 폴리네시아계 이주민들이 도착해 정착하면서 사회를 형성했으며, 특히 모아이(Moai)라 불리는 거대한 석상들을 제작·배치한 것으로 유명하다. 모아이는 부족(chiefdom) 지도자나 중요한 조상을 상징하며, 섬 전체에 걸쳐 권력과 신앙을 시각적으로 나타내는 역할을 했다. 이러한 조각과 건축 활동은 제한된 자원과 고립된 환경 속에서 복잡한 사회 조직, 노동 분업, 종교적·정치적 구조가 어떻게 발달했는지를 보여주는 중요한 증거로 평가된다. 또한, 고고학 연구를 통해 섬의 산림 파괴와 자원 고갈이 사회적 변화와 연결되었을 가능성이 제시되며, 이는 인간 활동과 환경의 상호작용을 탐구하는 인류학 연구에서도 중요한 사례로 활용된다.
Inca (잉카)	13세기부터 16세기까지 남아메리카 안데스(Andes) 지역에서 번성한 고대 제국이다. 수도 쿠스코(Cusco)를 중심으로 중앙집권적 통치 체계를 갖추었으며, 고도 지형을 활용한 계단식 농업(terrace farming)과 관개 시설로 곡물과 감자, 옥수수 등 농산물을 안정적으로 생산하였다. 16세기 초 스페인의 프란시스코 피사로(Francisco Pizarro) 등 정복자들의 침략과 질병으로 급속히 몰락하였다.
Mesopotamia (메소포타미아)	오늘날 이라크 대부분과 시리아 일부에 해당하는 지역으로, 티그리스강(Tigris)과 유프라테스강(Euphrates) 사이에서 발달한 고대 문명이다. 수메르(Sumer)는 기원전 4천 년경부터 독립적인 도시 국가들이 형성된 지역으로, 우루크(Uruk), 우르(Ur) 등 각 도시에서 신전과 왕권을 중심으로 한 정치·종교 체제가 발달했다. 수메르인들은 쐐기문자(cuneiform)를 개발했으며, 우르남무 법전과 리피트-이슈타르 법전 등 초기 법전을 통해 사회 질서를 유지했다. 농업과 관개 체계를 기반으로 도시 경제가 성장했으며, 장인과 상인의 조직, 신전 중심의 행정 구조를 통해 복잡한 사회 체계를 이루었다.
Native Americans (아메리카 원주민)	북아메리카 원주민 사회는 다양한 환경에 적응하며 여러 선사 문명을 형성하였다. 클로비스(Clovis) 문화는 약 1만 3천 년 전 중앙·남부 북미 지역에서 사냥과 채집을 중심으로 발달했으며, 날카로운 돌창과 화살촉으로 큰 동물을 사냥하는 기술이 특징이었다. 차코(Chaco) 문화는 현재의 뉴멕시코 지역에서 9~12세기경 발달한 문명으로, 거대한 석조 건축과 태양·별 관측을 활용한 정교한 천문 지식, 복잡한 도로망과 교역 체계가 특징이었다. 아나사지(Anasazi) 문화는 미국 남서부 지역에서 발달했으며, 절벽 주거(cliff dwelling), 물 관리 시스템과 건조 농업 등을 통해 건조한 환경에 적응하였다. 이들 문명은 지역적 환경과 자원에 따라 다양한 생활 방식과 사회 구조를 발전시켰으며, 후대 북미 원주민의 초기 농업, 건축, 사회 조직의 토대를 제공하였다.

Psychology (심리학)

인간의 심리 과정, 인지 오류, 그리고 인간 행동의 이론적 배경에 관한 지문이 주로 출제된다.

Bias (편향)	인간의 사고와 판단에 일관되게 나타나는 체계적인 오류를 의미한다. 이는 정보 처리 과정에서의 제한된 인지 능력으로 인해 발생하며, 종종 비합리적인 결정을 초래한다. 편향은 다양한 형태로 나타난다. 예를 들어 확증 편향(confirmation bias)은 기존의 신념을 강화하는 정보만을 선호하는 경향을 말하며, 후광 효과(halo effect)는 한 가지 긍정적인 특성이 다른 특성에 대한 평가에 영향을 미치는 현상을 의미한다. 또한 귀인 편향(attribution bias)은 타인의 행동 원인을 상황보다는 성격이나 의도에 귀속시키며 오해나 부정확한 평가를 초래할 수 있다. 편향은 때때로 빠른 판단을 요구하는 상황에서 유용할 수 있지만, 장기적으로는 비효율적이거나 부정확한 결정을 초래할 수 있다.
Child Psychology (아동심리학)	아동은 태어나면서부터 신체적, 인지적, 정서적 능력이 단계적으로 성장한다. 유아기(infancy)에는 감각과 운동 경험을 통해 세계를 인식하면서, 다른 대상이 눈에 보이지 않아도 계속 존재한다는 것을 인식하는 대상 영속성(object permanence)이 형성된다. 이어지는 초기 아동기에는 상징적 사고와 언어, 사회적 상호작용을 통한 사회성이 발달하고, 학습을 통한 기억과 주의가 향상된다. 중기 아동기에는 논리적 사고와 분류, 보존 개념 같은 구체적 조작(concrete operational) 능력이 생기고, 학교 교육을 통해 학습 전략과 자기조절이 성장한다. 청소년기에 들어서면 추상적 사고, 자아 정체성, 도덕성의 탐구가 이루어지며, 비판적 사고와 미래 계획 능력이 크게 발달한다.
Hypnosis (최면)	주의 집중과 암시(suggestion)를 통해 의식 상태를 변화시키는 현상이다. 이 상태에서는 피험자가 외부 자극이나 안내에 대해 평소보다 높은 수용성을 보이며, 감각, 기억, 행동, 통증 지각 등이 변할 수 있다. 심리학 연구에서는 최면을 인지적·정서적 조절(cognitive and emotional regulation)과 관련지어 분석하며, 의식의 선택적 집중과 자기암시(self-suggestion)의 메커니즘을 규명하려는 시도가 이루어진다. 최면을 활용하는 방법으로 통증 완화, 스트레스 관리, 행동 수정 등 다양한 응용이 연구되고 있으나, 개인의 암시 수용성(suggestibility)에 따라 효과가 달라질 수 있음이 관찰된다.
Psychology of Music (음악의 심리학)	음악은 정서와 행동에 영향을 주어 스트레스 감소, 통증 완화, 인지 기능 향상에 기여할 수 있다. 이는 도파민(dopamine) 등 신경전달물질(neurotransmitter)의 분비와 관련되어 있다. 또한 음악은 사회적 결속(social bonding)과 사회운동(social movements)에도 활용되며, 기억 회상과 생리 조절에도 도움을 준다. 음악치료(music therapy)는 임상적으로 우울증·불안 완화와 재활 치료 등에 쓰인다.
Risk Perception (위험 인식)	인간이 위험을 평가하고 판단하는 심리적 과정이다. 기억하기 쉽거나 인상적인 사건에 근거해 판단을 내리는 가용성 휴리스틱(availability heuristic) 등의 인지 편향, 나아가 미디어 보도 등에 따라 평가되는 위험은 실제 위험과 다르게 인식될 수 있다. 예를 들어 비행기는 통계적으로 자동차보다 안전하지만, 드물게 발생하는 큰 사고들 때문에 많은 사람들이 더 두려워한다. 문화적·경제적 요인 역시 영향을 미치며, 모험과 혁신을 중시하는 사회에서는 위험 감수(risk-taking)가 높고, 안전과 안정성을 중시하는 사회에서는 위험 회피(risk-avoidance)가 나타난다.
Signal Detection Theory (신호 탐지 이론)	인간이 자극을 인지할 때 실제로 의미 있는 정보(signal)와 주변의 방해되는 정보(noise)를 구별하는 과정을 설명하는 이론이다. 이 이론에 따르면, 관찰자가 신호가 실제로 존재하는지를 판단할 때, 그 결과는 자극에 대한 민감도(sensitivity)와 신호가 있다고 판단할 기준(criterion)에 따라 달라진다. 신호 탐지 이론은 올바른 탐지(hit), 잘못된 경보(false alarm), 놓침(miss), 올바른 거부(correct rejection)라는 네 가지 결과로 반응을 구분하며, 이는 지각, 의사결정, 의료 진단, 군사적 탐지와 같은 다양한 영역에서 활용된다.

■ Economics (경제학)

경제학의 핵심 이론과 경제 현상에 관한 지문이 주로 출제된다.

Agricultural Economics (농업경제학)	경제학 원리를 농업과 농촌 경제에 적용하여 자원의 효율적 배분과 정책 분석을 연구하는 학문이다. 농업 생산성(productivity), 농산물 시장(commodity market), 농촌 개발(rural development), 지속 가능한 농업(sustainable agriculture) 등 다양한 주제를 다루며, 농업 관련 정책과 경제적 의사결정에 중요한 기초를 제공한다.
Economic Miracle (경제 기적)	전쟁, 불황, 혹은 극심한 위기 이후 한 국가의 경제가 단기간에 급속히 성장하는 현상을 가리킨다. 대표적으로 제2차 세계대전 이후 패전국들의 사례가 있다. 이들은 국제 지원과 산업 정책을 바탕으로 빠른 경제 성장을 이루었다. 일본은 미국의 지원과 국내 저축을 바탕으로 수출 중심 산업화, 기술 혁신, 교육 투자 등을 추진하며 1950~70년대 고도성장을 달성했고, 세계 경제의 주요 강국으로 부상했다. 서독은 마셜 플랜(Marshall Plan)과 사회적 시장경제 체제 도입을 기반으로 '라인강의 기적'을 이루었다. 이탈리아 또한 산업화와 유럽 경제 공동체 참여를 통해 경제를 현대화하며 '이탈리아의 기적'이라 불리는 성장을 경험했다.
Multiplier Effect (승수 효과)	정부 지출이나 투자 등의 초기 지출(initial spending)이 최종적으로 전체 경제에서 그보다 더 큰 증가를 유발하는 현상을 가리킨다. 예를 들어 정부가 기반 시설 건설에 지출을 하면, 건설업체와 노동자에게 소득이 발생하고, 이들이 소비를 늘리면서 관련 산업 전반에 추가적인 수요가 생긴다. 이렇게 연쇄적으로 발생하는 소득과 소비 증가가 원래 지출보다 더 큰 경제적 파급 효과를 만들어내며, 이를 수치화한 것이 승수(multiplier)다. 승수 효과는 케인스 경제학(Keynesian economics)에서 특히 강조되며, 불황 시 재정 정책(fiscal policy)의 유효성을 설명하는 핵심 개념으로 활용된다. 다만 실제 승수 크기는 다양한 요인에 의해 제한될 수 있다.
Rational Behavior (합리적 행동)	개인이나 집단이 주어진 정보와 자원을 바탕으로 자신의 효용(utility)이나 이익을 극대화하기 위해 일관성 있게 선택하는 행위를 뜻한다. 이 가정은 고전 및 신고전파 경제학의 핵심 전제로, 수요·공급, 시장 균형, 게임 이론 등 다양한 분석의 기초가 되어 왔다. 그러나 실제 인간의 의사결정은 감정, 제한된 정보, 인지 편향(cognitive bias), 시간 제약 등에 의해 크게 영향받는다. 합리적 행동은 여전히 경제 분석의 유용한 틀이지만, 현실의 복잡성을 완전히 포착하기에는 한계가 있다는 점에서 지속적으로 보완이 이루어지고 있다. 행동경제학(behavioral economics)은 사람들이 종종 합리성에서 벗어난 선택을 한다는 점을 실험과 사례로 보여주며, 합리적 행동 가정의 보편성을 비판한다. 예를 들어, 사람들이 동일한 크기의 이익보다 손실을 더 크게 느끼고 회피하려는 경향인 손실 회피(loss aversion)처럼 사람들이 이익과 손실을 비대칭적으로 평가하거나 단기적 만족을 과도하게 중시하는 경향은 전통적 합리성 개념으로 설명하기 어렵다.

■ Sociology (사회학)

사회문화 환경에 따른 인간 상호작용의 방식과 규범에 관한 지문이 주로 출제된다.

Non-verbal Communication (비언어적 의사소통)	언어적 표현 없이 전달되는 모든 형태의 의사소통을 의미한다. 개인 간 신뢰 형성, 협상, 사회적 상호작용 등 다양한 사회적 상황에서 중요한 역할을 한다. 표정(facial expression), 몸짓(gesture), 시선(eye contact), 자세(posture), 신체적 거리, 목소리 톤 등 다양한 요소가 포함되며, 개인의 감정, 태도, 의도 등을 효과적으로 전달할 수 있다. 예를 들어 미소는 친근감과 호의, 찡그림은 불쾌감이나 반감을 나타내며, 손짓이나 고개 끄덕임은 동의 또는 강조를 표현하는 수단으로 사용된다. 또한, 비언어적 의사소통은 문화적 배경(cultural context)에 따라 의미가 달라질 수 있으며, 잘못 해석될 경우 오해나 갈등을 초래할 수도 있다.

HACKERS TEST

[01-05]

Imagined Communities

Benedict Anderson presented the concept of imagined communities in 1983 to argue that nations are artificial creations of shared belief, not pre-existing entities. He defined a nation as an imagined but sovereign political community. It is imagined because members picture a deep fellowship that binds them into a single "people" despite never meeting most fellow citizens.

According to Anderson, the spread of imagined communities relied on media and institutions. Newspapers standardized vernacular print-language and produced a shared sense of time as readers encountered the same reports each morning. Schools, railways, telegraph, and later radio and cinema similarly synchronized life. He also highlighted a state-driven triad of techniques: the census categorized populations and rendered them countable, the map fixed borders and projected territorial unity, and the museum curated artifacts into a continuous national past. Together, these practices made nations conceivable and governable.

In contemporary contexts, imagined communities continue to shape national identity through digital means. Television broadcasts, social media platforms, and online news create shared experiences and narratives across geographically dispersed populations. At the same time, digital media and the Internet also challenge the traditional notions of borders and sovereignty, gradually transforming how nations are imagined.

01 Why does Anderson describe nations as "imagined"?

Ⓐ To suggest that nations lack genuine institutional foundations
Ⓑ To emphasize that members feel unified despite not knowing each other personally
Ⓒ To argue that national identity stems from common ancestry and ethnicity
Ⓓ To show that governmental techniques merely uncover pre-existing communities

02 The word "sovereign" in the passage is closest in meaning to

Ⓐ concrete
Ⓑ powerful
Ⓒ traditional
Ⓓ independent

03 What role did newspapers play in creating imagined communities?

Ⓐ They replaced the telegraph as the main tool of information.
Ⓑ They established a uniform temporal experience for individuals.
Ⓒ They standardized spoken accents across regions.
Ⓓ They eliminated the need for regional radio reports.

04 What is suggested about digital media in relation to national identity?

Ⓐ It functions exactly like newspapers did in the nineteenth century.
Ⓑ It primarily encourages civic participation over cultural belonging.
Ⓒ It both reinforces and challenges traditional concepts of nationhood.
Ⓓ It prevents states from using census, maps, and museums effectively.

05 What is the relationship between paragraphs 2 and 3?

Ⓐ Paragraph 3 examines the limitations of the media techniques discussed in paragraph 2.
Ⓑ Paragraph 3 applies Anderson's framework from paragraph 2 to contemporary digital contexts.
Ⓒ Paragraph 3 provides background information on Anderson's theory introduced in paragraph 2.
Ⓓ Paragraph 3 suggests that the techniques in paragraph 2 are now irrelevant due to online platforms.

HACKERS TEST

[06-10]

Soft Power

Soft power refers to a country's ability to influence others through culture, values, and diplomacy rather than military or economic force. Popularized by political scientist Joseph Nye, the concept highlights how attraction can be more effective than coercion. Unlike hard power, which depends on the application of direct pressure, soft power shapes global perceptions subtly.

Culture plays a central role in soft power. Japan has extended its global presence through popular culture, cuisine, and technology, all of which captivate international audiences and enhance its image abroad. Similarly, France exerts soft power through fashion, food, and art, projecting an identity of elegance and creativity. These cultural exports boost tourism and trade while also building goodwill and shaping public opinion, allowing both nations to expand their influence.

Still, soft power has limitations. Cultural initiatives may encounter resistance if viewed as propaganda or threats to local traditions. Furthermore, sustaining soft power requires investment in education, cultural exchange, and diplomacy, which can be resource-intensive. Despite such challenges, soft power remains a vital tool for nations seeking lasting influence, as it encourages mutual respect and voluntary cooperation rather than conflict.

06 The word "coercion" in the first paragraph is closest in meaning to

Ⓐ concession
Ⓑ compulsion
Ⓒ negotiation
Ⓓ persuasion

07 What can be inferred about the effect of soft power?

Ⓐ It guarantees that all nations will adopt a country's cultural values.
Ⓑ It makes conventional diplomacy and negotiation unnecessary.
Ⓒ It redefines global viewpoints of a country in an indirect way.
Ⓓ It allows nations to shape public opinion in other countries through propaganda.

08 Why does the author mention Japan and France?

Ⓐ To demonstrate that cultural exports can serve as tools of influence
Ⓑ To illustrate how certain nations dominate global cultural markets
Ⓒ To argue that only technologically advanced nations develop soft power
Ⓓ To show that cultural attraction is more important than economic force

09 What can be concluded about paragraph 3?

Ⓐ It expands on the diplomatic strategies briefly mentioned earlier.
Ⓑ It highlights the challenges and limitations associated with soft power.
Ⓒ It elaborates on the cultural exports described earlier in the passage.
Ⓓ It introduces a new perspective that upholds the value of soft power.

10 Why might sustaining soft power be difficult for some countries?

Ⓐ It clashes with numerous local customs.
Ⓑ It requires a significant level of investment.
Ⓒ It depends too heavily on short-term trends.
Ⓓ It can only succeed when backed by military power.

HACKERS TEST

[11-15]

Jevons Paradox

The Jevons paradox is a counterintuitive phenomenon in economics, where improvements in technological efficiency can actually increase overall resource consumption instead of reducing it. Named after English economist William Stanley Jevons, the paradox was first observed with coal usage in nineteenth-century England. As steam engines became more efficient, coal demand rose because the reduced cost of operating steam engines encouraged greater use.

This paradox impacts modern resource management and environmental policy. **A** For example, greater fuel efficiency in cars may cause people to drive more, leading to higher total fuel consumption. **B** In agriculture, more efficient irrigation systems can result in greater crop production, ultimately increasing water use. **C** These responses illustrate that efficiency alone may not guarantee conservation. **D** Instead, it can change our behavior in ways that offset initial savings.

Addressing the Jevons paradox requires more than improving technology. Effective policies must pair efficiency gains with regulations or incentives that guide consumption. Without these measures, technological progress may accelerate resource depletion rather than slow it. Successful environmental policy requires recognizing that technological progress alone cannot ensure resource sustainability.

11 The word "offset" in the passage is closest in meaning to

Ⓐ heighten
Ⓑ substitute
Ⓒ counteract
Ⓓ control

12 Why does the author mention steam engines?

Ⓐ To provide an example that contrasts with more recent cases of fuel and water consumption
Ⓑ To suggest that industrialization helped solve the problem of limited resources
Ⓒ To introduce the origin of the idea that efficiency can sometimes increase resource use
Ⓓ To demonstrate that technologies of the past were more environmentally sustainable

13 There are four locations [■] in the passage that indicate where the following sentence could be added.

This effect is not limited to energy resources.

Where would the sentence best fit? Select a location [■] where the sentence could be added to the passage.

14 What is the relationship between paragraphs 2 and 3?

Ⓐ Paragraph 3 reinforces the examples given in paragraph 2 by providing additional cases of efficiency backfiring.
Ⓑ Paragraph 3 describes the characteristics of effective policies to respond to the problem described in paragraph 2.
Ⓒ Paragraph 3 disputes the claims in paragraph 2 by asserting that technological efficiency reduces resource consumption.
Ⓓ Paragraph 3 dismisses the concerns raised in paragraph 2 by highlighting technological progress as the solution.

15 What does the passage suggest about the role of technological progress in addressing the Jevons paradox?

Ⓐ It usually reduces overall consumption without government involvement.
Ⓑ It is sufficient on its own to prevent resource depletion.
Ⓒ It must be combined with measures to achieve resource sustainability.
Ⓓ It should be replaced with strict regulatory approaches to be effective.

HACKERS TEST

[16-20]

Megalithic Monuments

In many regions of the world, colossal stones were raised and positioned thousands of years ago by early societies, leaving behind monuments that stand as evidence of their engineering capabilities and collaboration efforts. These giant structures, known as megalithic monuments, vary in size, shape, and form. For example, some feature circular arrangements like Stonehenge, while others are rectangular like the temples of Malta.

Researchers have proposed many purposes for megalithic monuments. Some theories suggest they were used for burial rituals. Others believe these monuments played a role in religious ceremonies. There is also a theory based on their location and position that certain monuments were carefully aligned with solar or lunar cycles. They may have served as early astronomical observatories for tracking seasonal changes and celestial events.

To compensate for the lack of modern machinery and tools, building these monuments required advanced knowledge of geology, physics, and mathematics. Studies of the Dolmen de Menga in Spain reveal the sophisticated engineering techniques used to design sledges and counterweight systems to transport stones weighing up to 150 tons from a quarry 850 meters away. These massive stones were then positioned with such precision that the structure has remained standing for nearly six thousand years.

16 The word "celestial" in the passage is closest in meaning to

Ⓐ ancient
Ⓑ stellar
Ⓒ cultural
Ⓓ visible

17 What can be inferred about the societies that built megalithic monuments?

Ⓐ They operated formal administrative systems to allocate labor and resources.
Ⓑ They had established systems for large-scale cooperation.
Ⓒ They were inspired to create monuments for similar purposes.
Ⓓ They established trade alliances to secure stones from distant regions.

18 Why does the author mention Stonehenge and the temples of Malta?

Ⓐ To illustrate the structural diversity of megalithic monuments
Ⓑ To provide examples demonstrating sophisticated engineering techniques
Ⓒ To claim that ritual purposes outweighed engineering needs at many monuments
Ⓓ To propose that the differences in shape imply different purposes

19 Which of the following is NOT mentioned in the passage as a possible purpose of megalithic monuments?

Ⓐ Sites for burial rituals
Ⓑ Places for astronomical observation
Ⓒ Symbols of land ownership
Ⓓ Locations for religious ceremonies

20 What does the passage indicate about the Dolmen de Menga?

Ⓐ It was built near its quarry to facilitate the transport of stones.
Ⓑ It was carefully positioned in alignment with celestial cycles.
Ⓒ Its study is based on the remaining ruins since the structure is not intact.
Ⓓ Its construction involved advanced tools for hauling and balancing massive stones.

Answers p.489

4. Physical Science

TASK 3의 물리과학 지문에서는 주로 천문학, 화학, 물리학, 기상학, 지질학, 공학과 같은 세부 분야가 출제된다. 별의 진화, 원소의 반응과 물질의 성질, 에너지·힘·운동의 원리, 대기 순환과 기후 변화, 지구의 구성 요소와 지질학적 현상, 기술 발전과 구조 설계 등에 대한 탐구가 주요 주제이다.

■ Astronomy (천문학)

태양계, 행성, 천체에 관한 지문이 주로 출제된다.

Solar System (태양계)	태양을 중심으로 공전하는 8개의 행성과 다양한 작은 천체로 구성된 체계이다. 이 행성들은 크게 태양에 가까운 지구형 행성(terrestrial planets)과 태양에서 먼 거리에 있는 거대 행성으로 나뉜다. 지구형 행성(수성, 금성, 지구, 화성)은 주로 암석과 금속으로 이루어진 단단한 표면을 가지며, 크기는 작지만 밀도가 매우 높다. 거대 행성은 다시 거대 가스 행성(gas giant)과 거대 얼음 행성(ice giant)으로 나뉜다. 목성과 토성은 수소와 헬륨이 주성분인 거대 가스 행성으로 두꺼운 대기를 지닌다. 천왕성과 해왕성은 물, 메탄, 암모니아 등의 얼음 성분이 많아 거대 얼음 행성으로 분류된다.
Moon (달)	지구 주위를 도는 유일한 자연 위성이다. 달의 생성에 대한 가장 유력한 이론은 대충돌설(giant impact hypothesis)인데, 이는 약 45억 년 전 화성 크기의 천체가 원시 지구와 충돌했고, 그 충돌로 튕겨 나온 물질들이 모여 달이 형성되었다는 설명이다. 달 내부에서는 지구의 지진과 유사한 현상인 월진(moonquake)이 발생한다. 이 월진은 달의 지각이 미세하게 움직이거나 지구의 중력(조석력)에 의해 일어나는데, 이는 달의 내부 구조를 연구하는 데 중요한 단서가 된다.
Mars (화성)	태양계의 네 번째 행성이다. 과거에는 화성 표면에 액체 상태의 물이 존재했던 것으로 보이며, 현재도 지하에 액체 물이 있을 가능성이 과학자들에 의해 제기되고 있다. NASA 탐사선 퍼서비어런스(Perseverance)는 화성에서 생명체 존재 가능성을 시사하는 유기물과 퇴적층 구조를 관측했다. 또한, 일부 연구에서는 화성 지하 깊은 곳에 거대한 '지하 바다'가 있을 수 있다는 가능성도 발표되었다.
Jupiter (목성)	주로 수소와 헬륨으로 이루어진 거대 가스 행성으로, 내부에는 암석과 얼음으로 구성된 무거운 핵이 존재한다. 강력한 자기장과 대규모 소용돌이인 대적반(Great Red Spot)이 특징이다. 목성의 주요 위성 중 이오(Io)는 태양계에서 가장 활발한 화산 활동을 보인다. 또한 유로파(Europa)는 얼음으로 덮인 표면 아래에 액체 상태의 바다가 존재할 가능성이 높아 생명체 거주 가능성 연구의 중심지이며, 가니메데(Ganymede)와 칼리스토(Callisto)도 유사한 환경을 갖고 있다.
Supernova (초신성)	초신성은 거대한 별이 수명을 다하는 순간에 폭발하면서 막대한 에너지와 빛을 방출하는 현상이다. 이 폭발은 태양이 평생 방출하는 에너지보다 훨씬 큰 규모로 발생하며, 그 결과로 별의 외피가 우주 공간으로 흩어진다. 초신성은 새로운 원소를 생성하고 이를 우주로 퍼뜨려, 행성과 생명체의 구성 성분이 형성되는 데 중요한 역할을 한다. 또한 초신성의 폭발은 중성자별이나 블랙홀의 탄생으로 이어질 수 있어, 우주의 진화 과정에서 핵심적인 사건으로 여겨진다.

■ Chemistry (화학)

물질의 순환, 화학적 특성, 그리고 응용에 관한 지문이 주로 출제된다.

Nitrogen (질소)	식물 생장에 필수적인 영양소로 농업 생산에 중요한 역할을 한다. 자연에서는 대기 중 질소가 질소 고정(nitrogen fixation) 세균에 의해 암모니아로 전환된 후, 토양 미생물의 질산화(nitrification) 작용을 거쳐 식물이 이용 가능한 형태로 순환한다. 토양 내 질소는 미생물의 무기화·고착, 식물 흡수, 침출·탈질 등 여러 과정으로 이동·손실되며, 이를 충당하기 위해 질소 비료(nitrogen fertilizer)가 사용된다. 질소 비료는 크게 동물의 배설물이나 식물 잔재를 이용한 유기질 비료와, 공기 중의 질소를 화학적으로 합성해 만든 합성 질소 비료로 나뉜다. 합성 질소 비료의 투입은 작물의 생산성을 크게 높이지만, 비료 성분이 유출되어 수질 오염과 생태계 교란을 유발할 수도 있다.
Methane Hydrate (메테인 하이드레이트)	물 분자들이 얼음과 유사한 형태의 단단한 격자 구조를 형성하고, 그 안에 천연가스의 주성분인 메테인 분자가 갇혀 있는 형태의 물질이다. 겉으로는 얼음처럼 보이지만, 불을 붙이면 내부의 메테인 가스가 타오르며 불꽃을 만들어낸다. 이 모습이 마치 얼음이 타는 것처럼 보여서 흔히 '불타는 얼음'이라고 불린다. 메테인 하이드레이트는 낮은 온도와 높은 압력 조건에서만 안정성 있게 존재한다. 이러한 조건은 주로 수심이 깊은 바닷속 퇴적층이나 영구 동토층 아래에서 관찰된다. 이 물질이 중요하게 여겨지는 이유는 막대한 양의 메테인 가스를 포함하고 있기 때문이다. 전 세계적으로 매장된 메테인 하이드레이트의 양은 기존의 모든 화석 연료를 합친 것보다 더 많을 것으로 추정된다. 그러나 메테인은 이산화 탄소보다 강력한 온실가스이므로, 개발 과정에서 가스가 대기 중으로 방출되지 않도록 하는 친환경적인 기술 개발이 필수적이다.

■ Physics (물리학)

물리학의 기초가 되는 법칙, 그리고 실생활에서의 적용에 관한 지문이 주로 출제된다.

Electromagnetic Spectrum (전자기 스펙트럼)	전자기파가 파장(wavelength)과 진동수(frequency)에 따라 순서대로 배열된 것이다. 이 스펙트럼 중에서 가시광선(visible light)은 인간의 눈에 보이는 유일한 영역이다. 가시광선보다 파장이 긴 적외선(infrared)은 주로 물체의 온도 측정이나 열 감지 장비에 활용된다. 적외선보다 파장이 더 긴 마이크로파(microwave)는 무선 통신, 레이더, 전자레인지 등에 쓰인다. 마이크로파보다 더 파장이 긴 전자기파는 라디오파(radio waves)로 방송 통신과 무선 네트워크 등에 활용된다. 반대로 가시광선보다 파장이 짧은 자외선(ultraviolet)은 높은 에너지를 가져 살균, 소독, 화학 반응 촉진 등에 사용된다. 자외선보다 훨씬 더 짧은 파장을 가진 X선(X-ray)은 의료용 영상 촬영(엑스레이 촬영)과 물질 구조 분석에 활용되며, 가장 파장이 짧은 감마선(gamma ray)은 방사선 치료, 핵반응 연구, 살균 처리 등에 쓰인다.
Energy (에너지)	물리학적으로 일을 할 수 있는 능력을 가리킨다. 에너지는 다양한 형태로 존재하는데, 물체가 높은 곳에 있을 때와 같이 위치나 상태에 따라 저장될 수 있는 위치 에너지(potential energy)와 물체의 운동에 따라 나타나는 운동 에너지(kinetic energy) 등이 그 예이다. 에너지는 그 외에도 열·전기·화학 등 서로 다른 형태로 전환·전달되며, 연료에 저장된 전기 에너지나 화학 에너지와 같은 형태로 다양한 일을 가능하게 한다.

Meteorology (기상학)

기후의 변화 과정에 관한 지문이 주로 출제된다.

Jet Stream (제트 기류)	지구 상층 대기에서 발생하는 좁고 빠른 바람 띠로, 속도는 시속 100~400킬로미터에 달한다. 온도 차가 큰 지역, 특히 열대와 극지방 사이에서 더욱 뚜렷하게 나타난다. 제트 기류는 지상의 저기압과 고기압, 특히 사이클론(cyclone)의 경로와 발달에 영향을 주어 전 세계 기상 패턴과 날씨 변동을 결정하는 중요한 역할을 한다. 특히 북반구에서 제트 기류가 남쪽으로 파동을 그리며 요동칠 때, 북극 등 고위도에서 형성된 찬 공기가 남쪽으로 내려오고 제트 기류 상층에서의 발산(divergence)으로 인해 저기압 발달이 촉진되어 폭풍과 강수량 증가를 유발한다. 계절과 위도에 따라 위치와 세기가 변하며, 특히 겨울에는 극지와 적도 사이의 온도 차이가 커 속도가 증가한다. 최근에는 기후 변화로 북극이 더워지는 '북극 증폭(Arctic amplification)' 현상이 발생하면서 극지와 열대 기단 간 온도 차이가 줄어들고 있다. 이에 따라 제트 기류가 약화되고 있으며, 기상 현상의 이동이 느려져 폭염이나 집중호우 같은 극단적 기상 현상이 장기간 지속되는 현상이 증가하고 있다.

Geology (지질학)

지구의 구성 요소와 지질학적 작용에 관한 지문이 주로 출제된다.

Continental Drift (대륙이동설)	기상학자이자 지구물리학자인 알프레트 베게너(Alfred Wegener)는 과거 지구상의 모든 대륙이 판게아(Pangaea)라는 하나의 거대한 대륙이었으며, 이것이 분리되어 현재의 대륙들이 형성되고 이동해 왔다는 대륙 이동설의 개념을 제시했다. 대륙이 실제로 움직이는 원리에 대해서는 판구조론(plate tectonics)이 설명한다. 판구조론은 대륙 이동을 포함한 지각 운동의 원동력을 해양저 확장, 맨틀 대류(mantle convection), 판의 섭입에 따른 끌어당기는 힘(slab pull), 해저산맥에서의 압력(ridge push) 등으로 설명한다.
Glacier (빙하)	수천 년간 눈이 계속 쌓이고 그 압력으로 인해 압축되면서 형성된 거대한 얼음덩어리이다. 일단 형성된 빙하는 중력의 영향을 받아 매우 느린 속도로 산 아래나 해안 방향으로 움직인다. 빙하가 움직이는 이 과정에서 바닥의 암석을 깎아내고 운반하는 침식(erosion) 작용을 일으킨다. 빙하 내부에는 순수한 얼음 외에도 포집된 눈, 공기, 먼지 등이 포함되어 있으며, 밀도는 표면의 눈 상태에서 깊은 곳의 단단한 얼음으로 갈수록 점점 증가한다. 빙하가 바다에 이르면 끝부분이 분리되어 떨어져 나가는 빙하 붕괴(calving) 과정이 일어나며, 이렇게 떨어져 나온 얼음덩어리를 빙산(iceberg)이라 한다.
Groundwater (지하수)	비나 눈이 내린 후 지표면 아래의 토양이나 암석의 작은 틈과 공간에 스며들어 저장된 물이다. 이러한 지하수는 주로 대수층(aquifer)이라 불리는 지층에 저장되는데, 대수층은 공극률이 커서 물을 저장할 수 있고, 투수성이 높아 물이 이동할 수 있는 암석층이나 퇴적층이다. 지하수는 지표수보다 상대적으로 안정적인 수자원이지만, 너무 많은 양을 끌어다 쓰거나 외부 오염 물질이 유입되면 수위가 낮아지고 수질이 나빠질 수 있다.
Soil (토양)	땅 위의 암석이 물리적 및 화학적 풍화 과정을 거쳐 잘게 부서지고 분해되어 형성된 물질이다. 토양은 깊이에 따라 여러 수평층으로 구성된 토양 단면(soil profile)을 보이는데, 특히 표층에는 식물의 잔해가 분해되어 만들어진 부식물(humus)이 풍부하게 포함되어 있어 생물 서식에 매우 적합하다. 중력과 물의 작용으로 토양 입자가 깎여나가거나 이동하는 토양 침식은 자연적 과정으로서 토양의 형태와 분포를 변화시키는데, 침식이 과도하게 발생할 경우 표토 유실과 비옥도 저하를 초래해 토양의 건강과 생태계 유지에 부정적인 영향을 미친다.

Volcano (화산)	지구 내부의 뜨거운 물질인 마그마, 가스, 화산재 등이 지각의 틈을 통해 지표면으로 분출되는 현상, 또는 그로 인해 형성된 산과 같은 지형을 말한다. 마그마는 지하 깊은 곳에서 생성된 녹은 암석으로 규산염 함량에 따라 현무암질 마그마(basaltic magma), 안산암질 마그마(andesitic magma), 유문암질 마그마(rhyolitic magma)의 세 가지 유형으로 나뉘는데, 규산염 함량이 높을수록 점성이 커지고 유동성은 낮다. 마그마의 성질에 따라 화산 활동의 분출 양상과 최종적인 화산의 형태가 다양하게 나타난다. 마그마가 지표로 분출되어 땅 위로 나온 것을 용암(lava)이라 부르며, 이 용암은 냉각되면서 화산암(volcanic rock)으로 굳어진다.

■ Engineering (공학)

근대 기술의 발전 및 사회와 생활 구조에 대한 영향에 관한 지문이 주로 출제된다.

Clock (시계)	기계식 시계는 초기에는 수도원과 교회에서 종교 의식 시간을 알리는 용도로 사용되었으며, 14세기 이후에는 도시 광장과 시계탑에 설치되어 시민들의 일상 생활에도 영향을 미쳤다. 15~16세기에는 장인의 손으로 제작된 휴대용 시계와 개인용 시계가 등장하며 점차 상류층과 상업 계층으로 확산되었고, 17세기 이후 기술 발전으로 시계의 성능과 보급이 확대되었다. 본격적인 대량 생산과 중산층까지의 광범위한 보급은 19세기에 이루어졌다. 기계식 시계의 대중화는 시간 관리와 규칙적인 생활을 강조하는 사회적 변화를 촉발하였으며, 산업화와 근대 경제 체제에서 시간 개념을 체계화하는 데 중요한 역할을 했다. 또한, 정확한 시간 측정은 항해와 과학 연구에도 기여하며, 근대적 사회 질서와 생산성 향상에 영향을 미쳤다.
Lighting (조명)	전구(light bulb)의 발명은 19세기 후반 토머스 에디슨(Thomas Edison)과 다른 발명가들에 의해 이루어졌으며, 인공조명의 대중화를 가능하게 해 산업, 가정, 도시 환경 등 다양한 분야에서 생활과 문화에 큰 변화를 불러왔다. 미술관과 박물관에서는 조명의 강도와 유형이 작품의 보존과 감상에 직접적인 영향을 미친다. 종이, 안료, 섬유, 캔버스 등 유기 재료는 강한 빛에 장기간 노출되면 변색이나 손상이 발생할 수 있으므로, 미술관에서는 색감을 살리면서도 손상을 최소화하는 조도·스펙트럼 설계가 필요하다. 반면 박물관에서는 조명의 밝기를 조금 더 낮추거나 확산시키는 방식으로 고고학적 유물과 역사적 자료를 보호하며, 방문객이 세부 사항을 관찰할 수 있도록 조정한다.
Railroad (철도)	19세기 산업혁명 시대의 핵심 운송 수단으로, 원료와 상품, 사람을 대량으로 신속하게 이동시키며 산업 발전을 촉진했다. 영국에서 증기기관차(steam locomotive)의 상용화로 시작된 철도는 곧 미국과 독일 등지로 확산되었다. 미국에서는 19세기 중반 대륙횡단철도(Transcontinental Railroad)의 완공으로 서부 개척과 농산물·자원 수송이 가능해졌으며, 이는 산업화와 도시화, 노동력 이동을 가속했다. 독일에서는 철도망 구축이 공업 지역과 항구를 연결하며 중공업과 제철 산업의 성장을 뒷받침했고, 연방 국가 통합에도 기여했다. 철도는 경제적 기능뿐 아니라 사회문화적 영향력도 컸다. 도시와 농촌 간 교류가 활발해지고 관광과 여가 활동이 증가했으며, 시간표와 표준시간제 도입은 일상과 사회 질서에 변화를 불러왔다. 또한 철도는 군사적·전략적 중요성을 지니며 국가 발전과 정치적 역학에도 영향을 미쳤다.
Urban Engineering (도시공학)	도시의 공간, 기능, 미관을 체계적으로 설계하고 관리하는 분야이다. 근대 도시 개발은 19세기 산업화와 인구 급증을 배경으로 본격화되었으며, 특히 공중보건, 교통, 주거 환경 개선을 목표로 한 도시 개혁(reform)이 중심적 역할을 했다. 조르주외젠 오스만(Georges-Eugène Haussmann)의 프랑스 파리 재개발이 대표적 사례로, 좁은 골목과 비위생적 주거지를 철거하고 넓은 대로와 공원을 조성하여 도시 위생과 교통 효율을 높였다. 미국 뉴욕에서는 프레데릭 로 옴스테드(Frederick Law Olmsted)와 캘버트 보(Calvert Vaux)의 설계로 센트럴 파크(Central Park)가 조성되어 도시민에게 녹지 공간을 제공하고 사회적·문화적 활동을 촉진하였다.

HACKERS TEST

[01-05]

The History of Seismology

It was not until the nineteenth century that systematic efforts to scientifically understand and predict earthquakes were made. Researchers began documenting seismic activity and patterns in affected regions. Measurements of ground motion were taken using rudimentary instruments like pendulums.

By the late 1800s, seismology began to emerge as a formal scientific discipline. Early pioneers, such as John Milne, conducted studies of tremors and their propagation. Milne, often credited as a founder of modern seismology, helped develop the horizontal pendulum seismograph in the 1880s, which allowed for the continuous recording of ground movement. This enabled scientists to monitor earthquakes with increased accuracy. The continuous recording of seismic activity facilitated the identification of trends, laying the foundation for the development of predictive models in later decades.

Advancements in the twentieth and twenty-first centuries revolutionized the field. Scientists incorporated data from dense seismic networks, satellites, and sophisticated computer models to analyze fault stress and ground deformation. Recent technologies, such as real-time data sharing systems and AI-based algorithms, further enhance seismologists' capabilities. These tools make it possible to assess regional risks and issue timely warnings to residents. Nevertheless, making a precise prediction of the exact timing and location of an earthquake remains impossible.

01 What can be inferred about earthquake studies before the nineteenth century?

Ⓐ They focused on comparing earthquake effects across different regions.
Ⓑ They served as the foundation for the modern field of seismology.
Ⓒ They enabled people to predict earthquakes accurately.
Ⓓ They were not based on a formal scientific discipline.

02 The word "systematic" in the first paragraph is closest in meaning to

Ⓐ controversial
Ⓑ organized
Ⓒ academic
Ⓓ temporary

03 Which of the following is NOT mentioned in the passage as an advancement in early seismology?

Ⓐ The continuous recording of seismic activity
Ⓑ The identification of earthquake trends
Ⓒ The mapping of fault zones after earthquakes
Ⓓ The systematic study of tremor propagation

04 What is the relationship between paragraphs 2 and 3?

Ⓐ Paragraph 3 provides examples of the techniques mentioned in paragraph 2.
Ⓑ Paragraph 3 describes more advanced developments in the field introduced in paragraph 2.
Ⓒ Paragraph 3 challenges the effectiveness of the methods described in paragraph 2.
Ⓓ Paragraph 3 explains the limitations of the seismological advances discussed in paragraph 2.

05 What can be inferred about the horizontal pendulum seismograph?

Ⓐ It was employed by seismologists before the nineteenth century.
Ⓑ It was invented during a period of frequent earthquakes.
Ⓒ It was influenced by previous earthquake recording techniques.
Ⓓ It was primarily developed for use in laboratory settings.

HACKERS TEST

[06-10]

Oceanic Garbage Patches

Oceanic garbage patches are vast areas in the world's oceans where large amounts of floating debris accumulate due to ocean currents. These patches mainly consist of discarded fishing equipment, but also include bottles, bags, and other small plastic items. The most immense is the Great Pacific Garbage Patch, which is located between Hawaii and California.

These contaminated zones disrupt marine habitats and harm many organisms. Plastic waste in these zones is ingested by fish and marine mammals. This can cause injuries, starvation, and toxic chemical buildup. Some scientists note that garbage patches may also spread invasive species, as floating objects carry organisms across oceans.

Addressing this issue must begin with reducing plastic production, which drives the growth of garbage patches. Governments should implement policies that limit the use of single-use plastics. For cleanup and prevention, technologies like floating barriers can help collect existing debris, while improved recycling systems can prevent plastic from ever reaching the oceans. Ultimately, solving a problem of this global scale requires international cooperation and the collective action of all people.

06 The word "accumulate" in the passage is closest in meaning to

Ⓐ flow
Ⓑ transport
Ⓒ gather
Ⓓ divide

07 What is one way plastic waste can affect marine animals?

Ⓐ It impedes their ability to consume nutrients essential for survival.
Ⓑ It forces them to migrate to contaminated areas for new food sources.
Ⓒ It reduces their ability to detect predators due to visual obstruction.
Ⓓ It increases their vulnerability to diseases due to constant stress.

08 All of the following are true about oceanic garbage patches EXCEPT:

Ⓐ They are primarily comprised of commercial fishing gear.
Ⓑ They contain toxins that can accumulate within marine life.
Ⓒ They obstruct the natural circulation patterns of seawater.
Ⓓ They are expanding in size due to unstrained plastic production.

09 What can be inferred about invasive species?

Ⓐ They are the main victims of marine plastic waste.
Ⓑ They may use the garbage patches to spread to various regions.
Ⓒ Their diet consists of food sources from the ocean.
Ⓓ Their activity is most prominent in the waters near Hawaii.

10 What is the relationship between paragraphs 2 and 3?

Ⓐ Paragraph 3 discusses the sources of oceanic plastics compared to the risks in paragraph 2.
Ⓑ Paragraph 3 provides examples of the environmental impacts mentioned in paragraph 2.
Ⓒ Paragraph 3 explains possible solutions to the problems highlighted in paragraph 2.
Ⓓ Paragraph 3 outlines climate predictions that relate to the issues in paragraph 2.

HACKERS TEST

[11-15]

Arctic Tundra

The Arctic tundra is a vast treeless landscape located near the polar circle in North America and Eurasia. This area has persistently frigid temperatures, intense winds, and a surface layer of permafrost—a layer of soil that remains frozen throughout the year. This frozen ground makes it difficult for most plants to grow, resulting in simple vegetation like mosses, lichens, and small shrubs accounting for most plant life.

Despite its harsh conditions, the tundra ecosystem supports a wide variety of animal life. These creatures have a number of physical and behavioral adaptations that enable them to survive. Musk oxen, for example, have dense fur and a thick layer of fat to insulate their bodies against the cold. Other animals, such as caribou and geese, migrate south each fall to spend the winter in areas with milder climates.

The tundra ecosystem is facing significant environmental challenges. Human activity, including resource extraction and the burning of fossil fuels, directly threatens the region's fragile biological equilibrium. Furthermore, climate change is causing the permafrost to thaw. This thawing not only alters habitats for plants and animals but also jeopardizes global human health by releasing greenhouse gases and possibly reviving ancient pathogens.

11 The word "equilibrium" in the passage is closest in meaning to

   Ⓐ symmetry
   Ⓑ balance
   Ⓒ conflict
   Ⓓ equality

12 What is one adaptation of a tundra animal mentioned in the passage?

   Ⓐ Shedding fur annually
   Ⓑ Storing large amounts of fat
   Ⓒ Migrating to coastal areas
   Ⓓ Limiting movement during winter

13 All of the following are mentioned as environmental threats to the tundra EXCEPT

   Ⓐ Climate change
   Ⓑ Resource extraction
   Ⓒ Coastal erosion
   Ⓓ Energy generation

14 Why does the author mention ancient pathogens?

   Ⓐ To illustrate one of the potential global risks associated with climate change
   Ⓑ To explain how pathogens adapted to the frigid climate of the tundra
   Ⓒ To suggest that climate change is the primary cause of disease outbreaks
   Ⓓ To emphasize that pathogens were a major threat to ancient humans

15 What is the relationship between paragraphs 2 and 3?

   Ⓐ Paragraph 3 elaborates on the types of vegetation discussed in paragraph 2.
   Ⓑ Paragraph 3 challenges the adaptation strategies explained in paragraph 2.
   Ⓒ Paragraph 3 gives examples of the migratory patterns mentioned in paragraph 2.
   Ⓓ Paragraph 3 presents the dangers faced by the ecosystem described in paragraph 2.

HACKERS TEST

[16-20]

Tunguska Event

On June 30, 1908, a cataclysmic explosion that flattened trees over an area of approximately 2,000 square kilometers occurred near the Tunguska River in eastern Russia. Eyewitnesses saw the fireball from a distance of up to 800 kilometers, and seismic waves were detected as far away as Europe. The exact cause of the Tunguska Event is still unknown.

While scientists initially assumed an asteroid must have collided with Earth, this theory had one major flaw—no crater was ever discovered. The discrepancy led to many competing hypotheses, with a Russian geologist named Vladimir Epifanov suggesting that the explosion was caused by a gas such as methane, which ignited when it leaked into the air from an underground source.

The most likely explanation, however, is that the Tunguska Event involved an asteroid or a comet that exploded before it struck our planet. According to this theory, friction from contact with air molecules as the object passed through the atmosphere generated intense heat. When it was just several kilometers above the ground, the buildup of thermal energy triggered the detonation, sending out a massive shockwave that completely devastated the surrounding countryside.

16 The word "cataclysmic" in the first paragraph is closest in meaning to

Ⓐ notable
Ⓑ sudden
Ⓒ violent
Ⓓ diverse

17 Why does the author mention Europe?

Ⓐ To emphasize the remoteness of a region
Ⓑ To identify the discoverer of a phenomenon
Ⓒ To explain the immense size of a fireball
Ⓓ To show the significance of an occurrence

18 Why was the explanation involving an asteroid collision questioned?

Ⓐ A statement by a local witness was false.
Ⓑ A piece of physical evidence was absent.
Ⓒ A scientific experiment was inconclusive.
Ⓓ A different theory was persuasive.

19 To what did Vladimir Epifanov attribute the Tunguska Event?

Ⓐ The acceleration of a geological process
Ⓑ The development of an atmospheric anomaly
Ⓒ The collapse of an underground structure
Ⓓ The emission of a flammable substance

20 According to the third paragraph, what was a factor that contributed to the explosion?

Ⓐ An external energy source
Ⓑ A speed reduction
Ⓒ A temperature change
Ⓓ A chemical reaction

Answers p.492

5. Life Science

TASK 3의 생명과학 지문으로는 주로 생물학, 인지 과학, 생태학, 고생물학, 생리학, 환경과학 관련 주제가 출제되는데, 특히 생명체의 구조와 기능, 생명체와 환경 간의 상호작용, 현대 과학 연구 성과와 같은 내용을 다룬다.

■ Biology (생물학)

동물학, 미생물학에 관한 지문이 주로 출제된다.

1. Zoology (동물학)

Bird (새)	깃털, 날개, 부리를 특징으로 하는 척추동물로서, 알을 낳아 번식하며(oviparous) 대다수 종이 비행 능력을 지닌다. 조류는 혼자 살기도 하고, 짝을 이루어 새끼를 기르기도 하며, 무리를 이루기도 하는 등 매우 다양한 사회 구조를 보인다. 일부 종은 넓은 영역을 확보하여 타 개체의 접근을 차단하는데, 특히 번식 기간에는 영역성(territoriality)이 현저하게 증가하며, 수컷은 특정 행동을 통해 자신의 영역을 확립하고 경쟁 개체를 배척한다. 조류의 울음소리(vocalization)는 종별로 고유한 패턴을 나타내며, 무리 내 의사소통, 경계 신호, 먹이 위치 정보 공유 등 다양한 기능을 수행한다. 때때로 동일한 종 내에서도 지역적 차이를 나타내는데, 이는 개체의 학습 및 사회적 상호작용의 결과로 해석된다.
Bioluminescence (생물 발광)	해파리, 심해어, 반딧불이와 같은 생물체가 스스로 빛을 내는 현상이다. 이 빛은 이들 생물의 몸속에 있는 루시페린(luciferin)이라는 발광 물질과 반응을 돕는 효소인 루시페라아제(luciferase)의 작용으로 만들어진다. 루시페라아제가 루시페린과 산소의 결합 반응을 촉진하면 에너지가 나오는데, 이 에너지가 밝은 빛의 형태로 나오는 것이다. 생물 발광은 주로 짝짓기 신호, 포식자로부터 자신을 지키는 경고나 위장, 먹이 유인 등 생존에 필수적인 다양한 목적으로 활용된다. 생물 발광의 원리는 생명공학이나 의학 분야에서 폭넓게 응용되고 있다.
Frog (개구리)	개구리는 무미목(anura)에 속하는 양서류(amphibian)로서, 전 세계적으로 7,700여 종이 분포하는 것으로 알려져 있다. 대다수 종은 수생 환경에서 번식 주기를 시작한다. 개구리의 발성은 짝을 유인하거나 영역을 표시하는 핵심적 행동이다. 후두의 성대(또는 성막)를 통과하는 공기의 진동으로 생성되며, 울음주머니가 공명을 통해 소리를 증폭하고 전달 범위를 넓히는 역할을 한다. 한편, 울음주머니가 없는 종은 발성을 증폭시키지 못하여 비교적 미약한 소리를 낸다. 울음소리는 개구리의 종 구별에도 중요한 역할을 한다. 예를 들어, 미국봄청개구리(spring peeper)는 높은 음역의 휘파람 소리를 내는 것으로 유명하며, 봄철에 가장 먼저 발성을 시작하는 종 중 하나로 분류된다.

Galapagos Islands (갈라파고스 제도)	에콰도르 서부 해안에서 서쪽으로 약 1,000킬로미터 떨어진 태평양에 있는 화산 군도로, 독특한 생물 군집으로 유명하다. 이 제도의 종들은 각 섬의 환경에 적응하여 다양한 생태적 지위를 차지한다. 갈라파고스땅거북(Galapagos tortoise)은 최대 400킬로그램까지 자라며, 낮은 대사율과 체내 에너지·수분의 효율적 이용, 우기에 충분한 물과 먹이를 섭취하는 전략으로 건기를 견딘다. 바다이구아나(Marine iguana)는 도마뱀 중 유일하게 바다에서 먹이를 찾으며 해조류를 섭취한다. 갈라파고스핀치(Galapagos finches)는 섬마다 부리 모양과 크기가 달라 먹이 종류에 맞춰 진화했는데, 씨앗을 깨뜨리는 굵은 부리, 곤충을 잡기에 적합한 날카로운 부리, 꽃의 꿀을 빨기 위한 긴 부리 등으로 다양하게 분화되었다. 찰스 다윈(Charles Darwin)은 이러한 차이를 관찰하며 자연 선택(natural selection)의 개념을 발전시키는 데 중요한 영감을 얻었고, 이는 그의 진화론 정립에 핵심적인 역할을 했다.
Primates (영장류)	영장류는 포유류의 한 갈래로서, 큰 뇌 용량과 물건을 잡을 수 있는 정교한 손을 특징으로 한다. 이들은 열대 우림부터 사바나에 이르기까지 다양한 환경에 적응하며 진화해 왔다. 영장류의 핵심적인 능력 중 하나는 복잡한 문제 해결 능력이다. 침팬지는 나뭇가지를 가공해 흰개미를 잡거나 돌을 사용해 견과류를 깨뜨리는 등 도구 사용의 예시를 보이며, 일부 원숭이도 돌을 활용해 조개껍질을 여는 행동이 관찰된다. 또한, 이들의 복잡한 소통(communication) 능력은 다양한 발성과 몸짓을 통해 집단 내 협력과 강한 사회적 유대를 유지하는 핵심 기제이다.
Reptiles (파충류)	고생대 석탄기 후기(약 3억 1천만 년 전)에 등장한 척추동물로, 건조한 육지 환경에 적응하며 여러 특징이 생겼다. 가장 큰 혁신 중 하나는 양막(amnion)을 가진 알의 등장으로, 단단하거나 가죽질의 껍질이 알을 외부 충격과 건조로부터 보호해 수중이 아닌 육상에서도 번식이 가능하게 했다. 또한 파충류는 비늘로 덮인 피부를 통해 수분 손실을 최소화하며, 대부분 변온성(ectothermy)을 나타내어 외부 온도에 따라 체온이 달라진다. 이러한 특성은 에너지 소비를 줄이는 장점이 있지만, 활동성이 기온에 크게 의존한다는 제약도 있다. 파충류의 이러한 진화적 적응은 이후 조류와 포유류 진화의 기초가 되었으며, 중생대 동안 다양한 종으로 번성할 수 있는 토대를 마련했다.
Coral Reef (산호초)	작은 해양 동물인 산호(coral)들이 장기간에 걸쳐 형성한 복합적인 구조물이다. 개별 산호는 산호폴립(coral polyps)이라는 작은 자루 모양의 몸체로 구성되어 있으며, 이 폴립들은 해수에서 용해된 탄산칼슘(calcium carbonate)을 추출하여 골격을 생성한다. 산호초는 주로 얕은 열대 해역에 분포하며, 이 환경에서 대부분의 산호는 공생조류(zooxanthellae)와 공생 관계를 형성한다. 산호는 공생조류의 광합성 산물을 에너지원으로 삼아 성장한다. 산호초는 해안선을 파도로부터 보호하고, 다양한 어류에게 서식지를 제공하며, 높은 수준의 생물 다양성을 유지하는 등 생태계에서 핵심적인 기능을 수행한다.
Deep-sea Creatures (심해 생물)	태양광이 거의 도달하지 않는 깊은 수심에 서식하는 다양한 생물 집단을 총칭한다. 낮은 수온, 극도로 높은 수압, 그리고 제한적인 영양분이라는 심해의 환경 조건에 적응한 생물들은 특화된 형태적 및 생리적 구조를 발달시켰다. 주요 적응으로는 빛을 스스로 생성하는 생물 발광(bioluminescence), 에너지 소비를 최소화하는 느린 신진대사, 그리고 희소한 먹이를 포획하기 위한 큰 입과 날카로운 치아 등이 있다. 특히 일부 심해 미생물은 열수 분출공(hydrothermal vent) 주변에서 화학합성(chemosynthesis)을 수행하여 유기물을 합성하고 에너지를 획득한다.
Trout (송어)	연어과(Salmonidae)에 속하는 어류로, 일반적으로 기다란 유선형의 몸체를 특징으로 한다. 등 쪽은 주로 녹색 또는 갈색을, 배 쪽은 은백색을 나타낸다. 송어는 깨끗하고 산소 함량이 높은 물을 선호하며, 작은 하천, 대형 강, 호수 등의 민물 환경에서 분포하는데, 대체로 다양한 은신처, 자갈로 이루어진 강 바닥, 풍부한 먹이원, 그리고 청정한 바닥 조건을 갖춘 차가운 시냇물에서 안정적으로 서식한다. 갈색송어(Brown trout)와 같은 일부 종은 주변 수계 환경의 변화에 따라 민물과 바닷물을 오가며 생애 주기를 완성하는 회유성(diadromous) 어류이다.

2. Entomology (곤충학)

Bee (벌)	벌목(Hymenoptera)에 속하는 곤충군이며, 알려진 종은 약 20,000여 종에 달한다. 이들 중 다수는 꽃가루(pollen)와 꽃꿀(nectar)을 먹이로 삼아 식물의 주요 꽃가루 매개자 역할을 수행한다. 이 곤충군을 대표하는 것은 바로 꿀벌이다. 꿀벌 사회는 여왕벌(queen bee), 일벌(worker bee), 수벌(drone bee)의 세 계급으로 명확히 구분된다. 그러나 서식지 파괴, 농약 사용, 질병 등의 문제로 인해 꿀벌 개체 수가 급감하는 추세다. 특히 일벌들이 갑자기 벌집에서 사라지는 군집붕괴현상(colony collapse disorder)이 나타나 생태계와 농업에 심각한 영향을 미치고 있다. 꿀벌 외에도 다양한 종의 벌이 존재한다. 호박벌(bumblebee)은 여왕과 일벌이 계급을 이루는 소규모 사회를 형성하지만, 꿀을 저장하는 양은 비교적 적다. 어리호박벌(carpenter bee)과 같은 단생 벌(solitary bee)은 사회생활 없이 혼자 굴을 파고 알을 낳으며, 꽃가루를 저장하여 자손을 기른다. 한편, 알락꽃벌속(Nomada)에 속하는 벌들은 스스로 둥지를 짓지 않고 다른 벌의 둥지에 알을 낳아 숙주의 자원을 이용하는 독특한 습성이 있다.
Venomous Insects (독충)	독성 물질(venom)을 분비하여 먹이를 잡거나 자신을 방어하는 곤충군을 말한다. 대표적으로는 말벌(hornet)과 불개미(fire ant) 등이 있으며, 이들은 독침(stinger)이나 침샘을 통해 독을 전달한다. 독의 주요 사용 목적은 포식자 방어, 먹이 포획, 그리고 영역 경쟁이다. 일부 독충의 독은 인간에게도 심한 통증이나 알레르기 반응을 유발할 수 있다.

3. Botany (식물학)

Plant Self-defense (식물의 자기 방어)	식물은 포식자나 병원균 같은 위험으로부터 자신을 지키기 위해 다양한 방어 전략을 사용한다. 공격 전부터 갖추고 있는 방어책으로는 가시(thorn)나 털(trichome), 침입자가 뚫고 들어오기 어려운 두꺼운 세포벽 같은 물리적인 방어가 있다. 또한, 알칼로이드(alkaloid), 탄닌(tannin), 테르페노이드(terpenoid) 같은 화학적 방어 물질을 생산하여 맛이나 독성을 이용해 초식동물의 섭취를 막기도 한다. 이 외에도, 일부 식물은 상처를 입으면 특유의 냄새를 가진 휘발성(volatile) 화합물을 공중에 방출하는데, 이는 주변 식물들에게 위험을 알려 방어 태세를 갖추게 하거나 또는 자신을 공격하는 초식 동물의 천적을 유인한다.

4. Microbiology (미생물학)

Fungi (균류)	버섯, 효모, 곰팡이 등 여러 형태로 존재하는 진핵생물이다. 이들은 식물과는 달리 광합성(photosynthesis)을 하지 못하고 대신 외부에서 유기물(organic matter)을 흡수하여 에너지를 얻는다. 생태계에서 균류는 분해자로서 토양의 영양분 순환을 돕고 식물 뿌리와 공생하는 등 중요한 역할을 담당한다. 또한, 일부 균류는 항생제, 발효식품, 의약품 개발에도 유용하게 활용된다. 반면에 병원성 균류(pathogenic fungi)는 인간과 동물에게 질병을 일으키는 원인이 되기도 한다.
Microbiome (마이크로바이옴)	체내외에 서식하는 세균, 바이러스, 곰팡이 등 모든 미생물을 통틀어 일컫는 말이다. 이들은 소화(digestion), 면역(immunity), 기분 조절(mood regulation)과 같은 우리 몸의 다양한 기능을 수행한다. 특히 장내 세균은 음식 소화와 비타민 생산을 돕고, 일부는 장-뇌 축(gut-brain axis)을 통해 뇌 기능과 정신 건강에도 영향을 미친다. 식습관, 생활습관, 항생제 사용 등의 요인들이 미생물 균형에 큰 영향을 주는데, 이 균형이 깨지면 소화 문제, 면역력 약화를 초래할 수 있으며, 나아가 우울증이나 불안 증세와의 상관관계도 보고된 바 있다.

Vibrio Bacteria (비브리오균)	바닷물이나 강어귀처럼 염분이 있는 환경에 주로 서식하는 세균이다. 대표적인 종으로는 콜레라를 유발하는 비브리오 콜레라(Vibrio cholerae)와 식중독의 원인인 비브리오 파라헤모리티쿠스(Vibrio parahaemolyticus) 등이 있다. 이들 중 일부는 항생제 내성(antibiotic resistance)까지 획득하면서 치료가 점점 더 어려워지고 있다. 더욱이 해수 온도 상승과 염분 변화로 비브리오균의 밀도와 분포가 증가해 인간에게 감염될 가능성이 커지고 있다.

■ Cognitive Science (인지과학)

다양한 인지과학 연구와 관련된 지문이 주로 출제된다.

Cognitive Map (인지 지도)	인간과 동물이 공간 정보를 획득하고 저장하며, 회상하고 해독하는 정신적 구조를 말한다. 이는 심리학자 에드워드 톨먼(Edward Tolman)이 1940년대에 처음 정의했다. 인지 지도는 공간 및 기억과 밀접한 관련이 있는 두뇌 부위인 해마(hippocampus)를 통해 작동하며, 새로운 경험이나 경로 변화에 따라 끊임없이 동적으로 갱신된다. 이러한 인지 지도는 단순한 공간 인식뿐만 아니라 인간과 동물의 행동, 학습, 기억 등 여러 분야에서 핵심적인 개념으로 활용된다.
Mirror Test (거울 실험)	동물이 자기 자신을 인식할 수 있는지 확인하는 자기 인식(self-recognition) 평가 방법이다. 이 테스트는 동물이 몸에 표시를 한 다음 거울을 보여주는 방식으로 진행된다. 동물이 거울에 비친 표시를 인지하고 이를 직접 만지거나 제거하려는 행동을 보일 경우 자기 인식 능력이 있다고 판단한다. 일부 영장류, 돌고래, 코끼리, 그리고 특정 조류 등에서 이 테스트의 성공 사례가 보고되었다.

■ Ecology (생태학)

멸종, 도시화에 따른 생태계 파괴 등 생태 변화에 관한 지문이 주로 출제된다.

Ecological Succession (생태 천이)	일정한 지역에서 시간이 지남에 따라 생물군집과 생태계 구조가 변화하고 발달하는 과정이다. 초기 단계에서는 선구종(pioneer species)이라 불리는 환경 적응력이 높은 식물이나 미생물이 해당 지역을 먼저 점유한다. 특히 토양이 없는 환경에서 선구종은 토양 형성과 영양분 축적을 촉진한다. 이후 일차 천이나 이차 천이를 거치며 다양한 식물군과 동물군이 점차 정착하여 복잡한 구조를 갖춘 극상군집(climax community)에 도달한다. 생태 천이는 자연적 요인뿐만 아니라 외부 교란에 의해 영향을 받으며, 생태계의 다양성과 회복력에 중요한 역할을 한다.
Extinction (멸종)	특정 생물종이 지구상에서 완전히 사라지는 현상으로, 기후 변화, 다른 종과의 경쟁, 서식지 파괴, 환경 오염 등 여러 원인으로 인해 발생한다. 멸종은 생태계 균형에 큰 영향을 미치지만, 한편으로는 남아있는 종들에게 진화(evolution)하거나 새로운 적응(adaptation)을 할 기회를 제공하는 역할도 한다. 대멸종(mass extinction)은 지질학적으로 짧은 기간 동안 전 지구적으로 대부분의 종이 사라지는 현상이다. 과거에도 자연적인 대멸종 사건이 여러 차례 있었지만, 현재는 인간의 활동으로 인한 멸종 속도가 급격하게 증가하고 있다.
Tropical Rainforest (열대우림)	생물다양성(biodiversity)이 높은 곳으로, 여러 층으로 나뉜 식생 구조가 특징이다. 상층부의 거목들은 캐노피(canopy)를 형성하고, 그 아래에는 다양한 동식물이 서식하는 하층과 지면층이 존재한다. 열대우림의 토양은 영양분이 매우 부족하고 산성이지만, 유기물 분해가 빠르고 미생물 활동이 활발하여 영양분이 신속하게 재순환된다. 특히 나무 뿌리와 균류의 공생관계(mycorrhizae)는 토양 내 제한된 자원 흡수를 돕는다.

| Urbanization and Wildlife Population (도시화와 야생 생물 개체 수) | 도시화는 주로 토지 이용 변화와 기반 시설 확장으로 서식지 면적을 감소시키며, 빛 공해와 소음 등은 서식지의 질과 생태적 기능을 저하해 야생 생물에 부정적 영향을 준다. 이로 인해 야생 생물의 개체 수와 다양성이 영향받게 된다. 일부 적응력이 강한 종은 도심 환경에서 번성하지만, 특정 서식지에 특화된 종(habitat-specific species)은 개체 수가 급격히 줄어들 수 있다. 도시 생태계 연구는 이러한 변화를 이해하고, 인간 활동과 생물 다양성 보존 사이의 균형점을 찾는 데 필요한 중요한 정보를 제공한다. |

■ Paleontology (고생물학)

생명의 기원, 고대 생물, 멸종에 관한 지문이 주로 출제된다.

The Origin of Life (생명의 기원)	지구 생명은 원시 지구(primordial Earth)의 대기와 바다에 있던 물질이 자연 에너지와 반응하면서 생명의 기본 재료가 형성되며 시작되었다고 본다. 1953년에 진행된 Miller-Urey 실험은 메테인·암모니아·수소·수증기로 구성된 환원성 대기를 가정해 전기 방전을 가했을 때 여러 종류의 아미노산이 생성될 수 있음을 보여주었으며, 특별한 생명체나 효소 없이도 자연조건에서 생명체 기본 구성 요소가 만들어질 수 있다는 점을 시사했다. 이는 원시 지구의 번개나 화산 활동 같은 에너지가 이러한 반응을 일으켰을 가능성을 뒷받침한다.
Prehistoric Insects (선사시대 곤충)	약 3억 년 전 석탄기(Carboniferous)에는 지구 대기의 산소 농도가 오늘날보다 훨씬 높은 약 30~35%에 달했다. 산소가 풍부했던 이 시기에 곤충과 절지동물은 몸속에 산소를 더 효율적으로 공급할 수 있었고, 그 결과 거대한 형태로 성장할 수 있었다. 대표적인 예로는 날개폭이 약 70센티미터에 달하는 잠자리와 유사한 메가네우라(Meganeura), 그리고 길이가 약 2~2.5미터에 이르렀던 절지동물 아르트로플레우라(Arthropleura)가 있다. 그러나 페름기로 접어들면서 대기 중 산소 농도가 점차 감소하고, 육상 척추동물의 다양화로 생태계가 크게 변화했다. 이러한 환경 변화로 인해 산소 공급이 어려워지고 생태계의 균형이 바뀌면서, 거대 곤충들은 점차 지구상에서 사라지게 되었다.
Megafaunal Extinction (거대 동물 멸종)	가장 최근의 빙하기가 끝나가던 수만 년 전부터 약 1만 년 전 사이에 광범위하게 일어났다. 이 기간 북반구와 남반구 여러 지역에서 매머드(mammoth), 마스토돈(mastodon), 거대 나무늘보(giant sloths) 같은 대형 포유류를 포함한 다양한 거대 동물이 대규모로 사라졌다. 이 멸종의 원인에 대해서는 크게 세 가지 가설이 제시된다. 첫째는 인간이 지구상에 확산됨과 동시에 진행된 과도한 사냥, 즉 오버킬(overkill) 가설이다. 둘째는 빙하기에서 따뜻한 간빙기로 이어지는 기후 변화와 그에 따른 서식지 변화이다. 셋째는 인간의 사냥과 기후 변화의 영향이 결합된 복합적 요인이다. 지역과 종에 따라 결정적인 멸종 요인은 달랐지만, 이러한 대규모 멸종은 지구의 식생 구조, 탄소 순환, 그리고 생태계 전반에 걸쳐 장기적인 변화를 남겼다.
Dendrochronology (나이테 연대 측정법)	나무에 해마다 생기는 나이테(tree rings)를 분석하여 과거의 사건들을 시간 순서대로 연대 측정하고 해석하는 과학 분야다. 특히 과거의 기후(paleoclimate)나 기후의 변화 경향(climatic trends)을 연구하는 데 유용하다. 연구를 위해서는 먼저 나무껍질에서 중심까지 작은 원기둥 모양의 코어를 추출한 후, 실험실에서 나이테를 하나하나 세고 폭을 측정한다. 나이테의 폭은 그해의 강수량(precipitation)이나 기온 같은 외부 환경 조건에 크게 좌우된다. 즉, 환경이 좋으면 나이테가 넓고, 나쁘면 좁아진다. 이러한 원리를 이용해 나이테를 측정하면 수천 년에 걸친 기후 변화 기록을 역추적하여 알 수 있게 해준다.

■ Physiology (생리학)

신체의 다양한 작용에 관한 지문이 주로 출제된다.

Brain (뇌)	중추신경계(central nervous system)의 핵심 기관으로, 수많은 신경회로를 통해 우리 몸의 감각, 운동, 인지, 감정 기능을 통합하고 조절한다. 뇌는 크게 좌뇌와 우뇌로 나뉘는데, 좌뇌는 주로 언어 처리와 논리적 사고를 담당하고, 우뇌는 공간 인지(spatial perception), 주의 집중, 감성 기능에 더 관여한다. 그러나 대부분의 복잡한 인지 기능은 양쪽 반구의 협력을 통해 수행된다. 두 반구는 뇌량(corpus callosum)이라는 굵은 신경다발로 연결되어 서로 정보를 교환하며 협력한다. 뇌의 주요 구조로는 대뇌(cerebrum), 소뇌(cerebellum), 뇌간(brainstem)이 있다. 대뇌는 고차원적 사고, 기억, 의식적 행동을 담당하며, 특히 전두엽(frontal lobe)은 계획, 문제 해결, 운동 조절에 관여한다. 두정엽(parietal lobe)은 감각 정보 및 공간 인지 처리, 후두엽(occipital lobe)은 시각 처리, 측두엽(temporal lobe)은 청각과 기억 저장에 중요한 역할을 한다. 소뇌는 신체의 균형 유지와 운동 협응에 필수적이며, 뇌간은 심장 박동, 호흡 등 생명 유지 기능을 조절한다.
Circadian Rhythm (일주기 리듬)	약 24시간 주기로 반복되는 신체 내부의 자연스러운 시간 조절 체계이다. 이는 우리 몸의 생체 시계(biological clock) 역할을 한다. 이 리듬은 뇌의 깊숙한 곳인 시상하부(hypothalamus)에 있는 시교차상핵(suprachiasmatic nucleus, SCN)이 중심적으로 조절한다. 시교차상핵은 수면-각성 주기, 호르몬 분비, 체온 변화 등 다양한 생리 기능을 최적화하여 조절한다. 또한 일주기 리듬은 빛과 같은 외부 환경 신호에 의해 주기적으로 조정된다. 이를 통해 인간은 하루 주기에 맞춰 활동하고 휴식할 수 있도록 신체를 준비하는 것이다.
Sleep Patterns (수면 패턴)	인간의 수면은 약 90분 주기로 반복되는 수면 주기(sleep cycle)에 따라 이루어지며, 이는 비렘 수면(Non-Rapid Eye Movement)과 렘 수면(Rapid Eye Movement)을 포함한다. 비렘 수면은 세 단계로 나뉘며, 그중 제3단계(N3)는 깊은 수면 단계로, 신체 회복과 면역 기능 유지에 중요하다. 렘 수면은 눈동자가 빠르게 움직이는 단계로, 뇌 활동이 활발하고 이때 꿈을 꾼다. 또한 이 단계에서는 심장 박동과 호흡이 불규칙하다. 성인은 평균 7~9시간의 수면 동안 보통 4~6회의 수면 주기를 거친다. 이러한 수면은 위에 언급된 일주기 리듬에 따라 조절된다. 일부 동물 중에는 환경에 맞춰 수면 패턴이 진화한 경우도 있는데, 돌고래와 일부 조류는 단일 반구 수면(unihemispheric sleep)을 통해 뇌의 한쪽은 자면서도 다른 쪽은 깨어 있게 하여, 호흡과 포식자 감시를 유지할 수 있다.

■ Environmental Science (환경과학)

기후 변화, 환경 문제와 그 해결 방안에 관한 지문이 주로 출제된다.

Ocean Acidification (해양 산성화)	대기 중 이산화탄소 증가로 바닷물의 산성도가 높아지는 현상으로, 산호, 조개류, 플랑크톤 등 해양 생물에 큰 영향을 미친다. 산호는 골격 유지와 공생조류(zooxanthellae)와의 관계 유지가 어려워지고, 조개류와 플랑크톤은 껍데기 발달과 생존이 어려워져 해양 생태계와 양식업(aquaculture)에 영향을 준다. 이를 완화하기 위해 탄소 배출 감소, 해양 보호, 생물 적응 연구 등이 진행되고 있다.
Renewable Energy (재생에너지)	자연에서 지속적으로 공급되는 에너지원으로, 태양광, 풍력, 수력 등이 대표적이다. 이러한 에너지원은 화석 연료(fossil fuel)에 의존하지 않고 전력 생산을 가능하게 하며, 온실가스 배출 감소와 환경 영향 최소화 등 지속 가능성(sustainability) 측면에서 중요한 의미가 있다.

[01-05]

Keystone Species

Keystone species are organisms that have an impact on their ecosystem far greater than their numbers suggest. Ecologist Robert Paine developed this concept while studying starfish, the top predator in a tide pool ecosystem. He removed starfish from an ecosystem that had 14 other organisms. After three years, he observed that half the other species had died off. After 10 years, mussels, typically consumed by starfish, completely dominated the environment.

Keystone species can also play other roles in an ecosystem besides that of a predator. Beavers, for example, are habitat builders. Their dams support the healthy growth of wetlands teeming with life by limiting flooding, protecting against drought, and maintaining high water quality. Honeybees and other pollinating insects and birds play vital roles in the environment as well, helping to reproduce 80 percent of the world's plants, which serve as a key food source for countless herbivore species.

Protecting keystone species is a priority due to their large environmental impact. Efforts in Argentina demonstrate how they can be successfully preserved. Jaguars, which control prey populations that would otherwise overconsume vegetation, have been safeguarded in large national parks. A breeding program has stabilized their populations, which will help restore ecological balance.

01 The word "stabilized" in the passage is closest in meaning to

Ⓐ affected
Ⓑ secured
Ⓒ analyzed
Ⓓ ignored

02 What can be inferred about starfish?

Ⓐ Its numbers eventually dropped after three years.
Ⓑ Its absence reduced the survivability of other species.
Ⓒ It competed with mussels for the same food source.
Ⓓ It was killed off by the environment's top predator.

03 Which of the following is NOT mentioned as a way that beavers support wetland ecosystems?

Ⓐ Keeping flooding in check
Ⓑ Preventing droughts
Ⓒ Sustaining high water quality
Ⓓ Providing habitats to herbivores

04 According to the second paragraph, what vital role do some birds play in the environment?

Ⓐ They consume harmful insects.
Ⓑ Their nests protect other species.
Ⓒ They support plant reproduction.
Ⓓ Their presence indicates food sources.

05 What is the purpose of the third paragraph?

Ⓐ To illustrate the importance of certain prey populations
Ⓑ To show a successful case of protecting a keystone species
Ⓒ To describe an ecological issue found throughout Argentina
Ⓓ To celebrate the growth of keystone vegetation in national parks

HACKERS TEST

[06-10]

The Effects of Temperature on Sex Determination

In many reptiles, sex is determined not by genetics but by incubation temperature, in a process known as temperature-dependent sex determination. This mechanism involves a key enzyme, aromatase, that controls the balance of sex hormones. The enzyme's function is highly temperature-sensitive; specific temperatures during a critical developmental period can activate or suppress it. This directs the embryo's development toward male or female pathways, ultimately influencing sex ratios within the population. For example, in some turtle populations, warmer nest sites result in more female hatchlings.

Recent research on climate change shows that it may impact temperature-sensitive species. Elevated temperatures can lead to a disproportionate increase in females or males. As a result, many population groups could experience a decrease in their breeding activity. Researchers are testing intervention methods to address these issues. Techniques such as setting up sun shades above nests and relocating eggs to cooler areas are now being explored to prevent extreme sex imbalances. They are also carefully tracking the temperatures of eggs in the wild. Managing the influence of temperature on sex determination will be essential for the long-term survival of affected species.

06 The word "ultimately" in the passage is closest in meaning to

Ⓐ immediately
Ⓑ initially
Ⓒ finally
Ⓓ directly

07 What is indicated about aromatase?

Ⓐ Its function is modulated by thermal exposure during a key phase of development.
Ⓑ It steers development toward the male pathway as temperatures decrease.
Ⓒ Its activity is suppressed when the incubation temperature is lowered.
Ⓓ It is a secondary factor in the sex determination of reptiles.

08 What is an outcome of rising temperatures for some turtle populations?

Ⓐ An extension of the developmental period
Ⓑ A decrease in the hatching success rate
Ⓒ An increase in female offspring
Ⓓ A longer lifespan for newborn turtles

09 What can be inferred about climate change?

Ⓐ It will favor only male offspring.
Ⓑ It decreases the production of aromatase.
Ⓒ It halts the breeding activity of reptile populations.
Ⓓ It has the potential to skew the sex ratios of reptiles.

10 Which of the following is NOT mentioned as a method for helping temperature-sensitive species?

Ⓐ Installing shades to block sunlight
Ⓑ Relocating eggs to less heated environments
Ⓒ Placing lights around egg sites
Ⓓ Tracking the thermal conditions of eggs

HACKERS TEST

[11-15]

Hormonal Control

Hormonal control is an essential mechanism in the human body that helps regulate many fundamental processes. Hormones are chemical messengers produced by special glands and released into the bloodstream. They travel to different organs and tissues, carrying signals that initiate or suspend specific activities. For instance, erythropoietin, released by the kidneys, stimulates the production of red blood cells.

Hormonal regulation works through intercellular signaling. Every hormone seeks out target cells that possess complementary receptors. The binding of a hormone to its receptor initiates responses like promoting development, generating energy, or regulating the concentration of body fluids. This entire mechanism relies heavily on regulatory feedback. If the body detects an excess or deficiency of a particular substance, the secretion of hormones shifts to reestablish homeostasis. For instance, hormones from the thyroid gland manage the body's metabolic rate. When these levels become too elevated, signals inhibit further release; if they drop, output is boosted.

Hormonal control allows the body to adapt to changes in the environment and maintain steady internal conditions. This system permits the body to coordinate activities like growth, energy use, stress response, and repair. The precise action of hormones is vital for keeping all body systems in harmony and preventing disorders from developing.

11 The word "suspend" in the first paragraph is closest in meaning to

   Ⓐ monitor
   Ⓑ avoid
   Ⓒ stop
   Ⓓ preserve

12 What is the main function of erythropoietin?

   Ⓐ It stimulates muscle growth during physical activity.
   Ⓑ It regulates feedback loops for body fluid balance.
   Ⓒ It triggers the production of red blood cells.
   Ⓓ It removes dead blood cells from the organs.

13 What can be inferred about target cells?

   Ⓐ They bind with a matching hormone to start specific activities.
   Ⓑ They are able to produce any hormone needed by the body.
   Ⓒ They become inactive when exposed to hormones.
   Ⓓ They detect whether the amount of a substance is too much or too little.

14 What is indicated in the passage about regulatory feedback?

   Ⓐ It eliminates the need for special hormone glands.
   Ⓑ It adjusts hormone production to restore balance.
   Ⓒ It ensures that hormones only function temporarily.
   Ⓓ It prevents hormones from entering the bloodstream.

15 Why does the author mention the thyroid gland?

   Ⓐ To introduce a gland involved in bone and muscle growth
   Ⓑ To show how hormones are selectively targeted by metabolism
   Ⓒ To illustrate a disorder caused by a hormone imbalance
   Ⓓ To give an example of how a feedback mechanism operates

HACKERS TEST

[16-20]

Bird Territory

Birds establish territories to protect indispensable resources such as food and nesting sites. These territories are chosen and actively defended, especially during breeding season. Birds often establish territorial boundaries by singing or making visual displays. For instance, robins sing to warn off rivals, while red-winged blackbirds show their colorful wing patches to signal ownership.

Territory size differs depending on the type of bird. Hawks defend large areas due to their wide hunting range, while wrens and sparrows keep only a small zone around their nest. Some tropical hummingbirds defend flowering plants individually. Colonial birds, such as gulls, may only protect a tiny spot in crowded nesting sites.

Birds sometimes engage in physical conflicts to maintain their territorial boundaries. Common terns fiercely protect nesting areas in colonies, conducting coordinated aerial attacks to repel intruders. Similarly, northern mockingbirds engage in aerial attacks to defend their territories.

Some birds vary their territorial strategies to account for changes in resource availability. In coastal areas, oystercatchers aggressively chase intruders from feeding grounds at low tide. However, once the tide rises, these conflicts quickly diminish as the feeding area becomes submerged and food disappears.

16 The word "indispensable" in the first sentence is closest in meaning to

Ⓐ accessible
Ⓑ important
Ⓒ unusual
Ⓓ abundant

17 How do robins typically mark their territorial boundaries?

Ⓐ By building larger nests
Ⓑ By chasing other robins away
Ⓒ By producing songs
Ⓓ By gathering in large flocks

18 Why does the author mention wrens and sparrows?

Ⓐ To suggest that both types of birds share the same nesting areas
Ⓑ To explain why some birds do not establish territorial boundaries
Ⓒ To provide a contrast with a bird that maintains a large territory
Ⓓ To show how different types of birds defend their territories

19 What does the passage indicate about gulls?

Ⓐ They only protect a small area near their nest.
Ⓑ They select isolated locations for breeding.
Ⓒ They engage in aerial attacks to defend their territories.
Ⓓ They rely on solitary nesting to prevent competition.

20 How does the behavior of oystercatchers change once the tide rises?

Ⓐ They cooperate with other bird species.
Ⓑ They focus primarily on locating food.
Ⓒ They are more likely to defend nesting sites.
Ⓓ They are less prone to engage in conflict.

Answers p.495

무료 토플자료·유학정보 제공
goHackers.com

ACTUAL TEST

Hackers Updated TOEFL READING

ACTUAL TEST 1
ACTUAL TEST 2

ACTUAL TEST 1

TOEFL iBT READING

Module 1

During the test, the clock will show you how much time you have to finish Module 1.

You can click Next to move to the next question and click Back to go back to earlier questions in the same module.

During the test, you WILL NOT be able to return to Module 1 once you have started Module 2.

Fill in the missing letters in the paragraph.

Sweeping through Europe during the 14th century, the Black Death was a cataclysmic pandemic that altered the trajectory of European civilization. The ⁰¹pla____ was ⁰²respo_____ not ⁰³on___ for ⁰⁴t___ demise of ⁰⁵nea____ half the ⁰⁶ent____ population ⁰⁷b___ also ⁰⁸f___ triggering ⁰⁹ac____ labor ¹⁰shor_____ and sparking widespread social unrest. Consequently, the surviving workers found themselves in a position to negotiate higher wages, with many abandoning their feudal obligations in pursuit of improved economic prospects. These transformations laid the foundation for greater social mobility across the continent.

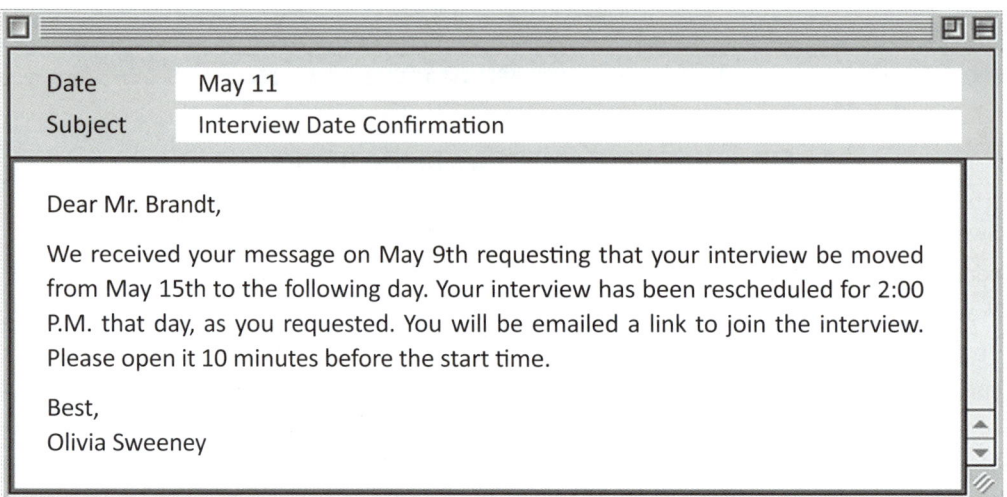

11 When is the date of the interview?

Ⓐ May 9th
Ⓑ May 11th
Ⓒ May 15th
Ⓓ May 16th

12 What can be inferred about Mr. Brandt's interview?

Ⓐ It will be conducted via an online conferencing platform.
Ⓑ It is a follow-up meeting from a previously held interview.
Ⓒ It had to be rescheduled due to a problem at the company.
Ⓓ It is for a high-level management position.

Read a text-message chain.

Elena Patel [9:15 A.M.]
Team, we need to finalize the presentation materials for next Tuesday's meeting. Let's make sure it is fully prepared and structured.

Sarah Kim [9:20 A.M.]
Got it! I'm working on the slides now. I'm focusing on the top three electric bicycles in our lineup.

Thomas Rivera [9:25 A.M.]
I'll include the rest in the handout materials I'm putting together. But I noticed some inconsistencies in the product specifications. Could someone please double-check those numbers?

Shawn Gibbs [9:30 A.M.]
You bet. I can verify those against the technical documentation later this morning, after I finish reviewing the budget report. I'm nearly done.

Elena Patel [9:35 A.M.]
Good catch, Thomas. Everyone, please carefully review your sections and make sure everything is accurate. The CEO will be sitting in on this presentation.

13 What is Thomas Rivera's responsibility?

Ⓐ Creating some slides
Ⓑ Preparing printed materials
Ⓒ Double-checking product specifications
Ⓓ Researching electric bicycles

14 What can be concluded about Shawn Gibbs?

Ⓐ He will need to finish slide preparation work by a deadline.
Ⓑ He will postpone reviewing the budget report.
Ⓒ He will not be free to do any extra work.
Ⓓ He will have time to take on an additional task.

15 At 9:35 A.M., what does Elena Patel most likely mean when she writes, "The CEO will be sitting in on this presentation"?

Ⓐ She believes the CEO has concerns about the team's abilities.
Ⓑ She will not be leading the meeting herself.
Ⓒ She wants the team's work to meet high standards.
Ⓓ She is pointing out that the CEO will attend this presentation only.

Chemosynthetic Communities

Most people are familiar with photosynthesis—the process by which plants use sunlight to produce energy. However, in the deepest parts of the ocean, where sunlight cannot penetrate, ecosystems thrive through chemosynthesis, which involves using chemicals instead of sunlight to produce food and nutrients. But how does chemosynthesis work?

At the foundation of these ecosystems are bacteria that convert chemicals like hydrogen sulfide into energy—much like plants convert sunlight. These chemosynthetic bacteria form the base of a complex food web that supports an array of bizarre creatures. Giant tube worms, some reaching lengths of eight feet, house these bacteria in specialized organs and receive nutrients in return. Certain species of clams and mussels have evolved symbiotic relationships with chemosynthetic bacteria, allowing them to flourish in harsh environments such as hydrothermal vents, where superheated water erupts from the seafloor.

What makes these chemosynthetic communities fascinating is their independence from solar energy, expanding the definition of what we consider habitable environments. The study of these communities may offer insights into how life might exist where sunlight is absent. For example, icy moons like Europa and Enceladus could support life based on these chemical reactions.

16 The word "penetrate" in the passage is closest in meaning to

  Ⓐ pierce
  Ⓑ dissolve
  Ⓒ reflect
  Ⓓ escape

17 Why do giant tube worms house chemosynthetic bacteria in specialized organs?

  Ⓐ They use the bacteria to filter toxins from the water.
  Ⓑ They help the bacteria reproduce more effectively.
  Ⓒ They receive nutrients produced by the bacteria.
  Ⓓ They make it possible for the bacteria to absorb chemicals.

18 All of the following are true about certain species of clams EXCEPT:

  Ⓐ They exist in areas where sunlight cannot reach.
  Ⓑ They can be found around hydrothermal vents.
  Ⓒ They generate chemical energy from superheated water.
  Ⓓ They have developed partnerships with some bacteria.

19 Why does the author mention icy moons?

  Ⓐ To suggest that chemosynthetic bacteria might have originated in space
  Ⓑ To compare the conditions on Earth's seafloor to those on celestial objects
  Ⓒ To provide an example of an environment where chemosynthesis is impossible
  Ⓓ To indicate that chemosynthetic ecosystems could provide clues about extraterrestrial life

20 What is the purpose of the third paragraph?

  Ⓐ It provides specific examples of the bacteria mentioned in paragraph 2.
  Ⓑ It explains the broader significance and implications of chemosynthetic communities.
  Ⓒ It contradicts the information about photosynthesis presented in paragraph 1.
  Ⓓ It concludes the passage by mentioning the difficulty of studying chemosynthetic communities.

End of Module 1

The first module of the Reading Section is now complete.
Module 2 will begin next.

TOEFL iBT READING

Module 2

During the test, the clock will show you how much time you have to finish Module 2.

You can click Next to move to the next question and click Back to go back to earlier questions in the same module.

Fill in the missing letters in the paragraph.

Octopuses are cephalopod mollusks with extraordinary physical and cognitive capabilities. They ⁰¹a__ known ⁰²f__ their ⁰³tent_____, which ⁰⁴gi___ them ⁰⁵pre_____ motor ⁰⁶con_____. This ⁰⁷distin_____ them ⁰⁸fr___ most ⁰⁹ot____ invertebrates. They ¹⁰c___ also alter the shape, color, and texture of their bodies, rendering themselves nearly invisible to predators. Observers have documented them engaging in sophisticated behaviors, such as escaping from highly secure enclosures, and they have the ability to recognize individual human faces. As a result, octopuses are regarded as evolution's most striking demonstration of complex intelligence outside of vertebrates.

Psychological Distance

Psychological distance explains how our mental representation of events shifts with perceived distance. This distance can be temporal (when), spatial (where), social (who), or hypothetical (likelihood). When events are psychologically distant, people tend to think abstractly, focusing on core features and broader patterns. Conversely, when events feel psychologically close, thinking becomes more concrete, with more emphasis being placed on details and contextual information.

Research demonstrates this theory's real-world relevance. In a study conducted by psychologists Yaacov Trope and Nira Liberman, participants made different choices depending on the time frame. When asked about events that would occur "next year," they prioritized desirability (why they would act), whereas for events that would occur "tomorrow," feasibility (how they would act) dominated. This pattern extends to consumer behavior—distant purchases focus on quality and benefits, while immediate ones stress price and convenience. This mental shift helps individuals make judicious decisions by adjusting their perspective.

The implications of psychological distance also apply to organizational strategy and public policy. Companies launching future products benefit from highlighting aspirational features, while immediate promotions should emphasize practicality. Similarly, policymakers can encourage greater citizen engagement and action by emphasizing the immediate and concrete aspects of climate change.

11. What does the passage mention as one result of perceiving an event as psychologically close?

    Ⓐ People focus on the likelihood of the event happening.
    Ⓑ People become concerned with how much time is available.
    Ⓒ People pay attention to specific details and context.
    Ⓓ People compare temporal and spatial information.

12. Why does the author mention Yaacov Trope and Nira Liberman's study?

    Ⓐ To show how psychological distance affects decision priorities
    Ⓑ To criticize a specific research methodology used in the study
    Ⓒ To explain why consumers prefer quality over price
    Ⓓ To argue that long-term planning is more effective than short-term planning

13. The word "judicious" in the passage is closest in meaning to

    Ⓐ confident
    Ⓑ sensible
    Ⓒ strategic
    Ⓓ impulsive

14. According to the passage, how can policymakers encourage citizen engagement?

    Ⓐ By highlighting concrete and material benefits
    Ⓑ By focusing on the immediate consequences
    Ⓒ By juxtaposing long-term impacts with short-term feasibility
    Ⓓ By comparing the effect across various aspects of life

15. What is the relationship between paragraphs 2 and 3?

    Ⓐ Paragraph 3 provides information that contradicts the research findings presented in paragraph 2.
    Ⓑ Paragraph 3 introduces an alternative theory that is related to the research described in paragraph 2.
    Ⓒ Paragraph 3 gives a detailed explanation of the study mentioned in paragraph 2.
    Ⓓ Paragraph 3 adds more applications of the pattern discussed in paragraph 2.

End of Module 2

The Reading Section is now complete.

Answers p.499

ual TEST 2

TOEFL iBT **READING**   Begin >

Module 1

During the test, the clock will show you how much time you have to finish Module 1.

You can click Next to move to the next question and click Back to go back to earlier questions in the same module.

During the test, you WILL NOT be able to return to Module 1 once you have started Module 2.

Fill in the missing letters in the paragraph.

The circulatory system is an essential physiological network within the human body. ⁰¹Th__ system, ⁰²wh____ is ⁰³orga_____ into ⁰⁴compo_____ such ⁰⁵a_ the ⁰⁶he____ and blood ⁰⁷ves_____, is divided ⁰⁸in___ two circuits, ⁰⁹bo___ serving ¹⁰crit_____ and specialized functions. One is pulmonary circulation, which transports deoxygenated blood to the lungs for gas exchange and returns oxygenated blood to the heart. The other, systemic circulation, distributes oxygen-rich blood from the heart to peripheral tissues and channels oxygen-depleted blood back to the cardiac chambers.

Fill in the missing letters in the paragraph.

Reverse psychology is a persuasive strategy in which an individual seeks to influence another's behavior by advocating for the contrary course of action. [11]Wh___ someone [12]i_ told [13]n___ to [14]eng____ in [15]parti_____ behaviors, it [16]c___ elicit [17]resis_____ and [18]inte_____ their [19]incli_____ to assert [20]th____ own autonomy. Although it constitutes a subtle form of manipulation, reverse psychology is typically regarded as innocuous when employed in low-stakes scenarios—for instance, when parents remark that their children need not eat their vegetables.

Read an email.

Date: August 10
Subject: Water Shutdown

Dear Tenant,

We regret to inform you that water service will be unavailable on August 15th from 9:00 A.M. to 2:00 P.M. We recommend that you store water in advance to cover your basic needs. This interruption is necessary in order to perform regular maintenance on the building's water pipes. We apologize for any inconvenience this may cause.

Sincerely,
Building Management

21 What is the main purpose of the email?

Ⓐ To schedule a tenant meeting about the building's water pipes
Ⓑ To request that tenants make an effort to conserve water
Ⓒ To inform tenants about new water billing procedures for the building
Ⓓ To notify tenants about upcoming maintenance work

22 Why must the service be interrupted?

Ⓐ To carry out routine upkeep on the plumbing system
Ⓑ To install new water meters in the units
Ⓒ To inspect a possible leak in the main water line
Ⓓ To upgrade the building's water pressure equipment

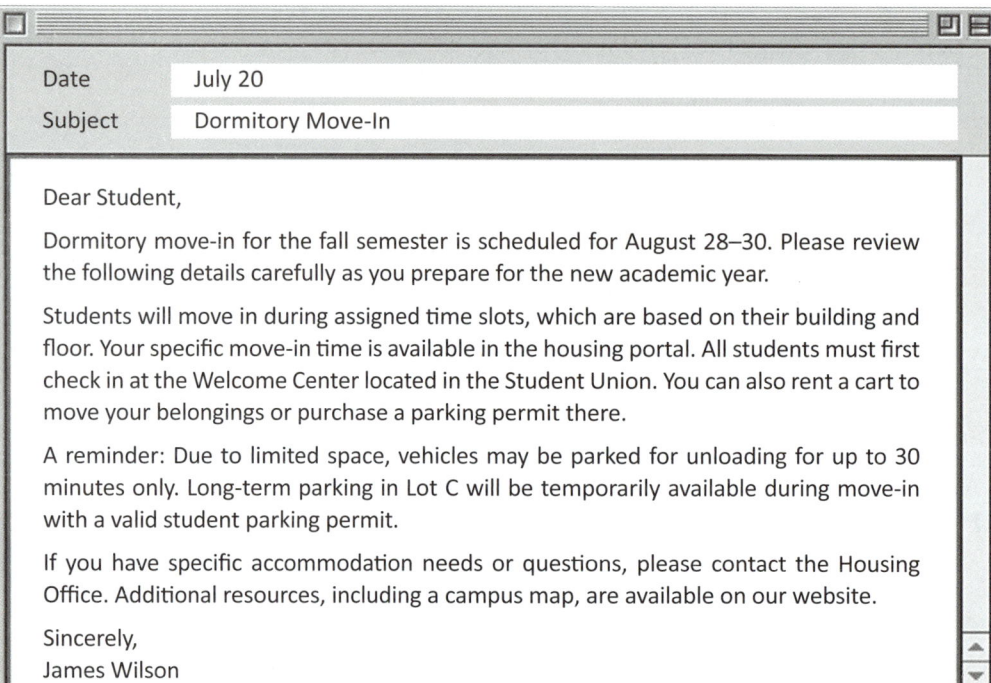

23 The email is most likely sent to

    Ⓐ Returning faculty members
    Ⓑ Future residents of campus housing
    Ⓒ Campus maintenance staff
    Ⓓ Students requesting parking permits

24 What will individuals do first during move-in?

    Ⓐ Submit a housing deposit
    Ⓑ Pick up a parking permit
    Ⓒ Attend a welcome seminar
    Ⓓ Complete a registration

25 What can be inferred about Lot C?

    Ⓐ It is not normally available for long-term student parking.
    Ⓑ It is difficult to find without a campus map.
    Ⓒ It is managed by the university's Housing Office.
    Ⓓ It is designated for loading and unloading only.

Read a social media post.

 **William Harris**

Are you looking to upgrade your tech skills? Tech Hub Academy now offers virtual coding workshops every Tuesday and Thursday evening! Our interactive sessions are perfect for beginners and intermediate learners who want to master programming fundamentals.

Learn from experienced instructors from leading tech companies who provide personalized feedback and guidance throughout each session. Small class sizes ensure that all students receive the attention and support they need. Many of our graduates have successfully transitioned into tech careers after completing our programs.

Register early to gain access to exclusive learning materials and coding resources worth $50. Plus, join our online community to connect with fellow learners and industry professionals for networking opportunities. Follow us on social media and share our program to receive a secret code for a 15% discount! Visit techhubacademy.com for more details and to secure your spot today.

LIKE   **COMMENT**

26 What is the main purpose of the post?

- Ⓐ To explain how coding skills support programming tasks
- Ⓑ To promote coding workshops offered by a tech training program
- Ⓒ To compare different levels of online learning courses
- Ⓓ To announce job openings in the tech industry

27 How will instructors support students?

- Ⓐ By providing them with supplementary resources
- Ⓑ By offering them one-on-one career counseling
- Ⓒ By giving them individual feedback and guidance
- Ⓓ By presenting them with a variety of job opportunities

28 Who will students meet in the online community?

- Ⓐ Tech Hub Academy instructors
- Ⓑ Previous program graduates
- Ⓒ Other students and tech professionals
- Ⓓ Hiring managers and job recruiters

Medieval Guilds

From the 11th to the 16th centuries, guilds flourished across Europe. These professional associations brought together those who practiced the same trade within a particular area.

Guilds operated within a hierarchy, allowing members to move upward based on experience. Youths trained as apprentices for several years before becoming journeymen capable of working for wages, and those talented enough could go on to become masters. However, achieving this status not only required the presentation of a "masterpiece" that met guild standards but also the funds to finance a workshop, tools, and a celebratory banquet. This was only one of many rules guilds had; wages were controlled, and workers were prohibited from forming their own associations, a restriction that led to revolts in Flanders and Florence.

Guild entry became increasingly difficult over time as established members raised membership fees. These fees helped fund administrative costs and provided services such as healthcare and funeral expenses for members. While the guild system limited competition and maintained high standards within the guilds, it also reinforced inequality. It served to protect the economic and social standing of those in charge, distancing them from workers who lacked the resources or skills to run their own businesses.

29 The word "hierarchy" in the passage is closest in meaning to

Ⓐ tradition
Ⓑ ranking
Ⓒ setting
Ⓓ routine

30 What is indicated in the passage about journeymen?

Ⓐ They received payment in exchange for their labor.
Ⓑ They trained apprentices as part of their job.
Ⓒ They used tools provided by the guild.
Ⓓ They were required to have their own workshop.

31 Why does the author mention the revolts in Flanders and Florence?

Ⓐ To highlight events that led to the decline of guilds
Ⓑ To show the consequence of workers forming their own associations
Ⓒ To suggest guild members in distinct regions communicated with one another
Ⓓ To demonstrate that guild members found guild regulations oppressive

32 How did the guild system benefit those in charge?

Ⓐ By providing them with an income from administrative work
Ⓑ By allowing them to establish the guild's quality standards
Ⓒ By safeguarding their financial and social status from competition
Ⓓ By exempting them from paying membership fees

33 Click on the sentence in paragraph 3 that identifies the specific benefits associated with the increased cost of guild admission.

Ⓐ Guild entry became increasingly difficult over time as established members raised membership fees.
Ⓑ These fees helped fund administrative costs and provided services such as healthcare and funeral expenses for members.
Ⓒ While the guild system limited competition and maintained high standards within the guilds, it also reinforced inequality.
Ⓓ It served to protect the economic and social standing of those in charge, distancing them from workers who lacked the resources or skills to run their own businesses.

End of Module 1

The first module of the Reading Section is now complete.
Module 2 will begin next.

Module 2

During the test, the clock will show you how much time you have to finish Module 2.

You can click Next to move to the next question and click Back to go back to earlier questions in the same module.

Fill in the missing letters in the paragraph.

Epigenetics offers a powerful link between lifestyle and genes. It ⁰¹demons_____ that ⁰²o___ environment, ⁰³di__, stress ⁰⁴lev____, and ⁰⁵ev__ age ⁰⁶c___ dramatically ⁰⁷infl_____ how ⁰⁸indiv_____ genes are ⁰⁹expr_____, without ¹⁰muta_____ the DNA sequence itself. Think of epigenetic marks as a memory system on the genome, recording our experiences. This means that two people with the same genetic makeup, like identical twins, can develop different health outcomes based on the adjustments their bodies make to their genes over time.

Pop Art and Consumerism

Pop art emerged in the United Kingdom in the mid-1950s in response to the consumer culture that dominated society following World War II. Artists in this movement drew inspiration for their works from everyday products, celebrities, and advertisements.

Pop art reached its peak in the 1960s, when American artists like Andy Warhol and Roy Lichtenstein famously embraced mass production techniques and transformed comic book imagery into large-scale paintings, before declining in influence during the 1970s as minimalism took over the art world. By treating mundane objects as worthy subjects for fine art, artists blurred the line between the "high" art typically encountered in a museum and the "low" art associated with advertising, challenging artistic conventions and inviting viewers to reconsider the value of familiar imagery.

■A Turning their artworks into commodities that could be bought, sold, and consumed was an extension of their stance toward consumerism. ■B In 1964, at an exhibition called The American Supermarket, fake goods such as velour-covered fruit and vegetables and Campbell's Soup tins were displayed for sale in New York's Bianchini Gallery. ■C However, instead of appearing like a traditional art gallery, the space resembled a real supermarket. ■D

11 According to the passage, pop art developed in the United Kingdom as a reaction to

Ⓐ the rise of consumerism
Ⓑ the elitism in the art world
Ⓒ the availability of new materials
Ⓓ the casualties of World War II

12 What is suggested about minimalism?

Ⓐ It rejected the use of mass production techniques.
Ⓑ It became the dominant art movement after pop art.
Ⓒ It drew inspiration from advertising and consumer culture.
Ⓓ It prompted artists to reconsider the value of familiar imagery.

13 Which of the following is NOT mentioned in the passage as an approach taken by pop artists?

Ⓐ Adopting manufacturing-style processes
Ⓑ Elevating common items to the level of fine art
Ⓒ Satirizing celebrities and commercial imagery
Ⓓ Using comic illustrations as the basis for large artworks

14 Why does the author mention The American Supermarket?

Ⓐ To show how artists in the 1960s were critical of the commercialization of art
Ⓑ To illustrate how pop artists applied their perspective on consumerism to their art
Ⓒ To provide evidence that the pop art movement reached its peak in the 1960s
Ⓓ To emphasize the importance of the exhibition to New York's pop art scene

15 There are four locations [■] in the passage that indicate where the following sentence could be added.

This provocative display of unconventional works created by prominent artists confronted the public with the eternal question, "What is art?"

Where would the sentence best fit? Select a location [■] where the sentence could be added to the passage.

End of Module 2

The Reading Section is now complete.

Hackers
Updated TOEFL
READING

TASK별
실전 필수 어휘

DAY 01 TASK 1 실전 필수 어휘
DAY 02 TASK 1 실전 필수 어휘
DAY 03 TASK 1 실전 필수 어휘
DAY 04 TASK 1 실전 필수 어휘
DAY 05 TASK 1 실전 필수 어휘
DAY 06 TASK 1 실전 필수 어휘
DAY 07 TASK 2 실전 필수 어휘
DAY 08 TASK 2 실전 필수 어휘
DAY 09 TASK 2 실전 필수 어휘
DAY 10 TASK 2 실전 필수 어휘

DAY 11 TASK 2 실전 필수 어휘
DAY 12 TASK 2 실전 필수 어휘
DAY 13 TASK 3 실전 필수 어휘
DAY 14 TASK 3 실전 필수 어휘
DAY 15 TASK 3 실전 필수 어휘
DAY 16 TASK 3 실전 필수 어휘
DAY 17 TASK 3 실전 필수 어휘
DAY 18 TASK 3 실전 필수 어휘
DAY 19 TASK 3 실전 필수 어휘
DAY 20 TASK 3 실전 필수 어휘

Day 01 — TASK 1 실전 필수 어휘

음성 바로 듣기 ▶

✅ TASK 1을 위해 필수적으로 알아야 할 어휘들이므로, 확실히 암기해 둡니다. 🎧 DAY01

☐	absorb [æbsɔ́ːrb]	흡수하다, 빨아들이다	☐	implementation [ìmpləməntéiʃən]	실행, 이행
☐	ambience [ǽmbiəns]	분위기	☐	indicator [índikèitər]	지표, 표시기
☐	ash [æʃ]	재, 화산재	☐	informed [infɔ́ːrmd]	정보에 입각한, 박식한
☐	barrier [bǽriər]	장벽, 방해물	☐	installment [instɔ́ːlmənt]	할부, 연재분
☐	blooming [blúːmiŋ]	꽃이 피는, 번영하는	☐	interruption [ìntərʌ́pʃən]	방해
☐	brilliance [bríljəns]	광채, 뛰어남	☐	invader [invéidər]	침입자, 침략자
☐	cave [keiv]	동굴, 굴	☐	landform [lǽndfɔːrm]	지형
☐	cognition [kɑːgníʃən]	인지, 인식	☐	lavish [lǽviʃ]	호화로운; 아낌없이 주다
☐	component [kəmpóunənt]	구성요소, 부품	☐	likewise [láikwàiz]	마찬가지로, 또한
☐	conservation [kàːnsərvéiʃən]	보존, 보호	☐	massive [mǽsiv]	거대한, 막대한
☐	creative [kriéitiv]	창조적인, 창의적인	☐	mitigation [mìtəgéiʃən]	완화, 경감
☐	crude [kruːd]	조잡한, 원유의	☐	offspring [ɔ́fspriŋ]	자손
☐	deity [déiəti]	신, 신격	☐	pattern [pǽtərn]	패턴, 양식
☐	departure [dipɑ́ːrtʃər]	출발, 이탈	☐	policy [pɑ́ləsi]	정책, 방침
☐	diet [dáiət]	식단	☐	proximity [prɑksíməti]	근접, 가까움
☐	drawback [drɔ́ːbæ̀k]	단점, 결점	☐	research [ríːsəːrtʃ]	연구; 연구하다
☐	dynamic [dainǽmik]	역동적인, 활동적인	☐	riverbed [rívərbèd]	강바닥
☐	efficiently [ifíʃəntli]	효율적으로	☐	sibling [síbliŋ]	형제자매
☐	engaging [ingéidʒiŋ]	매력적인, 흥미로운	☐	solution [səlúːʃən]	해결책, 용액
☐	erasure [iréiʃər]	삭제, 소거	☐	spontaneous [spɑntéiniəs]	자발적인, 자연발생적인
☐	esteem [istíːm]	존경; 존경하다	☐	structure [strʌ́ktʃər]	구조, 건물
☐	fabric [fǽbrik]	직물, 구조	☐	surpass [sərpǽs]	능가하다
☐	fertile [fɔ́ːrtl]	비옥한, 다산의	☐	technological [tèknəlɑ́dʒikəl]	기술의, 과학기술의
☐	foster [fɔ́ːstər]	육성하다	☐	threat [θret]	위협, 협박
☐	function [fʌ́ŋkʃən]	기능, 역할; 작동하다	☐	transparent [trænspǽərənt]	투명한
☐	genuine [dʒénjuin]	진짜의, 순수한	☐	undetectable [ʌnditéktəbl]	탐지할 수 없는
☐	government [gʌ́vərnmənt]	정부, 통치	☐	universe [júːnəvəːrs]	우주, 전체
☐	habitat [hǽbitæt]	서식지, 거주지	☐	usage [júːsidʒ]	사용법, 용법
☐	herd [həːrd]	무리, 떼	☐	viable [váiəbl]	실행 가능한
☐	illuminated [ilúːmənèitid]	조명된, 밝혀진	☐	warrior [wɔ́ːriər]	전사

Day 02   TASK 1 실전 필수 어휘

음성 바로 듣기 ▶

☑ TASK 1을 위해 필수적으로 알아야 할 어휘들이므로, 확실히 암기해 둡니다.   🎧 DAY02

☐ abundant [əbʌ́ndənt]	풍부한, 많은
☐ analysis [ənǽləsis]	분석, 해석
☐ attire [ətáiər]	복장; 차려입히다
☐ behavior [bihéivjər]	행동, 행위
☐ bond [band]	유대, 결속; 결속하다
☐ burden [bə́:rdn]	짐, 부담
☐ cavity [kǽvəti]	충치, 구멍
☐ coherent [kouhíərənt]	일관성 있는, 논리적인
☐ compress [kəmprés]	압축하다, 압착하다
☐ contemporary [kəntémpərèri]	현대의, 동시대의
☐ creature [krí:tʃər]	생물, 피조물
☐ crust [krʌst]	(지구의) 지각, 껍질
☐ deliberate [dilíbərət, dilíbərèit]	의도적인; 숙고하다
☐ descent [disént]	하강, 혈통
☐ discrepancy [diskrépənsi]	불일치, 차이
☐ downplay [dàunpléi]	축소하다, 경시하다
☐ earthly [ə́:rθli]	지상의, 세속적인
☐ elaborate [ilǽbərət, ilǽbərèit]	정교한; 자세히 설명하다
☐ ensure [inʃúər]	보장하다, 확실히 하다
☐ erratic [irǽtik]	불규칙한, 변덕스러운
☐ evidence [évədəns]	증거, 근거
☐ facial [féiʃəl]	얼굴의
☐ flammable [flǽməbl]	인화성의, 가연성의
☐ foul [faul]	더러운
☐ fundamental [fʌ̀ndəméntl]	기본적인, 근본적인
☐ geography [dʒiá:grəfi]	지리학, 지리
☐ groundbreaking [gráundbrèikiŋ]	획기적인, 선구적인
☐ harsh [hɑ:rʃ]	가혹한, 거친
☐ hind [haind]	뒤의, 후방의
☐ illusion [ilú:ʒən]	착각, 환상
☐ impractical [imprǽktikəl]	비실용적인
☐ indifference [indífərəns]	무관심
☐ ingenuity [ìndʒənjú:əti]	독창성, 재주
☐ insulate [ínsəlèit]	절연하다, 격리하다
☐ intolerance [intá:lərəns]	편협함, 불관용
☐ investment [invéstmənt]	투자, 출자
☐ landlocked [lǽndlɑ:kt]	내륙의, 바다가 없는
☐ layout [léiaut]	배치, 레이아웃
☐ location [loukéiʃən]	위치, 장소
☐ mechanical [məkǽnikəl]	기계의, 기계적인
☐ moderately [má:dərətli]	적당히, 비교적
☐ opaque [oupéik]	불투명한, 불분명한
☐ performer [pərfɔ́:rmər]	공연자, 연주자
☐ preserve [prizə́:rv]	보존하다, 보호하다
☐ quest [kwest]	탐구, 추구
☐ resilience [rizíljəns]	회복력, 탄력성
☐ rural [rúərəl]	농촌의, 시골의
☐ significantly [signífikəntli]	상당히, 현저하게
☐ sophisticated [səfístəkèitid]	정교한, 세련된
☐ stem [stem]	줄기; 비롯되다
☐ substandard [sʌ̀bstǽndərd]	기준 미달의
☐ survival [sərváivəl]	생존
☐ tectonic [tektá:nik]	지각구조의, 구조지질학의
☐ thrive [θraiv]	번영하다
☐ transportation [trænspərtéiʃən]	교통, 운송
☐ uneven [ʌní:vn]	고르지 않은
☐ unofficial [ʌnəfíʃəl]	비공식적인
☐ vaccination [væksənéiʃən]	예방접종
☐ victim [víktim]	피해자
☐ weather [wéðər]	날씨, 기후; 풍화시키다

Day 03 — TASK 1 실전 필수 어휘

TASK 1을 위해 필수적으로 알아야 할 어휘들이므로, 확실히 암기해 둡니다.

DAY03

access [ǽkses]	접근, 출입; 접근하다
ape [eip]	유인원, 원숭이
audience [ɔ́ːdiəns]	청중, 관중
beneficial [bènəfíʃəl]	유익한, 도움이 되는
boost [buːst]	증진시키다, 촉진하다
burgeon [bə́ːrdʒən]	급성장하다, 급증하다
century [séntʃəri]	세기, 100년
communication [kəmjùːnəkéiʃən]	의사소통, 통신
concentration [kànsəntréiʃən]	집중, 농도
contribution [kɑntribjúːʃən]	기여, 공헌
crisis [kráisis]	위기
cue [kjuː]	신호; 신호하다
delicate [délikət]	섬세한, 민감한
destruct [distrʌ́kt]	파괴하다
disparity [dispǽrəti]	격차, 불평등
downstream [dàunstríːm]	하류의; 하류로
ecological [ìkəláːdʒikəl]	생태학의, 생태계의
elevated [éləvèitid]	높은, 고상한
entertainer [èntərtéinər]	연예인, 오락가
eruption [irʌ́pʃən]	분출, 폭발
evoke [ivóuk]	불러일으키다, 환기시키다
factor [fǽktər]	요인, 인수
flaw [flɔː]	결함, 흠
foundation [faundéiʃən]	기초, 토대
fungus [fʌ́ŋɡəs]	균류, 곰팡이
gesture [dʒéstʃər]	몸짓
groundwork [ɡráundwə̀ːrk]	기초작업
hazard [hǽzərd]	위험, 장애
hotspot [háːtspɑːt]	중심지
imaging [ímidʒiŋ]	영상화, 화상진찰
impression [impréʃən]	인상
indispensable [ìndispénsəbl]	없어서는 안 될
injustice [indʒʌ́stis]	불평등, 부당함
intact [intǽkt]	온전한, 손상되지 않은
intricate [íntrikət]	복잡한, 정교한
island [áilənd]	섬
landscape [lǽndskèip]	경관, 풍경
league [liːɡ]	리그, 동맹
logical [láːdʒikəl]	논리적인, 합리적인
mental [méntl]	정신의, 마음의
multiple [mʌ́ltipəl]	다수의, 여러 개의
option [ɑ́pʃən]	선택, 옵션
period [píəriəd]	기간, 시대
probability [prɑ̀bəbíləti]	확률, 개연성
rapidly [rǽpidli]	빠르게, 급속히
resource [risɔ́ːrs]	자원, 자료
scope [skoup]	범위, 영역
skew [skjuː]	왜곡하다; 비뚤어진
source [sɔːrs]	근원, 출처
stench [stentʃ]	악취
superficial [sùːpərfíʃəl]	표면적인
swath [swɑθ]	긴 띠 모양의 지역
tentative [téntətiv]	잠정적인
tolerate [tɑ́lərèit]	관용하다, 견디다
triad [tráiæd]	세 개가 한 벌로 된 것
unexpected [ʌ̀nikspéktid]	예상치 못한
unrealistic [ʌ̀nriːəlístik]	비현실적인
vaguely [véiɡli]	막연히
visual [víʒuəl]	시각의, 눈에 보이는
weight [weit]	무게, 중량

Day 04   TASK 1 실전 필수 어휘

✅ TASK 1을 위해 필수적으로 알아야 할 어휘들이므로, 확실히 암기해 둡니다.

🎧 DAY04

☐ adapt [ədǽpt]	적응하다, 적합하게 하다
☐ architectural [à:rkitéktʃərəl]	건축의, 건축학의
☐ authentic [ɔ:θéntik]	진짜의, 진정한
☐ bias [báiəs]	편견, 치우침
☐ boredom [bɔ́:rdəm]	지루함
☐ capture [kǽptʃər]	포획하다; 포획
☐ challenge [tʃǽlindʒ]	도전, 과제; 도전하다
☐ community [kəmjú:nəti]	공동체, 지역사회
☐ conclusion [kənklú:ʒən]	결론, 끝
☐ cornerstone [kɔ́:rnərstòun]	초석, 기초
☐ criticism [krítəsìzm]	비판, 비평
☐ cultural [kʌ́ltʃərəl]	문화의, 문화적인
☐ demise [dimáiz]	죽음, 종말
☐ devastating [dévəstèitiŋ]	파괴적인, 치명적인
☐ distinct [distíŋkt]	뚜렷한, 별개의
☐ drastically [drǽstikəli]	급격히, 대폭
☐ economy [ikɑ́:nəmi]	경제, 경제체제
☐ elongate [ilɔ́:ŋgeit]	길게 하다, 연장하다
☐ environment [inváiərənmənt]	환경, 주변
☐ escalate [éskəlèit]	확대하다, 악화시키다
☐ evolution [èvəlú:ʃən]	진화, 발전
☐ faint [feint]	희미한, 약한
☐ fluctuation [flʌ̀ktʃuéiʃən]	변동, 요동
☐ fragile [frǽdʒəl]	부서지기 쉬운, 연약한
☐ gap [gæp]	틈, 격차
☐ giant [dʒáiənt]	거인; 거대한
☐ groupthink [grú:pθìŋk]	집단사고
☐ health [helθ]	건강
☐ humidity [hju:mídəti]	습도, 습기
☐ imminent [ímənənt]	임박한
☐ improve [imprú:v]	개선하다, 향상시키다
☐ infectious [infékʃəs]	전염성의, 감염성의
☐ innovation [ìnəvéiʃən]	혁신, 새로운 것
☐ intelligent [intélədʒənt]	지능적인, 똑똑한
☐ intriguing [intrí:giŋ]	흥미로운, 호기심을 자극하는
☐ jewelry [dʒú:əlri]	보석, 장신구
☐ lapse [læps]	경과, 실수; 경과하다
☐ legacy [légəsi]	유산, 유물
☐ manageable [mǽnidʒəbl]	관리할 수 있는, 다루기 쉬운
☐ migration [maigréiʃən]	이동, 이주
☐ navigate [nǽvəgèit]	항해하다, 길을 찾다
☐ origin [ɔ́:rədʒin]	기원, 출발점
☐ pierce [piərs]	꿰뚫다
☐ process [prɑ́ses]	과정, 공정; 처리하다
☐ ratio [réiʃou]	비율
☐ responsible [rispɑ́nsəbl]	책임감 있는, 신뢰할 수 있는
☐ seasonal [sí:zənl]	계절의, 계절적인
☐ soar [sɔ:r]	치솟다, 급등하다
☐ spark [spɑ:rk]	불러일으키다; 불꽃, 계기
☐ strain [strein]	긴장; 긴장시키다
☐ superior [supíəriər]	우수한; 상관
☐ symbiotic [sìmbaiɑ́:tik]	공생의, 상호의존적인
☐ texture [tékstʃər]	질감
☐ tradition [trədíʃən]	전통, 관습
☐ unclear [ʌnklíər]	불분명한
☐ unintended [ʌninténdid]	의도하지 않은
☐ unrelated [ʌnriléitid]	관련 없는
☐ various [vɛ́əriəs]	다양한, 여러 가지의
☐ vital [váitl]	생명의, 중요한
☐ wildlife [wáildlaif]	야생동물

Day 05   TASK 1 실전 필수 어휘

☑ TASK 1을 위해 필수적으로 알아야 할 어휘들이므로, 확실히 암기해 둡니다.

☐	adore [ədɔ́ːr]	숭배하다, 매우 좋아하다	☐	inaction [inǽkʃən]	활동하지 않음, 비활성
☐	arduous [ɑ́ːrdʒuəs]	고된, 힘겨운	☐	infinitely [ínfənətli]	무한히, 끝없이
☐	aware [əwéər]	인식하고 있는, 알고 있는	☐	insight [ínsàit]	통찰력, 이해
☐	blend [blend]	섞다; 혼합물	☐	internal [intə́ːrnl]	내부의, 안쪽의
☐	boundary [báundəri]	경계, 한계	☐	intruder [intrúːdər]	침입자
☐	cartography [kɑːrtɑ́grəfi]	지도학, 지도 제작술	☐	labor [léibər]	노동, 일
☐	classical [klǽsikəl]	고전의, 전통적인	☐	latitude [lǽtətjùːd]	위도
☐	competition [kàmpətíʃən]	경쟁, 대회	☐	legal [líːgəl]	법적인, 합법적인
☐	conflict [kɑ́nflikt, kənflíkt]	갈등, 충돌; 충돌하다	☐	manual [mǽnjuəl]	손의, 인력을 요하는; 안내서
☐	cosmic [kɑ́zmik]	우주의, 거대한	☐	mimic [mímik]	흉내 내다; 모조의
☐	critique [kritíːk]	비평; 비평하다	☐	network [nétwəːrk]	네트워크, 망
☐	cycle [sáikl]	순환, 주기	☐	output [áutpùt]	산출량, 결과물
☐	democracy [dimɑ́ːkrəsi]	민주주의	☐	planet [plǽnit]	행성
☐	developer [divéləpər]	개발자	☐	professional [prəféʃənl]	직업의; 전문가
☐	diverse [dáivəːrs]	다양한, 여러 가지의	☐	recycle [riːsáikl]	재활용하다
☐	dough [dou]	반죽	☐	retreat [ritríːt]	후퇴하다; 후퇴, 은둔처
☐	ecosystem [ìːkousístəm]	생태계	☐	sedimentary [sèdəméntəri]	퇴적의, 침적의
☐	empathize [émpəθàiz]	공감하다	☐	soil [sɔil]	토양, 흙
☐	epic [épik]	서사시의, 웅장한; 서사시	☐	specific [spisífik]	구체적인, 특정한
☐	essential [isénʃəl]	필수적인, 본질적인	☐	strategy [strǽtədʒi]	전략, 계획
☐	examine [igzǽmin]	조사하다, 검토하다	☐	supposedly [səpóuzidli]	소문에 따르면, 겉보기에
☐	feasibility [fìːzəbíləti]	실행 가능성, 실현 가능성	☐	sync [siŋk]	동조, 동기화; 맞추다
☐	formation [fɔːrméiʃən]	형성, 대형(배열)	☐	thematic [θimǽtik]	주제의, 주제와 관련된
☐	fragment [frǽgmənt]	조각; 조각내다	☐	trait [treit]	특성, 특징
☐	gear [giər]	장비, 기어; 준비하다	☐	underground [ʌ́ndərgraund]	지하의; 지하
☐	glimpse [glimps]	흘끗 봄, 일별; 흘끗 보다	☐	unintentional [əninténʃənəl]	고의가 아닌
☐	gutter [gʌ́tər]	하수구, 도랑	☐	unsettled [ʌnsétld]	불안정한
☐	heartbeat [hɑ́ːrtbiːt]	심장박동	☐	vary [vɛ́əri]	다양하다, 변화하다
☐	hypothesis [haipɑ́ːθəsis]	가설	☐	vivid [vívid]	생생한
☐	impact [ímpækt, impǽkt]	영향, 충격; 영향을 주다	☐	worldwide [wə́ːrldwaid]	전세계의; 전세계적으로

Day 06 TASK 1 실전 필수 어휘

☑ TASK 1을 위해 필수적으로 알아야 할 어휘들이므로, 확실히 암기해 둡니다.

☐ altitude [ǽltətjùːd]	고도, 높이	
☐ array [əréi]	배열; 배열하다	
☐ balance [bǽləns]	균형, 잔액; 균형잡다	
☐ blizzard [blízərd]	눈보라	
☐ breathing [bríːðiŋ]	호흡, 숨쉬기	
☐ casual [kǽʒuəl]	캐주얼한, 비공식적인	
☐ climate [kláimit]	기후, 풍토	
☐ complex [kəmpléks, kάmpleks]	복잡한; 복합체	
☐ consciousness [kάnʃəsnis]	의식, 자각	
☐ craft [kræft]	공예, 기술; 제작하다	
☐ crucial [krúːʃəl]	중요한, 결정적인	
☐ debunk [dibʌ́ŋk]	허구를 밝히다, 폭로하다	
☐ dense [dens]	밀도가 높은, 조밀한	
☐ diagnosis [dàiəgnóusis]	진단	
☐ divine [diváin]	신의, 신성한	
☐ dweller [dwélər]	거주자	
☐ education [èdʒukéiʃən]	교육, 학습	
☐ engage [ingéidʒ]	참여하다, 관여하다	
☐ era [íərə]	시대, 시기	
☐ establishment [istǽbliʃmənt]	설립, 확립, 기관	
☐ excessive [iksésiv]	과도한, 지나친	
☐ feat [fiːt]	위업, 기량	
☐ fossil [fάːsəl]	화석	
☐ framework [fréimwə̀rk]	틀, 체계	
☐ genius [dʒíːnjəs]	천재	
☐ glow [glou]	빛나다; 빛, 광채	
☐ habitable [hǽbitəbl]	살 수 있는, 거주 가능한	
☐ heightened [háitnd]	고조된, 증가된	
☐ identify [aidéntəfài]	식별하다, 확인하다	
☐ impediment [impédəmənt]	장애, 방해물	
☐ indelible [indéləbl]	지울 수 없는	
☐ information [ìnfərméiʃən]	정보	
☐ inspiration [ìnspəréiʃən]	영감, 감화	
☐ interpersonal [ìntərpə́ːrsənəl]	대인관계의, 사람 간의	
☐ intuitive [intjúːətiv]	직관적인	
☐ laden [léidn]	잔뜩 실은, 가득한	
☐ lava [lάːvə]	용암	
☐ lifestyle [láifstail]	생활양식	
☐ marine [məríːn]	해양의, 바다의	
☐ mission [míʃən]	임무, 사명	
☐ occasional [əkéiʒənəl]	가끔의, 우연한	
☐ outrage [áutreidʒ]	격분, 잔학행위; 격분시키다	
☐ plate [pleit]	판, 접시	
☐ profoundly [prəfáundli]	깊이, 심각하게	
☐ region [ríːdʒən]	지역, 지방	
☐ ritualistic [rìtʃuəlístik]	의식의, 의례적인	
☐ shift [ʃift]	이동하다; 변화, 교대	
☐ solid [sάlid]	고체의, 견고한; 고체	
☐ spectator [spékteitər]	관중	
☐ strikingly [stráikiŋli]	현저하게	
☐ suppress [səprés]	억압하다	
☐ task [tæsk]	과제, 업무	
☐ theory [θíːəri]	이론, 학설	
☐ transitional [trænzíʃənəl]	과도기의, 변화하는	
☐ underwater [ʌ̀ndərwɔ́ːtər]	수중의; 물속에서	
☐ unique [juːníːk]	독특한, 유일한	
☐ unwritten [ʌnrítn]	기록되지 않은	
☐ vast [væst]	광대한, 거대한	
☐ vulnerable [vʌ́lnərəbl]	취약한	
☐ yeast [jiːst]	효모	

Day 07 — TASK 2 실전 필수 어휘

☑ TASK 2를 위해 필수적으로 알아야 할 어휘들이므로, 확실히 암기해 둡니다. 🎧 DAY07

☐ accept [əksépt]	받아들이다, 수락하다		☐ link [liŋk]	연결; 연결하다
☐ adjustment [ədʒʌ́stmənt]	조정, 적응		☐ maximum [mǽksəməm]	최댓값; 최대의
☐ allocation [æ̀ləkéiʃən]	할당, 배분		☐ mindful [máindfəl]	주의 깊은, 염두에 두는
☐ appointment [əpɔ́intmənt]	약속, 임명		☐ objective [əbdʒéktiv]	목표; 객관적인
☐ artisan [ɑ́ːrtəzən]	장인, 기능공		☐ opportunity [ɑ̀pərtjúːnəti]	기회
☐ auditorium [ɔ̀ːditɔ́ːriəm]	강당, 청중석		☐ packet [pǽkit]	소포
☐ beautiful [bjúːtəfəl]	아름다운		☐ pastry [péistri]	페이스트리, 가루 반죽 과자
☐ booth [buːθ]	부스, (칸막이가 된) 작은 공간		☐ photography [fətɑ́grəfi]	사진술
☐ broken [bróukən]	부서진, 고장난		☐ post [poust]	우편, 게시물; 게시하다
☐ certificate [sərtífikət]	증명서, 자격증		☐ preparation [prèpəréiʃən]	준비
☐ chorus [kɔ́ːrəs]	합창단, 후렴		☐ procedure [prəsíːdʒər]	절차, 과정
☐ code [koud]	암호, 규칙		☐ quarter [kwɔ́ːrtər]	분기, 4분의 1
☐ compatibility [kəmpæ̀təbíləti]	호환성, 양립성		☐ recommendation [rèkəmendéiʃən]	추천
☐ confidential [kɑ̀nfədénʃəl]	기밀의, 비밀의		☐ reliability [rilàiəbíləti]	신뢰성
☐ conversation [kɑ̀ːnvərséiʃən]	대화, 회화		☐ renowned [rináund]	유명한, 저명한
☐ correspondence [kɔ̀ːrəspɑ́ːndəns]	통신, 서신		☐ resident [rézədənt]	거주자; 거주하는
☐ dental [déntl]	치과의, 치아의		☐ seat [siːt]	좌석; 앉히다
☐ discount [dískaunt]	할인; 할인하다		☐ server [sə́ːrvər]	서버, 웨이터
☐ drill [dril]	훈련, 드릴; 훈련하다		☐ shuttle [ʃʌ́tl]	셔틀; 왕복하다
☐ enhancement [inhǽnsmənt]	향상, 개선		☐ smock [smɑːk]	(화가 등의) 작업복
☐ exchange [ikstʃéindʒ]	교환; 교환하다		☐ speaker [spíːkər]	연사, 스피커
☐ exploration [èkspləréiʃən]	탐험, 탐사		☐ station [stéiʃən]	철도역, 방송국
☐ facility [fəsíləti]	시설, 설비		☐ subscription [səbskrípʃən]	구독
☐ furnished [fə́ːrniʃt]	가구가 비치된		☐ tenant [ténənt]	세입자
☐ guest [gest]	손님		☐ torrential [tɔːrénʃəl]	격류의, 폭우의
☐ heating [híːtiŋ]	난방		☐ unavailable [ʌ̀nəvéiləbl]	이용할 수 없는
☐ inconvenience [ìnkənvíːnjəns]	불편		☐ upper [ʌ́pər]	위쪽의, 상부의
☐ inquiry [ínkwəri]	문의, 조사		☐ vendor [véndər]	판매자, 공급업체
☐ invitation [ìnvitéiʃən]	초대		☐ volume [vɑ́ːljuːm]	볼륨, 양
☐ late [leit]	늦은; 늦게		☐ wastewater [wéistwɔ̀ːtər]	폐수

Day 08   TASK 2 실전 필수 어휘

■ TASK 2를 위해 필수적으로 알아야 할 어휘들이므로, 확실히 암기해 둡니다.   🎧 DAY08

☐ accommodation [əkàmədéiʃən]	숙박시설, 편의시설	
☐ admission [ədmíʃən]	입학, 입장	
☐ announce [ənáuns]	발표하다, 알리다	
☐ appreciate [əpríːʃièit]	감사하다, 인정하다	
☐ assistance [əsístəns]	도움, 지원	
☐ authorization [ɔ̀ːθərìzéiʃən]	권한, 인가	
☐ beverage [bévəridʒ]	음료	
☐ bottle [bάːtl]	병	
☐ cabin [kǽbin]	오두막, 선실	
☐ charge [tʃɑːrdʒ]	요금, 책임; 청구하다	
☐ citywide [sítiwàid]	시 전체의	
☐ collaborative [kəlǽbərèitiv]	협력적인, 공동의	
☐ completion [kəmplíːʃən]	완성, 완료	
☐ confirmation [kὰnfərméiʃən]	확인, 승인	
☐ cooking [kúkiŋ]	요리	
☐ coworker [kóuwə̀ːrkər]	동료	
☐ department [dipάːrtmənt]	부서, 학과	
☐ discussion [diskʌ́ʃən]	토론, 논의	
☐ due [djuː]	기한이 된, 마땅한	
☐ entrepreneur [ὰːntrəprənə́ːr]	기업가	
☐ excitement [iksáitmənt]	흥분, 자극	
☐ extension [iksténʃən]	연장, 확장	
☐ fascinating [fǽsənèitiŋ]	매혹적인, 흥미로운	
☐ gala [géilə]	축제, 경축 행사	
☐ guideline [gáidlàin]	지침	
☐ honor [άnər]	명예; 존경하다	
☐ indoor [índɔ̀ːr]	실내의	
☐ inspection [inspékʃən]	검사, 점검	
☐ involvement [invάːlvmənt]	관여, 참여	
☐ launch [lɔːntʃ]	출시하다; 출시	
☐ list [list]	목록; 나열하다	
☐ maybe [méibiː]	아마도	
☐ modification [mὰːdəfikéiʃən]	수정, 변경	
☐ offer [ɔ́ːfər]	제공하다; 제안	
☐ order [ɔ́ːrdər]	주문, 순서; 주문하다	
☐ painter [péintər]	화가, 페인트공	
☐ patron [péitrən]	후원자, 단골손님	
☐ picnic [píknik]	소풍, 피크닉	
☐ poster [póustər]	포스터	
☐ presentation [prìːzentéiʃən]	발표, 제시	
☐ program [próugræm]	프로그램; 프로그래밍하다	
☐ question [kwéstʃən]	질문; 질문하다	
☐ reference [réfərəns]	참고; 참조하다	
☐ remark [rimάːrk]	발언; 말하다	
☐ report [ripɔ́ːrt]	보고서; 보고하다	
☐ restriction [ristríkʃən]	제한	
☐ secure [sikjúər]	안전한; 확보하다	
☐ serving [sə́ːrviŋ]	1인분, 접대	
☐ sight [sait]	시야, 광경	
☐ smooth [smuːð]	부드러운; 부드럽게 하다	
☐ spot [spɑːt]	지점, 얼룩; 발견하다	
☐ stay [stei]	머물다; 체류	
☐ substitution [sʌ̀bstətjúːʃən]	대체	
☐ textile [tékstail]	직물; 직물의	
☐ tourism [túərizm]	관광업	
☐ understanding [ʌ̀ndərstǽndiŋ]	이해	
☐ upscale [ʌ́pskèil]	고급의	
☐ vessel [vésəl]	그릇, 선박	
☐ voluntary [vάːləntèri]	자발적인, 자원 봉사로 하는	
☐ webinar [wébinɑːr]	웨비나 (온라인 세미나)	

Day 09   TASK 2 실전 필수 어휘

☑ TASK 2를 위해 필수적으로 알아야 할 어휘들이므로, 확실히 암기해 둡니다.

🎧 DAY09

☐ accomplishment [əkámpliʃmənt]	성취, 업적	☐ local [lóukəl]	지역의, 현지의
☐ advance [ædvǽns]	앞서다, 발전하다; 진보	☐ meal [miːl]	식사
☐ annual [ǽnjuəl]	연간의, 매년의	☐ nominal [námənəl]	명목상의, 소액의
☐ approach [əpróutʃ]	접근하다; 접근법	☐ office [ɔ́ːfis]	사무실
☐ associate [əsóusièit]	동료; 연관시키다	☐ outdoor [áutdɔ̀ːr]	야외의
☐ automobile [ɔ̀ːtəməbíːl]	자동차	☐ paperwork [péipərwə̀ːrk]	서류작업
☐ billing [bíliŋ]	청구, 요금 부과	☐ payment [péimənt]	지불, 결제
☐ branch [bræntʃ]	가지, 지점	☐ platform [plǽtfɔːrm]	플랫폼, 연단
☐ cancellation [kænsəléiʃən]	취소	☐ preference [préfərəns]	선호
☐ charity [tʃǽrəti]	자선단체, 자선	☐ presenter [prizéntər]	발표자
☐ class [klæs]	수업, 계급	☐ project [prάːdʒekt, prədʒékt]	프로젝트; 투사하다
☐ collect [kəlékt]	수집하다, 모으다	☐ quiet [kwáiət]	조용한; 조용함
☐ complimentary [kàːmpləméntəri]	무료의, 칭찬의	☐ refreshment [rifréʃmənt]	다과, 음료수
☐ console [kənsóul]	위로하다	☐ reminder [rimáindər]	알림, 상기시키는 것
☐ coordinator [kouɔ́ːrdənèitər]	조정자, 코디네이터	☐ request [rikwést]	요청; 요청하다
☐ date [deit]	날짜	☐ routine [ruːtíːn]	일상; 일상적인
☐ destination [dèstənéiʃən]	목적지	☐ security [sikjúərəti]	보안, 안전
☐ document [dάkjumənt]	문서; 기록하다	☐ session [séʃən]	회기, 활동 시간
☐ eager [íːgər]	열망하는, 간절한	☐ sign [sain]	표지판; 서명하다
☐ equipment [ikwípmənt]	장비, 설비	☐ software [sɔ́ftwèər]	소프트웨어
☐ exercise [éksərsàiz]	운동, 연습; 운동하다	☐ square [skwɛər]	광장, 정사각형; 정사각형의
☐ extensive [iksténsiv]	광범위한, 대규모의	☐ storage [stɔ́ːridʒ]	저장
☐ feature [fíːtʃər]	특징; 특징으로 하다	☐ supervisor [súːpərvàizər]	감독자
☐ garbage [gάːrbidʒ]	쓰레기	☐ thorough [θə́ːrou]	철저한
☐ happen [hǽpən]	일어나다, 발생하다	☐ tracking [trǽkiŋ]	추적
☐ hour [auər]	시간	☐ unexpectedly [ʌ̀nikspéktidli]	예상치 못하게
☐ inform [infɔ́ːrm]	알리다, 통지하다	☐ utensil [juːténsəl]	도구, 식기
☐ installation [instəléiʃən]	설치	☐ vibrant [váibrənt]	활기찬
☐ item [áitəm]	항목, 품목	☐ volunteer [vὰːləntíər]	자원봉사자; 자원봉사하다
☐ lease [liːs]	임대; 임대하다	☐ wellness [wélnis]	건강, 건강 관리

Day 10   TASK 2 실전 필수 어휘

TASK 2를 위해 필수적으로 알아야 할 어휘들이므로, 확실히 암기해 둡니다.

🎧 DAY10

☐ account [əkáunt]	계정, 설명; 설명하다	
☐ affiliate [əfíliət, əfílièit]	계열사; 제휴하다	
☐ apartment [əpáːrtmənt]	아파트, 방	
☐ apron [éiprən]	앞치마	
☐ attach [ətǽtʃ]	첨부하다, 붙이다	
☐ availability [əvèiləbíləti]	이용가능성	
☐ biweekly [baiwíːkli]	격주의; 격주로	
☐ breakfast [brékfəst]	아침식사	
☐ career [kəríər]	경력, 직업	
☐ check [tʃek]	확인, 수표; 확인하다	
☐ classroom [klǽsruːm]	교실	
☐ comment [káment]	의견, 논평; 논평하다	
☐ comprehensive [kàmprihénsiv]	포괄적인, 종합적인	
☐ constructive [kənstrʌ́ktiv]	건설적인	
☐ copy [káːpi]	사본; 복사하다	
☐ deadline [dédlàin]	마감일	
☐ device [diváis]	장치, 기구	
☐ documentation [dàːkjumentéiʃən]	문서화, 서류	
☐ emergency [imə́ːrdʒənsi]	비상사태, 응급상황	
☐ evacuation [ivækjuéiʃən]	대피, 철수	
☐ expenditure [ikspénditʃər]	지출, 경비	
☐ external [ekstə́ːrnəl]	외부의, 외적인	
☐ fee [fiː]	수수료, 요금	
☐ glad [glæd]	기쁜, 즐거운	
☐ headquarters [hédkwɔ̀ːrtərz]	본부	
☐ iconic [aikáːnik]	상징적인	
☐ infringe [infríndʒ]	침해하다	
☐ intensive [inténsiv]	집중적인, 강도 높은	
☐ keynote [kíːnòut]	(연설 등의) 기조	
☐ least [liːst]	최소의; 최소로	

☐ lodge [lɑdʒ]	오두막; 머물다
☐ meeting [míːtiŋ]	회의, 만남
☐ notice [nóutis]	공지; 알아차리다
☐ open [óupən]	열린; 열다
☐ overview [óuvərvjùː]	개요, 전망
☐ parking [páːrkiŋ]	주차
☐ perfect [pə́ːrfikt, pərfékt]	완벽한; 완벽하게 하다
☐ playground [pléigràund]	놀이터
☐ preliminary [prilímənèri]	예비의, 초기의
☐ preside [prizáid]	주재하다, 사회를 보다
☐ prominently [práːmənəntli]	현저히, 눈에 띄게
☐ reading [ríːdiŋ]	읽기, 독서
☐ refund [ríːfʌnd]	환불; 환불하다
☐ remit [rimít]	송금하다
☐ requirement [rikwáiərmənt]	요구사항
☐ saving [séiviŋ]	절약, 저축
☐ segment [ségmənt]	부분, 구간
☐ setup [sétʌp]	설정, 설치
☐ sincerely [sinsíərli]	진심으로
☐ soothe [suːð]	달래다, 진정시키다
☐ staff [stæf]	직원
☐ streamline [stríːmlàin]	능률화하다, 간소화하다
☐ survey [sə́ːrvei]	조사; 조사하다
☐ tier [tir]	계층, 등급
☐ traffic [trǽfik]	교통
☐ university [jùːnəvə́ːrsəti]	대학교
☐ vacant [véikənt]	비어있는, 공석의
☐ viewer [vjúːər]	시청자, 관람자
☐ voucher [váutʃər]	교환권, 증빙서류
☐ workbook [wə́ːrkbuk]	연습문제집

Day 11 　　TASK 2 실전 필수 어휘

✅ TASK 2를 위해 필수적으로 알아야 할 어휘들이므로, 확실히 암기해 둡니다.　🎧 DAY11

□ achievement [ətʃíːvmənt]	성취, 달성
□ agenda [ədʒéndə]	의제, 일정
□ apologize [əpάlədʒàiz]	사과하다
□ arrangement [əréindʒmənt]	배치, 준비
□ attendee [ətèndíː]	참석자
□ available [əvéiləbl]	이용 가능한, 구할 수 있는
□ board [bɔːrd]	판자, 이사회; 탑승하다
□ breakthrough [bréikθrùː]	돌파구, 혁신
□ celebrate [séləbrèit]	축하하다, 기념하다
□ checking [tʃékiŋ]	확인, 점검
□ cleanup [klíːnʌ̀p]	청소, 정화
□ committee [kəmíti]	위원회
□ conduct [kəndʌ́kt, kʌ́ndʌkt]	수행하다; 행동
□ content [kάntent, kəntént]	내용; 만족하는
□ cordial [kɔ́ːrdʒəl]	진심어린, 따뜻한
□ dedicated [dédikèitid]	헌신적인, 전용의
□ dietary [dáiətèri]	식이의, 식단의
□ downtown [dàuntáun]	시내; 시내의
□ emotional [imóuʃənəl]	감정적인
□ evaluation [ivæ̀ljuéiʃən]	평가, 사정
□ expensive [ikspénsiv]	비싼
□ extra [ékstrə]	추가의; 여분
□ fellowship [félouʃìp]	친교, 장학금
□ graduate [grǽdʒuət, grǽdʒuèit]	졸업생; 졸업하다
□ healthcare [hélθkèər]	의료, 건강관리
□ inbox [inbὰːks]	수신함
□ ingredient [ingríːdiənt]	재료, 성분
□ interview [íntərvjùː]	면접; 면접하다
□ language [lǽŋgwidʒ]	언어
□ liable [láiəbl]	책임이 있는
□ magazine [mæ̀gəzíːn]	잡지
□ membership [mémbərʃìp]	회원자격, 회원 수
□ notification [nòutəfikéiʃən]	알림, 통지
□ opening [óupəniŋ]	개방, 개시, 빈자리
□ owner [óunər]	소유자
□ participant [pɑːrtísəpənt]	참가자
□ perform [pərfɔ́ːrm]	수행하다, 공연하다
□ playlist [pléilist]	재생목록
□ premiere [primíər]	초연; 초연하다
□ preview [príːvjùː]	미리보기; 미리 보다
□ provider [prəváidər]	공급자
□ receive [risíːv]	받다
□ regard [rigάːrd]	관심; 간주하다
□ remote [rimóut]	원격의, 멀리 떨어진
□ reschedule [rìːskédʒuːl]	일정을 변경하다
□ scenery [síːnəri]	경치, 풍경
□ selection [silékʃən]	선택, 선발
□ shareholder [ʃέərhòuldər]	주주
□ slot [slάːt]	자리, 시간대
□ souvenir [sùːvəníər]	기념품
□ stairwell [stέərwèl]	계단통 (계단이 나 있는 수직 공간)
□ street [stríːt]	거리
□ swap [swάːp]	교환하다; 교환
□ timeline [táimlàin]	연대표
□ treat [tríːt]	대우하다; 대접
□ untapped [ʌ̀ntǽpt]	개발되지 않은
□ vegan [víːgən]	비건 (엄격 채식주의자)
□ viewpoint [vjúːpɔint]	관점
□ warehouse [wέərhàus]	창고
□ workout [wə́ːrkàut]	운동

Day 12 — TASK 2 실전 필수 어휘

☑ TASK 2를 위해 필수적으로 알아야 할 어휘들이므로, 확실히 암기해 둡니다.

☐ acquaint [əkwéint]	익숙하게 하다, 소개하다		☐ maintenance [méintənəns]	유지보수, 관리
☐ ahead [əhéd]	앞에, 미리		☐ milestone [máilstòun]	이정표, 중요한 단계
☐ appetizer [ǽpitàizər]	애피타이저, 전채요리		☐ notify [nóutəfài]	통지하다, 알리다
☐ arrival [əráivəl]	도착		☐ operate [ápərèit]	운영하다, 작동시키다
☐ audit [ɔ́:dit]	(회계) 감사; (회계를) 감사하다		☐ package [pǽkidʒ]	포장된 것, 소포; 포장하다
☐ basis [béisis]	기초, 근거		☐ participation [pɑːrtìsəpéiʃən]	참여
☐ booking [búkiŋ]	예약		☐ permit [pərmít, pə́:rmit]	허가하다; 허가증
☐ brochure [brouʃúər]	안내책자		☐ ponder [pɑ́:ndər]	생각하다, 숙고하다
☐ celebration [sèləbréiʃən]	축하, 기념		☐ premium [prí:miəm]	상금, 할증금; 고급의
☐ chef [ʃef]	요리사		☐ prior [práiər]	이전의; 미리
☐ client [kláiənt]	고객, 의뢰인		☐ purchase [pə́:rtʃəs]	구매하다; 구매
☐ company [kʌ́mpəni]	회사, 방문객		☐ recipient [risípiənt]	수신자, 수혜자
☐ conference [kɑ́nfərəns]	회의, 학술대회		☐ registration [rèdʒistréiʃən]	등록
☐ contributor [kəntríbjutər]	기여자, 공헌자		☐ renew [rinjú:]	갱신하다, 새롭게 하다
☐ corner [kɔ́:rnər]	모퉁이, 구석		☐ reservation [rèzərvéiʃən]	예약
☐ demonstration [dèmənstréiʃən]	시연, 증명		☐ scheduling [skédʒu:liŋ]	일정 계획
☐ dining [dáiniŋ]	식사		☐ serene [sərí:n]	평온한, 고요한
☐ draft [dræft]	초안; 작성하다		☐ shipment [ʃípmənt]	배송
☐ endorse [indɔ́:rs]	지지하다, 보증하다		☐ smell [smel]	냄새; 냄새 맡다
☐ exam [igzǽm]	시험		☐ spacious [spéiʃəs]	넓은, 여유있는
☐ expert [ékspə:rt]	전문가; 전문의		☐ stall [stɔ:l]	가판대; 지연시키다
☐ facilitator [fəsílətèitər]	진행자, 조력자		☐ submission [səbmíʃən]	제출
☐ fitness [fítnis]	건강, 적합성		☐ technician [tekníʃən]	기술자
☐ grand [grænd]	웅장한, 거대한		☐ timing [táimiŋ]	타이밍, 시기
☐ hear [hiər]	듣다		☐ trendy [tréndi]	유행하는
☐ include [inklú:d]	포함하다		☐ upbeat [ʌ́pbì:t]	낙관적인
☐ inhabitant [inhǽbətənt]	거주자, 주민		☐ vehicle [ví:ikl]	차량, 운송수단
☐ inventory [ínvəntɔ̀:ri]	재고, 목록		☐ visit [vízit]	방문하다; 방문
☐ laptop [lǽptɑ:p]	노트북		☐ wary [wɛ́əri]	조심하는
☐ lighting [láitiŋ]	조명		☐ workplace [wə́rkplèis]	직장

Day 13 — TASK 3 실전 필수 어휘

TASK 3를 위해 필수적으로 알아야 할 어휘들이므로, 확실히 암기해 둡니다.

🎧 DAY13

□ aberrant [əbérənt]	일탈한, 도리를 벗어난
□ acidification [əsìdəfikéiʃən]	산성화
□ aerial [ɛ́əriəl]	공중의, 항공의
□ ailment [éilmənt]	질병, 불편함
□ allude [əlúːd]	암시하다, 언급하다
□ angular [ǽŋgjulər]	각진, 각도의
□ aqueduct [ǽkwədʌkt]	수도교, 도수로
□ astonishing [əstániʃiŋ]	놀라운
□ awakening [əwéikəniŋ]	각성, 깨어남
□ brine [brain]	염수
□ carcass [káːrkəs]	사체
□ civilization [sìvəlaizéiʃən]	문명, 문화
□ collectivist [kəléktivìst]	집단주의자; 집단주의의
□ compel [kəmpél]	강요하다, ~하게 만들다
□ congestion [kəndʒéstʃən]	혼잡, 막힘
□ contraction [kəntrǽkʃən]	수축, 단축
□ counterintuitive [kàuntərintjúːitiv]	직관에 반하는
□ decomposer [dìːkəmpóuzər]	분해자
□ demographic [dèməgrǽfik]	인구통계학의; 인구
□ detrimental [dètrəméntl]	해로운
□ dissociate [disóuʃièit]	분리하다, 분리되다
□ electronic [ìlektrάːnik]	전자의
□ equitable [ékwətəbl]	공정한, 공평한
□ expedite [ékspədàit]	신속히 처리하다, 촉진하다
□ fertility [fərtíləti]	생식력, 비옥함
□ flourish [fləˊːriʃ]	번성하다; 번영, 현란한 동작
□ frailty [fréilti]	허약함, 약점
□ hallucination [həlùːsənéiʃən]	환각
□ heritage [héritidʒ]	유산
□ hospitable [háːspitəbl]	환대하는, 친절한, 쾌적한

□ imbalance [imbǽləns]	불균형
□ impulse [ímpʌls]	충동
□ inheritance [inhérətəns]	상속, 유산
□ intellectual [ìntəléktʃuəl]	지적인; 지식인
□ irritability [ìrətəbíləti]	과민성, 예민함
□ lineage [líniidʒ]	혈통, 계보
□ malfunction [mælfʌ́ŋkʃən]	오작동; 오작동하다
□ marital [mǽrətl]	결혼의, 부부의
□ meadow [médou]	초원
□ metabolism [mətǽbəlìzm]	신진대사
□ molecule [máːləkjùːl]	분자
□ newfound [nùːfáund]	새로이 얻은
□ perception [pərsépʃən]	지각, 인식
□ pesticide [péstisàid]	살충제
□ physiological [fìziəlάdʒikəl]	생리학적인
□ premature [prìːmətʃúər]	시기상조의, 조기의
□ prominent [prάmənənt]	돌출한, 유명한
□ rally [rǽli]	집회; 집결하다
□ reestablish [rìːistǽbliʃ]	재설립하다, 회복시키다
□ repel [ripél]	물리치다, 격퇴하다
□ residual [rizídʒuəl]	잔여의
□ ritual [rítʃuəl]	의식; 의식의
□ sanctuary [sǽŋktʃuèri]	보호구역, 성소, 피난처
□ sedentary [sédntèri]	앉아서 하는, 정착성의
□ shrub [ʃrʌb]	관목
□ solitary [sάlətèri]	고독한, 혼자의
□ starvation [stɑːrvéiʃən]	굶주림
□ teeming [tíːmiŋ]	바글거리는, 풍부한
□ tragedy [trǽdʒədi]	비극
□ tumor [tjúːmər]	종양

Day 14 — TASK 3 실전 필수 어휘

✅ TASK 3를 위해 필수적으로 알아야 할 어휘들이므로, 확실히 암기해 둡니다.

🎧 DAY14

☐ abrasion [əbréiʒən]	마모, 찰과상		☐ interject [ìntərdʒékt]	(말을) 끼어들다
☐ aesthetic [esθétik]	미적인; 미학		☐ isolation [àisəléiʃən]	고립, 격리
☐ aloft [əlɔ́ːft]	공중에, 높이		☐ landfall [lǽndfɔ̀l]	상륙
☐ anthology [ænθάːlədʒi]	선집, 모음집		☐ linear [líniər]	직선의, 선형의
☐ architecture [άːrkitèktʃər]	건축학, 건축		☐ longevity [lɑːndʒévəti]	장수, 수명
☐ astounding [əstáundiŋ]	놀라운		☐ mammal [mǽməl]	포유류
☐ awareness [əwέərnis]	인식, 자각		☐ marketer [mάːrkitər]	마케터
☐ caregiver [kέərgìvər]	돌봄제공자, 간병인		☐ meager [míːgər]	빈약한, 부족한
☐ clan [klæn]	씨족, 가문		☐ misfiring [mìsfáiəriŋ]	점화 불량, 실패
☐ collision [kəlíʒən]	충돌		☐ monument [mάːnjumənt]	기념물
☐ congregate [kάːŋgrigèit]	모이다, 집합하다		☐ niche [nitʃ]	적소, 틈새
☐ convergence [kənvə́ːrdʒəns]	수렴, 집중		☐ parsimonious [pὰːrsəmóuniəs]	인색한
☐ counterpart [káuntərpὰːrt]	상대방, 대응물		☐ perfection [pərfékʃən]	완전, 완벽
☐ cult [kʌlt]	종파, 숭배		☐ petition [pətíʃən]	청원; 청원하다
☐ depict [dipíkt]	묘사하다, 그리다		☐ pioneer [pàiəníər]	개척자; 개척하다
☐ disdain [disdéin]	경멸; 경멸하다		☐ policymaker [pάːləsimèikər]	정책입안자
☐ dissolve [dizάːlv]	용해하다, 해산하다		☐ precipitation [prisìpətéiʃən]	강수량, 침전
☐ ensue [insúː]	뒤따르다, 결과로 일어나다		☐ preservative [prizə́ːrvətiv]	방부제; 보존하는
☐ ergonomic [ə̀ːrgənάːmik]	인체공학의		☐ prone [proun]	경향이 있는, 엎드린
☐ expedition [èkspədíʃən]	탐험, 원정, 신속		☐ ramification [ræməfikéiʃən]	파생 결과, 파문
☐ fertilizer [fə́ːrtəlàizər]	비료		☐ refinement [riːfáinmənt]	정제, 세련, 개선
☐ flourishing [flə́ːriʃiŋ]	번영하는, 융성한		☐ repetition [rèpətíʃən]	반복
☐ freshwater [fréʃwɔ̀ːtər]	민물; 민물의		☐ resurface [rìːsə́ːrfis]	다시 나타나다
☐ gentrification [dʒèntrəfikéiʃən]	젠트리피케이션		☐ robust [roubʌ́st]	강건한, 견고한
☐ haphazard [hæphǽzərd]	되는대로의; 무계획적으로		☐ sanitation [sæ̀nitéiʃən]	위생, 환경미화
☐ heuristic [hjuərístik]	학생 스스로 발견하게 하는		☐ segregation [sègrigéiʃən]	분리, 격리
☐ household [háushòuld]	가정; 가정의		☐ sovereign [sάvərən]	주권의; 군주
☐ imperative [impérətiv]	필수적인; 명령		☐ suburb [sʌ́bəːrb]	교외
☐ incongruity [ìnkəŋgrúːəti]	부조화		☐ transfer [trænsfə́ːr, trǽnsfər]	이동시키다; 이동
☐ inhibit [inhíbit]	억제하다, 막다		☐ undeniably [ʌ̀ndináiəbli]	부인할 수 없이

Day 15 — TASK 3 실전 필수 어휘

TASK 3를 위해 필수적으로 알아야 할 어휘들이므로, 확실히 암기해 둡니다.

DAY15

- absorbent [æbsɔ́ːrbənt] 흡수성의; 흡수제
- activist [ǽktəvist] 활동가
- affluent [ǽfluənt] 부유한, 풍부한
- amenity [əménəti] 편의시설, 쾌적함
- anthropomorphism [æ̀nθrəpəmɔ́ːrfizm] 의인법, 의인화
- arid [ǽrid] 건조한, 불모의
- asylum [əsáiləm] 피난처, 보호 시설, 망명
- biodiversity [bàioudivə́ːrsəti] 생물다양성
- buildup [bíldʌp] 축적, 증강
- chromosome [króuməsòum] 염색체
- clot [klɑːt] 응고, 덩어리; 응고하다
- colossal [kəlásəl] 거대한, 엄청난
- competitor [kəmpétətər] 경쟁자
- connectivity [kɑ̀ːnektívəti] 연결성
- convey [kənvéi] 전달하다, 운반하다
- counterweight [káuntərwèit] 균형추
- cultivation [kʌ̀ltəvéiʃən] 경작, 양성
- deduce [didjúːs] 추론하다, 연역하다
- deplete [diplíːt] 고갈시키다, 소모하다
- digestion [daidʒéstʃən] 소화
- disengagement [dìsengéidʒmənt] 이탈, 분리
- distract [distrǽkt] 주의를 돌리다
- elevation [èləvéiʃən] 고도, 상승, 입면도
- entail [intéil] 수반하다, 필요로 하다
- evaporation [ivæ̀pəréiʃən] 증발
- extinction [ikstíŋkʃən] 멸종, 소멸
- feudalism [fjúːdlìzm] 봉건주의
- geographic [dʒìːəgrǽfik] 지리적인
- hull [hʌl] 선체, 껍질
- imperial [impíəriəl] 제국의, 황실의
- indigenous [indídʒənəs] 토착의, 원주민의
- inhospitable [inhɑ́spitəbl] 불친절한, 살기 어려운
- interlock [ìntərlɑ́k] 맞물리다, 결합하다
- itinerant [aitínərənt] 순회하는, 떠돌아다니는
- landmark [lǽndmɑːrk] 이정표, 명소
- lingering [líŋɡəriŋ] 오래 남는, 지속하는
- manifest [mǽnəfèst] 명백한; 나타내다
- marvel [mɑ́ːrvəl] 경이; 감탄하다
- medicament [mədíkəmənt] 약제
- meticulous [mətíkjuləs] 세심한, 꼼꼼한
- missionary [míʃənèri] 선교사
- multidisciplinary [mʌ̀ltidísəplənèri] 다학제의, 학제간의
- nourishment [nə́ːriʃmənt] 영양분, 음식물
- oscillate [ɑ́ːsəlèit] 진동하다, 동요하다
- pasture [pǽstʃər] 목초지; 방목하다
- performance [pərfɔ́ːrməns] 수행, 성과, 공연
- precursor [prikə́ːrsər] 선구자
- prevalent [prévələnt] 널리 퍼진
- propaganda [prɑ̀ːpəɡǽndə] 선전
- quantification [kwɑ̀ːntəfəkéiʃən] 수량화
- ravage [rǽvidʒ] 황폐하게 하다; 파괴, 피해
- replenish [ripléniʃ] 보충하다
- resurgence [risə́ːrdʒəns] 부활, 재기
- rudimentary [rùːdəméntəri] 기초적인, 미숙한
- stealth [stelθ] 은밀함
- susceptible [səséptəbl] 영향받기 쉬운
- temporal [témpərəl] 시간의, 일시적인
- transient [trǽnʃənt] 일시적인
- undercurrent [ʌ́ndərkə̀ːrənt] 저류, 잠재적 경향
- vernacular [vərnǽkjulər] 방언; 토착의

Day 16   TASK 3 실전 필수 어휘

☑ TASK 3를 위해 필수적으로 알아야 할 어휘들이므로, 확실히 암기해 둡니다.   🎧 DAY16

☐ abundance [əbʌ́ndəns]	풍부함, 다량
☐ adaptation [æ̀dəptéiʃən]	적응, 각색
☐ affordability [əfɔ̀ːrdəbíləti]	구매가능성, 적정가격
☐ alienation [èiljənéiʃən]	소외, 분리
☐ amphibian [æmfíbiən]	양서류
☐ anxiety [æŋzáiəti]	불안, 염려
☐ bipedalism [baipédlìzm]	이족보행
☐ byproduct [báiprὰːdəkt]	부산물
☐ cataclysmic [kæ̀təklízmik]	대격변의, 파멸적인
☐ chronic [krάnik]	만성의, 지속적인
☐ coarse [kɔːrs]	거친, 조악한, 상스러운
☐ column [kάləm]	기둥, 열(세로 줄)
☐ compulsion [kəmpʌ́lʃən]	강박, 충동
☐ consensus [kənsénsəs]	합의, 의견 일치
☐ conveyance [kənvéiəns]	운반, 운송 수단, 양도
☐ countryside [kʌ́ntrisàid]	시골, 농촌
☐ cumbersome [kʌ́mbərsəm]	다루기 힘든, 거추장스러운
☐ depletion [diplíːʃən]	고갈, 감소
☐ dilute [dilúːt]	희석하다; 묽은
☐ disorder [disɔ́ːrdər]	무질서, 장애
☐ distressed [distrést]	고통받는, 낡은
☐ embellish [imbéliʃ]	장식하다, 미화하다
☐ extraterrestrial [èkstrətəréstriəl]	지구 밖의, 외계의
☐ fiber [fáibər]	섬유, 식이섬유
☐ formative [fɔ́ːrmətiv]	형성기의
☐ frigid [frídʒid]	극도로 추운
☐ geology [dʒiάːlədʒi]	지질학
☐ harpoon [hɑːrpúːn]	작살; 작살로 잡다
☐ hibernation [hàibərnéiʃən]	동면, 겨울잠
☐ impermanence [impə́ːrmənəns]	무상함, 일시성
☐ industrialization [indʌ̀striəlizéiʃən]	산업화
☐ inscription [inskrípʃən]	비문, 새김
☐ intermittent [ìntərmítnt]	간헐적인
☐ juvenile [dʒúːvənl]	청소년의; 청소년
☐ landmass [lǽndmæ̀s]	대륙, 육지
☐ longstanding [lɔ́ŋstæ̀ndiŋ]	오래된, 지속적인
☐ manifesto [mæ̀nəféstou]	선언문, 강령
☐ masses [mǽsiz]	대중, 민중
☐ medication [mèdəkéiʃən]	약물, 투약
☐ meticulously [mətíkjuləsli]	세심하게
☐ novelty [nάːvəlti]	새로움, 색다른 물건
☐ ostensibly [asténsəbli]	표면상, 겉으로는
☐ peril [pérəl]	위험
☐ phenomenon [finάmənὰn]	현상
☐ pivotal [pívətl]	중추적인, 핵심적인
☐ pollutant [pəlúːtnt]	오염물질
☐ predecessor [prédəsesər]	전임자, 조상
☐ probe [proub]	탐사선; 조사하다
☐ propagation [prὰpəgéiʃən]	전파, 번식
☐ quarry [kwɔ́ːri]	채석장, 사냥감
☐ refraction [rifrǽkʃən]	굴절
☐ replicate [réplikèit]	복제하다
☐ rugged [rʌ́gid]	울퉁불퉁한, 험준한, 튼튼한
☐ skepticism [sképtəsìzm]	회의주의
☐ spatial [spéiʃəl]	공간의
☐ symmetry [símətri]	대칭
☐ tenet [ténit]	신조, 교리
☐ transnational [trænsnǽʃənəl]	초국가적인
☐ unearth [ʌnə́ːrθ]	발굴하다, 밝혀내다
☐ vigilant [vídʒələnt]	경계하는

Day 17 — TASK 3 실전 필수 어휘

TASK 3를 위해 필수적으로 알아야 할 어휘들이므로, 확실히 암기해 둡니다.

DAY17

- accelerate [æksélərèit] 가속하다, 촉진하다
- adjacent [ədʒéisnt] 인접한
- afterlife [ǽftərlàif] 사후세계, 내세
- alignment [əláinmənt] 정렬, 일치
- amputation [æmpjutéiʃən] 절단
- appealing [əpíːliŋ] 매력적인, 호소력 있는
- augment [ɔːgmént, ɔ́ːgment] 증가시키다; 증가(분)
- bleach [bliːtʃ] 표백하다; 표백제
- bystander [báistændər] 구경꾼, 방관자
- catalyst [kǽtəlist] 촉매
- chronological [krànəláːdʒikəl] 연대순의, 시간순의
- concession [kənséʃən] 양보, 인정
- constraint [kənstréint] 제약, 강제
- conviction [kənvíkʃən] 확신, 유죄 판결
- courtship [kɔ́ːrtʃip] 구애
- cumulative [kjúːmjulətiv] 누적의, 축적된
- deficiency [difíʃənsi] 결핍, 부족
- deposit [dipázit] 보증금; 입금하다
- diplomacy [diplóuməsi] 외교
- disposition [dìspəzíʃən] 성향, 배치
- domesticate [dəméstikèit] 길들이다, 가축화하다
- embodiment [imbádimənt] 구현, 화신
- ephemeral [iférməl] 수명이 짧은, 일시적인
- excavation [èkskəvéiʃən] 발굴
- fortification [fɔ̀ːrtəfikéiʃən] 요새화, 강화
- hemisphere [hémisfìər] 반구
- hierarchy [háiərɑ̀ːrki] 계층 구조, 서열
- impermeable [impə́ːrmiəbl] 불침투성의
- inexplicably [inéksplikəbli] 설명할 수 없게
- instantaneous [ìnstəntéiniəs] 즉각적인
- intestine [intéstin] 내장, 창자
- juxtapose [dʒʌ̀kstəpòuz] 병치하다, 나란히 두다
- legislation [lèdʒisléiʃən] 법률, 입법
- literacy [lítərəsi] 문해력, 읽고 쓸 줄 아는 능력
- manuscript [mǽnjuskrìpt] 원고, 필사본
- masterpiece [mǽstərpìs] 걸작
- mitigate [mítəgèit] 완화하다
- necessitate [nəsésətèit] 필요로 하다, 요구하다
- noxious [náːkʃəs] 유해한, 유독한
- painstakingly [péinstèikiŋli] 공들여, 세심하게
- permeate [pə́ːrmièit] 스며들다, 퍼지다
- philosophy [filáːsəfi] 철학
- placate [pléikeit] 달래다, 누그러뜨리다
- predicament [pridíkəmənt] 곤경, 궁지
- profitability [pràːfitəbíləti] 수익성
- quintessence [kwintésns] 정수, 전형
- reclamation [rèkləméiʃən] 개간, 매립, 재생
- refute [rifjúːt] 반박하다, 논박하다
- repository [ripáːzətɔ̀ːri] 저장소, 보관소
- retrain [riːtréin] 재교육하다
- rupture [rʌ́ptʃər] 파열; 파열시키다
- scholar [skáːlər] 학자
- sewage [súːidʒ] 하수, 오물
- societal [səsáiətl] 사회의
- speculation [spèkjuléiʃən] 추측, 투기
- stimulate [stímjulèit] 자극하다, 촉진하다
- synthetic [sinθétik] 합성의, 인조의
- territory [térətɔ̀ːri] 영토, 구역
- traverse [trǽvəːrs] 가로지르다; 횡단
- virtue [və́ːrtʃuː] 미덕, 장점

Day 18 — TASK 3 실전 필수 어휘

✓ TASK 3를 위해 필수적으로 알아야 할 어휘들이므로, 확실히 암기해 둡니다. 🎧 DAY18

☐ administrative [ædmínəstrèitiv]	행정의, 관리의
☐ alleviate [əlí:vièit]	완화하다, 경감하다
☐ anatomy [ənǽtəmi]	해부학
☐ appliance [əpláiəns]	가전제품, 기구
☐ aspiration [æspəréiʃən]	열망, 포부
☐ autonomy [ɔ:tánəmi]	자율성, 독립성
☐ blindly [bláindli]	맹목적으로
☐ calibration [kæləbréiʃən]	보정, 교정
☐ catastrophic [kætəstráfik]	재앙의, 파멸적인
☐ circuit [sə́:rkit]	회로, 순환
☐ coercion [kouə́:rʃən]	강제, 강압
☐ commence [kəméns]	시작하다
☐ concrete [kánkri:t]	구체적인; 콘크리트
☐ contamination [kəntæmənéiʃən]	오염
☐ cosmetic [kɑzmétik]	미용의; 화장품
☐ covertly [kʌ́vərtli]	은밀히, 남몰래
☐ dairy [déəri]	유제품; 낙농의
☐ deforestation [di:fɔ:ristéiʃən]	삼림벌채, 산림파괴
☐ deprecate [déprikèit]	반대하다, 폄하하다
☐ disprove [disprú:v]	반증하다, 틀림을 입증하다
☐ embryo [émbriòu]	배아
☐ epitaph [épitæf]	묘비명
☐ exhaust [igzɔ́:st]	고갈시키다; 배기가스
☐ fasting [fǽstiŋ]	단식; 단식의
☐ fission [fíʃən]	(핵)분열; 분열하다
☐ fraction [frǽkʃən]	분수, 일부분
☐ furry [fə́:ri]	털이 많은
☐ goodwill [gùdwíl]	선의, 호의
☐ hygiene [háidʒi:n]	위생
☐ implication [ìmplikéiʃən]	함의, 영향, 연루
☐ instinctively [instíŋktivli]	본능적으로
☐ invasive [invéisiv]	침습성의, 침입하는
☐ kaleidoscopic [kəlàidəskɑ́:pik]	만화경 같은, 변화무쌍한
☐ meditation [mèditéiʃən]	명상
☐ millennium [miléniəm]	천년(간)
☐ mobility [moubíləti]	이동성, 유동성
☐ negotiation [nigòuʃiéiʃən]	협상
☐ nutrient [njú:triənt]	영양소
☐ paleontology [pèiliantálədʒi]	고생물학
☐ pendulum [péndʒuləm]	진자, 추
☐ personnel [pə̀:rsənél]	인사, 직원
☐ placement [pléismənt]	배치, 취업
☐ portrait [pɔ́:rtrit]	초상화
☐ predictably [pridíktəbli]	예상대로, 예측 가능하게
☐ profound [prəfáund]	깊은, 심오한
☐ prosperity [prɑspérəti]	번영
☐ quota [kwóutə]	할당량
☐ recognizable [rékəgnàizəbl]	알아볼 수 있는
☐ reminiscent [rèmənísnt]	~을 연상시키는
☐ reproduction [rìprədʌ́kʃən]	번식, 재생산
☐ safeguard [séifgà:rd]	보호장치; 보호하다
☐ sculpture [skʌ́lptʃər]	조각; 조각하다
☐ sewer [sú:ər]	하수도
☐ socioeconomic [sòusiouèkənɑ́:mik]	사회경제적인
☐ spiritually [spíritʃuəli]	정신적으로
☐ stunted [stʌ́ntid]	발육이 저해된, 왜소한
☐ systemic [sistémik]	체계적인
☐ tribal [tráibl]	부족의, 종족의
☐ unparalleled [ʌnpǽrəleld]	비할 데 없는
☐ weaponry [wépənri]	무기

Day 19 TASK 3 실전 필수 어휘

✅ TASK 3를 위해 필수적으로 알아야 할 어휘들이므로, 확실히 암기해 둡니다.   🎧 DAY19

☐	accretion [əkríːʃən]	축적, 부착	☐	inflammation [ìnfləméiʃən]	염증
☐	adolescence [ædəlésns]	청소년기	☐	insurmountable [ìnsərmáuntəbl]	극복할 수 없는
☐	aggressive [əgrésiv]	공격적인, 적극적인	☐	irregularity [irègjulǽrəti]	불규칙성
☐	alliance [əláiəns]	동맹, 연합	☐	keystone [kíːstòun]	쐐기돌, 핵심
☐	apprehensive [æprihénsiv]	걱정하는, 우려하는	☐	lifespan [láifspæn]	수명
☐	auxiliary [ɔːgzíljəri]	보조의; 보조기구, 보조자	☐	mating [méitiŋ]	교미, 짝짓기
☐	callousness [kǽləsnəs]	냉담함, 무정함	☐	megalithic [mègəlíθik]	거석의
☐	celestial [səléstʃəl]	천체의, 하늘의	☐	modulate [mάdʒulèit]	조절하다, 변조하다
☐	circulation [sə̀ːrkjuléiʃən]	순환, 유통	☐	neural [njúərəl]	신경의
☐	cognitive [kάgnətiv]	인지의, 인식의	☐	nutrition [njuːtríʃən]	영양
☐	communal [kəmjúːnəl]	공동의, 공공의	☐	pancreas [pǽnkriəs]	췌장
☐	concurrently [kənkə́ːrəntli]	동시에	☐	people [píːpl]	사람들; (사람을) 거주시키다
☐	contemplation [kɑ̀ntəmpléiʃən]	숙고, 명상	☐	perspiration [pə̀ːrspəréiʃən]	땀, 발한
☐	cosmology [kɑːzmάːlədʒi]	우주론, 우주학	☐	phrase [freiz]	구문; 표현하다
☐	debris [dəbríː]	잔해, 쓰레기	☐	plagiarism [pléidʒərìzm]	표절
☐	deformation [dìːfɔːrméiʃən]	변형, 기형	☐	postwar [pòustwɔ́ːr]	전후의
☐	desiccate [désikèit]	건조시키다	☐	predictive [pridíktiv]	예측의
☐	discern [disə́ːrn]	식별하다, 알아차리다	☐	progression [prəgréʃən]	진행, 발전
☐	dispute [dispjúːt]	논쟁; 논쟁하다	☐	protest [próutest, prətést]	항의; 항의하다
☐	emission [imíʃən]	배출, 방출	☐	radiation [rèidiéiʃən]	방사선, 복사
☐	epoch [épək]	(역사의) 시대, 획기적 시기	☐	rectangular [rektǽŋgjulər]	직사각형의
☐	existential [èɡzisténʃəl]	실존의, 존재의	☐	remoteness [rimóutnis]	외딴 곳, 멀리 떨어져 있음
☐	fatigue [fətíːg]	피로	☐	reservoir [rézərvwɑːr]	저수지
☐	fissure [fíʃər]	균열, 틈	☐	secrete [sikríːt]	분비하다, 숨기다
☐	fracture [frǽktʃər]	골절, 균열	☐	sociopolitical [sòusiəpəlítikəl]	사회정치적인
☐	fusion [fjúːʒən]	융합	☐	spore [spɔːr]	포자
☐	herder [hə́ːrdər]	목축업자, 양치기	☐	sublime [səbláim]	숭고한, 웅장한; 숭고함
☐	hoax [houks]	속임수, 거짓 정보	☐	tantalizing [tǽntəlàiziŋ]	감질나게 하는, 매혹적인
☐	hyperactive [hàipərǽktiv]	과민한, 지나치게 활동적인	☐	topography [təpάːgrəfi]	지형, 지형학
☐	impressive [imprésiv]	인상 깊은	☐	trillion [tríljən]	조 (단위)

Day 20 — TASK 3 실전 필수 어휘

TASK 3를 위해 필수적으로 알아야 할 어휘들이므로, 확실히 암기해 둡니다.

☐ accumulate [əkjúːmjulèit]	축적하다, 모으다
☐ adversity [ædvə́ːrsəti]	역경, 곤경
☐ agriculture [ǽgrəkÀltʃər]	농업, 농학
☐ allot [əláːt]	할당하다, 배정하다
☐ anecdote [ǽnikdòut]	일화
☐ aquatic [əkwǽtik]	수중의, 물의
☐ avian [éiviən]	조류의; 새
☐ brewing [brúːiŋ]	(맥주) 양조
☐ census [sénsəs]	인구조사
☐ civic [sívik]	시민의, 시의
☐ commute [kəmjúːt]	통근하다; 통근
☐ confront [kənfrÁnt]	직면하다, 맞서다
☐ counteract [kàuntərǽkt]	상쇄하다, 대항하다
☐ decode [diːkóud]	해독하다, 복호화하다
☐ degeneration [didʒènəréiʃən]	퇴화, 악화
☐ deter [ditə́ːr]	저지하다, 단념시키다
☐ discourse [dískɔːrs]	담론, 강연
☐ disruption [disrÁpʃən]	혼란, 중단
☐ emulate [émjulèit]	모방하다, 견주다
☐ equator [ikwéitər]	적도
☐ exonerate [igzáːnərèit]	면죄하다, 혐의를 벗기다
☐ fleet [fliːt]	함대, 차량단
☐ fragility [frədʒíləti]	깨지기 쉬움, 취약성
☐ grocery [gróusəri]	식료품
☐ hereditary [hərédətèri]	유전의, 세습의
☐ horizontal [hɔ̀ːrəzáːntl]	수평의
☐ improvisational [impràːvəzéiʃənəl]	즉흥적인
☐ irrigation [irəgéiʃən]	관개, 관수
☐ kinship [kínʃip]	친족관계, 유대감
☐ lime [laim]	석회
☐ livelihood [láivlihud]	생계
☐ magnetism [mǽgnətìzm]	(자석의) 자기
☐ marginally [máːrdʒinli]	약간, 미미하게
☐ matriarch [méitriàːrk]	여성 우두머리
☐ memorable [mémərəbl]	기억할 만한
☐ neurotransmitter [njùəroutrænsmítər]	신경 전달 물질
☐ obligation [àːbləgéiʃən]	의무
☐ paradox [pǽrədàks]	역설, 모순
☐ percent [pərsént]	퍼센트; 백분율의
☐ pest [pest]	해충
☐ physical [fízikəl]	물리적인, 신체의
☐ potent [poutnt]	강력한, 효력있는
☐ prehistoric [prìːhistɔ́ːrik]	선사시대의
☐ prolific [prəlífik]	다산의, 다작의, 풍부한
☐ provoke [prəvóuk]	자극하다, 도발하다
☐ rainfall [réinfɔ̀ːl]	강우량, 비
☐ recycling [rìːsáikliŋ]	재활용
☐ renewable [bènəfíʃəl]	재생 가능한
☐ reshape [rìːʃéip]	재구성하다
☐ rhythm [ríðm]	리듬
☐ salient [séiliənt]	두드러진, 현저한
☐ sectional [sékʃənəl]	부분의, 구역의
☐ soliloquy [səlíləkwi]	독백
☐ spur [spəːr]	가시, 박차; 자극하다
☐ subside [səbsáid]	가라앉다, 진정되다, 줄다
☐ taxing [tǽksiŋ]	고된, 힘든
☐ totem [tóutəm]	토템 (신성시되는 상징물)
☐ trustworthiness [trÁstwəːrðinis]	신뢰성
☐ vandalism [vǽndəlìzm]	기물파손
☐ workforce [wə́ːrkfɔ̀ːrs]	노동력

MEMO

기본에서 실전까지 NEW 토플 리딩 완벽 대비

HACKERS
Updated
TOEFL
READING

개정 6판 4쇄 발행 2026년 2월 2일
개정 6판 1쇄 발행 2025년 11월 7일

지은이	David Cho	언어학 박사, 前 UCLA 교수, 해커스 어학연구소 공저
펴낸곳	(주)해커스 어학연구소
펴낸이	해커스 어학연구소 출판팀

주소	서울특별시 서초구 강남대로61길 23 (주)해커스 어학연구소
고객센터	02-537-5000
교재 관련 문의	publishing@hackers.com
동영상강의	HackersIngang.com

ISBN	978-89-6542-653-0 (13740)
Serial Number	06-04-01

저작권자 ⓒ 2025, David Cho, 해커스 어학연구소
이 책 및 음성파일의 모든 내용, 이미지, 디자인, 편집 형태에 대한 저작권은 저자에게 있습니다.
서면에 의한 저자와 출판사의 허락 없이 내용의 일부 혹은 전부를 인용, 발췌하거나 복제, 배포할 수 없습니다.

외국어인강 1위,
해커스인강(HackersIngang.com)
해커스인강

- 실전 감각을 극대화하는 **iBT 리딩 실전모의고사**
- 효과적인 리딩 학습을 돕는 **단어암기 MP3**
- 해커스 토플 스타강사의 **본 교재 인강**

전세계 유학정보의 중심,
고우해커스(goHackers.com)
고우해커스

- 토플 보카 외우기, 토플 스피킹/라이팅 첨삭 게시판 등 무료 학습 콘텐츠
- 고득점을 위한 **토플 공부전략 강의**
- 국가별 대학 및 전공별 정보, 유학 Q&A 게시판 등 다양한 유학정보

[외국어인강 1위] 헤럴드 선정 2018 대학생 선호브랜드 대상 '대학생이 선정한 외국어인강' 부문 1위

전세계 유학정보의 중심
고우해커스

goHackers.com

HACKERS

Updated
TOEFL

READING

정답·해석·정답단서

2026년 1월 21일
NEW TOEFL
완벽 대비

해커스 어학연구소

HACKERS
Updated
TOEFL
READING

정답·해석·정답단서

DIAGNOSTIC TEST

p.21

01 types	02 across	03 regions
04 differences	05 environmental	06 These
07 in	08 influence	09 vegetation
10 each	11 ⓒ	12 ⓑ
13 Ⓐ	14 Ⓒ	15 Ⓓ
16 Ⓒ	17 Ⓑ	18 Ⓓ
19 Ⓒ	20 Ⓐ	

[01-10]

토양은 지상 생태계의 토대를 형성하기 때문에 가장 필수적인 자원 중 하나임에도 불구하고 흔히 간과되는 천연자원이다. 토양의 유형은 환경 조건의 차이로 인해 여러 지역에 걸쳐 다르게 나타난다. 이러한 차이는 결과적으로 뚜렷하게 다른 각 지역 내에서 식물 및 농부들이 경작하는 작물에 영향을 준다. 토양 지리를 이해하는 것은 전 세계에서 계획자들이 지속 가능한 토지 이용, 효과적인 농업 관행, 그리고 환경 보전 노력에 대해 정보에 입각한 결정을 내리는 데 도움을 준다.

overlook [òuvərlúk] 간과하다   terrestrial [təréstriəl] 지상의
environmental [invàiərənméntl] 환경의
vegetation [vèdʒətéiʃən] 식물   distinct [distíŋkt] 뚜렷한
cultivate [kʌ́ltəvèit] 경작하다   sustainable [səstéinəbl] 지속 가능한
agricultural [ægrikʌ́ltʃərəl] 농업의
conservation [kànsərvéiʃən] 보전

[11-12] 이메일을 읽으시오.

날짜: 2월 20일
제목: City 박물관 멤버십

Ms. Miller께,

¹¹귀하의 City 박물관 연간 회원권이 곧 만료될 예정이므로, 혜택을 계속 유지하시려면 3월 31일까지 갱신해주시기 바랍니다. 올해, 회원 여러분께서는 특별 전시회 초대권을 받으실 것입니다. 최근 출시된 저희의 모바일 애플리케이션 독점으로 15% 할인이 가능하니, ¹²애플리케이션을 다운로드받고 이 특가를 활용하시는 것을 권장드립니다.

Ava Mitchell 드림

expire [ikspáiər] 만료되다   invitation [ìnvitéiʃən] 초대권, 초대장
exclusively [iksklúːsivli] 독점으로, 배타적으로

11 Main Purpose Question

이메일의 주된 목적은 무엇인가?
Ⓐ 박물관 프로그램의 갱신을 알리기 위해
Ⓑ 회원을 특별 행사에 초대하기 위해
☑ 박물관 회원권을 계속 유지하는 것에 대해 상기시키기 위해
Ⓓ 박물관의 큐레이터 일자리를 광고하기 위해

12 Detail Question

Ms. Miller가 하도록 조언받는 것은 무엇인가?
Ⓐ 혜택을 활용한다
☑ 기기에 프로그램을 설치한다
Ⓒ 전시회를 보기 위해 박물관을 방문한다
Ⓓ 온라인으로 지불금을 낸다

[13-15] 이메일을 읽으시오.

제목: 건강 워크숍 시리즈

Ms. Johnson께,

¹³3월 12일부터 14일까지 Grand Convention Center에서 개최되는 저희의 종합 건강 워크숍 시리즈에 귀하를 초청하게 되어 기쁩니다.

¹⁴올해의 초점은 "영양, 피트니스, 그리고 마음챙김의 통합"입니다. 본 행사는 존경받는 ¹⁴영양학자 Sarah Williams 박사의 주요 발표와 더불어, 네 개의 역동적인 전문가 패널 토론 및 상호 작용적인 쌍방향 실습형 세션을 특징으로 할 것입니다. 전체 일정은 곧 공유될 것입니다.

또한 ¹⁵인기 있었던 참가자 쇼케이스를 다시 진행하는데, 이곳에서 참석자들이 자신만의 건강한 조리법이나 신체 단련 루틴을 공유하실 수 있습니다. 쇼케이스에 참여를 원하신다면, 2월 25일까지 조직팀에 간단한 제안서를 보내주시기 바랍니다.

Michael Hughes 드림

extend an invitation 초청하다, 초대장을 보내다
comprehensive [kàmprihénsiv] 종합적인
nutrition [njuːtríʃən] 영양
integration [ìntəgréiʃən] 통합   esteemed [istíːmd] 존경받는
nutritionist [njuːtríʃənist] 영양학자
hands-on [hæ̀ndz-áːn] 실습형의, 직접 해보는
attendee [ətèndíː] 참석자

13 Main Purpose Question

이메일의 주된 목적은 무엇인가?
☑ Ms. Johnson을 건강 워크숍에 초대하기 위해
Ⓑ 다가오는 건강 행사의 일정을 제공하기 위해
Ⓒ 지난 참가자들로부터 의견을 수집하기 위해
Ⓓ 참가자 쇼케이스 세션의 우승자를 발표하기 위해

14 Detail Question

Sarah Williams 박사는
Ⓐ 패널 토론을 진행할 것이다
Ⓑ 실습형 워크숍을 가르칠 것이다
☑ 건강에 관한 주요 발표를 할 것이다
Ⓓ 참가자 쇼케이스에 제출된 것들을 심사할 것이다

어휘   moderate [mádərèit] 진행하다, ~의 의장 역할을 맡다

15 Inference Question

참가자 쇼케이스 세션에 대해 추론할 수 있는 것은?
Ⓐ 2월 25일에 개최될 것이다.
Ⓑ 영양 전문가만을 위한 것이다.
Ⓒ 추가 요금 지불이 필요하다.
Ⓓ 이전 워크숍에서도 제공된 적이 있다. ✓

[16-20]

도시 환경에서의 문화 장소 만들기

문화 장소 만들기는 도시 계획에서 새롭게 떠오르는 접근법으로, 예술 및 문화 활동을 통합하여 공공 공간을 변화시키는 관례를 의미한다. 기존 환경에 문화적 표현을 통합함으로써, 성공적인 문화 장소 만들기는 지역 공동체의 참여와 문화적 교류를 촉진할 수 있다.

연구에 따르면, 성공적인 문화 장소 만들기 사업은 일반적으로 예술가, 주민, 지역 정부 간의 협력적 동반자 관계를 수반한다. 예를 들어, Milwaukee의 Beerline Trail 사업은 버려진 철도 회랑을 조각품, 주민이 함께 사용하는 테이블, 조명, 공연 공간이 어우러진 활기찬 공공장소로 탈바꿈시켰으며, 이 모든 것은 주민들과 함께 공동으로 설계되었다. [17]이 프로젝트는 포용적인 도시 공간 재생의 대표적인 성공 사례로 평가된다. 그러나 여전히 중요한 과제들이 남아 있다. [18/19]그중 가장 시급한 문제 중 하나는 새로운 투자와 더 부유한 주민이 유입될 때 흔히 원주민의 이주가 발생한다는 점이다.

[19]그럼에도 불구하고, 문화 장소 만들기는 예술적 혁신과 공동체 보존 간의 균형을 추구할 수 있다. 그것의 장기적 지속 가능성은 이 균형을 유지하는 데 달려있다. [20]Boston의 Dudley Square에서는 Dudley Street 지역 이니셔티브(DSNI)가 장소 만들기 전략과 저렴한 주택 정책을 결합하였다. 이 사업은 과거에 방치되었던 지역에 저가 주택을 창출함으로써 지역의 안정화를 이루고, [20]주민의 이주를 방지했으며, 다양한 주민들이 공동 소유 의식과 집단 정체성을 형성할 수 있는 공간을 조성하였다.

---

emerging[imə́ːrdʒiŋ] 새롭게 떠오르는
incorporate[inkɔ́ːrpərèit] 통합하다
transform[trænsfɔ́ːrm] 변화시키다
integrate[íntəgrèit] 통합하다
foster[fɔ́ːstər] 촉진하다 engagement[ingéidʒmənt] 참여
involve[inválv] 수반하다 corridor[kɔ́ːridər] 회랑, (좁고 긴) 통로
sculpture[skʌ́lptʃər] 조각품 regard[rigáːrd] 평가하다, 간주하다
representative[rèprizéntətiv] 대표적인
inclusive[inklúːsiv] 포용적인 pressing[présiŋ] 시급한
displacement[displéismənt] 이주 affluent[ǽfluənt] 부유한
preservation[prèzərvéiʃən] 보존 affordable[əfɔ́ːrdəbl] 저렴한
stabilize[stéibəlàiz] 안정화하다 diverse[dáivəːrs] 다양한

16 Vocabulary Question

지문의 단어 "engagement"와 의미상 가장 유사한 것은?
Ⓐ 정체성
Ⓑ 창의성
Ⓒ 참여 ✓
Ⓓ 약속

어휘 identity[aidéntəti] 정체성 creativity[krìːeitívəti] 창의성
participation[pɑːrtìsəpéiʃən] 참여
appointment[əpɔ́intmənt] 약속

17 Inference Question

지문은 Milwaukee의 Beerline Trail 사업에 대해 무엇을 암시하는가?
Ⓐ 주민들이 설계 과정에 개입하지 못하게 하였다.
Ⓑ 성공적인 지역사회 협력의 사례이다. ✓
Ⓒ 새로운 철도 회랑 건설을 주된 목표로 하였다.
Ⓓ 주민들의 작품만을 활용하였다.

어휘 prevent[privént] 못하게 하다
collaboration[kəlæbəréiʃən] 협력 aim[eim] 목표로 하다

18 Fact Question

지문은 문화 장소 만들기에 대해 무엇을 명시하는가?
Ⓐ 주로 정부 기관이 주도하는 사업이다.
Ⓑ 오직 지역 예술가의 예술적 기여만을 포함한다.
Ⓒ 지역 주민의 예술 감상 능력 향상을 목표로 한다.
Ⓓ 기존 지역 주민의 이주를 유발할 수 있다. ✓

어휘 appreciation[əprìːʃiéiʃən] 감상 능력, 감상

19 Rhetorical Purpose Question

2단락과 3단락의 관계는?
Ⓐ 3단락은 2단락에 서술된 생각을 뒷받침하는 근거를 제시한다.
Ⓑ 3단락은 2단락에 소개된 도전 과제에 대한 논의를 확장한다.
Ⓒ 3단락은 2단락에 제기된 문제들에 대한 해결책을 제시한다. ✓
Ⓓ 3단락은 2단락에 소개된 개념의 장기적 영향을 고찰한다.

20 Rhetorical Purpose Question

글쓴이는 왜 Dudley Street 지역 이니셔티브를 언급하는가?
Ⓐ 원주민이 확실히 포함되게끔 하는 방법을 보여주기 위해 ✓
Ⓑ 전통적 도시 설계 접근법을 비판하기 위해
Ⓒ 문화 장소 만들기의 재정적 이점을 입증하기 위해
Ⓓ 정부 자금 지원의 중요성을 강조하기 위해

TASK 1 | Complete the Words

Section I Blank Types

1. Intuitive Blanks

HACKERS PRACTICE p.38

01 can
02 must
03 into
04 deal
05 light
06 subject, from
07 only, But
08 essential, ecosystems
09 investigate, interventions
10 serve, bring
11 challenge, scenario, whether
12 Unlike, which, succession
13 geological, away, enormous
14 focused, gases, pose
15 leadership, make, risk
16 When, confidence, chain, reputation
17 intentions, understanding, that, literature
18 for, conservation, roots, other
19 foundational, philosophy, voluntarily, authority
20 rather, result, decision, represents

01
소셜 미디어는 대중의 의견에 영향을 미치고, 트렌드를 형성하며, 교육과 사회 운동을 위한 기회를 제공할 수 있다.

어휘 opportunity[ɑ̀pərtjúːnəti] 기회
activism[ǽktəvìzm] 사회 운동, 행동주의

02
대규모 실험을 시작하기 전에, 연구팀은 의욕적이면서도 실증적으로 측정 가능한 목표를 설정해야 한다.

어휘 initiate[iníʃièit] 시작하다 ambitious[æmbíʃəs] 의욕적인
empirically[impírikəli] 실증적으로, 경험적으로

03
토목 공학은 과학과 수학이 어떻게 물리적 구조물로 변환되는지를 보여준다.

어휘 translate[trænsléit] 변환되다, 바뀌다

04
정치 이론에서 가장 중심적인 난제는 개인의 자유와 공동체적 사회 질서의 요구 사이의 긴장을 어떻게 다룰지이다.

어휘 tension[ténʃən] 긴장 communal[kəmjúːnəl] 공동체의

05
1930년대의 역사적 거래 데이터를 분석함으로써, 경제학자들은 금융 위기와 장기적인 시장 침체를 악화시키는 요인들을 밝히기를 바랐다.

어휘 exacerbate[igzǽsərbèit] 악화시키다
prolonged[prəlɔ́ːŋd] 장기적인

06
구술 기록은 특유의 난제를 제기하는데, 이는 인간 기억의 불완전함, 과거에 대한 개인적 해석, 그리고 인터뷰 대상자의 현재 관점에서 비롯되는 잠재적 편향에 영향을 받는다는 점이다.

어휘 fallibility[fæ̀ləbíləti] 불완전함, 오류를 범하기 쉬움
personal[pə́ːrsənl] 개인적인 bias[báiəs] 편향

07
사람들은 때때로 블록버스터 트렌드가 제작사들로 하여금 대중적 매력이 있는 작품에만 집중하도록 만든다고 비판한다. 하지만 블록버스터는 여전히 대중문화를 형성하고 영화 시장을 이끈다.

어휘 criticize[krítəsàiz] 비판하다

08
높은 생물 다양성은 건강한 생태계를 위해 필수인데, 이는 그것이 환경적 스트레스 요인에 대한 회복력을 증가시키고, 수분 및 영양분 순환과 같은 자연 과정의 안정성을 보장하기 때문이다.

어휘 resilience[rizíljəns] 회복력
environmental[invàiərənméntl] 환경적인
pollination[pɑ̀lənéiʃən] 수분 nutrient[njúːtriənt] 영양분

09
역학자들은 질병의 양상을 조사하고, 위험 요소를 식별하며, 전염병의 원인을 파악하여 공중 보건 개입에 필요한 정보를 제공한다. 이 분야는 전염병 발생부터 장기적인 건강 상태에 이르는 모든 데이터에 통계적 방법을 사용하여 분석한다.

어휘 risk factor 위험 요소 epidemic[èpədémik] 전염병
statistical[stətístikəl] 통계적인 infectious[infékʃəs] 전염성의

10
산업 혁명이 보여주는 것과 같이, 기술 혁신은 엄청난 사회적 변화를 가져오는 강력한 촉매 역할을 한다.

어휘 catalyst[kǽtəlist] 촉매 profound[prəfáund] 엄청난, 심오한
exemplify[igzémpləfài] (예시로) 보여주다

11

악명 높은 트롤리 문제는 도덕적 직관을 시험하고 도전하도록 설계된 윤리학의 사고 실험이다. 기본적인 시나리오는 폭주하는 트롤리를 다섯 명을 죽이게 될 선로에서 한 명만 죽이게 될 선로로 전환하기 위해 레버를 당길지 말지를 결정하는 것을 포함한다.

어휘 **trolley**[tráli] 트롤리(전차) **intuition**[ìntju:íʃən] 직관
divert[divɜ́:rt] 전환하다, 방향을 바꾸게 하다
runaway[rʎnəwei] 폭주하는, 제어가 안 되는

12

화성은 음을 동시에 조합하여 화음과 그것들 간의 관계를 형성하는 것을 수반한다. 음의 선형적 연속인 멜로디와 달리, 화성은 음악의 수직적 측면에 초점을 맞춘다.

어휘 **simultaneously**[sàiməltéiniəsli] 동시에
relationship[riléiʃənʃip] 관계 **linear**[líniər] 선형적인
succession[səkséʃən] 연속 **vertical**[vɜ́:rtikəl] 수직적인

13

침식은 바람, 물, 또는 얼음과 같은 자연적인 힘으로 토양과 암석 물질이 마모되어 운반되는 지질학적 과정이다. 수천 년에 걸쳐, 움직이는 물과 빙하 작용은 지형에 강력한 영향을 미쳐, 계곡을 깎아내고 막대한 양의 퇴적물을 운반할 수 있다.

어휘 **erosion**[iróuʒən] 침식 **geological**[dʒìəlá:dʒɪkəl] 지질학의
wear away 마모시키다 **glaciation**[glèiʃiéiʃən] 빙하 작용
carve[kɑ:rv] 깎아내다 **sediment**[sédəmənt] 퇴적물

14

전 세계적인 노력은 이제 온실가스의 배출을 완화하기 위한 전략 개발에 집중되어 있는데, 현재의 궤적이 계속 미래 지구의 안정성에 중대한 위협을 가하고 있기 때문이다.

어휘 **mitigate**[mítəgèit] 완화하다 **emission**[imíʃən] 배출
trajectory[trədʒéktəri] 궤적 **stability**[stəbíləti] 안정성

15

효과적인 리더십은 불확실한 상황에서 결정을 내릴 수 있는 능력을 필요로 하며, 비록 그것이 때때로 입증되지 않은 전략으로 위험을 감수해야 함을 의미할지라도 그러하다.

어휘 **effective**[iféktiv] 효과적인 **uncertainty**[ʌnsɜ́:rtənti] 불확실성
unproven[ʌnprú:vən] 입증되지 않은 **strategy**[strǽtədʒi] 전략

16

기업이 홍보 위기에 직면할 때, 커뮤니케이션 팀은 투자자 신뢰의 상실을 막기 위해 올바른 메시지를 전달해야 한다. 추측이 유포되도록 허용하는 것은 미디어에서 부정적인 연쇄 반응을 일으켜, 기업의 평판을 급속도로 훼손할 수 있다.

어휘 **public relations** 홍보 **deliver**[dilívər] 전달하다
speculation[spèkjuléiʃən] 추측 **circulate**[sɜ́:rkjəleit] 유포되다
erode[iróud] 훼손하다 **reputation**[rèpjutéiʃən] 평판

17

일부 비평가들은 저자의 의도가 텍스트에 대한 우리의 이해를 이끌어야 한다고 믿는 반면, 다른 이들은 일단 출판되면 문학은 그 자체의 생명을 얻는다고 주장한다.

어휘 **intention**[inténʃən] 의도

18

대나무는 환경 보전에 중요하다. 그것의 강한 뿌리는 토양 침식을 방지하는 데 도움을 준다. 또한 토양의 오염 물질을 흡수하여, 다른 식물들이 대나무 근처에서 더 쉽게 자랄 수 있도록 할 수 있다.

어휘 **crucial**[krú:ʃəl] 중요한 **conservation**[kànsərvéiʃən] 보전
absorb[æbsɔ́:rb] 흡수하다 **pollutant**[pəlú:tnt] 오염 물질

19

사회 계약의 개념은 정치 철학의 기초가 되는 사상으로, 개인들이 자발적으로 자신들의 자유 일부를 포기하고, 남은 권리의 보호와 사회 질서의 유지를 대가로 통치자나 정부의 권위에 복종한다고 가정한다.

어휘 **contract**[kántrækt] 계약
foundational[faundéiʃənl] 기초가 되는
postulate[pástʃuleit] 가정하다 **surrender**[səréndər] 포기하다

20

기회비용은 상품의 화폐적 가격이 아니라, 결정을 내린 결과로 포기해야 하는 차선책의 가치이다. 개인, 기업, 또는 정부에 의한 모든 선택은 교환 조건을 수반하며, 기회비용은 이때 이루어지는 진짜 희생에 해당한다.

어휘 **alternative**[ɔ:ltɜ́:rnətiv] 대안 **forgo**[fɔ:rgóu] 포기하다
trade-off[tréidɔ̀:f] (타협을 위한) 교환 조건
sacrifice[sǽkrəfàis] 희생

HACKERS TEST

01 plays	02 role	03 the
04 of	05 memories	06 organization
07 experiences	08 becomes	09 during
10 that		
11 of	12 characteristic	13 is
14 possible	15 see	16 with
17 eyes	18 instead	19 out
20 locations		
21 increased	22 on	23 vehicles
24 makes	25 streets	26 resulting
27 delays	28 accidents	29 building
30 roads		
31 form	32 wind	33 is
34 enough	35 transport	36 particles
37 accumulate	38 obstacles	39 shape
40 determined		

[01-10]

해마는 뇌의 측두엽 깊숙한 곳에 있는 작고 구부러진 영역이다. 해마는 새로운 기억의 창조와 경험의 조직화에 역할을 한다. 해마는 정보를 학습하거나 특정 사건을 회상하는 것과 관련된 작업을 수행하는 동안 활성화된다. 이 영역의 손상은 부상 이후의 사건을 기억하는 능력을 약화시킬 수 있다. 그러므로 부상 후의 환자 및 그 밖의 기억 관련 장애를 겪는 사람들을 치료하려면 해마에 대한 더 많은 연구와 이해가 필요하다.

hippocampus[hìpəkǽmpəs] 해마 temporal lobe 측두엽
organization[ɔ̀ːrɡənizéiʃən] 조직화 damage[dǽmidʒ] 손상
ability[əbíləti] 능력 injury[índʒəri] 부상

[11-20]

블랙홀은 중력이 매우 강해서 빛조차도 탈출할 수 없는 우주의 영역이다. 이러한 특징 때문에, 우리 눈으로 블랙홀을 볼 수는 없다. 대신 천문학자들은 블랙홀이 근처의 별과 기체에 미치는 영향을 관찰하여 블랙홀의 위치를 파악한다. 블랙홀이 주변 환경에 미치는 영향은 은하가 어떻게 형성되는지와 같은 우주에 대한 새로운 사실을 천문학자들이 발견하는 데 도움을 준다. 이것이 바로 블랙홀 연구가 천문학에서 중요한 연구 분야가 되는 이유이다.

gravity[ɡrǽvəti] 중력 characteristic[kæ̀riktərístik] 특징
astronomer[əstrάnəmər] 천문학자 figure out 파악하다
location[loukéiʃən] 위치 observe[əbzə́ːrv] 관찰하다

[21-30]

급속도로 성장하는 도시들이 직면하는 주요 과제 중 하나는 교통 체증이다. 개인 차량에 대한 의존도가 증가하면서 점차 거리를 혼잡하게 만들고, 이는 지연과 사고를 초래한다. 단순히 더 많은 도로를 건설하는 것은 교통 체증을 줄이지 못할 수도 있는데, 이는 더 많은 사람들이 운전하기를 선택하도록 야기할 수 있기 때문이다. 더 나은 해결책은 대중교통 시스템을 개선하는 것으로서, 대중교통은 더 적은 도로 공간을 사용하여 훨씬 더 많은 사람들을 수송한다. 효율적인 대중교통 네트워크는 체증을 줄일 뿐만 아니라 도시 생활의 전반적인 질을 향상시킨다.

traffic congestion 교통 체증 reliance[riláiəns] 의존(도)
reduce[ridjúːs] 줄이다 public transit 대중교통
efficient[ifíʃənt] 효율적인 improve[imprúːv] 향상시키다

[31-40]

사구는 모래가 퇴적되어 생성된 지형으로, 일반적으로 사막과 해안 지역에서 발견된다. 사구는 바람 에너지가 모래 입자를 운반할 만큼 높을 때 형성되며, 이 입자들이 장애물 주변에 축적된다. 사구의 모양은 바람의 방향, 풍속, 모래의 가용성과 같은 요인들에 의해 결정된다. 초승달 모양의 사구는 한 방향에서 꾸준한 바람이 불고 모래 공급이 제한적일 때 형성된다. 이와 대조적으로, 중심점에서 다수의 팔이 뻗어 나가는 특징을 가진 별 모양 사구는 여러 방향에서 부는 바람과 풍부한 모래 공급이 있는 위치에서 형성된다.

dune[djuːn] 사구 deposition[dèpəzíʃən] 퇴적
particle[pάːrtikəl] 입자 accumulate[əkjúːmjulèit] 축적되다
obstacle[άbstəkl] 장애물 determine[ditə́ːrmin] 결정하다
availability[əvèiləbíləti] 가용성 crescent[krésnt] 초승달

radiate[réidièit] 뻗어 나가다 abundant[əbʌ́ndənt] 풍부한

2. Contextual Blanks

HACKERS PRACTICE p.48

01 prevent 02 primary 03 examine
04 mechanized 05 observations
06 observatories, benefit 07 fluent, access
08 desires, finite 09 various, express
10 context, meaning
11 states, speed, direction
12 divided, includes, consists
13 change, relation, toward
14 distinct, complement, details
15 impact, healthy, entire
16 supply, demand, principle, interaction
17 behavior, satisfaction, incentives, praise
18 fixed, emerge, analyze, cognitive
19 Modern, distant, raising, unique
20 factors, climate, subtle, gradual

01

권력의 집중을 막고 자유를 보호하기 위해, 많은 현대 민주주의 국가들은 삼권분립 원칙을 채택하고 있다.

어휘 concentration[kὰnsəntréiʃən] 집중 authority[əθɔ́ːrəti] 권력
protect[prətékt] 보호하다 liberty[líbərti] 자유
adopt[ədάpt] 채택하다 separation[sèpəréiʃən] 분립, 분리

02

역사학자에게 중요한 과제는 1차 사료와 2차 사료를 구별하는 것인데, 이 구별이 곧 증거의 신뢰성과 직접성을 결정하기 때문이다.

어휘 distinguish[distíŋɡwiʃ] 구별하다 distinction[distíŋkʃən] 구별
reliability[rilàiəbíləti] 신뢰성 evidence[évədəns] 증거

03

Kant는 우리가 우리의 행위를 그 결과에 기초해서가 아니라, 그것을 이끄는 보편적인 원칙, 즉 정언 명령에 근거하여 고찰할 것을 촉구한다.

어휘 consequence[kάnsəkwèns] 결과 principle[prínsəpl] 원칙

04

증기기관의 도입 이후, 섬유 생산은 점점 더 기계화되었다.

어휘 textile[tékstail] 섬유

05

연역적 추론은 일반적인 법칙에서 시작하지만, 귀납적 추론은 특정한 관찰에서 시작한다.

어휘 **deductive**[didʌ́ktiv] 연역적인 **inductive**[indʌ́ktiv] 귀납적인

06

관측소를 높은 고도에 짓는 것은 대기 간섭을 최소화하고 선명한 천문 데이터를 포착하는 데 필수적이다. 높은 장소는 희박한 공기, 적은 광공해, 낮은 습도의 이점을 누리며, 이 모든 것이 우수한 관측 조건에 기여한다.

어휘 **observatory**[əbzá:rvətɔ́:ri] 관측소, 천문대
altitude[ǽltətjù:d] 고도 **atmospheric**[æ̀tməsférik] 대기의
astronomical[æ̀strənámikəl] 천문의 **pollution**[pəlú:ʃən] 공해
humidity[hju:mídəti] 습도

07

광범위한 디지털화가 도래하기 전에는, 고대 북유럽어에 유창하지 않은 학자들은 바이킹 시대 연구의 원본 사료에 접근하기 어려웠고, 오직 번역되고 흔히 여과된 2차 자료에만 의존해야 했다.

어휘 **advent**[ǽdvent] 도래 **digitization**[dìdʒətəzéiʃən] 디지털화
Old Norse 고대 북유럽어 **translate**[trænsléit] 번역하다
filter[fíltər] 여과하다, 거르다

08

인간의 욕구와 필요는 거의 무한하지만, 그러한 욕구를 충족시키기 위해 사용할 수 있는 자원(시간, 토지, 노동, 자본)은 유한하다.

어휘 **virtually**[vɔ́:rtʃuəli] 거의, 사실상 **limitless**[límitlis] 무한한
finite[fáinait] 유한한

09

예술은 다양한 창조적 매체를 포함한다. 예를 들어, 문학, 음악, 회화는 아이디어를 표현하기 위해 각기 다른 기법을 사용한다.

어휘 **medium**[mí:diəm] 매체(pl. media)

10

맥락을 제공하는 것은 역사학자에게 중요하다. 이는 그들이 배경과 주변 상황을 명확하게 묘사함으로써 의미를 구성한다는 것을 뜻한다.

어휘 **delineate**[dilínièit] 묘사하다, 기술하다
surrounding[səráundiŋ] 주변의, 주위의

11

Newton의 제1 운동법칙은 정지 상태에 있는 물체는 정지 상태를 유지하고, 운동 상태에 있는 물체는 불균형적인 외부 힘의 작용을 받지 않는 한 같은 속도와 같은 방향으로 운동 상태를 유지한다는 것이다.

12

문화는 일반적으로 두 가지 주요 범주로 나뉘는데, 하나는 사상과 태도를 포함하는 비물질문화이고, 다른 하나는 도구와 건축물과 같이 만질 수 있는 인공물로 구성된 물질문화이다.

어휘 **nonmaterial**[nànmətíəriəl] 비물질적인 **attitude**[ǽtitjù:d] 태도
tangible[tǽndʒəbl] 만질 수 있는 **artifact**[á:rtəfæ̀kt] 인공물, 유물
architecture[á:rkitèktʃər] 건축물

13

Doppler 효과는 파동의 근원으로부터 상대적으로 움직이는 관찰자에 대하여 파동의 주파수나 파장에 변화가 생기는 것을 설명한다. 예를 들어, 천체가 지구 쪽으로 움직일 때 빛의 파장은 압축되고, 멀어질 때 파장은 늘어난다.

어휘 **frequency**[frí:kwənsi] 주파수 **wavelength**[wéivlèŋθ] 파장
celestial[səléstʃəl] 천체의 **compress**[kəmprés] 압축하다
stretch[stretʃ] 늘리다

14

현대 연구는 서로 보완하면서 뚜렷하게 다른 방법론들에 의존한다. 예를 들어, 양적 연구는 광범위한 통계적 패턴을 규명하지만 깊이가 부족한 반면, 질적 연구는 풍부한 세부 정보를 제공하지만 일반화하기 어렵다.

어휘 **complement**[kámpləmənt] 서로 보완하다
quantitative[kwántətèitiv] 양적인
qualitative[kwálitèitiv] 질적인
generalizability[dʒènərəlɑizəbíləti] 일반화 가능성

15

지속 가능한 디자인은 자원을 효율적으로 사용하고, 건강한 환경을 조성하며, 에너지 소비를 줄임으로써 건물이 환경에 미치는 부정적인 영향을 최소화하는 것을 추구한다. 이러한 접근 방식은 재료 조달부터 건설, 운영, 그리고 최종적인 철거 또는 재사용까지 건물의 전체 생애 주기를 고려한다.

어휘 **efficiently**[ifíʃəntli] 효율적으로
consumption[kənsʌ́mpʃən] 소비 **demolition**[dèməlíʃən] 철거

16

수요와 공급의 법칙은 시장 경제학의 근본적인 원리이며, 자원의 가용성과 그 자원을 향한 욕구 사이의 상호작용을 설명한다.

어휘 **demand**[dimǽnd] 수요 **bedrock**[bédrɑk] 근본적인
availability[əvèiləbíləti] 가용성

17

동기 부여는 목표를 향한 사람의 행동을 시작하고, 방향을 잡고, 지속시키는 과정이다. 이는 내적인 만족에 의해 움직이거나 보상이나 찬사와 같은 외적인 유인에 의해 힘을 얻을 수 있다.

어휘 **motivation**[mòutəvéiʃən] 동기 부여
incentive[inséntiv] 유인, 장려책 **praise**[preiz] 찬사

18

언어는 고정된 시스템이 아니라 끊임없이 진화하는 시스템이다. 새로운 단어가 출현하고, 오래된 형태는 사라지며, 시간이 지남에 따라 의미가 변화한다. 언어학자들은 인지적 과정과 사회적 역동성 모두를 이해하기 위해 이러한 변화를 분석한다.

어휘 **constantly**[kánstəntli] 끊임없이 **emerge**[imɔ́:rdʒ] 출현하다
cognitive[kágnətiv] 인지적인

19

지구상과 우주에 있는 현대적인 망원경은 과학자들이 멀리 떨어진 은하,

성운, 그리고 다른 별 주위를 도는 외계 행성들을 관찰할 수 있게 한다. 이러한 외계 행성의 발견은 외계 생명체에 대한 탐색을 강화했고, 지구가 유일무이한지에 대한 질문을 제기했다.

어휘 observe[əbzə́ːrv] 관찰하다
nebula[nébjələ] 성운(pl. nebulae)
extraterrestrial[èkstrətəréstriəl] 외계의

20

롱 뒤레(장기 지속)라는 개념은 지리, 기후 패턴, 인구 통계와 같이 느리게 움직이는 구조적 요인들의 깊은 영향을 강조하는데, 이는 여러 세대에 걸쳐 문명을 형성한다. 이 미묘하고 점진적인 변화의 시기는 많은 학자에 의해 헤드라인을 장식하는 극적이고 즉각적인 사건들보다 인간 역사에서 더 근본적인 것으로 여겨진다.

어휘 structural[strʌ́ktʃərəl] 구조적인 geography[dʒiáːgrəfi] 지리
demographics[dèməgrǽfiks] 인구 통계
instantaneous[ìnstəntéiniəs] 즉각적인

HACKERS TEST
p.52

01 describes	02 where	03 attempt
04 censor	05 remove	06 information
07 causing	08 to	09 even
10 widely		
11 foster	12 among	13 groups
14 provide	15 protection	16 abuse
17 discrimination	18 vulnerable	19 Every
20 strives		
21 massive	22 driven	23 career
24 and	25 better	26 of
27 creates	28 centers	29 innovation
30 now		
31 this	32 practice	33 raised
34 concern	35 toxic	36 on
37 produce	38 substances	39 have
40 chronic		

[01-10]

Streisand 효과는 검열의 역설을 드러내는 현상이다. 이는 사람들이 특정 정보를 검열하거나 삭제하려고 시도할 때, 오히려 그 정보가 원래보다 훨씬 더 광범위하게 확산되도록 만드는 상황을 설명한다. 이 효과는 자신의 Malibu 자택 항공사진을 웹사이트에서 내리도록 법적 조치를 취했던 Barbra Streisand의 이름을 따서 명명되었다. 그녀의 조치는 역설적으로 그 사진들에 대한 대중의 엄청난 관심을 불러일으켰고, 그 사진들은 400,000회 넘게 조회되었다. 이는 반발심이라는 심리학적 개념을 보여주는데, 자유에 대한 억압이 사람들로 하여금 그 자유를 회복하도록 강하게 몰아붙이는 것이다.

phenomenon[finámənàn] 현상 censorship[sénsərʃip] 검열
describe[diskráib] 설명하다 attempt[ətémpt] 시도하다
censor[sénsər] 검열하다 aerial[ɛ́əriəl] 항공의
ironically[airánikəli] 역설적으로 reactance[riǽktəns] 반발
suppression[səpréʃən] 억압 impel[impél] 강하게 몰아붙이다
restore[ristɔ́ːr] 회복하다

[11-20]

인권은 국적, 성별, 배경과 관계없이 모든 사람이 누릴 자격이 있는 기본적인 자유이다. 인권은 다양한 집단 사이의 평등을 증진하고, 취약한 사람들에 대한 학대와 차별로부터의 필수적인 보호를 제공한다. 모든 정부는 이러한 권리가 지켜지도록 노력한다. 인권을 보호하기 위해 국제 조약과 국내 법률이 마련되어 있다. 시민들은 이러한 권리가 침해될 때 그 권리를 옹호할 수도 있다. 인권을 이해함으로써, 사람들은 불의를 인식하고 모두에게 이익이 되는 더 공정한 사회를 향해 나아갈 수 있다.

entitle[intáitl] 자격을 주다 foster[fɔ́ːstər] 증진시키다
abuse[əbjúːz] 학대 discrimination[diskrìmənéiʃən] 차별
vulnerable[vʌ́lnərəbl] 취약한 strive[straiv] 노력하다
uphold[ʌphóuld] 지키다 advocate[ǽdvəkət] 옹호하다

[21-30]

도시화는 전 세계적으로 사람들이 시골 지역을 떠나 확장하는 도시로 유입되도록 이끈다. 더 많은 직업 기회와 더 높은 삶의 질에 의해 촉진된 이 거대한 이동은 혁신의 활기찬 중심지를 만든다. 도시들은 이제 경제 활동의 주요 동력으로서, 기술 발전과 사회 진보를 촉진하는 역할을 한다. 그러나, 이러한 급격한 성장은 또한 신중한 계획과 해결책을 요구하는 지속 가능성 문제 및 사회적 불평등을 포함한 과제들을 제시한다.

urbanization[əˌrbənizéiʃən] 도시화 rural[rúərəl] 시골의
vibrant[váibrənt] 활기찬 center[séntər] 중심지
innovation[ìnəvéiʃən] 혁신 foster[fɔ́ːstər] 촉진하다
sustainability[səstèinəbíləti] 지속 가능성
thoughtful[θɔ́ːtfəl] 신중한, 사려 깊은

[31-40]

현대 농업에서 농약의 사용은 작물 수확량을 크게 늘리고 식량 안보를 개선했다. 그러나, 이러한 광범위한 관행은 신선한 농산물 위에 남는 독성 잔류물에 관한 상당한 우려를 제기했다. 이러한 물질들은 장기적이고 만성적인 영향이 있을 수 있다. 따라서, 전 세계 규제 기관들은 효과적인 해충 방제의 필요성과 공중 보건 보호의 의무 사이에서 균형을 맞추고 있다. 이들은 수확된 농산물을 검사하여 잔류 유해 화학물질을 탐지하고 측정하는 엄격한 모니터링을 시행했다. 또한 지속 가능한 농업 관행을 지원하기 위해 농약의 최대 허용 수준을 규정하는 엄격한 잔류 허용 기준을 시행한다.

application[æ̀pləkéiʃən] 사용 pesticide[péstisàid] 농약, 살충제
yield[jiːld] 수확량 practice[prǽktis] 관행
considerable[kənsídərəbl] 상당한 residue[rézədjùː] 잔류물
produce[prədjúːs] 농산물 substance[sʌ́bstəns] 물질
chronic[kránik] 만성적인 regulatory[régjulətɔ̀ːri] 규제의
imperative[impérətiv] 의무 stringent[stríndʒənt] 엄격한

Section II Passage Topics

1. Humanities

HACKERS TEST
p.58

01 era	02 characterized	03 renewed
04 in	05 culture	06 started
07 flourishing	08 art	09 science
10 like		
11 symbols	12 represent	13 concepts
14 sounds	15 image	16 resembles
17 ear	18 meaning	19 listen
20 corresponds		
21 around	22 world	23 similar
24 stages	25 of	26 specific
27 they	28 learning	29 first
30 progress		
31 is	32 from	33 generation
34 another	35 spoken	36 These
37 teach	38 lessons	39 explain
40 phenomena		

[01-10]

르네상스는 14세기부터 17세기까지의 유럽 역사의 한 시기였다. 이 시대는 고전 문화에 대한 새로워진 관심으로 특징지어진다. 이는 예술과 과학의 번성을 촉발했다. 레오나르도 다빈치나 미켈란젤로 같은 예술가들은 인간의 잠재력을 기리는 걸작들을 창조했고, 동시에 합리성의 출현은 전통적인 믿음에 도전했다. 르네상스는 사상과 사회에 큰 변화를 불러왔으며, 대항해 시대와 과학 혁명을 위한 길을 열었다. 인본주의와 경험적 탐구에 대한 강렬한 집중은 르네상스를 근대의 시작으로 기록되게 했다.

era[íərə] 시대   characterize[kǽrəktəraiz] 특징짓다
renewed[rinjúːd] 새로워진, 새로운   flourishing[fləˈriʃiŋ] 번성
masterpiece[mǽstərpìːs] 걸작   potential[pəténʃəl] 잠재력
rationality[ræ̀ʃənǽləti] 합리성   traditional[trədíʃənl] 전통적인
belief[bilíːf] 믿음   humanism[hjúːmənìzm] 인본주의
empirical[impírikəl] 경험적인   dawn[dɔːn] 시작

[11-20]

세계 최초의 문자 체계 중 하나는 고대 이집트인들에 의해 기원전 약 3000년에 상형문자라고 불리는 그림들을 사용하여 개발되었다. 상형문자 기호들은 개념과 소리 모두를 나타낼 수 있다. 귀를 닮은 이 미지는 '듣다'라는 의미가 있으며, 자음 'j', 'd', 'n'에 해당한다. 이처럼 다층적인 의미는 현대 언어학자들이 상형문자를 이해하는 것을 극도로 어렵게 만들었다. 이 문자는 연구자들이 상형문자와 그리스 문자로 똑같은 텍스트가 포함된 로제타석이라는 유물을 연구하여 마침내 해독했던 1822년까지 미스터리로 남아있었다.

hieroglyph[háiərəglìf] 상형문자   symbol[símbəl] 기호
represent[rèprizént] 나타내다   resemble[rizémbl] 닮다
meaning[míːniŋ] 의미   correspond[kɔ̀ːrəspάːnd] 해당하다
linguist[líŋgwist] 언어학자   decipher[disáifər] 해독하다
artifact[άːrtəfækt] 유물   exact[igzǽkt] 똑같은

[21-30]

언어 습득은 인간이 언어를 이해하고 만들어내는 능력을 발달시키는 과정을 포함한다. 전 세계의 아이들은 어떤 특정 언어를 배우는지에 관계없이 유사한 발달 단계를 따른다. 그들은 먼저 옹알이를 하고, 단어로 나아가며, 결국 복잡한 문장을 구성한다. 연구는 인간이 다른 종들과 우리를 구별하는 특성인 언어에 대한 선천적인 능력을 가지고 있음을 시사한다. 이 선천적인 능력은 습득 과정을 안내하는, 흔히 '보편 문법'이라고 불리는 생물학적 성질을 시사한다.

acquisition[æ̀kwəzíʃən] 습득
developmental[divèləpméntl] 발달의   babble[bǽbl] 옹알이하다
progress[prάgres] 나아가다   construct[kənstrʌ́kt] 구성하다
innate[inéit] 선천적인   distinguish[distíŋgwiʃ] 구별하다
predisposition[prìːdispəzíʃən] 성질, 성향

[31-40]

민간전승은 사람들의 집단이 공유하는 전통적인 이야기, 관습, 믿음의 집합이다. 이것은 입으로 하는 말을 통해 한 세대에서 다른 세대로 전달된다. 이러한 이야기들은 도덕적 교훈을 가르치고, 자연 현상을 설명하는 데 도움을 주며, 사람들에게 문화적 정체성을 부여한다. 많은 민속 이야기들은 상상의 인물, 마법의 물건, 또는 말하는 동물들을 사용하여 이야기를 재미있게 만든다. 이러한 전통은 공동체를 하나로 모으고 공유된 가치를 계속 존속시키는 데 기여한다.

folklore[fóuklɔ̀ːr] 민간전승   traditional[trədíʃənl] 전통적인
custom[kʌ́stəm] 관습   generation[dʒènəréiʃən] 세대
moral[mɔ́ːrəl] 도덕적인   lesson[lésn] 교훈
phenomenon[finάmənὰn] 현상
imaginary[imǽdʒəneri] 상상의

2. Arts

HACKERS TEST
p.62

01 unique	02 was	03 from
04 creative	05 of	06 traditions
07 powerful	08 by	09 based
10 their		

11 subjects	12 broken	13 rearranged
14 abstract	15 that	16 emphasized
17 perspectives	18 argue	19 these
20 captured		
21 film	22 can	23 recorded
24 projected	25 relies	26 the
27 living	28 between	29 actors
30 audience		
31 structures	32 solid	33 imposing
34 they	35 bold	36 and
37 exposed	38 such	39 concrete
40 architecture		

[01-10]

재즈는 깊은 역사와 독특한 특징으로 인정받는 매우 영향력 있는 음악 스타일이다. 이 고유한 장르는 다양한 전통의 창조적인 융합에서 탄생했으며, 이는 예술가들이 자신의 문화적 배경을 기반으로 한 강력한 표현이었다. 이들 음악가의 작업은 다양한 민족 유산에 깊이 뿌리를 두면서도 완전히 새로운 음악을 낳았고, 전 세계적으로 빠르게 추종자들을 끌어모았다. 오늘날 널리 연주되고 사랑받으며, 표현이 풍부한 이 장르는 이후 R&B, 펑크, 프로그레시브 록을 포함한 수많은 다른 음악 스타일을 형성하고 영향을 주었다.

influential [ìnfluénʃəl] 영향력 있는
recognize [rékəgnàiz] 인정하다   distinctive [distíŋktiv] 독특한
diverse [dáivə:rs] 다양한   tradition [trədíʃən] 전통
powerful [páuərfəl] 강력한   ethnic [éθnik] 민족의
heritage [héritidʒ] 유산   expressive [iksprésiv] 표현이 풍부한

[11-20]

Pablo Picasso와 Georges Braque의 영향력 있는 작품들이 주된 예시인 입체파는 흔히 가장 중요한 현대 미술 운동 중 하나라고 일컬어진다. 소재들은 나뉘고 재배열되어 여러 관점을 동시에 강조하는 추상적인 형태로 나타났다. 비평가들은 이러한 기법들이 산업화와 제1차 세계대전으로 이어진 긴장을 포함하여 20세기 초의 분위기를 포착했다고 주장한다. 따라서 입체파는 그 시대를 이상적으로 대표하는 것으로 간주된다.

cubism [kjú:bizm] 입체파   exemplify [igzémpləfài] 예시하다
hail [heil] 일컬어지다   subject [sʌ́bdʒikt] 소재
abstract [ǽbstrækt] 추상적인   emphasize [émfəsàiz] 강조하다
perspective [pərspéktiv] 관점   tension [ténʃən] 긴장
representation [rèprizentéiʃən] 대표하는 것, 대표자

[21-30]

연극은 다양한 형태 속에서 전 세계 인류 문화의 중심적인 부분이었다. 녹화되고 영사될 수 있는 영화와 달리, 연극은 공유된 공간에서 배우와 관객 사이의 즉각적이고 살아있는 연결에 의존한다. 이 상호작용은 복제될 수 없는 에너지와 즉흥성을 가능하게 하여, 각 공연을 단 하나의 반복 불가능한 사건으로 만든다. 연극이 물리적 현존에 의존한다는 것은 조명, 무대 디자인, 음향이 유기적으로 경험되어 관객의 감정적, 지적 참여에 직접적으로 영향을 미친다는 것을 의미하기도 한다.

project [prədʒékt] 영사하다   rely [rilái] 의존하다
immediate [imí:diət] 즉각적인
spontaneity [spàntəní:əti] 즉흥성, 자발성
replicate [répləkèit] 복제하다   reliance [riláiəns] 의존
presence [prézns] 현존   engagement [ingéidʒmənt] 참여

[31-40]

브루탈리즘은 20세기 중반에 등장했으며, 장식 요소보다 실용적인 디자인을 우선시한다. 브루탈리스트 구조물은 대담한 형태와 콘크리트와 같은 노출된 날것의 재료를 사용하기 때문에 견고하고 위압적이다. 브루탈리스트 건축은 특히 공공 기관에서 개방성 및 집단적 이익과 같은 사회적 목표를 촉진하기 위해 단순한 형태를 강조하는 건물을 개발하고자 했다. 브루탈리즘에 대한 의견은 다양하지만, 이는 현대 건축에서 아름다움과 디자인에 대한 전통적인 관념에 도전한 영향력 있는 운동으로 남아있다.

emerge [imə́:rdʒ] 등장하다   prioritize [praió:rətàiz] 우선시하다
practical [prǽktikəl] 실용적인   decorative [dékərətiv] 장식의
structure [strʌ́ktʃər] 구조물   solid [sálid] 견고한
imposing [impóuziŋ] 위압적인, 인상적인
bold [bould] 두드러진, 대담한   exposed [ikspóuzd] 노출된
promote [prəmóut] 촉진하다   collective [kəléktiv] 집단적인
institution [ìnstitú:ʃən] 기관   notion [nóuʃən] 관념

3. Social Science

HACKERS TEST

01 guide	02 behaviors	03 members
04 societies	05 maintain	06 within
07 group	08 instance	09 is
10 common		
11 inherently	12 alignment	13 their
14 and	15 Discrepancy	16 what
17 believes	18 how	19 behaves
20 about		
21 innovation	22 stronger	23 which
24 only	25 agriculture	26 construction
27 also	28 warfare	29 complex
30 systems		

31 increase	32 companies	33 assess
34 cost	35 expense	36 producing
37 additional	38 of	39 Similarly
40 government		

[01-10]

사회 규범은 공동체 내에서 용인되는 행동 방식에 대한 공통의 이해를 나타낸다. 이는 사회 구성원들의 행동을 지도하고 집단 내의 질서를 유지한다. 예를 들어, 많은 곳에서 버스 정류장에서 줄을 서는 것은 흔히 기대되는 것이며, 이는 대기 승객들 사이의 공정성을 보장한다. 규범은 사람들이 일상에서 상호작용하고 선택하는 방식을 형성한다. 사회 규범을 따름으로써, 사람들은 더 연결된 느낌을 받고, 다른 사람들과 더 강력한 사회적 유대를 형성한다.

norm[nɔːrm] 규범　acceptable[əkséptəbl] 용인되는
conduct[kándʌkt] 행동 방식　behavior[bihéivjər] 행동
maintain[meintéin] 유지하다　group[gruːp] 집단
expectation[èkspektéiʃən] 기대　fairness[fɛ́ərnis] 공정성
passenger[pǽsəndʒər] 승객　interact[ìntərǽkt] 상호작용하다

[11-20]

인지 부조화는 개인의 가치관이 새로운 정보와 상충할 때 발생하는 정신적 불편 상태를 말한다. 사람들은 본질적으로 자신의 사고와 행동의 일치를 추구한다. 자신이 믿는 것과 행동하는 방식 사이의 불일치는 정신적 고통을 초래한다. 이러한 불안을 완화하기 위해, 개인은 자신의 행동을 정당화하거나 자신의 견해에 도전하는 정보를 부정하기도 한다. 이러한 부조화의 정도는 상충하는 요소들이 자신의 자아 개념 및 가치관의 핵심일 때 가장 크다. 이 심리적 과정은 개인적인 결정부터 사람들이 새로운 정보를 해석하는 방식에 이르기까지 일상생활의 여러 측면에 영향을 미친다.

dissonance[dísənəns] 부조화　conflict[kənflíkt] 상충하다
inherently[inhérəntli] 본질적으로　alignment[əláinmənt] 일치
discrepancy[diskrépənsi] 불일치　behave[bihéiv] 행동하다
distress[distrés] 고통　mitigate[mítəgèit] 완화하다
magnitude[mǽgnətjùːd] 정도, 크기

[21-30]

청동기 시대는 우수한 도구, 무기, 장식품 제작에 청동의 광범위한 채택이 특징인 인류 역사의 중대한 시기였다. 이 혁신은 더 강력한 도구를 낳았고, 이는 농업과 건설을 진전시켰을 뿐만 아니라, 전쟁도 변모시켰다. 그 결과, 복잡한 사회 시스템이 발전하기 시작했고, 공동체 내에 전문화된 역할이 확립되어 노동과 필수 자원의 효율적인 조직화를 강화했다. 청동기 시대는 그 이전 신석기 시대와 그 이후의 초기 선진 문명의 출현 사이에서 중요한 가교 역할을 하며, 주요 문화적, 기술적 진보의 토대를 마련했다.

pivotal[pívətl] 중대한　adoption[ədápʃən] 채택
decorative[dékərətiv] 장식의　implement[ímpləmènt] 도구
agriculture[ǽgrəkʌ̀ltʃər] 농업　construction[kənstrʌ́kʃən] 건설
enhance[inhǽns] 강화하다, 증진하다　efficient[ifíʃənt] 효율적인
organization[ɔ̀ːrɡənizéiʃən] 조직화, 구성
Neolithic[nìːəlíθik] 신석기의　subsequent[sʌ́bsikwənt] 그 이후의
civilization[sìvəlaizéiʃən] 문명

[31-40]

경제학은 개인과 사회가 제한된 자원에 직면하여 어떻게 결정을 내리는지를 탐구한다. 수익성을 높이기 위해, 기업은 한계 비용, 즉 산출물 한 단위를 추가로 생산하는 데 드는 비용을 평가해야 한다. 마찬가지로, 정부는 연간 예산의 상당 부분을 한 가지 주요 공공 부문 계획에 할당할지, 다른 계획에 할당할지를 두고 효용을 따져 보아야 한다. 이처럼 계산된 결정은 경제 주체들이 자원을 어떻게 배분하는지를 반영하며, 시장 행동과 국내총생산과 같은 지표 모두에 영향을 미친다. 경제 모델은 정량적 데이터와 행동 통찰을 사용하여 시장 동향을 예측하고 정책 효과를 평가한다.

profitability[prɑ̀fitəbíləti] 수익성　assess[əsés] 평가하다
produce[prədjúːs] 생산하다　additional[ədíʃənl] 추가의
government[gʌ́vərnmənt] 정부　utility[juːtíləti] 효용, 유용성
allocate[ǽləkèit] 할당하다　budget[bʌ́dʒit] 예산
initiative[iníʃiətiv] 계획　calculate[kǽlkjulèit] 계산하다
indicator[índikèitər] 지표　quantitative[kwántətèitiv] 정량적인
forecast[fɔ́ːrkæ̀st] 예측하다　evaluate[ivǽljuèit] 평가하다

4. Physical Science

HACKERS TEST　p.70

01 requires	02 particular	03 configuration
04 heat	05 abundant	06 and
07 tightly	08 underground	09 that
10 pressure		
11 material	12 generated	13 in
14 course	15 producing	16 power
17 involves	18 reactions	19 emit
20 amounts		
21 form	22 strong	23 winds
24 water	25 high	26 extremely
27 regions	28 clouds	29 freeze
30 grow		
31 giant	32 heavier	33 the
34 exhaust	35 fuel	36 core
37 What	38 is	39 sphere
40 densely		

[01-10]

계속해서 흐르는 평범한 온천과 달리, 간헐천은 간헐적이며 강력한 분출로 정의된다. 간헐천은 특정한 지질학적 구조를 필요로 하는데, 열원, 풍부한 물, 그리고 압력이 축적될 수 있도록 하는 단단히 좁은

지하 배관 체계이다. 이 구조는 과열된 물이 더 이상 억제되지 못하고 표면 아래의 불안정한 상태를 반영하는 특유의 물과 증기 기둥 형태로 분출될 때까지 붙잡아 둔다. 분출 중에 방출되는 엄청난 힘은 간헐천을 지구상에서 가장 역동적인 열수 특성 중 하나로 만든다.

geyser[gáizər] 간헐천 intermittent[ìntərmítnt] 간헐적인
require[rikwáiər] 필요로 하다 particular[pərtíkjulər] 특정한
configuration[kənfìgjuréiʃən] 구조 abundant[əbʌ́ndənt] 풍부한
constricted[kənstríktid] 좁은, 수축된
underground[ʌ́ndərgraund] 지하의 contain[kəntéin] 억제하다
volatile[válətil] 불안정한 eruption[irʌ́pʃən] 분출
hydrothermal[hàidrəθə́:rməl] 열수의

[11-20]

핵연료가 사용된 후 남는 잔류물은 핵폐기물로 알려져 있다. 이 물질은 주로 전력 생산 과정에서 생성되는데, 이 과정은 막대한 양의 에너지를 방출하는 핵 반응을 포함한다. 이 폐기물이 수천 년 동안 위험한 특성을 유지할 수 있다는 점을 고려할 때, 전 세계 사회의 중요한 과제는 인간 집단과 자연 서식지 모두를 지속적인 피해로부터 보호하기 위한 안전한 장기 처분 전략을 개발하는 것이다. 일반적인 방법에는 고준위 방사성 물질을 지구 표면 깊숙한 곳에 특수 제작된 지질학적 저장소에 배치하는 것이 포함된다.

residue[rézədjù:] 잔류물 nuclear fuel 핵연료
material[mətíəriəl] 물질 generate[dʒénərèit] 생성하다
produce[prədjú:s] 생산하다 involve[inválv] 포함하다
emit[imít] 방출하다 tremendous[triméndəs] 막대한
perilous[pérələs] 위험한 disposal[dispóuzəl] 처분
repository[ripázətɔ́:ri] 저장소

[21-30]

우박은 뇌우 구름에서 떨어지는 우박 알갱이라고 불리는 고체 얼음 구로 구성된 강수 형태이다. 우박은 강한 상승 기류가 물방울을 구름의 극도로 차가운 지역으로 끌어올릴 때 형성된다. 우박 알갱이가 상승 기류가 지탱할 수 없을 만큼 무거워질 때까지 과냉각된 물과 충돌하고 이를 모으면서 얼어붙고 크기가 커진다. 우박은 작은 완두콩 크기의 알갱이부터 골프공 크기 또는 그 이상에 이르기까지 크기가 다양할 수 있으며, 농작물과 재산에 큰 위협이 된다.

hail[heil] 우박 precipitation[prisìpətéiʃən] 강수
hailstone[héilstoun] 우박 알갱이 updraft[ʌ́pdræft] 상승 기류
droplet[dráplit] 방울 collide[kəláid] 충돌하다
pellet[pélit] 알갱이 property[prápərti] 재산

[31-40]

중성자별은 질량이 큰 별의 생애주기에서 마지막 단계를 나타내는 별의 잔해이다. 태양보다 더 무거운 거대 별들이 자신들의 연료를 다 소모하면, 그 중심핵은 내부로 붕괴한다. 남는 것은 중력이 양성자와 전자를 함께 짓눌러 거의 전적으로 중성자로만 이루어진 덩어리를 이룰 만큼 밀도가 극도로 높은 구체이다. 이 별들은 지름이 약 12마일(20킬로미터)에 불과하지만, 태양보다 더 많은 질량을 포함한다. 이는 중성자별 단 한 티스푼이 수십억 톤의 무게가 나간다는 것을 의미한다.

neutron[njú:trɑn] 중성자 stellar[stélər] 별의

remnant[rémnənt] 잔해, 남은 부분 exhaust[igzɔ́:st] 소모하다
fuel[fjuəl] 연료 implode[implóud] 내부로 붕괴하다
sphere[sfiər] 구체 proton[próutɑn] 양성자
electron[iléktrɑn] 전자 mass[mæs] 덩어리, 질량
diameter[daiǽmətər] 지름 weigh[wei] 무게가 나가다

5. Life Science

HACKERS TEST p.74

01 simple	02 lack	03 structures
04 in	05 advanced	06 They
07 rapidly	08 allows	09 to
10 quickly		
11 alter	12 through	13 process
14 as	15 modification	16 techniques
17 possible	18 introduction	19 desirable
20 into		
21 hunt	22 at	23 using
24 exceptional	25 abilities	26 locate
27 target	28 of	29 predators
30 silently		
31 mechanism	32 with	33 distress
34 alerting	35 nervous	36 which
37 secretes	38 chemical	39 into
40 bloodstream		

[01-10]

박테리아는 지구상의 거의 모든 환경에 존재하는 매우 작은 단세포 유기체이다. 이 단순한 미생물들은 더 진화된 세포에서 발견되는 복잡한 구조를 갖추고 있지 않다. 이들은 빠르게 번식하며, 이로 인해 변화하는 환경에 신속하게 적응할 수 있다. 일부 종은 폐렴이나 결핵 같은 질병을 일으키는 반면, 다른 종은 소화나 항생제 생산을 돕는 등 이로운 역할을 한다. 30,000종이 넘게 확인되어 있으며, 박테리아는 생명의 세 가지 주요 영역 중 하나에 해당한다.

microscopic[màikrəskápik] 미세한
organism[ɔ́:rgənizm] 유기체 simple[símpl] 단순한
structure[strʌ́ktʃər] 구조 reproduce[rì:prədjú:s] 번식하다
adapt[ədǽpt] 적응하다 disease[dizí:z] 질병
pneumonia[njumóunjə] 폐렴 tuberculosis[tjubə̀:rkjulóusis] 결핵
digestion[didʒéstʃən] 소화

[11-20]

유전자는 생물의 특성을 결정하는 정보를 전달하며 유전의 근본이 되는 생물학 단위이다. 과학자들은 유전자 변형이라고 알려진 과정을 통해서 이들을 변형시킨다. 정교한 기술은 식물과 동물에서부터 박테리아에 이르기까지 다양한 유기체에 원하는 특성을 도입하는 것을 가능하게 한다. 이는 연구자들이 농업과 의학과 같은 분야의 주요 문제에 대한 해결책을 개발할 수 있도록 한다. 그러나, 유전자 변형이 더욱 널리 퍼지면서, 그것이 사회와 환경에 미치는 영향에 대한 논쟁을 계속해서 불러일으키고 있다.

gene[dʒiːn] 유전자　**fundamental**[fʌ̀ndəméntl] 근본적인
biological[bàiəládʒikəl] 생물학적인　**heredity**[hərédəti] 유전
alter[ɔ́ːltər] 변형시키다　**genetic modification** 유전자 변형
sophisticated[səfístəkèitid] 정교한
introduction[ìntrədʌ́kʃən] 도입
desirable[dizáiərəbl] 원하는, 바람직한

[21-30]

올빼미는 전 세계의 다양한 서식지에서 발견되는 야행성 조류이다. 이들은 주로 밤에 사냥하며, 뛰어난 감각 능력을 사용하여 목표물의 위치를 파악한다. 이 포식자들 중 다수는 조용히 비행하여, 사냥당하는 동물들이 그것들을 알아차릴 가능성을 줄인다. 크고 정면을 향한 눈과, 머리를 최대 270도까지 회전할 수 있다는 사실이 이 독특한 새의 특징이다. 이들의 특징과 신비로운 야간 습성은 많은 문화권에서 수많은 신화와 전설에 영감을 주었다.

nocturnal[naːktə́ːrnl] 야행성의　**diverse**[dáivəːrs] 다양한
habitat[hǽbitæt] 서식지　**exceptional**[iksépʃənl] 뛰어난
sensory[sénsəri] 감각의　**locate**[lóukeit] 위치를 파악하다
predator[prédətər] 포식자　**silently**[sáiləntli] 조용히
habit[hǽbit] 습성

[31-40]

위험에 직면했을 때, 사람의 몸은 투쟁-도피 반응이라고 알려진 여러 생리적 변화를 신속하게 시작한다. 이 메커니즘은 신경계에 경고하는 조난 신호로 시작되며, 이는 화학 물질인 아드레날린을 즉시 혈류 속으로 분비한다. 전신을 순환하며, 아드레날린은 폐 용량 확장을 유발하고 심장 박동을 가속한다. 그 결과 발생하는 산소의 급증은 준비 태세를 향상시키는 에너지의 분출을 제공하며, 이로써 사람이 위협에 성공적으로 대처하거나 위협으로부터 도망칠 수 있는 능력을 증가시킨다.

swiftly[swíftli] 신속하게　**initiate**[iníʃièit] 시작하다
physiological[fìziəládʒikəl] 생리적인　**response**[rispáns] 반응
mechanism[mékənìzm] 메커니즘　**alert**[ələ́ːrt] 경고하다
nervous[nə́ːrvəs] 신경의　**secrete**[sikríːt] 분비하다
chemical[kémikəl] 화학 물질　**bloodstream**[blʌ́dstriːm] 혈류
lung[lʌŋ] 폐　**capacity**[kəpǽsəti] 용량　**surge**[səːrdʒ] 급증
enhance[inhǽns] 향상시키다　**flee**[fliː] 도망치다

TASK 2 | Read in Daily Life

Section I Question Types

1. Main Topic/Purpose Questions

Example p.83

공지를 읽으시오.

> 12월 10일부터 학생들은 새로운 온라인 시스템을 통해 재학 증명서 및 그밖의 문서를 이용할 수 있게 될 것입니다. 학생 ID 번호로 로그인하여 문서를 다운로드하고 인쇄하십시오. 12월 9일 이후로는 더 이상 실물 사본이 발급되지 않습니다. 문의사항이 있으면, 학적과로 연락하십시오.
>
> **access** [ǽkses] 이용하다, 접근하다
> **enrollment certificate** 재학 증명서　**physical** [fízikəl] 물리적인
> **registrar** [rédʒistrɑ̀:r] (대학의) 학적 담당 사무원

공지의 주된 목적은 무엇인가?
Ⓐ 신입생들에게 문서 발급 절차를 안내하기 위해
Ⓑ 학사 일정의 변경 사항을 공지하기 위해
Ⓒ 시스템 오작동에 대해 사과하기 위해
☑ 학생들에게 새로운 문서 입수 방법을 알리기 위해

HACKERS PRACTICE p.84

01 Ⓑ　02 Ⓒ　03 Ⓐ　04 Ⓑ

01 Main Purpose Question

이메일을 읽으시오.

> 제목: 회신: 그림 워크숍
>
> Ms. Simons께,
>
> 귀하의 5월 27일 정물화 그림 워크숍 자리가 확정되었습니다. 준비해 오실 것은 앞치마뿐입니다. 다른 모든 준비물인 물감, 붓, 그리고 캔버스는 도착해서 바로 사용하실 수 있도록 미리 준비해 놓겠습니다.
>
> Francisco Mondi 드림
>
> **still life** 정물화　**confirm** [kənfə́:rm] 확정하다
> **apron** [éiprən] 앞치마　**supply** [səplái] 준비물, 물품

이메일의 주된 목적은 무엇인가?
Ⓐ 결제 세부사항을 명시하기 위해
☑ 등록을 확정하기 위해
Ⓒ 등록 혜택을 설명하기 위해
Ⓓ 새로운 강사를 소개하기 위해

어휘　**registration** [rèdʒistréiʃən] 등록

02 Main Purpose Question

광고를 읽으시오.

> 즉시 입주 가능
>
> 침실 네 개, 욕실 두 개인 이 주택은 현재 Kingswood 택지 구역에서 매물로 나와 있습니다. 이 주택은 최근 보수를 마쳤고, 새 가전을 갖춘 현대식 주방, 널찍한 개방형 구조, 스파 스타일의 안방 욕실이 특징입니다. 이 주택은 또한 전문적으로 조경이 되었으며 큰 수영장과 온수 욕조가 있는 아름다운 뒷마당을 갖추고 있습니다.
>
> 새 소유주는 이 도시 최고의 학교, 소매점, 대중교통은 물론 전용 호수, 커뮤니티 센터, 복합 체육시설을 비롯한 Kingswood 택지 구역의 모든 편의시설을 쉽게 이용하실 수 있습니다. 가격은 겨우 275,000달러로, 주택과 생활 방식을 향상하려는 가족에게 훌륭한 기회입니다. 더 많은 정보를 원하시면, 555-0872로 Margaret Benes에게 전화하세요.
>
> **subdivision** [sʌ̀bdivíʒən] 택지 구역, 구획
> **feature** [fí:tʃər] 특징으로 하다
> **appliance** [əpláiəns] 가전, 가정용 기기
> **master bathroom** 안방 욕실　**property** [prɑ́pərti] 주택, 건물
> **access** [ǽkses] 이용(접근) 기회　**retail outlet** 소매점
> **amenity** [əménəti] 편의시설

광고의 주된 목적은 무엇인가?
Ⓐ 새롭게 열린 택지 구역을 홍보하기 위해
Ⓑ 주택 가격 인하를 발표하기 위해
☑ 판매중인 주택을 소개하기 위해
Ⓓ 몇 가지 개조 사항을 강조하기 위해

03 Main Purpose Question

공지를 읽으시오.

> 소중한 고객 여러분께,
>
> 저희 옥상 정원은 정기 유지보수를 위해 5월 25일부터 6월 1일까지 휴장합니다. 정원이 계속해서 모든 분께 안전하고 즐거운 공간이 될 수 있게 하도록 매일 안전 점검을 하고 새 꽃을 심겠습니다. 6월 2일에 여러분을 다시 맞이하기를 기대합니다!
>
> **maintenance** [méintənəns] 유지보수
> **pleasant** [plézənt] 즐거운, 쾌적한

공지의 주된 목적은 무엇인가?
☑ 방문객들에게 시설의 임시 폐쇄를 알리기 위해
Ⓑ 방문객들을 새로 단장한 옥상 정원으로 초대하기 위해
Ⓒ 직원들에게 일정을 공지하기 위해
Ⓓ 재개장 행사를 홍보하기 위해

어휘　**closure** [klóuʒər] 폐쇄, 휴업

04 Main Purpose Question

이메일을 읽으시오.

제목: 테니스 레슨 일정 변경 요청

Mr. Lin께,

테니스 레슨 일정을 변경하고자 연락드리는데, 그것이 현재는 이번 주 수요일인 5월 6일 오후 5시에 예약되어 있습니다. 안타깝게도, 업무 약속이 생겨서 예정된 시간에 참석할 수 없습니다.

제 레슨을 이번 주 금요일인 5월 8일 오전 10시로 옮길 수 있는지를 알고 싶습니다. 해당 시간이 불가능하다면, 금요일 오후 4시 이후에도 언제든지 가능합니다. 또한 금요일에 시간이 안 되신다면 대체 강사를 추천해 주실 수 있으면 감사하겠습니다.

양해해 주셔서 감사합니다.

Laura Mondale 드림

---
commitment [kəmítmənt] 책무, 약속   come up 생기다, 발생하다
alternative [ɔːltə́ːrnətiv] 대체의

Ms. Mondale이 Mr. Lin에게 연락하는 이유는?
Ⓐ 회원권을 해지하기 위해
☑ 레슨 일정을 변경하기 위해
Ⓒ 테니스 레슨에 등록하기 위해
Ⓓ 테니스 코트를 예약하기 위해

HACKERS TEST

p.86

01 Ⓒ	02 Ⓓ	03 Ⓒ	04 Ⓐ	05 Ⓐ
06 Ⓒ	07 Ⓑ	08 Ⓑ	09 Ⓒ	10 Ⓑ
11 Ⓓ	12 Ⓒ	13 Ⓓ	14 Ⓐ	15 Ⓒ

[01-02] 이메일을 읽으시오.

수신: Eva Parker <e.parker@pmail.com>
발신: Brett Lewis <customerservice@cvhotel.com>
날짜: 5월 27일
제목: 회신: 요청

Ms. Parker께,

01**귀하께서 요청하신 변경 사항을 처리할 수 있었습니다.** 이제 6월 1일부터 8일까지의 곧 다가올 숙박 기간 동안 디럭스 룸 대신 스위트룸을 이용하실 수 있습니다. 비용은 원래 지불하신 금액보다 1박당 45달러가 추가됩니다. 02**체크인 시 차액을 결제해 주시기 바랍니다.**

Brett Lewis 드림

---
upcoming [ʌ́pkʌ̀miŋ] 곧 다가올

01 Main Purpose Question

이메일의 주된 목적은 무엇인가?
Ⓐ 계절 판촉 행사를 설명하기 위해
Ⓑ 객실 선호도를 확인하기 위해
☑ 예약 변경을 확정하기 위해
Ⓓ 고객 불만을 처리하기 위해

어휘 preference [préfərəns] 선호도
      complaint [kəmpléint] 불만, 불평

02 Detail Question

Mr. Lewis는 Ms. Parker에게 무엇을 요청하는가?
Ⓐ 안내 데스크 직원에게 전화한다
Ⓑ 영수증 사본을 제공한다
Ⓒ 숙박 기간을 명시한다
☑ 미결제 잔액을 지불한다

어휘 outstanding balance 미결제 잔액

[03-04] 공지를 읽으시오.

입주민 여러분께,

4월 6일 오전 10시부터 오후 1시까지 B동 외부 03**창문 청소가 진행됩니다.** 안전과 철저한 청소를 위해 이 시간 동안 창문을 닫아 주시기 바랍니다. 또한, 04**식물이나 장식품 등 모든 개인 물품은 창틀에서 치워 주시기 바랍니다.**

---
take place 진행되다, 발생하다   thorough [θə́ːrou] 철저한
windowsill [wíndousìl] 창틀

03 Main Purpose Question

공지의 주된 목적은 무엇인가?
Ⓐ 입주민들에게 청소 계획 지원을 요청하기 위해
Ⓑ 건물 정책의 일시적 변경을 입주민들에게 알리기 위해
☑ 예정된 창문 청소를 입주민들에게 알리기 위해
Ⓓ 시설 내 신규 설비에 대한 세부사항을 제공하기 위해

어휘 temporary [témpərèri] 일시적인   installation [ìnstəléiʃən] 설비

04 Intention Question

공지에서 개인 물품을 언급하는 이유는 무엇인가?
☑ 창틀에서 치워야 하는 것을 안내하기 위해
Ⓑ 입주민들에게 해당 물품들이 건물 내에서 허용되지 않음을 알리기 위해
Ⓒ 청소팀이 파손에 대해 책임지지 않음을 설명하기 위해
Ⓓ 소지품을 임시로 보관할 지정 구역을 명시하기 위해

어휘 responsible [rispánsəbl] 책임이 있는
      designated [dézignèitid] 지정된   possession [pəzéʃən] 소지품

[05-06] 포스터를 읽으시오.

BELLE AND THE BEASTS
Red Rock 아레나에서의
라이브 콘서트

05**펑크 밴드가 새 앨범의 히트곡들을 연주하는 것을 즐기세요**

날짜:
8월 11일 토요일
오후 6시에 입장
오후 7시에 공연 시작

티켓:
06**현장 구매 45달러**
온라인 예매 35달러
www.redrockarena.com/tickets

05 Main Purpose Question
포스터의 주된 목적은 무엇인가?
- ☑ⒶⒶ 음악 공연을 홍보하기 위해
- Ⓑ 새 앨범을 발표하기 위해
- Ⓒ 지역 밴드를 광고하기 위해
- Ⓓ 연락처 정보를 제공하기 위해

06 Detail Question
할인받는 방법은 무엇인가?
- Ⓐ 아레나를 방문함으로써
- Ⓑ 일찍 도착함으로써
- ☑Ⓒ 웹사이트를 이용함으로써
- Ⓓ 팬클럽에 가입함으로써

[07-09] 소셜 미디어 게시물을 읽으시오.

Adam Lancaster

저는 자전거로 도시를 탐험하는 것을 좋아합니다. 숨겨진 장소들을 발견하면서 얼굴에 스치는 바람을 느끼는 것에는 뭔가 특별한 것이 있습니다. 지난 여름, 저는 [08]**암스테르담을 자전거로 돌아다니면서 일주일을 보냈는데, 정말 놀라웠습니다**. 자전거로 돌아다니지 않았더라면 절대 알아채지 못했을 작은 카페들, 아름다운 공원들, 그리고 조용한 운하들을 발견했습니다.

[07]**만약 제 경험이 여러분에게 영감을 주었다면, 여러분만의 도시 자전거 여행을 계획하기 전에 고려해야 할 실용적인 팁들이 있습니다.** 여러분의 자전거 타기를 순조롭고 즐겁게 만들 방법을 찾아야 할 것입니다. 많은 대여점이 일일 또는 주간 옵션을 제공하므로, 자신의 자전거를 가져오기보다는 현지에서 자전거를 대여하는 것을 추천합니다. [09]**자전거 특화 앱을 사용하면 번잡한 도로를 피하고 시간을 최대한 활용하는 데 도움이 될 수 있습니다.** 안전도 염두에 두어야 합니다. 현지 교통 규칙과 자전거 도로 표지판을 반드시 따르고, 헬멧과 반사 장비를 착용하세요.

inspire[inspáiər] 영감을 주다, 격려하다
practical[præktikəl] 실용적인, 현실적인
figure out 찾다, 생각해 내다
make the most of 최대한 활용하다 **reflective**[rifléktiv] 반사하는

---

07 Main Purpose Question
게시물의 주된 목적은 무엇인가?
- Ⓐ 저자의 자전거 타기 선호 사항을 상세히 설명하기 위해
- ☑Ⓑ 실용적인 자전거 여행 팁을 공유하기 위해
- Ⓒ 유럽 도시들에서의 자전거 타기 역사를 설명하기 위해
- Ⓓ 다양한 자전거 대여 서비스들을 비교하기 위해

어휘 **preference**[préfərəns] 선호 사항

08 Intention Question
게시물에서 암스테르담을 언급하는 이유는 무엇인가?
- Ⓐ 그 도시의 가장 선호되는 장소들을 나열하기 위해
- ☑Ⓑ 훌륭한 도시 자전거 타기 경험의 예시를 제공하기 위해
- Ⓒ 이상적인 도시 자전거 여행 목적지를 소개하기 위해
- Ⓓ 암스테르담이 유럽 최고의 자전거 도로를 가지고 있음을 보여주기 위해

어휘 **destination**[dèstənéiʃən] 목적지

09 Inference Question
자전거 특화 앱에 대해 추론할 수 있는 것은?
- Ⓐ 주로 자전거를 미리 예약하는 데 사용된다.
- Ⓑ 자전거 타는 사람들이 이용하기 쉬운 카페와 공원을 나열한다.
- ☑Ⓒ 실시간 도로 정보를 제공한다.
- Ⓓ 자전거 대여 결제를 하는 데 꼭 필요하다.

[10-12] 기사를 읽으시오.

Riverdale—[10]**다국적 반도체 제조사 Trimark 반도체가 어제 최신 공장의 준공식을 개최했다.** Riverdale 공업 지대에 있는 이 새 시설은 스마트폰, 컴퓨터, 기타 전자기기용 마이크로칩을 생산할 것이다.

[11]**Trimark의 회장 Carl Grove**는 회사의 새로운 12,000제곱미터 규모 공장 준공식에 참석해 이것은 회사의 Riverdale에 대한 투자의 시작에 불과하다고 밝혔다. "이 공장은 우리가 이 지역에 계획한 복합단지의 첫 부분일 뿐입니다. 궁극적으로, 국제 본사를 포함해 저희의 사업 전체를 이 지역으로 이전할 계획입니다."

Riverdale 시장 Karen Beatty는 회사와 대표들의 Riverdale에 대한 약속에 감사를 표했다. [12]**그녀는 4,000개 이상의 일자리 직접 창출 등 이 기업의 결정이 가져올 경제적 영향을 강조했다.** Beatty 시장은 회사의 조치를 인정해 Mr. Grove에게 특별 시민 공로상을 수여했다.

semiconductor[sèmikəndʌ́ktər] 반도체
industrial[indʌ́striəl] 공업의   **be on hand** 참석하다, 참가하다
operation[àpəréiʃən] 사업, 기업
headquarters[hédkwɔ̀:rtərz] 본사
representative[rèprizéntətiv] 대표자 **civic**[sívik] 시민의

---

10 Main Topic Question
기사는 무엇에 관한 것인가?
- Ⓐ 스마트폰 출시
- ☑Ⓑ 제조 시설
- Ⓒ 건설 계획
- Ⓓ 시 주관 행사

11 Detail Question
Carl Grove는 누구인가?
- Ⓐ 시 공무원
- Ⓑ 공장 근로자
- Ⓒ 기업 투자자
- ☑Ⓓ 기업 경영자

12 Inference Question
기사로부터 이 회사에 관해 추론할 수 있는 것은?
- Ⓐ 다른 공장들을 폐쇄했다.
- Ⓑ Riverdale에서 설립되었다.
- ☑Ⓒ 향후 지역 채용을 더 많이 할 것이다.
- Ⓓ 시로부터 인센티브를 받고 있다.

[13-15] 소셜 미디어 게시물을 읽으시오.

Chloe Winchester

[13]**드디어 Birchwood에서 새 아파트를 구했어요!** 이곳에서 집을 구하는 것은 쉬운 일이 아니었어요. 아파트들을 거의 즉시 덥석 사

가기 때문에, 이 기회가 생겼을 때 빠르게 움직여야 했어요. 그것은 어느 조용한 건물 5층에 있는 아늑하고 밝은 침실 하나짜리 아파트예요. ¹⁴이 아파트를 선택한 이유는 Oak가 버스 정류장에서 몇 걸음 거리에 편리하게 자리 잡고 있기 때문이에요.

입주는 신났지만, 새로운 동네에 적응하는 것이 조금 초조하네요. 근처 거리들을 답사하고 지역 상점들을 둘러보고 있어요. 지금까지 가장 흥미로운 점 중 하나는 길 건너편에 있는 매력적인 카페로, 아침 식사를 하기에 안성맞춤이에요. 근처에 몇 개의 피트니스 센터도 발견했어요. 매일 세탁하는 것을 걱정하고 싶지 않아서 ¹⁵지금은 믿을 만한 세탁 서비스를 찾고 있어요.

이 새로운 시기는 가능성으로 가득 찬 것 같아요. Birchwood가 제공할 모든 것을 보는 것이 기대돼요!

secure [sikjúər] 구하다, 얻어 내다
opportunity [ὰpərtjúːnəti] 기회 cozy [kóuzi] 아늑한
nerve-wracking [nɔ́ːrvrækiŋ] 초조하게 하는
adjust [ədʒʌ́st] 적응하다

13 Main Purpose Question

게시물의 주된 목적은 무엇인가?
Ⓐ 아파트 건물의 편의시설을 설명하기 위해
Ⓑ 지역 주택 시장에 대한 상세한 분석을 제공하기 위해
Ⓒ 지역 상점 추천을 요청하기 위해
☑ 성공적인 아파트 찾기를 알리기 위해

14 Detail Question

Ms. Winchester는 왜 이 아파트를 선택했는가?
☑ 대중교통 접근이 편리하다.
Ⓑ 임대료가 근처의 다른 세대들보다 훨씬 저렴했다.
Ⓒ 밝고 아늑하다.
Ⓓ 조용한 환경에 위치해 있다.

15 Detail Question

Ms. Winchester가 현재 찾고 있는 것은?
Ⓐ 지역 버스 노선 정보
Ⓑ 아침식사 메뉴가 있는 카페
☑ 믿을 수 있는 세탁 서비스
Ⓓ 좋은 장비를 갖춘 체육관

2. Detail Questions

Example p.93

공지를 읽으시오.

6월 11일 수요일 오전 9시부터 오후 6시 사이에 사무실 건물 전체의 전기 시스템 점검이 예정되어 있습니다. 이 시간 동안, 건물 전원이 차단될 예정입니다. 이날 모든 직원은 재택근무를 해야 할 것입니다.

inspection [inspékʃən] 점검

전기 시스템 점검은 언제 시작되는가?
☑ 6월 11일 오전 9시

Ⓑ 6월 11일 오후 6시
Ⓒ 6월 12일 오전 9시
Ⓓ 6월 12일 오후 6시

HACKERS PRACTICE p.94

01 Ⓓ   02 Ⓒ   03 Ⓑ   04 Ⓒ

01 Detail Question

이메일을 읽으시오.

제목: 독점 초대

Ms. Gray께,

저희 새로운 조각 전시회의 독점 미리보기 행사에 귀하를 초대하고 싶습니다. **행사는 4월 8일 월요일 오후 6시에 열릴 예정입니다.** 4월 6일 오후 5시 30분까지 참석 여부를 회신해 주시기를 정중히 부탁드립니다. 귀하의 비평가로서의 식견을 공유해 주실 수 있다면 저희로서는 영광이겠습니다.

Oliver Chan
관장, Winslow Artspace

exclusive [iksklúːsiv] 독점적인, 배타적인
sculpture [skʌ́lptʃər] 조각, 조각품
RSVP [áːrèsvìːpíː] (초대에) 회신하다 insight [ínsàit] 식견, 통찰

전시회 미리보기는 언제 예정되어 있는가?
Ⓐ 4월 6일 오후 5시 30분
Ⓑ 4월 6일 오후 6시
Ⓒ 4월 8일 오후 5시 30분
☑ 4월 8일 오후 6시

02 Detail Question

메시지 대화문을 읽으시오.

Mary Crockett (오전 10:00)
모두 좋은 아침이에요. **우리 미용실에 새 접수 담당자를 채용했다는 것을 모두에게 알리고자 해요.** 그녀는 월요일부터 일을 시작해요.

Hiro Yamamoto (오전 10:05)
좋은 소식이네요. 지난 2주 동안 접수 담당자 없이 정말 힘들었어요.

Cindy Sullivan (오전 10:10)
맞아요. 고객 머리 하면서 전화도 받고 손님들도 맞이해야 해서 꽤 스트레스였어요.

Meghan Tran (오전 10:15)
동의해요. 월요일 문 열기 전에 작은 환영 파티를 해야 할 것 같네요.

Mary Crockett (오전 10:20)
좋은 생각이에요. **문 열기 30분 전에 들어와요.** 옆 제과점에서 페이스트리를 좀 사 올게요.

Meghan Tran (오전 10:21)
완벽해요. 갈게요. 커피도 사 올게요.

receptionist [risépʃənist] 접수 담당자

월요일에 모두 미용실에 일찍 나올 이유는 무엇인가?
Ⓐ 일을 일찍 시작하기 위해
Ⓑ 페이스트리를 만들기 위해

ⓒ 새 직원을 맞이하기 위해
ⓓ 고객의 요구를 충족하기 위해

03 Detail Question

이메일을 읽으시오.

> 제목: 일정 변경 – RN 218 항공편
>
> Mr. Martel께,
>
> 귀하의 항공편인 RN 218편이 원래 일정보다 50분 빠른 오전 7시 45분 출발로 일정이 변경되었습니다. 계정에서 새로운 여행 일정을 확인해 주시기 바랍니다. 새로운 시간이 귀하와 맞지 않는다면, **저희 웹사이트에서** 24시간 이내에 다른 항공편으로 변경하거나 **환불을 요청**하실 수 있습니다.
>
> Clara Wilson 드림
> 고객 서비스 담당자, Kairos 항공사
>
> **flight**[flait] 항공편   **depart**[dipá:rt] 출발하다, 떠나다
> **itinerary**[aitínərèri] 여행 일정

Mr. Martel은 어떻게 환불을 요청할 수 있는가?
ⓐ 고객 상담실에 이메일을 보냄으로써
☑ 항공사 웹사이트를 방문함으로써
ⓒ 공항 발권 데스크에 전화함으로써
ⓓ 자동 환불을 기다림으로써

어휘 **reimbursement**[rì:imbə́:rsmənt] 환불, 상환

04 Detail Question

소셜 미디어 게시물을 읽으시오.

> 모든 책 애호가에게 외칩니다! 이번 주 목요일, 지역 작가들과 함께하는 저녁을 위해 The Inkpot Café로 오세요. 제가 행사를 안내하고 모든 분이 참여하도록 각 작가와 짧은 질의응답 시간을 진행하겠습니다.
>
> **특히 Marissa Keane 작가를 모시게 되어 기쁜데, 그녀는** 비평가들의 찬사를 받은 소설 Echoes of the Gilded Age의 **집필 과정에 대한 특별 발표를 할 것입니다.** 그녀는 아이디어의 초기 영감부터 최종 편집까지 자신의 창작 여정에 대한 개인적 식견을 공유할 것입니다.
>
> 개장은 오후 6시이며, 행사는 오후 6시 30분부터 8시까지 진행됩니다. 미리 알려드리자면, 좌석은 선착순이며, 좌석이 다 찬 뒤에는 입석도 준비되어 있습니다. 또한, 자막과 함께 전체 행사를 실시간 스트리밍할 예정입니다. 링크는 오후 5시 30분에 여기에 게시될 것입니다.
>
> **host**[houst] 진행하다, 주최하다   **involve**[inválv] 참여시키다
> **acclaimed**[əkléimd] 찬사 받는   **insight**[ínsàit] 식견, 통찰
> **heads-up**[hédʌp] 알림, 경고   **first come, first served** 선착순
> **standing room** 입석   **caption**[kǽpʃən] 자막

Marissa Keane은
ⓐ 자신의 소설 속 한 구절을 읽을 것이다
ⓑ 행사와 질의응답을 안내할 것이다
☑ 자신의 집필 과정에 대해 이야기할 것이다
ⓓ 자신의 책에 사인해 줄 것이다

어휘 **passage**[pǽsidʒ] 구절, 통로

HACKERS TEST   p.96

01 ⓑ	02 ⓓ	03 ⓒ	04 ⓑ	05 ⓓ
06 ⓓ	07 ⓑ	08 ⓒ	09 ⓒ	10 ⓒ
11 ⓓ	12 ⓓ	13 ⓓ	14 ⓓ	15 ⓒ

[01-02] 표지판을 읽으시오.

> 고객 여러분께 알림
>
> ⁰¹5월 10일부터 14일까지, Wallace 백화점은 휴업합니다. ⁰¹이 기간 동안 저희 건물에 새로운 화재 경보 및 스프링클러 시스템이 설치될 예정입니다. 불편에 대해 보상해 드리고자, 모든 고객님께 10달러 디지털 상품권을 드립니다. ⁰²**상품권을 이용하시려면 저희 모바일 앱을 다운로드하시면 됩니다.**
>
> **inconvenience**[ìnkənví:njəns] 불편   **gift certificate** 상품권

01 Detail Question

표지판에 따르면, 5월에 무슨 일이 일어날 것인가?
ⓐ 내부 장식을 다시 하는 계획이 시작될 것이다.
☑ 안전 장비가 설치될 것이다.
ⓒ 건물 안전 점검이 시행될 것이다.
ⓓ 비상 절차가 시험될 것이다.

어휘 **redecorate**[rì:dékəreit] 내부 장식을 다시 하다
inspection[inspékʃən] 점검   **procedure**[prəsí:dʒər] 절차

02 Detail Question

고객들은 어떻게 상품권을 받을 수 있는가?
ⓐ 웹사이트에 접속함으로써
ⓑ 양식을 다운로드함으로써
ⓒ 직원에게 이야기함으로써
☑ 애플리케이션을 설치함으로써

[03-04] 광고를 읽으시오.

> 피아노 판매합니다. 거의 사용하지 않은 Stonebrook & Sons 그랜드 피아노로 상태가 매우 좋습니다. 초보자와 숙련된 연주자 모두에게 알맞습니다. ⁰³ᴬ**배송**, ⁰³ᴮ**가정 내 설치**, ⁰³ᴰ**전문 조율** 포함하여 3,900달러. ⁰⁴**더 많은 정보는 Vintage Tone Emporium을 방문**하시거나 555-2841로 전화하시기 바랍니다.
>
> **condition**[kəndíʃən] 상태   **tuning**[tjú:niŋ] 조율

03 Detail Question

피아노 가격에 포함되지 않은 것은 무엇인가?
ⓐ 배송 비용
ⓑ 가정 내 설치
☑ 연장된 보증
ⓓ 음향 조정

어휘 **placement**[pléismənt] 설치, 배치
warranty[wɔ́:rənti] 보증

04 Inference Question

광고로부터 이 피아노에 관해 추론할 수 있는 것은?
Ⓐ 현재 창고에 있다.
Ⓑ 사업체가 판매하고 있다. ✓
Ⓒ 전문가가 소유했었다.
Ⓓ 당일 배송이 가능하다.

어휘 **storage**[stɔ́:ridʒ] 창고, 보관소

[05-06] 영수증을 읽으시오.

Nelson Office Furniture

고객: Brad Wilcox 주문: 93809
날짜: 7월 7일 ⁰⁵매장번호: 009

품목	수량	가격
Lyman 책상	4	350.00달러
Neo 의자	4	125.00달러
⁰⁶500달러 미만 주문에는 25달러의 배송비가 부과됩니다.	배송	해당 없음
	세금	45.00달러
	⁰⁶**총합**	**520.00달러**

www.nelsonoffice.com을 방문하여 의견을 남기고
Nelson 로열티 클럽 회원에 가입하세요.

05 Inference Question

Nelson Office Furniture에 대해 암시된 것은?
Ⓐ 온라인 주문에 할인을 제공한다.
Ⓑ 7월 7일에 배송을 보냈다.
Ⓒ 새로운 제품 라인을 출시했다.
Ⓓ 여러 지점을 운영한다. ✓

06 Detail Question

Mr. Wilcox가 배송비를 부과받지 않은 이유는?
Ⓐ 로열티 클럽 회원이 되었다.
Ⓑ 제품에 대한 후기를 게시했다.
Ⓒ 매장에서 주문품을 가져갔다.
Ⓓ 최소 구매액을 충족했다. ✓

[07-09] 이메일을 읽으시오.

제목: Morris Tower

Ms. Porter께,

⁰⁷지난주 이메일에서 귀하의 직원 중 한 명을 Morris Tower로 보내달라고 요청했습니다. 하지만 아직 회신받지 못했습니다. 가능한 한 빨리 필요한 조치를 해주실 수 있을까요? ⁰⁸로비의 에어컨이 작동하지 않는다는 임차인들의 불만을 여러 차례 접수했습니다. 그리고 현재의 폭염을 고려할 때, 상황은 아마 더 악화되기만 할 것 같습니다. 귀하의 기술자 중 한 명이 토요일에 올 수 있다면 감사하겠습니다. 저는 오전 9시부터 11시 30분까지 부재하겠지만, ⁰⁹정오에 귀하의 직원을 만날 수 있습니다. 제가 개인적인 일로 오후 1시 30분에 나가야 하므로 오후 늦은 시간은 불가능하다는 점을 참고해 주시기 바랍니다.

Samuel Collins 드림
건물 관리자
Morris Tower

어휘 **employee**[implɔ́ii:] 직원 **necessary**[nésəsèri] 필요한
arrangement[əréindʒmənt] 조치, 처리 방식
tenant[ténənt] 임차인, 세입자

07 Main Purpose Question

Mr. Collins가 Ms. Porter에게 이메일을 보낸 이유는?
Ⓐ 현황 보고서를 제공하기 위해
Ⓑ 요청한 사항에 대해 더 알아보기 위해 ✓
Ⓒ 약속을 변경하기 위해
Ⓓ 지연에 대해 사과하기 위해

어휘 **apologize**[əpálədʒàiz] 사과하다

08 Detail Question

임차인들이 무엇에 대해 불만을 제기했는가?
Ⓐ 유지보수 계획이 취소되었다.
Ⓑ 건물에 청소가 필요하다.
Ⓒ 기기가 제대로 작동하지 않고 있다. ✓
Ⓓ 출입구가 막혔다.

어휘 **malfunction**[mælfʌ́ŋkʃən] 제대로 작동하지 않다

09 Detail Question

Mr. Collins는 토요일 몇 시에 만나고 싶어 하는가?
Ⓐ 오전 9시
Ⓑ 오전 11시 30분
Ⓒ 오후 12시 ✓
Ⓓ 오후 1시 30분

[10-12] 광고를 읽으시오.

여름 특가

Titan 산맥의 중심에 있는 Pine Ridge 산장은 세계적인 수준의 스키로 유명할 뿐만 아니라 훨씬 더 많은 것을 제공합니다. 여름 방문객들은 하이킹, ¹⁰낚시, 급류 래프팅, 그 밖의 다양한 활동을 즐길 수 있습니다!

여름 여행을 더욱 근사하게 만들기 위해, 4월 30일까지 예약되는 6월에서 9월 사이의 숙박에 대해 모든 객실에 여행 기간에 따라 최대 50퍼센트까지 할인이 제공됩니다.*

숙박 기간	할인율
1-2박	15퍼센트
3-4박	25퍼센트
5-6박	35퍼센트
¹¹7박 이상	50퍼센트

예약을 하시려면, 산장의 예약 전화 801-555-7453으로 직접 전화하시거나 www.pine-ridge.com을 방문하세요. ¹²대규모 단체를 위한 특별 예약을 하시거나, 본 건물에서 비공개 행사를 예약하시려면, EvanS@pine-ridge.com으로 ¹²영업 책임자 Evan Singleton에게 연락하시기 바랍니다.

*객실 상황에 따라 달라질 수 있음. 독립기념일 주말에는 할인이 유효하지 않음.

어휘 **book**[buk] 예약하다 **duration**[djuréiʃən] 기간
property[prápərti] 건물, 재산 **valid**[vǽlid] 유효한, 타당한

10 Inference Question

Pine Ridge 산장에 대해 추론할 수 있는 것은?
Ⓐ 여름에만 개장한다.
Ⓑ 수익이 줄어들었다.
✓ 수로 근처에 위치해 있다.
Ⓓ 주로 외국 손님의 수요에 맞춘다.

11 Detail Question

2주 동안 숙박하는 고객들은 얼마나 할인받는가?
Ⓐ 15퍼센트
Ⓑ 25퍼센트
Ⓒ 35퍼센트
✓ 50퍼센트

12 Detail Question

개인 행사를 위한 장소는 어떻게 마련될 수 있는가?
Ⓐ 전화번호로 전화함으로써
Ⓑ 직접 건물을 방문함으로써
Ⓒ 웹사이트에 접속함으로써
✓ 영업 담당자에게 연락함으로써

[13-15] 양식을 읽으시오.

> ¹³세계 디지털 뱅킹 서밋 등록
>
> 등록 데스크는 매일 오전 8시에 문을 엽니다. ¹⁴명찰을 받으려면 이 메일 확인서를 제시해 주십시오. 기조연설과 메인 세션 참석은 등록에 포함되어 있습니다. ¹⁵개인 워크숍은 별도의 사전 등록이 필요합니다. 콘퍼런스는 매일 오전 9시부터 오후 5시 30분까지 진행되며, 하루 종일 인적 네트워크 형성 기회가 제공됩니다.
>
> | 참석자 ID 번호: 2409 | 참석자: Samantha Hargrove |
> |---|---|
> | 조직: Zenith 투자 그룹 | 참석 일자: 4월 14일 – 4월 16일 |

registration [rèdʒistréiʃən] 등록
confirmation [kànfərméiʃən] 확인서
badge [bædʒ] 명찰, 신분증   keynote speech 기조연설

13 Main Purpose Question

이 양식의 용도는 무엇인가?
Ⓐ 기조연설자 역할 신청
Ⓑ 네트워크 장비 요청
Ⓒ 후원 프로그램 참가
✓ 콘퍼런스 등록

14 Detail Question

참가자들이 등록 데스크에 가져와야 하는 것은 무엇인가?
Ⓐ 명함
Ⓑ 사진이 있는 신분증
Ⓒ 여권
✓ 이메일 확인서

15 Detail Question

별도 등록이 필요한 활동은 무엇인가?
Ⓐ 기조연설
Ⓑ 메인 세션
✓ 개인 워크숍
Ⓓ 인적 네트워크 형성 기회

3. Fact/Negative Fact Questions

Example   p.103

공지를 읽으시오.

> 제목: 시험 시간표 변경
>
> 학생 여러분,
>
> 학교 시험 일정이 변경되었습니다. 모든 기말고사는 6월 3일부터 6월 10일까지 매일 오전 9시에 B동에서 진행됩니다. **본인의 특정 과목 및 좌석 배치에 관해서는 강의 포털에서 확인해 주십시오.** 시험 시간이 충돌할 경우, 즉시 학사지원처로 이메일을 보내십시오. 시험 장소나 날짜에 관한 추가 변경 사항이 생기면, 이메일을 통해 알려드리겠습니다. 저희는 공정하고 체계적인 시험 절차를 유지하기 위해 노력하고 있습니다. 협조해 주셔서 감사합니다.

specific [spisífik] 특정한   arrangement [əréindʒmənt] 배치
conflict [kánflikt] 충돌, 불일치   immediately [imí:diətli] 즉시

좌석 배치에 대해 명시된 것은?
Ⓐ 시험 전에 변경될 수 있다.
Ⓑ 시험마다 다르다.
✓ 강의 포털에서 확인할 수 있다.
Ⓓ 학생들이 선택한다.

HACKERS PRACTICE   p.104

01 Ⓑ   02 Ⓐ   03 Ⓓ   04 Ⓒ

01 Fact Question

공지를 읽으시오.

> 새로운 셔틀버스 서비스가 8월 25일 시작됩니다. 버스는 오전 7시부터 오후 7시까지 Downsview 역과 시청 사이에서 운영되며, 30분마다 운행합니다. 이 서비스는 평일에만 이용 가능하다는 점을 참고하시기 바랍니다. 예약은 필요 없으며, **서비스 이용에 요금이 부과되지 않습니다.**

공지가 셔틀버스 서비스에 대해 명시하는 것은?
Ⓐ 사전 예약이 필요하다.
✓ 무료로 이용할 수 있다.
Ⓒ 주말에만 운영된다.
Ⓓ 한 시간에 한 번 제공된다.

02 Fact Question

광고를 읽으시오.

> 저희는 **Green Plate로 식물성 식품 산업에 진출하면서** 간편식 솔루션의 새 시대를 열고 있습니다. 저희의 식품 분야 전문 기술을 바탕으로, 각 Green Plate 식사는 뛰어난 맛과 균형 잡힌 영양을 고려해 설계되었습니다. 3월 24일까지 가입하시고 첫 2주 체험 키트

를 35퍼센트 할인받으세요.

prepared meal 간편식, 미리 조리된 식품
expertise[èkspərtíːz] 전문 기술, 전문 지식
exceptional[iksépʃənl] 뛰어난 nutrition[njuːtríʃən] 영양
subscribe[səbskráib] 가입하다, 구독하다

광고가 Green Plate 식사에 대해 명시하는 것은?
- (A) 주로 식물로 구성되어 있다. ✓
- (B) 소비자가 직접 요리해야 한다.
- (C) 주요 슈퍼마켓에서 판매된다.
- (D) 고객들에게 무료로 배송된다.

03 Fact Question

공지를 읽으시오.

고객 여러분께,

시스템 업그레이드가 예정되어 있어, 3월 27일 토요일 오후 9시부터 오후 11시까지 저희 온라인 뱅킹 서비스를 이용하실 수 없습니다. 저희는 고객 여러분이 모든 긴급한 온라인 거래를 이 기간 이전에 완료하시기를 권장합니다. ATM 서비스는 영향받지 않습니다.

unavailable[ʌ̀nəvéiləbl] 이용할 수 없는
urgent[ə́ːrdʒənt] 긴급한 transaction[trænzǽkʃən] 거래, 처리

3월 27일 밤의 온라인 뱅킹 서비스에 대해 명시된 것은?
- (A) 경고 메시지를 표시할 것이다.
- (B) 기업 고객들만 이용 가능할 것이다.
- (C) 입금을 받지 않을 것이다.
- (D) 이용할 수 없을 것이다. ✓

어휘 deposit[dipázit] 입금

04 Negative Fact Question

기사를 읽으시오.

Elmhurst—Elmhurst시가 다가오는 선거를 준비하고 있다. ^A^11월 5일에 주민들은 세 번의 임기를 마치고 은퇴하는 Sandra Moretti를 대신할 ^B^새 시장을 선출하기 위해 투표함으로 갈 것이다.

^C^열두 명이 넘는 후보가 시장 자리를 놓고 겨루며, 경쟁은 뜨거워졌다. 현재 선두는 지역 사업가 David Smith이다. 최근 여론조사에 따르면 Mr. Smith는 가장 근접한 경쟁자인 시의회 의장 Annie Tobin보다 5포인트 앞서 있다. 그러나, ^D^당선 후보는 전체 투표수의 최소 50퍼센트를 획득해야 한다는 선거 규정 때문에 이 경쟁은 두 사람 간 결선투표로 이어질 가능성이 크다. 두 번째 선거가 필요할 경우, 이는 12월 10일에 실시될 것이다.

election[ilékʃən] 선거 resident[rézədənt] 주민
ballot box 투표함 mayor[méiər] 시장
candidate[kǽndidèit] 후보 vie[vai] 겨루다, 다투다
run-off election 결선투표 electoral[iléktərəl] 선거의

다음 중 선거에 대해 사실이 아닌 것은?
- (A) 11월에 실시될 것이다.
- (B) 시 공직을 위한 것이다.
- (C) 24명의 후보가 있다. ✓
- (D) 당선자는 과반수 득표가 필요하다.

HACKERS TEST p.106

01	D	02	D	03	C	04	B	05	D
06	B	07	D	08	D	09	D	10	B
11	C	12	C	13	A	14	D	15	C

[01-02] 이메일을 읽으시오.

제목: 유지보수 점검

주민 여러분께,

^02^연례 유지보수 점검이 11월 11일에 실시될 예정임을 다시 알려 드립니다. 해결해야 할 문제점을 찾기 위해 ^01^건물 직원이 각 아파트를 방문해야 합니다. 귀하의 세대에 이들이 들어갈 수 있도록 해 주십시오. 협조에 감사드립니다.

Stan Leighton 드림
건물 관리인

maintenance[méintənəns] 유지보수
inspection[inspékʃən] 점검 address[ədrés] 해결하다, 처리하다
superintendent[sùːpərinténdənt] 관리인, 감독관

01 Main Purpose Question

이 이메일의 주된 목적은 무엇인가?
- (A) 점검 일정의 변경을 알리기 위해
- (B) 세대 내의 유지보수 문제들을 보고하도록 주민들에게 요청하기 위해
- (C) 직원들에게 건물 유지보수 점검에 대해 알리기 위해
- (D) 건물 직원들이 세대에 들어갈 수 있도록 해 줄 것을 주민들에게 상기시키기 위해 ✓

02 Fact Question

이메일이 점검에 대해 명시하는 것은?
- (A) 자발적이다.
- (B) 11일이 소요될 것이다.
- (C) 안전 문제에 관한 것이다.
- (D) 매년 일어난다. ✓

[03-04] 기사를 읽으시오.

인기있는 지역 야구단 Dallas Tigers가 3월 15일 시즌 첫 경기를 준비하고 있다. ^03^지난 시즌 Houston Hurricanes를 리그 챔피언십으로 이끈 감독 Brian Radcliffe는 새 팀과 계약을 체결하게 되어 매우 기뻐했다. ^04^그는 최근 인터뷰에서 "올해 우리는 좋은 성적을 낼 것이라고 확신하고, 특히 스타 투수 Davis Wilkins의 막판 합류로 더욱 그렇다"라고 말했다. "모든 선수가 열심히 훈련하고 있고, 로커 룸 안에는 높은 자신감이 감돌고 있다."라고 그는 덧붙였다.

팬들에게 감사의 뜻을 표하기 위해, 팀은 3월 15일 경기에 가장 먼저 도착한 100명에게 무료 야구 모자를 나눠 줄 것이다. 이 중 하나를 원한다면, 경기 시작 최소 한 시간 전에 경기장에 도착해야 한다.

opener[óupənər] 첫 경기, 개시 contract[kántrækt] 계약
confidence[kánfədəns] 자신감
appreciation[əprìːʃiéiʃən] 감사 hand out 나눠 주다

03 Inference Question
Mr. Radcliffe에 대해 추론할 수 있는 것은?
Ⓐ 팀에서 감독 역할을 해본 적이 없다.
Ⓑ Dallas에서 야구를 했었다.
☑ 최근에 Houston Hurricanes를 떠났다.
Ⓓ 아직 계약을 체결하지 않았다.

04 Fact Question
Dallas Tigers에 대해 명시된 것은?
Ⓐ 리그 우승을 차지했다.
☑ 새 선수를 영입했다.
Ⓒ 로커 룸을 개선했다.
Ⓓ 훈련을 연기했다.

어휘 postpone [poustpóun] 연기하다

[05-06] 광고를 읽으시오.

당신의 안전을 당신의 손으로 지키십시오
⁰⁶ᴬ전 육군 교관이자 경비 전문가 Matthew Bates와 함께하는
⁰⁵호신술 개인 교습에 등록하십시오.
- ⁰⁶ᴰ30년이 넘는 군과 민간 강의 경력
- ⁰⁶ᴮ90분 수업 한 회당 40달러
- ⁰⁶ᶜ개인의 필요와 능력에 맞게 맞춤 설계된 수업

더 많은 정보는 555-2327로 문의하십시오.

instructor [instrʌ́ktər] 교관, 강사   tailor [téilər] 맞춤 설계하다
---

05 Main Topic Question
이 광고는 무엇을 홍보하는가?
Ⓐ 군 복무
Ⓑ 경비 시스템
Ⓒ 단체 피트니스 수업
☑ 호신술 훈련

06 Negative Fact Question
다음 중 Matthew Bates에 대해 사실이 아닌 것은?
Ⓐ 육군에 있었다.
☑ 1시간에 40달러를 받는다.
Ⓒ 각 고객에 따라 서비스를 맞춘다.
Ⓓ 30년이 넘는 경력이 있다.

[07-09] 이메일을 읽으시오.

수신: Ray Carson <r.carson@dmail.com>
발신: Myra Adams <m.adams@bedforddept.com>
날짜: 6월 3일
제목: 회신: 지원서

Mr. Carson께,

이곳 Bedford 백화점의 Collingwood 지점에서 귀하에게 부점장 자리를 제의하기로 했음을 알려드리게 되어 기쁩니다. ⁰⁷귀하의 폭넓은 관련 경력을 고려할 때, 이 역할에서 성공하시리라 확신합니다. 지난주 면접에서 논의한 바와 같이, ⁰⁸시작일은 7월 5일입니다. 첫 날에는 4시간 오리엔테이션에 참여하실 것입니다. 이 시간 동안, 당사 정책과 귀하가 수행할 다양한 업무에 대해 익히실 것입니다. ⁰⁹다음 주에 당사 인사팀 구성원인 Brenda Weatherford와 만나 주시기 바랍니다. 그녀는 귀하와 함께 고용 계약서를 검토하고, 가지고 계실 어떤 질문이든 답변해 드릴 것입니다. 편하신 날짜와 시간을 알려 주시기 바랍니다.

Myra Adams 드림

inform [infɔ́:rm] 알리다, 통지하다   offer [ɔ́:fər] 제의하다
branch [bræntʃ] 지점, 나뭇가지   extensive [iksténsiv] 폭넓은
relevant [réləvənt] 관련 있는   confident [kánfədənt] 확신하는
thrive [θraiv] 성공하다, 번창하다
participate [pɑːrtísəpèit] 참여하다
---

07 Inference Question
Mr. Carson에 대해 추론할 수 있는 것은?
Ⓐ 다른 지점으로 전근했다.
Ⓑ 시작일 변경을 요청했다.
Ⓒ 6월에 지원서를 제출했다.
☑ 이전에 소매점에서 근무했다.

어휘 transfer [trænsfə́:r] 이적하다, 이동하다

08 Detail Question
7월 5일에 일어날 것은?
Ⓐ 회사 정책이 개정된다.
Ⓑ 채용 면접이 시행된다.
☑ 교육 과정이 진행된다.
Ⓓ 팀장이 발표된다.

09 Fact Question
이메일이 Ms. Weatherford에 대해 명시하는 것은?
Ⓐ 경영팀의 일원이다.
☑ Mr. Carson과 법적 합의를 논의할 것이다.
Ⓒ 오리엔테이션의 진행자이다.
Ⓓ Mr. Carson의 직속 관리자가 될 것이다.

[10-12] 소셜 미디어 게시물을 읽으시오.

Riverside시 @RiversideCity | 4월 21일

¹⁰행사가 있는 날이 빠르게 다가오고 있습니다. 52회 Riverside Fun Run까지 이제 고작 14일 남았어요! 준비되셨나요?

1년에 한번 열리는 이 경주는 달리기를 원하든, 걷기를 원하든, 휠체어를 타기를 원하든, 참가를 원하는 모든 분께 열려 있습니다. 참가자는 5킬로미터 또는 10킬로미터 코스, 혹은 풀 마라톤 중에서 선택할 수 있습니다. 각 우승자에게는 경주별로 트로피가 수여되며 참여하신 모든 분은 참가증서와 물병, 티셔츠를 받습니다.

그러나 경주에 참여하지 않아도 즐거울 수 있습니다. ¹¹라이브 음악, 지역 노점상 소개, 그리고 어린이를 위한 특별 놀이 공간도 마련됩니다.

¹²행사는 5월 5일 오전 8시에 시청에서 시작됩니다.

등록은 4월 30일까지 가능합니다.

등록비: 25달러

행사로 모금된 모든 수익은 어려움에 처한 아동, 노인, 가정을 위해 음식을 제공하는 시의 프로그램을 지원하는 데 사용될 것입니다.

> participate[pɑːrtísəpèit] 참가하다
> certificate[sərtífikət] 증서, 자격증
> registration[rèdʒistréiʃən] 등록 proceeds[próusiːdz] 수익

10 Main Purpose Question

게시물의 주된 목적은 무엇인가?
Ⓐ 일정 변경을 알리기 위해
✅ 다가오는 행사를 홍보하기 위해
Ⓒ 사람들이 달리기를 해보도록 장려하기 위해
Ⓓ 자선 모금을 위해

11 Fact Question

Riverside Fun Run에 대해 명시된 것은?
Ⓐ 처음으로 개최된다.
Ⓑ 오직 하나의 정해진 코스 거리만을 제공한다.
✅ 부대 행사들이 함께 진행된다.
Ⓓ 어린이를 위한 특별 경주를 포함한다.

12 Detail Question

경주는 언제 열리는가?
Ⓐ 4월 21일
Ⓑ 4월 30일
✅ 5월 5일
Ⓓ 5월 10일

[13-15] 메시지 대화문을 읽으시오.

> Mitch Henderson (오후 2:30)
> Melville Industries사 계약 관련 ¹³고객 프레젠테이션이 금요일로 잡혀 있어요. 저에게 진행 상황을 알려주시겠어요?
>
> Rachel Norton (오후 2:33)
> 저는 재무 예측 섹션을 완료했어요. ¹⁵ᴮ우리 자동화 시스템을 도입하면 그들이 첫해만 해도 운영비를 5퍼센트 절감할 수 있음을 비용 분석이 증명해요.
>
> Brandon West (오후 2:36)
> 기술 사양서는 완성됐어요. ¹⁵ᴰ로봇 유닛과 센서 네트워크 구성 요소를 포함해 ¹⁵ᴬ설치 단계별 상세 일정도 넣었어요.
>
> Catherine Walsh (오후 2:40)
> 저는 위험 평가 보고서 초안을 작성 중이에요. 자동화 컨베이어 시스템에 잠재적인 안전 규정 준수 문제가 있을 수 있음을 확인해서, 기술 문서를 다시 검토할 계획이에요.
>
> Brandon West (오후 2:43)
> 무엇이 필요한지 알려 주세요, Catherine. 최신 데이터를 보내드릴 수 있어요.
>
> Mitch Henderson (오후 2:45)
> 좋아요. 모든 것이 맞춰지도록, 목요일 오후 3시에 전체 리허설을 잡죠.

> projection[prədʒékʃən] 예측, 견적
> implement[ímpləmènt] 도입하다
> specification[spèsəfikéiʃən] 사양서, 설명서
> assessment[əsésmənt] 평가
> compliance[kəmpláiəns] 규정 준수

13 Main Purpose Question

이 메시지 대화문의 주된 목적은 무엇인가?
✅ 고객 프레젠테이션 준비 상황을 이해하기 위해
Ⓑ 현재 프로젝트의 예산 조정을 논의하기 위해
Ⓒ 팀원들과 분기 실적 목표를 점검하기 위해
Ⓓ 프로젝트 관리를 위한 정기 팀 회의 일정을 잡기 위해

14 Intention Question

오후 2시 40분에 Ms. Walsh가 "I'm planning to revisit the technical documents"라고 쓸 때 무엇을 암시하는가?
Ⓐ 기술 사양서가 잘못되었다고 생각한다.
Ⓑ 일부 장비를 직접 점검하려 한다.
Ⓒ 위험 평가를 금요일까지 미루려 한다.
✅ 기술 사양서를 재검토해야 한다.

어휘 in person 직접 re-examine[riːigzǽmin] 재검토하다

15 Negative Fact Question

다음 중 자동화 시스템에 대해 사실이 아닌 것은?
Ⓐ 여러 단계 설치가 필요하다.
Ⓑ 운영 지출을 낮출 것으로 예상된다.
✅ 이전에 안전 문제로 언급된 적이 있다.
Ⓓ 기계화된 장비를 포함한다.

4. Vocabulary Questions

Example p.113

기사를 읽으시오.

> 재생 가능한 방식으로 전기를 생산하는 비용이 지난 10년간 급락하면서, 시장 역학 관계를 근본적으로 변화시켰다. 집중적인 연구 개발로 추진된 기술 발전은 태양광 패널과 풍력 터빈을 훨씬 더 효율적으로 만들었으며, 생산 및 설치 비용도 상당히 낮췄다. 이는 전 세계의 소비자, 기업, 그리고 전체 전력망에 있어 청정 에너지를 전통적인 탄소 집약적 발전원에 비해 점점 더 매력적이고 흔히 더 저렴한 대안이 되게 한다. 이제 시장의 동력은 결정적으로 재생 에너지 쪽으로 향하고 있다.

> plummet[plʌ́mit] 급락하다
> fundamentally[fʌ̀ndəméntli] 근본적으로
> improvement[imprúːvmənt] 발전
> compelling[kəmpéliŋ] 매력적인
> alternative[ɔːltə́ːrnətiv] 대안 utility grid 전력망, 급전망
> momentum[mouméntəm] 동력

지문의 단어 "plummeted"와 의미상 가장 유사한 것은?
Ⓐ 애썼다
✅ 감소했다
Ⓒ 망설였다
Ⓓ 약화되었다

HACKERS PRACTICE p.114

01 ⓑ 02 ⓒ 03 ⓓ 04 ⓓ

01 Vocabulary Question

이메일을 읽으시오.

제목: 모바일 결제 파트너십

Mr. Reilly께,

어제 만나 주셔서 감사합니다. 귀사가 새로운 모바일 결제 애플리케이션을 공동 개발하는 파트너십에 열려 있다는 소식을 듣고 매우 기뻤습니다. 저는 이 프로젝트가 우리 두 회사 모두에게 수익성이 좋은 프로젝트가 될 것으로 생각합니다.

Sumin Na 드림

---
lucrative [lú:krətiv] 수익성이 좋은

마지막 문장의 단어 "lucrative"와 의미상 가장 유사한 것은?
Ⓐ 협력적인
Ⓑ 수익성이 있는 ✓
Ⓒ 힘든
Ⓓ 위험한

어휘 cooperative [kouá:pərətiv] 협력적인
profitable [prá:fitəbl] 수익성이 있는 arduous [á:rdʒuəs] 힘든

02 Vocabulary Question

이메일을 읽으시오.

제목: 숙박 시설

담당자님께,

몬트리올 시내에 있는 귀 호텔의 객실 숙박 가능 여부에 대한 정보를 더 얻고 싶습니다.

저는 근처 Monterra Industries사 본사에서 근무합니다. 저희는 회의를 위해 해외 고객들이 묵게 할 것인데, 10월 6일부터 10월 14일까지 그들이 묵을 숙박 시설을 확보해야 합니다. 손님은 총 여섯 명이지만, 두 명은 커플이므로 다섯 개의 객실이 필요합니다. 가능하다면 스위트룸이면 좋겠습니다.

이 기간의 숙박 가능 여부를 확인해 주시고, 빈 객실이 있다면 어떤 종류의 객실인지, 공항 셔틀 서비스 비용을 포함하여 전체 가격이 얼마가 될지 알려주십시오. 곧 답변을 듣기를 바랍니다.

Jim Taylor

---
accommodation [əkàmədéiʃən] 숙박 시설
vacancy [véikənsi] 빈 방, 공석

세 번째 문단의 단어 "vacancies"와 의미상 가장 유사한 것은?
Ⓐ 시설
Ⓑ 강당
Ⓒ 공실 ✓
Ⓓ 예약

어휘 facility [fəsíləti] 시설 reservation [rèzərvéiʃən] 예약

03 Vocabulary Question

이메일을 읽으시오.

제목: 주문 확인

Mr. Osborne께,

필요한 사무 장비 구매에 OfficeMate를 선택해 주셔서 감사합니다. 귀하의 주문을 접수했으며, 요청하신 대로 새로운 XJ-2200 프린터의 발송을 신속하게 처리할 것입니다. 늦어도 내일 저녁까지는 받으실 것입니다.

Katy Griffin, 고객 서비스 담당자

---
equipment [ikwípmənt] 장비, 용품
expedite [ékspədàit] 신속히 처리하다

두 번째 문장의 단어 "expedite"와 의미상 가장 유사한 것은?
Ⓐ 보장하다
Ⓑ 처리하다
Ⓒ 검토하다
Ⓓ 서둘러 하다 ✓

어휘 hasten [heisn] 서둘러 하다

04 Vocabulary Question

소셜 미디어 게시물을 읽으시오.

저는 방금 Marrakesh Café에서 돌아왔는데, 이곳이 이 도시에서 제가 가장 좋아하는 새로운 식당이 될 수도 있을 것 같습니다. 다른 곳에서 찾을 수 있는 식당과는 다릅니다.

제가 들어선 순간부터, 아늑한 분위기와 친절한 직원들이 저로 하여금 환영받는 느낌을 받게 했습니다. 식당에 가는 것보다 친구 집을 방문하는 것 같았습니다.

모로코에 한 번 가본 적이 있어서, 카사블랑카에서 먹었던 제가 가장 좋아하는 요리인 양고기 타진을 주문하고 싶었습니다. 아쉽게도, 그날은 이미 다 팔렸습니다. 종업원이 괜찮아보이는 다른 음식들을 제안해 주었습니다. 결국 저는 *ferakh maamer*라는 이름의, 속을 채운 닭고기 요리를 주문했습니다. 너무 맛있어서, 사실 처음 골랐던 메뉴가 없었던 것이 기뻤습니다.

새롭고 맛있는 것을 시도해 보고 싶다면, Marrakesh Café에 들러보세요! 화요일을 제외하고 매일 오전 11시부터 오후 11시까지 영업합니다.

---
cozy [kóuzi] 아늑한, 친밀한 ambiance [ǽmbiəns] 분위기, 환경
suggestion [səgdʒéstʃən] 제안 stuffed [stʌft] 속을 채운

두 번째 문단의 단어 "ambiance"와 의미상 가장 유사한 것은?
Ⓐ 장소
Ⓑ 가구
Ⓒ 장식
Ⓓ 분위기 ✓

어휘 furniture [fə́:rnitʃər] 가구
atmosphere [ǽtməsfiər] 분위기, 대기

HACKERS TEST   p.116

01 ⓒ	02 Ⓐ	03 ⓒ	04 Ⓐ	05 Ⓑ
06 Ⓑ	07 Ⓐ	08 ⓒ	09 ⓒ	10 ⓒ
11 Ⓓ	12 Ⓑ	13 ⓒ	14 Ⓐ	15 Ⓓ

[01-02] 이메일을 읽으시오.

제목: 회의 시간 변경

직원 여러분께,

⁰¹오늘 오후 회의는 사무실 밖에 있는 인원의 수로 인해 내일 아침으로 연기되겠습니다. 오전 10시에 회의실에서 모여 주시기 바라며, 프로젝트 최신 정보를 검토할 수 있도록 가져오는 것을 잊지 마세요. 감사합니다.

Max Lipscott, 팀장

postpone [poustpóun] 연기하다   go over 점검하다, 검토하다

01 Main Purpose Question

이메일의 주된 목적은 무엇인가?
Ⓐ 결근을 알리기 위해서
Ⓑ 요구 사항을 상기시키기 위해서
✓ⓒ 일정 변경을 알리기 위해서
Ⓓ 참석 여부를 문의하기 위해서

어휘 absence [ǽbsəns] 결근, 부재

02 Vocabulary Question

지문의 어구 "go over"와 의미상 가장 유사한 것은?
✓Ⓐ 검토하다
Ⓑ 완료하다
ⓒ 회피하다
Ⓓ 지연시키다

[03-04] 공지를 읽으시오.

FitPlus 회원 여러분에게 알림:

⁰⁴실내 달리기 트랙이 5월 1일부터 6월 11일까지 재단장을 위해 폐쇄됨을 알려드립니다. 이 동안, **⁰⁴야외 달리기 트랙**이나 체육관의 다른 시설을 이용하실 것을 회원 여러분께 권장합니다.

advise [ədváiz] 알리다, 조언하다
refurbishment [rifə́ːrbiʃmənt] 재단장

03 Vocabulary Question

지문의 단어 "refurbishment"와 의미상 가장 유사한 것은?
Ⓐ 복구
Ⓑ 위생 관리
✓ⓒ 수리
Ⓓ 확장

어휘 restoration [rèstəréiʃən] 복구
     sanitation [sæ̀nitéiʃən] 위생 관리, 위생

04 Inference Question

FitPlus에 대해 추론할 수 있는 것은?
✓Ⓐ 여러 개의 달리기 구역이 있다.
Ⓑ 모든 달리기 수업을 취소할 것이다.
ⓒ 회원들은 할인을 받을 것이다.
Ⓓ 수업들은 야외에서 진행될 것이다.

[05-06] 포스터를 읽으시오.

기술 일자리의 날

기술 분야에서 일자리를 찾고 계신가요? 그렇다면 기술 일자리의 날에 오세요!

⁰⁶수백 개의 기술 기업이 이곳에서 하드웨어 개발, 프로그래밍, AI 및 그밖의 분야의 일자리를 위한 **예비 지원자를 찾고 있을 것입니다**!

날짜: 7월 10일 토요일
장소: Abramson 센터, 442번지 Northwood가

prospective [prəspéktiv] 예비의, 장래의
candidate [kǽndidèit] 지원자, 후보

05 Vocabulary Question

지문의 단어 "prospective"와 의미상 가장 유사한 것은?
Ⓐ 자격을 갖춘
✓Ⓑ 잠재적인
ⓒ 평판이 좋은
Ⓓ 경험이 많은

어휘 qualified [kwáləfàid] 자격을 갖춘
     reputable [répjətəbəl] 평판이 좋은

06 Inference Question

포스터가 기술 일자리의 날에 대해 암시하는 것은?
Ⓐ 며칠에 걸쳐 개최될 것이다.
✓Ⓑ 수많은 고용주를 만날 기회를 제공할 것이다.
ⓒ 프로그래밍에 대한 강연을 포함한다.
Ⓓ 연례 행사이다.

어휘 numerous [njúːmərəs] 수많은

[07-09] 기사를 읽으시오.

Potterton, 3월 28일—Potterton 시는 **⁰⁷올해 4월 13일에 시작되는 연례 튤립 축제**를 준비하고 있다. 일주일간 진행되는 이 행사는 도시 전역에 약 60만 송이의 선명한 꽃이 피어나는 것을 기념한다.

⁰⁹ᴮ정원 투어, 봄 시장, 튤립꽃으로 장식된 자동차와 장식 차량을 특색으로 하는 Main가 튤립 퍼레이드에 더해, 방문객들은 처음으로 축제 마당을 기대할 수 있다. 올해 Holmes 공원에는 **⁰⁹ᴬ다양한 놀이기구**와 게임이 설치될 예정이다. **⁰⁹ᴰ매일 밤 라이브 음악과 불꽃놀이**도 열릴 것이다.

시 당국은 이 확대된 선택지들이 지난 참석 기록을 깨고, 잠재적으로 백만 명의 참석자를 넘게 하기를 희망한다. Davies 시장에 따르면, 이는 이 축제를 Potterton의 가장 큰 관광 명소로 만들고 지역 경제에 1억 달러가 넘는 수익을 가져다줄 것이다.

celebrate[séləbrèit] 기념하다, 축하하다
vehicle[ví:ikl] 자동차, 차량   float[flout] 장식 차량
attendee[ətèndí:] 참석자   draw[drɔ:] 이목을 끄는 것

07 Main Topic Question
기사는 주로 무엇에 관한 것인가?
☑ 올해 튤립 축제의 주요 내용
Ⓑ Potterton의 유명한 관광 명소
Ⓒ 튤립 꽃의 생태
Ⓓ Potterton 관광 정책의 역사

08 Vocabulary Question
첫 번째 문단의 단어 "vibrant"와 의미상 가장 유사한 것은?
Ⓐ 튼튼한
Ⓑ 고유의
☑ 색채가 풍부한
Ⓓ 극적인

어휘 native[néitiv] 고유의, 토종의

09 Detail Question
방문자들이 경험하지 못할 것은?
Ⓐ 놀이기구 타기
Ⓑ 정원 방문하기
☑ 튤립 재배법 배우기
Ⓓ 야간 공연 즐기기

[10-12] 이메일을 읽으시오.

제목: 자판기

담당자께,

¹⁰저희 아파트 건물에 있는 자판기에 대한 즉각적인 서비스를 요청드리기 위해 오늘 이 메일을 씁니다. 지난 몇 주 동안, 비접촉결제 기능이 반응하지 않아, 비현금 결제를 받을 수 없습니다. 대다수 입주민이 카드나 휴대전화로 자판기에서 스낵을 결제하기를 선호하기 때문에 불만을 많이 접수했습니다. 이는 저희에게 큰 매출 손실도 발생시키고 있습니다.

가능한 한 빨리 자판기를 수리하기 위한 서비스 방문 일정을 잡고자 합니다. ¹²저희 관리사무소는 평일 오전 9시부터 오후 5시까지 운영하므로 이 시간대가 가장 편하지만, 필요하다면 다른 시간에도 직원이 귀사의 기술자를 자판기까지 동행하도록 조치할 수 있습니다.

본 사안에 신속히 관심을 가져 주셔서 감사합니다.

Steven Slotkin, 건물 관리자
¹²Moore Point 아파트

vending machine 자판기   immediate[imí:diət] 즉각적인
unresponsive[ʌ̀nrispánsiv] 반응하지 않는
complaint[kəmpléint] 불만
escort[iskɔ́:rt] 동행하다   prompt[prɑmpt] 신속한

10 Main Purpose Question
이메일의 주된 목적은 무엇인가?
Ⓐ 현금 결제를 요청하기 위해
Ⓑ 신용카드 선택지를 강조하기 위해
☑ 긴급 수리 서비스를 요청하기 위해
Ⓓ 기계의 위치를 설명하기 위해

11 Vocabulary Question
첫 번째 문단의 단어 "unresponsive"와 의미상 가장 유사한 것은?
Ⓐ 조용한
Ⓑ 휴지 상태의
Ⓒ 연결이 끊긴
☑ 작동하지 않는

어휘 dormant[dɔ́:rmənt] 휴지 상태의, 동면중의
nonfunctional[nɑ̀nfʌ́ŋkʃənəl] 작동하지 않는

12 Detail Question
Mr. Slotkin은 어떤 종류의 업체에서 일하는가?
Ⓐ 신용카드 회사
☑ 주택 제공 업체
Ⓒ 기계 제작소
Ⓓ 스낵 제조사

[13-15] 공지를 읽으시오.

Hudson Tower 입주민 여러분께 알림

여러 세입자가 주차 공간을 찾는 데 어려움이 있다는 정식 항의서를 제출했습니다. 이 문제를 해결하기 위해, 건물의 주차 정책에 다음과 같은 변경 사항을 시행할 것입니다:

- ¹⁴7월 3일부터, 각 세대에는 무료로 1개의 주차 공간이 배정됩니다. 이 날짜까지 행정 사무실을 방문하여 주차 공간을 확정해 주시기 바랍니다. 세대당 추가 1개 공간을 월 65달러에 지정할 수 있습니다. 추가 공간의 수에는 제한이 있으며, 선착순으로 배정됨에 주의하십시오.
- ¹⁵주차 시설의 최상층(총 30개 공간)은 방문객 전용 주차 구역으로 지정됩니다. 이곳에 주차하는 차량은 임시 주차 허가증을 드러내야 하며, 허가증은 우리 건물 부지 입구의 보안 요원이 발급합니다.

이 사안에 대한 여러분의 이해에 감사드립니다.

tenant[ténənt] 세입자   submit[səbmít] 제출하다
implement[ímpləmènt] 시행하다, 실시하다
assign[əsáin] 배정하다   reserve[rizə́:rv] 지정하다, 예약하다
allocate[ǽləkèit] 배정하다   designate[dézignèit] 지정하다

13 Vocabulary Question
첫 번째 문단의 단어 "submitted"와 의미상 가장 유사한 것은?
Ⓐ 항소했다
Ⓑ 집행했다
☑ 제출했다
Ⓓ 생성했다

어휘 appeal[əpí:l] 항소하다   enforce[infɔ́:rs] 집행하다

14 Detail Question
세입자들이 7월 3일까지 해야 하는 것은?
☑ 지정 주차 공간을 요청한다
Ⓑ 행정 사무실에서 수수료를 지불한다

ⓒ 보안 요원에게 방문객 이름을 제공한다
ⓓ 추가 공간 가용 여부를 확인한다

15 Inference Question

주차 시설의 최상층에 대해 결론지을 수 있는 것은?
ⓐ 건물 직원 전용으로 지정될 것이다.
ⓑ 현재 장비 보관에 사용되고 있다.
ⓒ 수용량을 최대한 활용하기 위해 보수 중이다.
✓ⓓ 입주민 차량의 출입이 금지될 것이다.

어휘 capacity[kəpǽsəti] 수용력, 용량
      off-limits[ɑ́flímits] 출입 금지의

5. Inference Questions

Example
p.123

공지를 읽으시오.

> 대학 체육관은 9월 5일부터 대규모 개선 프로젝트를 시작하며 10월 25일까지 완료할 것으로 예상됩니다. 이 프로젝트는 새로운 장비를 설치하고, 웨이트 룸을 확장하며, 단체 피트니스 전용 스튜디오를 추가하는 것을 목표로 합니다. **체육관은 매년 겨울 방학마다 소규모 유지보수 및 개선을 진행합니다.** 하지만, 이번 대규모 개선은 최근 캠퍼스 내 피트니스 수요에 대한 설문조사 후에 계획되었습니다. 이 기간, 체육관의 모든 시설은 폐쇄됩니다. 예정된 수업과 팀 훈련은 대체 장소에서 진행될 것이며, 영향받는 참가자들은 개별 통지를 받을 것입니다. 진행 상황에 대한 정기 업데이트는 대학 웹사이트를 통해 공지될 예정입니다.

equipment[ikwípmənt] 장비 dedicated[dédikèitid] 전용의
maintenance[méintənəns] 유지보수
notification[nòutəfikéiʃən] 통지

체육관 시설에 대해 추론할 수 있는 것은?
✓ⓐ 매년 정기적인 개선 작업을 거친다.
ⓑ 작업 후에 상당히 넓어질 것이다.
ⓒ 개선 후 이용 가능한 유일한 체육관이 될 것이다.
ⓓ 수업에 사용되지 않는다.

HACKERS PRACTICE
p.124

01 ⓑ   02 ⓑ   03 ⓓ   04 ⓒ

01 Inference Question

공지를 읽으시오.

> 고객 여러분께 알립니다
>
> **공급이 제한적인 관계로, 최근 출시된 PlayBox 비디오 게임 콘솔은 1인당 1대로 구매가 제한됩니다.** 더 많은 고객님께서 이 제품을 구매하실 기회를 보장하기 위해 노력하는 동안, 양해해 주셔서 감사합니다.

ensure[inʃúər] 보장하다, 반드시 ~하게 하다
purchase[pə́ːrtʃəs] 구입하다

PlayBox 비디오 게임 콘솔에 대해 추론할 수 있는 것은?
ⓐ 이전 모델을 대체한다.
✓ⓑ 수요가 높다.
ⓒ 사전 예약이 필요하다.
ⓓ 한 사람만 플레이할 수 있다.

02 Inference Question

이메일을 읽으시오.

> 수신: meganwoods@hmail.com
> 발신: careers@globaltechsolutions.com
> 제목: 면접 초청
>
> Ms. Woods께,
>
> **GlobalTech Solutions사의 마케팅 전문가 직무에 관심을 기울여주셔서 감사합니다.** 저희는 귀하의 디지털 마케팅 경력에 깊은 인상을 받았으며, 지원서에 대해 더 논의하고자 귀하를 면접에 모시고자 합니다. 당사는 디지털 영향력을 확대함에 따라 **공석을 채울 재능 있는 인재를 적극적으로 찾고 있으며,** 귀하의 프로필이 당사의 요구와 잘 부합합니다.
>
> 면접 일정은 2월 22일 목요일 오후 3시에 잡고자 합니다. 면접은 Venture Plaza 500번지의 Apex 빌딩에 있는 당사 사무실에서 진행될 것입니다. 면접에서는 귀하의 자격, 이전 경험, 직무 이해도를 살펴볼 것입니다. 또한 봉급과 예상 입사일에 대해서도 논의할 것입니다.
>
> 가능하신지 확인해 주십시오. 대면 참석이 불가능하다면, 그 대신 저희가 화상 면접을 준비할 수 있습니다. 빠른 회신을 기다리겠습니다.
>
> Cassian Walker 드림

impress[imprés] 깊은 인상을 주다
application[æ̀pləkéiʃən] 지원서   presence[prézns] 영향력, 존재
qualification[kwɑ̀ːləfikéiʃən] 자격
compensation[kɑ̀mpənséiʃən] 봉급, 보상

GlobalTech Solutions사의 마케팅 전문가 직무에 대해 추론할 수 있는 것은?
ⓐ 넓은 범위의 출장이 요구된다.
✓ⓑ 현재 공석이다.
ⓒ 유연 근무 시간을 제공한다.
ⓓ 관리직이다.

어휘 managerial[mæ̀nidʒíəriəl] 관리의

03 Inference Question

공지를 읽으시오.

> 리콜 주의
>
> 오염 가능성으로 인해, **12월 10일에 제조된 모든 Lindendale Farms 소시지가 리콜 중입니다.** 어떠한 경우에도 이 제품을 섭취하지 말도록 고객님들께 주의드립니다. 이 제조일자가 표시된 소시지를 구매처로 다시 가져오시면 개봉 여부와 관계없이 새 상품으로 교환해 드립니다.

contamination[kəntæ̀mənéiʃən] 오염
manufacture[mæ̀njufǽktʃər] 제조하다
under any circumstances 어떠한 경우에도

Lindendale Farms 소시지에 대해 추론할 수 있는 것은?
Ⓐ 개봉되었다면 반품할 수 없다.
Ⓑ 구매자가 폐기해야 한다.
Ⓒ 단 한 곳의 매장에서만 판매된다.
☑ 다른 날에 제조되었으면 섭취할 수 있다.

어휘 destroy [distrɔ́i] 폐기하다, 파괴하다

04 Inference Question
소셜 미디어 게시물을 읽으시오.

> Erin McCarthy
>
> **지난주, 저는 시의 일요 걷기 투어 프로그램에 참여했습니다.** 익숙한 거리들을 새로운 관점에서 경험하는 방법이었습니다. 저희는 오래된 건축물이 지난 세대들의 이야기를 들려주는 역사적인 동네들을 거닐었습니다. 다채로운 벽화는 만약 벽화가 없었더라면 평범했을 거리에 창의성과 특색을 더했습니다. 신진 예술가들의 흥미로운 작품을 전시한 야외 갤러리도 방문했습니다.
>
> 이 투어는 도시 경계를 벗어나지 않고도 신체 활동, 답사, 사회적 교류의 결합을 제공했습니다. 거의 8킬로미터를 걸으면서, 저는 활력이 솟기도 했고 사색에 잠기기도 했습니다. 가이드가 도시 역사에 대한 흥미로운 통찰을 공유했으며, 단체 점심으로 마무리하며 따뜻하고 공동체적인 분위기가 더해졌습니다.
>
> **경로가 매주 바뀌므로**, 언제나 새롭게 발견할 것이 있습니다. 잘 알고 있다고 생각한 도시의 숨은 구석을 발견할 방법을 찾고 있다면, 한번 시도해 보시기 바랍니다! 시 웹사이트를 통해 이 행사에 온라인으로 쉽게 등록하실 수 있습니다.
>
> light [lait] 관점, 견해
> historic [histɔ́rik] 역사적인, 역사적으로 중요한
> architecture [ά:rkitèktʃər] 건축물
> intriguing [intríːɡiŋ] 흥미로운
> emerging [imə́:rdʒiŋ] 신진의, 신흥의
> fascinating [fǽsənèitiŋ] 흥미로운, 매력적인

시의 걷기 투어에 대해 추론할 수 있는 것은?
Ⓐ 저녁 시간대에 제공된다.
Ⓑ 참가자들은 간식을 직접 가져와야 한다.
☑ 매주 진행된다.
Ⓓ 가이드들은 역사 자격증이 있다.

어휘 certify [sə́:rtəfài] 자격증을 주다

HACKERS TEST
p.126

01 Ⓒ	02 Ⓓ	03 Ⓐ	04 Ⓒ	05 Ⓓ
06 Ⓑ	07 Ⓒ	08 Ⓓ	09 Ⓒ	10 Ⓓ
11 Ⓐ	12 Ⓑ	13 Ⓑ	14 Ⓑ	15 Ⓒ

[01-02] 기사를 읽으시오.

> Baytown—Jefferson가가 Founder's Day 퍼레이드로 인해 7월 10일 토요일 오전 9시부터 오후 6시까지 폐쇄된다. 01운전자들은 우회 경로를 계획해야 한다. 02행사에 참석할 예정인 사람들에게는 지하철 이용이 권장된다.

> alternative route 우회 경로

01 Detail Question
운전자들에게 권고되는 것은?
Ⓐ 아침 일찍 출발한다
Ⓑ 퍼레이드 경로 근처에 주차한다
☑ 폐쇄된 도로를 피한다
Ⓓ 대신 지하철을 탄다

02 Inference Question
Founder's Day 퍼레이드에 대해 추론할 수 있는 것은?
Ⓐ 많은 사람들이 참석할 것으로 예상된다.
Ⓑ Baytown 전역에서 열린다.
Ⓒ 경로가 달라질 것으로 예상된다.
☑ 장소는 지하철역으로부터 접근 가능하다.

어휘 attend [əténd] 참석하다   vary [vέəri] 달라지다, 각기 다르다

[03-04] 송장을 읽으시오.

> 송장:
>
> Premier Solutions사
> 482번지 S. Washington가
> 555-2123
>
> 송장 번호: 0148-249150
> 날짜: 2월 4일
> 청구 대상: Peak Energy Consultants사
>
> | 서비스 | 요금 | 총액 |
> |---|---|---|
> | 03/04네트워크 설치 | 250달러/시간 | 2,500달러 |
> | 04시스템 교육 (단체) | 200달러/시간 | 600달러 |
> | 총액: | | 3,100달러 |
>
> 약관: 지불은 30일 내 이루어져야 합니다. 연체금에는 수수료 10퍼센트가 매겨집니다.
>
> Premier Solutions사를 선택해 주셔서 감사합니다

어휘 assess [əsés] (세금 등을) 매기다, 할당하다

03 Detail Question
Peak Energy Consultants사가 구매한 서비스의 종류는?
☑ 네트워크 설치
Ⓑ 개인 교육
Ⓒ 결제 처리
Ⓓ 에너지 컨설팅

04 Inference Question
Premier Solutions에 대해 추론할 수 있는 것은?
Ⓐ 단체 할인을 제공한다.
Ⓑ 에너지 효율적인 시스템을 전문으로 한다.
☑ IT 기업이다.
Ⓓ 다양한 결제 수단을 받는다.

어휘 specialize [spéʃəlàiz] 전문으로 하다

[05-06] 공지를 읽으시오.

수신: 전 직원
제목: 휴가 신청
날짜: 8월 15일

05 9월 1일부터, 휴가 신청의 최소 사전 통지 기간이 2주에서 3주로 늘어납니다. 목적은 프로젝트에 대한 지장을 최소화하는 것입니다. 문의 사항이 있으면 06 저희 팀원 Jared Andrews에게 말해 주십시오. 저희 사무실은 403호에 있습니다. 감사합니다.

Violet Parson
06 인사팀 관리자

disruption [disrʌ́pʃən] 지장, 붕괴

05 Main Purpose Question

공지의 주된 목적은 무엇인가?
Ⓐ 프로젝트 마감일을 연장하기 위해
Ⓑ 부서 목표를 소개하기 위해
Ⓒ 상태 업데이트를 요청하기 위해
☑ 정책 변경을 발표하기 위해

06 Inference Question

Mr. Andrews에 대해 추론할 수 있는 것은?
Ⓐ 최근에 새 사무실로 옮겼다.
☑ 인사팀 소속이다.
Ⓒ Ms. Parson의 직속 상사이다.
Ⓓ 다른 직책으로 발령되었다.

[07-09] 기사를 읽으시오.

박물관이 Cajun 문화와 역사를 선보이다

8월 28일—07 Beaumont Heritage 재단은 이 지역 Acadian 사람들의 역사에 초점을 맞춘 시설인 Museum of Cajun Culture를 새로 개관했다. 새 박물관은 이 집단이 캐나다 동부에서 추방된 때부터 오늘날까지의 흔적을 짚는 희귀 문서, 사진, 유물의 전시를 특징으로 한다.

08 1765년에 세워진 농지에 있는 완전히 복원된 전통 가옥에 자리한 이 박물관은 초기 정착민들의 삶이 어떠했는지 방문객들이 직접 볼 수 있는 관람 기회를 제공한다. 시대 의상을 갖춰 입은 직원들은 그들이 마주한 야생의 환경을 길들이는 일이 얼마나 어려웠을지를 보여 주기 위한 시연도 한다.

재단은 이 박물관이 이 지역의 고유한 역사에 관심 있는 방문객들을 끌어들이고 지역 주민들의 문화적 자긍심에 불을 붙이기를 바란다. 화요일부터 일요일까지, 오전 10시부터 오후 6시까지 운영하며, 지역 및 전국 공휴일에는 특별 행사를 제공한다.

showcase [ʃóukeis] 선보이다 foundation [faundéiʃən] 재단
artifact [ά:rtəfækt] 유물 expulsion [ikspʌ́lʃən] 추방
homestead [hóumsted] (과거 미국의) 정부 공여 농지
settler [sétlər] 정착민 tame [teim] 길들이다

07 Main Topic Question

기사의 주제는 무엇인가?
Ⓐ 지역의 역사
Ⓑ 독특한 지역 문화
Ⓒ 최근에 발견된 유물 몇 점
☑ 새로 개관한 박물관

08 Inference Question

기사로부터 초기 정착민에 대해 추론할 수 있는 것은?
Ⓐ 여러 지역에서 왔다.
Ⓑ 이 지역을 살기 쉬운 곳이라고 여겼다.
Ⓒ 다른 지역 문화와 섞였다.
☑ 18세기에 도착했다.

09 Vocabulary Question

마지막 문단의 단어 "ignite"와 의미상 가장 유사한 것은?
Ⓐ 준비하다
Ⓑ 정의하다
☑ 깨우다
Ⓓ 확인하다

어휘 define [difáin] 정의하다 verify [vérəfài] 확인하다

[10-12] 웹페이지를 읽으시오.

www.tastetheworld.com/Blog

| 홈 | 블로그 | 정보 | 연락처 |

이곳 Scarborough에서 맛있는 세계 음식을 찾는 걸 좋아하신다면, 좋은 소식이 있어요. 10 도심의 Lincoln가에 Samarkand Palace라는 새 중앙아시아 식당이 문을 열었어요.

저는 예전엔 중앙아시아 요리를 잘 몰랐는데 첫 방문 이후로 푹 빠졌어요. 제가 먹어 본 모든 메뉴가 맛있었을 뿐 아니라 11 이 도시 치고 가격도 부담 없었어요. 남편과 저는 샐러드와 딥 네 가지, 빵 두 가지, 수프, 만두, 속을 채운 양배추, 양꼬치 여러 개를 주문했는데, 그날 밤 계산서가 40달러도 안 나왔어요!

분위기와 직원들도 언급할 만했어요. 가게 전체가 전통 우즈베키스탄 건물처럼 꾸며져 있고 곳곳에 아름다운 타일들이 있어요. 직원들은 엄청 도움이 되었고, 모든 요리가 무엇인지 시간을 들여 설명해 주셨어요. 12 식사 후에는 무료 디저트도 주셨어요. 10 Samarkand Palace에 한 번 가 보세요!

affordable [əfɔ́:rdəbl] (가격이) 부담 없는
dumpling [dʌ́mpliŋ] 만두 stuff [stʌf] 속을 채우다
skewer [skjú:ər] 꼬치 atmosphere [ǽtməsfìər] 분위기

10 Main Purpose Question

페이지의 주된 목적은 무엇인가?
Ⓐ 외국 요리를 논하기 위해
Ⓑ 도시의 식당 문화를 평가하기 위해
Ⓒ 아시아 요리 레시피를 제공하기 위해
☑ 새로 문을 연 식당을 추천하기 위해

11 Inference Question

시도해 본 음식들에 대해 추론할 수 있는 것은?
☑ 가격이 다른 곳보다 더 저렴했다.
Ⓑ 소량으로 제공되었다.
Ⓒ 모든 요리에 양고기가 들어 있었다.
Ⓓ 직원들이 추천한 메뉴였다.

12 Detail Question

무료로 제공된 것은 무엇인가?
Ⓐ 장식용 타일
Ⓑ 달콤한 음식 ✓
Ⓒ 우즈베키스탄 음식 안내서
Ⓓ 전통 접시

[13-15] 기사를 읽으시오.

> 최근 기자회견에서 [13]Roberts 시장은 Anderson 공원 옆 부지에 500세대 아파트 단지 건설 승인이 시 의회에 의해 내려졌다고 발표했다. 개발업자는 3월 28일에 공사를 시작할 예정이다. Roberts 시장은 이 프로젝트가 도시에 새로운 주민과 기업을 끌어들일 것이라고 주장했다. [14]"제 임기가 끝나고 제가 정계에서 은퇴하기 전에 이 개발을 시작할 수 있었던 것이 매우 자랑스럽습니다"라고 그녀는 설명했다.
>
> 그녀의 기쁨에도 불구하고, Mulberry Heights 지역의 많은 주민들은 교통 혼잡 증가와 기타 문제를 초래할 것이라고 주장하며 이 프로젝트에 반대 의사를 표명했다. [15]이에 대응하여, 시 정부는 웹사이트에 설문을 게시했으며 Mulberry Heights에 거주하는 모든 사람에게 이를 작성해 달라고 요청하고 있다. 이들의 의견이 검토된 뒤, 우려를 해소하기 위한 정책이 고려될 것이다.
>
> **press conference** 기자회견 **approval**[əprúːvəl] 승인, 허가
> **property**[prápərti] 부지, 토지, 부동산
> **grant**[grænt] 승인을 내리다 **city council** 시 의회
> **retirement**[ritáiərmənt] 은퇴 **traffic congestion** 교통 혼잡

13 Main Topic Question

기사의 주제는 무엇인가?
Ⓐ 여가 시설 개장
Ⓑ 주택 단지 건설 ✓
Ⓒ 정부 정책 개정
Ⓓ 부지 점검 결과

14 Inference Question

Roberts 시장에 대해 추론할 수 있는 것은?
Ⓐ Anderson 공원 옆의 토지를 소유하고 있다.
Ⓑ 재선에 출마할 계획이 없다. ✓
Ⓒ 내년에 Mulberry Heights를 떠나려 한다.
Ⓓ 시 의회의 지지를 받지 못한다.

15 Detail Question

Mulberry Heights 지역 주민들이 요청받은 것은?
Ⓐ 웹사이트에서 의견을 읽는다
Ⓑ 회의에 참여한다
Ⓒ 설문지를 작성한다 ✓
Ⓓ 사업 제안을 검토한다

어휘 **questionnaire**[kwèstʃənέər] 설문지

---

6. Intention Questions

Example p.133

공지를 읽으시오.

> 서쪽 건물 뒤편 주차장이 정기 유지보수 작업으로 인해 8월 16일 토요일에 폐쇄될 예정임을 알려드립니다. 모든 차량은 금요일 저녁 8시까지 이동해야 합니다. 주차장은 일요일 오전 6시에 다시 개방됩니다. 이 동안, 직원과 방문객은 동쪽 주차장을 이용해야 합니다. 협조해 주셔서 감사합니다.
>
> **advise**[ədváiz] 알리다 **routine**[ruːtíːn] 정기적인, 일상적인
> **maintenance**[méintənəns] 유지보수
> **vehicle**[víːikl] 차량

공지에서 동쪽 주차장을 언급하는 이유는 무엇인가?
Ⓐ 유지보수 직원에게 길을 안내하기 위해서
Ⓑ 특별 행사에 대해 알리기 위해서
Ⓒ 주차 요금 변경을 설명하기 위해서
Ⓓ 대체 주차장을 제안하기 위해서 ✓

HACKERS PRACTICE p.134

01 Ⓒ   02 Ⓑ   03 Ⓓ   04 Ⓐ

01 Intention Question

이메일을 읽으시오.

> 제목: 음식 공급 확인
>
> Ms. Leigh께,
>
> 목요일 워크숍용 음식 공급 주문을 확인하는 바입니다. 모든 식이 제한사항이 정확하게 높은 품질로 충족되도록, **오늘 오후 5시까지 모든 최신 정보를 보내주시기 바랍니다.** 저희 주방에서는 오늘 저녁 최종 확인이 필요합니다. 신속한 답변에 감사드립니다.
>
> Derek Halloway
>
> **dietary**[dáiətèri] 식이의, 음식물의 **restriction**[ristríkʃən] 제한사항

Mr. Halloway가 "the final confirmation this evening"이 필요하다고 언급한 것은 그의 태도에 대해 무엇을 암시하는가?
Ⓐ Ms. Leigh가 최신 정보 제공을 잊을까 걱정한다.
Ⓑ 요청된 식사 품질을 달성할 수 없을까 우려한다.
Ⓒ 최종 마감시한을 강조하고 싶어 한다. ✓
Ⓓ 지정된 마감시한을 훨씬 넘겨서도 변경사항을 기꺼이 받아들이려 한다.

02 Intention Question

메시지 대화문을 읽으시오.

> Madison Bennett (오후 1:00)
> 안녕하세요, 팀 여러분. 데이터 문해력 교육 세션이 다음 주 화요일임을 상기시켜 드려요. 모든 준비 과제가 월요일 오전까지 완료되도록 해주세요.
>
> Liam King (오후 1:05)
> 알겠어요, Madison. 저는 '데이터의 편향과 윤리적 고려 사항' 부분을 마무리 중이고, 오늘 업로드할게요.

Riley Hayes (오후 1:10)
저는 월요일 오전까지 '인터랙티브 데이터 스토리텔링' 사례 연구 준비를 마무리하고 모두와 공유할게요.

Noah Cardew (오후 1:15)
금요일에 사외 미팅이 있지만, 주말 동안 기본 데이터 분석 기법 슬라이드 통합 작업을 완료할게요.

Madison Bennett (오후 1:20)
모두 매우 선제적으로 움직여줘서 고마워요! **여러분의 노력 덕분에 교육 전에 모든 내용을 검토할 시간을 확보할 수 있겠어요.**

literacy[lítərəsi] 문해력   bias[báiəs] 편향
ethical[éθikəl] 윤리적인   consideration[kənsìdəréiʃən] 고려 사항
case study 사례 연구   integrate[íntəgrèit] 통합하다
proactive[pròuǽktiv] 선제적인, 사전 대책을 마련하는

오후 1시 20분에 Ms. Bennett이 "Thank you all for being so proactive"라고 쓸 때, 이는 무엇을 의미할 가능성이 가장 높은가?
Ⓐ 팀이 작업을 더 빨리 끝내도록 촉구하고 있다.
✓ 팀의 마감 전에 일을 끝내려는 계획들을 칭찬하고 있다.
Ⓒ 팀이 메시지를 신속히 보낸 것에 감사하고 있다.
Ⓓ 팀이 기꺼이 선택적 친목 모임에 참석하려는 것을 고마워하고 있다.

어휘 urge[ə:rdʒ] 촉구하다   commend[kəménd] 칭찬하다, 추천하다
promptly[prámptli] 신속히, 지체 없이

03 Intention Question

기사를 읽으시오.

GIA Express 개통 예정

Greenville—시 교통국장은 새로운 공항철도 노선이 6월 1일 월요일에 개통될 것이라고 발표했다. 이 서비스는 Greenville 국제공항(GIA)과 도시의 중앙 교통 허브를 연결할 것인데, 승객들은 **교통 허브에서 주요 지하철 시스템이나 전국 철도 및 버스 네트워크로 갈아탈 수 있다.**

GIA Express는 직통 서비스만 제공하며 40마일 구간을 15분 이내에 주파할 것이다. 열차는 오전 5시부터 오후 11시까지 양방향으로 20분 간격으로 출발할 것이다. 승차권은 1인당 편도 10달러, 왕복 18달러이다. 10세 미만 어린이, 고령자, 장애인에게는 모든 운임에서 2달러 할인이 제공된다.

disabled[diséibld] 장애가 있는

이 문맥에서 'transportation hub'라는 용어는 무엇을 의미할 가능성이 가장 높은가?
Ⓐ 사람들이 교통수단을 예약할 수 있는 장소
Ⓑ 국제 교통 서비스가 제공되는 장소
Ⓒ 교통 관련 임원들이 근무하는 장소
✓ 다양한 교통수단들이 모이는 장소

04 Intention Question

기사를 읽으시오.

현지 금융 기술 강자인 Nexus Data Solutions사가 어제 프랑크푸르트에 기반을 둔 Pinnacle Consulting사와 기술협력을 발표했다. 이번 전략적 조치로 Nexus Data는 금융 부문의 디지털 보안 표준을 선도하는 데 주력하는 전문 팀을 통합해 사이버 위험과 규정 준수 역량을 강화하게 된다. 이 전략적 통합을 준비하기 위해 One North에 있는 Nexus Data의 주요 개발 시설이 대규모 업그레이드를 앞두고 있다.

Nexus Data Solutions사는 주요 중앙은행을 대상으로 한 글로벌 보안 감사에서 세 차례 연속 경쟁사들을 꾸준히 능가하며 세계적인 평판을 확고히 했다. 그러나, **이 회사의 첫 프로젝트가 지역 비영리단체를 위한 안전한 데이터 관리 플랫폼을 개발하는 무상 봉사 계획이었다는 사실을 인식하는 사람은 많지 않은데, 이 회사는 뭄바이에 있는 소규모 독립 보조금 재단을 통해 이 유산을 계속해서 존중하고 있다.**

powerhouse[páuərhaus] 강자, 유력 기관
alliance[əláiəns] 협력, 동맹   strategic[strətí:dʒik] 전략적인
bolster[bóulstər] 강화하다, 북돋우다
compliance[kəmpláiəns] 규정 준수
integration[ìntəgréiʃən] 통합   reputation[rèpjutéiʃən] 평판
audit[ɔ́:dit] 감사   pro-bono[proubóunou] 무상의
initiative[iníʃiətiv] 계획, 진취성   grant[grænt] 보조금

기사는 왜 보조금 재단을 언급하는가?
✓ 회사의 무상 봉사에 대한 헌신을 인정하기 위해
Ⓑ Pinnacle Consulting사와의 기술협력의 근거를 설명하기 위해
Ⓒ 금융 부문에서 회사의 미래 수익 성장을 예측하기 위해
Ⓓ One North 시설의 주요 물리적 업그레이드를 설명하기 위해

어휘 commitment[kəmítmənt] 헌신, 약속
rationale[ræ̀ʃənǽl] 근거, 이유   revenue[révənjù:] 수익

HACKERS TEST   p.136

01 Ⓓ	02 Ⓐ	03 Ⓐ	04 Ⓒ	05 Ⓓ
06 Ⓐ	07 Ⓓ	08 Ⓐ	09 Ⓒ	10 Ⓒ
11 Ⓓ	12 Ⓑ	13 Ⓒ	14 Ⓐ	15 Ⓐ

[01-02] 공지를 읽으시오.

분실물 보관소 절차

개인 소지품을 잃어버린 경우, **01즉시 보안 사무소에 가서 신고서를 작성하시기 바랍니다. 02공식 양식을 작성하고 상세한 설명을 제공해야 합니다.** 이 단계는 신속한 수색을 시작하고 회수를 보장하는 데 필요합니다.

lost and found 분실물 보관소
misplace[mispléis] 잃어버리다, 잘못 놓다
initiate[iníʃièit] 시작하다, 착수시키다

01 Intention Question

공지는 왜 보안 사무소를 언급하는가?
Ⓐ 사무소의 일일 근무 시간을 설명하기 위해
Ⓑ 신고서 작성 비용을 명시하기 위해
Ⓒ 연락처 정보를 제공하기 위해
✓ 독자들에게 신고서를 작성할 장소를 알려주기 위해

02 Detail Question

신속한 수색을 시작하기 위해 사람들이 해야 할 일은 무엇인가?
✓ 공식 양식을 작성한다

Ⓑ 경찰에 신고한다
Ⓒ 관리자에게 전화한다
Ⓓ 온라인으로 분실물 목록을 확인한다

[03-04] 이메일을 읽으시오.

제목: 청구서 재검토

PrintMaster사 청구 팀께,

"ProPrint" 프린터 50대에 대한 청구서를 받았습니다. ⁰⁴청구서에는 배송비가 125달러로 기재되어 있는데, 이에 반해 견적 금액은 50달러였습니다. ⁰⁴다른 잠재적 오류가 있는지 전체 청구서를 재확인한 후 수정된 청구서를 발행해 주시기 바랍니다. 수정된 청구서를 받으면 결제를 진행하겠습니다.

Emma Carrow 드림
Acme Technologies사

---

shipping fee 배송비, 운송료 **revise** [riváiz] 수정하다, 변경하다

03 Vocabulary Question
지문의 단어 "quoted"와 의미상 가장 유사한 것은?
☑ 견적의
Ⓑ 지나친
Ⓒ 최종 확정된
Ⓓ 연체된

04 Intention Question
Ms. Carrow가 "수정된 청구서를 받으면 결제를" 진행하겠다고 말한 것은 그녀의 태도에 대해 무엇을 암시하는가?
Ⓐ 배송 주소가 잘못 입력되었음을 지적하고 있다.
Ⓑ 견적 금액에 대해 불만을 표현하고 있다.
☑ 추가적인 오류들이 청구서에 포함되어 있을 수 있음을 보여주고 있다.
Ⓓ 배송 할인이 적용되지 않았음을 시사하고 있다.

[05-06] 표지판을 읽으시오.

가을 도서전

Regency Books의 가을 도서전에서 당신의 다음 애독서가 될 책을 찾아보세요!

날짜: 10월 3일, 금요일 – 10월 5일, 일요일

장소: 1724-E번지 2번가

⁰⁵ᴬ모든 도서(신품과 중고), ⁰⁵ᴮ선물 패키지, ⁰⁵ᶜ문구류 재고에 대해 큰 할인 제공

저희의 보유 도서 목록을 둘러보러 오세요, 무엇을 발견하게 될지 모르거든요!

---

stationery [stéiʃənèri] 문구류
inventory [ínvəntɔ̀ːri] (상품 등의) 목록

05 Detail Question
행사에 포함되지 않을 것은 무엇인가?
Ⓐ 중고 도서
Ⓑ 선물 세트
Ⓒ 글쓰기 용품
☑ 전자책 기기

06 Intention Question
이 문맥에서 "great deals"라는 표현은 무엇을 의미할 가능성이 가장 높은가?
☑ 저렴한 가격
Ⓑ 많은 수량
Ⓒ 독점 혜택
Ⓓ 좋은 해결책

[07-09] 메시지 대화문을 읽으시오.

Melissa Watson (오전 9:40)
안녕하세요, 팀원 여러분. 모바일 결제 시스템 개선 제안에 대한 발표가 다음 주 금요일이라는 점을 유념해 주세요. 최종 슬라이드와 시연은 완전히 준비되었나요?

Ben Klein (오전 9:45)
기술 통합 슬라이드는 완성되었고, ⁰⁹ᴬ새로운 결제 흐름 시연은 원활하게 실행돼요. 파일들은 공유 드라이브에 있어요.

Lisa Payne (오전 9:50)
사용자 경험에 대한 개선 사항이 명확하게 강조되었어요. 저는 또한 ⁰⁹ᴮ새로운 인터페이스로 향상된 사용자 의견에도 중점을 둘게요.

Melissa Watson (오전 9:55)
고마워요, Ben, Lisa. Vanessa, 보안 부분은 어떤가요?

Vanessa Reed (오전 9:57)
저는 ⁰⁸거래 오류를 극적으로 줄여줄 ⁰⁹ᴰ보안 업그레이드를 강조할게요. 또한 향후 사용자 증가에 관한 질문들도 다루겠습니다.

Melissa Watson (오전 10:01)
완벽해요. 경영진에게 깊은 인상을 줄 수 있겠어요. 오후 3시에 준비 세션을 위해 회의실에서 만나요.

---

proposal [prəpóuzəl] 제안, 제의 **integration** [ìntəgréiʃən] 통합
transaction [trænzækʃən] 거래, 처리

07 Intention Question
오전 10시 1분에 Melissa Watson이 "That should impress the executive team"이라고 쓸 때, 이는 무엇을 의미할 가능성이 가장 높은가?
Ⓐ 경영진이 보안 문제에 관심을 가져야 한다고 생각한다.
Ⓑ 발표 슬라이드가 미완성된 것에 대해 염려하고 있다.
Ⓒ 팀이 사용자 만족도에 대한 자료를 더 추가해야 함을 내비치고 있다.
☑ 내용이 매우 좋은 반응을 얻을 것이라고 믿는다.

08 Inference Question
모바일 결제 시스템에 대해 추론할 수 있는 것은?
☑ 현재 결제 오류가 발생하기 쉽다.
Ⓑ 결제를 처리하기 위해 특별한 하드웨어 장치가 필요하다.
Ⓒ 인터페이스가 사용자 불만족의 주된 원인이다.
Ⓓ 디자인은 경쟁사의 플랫폼을 기반으로 하고 있다.

어휘 **prone** [proun] ~하기 쉬운

09 Detail Question

모바일 결제 시스템에서 업데이트되지 않을 것은 무엇인가?
Ⓐ 결제 과정
Ⓑ 사용자 인터페이스
✓ Ⓒ 환불 관리 시스템
Ⓓ 보안 시스템

[10-12] 공지를 읽으시오.

> [10]안전한 드론 비행을 장려하기 위해, 시 정부는 Elmford 공원을 취미용 드론 사용 구역으로 지정했습니다. [11B]비행은 매일 오전 9시부터 일몰까지 허용되며, 무게 55파운드 미만의 드론만 허용됩니다.
>
> [11A]경계 표지 안쪽에서만 조종해 주세요. 안전을 위해, 장비의 고도는 120미터 미만으로 유지하고, 항상 눈으로 직접 볼 수 있는 상태를 유지하고, 사람들 위로는 비행하지 마십시오. 또한, 상황 인지를 유지할 수 있도록 주변 소리나 시야를 차단하는 헤드셋 사용을 피하십시오. 그리고, 모두가 편안하게 공간을 공유할 수 있도록 [11C]다른 이용자들에게 양보해 주십시오.
>
> 공원 및 드론 사용과 관련된 전체 규정 및 규제 목록은 cityofelmford.gov/parks에서 확인하세요.
>
> promote[prəmóut] 장려하다, 촉진하다
> designate[dézignèit] 지정하다
> recreational[rèkriéiʃənəl] 취미의, 오락의
> altitude[ǽltətjù:d] 고도   regulation[règjuléiʃən] 규제, 규정

10 Main Purpose Question

공지의 주된 목적은 무엇인가?
Ⓐ 전문 드론 사진 워크숍을 홍보하기 위해
Ⓑ 새로운 시 전역 드론 규제를 주민들에게 알리기 위해
✓ Ⓒ 공원에서의 취미용 드론 사용 규정을 제공하기 위해
Ⓓ 곧 있을 드론 축제를 알리기 위해

11 Detail Question

Elmford 공원에서 드론 조종자에게 요구되지 않는 것은?
Ⓐ 표시된 경계 내에 머무르는 것
Ⓑ 지정된 시간 동안에만 조종하는 것
Ⓒ 다른 사람들이 해당 구역을 사용하도록 허용하는 것
✓ Ⓓ 드론 조종자로서 등록하는 것

12 Intention Question

이 문맥에서 "maintain visual line of sight"라는 표현은 무엇을 의미할 가능성이 가장 높은가?
Ⓐ 드론이 비행하는 동안 다른 사람들이 지켜보도록 허용한다
✓ Ⓑ 항상 드론을 눈으로 볼 수 있는 범위에 둔다
Ⓒ 쌍안경을 사용해 시야 거리를 늘린다
Ⓓ 다른 공원 방문자의 시야에서 드론을 보이지 않게 한다

[13-15] 메시지 대화문을 읽으시오.

> Jessica Martinez (오후 3:15)
> 지역 마케팅 회의가 다음 달이에요. 모두의 진행 상황에 관한 최신 정보를 알려 주세요.
>
> Robert Chang (오후 3:18)
> 저는 시장 동향에 대한 개회 세션을 준비했어요. 슬라이드에는 3분기 분석과 업계 예측이 포함되어 있어요.
>
> Amanda Foster (오후 3:22)
> 고객 주의 끌기 전략에 대한 제 세션은 준비되었어요. 오후 2시까지 회의실에 상호작용형 디스플레이 설치가 필요해요.
>
> Emilio Santos (오후 3:25)
> [13]인맥 교류 점심식사가 준비되었어요. [15]참석자 150명분 식사 준비가 확정되었고, 장소 배치도 끝났어요.
>
> Jessica Martinez (오후 3:28)
> 모두 잘하고 있네요. Emilio, 기조연설자로부터 확답은 받았나요?
>
> Emilio Santos (오후 3:30)
> Dr. Newsom의 개인 일정에 관해 아직 기다리고 있어요. 그녀의 비서가 내일 아침까지 확답을 준다고 했어요.
>
> Jessica Martinez (오후 3:33)
> [14]대안을 준비해 둬야겠어요. 작년 회의가 우리에게 교훈을 가르쳐줬으니까요.
>
> regional[rí:dʒənəl] 지역의   forecast[fɔ́:rkæst] 예측, 예상
> engagement[ingéidʒmənt] 주의 끌기, 관심

13 Detail Question

Mr. Santos가 맡은 일은 무엇인가?
Ⓐ 세션을 위한 상호작용형 디스플레이를 설치하는 것
Ⓑ 기조연설자의 여행 준비를 담당하는 것
✓ Ⓒ 인맥 교류 점심식사를 준비하는 것
Ⓓ 회의실 예약을 확정하는 것

14 Intention Question

오후 3시 33분에 Ms. Martinez가 "Last year's conference taught us a lesson"라고 쓸 때, 무엇을 암시하는가?
✓ Ⓐ 대안 준비가 필요한 어려움에 직면했었다.
Ⓑ 회의 세부 계획을 모두 원활하게 관리했었다.
Ⓒ 참가자들로부터 긍정적인 피드백을 받았었다.
Ⓓ 다른 연설자들로부터 유용한 발표 기술을 배웠었다.

어휘 logistics[loudʒístiks] 세부 계획

15 Inference Question

회의에 대해 추론할 수 있는 것은?
✓ Ⓐ 150명의 참석자가 있을 것이다.
Ⓑ 온라인 웨비나이다.
Ⓒ 장소가 변경되었다.
Ⓓ 기조연설자가 참석을 취소했다.

Section II Passage Types

1. Email

Example
p.145

이메일을 읽으시오.

수신: danielspencer@sqmail.com
발신: susanbaxter@sqmail.com
날짜: 8월 11일
제목: 부서 회의

Mr. Spencer께,

8월 25일 월요일 오후 2시, 본사 회의실 B에서 예정된 ¹곧 있을 부서 회의를 알려드리기 위해 이 이메일을 씁니다.

이번 회의는 하반기 예산 배정 마무리에 관해 다루고 프로젝트 일정 업데이트 사항을 검토할 예정입니다.

²최신 예산 보고서 사본을 지참하시고 현재 진행 중인 사업에 대한 진척 상황을 논의할 준비를 해 주십시오.

안건에 포함하고 싶은 특정 주제가 있다면, 8월 22일 금요일까지 저에게 이메일로 보내주시기 바랍니다. 질문이나 궁금한 사항은 555-1147로 저에게 연락 주십시오.

Susan Baxter 드림

department [dipá:rtmənt] 부서   notify [nóutəfài] 알리다
budget [bʌ́dʒit] 예산   allocation [æ̀ləkéiʃən] 배정
initiative [iníʃiətiv] 사업   agenda [ədʒéndə] 안건

1 Main Purpose Question
이메일의 주된 목적은 무엇인가?
Ⓐ 회의의 세부 사항을 설명하기 위해
Ⓑ 새로운 사무실 정책을 발표하기 위해
Ⓒ 보고서에 대한 의견을 요청하기 위해
Ⓓ 예산 결정을 확정하기 위해

2 Detail Question
Mr. Spencer가 지참해야 하는 것은?
Ⓐ 연간 보고서
Ⓑ 새로운 사업 제안서
Ⓒ 최근의 예산 개요
Ⓓ 진행 보고서

HACKERS TEST
p.146

01 Ⓐ	02 Ⓒ	03 Ⓑ	04 Ⓓ	05 Ⓐ
06 Ⓑ	07 Ⓐ	08 Ⓑ	09 Ⓐ	10 Ⓓ
11 Ⓑ	12 Ⓐ	13 Ⓐ	14 Ⓑ	15 Ⓐ

[01-02] 이메일을 읽으시오.

수신: KevinL@timemail.com
발신: ChefKen@MoltoBeneRest.com
날짜: 8월 1일
제목: 견습 프로그램

안녕하세요 Kevin,

당신의 인상적인 면접에 뒤이어, 저희 견습 프로그램의 ⁰¹일자리를 당신에게 공식적으로 제안하게 되어 기쁩니다. ⁰²이 프로그램은 9월 1일부터 11월 30일까지 진행될 것입니다. 논의했던 바와 같이, 본 역할은 유급직이며 20달러의 시급이 지급됩니다. 8월 10일까지 수락 여부를 확정해 주시기 바랍니다.

Ken Cuccio 드림
총괄 주방장
Molto Bene 식당

apprenticeship [əpréntəsʃip] 견습직, 수습 기간
impressive [imprésiv] 인상적인, 인상 깊은
acceptance [əkséptəns] 수락, 받아들임

01 Main Purpose Question
이메일의 주된 목적은 무엇인가?
Ⓐ 지원자에게 일자리를 제의하기 위해
Ⓑ 고용 기간을 논의하기 위해
Ⓒ 후속 면접을 정하기 위해
Ⓓ 필요 물품 목록을 제공하기 위해

02 Detail Question
프로그램의 첫날은 언제인가?
Ⓐ 8월 1일
Ⓑ 8월 10일
Ⓒ 9월 1일
Ⓓ 11월 30일

[03-04] 이메일을 읽으시오.

제목: 귀하의 댄스 수업 일정 변경

Mr. Clark께,

귀하가 등록하신 10월 26일 오후 5시 ⁰³댄스 수업이 갑작스러운 강사 개인 일정과의 충돌로 인해 일정 변경되었습니다. ⁰⁴수업은 이제 10월 28일 오후 6시에 진행될 것입니다. 이 새로운 시간이 귀하에게 맞지 않다면, 등록비는 전액 환불될 것입니다.

Sophie Allen 드림

conflict [kɑ́nflikt] 충돌, 갈등   instructor [instrʌ́ktər] 강사

03 Detail Question
댄스 수업이 일정 변경된 이유는?
Ⓐ 댄스 연습장에 긴급한 수리가 필요했다.
Ⓑ 강사에게 예상치 못한 일정 변경이 있었다.
Ⓒ 등록자 수가 적어서 원래 수업이 취소되었다.
Ⓓ 댄스 연습장에 다른 행사와 일정 충돌이 있었다.

어휘 unexpected [ʌ̀nikspéktid] 예상치 못한
      enrollment [inróulmənt] 등록자 수

04 Detail Question
댄스 수업의 변경된 일시는 언제인가?
Ⓐ 10월 26일 오후 5시
Ⓑ 10월 26일 오후 6시
Ⓒ 10월 28일 오후 5시
✓Ⓓ 10월 28일 오후 6시

[05-06] 이메일을 읽으시오.

수신: Service@ForthAir.com
발신: ABKant@mailape.com
날짜: 8월 9일
제목: 수하물 보상

관계자분께,

저는 05 8월 7일 항공편의 제 06 위탁 수하물을 아직 받지 못했습니다. 다행히, 06 기내 반입 가방에 갈아입을 옷 몇 벌이 있었지만, 떨어져 가고 있습니다. 내일까지 보상받을 수 있을지 알고 싶습니다.

Abigail Kant 드림

checked baggage 위탁 수하물
carry-on[kérian] 기내 반입 가방

05 Detail Question
Ms. Kant의 항공편은 언제였는가?
✓Ⓐ 8월 7일
Ⓑ 8월 8일
Ⓒ 8월 9일
Ⓓ 8월 10일

06 Inference Question
Ms. Kant에 대해 추론할 수 있는 것은?
Ⓐ 자주 이용하는 고객이다.
✓Ⓑ 여러 가방을 가지고 있었다.
Ⓒ 이미 지불금을 받았다.
Ⓓ 비싼 옷을 샀다.

어휘 **regular customer** 자주 이용하는(단골) 고객

[07-09] 이메일을 읽으시오.

제목: ATM 정비 요청
SmartATM 서비스 그룹 지원팀께,

Turner Plaza 지점 로비 ATM(장비 번호 4721)에 대한 07 긴급 정비 요청입니다. 오늘 오전 대략 9시 15분부터, 이 장비가 09 모든 출금 시도에 작동하지 않고 있으며, 현금이 충분히 채워져 있음에도 불구하고 "거래를 처리할 수 없음 - 지원팀에 문의"라는 오류를 표시하고 있습니다. 잔액 조회와 같은 다른 기능들은 여전히 정상적으로 작동하고 있습니다.

이 고장은 저희의 아침 피크 시간대 서비스를 심각하게 방해하고 있습니다. 08 이러한 혼란에 대응하기 위해, 현재 저희는 고객들을 저희 은행 인근 지점들로 안내하고 있습니다.

이 문제를 진단하고 수리할 기술자의 파견이 필요합니다. 예상 도착 시간을 확인해 주시기 바랍니다.

파견 시, 조정을 위해 1-555-3321-7890으로 제게 바로 연락 바랍니다. 신속한 관심에 감사드립니다.

Emily Carter 드림
지점 운영 관리자
Continental Bridge 은행

urgent[ɚ́ːrdʒənt] 긴급한
approximately[əpráksəmətli] 대략, 거의
withdrawal[wiðdrɔ́ːəl] 출금, 회수
transaction[trænzǽkʃən] 거래   **balance**[bǽləns] 잔고, 잔액
dispatch[dispǽtʃ] 파견, 발송   **diagnose**[dáiəgnòus] 진단하다
coordination[kouɔ̀ːrdənéiʃən] 조정, 조화

07 Main Purpose Question
이메일의 주된 목적은 무엇인가?
✓Ⓐ 시스템 오류로 인해 신속한 정비를 요구하기 위해
Ⓑ 고객 서비스 처리를 위한 전략의 윤곽을 그리기 위해
Ⓒ 고장난 기계 수리에 대한 조언을 구하기 위해
Ⓓ 정기 점검 일정을 잡기 위해

어휘 **outline**[áutlàin] ~의 윤곽을 그리다

08 Detail Question
Turner Plaza 지점이 이메일을 보내기 전에 한 일은 무엇인가?
Ⓐ 오류 코드를 기록하기 위해 지원 번호로 연락했다.
✓Ⓑ 고객들을 대체 은행 지점들로 안내했다.
Ⓒ 기술자의 예상 도착 시간 확인을 받았다.
Ⓓ ATM 장비에 대해 철저한 검토를 시행했다.

09 Inference Question
로비 ATM에 대해 추론할 수 있는 것은 무엇인가?
✓Ⓐ 현금 지급과 관련된 부품이 고장났다.
Ⓑ 네트워크 정지로 인해 현재 서비스가 중단되었다.
Ⓒ 현금이 떨어져서 돈을 지급할 수 없다.
Ⓓ 기술자에 의해 오늘 완전히 교체될 예정이다.

어휘 **dispense**[dispéns] 지급하다, 나눠 주다
      be out of service 서비스가 중단되다
      outage[áutidʒ] 공급 정지, 정전

[10-12] 이메일을 읽으시오.

날짜: 7월 7일
제목: Verona 소파 배송일 변경

Mr. Pryce께,

최근 주문하신 Verona 소파에 관해 이메일을 씁니다. 안타깝게도, 예상치 못한 공급망 지장으로 인해, 11 예상 배송일이 7월 16일에서 **7월 28일로 변경되었습니다**.

이러한 불편을 끼쳐 죄송합니다. 이 예상치 못한 변경에 대해 10 보상하기 위해, 5퍼센트 환불을 제공해 드리며, 이는 원래 결제하신 수단으로 다시 입금될 것입니다. 이 정산은 오늘 자동으로 처리되고 있으며, 3~5영업일 내에 계좌에 입금이 반영되는 것을 확인하실 수 있을 것입니다. 이것은 기존의 보증이나 지원 서비스에 영향을 주지 않을 것입니다.

12 **주문을 완전히 취소하고 싶으시면, 7월 21일까지 이 이메일에 회신해 주시기 바랍니다.**

고객님의 만족이 저희의 우선 사항이며, 저희는 이 문제를 신속하게 해결하기 위해 최선을 다하고 있습니다. 이해해 주셔서 감사합니다.

Sarah Lee 드림

unforeseen [ʌnfɔːrsíːn] 예상치 못한, 뜻밖의
disruption [disrʌ́pʃən] 지장, 중단, 붕괴
estimated [éstəmeitid] 예상된, 추측의
credit [krédit] 입금하다 adjustment [ədʒʌ́stmənt] 정산, 조정
priority [praiɔ́ːrəti] 우선 사항, 우선권

10 Detail Question
회사가 제공하기로 한 것은?
Ⓐ 배송 회사를 변경한다
Ⓑ 제품 보증을 연장한다
Ⓒ 향후 구매에 대해 할인한다
✓Ⓓ 금전적 보상을 제공한다

11 Detail Question
원래의 배송 날짜는 언제였는가?
Ⓐ 7월 7일
✓Ⓑ 7월 16일
Ⓒ 7월 21일
Ⓓ 7월 28일

12 Detail Question
Mr. Pryce가 주문을 취소하기 위해 해야 하는 것은 무엇인가?
✓Ⓐ 이메일을 보낸다
Ⓑ 판매원에게 전화한다
Ⓒ 가게를 방문한다
Ⓓ 온라인 양식을 작성한다

[13-15] 이메일을 읽으시오.

제목: 예정된 에어컨 점검 (9월 19일)

Ms. Jackson께,

¹³본 이메일은 9월 19일 귀하의 세대에 예정된 에어컨 유지보수 서비스를 확정하기 위한 것입니다. CoolPro Air Conditioning의 ¹⁵기술자들이 오전 9시와 오전 11시 사이에 도착할 예정입니다. 그들은 도착 약 30분 전에 귀하에게 전화할 것입니다.

기술자들을 돕기 위해, ¹⁴ᶜ에어컨 본체 주변에 최소 3피트를 깨끗하게 해주시고 ¹⁴ᴬ귀중품을 미리 안전하게 보관해 주십시오. 안전을 위해, 그들은 시작하기 전에 전원을 끌 것입니다. 서비스에는 배수 시스템 테스트, 그리고 필요한 경우 공기 필터 교체가 포함됩니다.

¹⁴ᴰ이 시간이 불편하시다면, 저희가 일정을 조정할 수 있도록 9월 12일 오후 5시까지 이메일이나 전화로 저희에게 알려주십시오. 서비스 후에는, 완료된 작업을 자세히 설명하는 알림 태그나 서비스 요약서가 남겨질 것입니다.

Leo Koval 드림
East Corner 아파트

maintenance [méintənəns] 유지보수
approximately [əpráksəmətli] 약, 거의
drainage [dréinidʒ] 배수

13 Main Purpose Question
이메일의 주된 목적은 무엇인가?
✓Ⓐ 에어컨 서비스 예약을 확정하기 위해
Ⓑ 에어 필터 교체 방법을 설명하기 위해
Ⓒ 에어컨 서비스 비용 지불을 요청하기 위해
Ⓓ 에어컨에 관한 안전 지침을 제공하기 위해

14 Detail Question
Ms. Jackson이 요청 받지 않은 것은?
Ⓐ 개인 물품을 미리 치운다
✓Ⓑ 서비스 중에 아파트를 비운다
Ⓒ 에어컨 주변 공간을 깨끗하게 한다
Ⓓ 시간이 안 맞는다면 사무소에 연락한다

어휘 put away 치우다 vacate [véikeit] 비우다

15 Detail Question
기술자들이 Ms. Jackson에게 연락할 수 있는 가장 빠른 시간은 언제인가?
✓Ⓐ 9월 19일, 오전 8시 30분
Ⓑ 9월 19일, 오전 9시
Ⓒ 9월 19일, 오전 10시 30분
Ⓓ 9월 19일, 오전 11시

2. Text-Message Chain

Example
p.153

메시지 대화문을 읽으시오.

Nina Park (오전 9:00)
좋은 아침이에요, 팀 여러분! 다시 알려드려요. 금요일 회의에 사용할 모든 투자자 발표 슬라이드와 시연 영상은 목요일까지 마무리되어야 해요.

Mohammed Aziz (오전 9:05)
수요일까지 ¹슬라이드 디자인을 끝내고 초기 의견을 받기 위해 슬라이드 디자인을 보낼게요.

Marco Enriquez (오전 9:09)
저는 지난달 베타 테스트에서 업데이트된 사용자 의견을 모으고, 시연 영상의 요점들을 강조할게요.

Nina Park (오전 9:12)
좋아요. 그리고 장비 호환성도 사전에 다시 한번 확인해야 해요. 지난달 웨비나에서 무슨 일이 있었는지 기억합시다.

Marco Enriquez (오전 9:15)
²네, 지난달 웨비나 때 약간의 문제가 있었죠. 제가 수요일까지 모든 장비에 대한 철저한 호환성 점검을 진행할게요.

Nina Park (오전 9:20)
훌륭해요, 팀 여러분! 우리 함께 완벽한 발표를 해낼 수 있을 거라고 확신해요.

investor [invéstər] 투자자
compatibility [kəmpætəbíləti] 호환성
webinar [wébinɑːr] 웨비나(인터넷 세미나)
glitch [glitʃ] 문제, 결함 thorough [θə́ːrou] 철저한
deliver [dilívər] 제공하다 flawless [flɔ́ːlis] 완벽한

1 Detail Question

Mr. Aziz의 책무는?
Ⓐ 사용자 의견 수집하기
Ⓑ 슬라이드 디자인 마무리하기 ✓
Ⓒ 발표 슬라이드에 대한 의견 보내기
Ⓓ 시연 영상을 발표하기

2 Intention Question

오전 9시 12분에 Ms. Park이 "Remember what happened with the webinar last month"라고 쓸 때, 그녀가 의미하는 것은?
Ⓐ 기술적 문제가 다시는 발생하지 않도록 확실히 하고 싶어 한다. ✓
Ⓑ 다가오는 회의 일정을 변경할 것을 제안하고 있다.
Ⓒ 지난달 웨비나가 불필요했다고 생각한다.
Ⓓ 이번에는 장비 호환성 검사를 건너뛰기를 원한다.

HACKERS TEST   p.154

01	Ⓓ	02	Ⓑ	03	Ⓒ	04	Ⓓ	05	Ⓐ
06	Ⓒ	07	Ⓒ	08	Ⓓ	09	Ⓑ	10	Ⓑ
11	Ⓓ	12	Ⓒ	13	Ⓒ	14	Ⓐ	15	Ⓑ

[01-02] 메시지 대화문을 읽으시오.

Sam Howe   오전 10:14
안녕하세요, 팀 여러분. 저희 재정 보고서 마감 기한이 바뀌었다는 것을 모두에게 다시 한번 알리고 싶어요. 월요일이 이제 휴일이 되어서, 금요일까지 모든 것을 완료해야 해요.

Grace Malone   오전 10:16
상기시켜주셔서 감사해요. 저는 모든 데이터 수집을 거의 끝냈어요. 오늘 오후에 Jacob에게 보낼게요. ⁰¹그가 수요일까지 보고서와 발표 자료에 필요한 그래프를 만들 수 있기를 바라요.

Jacob Cho   오전 10:17
그건 문제없을 것 같아요. ⁰¹만드는 데 몇 시간밖에 안 걸려요.

Tanner Gonzalez   오전 10:21
완벽하네요. 완성되는 대로 저에게 보내주시면 ⁰²제가 모든 것을 편집하고 인쇄할게요.

Sam Howe   오전 10:25
모두 고마워요. 모든 것이 처리된 것 같고 시간에 맞춰 끝낼 수 있을 것 같아요.

financial [fainǽnʃəl] 재정의, 금융의
compile [kəmpáil] 수집하다, 편집하다   material [mətíəriəl] 자료
handle [hǽndl] 처리하다, 다루다

01 Intention Question

오전 10시 17분에 Jacob Cho가 "That shouldn't be a problem"이라고 쓸 때, 그가 의미하는 것은?
Ⓐ Ms. Malone의 말에 동의한다.
Ⓑ 이미 작업을 완료했다.
Ⓒ 기꺼이 잔업을 하려고 한다.
Ⓓ 수요일까지 끝낼 수 있다. ✓

어휘 accomplish [əkάmpliʃ] 완료하다, 완수하다

02 Inference Question

Tanner Gonzalez에 대해 추론할 수 있는 것은?
Ⓐ 가장 최근에 들어온 팀원이다.
Ⓑ 자료를 수정할 것이다. ✓
Ⓒ 추가 시간이 필요하다.
Ⓓ 자료를 발표할 것이다.

[03-04] 메시지 대화문을 읽으시오.

Marc Bishop [오후 1:11]
⁰³우리 부서장님께서 월요일 예산 발표에 참석하실 수 없어요. 시카고에서 고객과 미팅이 있어서 화요일이 되어서야 돌아오실 거예요. ⁰³그가 돌아온 다음 날까지 발표를 미뤄야 할 것 같아요.

Danielle Newman [오후 1:13]
네. ⁰⁴그날 오후 2시부터 4시까지 메인 회의실을 예약하죠.

Liu Zhou [오후 1:15]
방금 예약 일정을 확인했어요. 마케팅팀이 워크숍을 계획해 놓았어요. ⁰⁴우리는 대신 오전에 발표해야 하겠어요. 오전 10시에 시작할 수 있어요.

Marc Bishop [오후 1:16]
괜찮네요. 그리고 준비할 시간이 며칠 더 있으니까, 발표를 어떻게 개선할지 고려해야 해요.

Danielle Newman [오후 1:18]
제가 차트의 모든 데이터를 검토해서 모든 것이 정확한지 확인하면 어떨까요?

Liu Zhou [오후 1:20]
좋아요. 그렇게 하시는 동안, 저는 유인물에 개선할 점이 있는지 볼게요.

department [dipά:rtmənt] 부서, 부처   attend [əténd] 참석하다
budget [bʌ́dʒit] 예산, 비용   push back 미루다
reserve [rizə́:rv] 예약하다
go through 검토하다, 살펴보다   accurate [ǽkjurət] 정확한

03 Detail Question

Mr. Bishop이 발표 연기를 제안하는 이유는?
Ⓐ 출장을 계획하고 있다.
Ⓑ 고객과 만나야 한다.
Ⓒ 관리자의 참석을 원한다. ✓
Ⓓ 예산을 수정하려고 한다.

04 Intention Question

오후 1:15분에 Ms. Zhou가 "The marketing team has a workshop planned"라고 쓸 때 무엇을 암시하는가?
Ⓐ 그룹 프로젝트가 취소되었다.
Ⓑ 주간 일정이 업데이트되었다.
Ⓒ 교육 세션이 유용할 것이다.
Ⓓ 회의 공간을 사용할 수 없다. ✓

[05-06] 메시지 대화문을 읽으시오.

Genet Tesfaye [오후 6:00]
Saffron Table에 연락해 주셔서 감사합니다. 오늘 무엇을 도와드릴까요?

Aarav Sharma [오후 6:01]
이번 주 금요일 오후 7시에 예약하고 싶어요.

Genet Tesfaye [오후 6:02]
죄송하지만, 이번 주 금요일 저녁은 예약이 다 찼습니다. 하지만, 현재 목요일 오후 8시에는 예약 가능합니다. 05마침 그날이 저희의 '와인 & 애피타이저 특별 밤'으로, 05/06모든 애피타이저와 일부 와인에 5퍼센트 할인을 제공합니다.

Aarav Sharma [오후 6:03]
그렇다면, 목요일 오후 8시로 할게요.

Genet Tesfaye [오후 6:05]
몇 분이 오실 예정인가요?

Aarav Sharma [오후 6:07]
2인 테이블로 부탁드려요.

Genet Tesfaye [오후 6:09]
감사합니다. 목요일 오후 8시 2인 테이블 예약이 확정되었습니다. 할인 혜택은 적용 가능한 품목에 자동으로 적용됩니다.

Aarav Sharma [오후 6:10]
좋아요.

assist[əsíst] 돕다   reservation[rèzərvéiʃən] 예약
apologize[əpɑ́lədʒàiz] 사과하다   book[buk] 예약하다
happen[hǽpən] 공교롭게(우연히) ~하다
apply[əplái] 적용하다   eligible[élidʒəbl] 적용 가능한, 자격이 있는

05 Intention Question

Ms. Tesfaye가 "Wine & Appetizer Special night"를 언급한 것은 그녀의 태도에 대해 무엇을 암시하는가?
☑ 고객에게 할인이 매력적으로 느껴질 수 있다고 생각한다.
Ⓑ 고객이 더 많은 음식과 음료를 주문하도록 권유하려 한다.
Ⓒ 고객이 주말에 방문하도록 권장하고 있다.
Ⓓ 목요일에 레스토랑이 얼마나 인기 있는지 강조하고 싶어 한다.

어휘 dissatisfied[dissǽtisfàid] 불만족한
popularity[pɑ̀:pjulǽrəti] 인기

06 Intention Question

이 문맥에서 'eligible items'라는 표현은 무엇을 의미할 가능성이 가장 높은가?
Ⓐ 그날 저녁에 주문 가능한 모든 음식과 음료 품목
Ⓑ 메뉴에서 가장 비싼 품목
☑ 특가 판매에 해당하는 애피타이저와 와인
Ⓓ 목요일에 제공되는 메인 코스

[07-09] 메시지 대화문을 읽으시오.

Dana Scott [오후 2:00]
좋은 오후예요, 팀 여러분. 09D의뢰인이 GlowHerb 제품군을 위한 우리의 포장 초안을 검토했고 제품의 이점과 천연 성분을 더 잘 부각하는 두 가지 추가 선택지를 요청했어요.

Natalie Jones [오후 2:05]
07/09D현재의 라벨을 편집해서 "유기농"과 "비건" 성분을 강조하여 더 눈에 띄게 할게요.

Paul Dunaway [오후 2:10]
새로운 디자인 콘셉트를 생각해서 금요일까지 초안을 보낼게요. 09A"진정"과 "수분 공급" 이점을 강조해야 할까요?

Dana Scott [오후 2:15]
09A네, 그런 효능들을 부각하세요. 또한, 의뢰인은 그 이점들을 시각적으로 나타내기 위해 09C제품의 질감과 자연스러운 외관을 특징적으로 보여주기를 원했어요.

Paul Dunaway [오후 2:20]
그렇게 하려면, 제품의 고해상도 이미지가 더 필요해요. 08제가 의뢰인에게 직접 연락해서 요청해야 할까요?

Dana Scott [오후 2:25]
그들에게 연락하는 일은 제가 주도할게요.

draft[dræft] 초안   ingredient[ingríːdiənt] 성분, 구성 요소
emphasis[émfəsis] 강조   come up with 생각해내다
soothe[suːð] 진정시키다, 달래다
hydrate[háidreit] 수분을 공급하다   texture[tékstʃər] 질감, 감촉
high-resolution[hàirèzəlúːʃən] 고해상도의
reach out 연락을 취하다

07 Fact Question

Natalie Jones는 무엇을 명시하는가?
Ⓐ 현재 디자인이 이미 핵심 성분들을 충분히 특색으로 삼는다고 생각한다.
Ⓑ 새로운 라벨 선택지에 대해 의뢰인과 상담하는 것부터 시작할 것이다.
☑ 제품 구성 요소를 더 잘 부각하기 위해 포장을 수정할 것이다.
Ⓓ 새로운 포장 콘셉트를 디자인하는 일을 맡고 있다.

08 Intention Question

오후 2시 25분에 Dana Scott이 "I'll take the lead on reaching out for those"라고 쓸 때, 이는 무엇을 의미할 가능성이 가장 높은가?
Ⓐ 의뢰인이 이미지를 가지고 자신에게 연락하기를 기다릴 것이다.
Ⓑ Paul이 이미지를 요청하는 것을 잊을까 걱정한다.
☑ 의뢰인에게 연락해서 이미지를 요청할 사람은 자신이다.
Ⓓ 이미지를 요청하기 전에 디자인 콘셉트에 집중할 것이다.

09 Detail Question

의뢰인은 포장 디자인에서 자신들 제품의 다음 측면 중 이것을 제외하고 모두를 강조하고자 한다.
Ⓐ 치유 효능
☑ 가격
Ⓒ 물리적 질감
Ⓓ 성분

[10-12] 메시지 대화문을 읽으시오.

Lena Thompson [오전 8:45]
10다음 주 우리의 혁신 쇼케이스를 위해, 협력사 손님들이 올 거예요.

Maya Patel [오전 8:46]
방문객들을 위한 특별 주차 제도가 있나요?

Lena Thompson [오전 8:47]
11동쪽 주차장의 자리들이 손님 전용으로 지정될 거예요. 안내판이 설치될 것이고, 우리 보안팀이 도움을 줄 거예요.

Julio Rivera [오전 8:50]
저는 런던에서 올 고객인 Sophia Baumgartner가 있어요. 그녀가 도착했을 때 어디로 가라고 말해야 할까요?

Lena Thompson [오전 8:52]
프론트 데스크로 가서 등록하라고 말하세요. ¹²우리 직원 중 한 명이 그녀를 지정석까지 안내할 거예요.

Joshua O'Connor [오전 8:55]
내일 우리가 특별 배지를 차야 하나요?

Lena Thompson [오전 8:57]
아니요, 하지만 전 직원용 서쪽 출입구를 이용하시고 항상 보안 카드를 지참해 주세요.

arrangement [əréindʒmənt] 제도, 배치, 준비
reserve [rizə́:rv] 지정하다, 유보하다
check in 등록하다, (도착했다고) 알리다 **escort** [iskɔ́:rt] 안내하다

10 Fact Question
다음 중 혁신 쇼케이스에 대해 사실인 것은?
Ⓐ 손님들의 발표가 있을 것이다.
Ⓑ 직원이 아닌 사람들이 많이 참석할 것이다. ✓
Ⓒ 모든 직원에게 특별 배지 착용이 요구될 것이다.
Ⓓ 런던에서 개최될 것이다.

11 Intention Question
이 문맥에서 'parking arrangements'라는 표현은 무엇을 의미할 가능성이 가장 높은가?
Ⓐ 지정된 자리에 자신의 차를 주차하는 행위
Ⓑ 회사 부지 내 주차에 대한 서면 규칙과 벌금
Ⓒ 주차장의 건설과 유지보수
Ⓓ 주차 공간을 조직하기 위한 세부사항이나 계획 ✓

12 Inference Question
Sophia Baumgartner에 대해 추론할 수 있는 것은?
Ⓐ 일반 직원들이 먼저 차를 주차할 때까지 기다려야 할 것이다.
Ⓑ Mr. Rivera에 의해 안내받을 것이다.
Ⓒ 도착하면 지정된 구역에 앉을 것이다. ✓
Ⓓ 동쪽 주차장에서 등록할 것이다.

[13-15] 메시지 대화문을 읽으시오.

James Holloway [오후 1:00]
예상치 못한 고객 문제 때문에, 저희 ATAC Tech Summit 대표단을 5명에서 3명으로 줄여야 해요. 남은 대표는 Alex, Maria, 그리고 저예요.

Alex Wright [오후 1:03]
그럼 저희 목표에 큰 영향이 있어요. ¹³다른 두 명의 팀원이 두 건의 최우선 판매 회사 미팅에 중점을 두고 있었고, Maria와 저는 AI 관련 발표를 준비 중이었어요.

James Holloway [오후 1:05]
¹³이제 그 거래들을 확보하는 것이 최우선 과제예요. 당신이 그 일을 맡아주세요, Alex. 수정된 업무 목록을 확정하기 위해 오후 3시에 화상 회의로 만나요.

Maria Perez [오후 1:07]
알겠어요. 그동안에, ¹⁴/¹⁵두 팀원의 환불 불가능한 비용을 나중에 사용할 수 있는 크레딧으로 전환할 수 있는지 항공사와 호텔에 연락해 볼까요?

James Holloway [오후 1:08]
좋은 지적이에요. ¹⁴얼마나 지킬 수 있는지 오후 3시 회의 전에 저에게 알려주세요.

delegation [dèləgéiʃən] 대표단, 위임 **reduce** [ridjú:s] 줄이다
priority [praiɔ́:rəti] 우선 사항 **vendor** [véndər] 판매 회사
revise [riváiz] 수정하다 **convert** [kənvə́:rt] 전환하다
salvage [sǽlvidʒ] 지키다, 구조하다

13 Inference Question
Alex Wright에 대해 추론할 수 있는 것은?
Ⓐ 사무실에 남아 있을 것이다.
Ⓑ 회사 재정에 대한 보고서를 준비할 것이다.
Ⓒ 판매 회사 미팅에 참석할 것이다. ✓
Ⓓ 다음 주 고객 미팅을 위해 출장을 갈 것이다.

14 Detail Question
화상 회의 전에 Maria Perez가 할 것은 무엇인가?
Ⓐ 재정 손실을 최소화하기 위해 서비스 제공업체에 연락한다 ✓
Ⓑ 고객의 예상치 못한 위기를 관리한다
Ⓒ 세 명의 대표를 선택한다
Ⓓ 프레젠테이션을 준비한다

15 Intention Question
오후 1시 08분에 James Holloway가 "Good catch"라고 쓸 때, 이는 무엇을 의미할 가능성이 가장 높은가?
Ⓐ Alex가 실수를 저질렀다는 것에 동의한다.
Ⓑ 간과되었던 업무를 확인한 것에 대해 Maria를 칭찬하고 있다. ✓
Ⓒ 최우선 판매 회사에 연락하라고 Maria에게 상기시키고 있다.
Ⓓ Maria가 사전에 회의실을 예약해 놓은 것을 인정하고 있다.

어휘 **compliment** [kɑ́:mpləmənt] 칭찬하다

3. Notice

Example
공지를 읽으시오.

입주민 여러분께,

10월 28일 오전 10시부터 오후 12시까지 ¹정기 해충 방제가 실시될 예정임을 알려드립니다.

입주민 여러분의 안전을 위해, 작업이 진행되는 동안 ²ᴬ아파트에서 퇴실해 주시기 바랍니다. 아울러, ²ᶜ모든 식료품을 밀봉된 용기에 보관해 주시고 ²ᴰ창문을 모두 닫고 잠갔는지 확인해 주시기 바랍니다.

conduct [kəndʌ́kt] 실시하다 **vacate** [véikeit] 퇴실하다
container [kəntéinər] 용기 **ensure** [inʃúər] 확인하다

1 Main Purpose Question
공지의 주된 목적은?
Ⓐ 건물 관리 변경 사항을 설명하기 위해
Ⓑ 예정된 해충 방제를 공지하기 위해 ✓

Ⓒ 건물 외부 청소를 알리기 위해
Ⓓ 엘리베이터 점검을 통보하기 위해

2 Detail Question

입주민들이 요구받지 않은 사항은?
Ⓐ 집을 일시적으로 비운다
✅ 아파트를 미리 청소한다
Ⓒ 음식물을 밀폐 용기에 보관한다
Ⓓ 건물의 모든 창문을 닫는다

HACKERS TEST   p.162

01 Ⓒ	02 Ⓑ	03 Ⓒ	04 Ⓒ	05 Ⓑ
06 Ⓐ	07 Ⓒ	08 Ⓑ	09 Ⓒ	10 Ⓑ
11 Ⓓ	12 Ⓒ	13 Ⓐ	14 Ⓓ	15 Ⓐ

[01-02] 공지를 읽으시오.

> Sunset가의 공사로 인해, ⁰¹직원 셔틀은 1월 28일부터 2월 2일까지 임시로 이 도로를 우회할 예정입니다. 대신 ⁰²한 블록 서쪽에 있는 Maple가를 이용할 것입니다. 직원 여러분들은 대체 경로를 따라 설치된 임시 정류장에서 승차하시기 바랍니다. 불편을 끼쳐 죄송합니다.
>
> bypass[báipæːs] 우회하다, 건너뛰다   board[bɔːrd] 승차하다

01 Main Purpose Question

공지의 주된 목적은 무엇인가?
Ⓐ 새로운 버스 서비스 도입을 발표하기 위해
Ⓑ 도로의 공사 계획을 설명하기 위해
✅ 직원들에게 임시 경로 변경을 알리기 위해
Ⓓ 도로의 교통 체증에 대해 경고하기 위해

02 Detail Question

직원들에게 권고되는 것은?
Ⓐ 공사가 끝날 때까지 이동을 미룬다
✅ 한 블록 서쪽의 버스 정류장을 이용한다
Ⓒ 대체 교통수단을 찾는다
Ⓓ 공사 일정을 확인한다

[03-04] 표지판을 읽으시오.

> TRES CHIC BOUTIQUE
> 개점!
>
> 이번 주 토요일에 저희의 개점을 축하해 주세요!
>
> 장신구 10~20퍼센트, ⁰⁴의류 품목 25퍼센트, 향수 30퍼센트 할인 혜택을 받으세요.
>
> 오전 9시에 문을 열며 ⁰³선착순 100명의 고객에게는 무료 토트백을 드립니다!
>
> 영업시간:
> 월요일-금요일: 오전 10시 - 오후 9시
> 토요일-일요일: 오전 9시 - 오후 10시

03 Detail Question

고객들이 어떻게 무료 토트백을 받을 수 있는가?
Ⓐ 최소 금액 이상 구매함으로써
Ⓑ 특정 향수를 구매함으로써
✅ 매장에 일찍 감으로써
Ⓓ 매장에 연락함으로써

04 Detail Question

셔츠는 할인이 얼마나 되는가?
Ⓐ 10퍼센트
Ⓑ 20퍼센트
✅ 25퍼센트
Ⓓ 30퍼센트

[05-06] 포스터를 읽으시오.

> CITY FITNESS 이전
>
> 회원님들께 더 나은 서비스를 제공하기 위해 ⁰⁵더 큰 장소로 이전합니다.
>
> 새 위치: San Pedro 쇼핑센터, 133번지 East Elm로
> 개장일: 10월 1일 월요일
>
> ⁰⁶회원권은 자동으로 새 위치로 이전됩니다.
>
> 질문이나 우려사항이 있다면, 555-8210으로 전화해 주십시오.

05 Detail Question

이전 이후 무엇이 바뀔 것인가?
Ⓐ 회원권 가격
✅ 시설의 크기
Ⓒ 운영 시간
Ⓓ 시설 직원

06 Inference Question

회원들에 대해 추론할 수 있는 것은?
✅ 재등록할 필요가 없다.
Ⓑ 10월 1일까지 답변해야 한다.
Ⓒ 여러 위치 중에서 선택할 수 있다.
Ⓓ 전화번호로 전화해야 한다.

[07-09] 공지를 읽으시오.

> 단기 임대 숙소 등록
>
> ⁰⁷모든 호스트는 11월 1일 금요일까지 단기 임대 숙소를 등록해야 합니다. 등록하지 않을 경우 11월 2일부터 이를 따르지 않은 건물에 대해 하루 최대 500달러의 벌금이 부과됩니다. 또한, 호스트들은 모든 숙박시설 광고에 시 등록 번호를 표시해야 합니다.
>
> 단기 임대 숙소 등록은 온라인으로 또는 방문하여 가능합니다. 제출 시 75달러의 수수료를 납부해야 합니다.
>
> 온라인 등록: brookdale.gov/short_term_rentals를 방문하십시오. 필요한 서류에는 ⁰⁹ᴰ사진이 있는 신분증, ⁰⁹ᴬ가장 최근의 재산세 고지서, 주차 공간 배치, ⁰⁹ᴮ평면도가 포함됩니다.
>
> 방문 등록: 평일 오전 9시부터 오후 5시까지 시청 204호실에서 등록하십시오. 온라인 등록과 동일한 서류를 가져오시기 바랍니다.
>
> ⁰⁸온라인 신청은 모든 필요 서류와 결제가 접수된 후 3-5영업일

이내에 처리됩니다. 방문 신청은 직원이 기록을 수동으로 입력해야 하므로 최대 7영업일이 소요될 수 있습니다.

short-term[ʃɔːrtə́ːrm] 단기의 rental[réntl] 임대 물건
registration[rèdʒistréiʃən] 등록
noncompliant[nànkəmpláiənt] 따르지 않는
property[prɑ́pərti] 건물, 부동산
accommodation[əkɑ̀mədéiʃən] 숙박시설
in person 방문하여, 직접 up to 최대 ~까지
manually[mǽnjuəli] 수동으로

07 Main Purpose Question

공지의 주된 목적은 무엇인가?
Ⓐ 단기 임대 숙소에 대한 세금 인상을 발표하기 위해
Ⓑ 숙박시설의 주차 규정을 설명하기 위해
☑ 필수적인 절차에 대한 안내를 제공하기 위해
Ⓓ 추천 숙박시설을 홍보하기 위해

어휘 tax[tæks] 세금 promote[prəmóut] 홍보하다

08 Inference Question

온라인 등록에 대해 결론지을 수 있는 것은?
Ⓐ 방문 등록보다 더 적은 서류가 필요하다.
☑ 직원의 수동 기록 입력이 필요하지 않다.
Ⓒ 11월 1일 마감일 이후에도 제출할 더 많은 시간을 허용한다.
Ⓓ 모든 신청자에게 무료이다.

09 Detail Question

다음 중 호스트들에게 요구되지 않는 것은 무엇인가?
Ⓐ 재산세 고지서
Ⓑ 평면도
☑ 보험 증명서
Ⓓ 사진이 있는 신분증

[10-12] 공지를 읽으시오.

중환자실(ICU) 방문객을 위한 공지

¹⁰다음 지침을 따라주십시오. 여러분의 협조는 환자의 회복과 안전에 매우 중요합니다.

1. 방문 시간: 방문 시간은 엄격히 준수됩니다. 오전 11:00부터 오후 12:00까지와 오후 6:00부터 7:00까지입니다.
2. 감염 관리: 질병 증상(감기, 독감, 발열, 기침)이 있다면, 중환자실에 들어가지 마십시오.
3. 손 위생: ¹¹중환자실 출입 전과 나갈 때, 반드시 손을 철저히 소독해야 합니다. 비치된 소독용 젤을 사용하십시오.
4. 개인 물품: 환자의 안전과 감염 관리를 위해, 최소한의 개인 물품만 허용됩니다. ¹²ᴮ외부 음식과 음료는 엄격히 금지됩니다. ¹²ᴬ/ᴰ모든 큰 코트와 가방(예: 배낭, 쇼핑백)은 병동 밖에 두고 오십시오.
5. 소음: 복도와 환자실에서는 조용히 말하고 대화를 간단히 해주십시오. ¹²ᶜ방해를 방지하기 위해 모든 휴대전화를 무음으로 설정하거나 꺼주십시오.

intensive care unit 중환자실, 집중 치료 병동
cooperation[kouɑ̀ːpəréiʃən] 협조 patient[péiʃənt] 환자
strictly[stríktli] 엄격히 observe[əbzə́ːrv] 준수하다, 지키다
infection[infékʃən] 감염 symptom[símptəm] 증상
illness[ílnis] 질병 sanitize[sǽnitàiz] 소독하다
antiseptic[æntəséptik] 소독용의 prohibit[prəhíbit] 금지하다
disturbance[distə́ːrbəns] 방해

10 Main Purpose Question

공지의 주된 목적은 무엇인가?
Ⓐ 중환자실 시설을 광고하기 위해
☑ 환자의 안전과 회복을 보장하는 지침을 제공하기 위해
Ⓒ 중환자실에서의 자원봉사 기회를 홍보하기 위해
Ⓓ 의료 장비 사용법을 설명하기 위해

11 Intention Question

공지에서 소독용 젤을 언급하는 이유는?
Ⓐ 중증 환자에게 사용되는 약품의 예시를 들기 위해
Ⓑ 중환자실에서 금지된 품목을 명시하기 위해
Ⓒ 방문객에게 각자의 손 소독제를 가져오도록 요청하기 위해
☑ 방문객에게 손을 세정하는 방법을 지시하기 위해

어휘 sanitizer[sǽnitàizər] 소독제, 살균제

12 Detail Question

방문객이 중환자실에 가져갈 수 있는 것은?
Ⓐ 배낭
Ⓑ 커피
☑ 휴대전화
Ⓓ 큰 코트

[13-15] 공지를 읽으시오.

입주민 여러분,

최근 화재 위험과 관련된 안전 우려에 따라, 관리단은 전동 자전거와 전동 스쿠터를 포함한 ¹³개인 전동 이동 수단 충전에 관한 단지 규정을 다시 한번 안내드립니다. 이러한 전동 이동수단의 충전은 각 세대 내부, 발코니, 공용 구역, 계단실에서 금지됩니다.

개인 전동 이동 수단은 화재 안전 설비와 적절한 환기 시설을 갖춘 지정 충전소에서만 충전해야 합니다. 충전소들은 야외 주차장(관리 사무소 본관 근처)과 정문 인근에 있습니다. ¹⁵가까운 시일 내에 더 많은 곳이 추가될 예정입니다.

인가되지 않은 구역에서 개인 이동 장비를 충전하다가 발각되는 입주민은 우선 서면 경고를 받습니다. ¹⁴반복적인 불이행 시 임대차 계약서에 나와 있는 바와 같이 추가 징계 조치로 이어집니다. 최근 이 문제로 한 입주민의 임대차 갱신을 거부한 바 있음을 유념하시기 바랍니다.

모든 입주민의 안전을 위한 협조에 감사드립니다.

complex[kəmpléks] 단지, 복합 건물
vehicle[víːikl] 이동(운송) 수단 prohibit[prəhíbit] 금지하다
individual[ìndəvídʒuəl] 각각의, 개별의
stairwell[stέərwel] 계단실 designated[dézignèitid] 지정된
equip[ikwíp] (시설을) 갖추다 ventilation[vèntəléiʃən] 환기
unauthorized[ʌnɔ́ːθəràizd] 인가되지 않은
noncompliance[nànkəmpláiəns] 불이행, 따르지 않음
disciplinary[dísəplənèri] 징계의 refuse[rifjúːz] 거부하다

13 Main Purpose Question
공지의 주된 목적은 무엇인가?
- Ⓐ 입주민들에게 규정을 상기시키기 위해 ✓
- Ⓑ 새로운 충전소 개장을 공지하기 위해
- Ⓒ 화재 안전 장비 사용법을 설명하기 위해
- Ⓓ 임대차 갱신 절차를 안내하기 위해

14 Detail Question
인가되지 않은 구역에서 전동 이동 수단을 반복적으로 충전하면 무엇이 일어날 수 있는가?
- Ⓐ 벌금을 부과받을 수 있다.
- Ⓑ 서면 경고를 받을 수 있다.
- Ⓒ 기기가 압수될 수 있다.
- Ⓓ 임대차 갱신이 거부될 수 있다. ✓

어휘 confiscate[kάnfəskèit] 압수하다

15 Inference Question
관리사무소에 대해 무엇을 추론할 수 있는가?
- Ⓐ 조만간 더 많은 충전소를 세울 계획이다. ✓
- Ⓑ 전동 이동 수단 충전에 대한 민원을 접수했다.
- Ⓒ 정문 근처에 자리잡고 있다.
- Ⓓ 최근에 화재 피해를 당했다.

4. Advertisement

Example
p.169

광고를 읽으시오.

Horizon Haven 리조트
Horizon Haven 리조트의 6월 15일에 있을 성대한 재개장 소식을 알려드리게 되어 기쁩니다. 오셔서 건강과 평온함의 안식처를 찾아보세요.

깨끗한 해변을 따라 자리 잡은 저희 리조트는 무성한 열대 정원과 바다 전망을 갖춘 평화로운 환경을 제공합니다. 새롭게 업그레이드된 스위트룸에는 ¹완벽하게 설비가 갖춰진 주방, 넓은 욕실, 전용 테라스가 포함되어 있습니다.

다른 시설은 다음과 같습니다:
· 마사지, 얼굴 관리, 웰니스 트리트먼트를 제공하는 현장 스파
· 현지에서 공급된 식재료를 사용한 유기농 식사 선택지
· 피트니스 센터 및 야외 수영장 이용
· 예약 가격에 설비 및 리조트 이용료가 완전히 포함됨
· 새 리넨, 목욕 가운 및 웰니스 키트 제공
· 리조트 전역에서 이용 가능한 고속 Wi-Fi

오늘 당신의 건강 휴가를 예약하세요! ²5월 5일까지 예약을 확정하시고 15퍼센트 할인받으세요. 날짜를 예약하려면, http://www.horizonhavenresort.com/reservation을 방문하세요.

sanctuary[sǽŋktʃuèri] 안식처 serenity[sərénəti] 평온함
nestle[nésl] 자리잡다 pristine[prísti:n] 깨끗한
tranquil[trǽŋkwil] 평화로운 lush[lʌʃ] 무성한
spacious[spéiʃəs] 넓은 organic[ɔ:rgǽnik] 유기농의
ingredient[ingrí:diənt] 식재료 utility[ju:tíləti] 설비

1 Inference Question
Horizon Haven 리조트에 대해 추론할 수 있는 것은?
- Ⓐ 인터넷 접속을 위한 특별 구역을 제공한다.
- Ⓑ 개인 트레이닝 수업을 제공한다.
- Ⓒ 투숙객들이 객실에서 음식을 조리할 수 있도록 허용한다. ✓
- Ⓓ 일부 설비에 대해 추가 요금을 요구한다.

2 Detail Question
할인을 받기 위해 언제까지 예약해야 하는가?
- Ⓐ 5월 5일 ✓
- Ⓑ 5월 15일
- Ⓒ 6월 5일
- Ⓓ 6월 15일

HACKERS TEST
p.170

01 Ⓐ	02 Ⓓ	03 Ⓐ	04 Ⓓ	05 Ⓐ
06 Ⓑ	07 Ⓒ	08 Ⓓ	09 Ⓑ	10 Ⓑ
11 Ⓒ	12 Ⓐ	13 Ⓐ	14 Ⓓ	15 Ⓐ

[01-02] 광고를 읽으시오.

봄 학기 할인을 위해 이번 주에 캠퍼스 서점에 들러보세요! 모든 중고 교과서는 30퍼센트 저렴하게, 새 책과 컴퓨터 소프트웨어는 20퍼센트 저렴하게 구입하세요. 또한 모든 학교 브랜드 의류는 최대 반값까지 할인받을 수 있습니다. ⁰²100달러 넘게 구매하시면 무료 커피 머그잔을 드립니다!

semester[siméstər] 학기 apparel[əpǽrəl] 의류

01 Vocabulary Question
지문의 어구 "swing by"와 의미상 가장 유사한 것은?
- Ⓐ 방문하다 ✓
- Ⓑ 연락하다
- Ⓒ 답사하다
- Ⓓ 뒤따르다

02 Detail Question
조건을 충족하는 구매 시 무료로 제공되는 품목은 무엇인가?
- Ⓐ 중고 교과서
- Ⓑ 학교 브랜드 의류
- Ⓒ 컴퓨터 소프트웨어
- Ⓓ 커피잔 ✓

어휘 qualify[kwάləfài] 조건을 충족하다, 자격이 되다

[03-04] 광고를 읽으시오.

언어 교환
다른 언어 말하기를 연습하고 싶으신가요? 그렇다면 ⁰³매주 금요일 오후 7시에 Central Brew 카페에서 열리는 언어 교환의 밤에 오세요. 세계 각지에서 온 사람들이 참여하여 자신의 모국어를 다른 사람들과 공유합니다. ⁰⁴5달러 입장료에는 저녁 내내 커피, 차, 그리

고 간단한 음식이 포함됩니다.

participate [pɑːrtísəpèit] 참여하다
finger food (손으로 쉽게 집을 수 있는) 간단한 음식

03 Fact Question
행사에 대해 명시된 것은?
ⓐ 일주일에 한 번 열린다. ✓
ⓑ 수년간 개최되어 왔다.
ⓒ 정기적으로 장소를 바꾼다.
ⓓ 재미있는 외국어 게임이 있다.

04 Detail Question
5달러 요금에 포함되지 않는 것은 무엇인가?
ⓐ 행사 입장
ⓑ 무료 음료
ⓒ 무료 간식
ⓓ 연습 교재 ✓

어휘 complimentary [kàːmpləméntəri] 무료의

[05-06] 광고를 읽으시오.

05 새로운 피트니스 강좌

05 커뮤니티 센터에서 모든 주민을 위한 **무료 피트니스 강좌를 제공할 것입니다**. 제공되는 강좌는 요가와 필라테스부터 댄스와 근력 운동에 이를 것입니다. 각 강좌는 한 시간 동안 진행됩니다. 공간이 제한되어 있으므로, 가능한 한 빨리 06 **센터 프론트 데스크를 방문하여 등록하십시오**.

register [rédʒistər] 등록하다

05 Main Topic Question
광고가 홍보하는 것은 무엇인가?
ⓐ 커뮤니티 센터의 건강 관리 프로그램 ✓
ⓑ 주민들을 위한 무료 장비 대여
ⓒ 지역 스포츠 토너먼트 및 대회
ⓓ 영양 워크숍 및 식단 계획

어휘 equipment [ikwípmənt] 장비 nutrition [njuːtríʃən] 영양

06 Detail Question
주민들은 어떻게 등록할 수 있는가?
ⓐ 첫 번째 수업에 참석함으로써
ⓑ 센터의 프론트 데스크를 방문함으로써 ✓
ⓒ 학생회관을 방문함으로써
ⓓ 센터의 웹사이트에 접속함으로써

[07-09] 광고를 읽으시오.

세계를 배우세요

다른 나라로 긴 여행을 떠나는 꿈을 꾸고 계신가요? 해외 학기 프로그램이 현재 학업을 중단하지 않고도 여러분의 꿈을 실현시켜 드릴 수 있습니다. 이 흥미진진한 프로그램은 학생들이 일본, 이탈리아, 호주를 포함한 50개국이 넘는 파트너 대학교에서 한 학기 동안 공부하면서 현지 문화에 몰입할 수 있게 해줍니다. 07 **참가자들은 수강**하는 모든 과목에 대해 정규 학점을 취득하며 문화 여행을 통해 강의실 밖에서 배울 기회를 얻습니다.

08A **수업료**, 08C **식사**, 08B **건강보험**, 08C **홈스테이를 포함한 프로그램 비용**은 저렴하며, 09 **일부 학생들은 전체 비용을 보장하는 보조금 및 기타 재정 지원 패키지 자격이 있을 수도 있습니다**. 프로그램에 대해 더 자세히 알아보시려면, 6월 13일 월요일 오전 10시에 Fletcher Hall에서 열리는 오리엔테이션 세션에 참석하세요. 놀라운 여정의 첫걸음이 될 수도 있습니다!

abroad [əbrɔ́ːd] 해외로 interrupt [ìntərʌ́pt] 중단하다
immerse [imə́ːrs] 몰입하다 excursion [ikskə́ːrʒən] 여행, 소풍
cover [kʌ́vər] (비용을) 보장하다, 포함하다 tuition [tjuːíʃən] 수업료
affordable [əfɔ́ːrdəbl] 저렴한, 가격이 알맞은
qualify [kwɑ́ləfài] 자격이 되다 grant [grænt] 보조금

07 Detail Question
이 프로그램의 이점은?
ⓐ 학기 사이에 진행된다.
ⓑ 여러 나라로 여행할 수 있게 해준다.
ⓒ 학업에 대한 학점을 제공한다. ✓
ⓓ 전적으로 교실 밖에서 진행된다.

08 Detail Question
프로그램 비용에 포함되지 않는 것은?
ⓐ 수업료
ⓑ 건강보험
ⓒ 음식과 숙박
ⓓ 여행 경비 ✓

09 Inference Question
이 프로그램에 대해 추론할 수 있는 것은?
ⓐ 1년 중 한 학기 동안만 진행된다.
ⓑ 일부 참가자들에게는 무료이다. ✓
ⓒ 학생들이 외국어를 구사할 것을 요구한다.
ⓓ 6월 13일에 시작된다.

[10-12] 광고를 읽으시오.

우수 관리자 워크숍

오늘날의 역동적인 비즈니스 환경에서, 효과적인 관리는 조직 성공의 핵심입니다. 리더십 기술을 향상하고 더 나은 성과를 끌어내려면, 우수 관리자 워크숍에 등록하세요.

본 워크숍은 1월 15일 화요일 오전 9시부터 오후 5시까지 Innovation Valley Center에서 진행되며, 운영, 재무, 인사, 영업 등 다양한 부서의 감독자와 관리자를 위해 기획되었습니다.

이번 워크숍은 업계를 선도하는 컨설턴트로부터 직접 현대적인 리더십 전략, 갈등 해결, 성과 코칭, 그리고 효과적인 위임에 대한 식견을 얻을 결정적인 기회입니다. 명확한 목표 설정 능력에 숙달해야 하든, 건설적인 피드백을 제공하는 방법을 배워야 하든, 저희 전문 조력자들이 그 방법을 알려드릴 것입니다.

11 **미래 업무 환경을 헤쳐 나가는 데 도움이 되도록**, 10 **워크숍은 올해 처음으로** 디지털 전환과 12 **원격 팀 관리에 대한 전문 과정도 포함**합니다. 이 중요한 전문성 개발 기회를 놓치지 마십시오.

environment [inváiərənmənt] 환경
organizational [ɔ̀ːrgənizéiʃənəl] 조직의
elevate [éləvèit] 향상하다, 올리다   enroll [inróul] 등록하다
managerial [mæ̀nidʒíəriəl] 관리의, 운영의
supervisor [súːpərvàizər] 감독자   department [dipɑ́ːrtmənt] 부서
crucial [krúːʃəl] 결정적인   conflict [kɑ́nflikt] 갈등
resolution [rèzəlúːʃən] 해결   delegation [dèləgéiʃən] 위임
facilitator [fəsílətèitər] 조력자, 촉진자
module [mɑ́dʒuːl] 과정, 학습 단위
transformation [trænsfərméiʃən] 변화

10 Inference Question
워크숍에 대해 추론할 수 있는 것은?
Ⓐ 주로 재무 및 영업에 초점을 맞출 것이다.
☑ 이전에 개최된 적이 있다.
Ⓒ 참석자들은 상세한 전문 포트폴리오를 가져와야 한다.
Ⓓ 주요 목표는 관리자가 새로운 일자리를 찾도록 돕는 것이다.

11 Intention Question
광고는 왜 전문 과정을 언급하는가?
Ⓐ 전문적인 IT 교육의 필요성을 강조하기 위해
Ⓑ 참석자들에게 필수 조건을 알려주기 위해
☑ 워크숍의 추가적인 이점을 제공하기 위해
Ⓓ 회사의 운영 구조에 필요한 변화를 설명하기 위해

어휘   prerequisite [priːrékwəzit] 필수 조건

12 Detail Question
참석자들이 배우게 될 것은?
☑ 사무실 밖에서 일하는 직원을 감독하는 방법
Ⓑ 효율적인 성과 검토 시스템을 제공하는 방법
Ⓒ 팀원 간의 의사소통을 촉진하는 방법
Ⓓ 디지털 전환에 대한 공식 인증서를 받는 방법

[13-15] 광고를 읽으시오.

> **Cozy Corner**
>
> ¹³Cozy Corner에서 열정적인 정규직 및 시간제 직원을 모집합니다.
>
> 담당 업무는 주문 접수, 서빙, 음료 제조, 결제 처리, 청소를 포함하여 식사 경험의 모든 측면을 아우릅니다.
>
> 자격 요건 및 보상:
> · 장시간 서 있을 수 있는 능력
> · 사전 경험은 도움이 되지만 필수는 아님 (수습 직원 환영!)
> · ¹⁴야간 및 주말 근무를 포함한 유연한 근무 가능 시간
> · 시간당 15.00달러의 경쟁력 있는 초봉에 팁 별도 지급
>
> ¹⁵모든 신규 채용 직원은 채용일로부터 30일 이내에 필수 식품 안전 인증서를 제출해야 합니다.
>
> 지원하시려면: 월요일부터 금요일까지 오후 2시에서 4시 사이에 이력서를 지참하고 ¹³식당을 방문하십시오.

enthusiastic [inθùːziǽstik] 열정적인   aspect [ǽspekt] 측면
payment [péimənt] 결제, 지불
requirement [rikwáiərmənt] 자격 요건
compensation [kɑ̀mpənséiʃən] 보상

trainee [treiníː] 수습 직원   competitive [kəmpétətiv] 경쟁력 있는
certification [sə̀ːrtəfikéiʃən] 인증서

13 Main Topic Question
광고가 홍보하는 것은?
☑ 지역 식당의 구인
Ⓑ 고객 서비스 기술에 대한 교육 과정
Ⓒ 식품 안전에 관한 단기 강좌
Ⓓ 식당의 새로운 메뉴

14 Inference Question
Cozy Corner에 대해 추론할 수 있는 것은?
Ⓐ 오후 2시에서 4시 사이에는 영업하지 않는다.
Ⓑ 경험이 있는 직원만 고용한다.
Ⓒ 가장 인기 있는 품목은 음료이다.
☑ 직원들은 밤과 주말에만 일할 수도 있다.

15 Intention Question
광고는 왜 식품 안전 인증서를 언급하는가?
☑ 채용 요건을 명시하기 위해서
Ⓑ 교육이 가능함을 알리기 위해서
Ⓒ 보상 패키지를 제안하기 위해서
Ⓓ 지원 방법을 안내하기 위해서

5. Social Media Post

Example   p.177

소셜 미디어 게시물을 읽으시오.

> **Marie Sanders**
>
> 책을 사랑하는 분들, 준비하세요! ¹지역 도서 박람회가 곧 다가오는데, 이번에는 그 어느 때보다 더 규모가 크고 좋을 거예요. 이번 주 토요일에 지역 커뮤니티 센터를 방문하여 독서의 소박한 즐거움을 함께 기념하세요.
>
> 모든 독자를 위한 것들이 있어요. 사랑받는 고전과 베스트셀러 그래픽 노블부터 아이들을 위한 최신 그림책에 이르기까지 모든 것이 있는 수십 개의 테이블을 둘러보세요. 또한 미스터리, 회고록, 공상 과학 소설처럼 활기찬 ²ᴬ주제별 섹션에서 여러분이 가장 좋아하는 장르를 탐색할 수도 있습니다.
>
> 책 외에도, 다양한 체험 활동을 즐겨보세요. 스토리텔링 모임, ²ᴰ재미있는 책갈피 만들기 코너, 그리고 ²ᴮ독특한 소장품을 위한 입찰식 경매가 마련되어 있어요. 친절한 자원봉사자들이 여러분이 찾는 것을 정확히 찾을 수 있도록 도울 거예요.
>
> 모든 수익금은 우리 도서관의 문해력 프로그램을 지원하는 데 사용됩니다. 친구들을 데려와서 여러분이 가장 좋아하는 추천 도서를 공유해 주세요. 그곳에서 여러분을 만날 수 있기를 기대해요!

graphic novel 그래픽 노블(만화의 형태로 된 소설)
memoir [mémwɑːr] 회고록
interactive [ìntərǽktiv] 체험의, 상호적인
silent auction 입찰식 경매(팻말을 들어 입찰하는 경매)
collectible [kəléktəbl] 소장품
proceeds [próusiːdz] 수익금   literacy [lítərəsi] 문해력

1 Main Purpose Question

이 게시물의 주된 목적은 무엇인가?
Ⓐ 다양한 문학 장르를 비교하기 위해
Ⓑ 도서 박람회 자원봉사자를 모집하기 위해
Ⓒ 지역 사회의 문해력 문제를 강조하기 위해
✓Ⓓ 지역 도서 박람회를 홍보하기 위해

2 Detail Question

방문객들이 경험하지 못할 것은?
Ⓐ 주제별 섹션을 탐색하는 것
Ⓑ 경매에서 입찰하는 것
✓Ⓒ 도서 사인회에 참석하는 것
Ⓓ 책갈피를 만드는 것

03 Detail Question

공연은 어디에서 열렸는가?
Ⓐ 콘서트홀에서
✓Ⓑ 공원에서
Ⓒ 록 클럽에서
Ⓓ 경기장에서

04 Inference Question

콘서트에 대해 추론할 수 있는 것은?
✓Ⓐ 이후에 더 많은 콘서트가 이어질 것이다.
Ⓑ 다양한 음악 장르를 포함했다.
Ⓒ 여러 지역의 밴드들을 끌어모았다.
Ⓓ 전문적인 안무가 특징이었다.

어휘 dance routine 안무, 정해진 춤 동작

[05-06] 소셜 미디어 게시물을 읽으시오.

> City of Temple @TempleOfficial | 목요일, 5월 1일
>
> Temple 주민 여러분께 알려드려요! 우리 시를 깨끗하고 푸르게 유지하는 데 도움이 되도록 쓰레기 수거 일정이 변경되었습니다!
>
> 새로운 수거 일정:
>   일반 쓰레기: 매주 화요일과 금요일에 수거
>   음식물 찌꺼기: 목요일에만 수거
>   ⁰⁵재활용품: 수요일에만 수거
>
> 색상 안내(헷갈리지 않게 꼭 확인해 주세요!):
>   검은색 쓰레기통: 일반 쓰레기
>   ⁰⁶초록색 쓰레기통: 퇴비 및 음식물 찌꺼기(남은 음식물 포함!)
>   파란색 쓰레기통: ⁰⁵재활용품(음식물 상자 및 음료 캔 포함)
>
> 함께 협력하여 우리 동네를 깔끔하게 유지해 주심에 감사합니다!
>
> #TempleCares #WasteCollection #CityUpdate

heads-up [hédzʌp] 알림 resident [rézədənt] 주민
scrap [skræp] 음식물 찌꺼기 leftover [léftouvər] 남은 음식물
pitch in 협력하다 tidy [táidi] 깔끔한

HACKERS TEST   p.178

01 Ⓓ	02 Ⓒ	03 Ⓑ	04 Ⓐ	05 Ⓑ
06 Ⓐ	07 Ⓐ	08 Ⓑ	09 Ⓑ	10 Ⓒ
11 Ⓒ	12 Ⓐ	13 Ⓑ	14 Ⓒ	15 Ⓓ

[01-02] 소셜 미디어 게시물을 읽으시오.

> Tyler Banks @tylerrides | 4월 10일
>
> Plymouth Pedal Pushers 자전거 동호회에서 ⁰¹/⁰²첫 라이딩을 다녀왔어요. 정말 재미있었어요! 오늘 라이딩에는 40명이 넘는 참가자가 있었어요. 25킬로미터를 달리는 동안 아름다운 풍경을 많이 볼 수 있었어요. 5월 1일에 있을 다음 라이딩이 정말 기대돼요!

01 Main Purpose Question

게시물의 주된 목적은 무엇인가?
Ⓐ 자전거 타기 동호회를 홍보하기 위해
Ⓑ 다가오는 여행을 광고하기 위해
Ⓒ 자전거 안전 수칙을 알려주기 위해
✓Ⓓ 자전거 라이딩을 묘사하기 위해

02 Inference Question

Tyler Banks에 대해 암시된 것은?
Ⓐ 새 자전거를 마련했다.
Ⓑ Plymouth에 산다.
✓Ⓒ 최근 한 동호회에 가입했다.
Ⓓ 풍경 사진을 찍었다.

[03-04] 소셜 미디어 게시물을 읽으시오.

> MillervilleEvents.com/Blog
>
> Millerville의 ⁰³/⁰⁴여름 시리즈 중 첫 번째 공개 콘서트가 어젯밤 Pine Tree 공원에서 열렸는데, 정말 열정적인 분위기였어요! 지역 록밴드들이 약 5시간 동안 공연하며, 엄청난 인파를 끌어모았습니다. 많은 사람들이 광장에서 음악을 듣고 춤을 추며 피크닉을 즐기는 모습이 보였습니다.

atmosphere [ǽtməsfiər] 분위기
electric [iléktrik] 열정적인, 열광케 하는   draw [drɔː] 끌어모으다

05 Detail Question

음식물 상자는 언제 수거되는가?
Ⓐ 화요일에
✓Ⓑ 수요일에
Ⓒ 목요일에
Ⓓ 금요일에

06 Detail Question

주민들은 남은 음식물을 어떻게 처리해야 하는가?
✓Ⓐ 초록색 쓰레기통에 넣는다
Ⓑ 일반 쓰레기에 추가한다
Ⓒ 매일 버린다
Ⓓ 검은 봉투로 싼다

[07-09] 소셜 미디어 게시물을 읽으시오.

> 중대 발표
>
> 먼저 저희 Bao Wow 팝업 행사들에 보여주신 성원에 대해 모두에게 감사드려요. 저희 퓨전 번에 대한 반응이 너무 긍정적이어서,

큰 결정을 내렸습니다. ⁰⁷푸드트럭을 구입하기로 했어요!

다음 달부터, Bao Wow는 ⁰⁸2번가 푸드트럭 공원(시립 부두 맞은편 2번가 2824번지)에 자리를 잡을 것이에요. 베스트셀러인 한국식 치킨 번과 멕시코식 스트리트 콘 번을 포함해, 팝업 행사에서 인기 있었던 모든 번들을 제공할 예정이며, 여러 흥미로운 새 선택지와 주간 특선 메뉴도 추가할 거예요.

개업을 기념해서, ⁰⁹저희 소셜 미디어 팔로워들에게 처음 2주 동안 20퍼센트 할인을 제공할 예정이에요. 할인받기 위해서는 저희를 팔로우하고 있다는 것만 보여주시면 됩니다.

다음 달에 만나요!!!

first off 먼저 **reception** [risépʃən] 반응
positive [pɑ́:zətiv] 긍정적인 **celebrate** [séləbrèit] 기념하다
discount [dískaunt] 할인

07 Inference Question

Bao Wow에 대해 추론할 수 있는 것은?
Ⓐ 고정된 장소가 없다. ✓
Ⓑ 현재 연회용 음식을 제공한다.
Ⓒ 비평가들로부터 긍정적인 평을 받았다.
Ⓓ 전통 중국 음식을 제공한다.

어휘 **permanent** [pɑ́:rmənənt] 고정된, 영구적인

08 Detail Question

2번가 2824번지에는 무엇이 있는가?
Ⓐ 시립 부두
Ⓑ 새로운 레스토랑
Ⓒ 팝업 행사장
Ⓓ 푸드트럭 단지 ✓

09 Detail Question

할인받기 위해 고객들이 해야 하는 것은?
Ⓐ 20달러가 넘는 음식을 구매한다
Ⓑ 계정을 팔로우하고 있음을 증명한다 ✓
Ⓒ 소셜 미디어 게시물을 작성한다
Ⓓ 할인 쿠폰을 제시한다

[10-12] 웹페이지를 읽으시오.

www.gleemanbistro.com

| 정보 | 예약 | 리뷰 | 연락처 |

고객명: Janice Waters
방문 날짜: 6월 15일

제 고객 중 한 분이 Gleeman's 식당에 한번 가보라고 추천해주셨습니다. ¹⁰그래서 제 동료가 관리자 직급으로 승진했을 때, 이 레스토랑에서 작은 파티를 개최했습니다. 저희가 아마 꽤 시끄러울 것이라는 걸 알고 있어서, ¹¹저희만의 식사 공간을 위해 추가로 30달러를 지불하기로 결정했습니다. 저희가 앉은 방은 넓고 편안했습니다.

거의 모든 것이 만족스러웠습니다. ¹²ᶜ주문한 음식은 잘 조리되었고, ¹²ᴮ종업원도 매우 유능했습니다. ¹²ᴬ제가 불만을 가진 유일한 점은 주차장이 꽤 작다는 것입니다. 실제로 자리를 얻기 위해 다른 손님이 떠나기를 기다려야 했습니다. 하지만 이것은 사소한 문제였습니다. 또한 ¹²ᴰ가격이 매우 합리적이었다는 점도 언급해야겠습니다.

bistro [bístrou] (작은) 식당 **colleague** [kɑ́li:g] 동료
supervisor [sú:pərvàizər] 관리자
organize [ɔ́:rgənàiz] 개최하다 **spacious** [spéiʃəs] 넓은
satisfaction [sæ̀tisfǽkʃən] 만족
reasonable [rí:zənəbl] 합리적인

10 Detail Question

Ms. Waters가 Gleeman's 식당을 방문한 이유는?
Ⓐ 은퇴 파티에 참석하기 위해
Ⓑ 고객과 만나기 위해
Ⓒ 승진을 축하하기 위해 ✓
Ⓓ 가족 행사에 참여하기 위해

어휘 **retirement** [ritáiərmənt] 은퇴

11 Detail Question

손님들에게 무엇에 대해 추가 요금이 부과되는가?
Ⓐ 배달 서비스
Ⓑ 주차 공간
Ⓒ 개별 방 ✓
Ⓓ 특별 요리

12 Detail Question

Ms. Waters가 만족하지 못했던 것은
Ⓐ 시설의 크기 ✓
Ⓑ 직원의 능력
Ⓒ 음식의 품질
Ⓓ 식사의 비용

[13-15] 소셜 미디어 게시물을 읽으시오.

¹³연례 Willow Creek 지역 과학 박람회는 완벽한 성공이었고, 지역적으로 성장하는 과학 탐구 정신을 보여주었습니다. ¹⁴커뮤니티 센터는 Willow Creek과 그 주변 지역의 청소년들이 노력을 쏟아부은 프로젝트들을 공유하면서 전염성 있는 에너지로 가득 찼습니다.

이 행사에서는 ¹⁵ᴬ역동적인 태양계 모형들부터 ¹⁵ᴮ지속가능한 지역 농업에 관해 예리하고 잘 연구된 실험까지, 놀랍도록 다양한 프로젝트들이 선을 보였습니다. 또 다른 주목할 만한 프로젝트는 지역 폐기물 관리 문제를 해결하기 위해 설계된 ¹⁵ᶜ스마트 재활용 분류 장치였습니다. 전시품들의 창의성과 기발함은 지역 공학자들과 과학자들이 진행한 심사를 꽤 어렵게 만들었습니다.

경쟁을 넘어서, 이 박람회는 훌륭한 지역 행사였습니다. 부모들과 이웃들이 함께 모여 참가자들을 응원했습니다. 이 날은 Willow Creek 내의 커다란 잠재력을 보여주었습니다. 모든 참가자 여러분 매우 잘했어요!

absolute [ǽbsəlù:t] 완벽한, 절대적인
showcase [ʃóukeis] 보여주다
thrive [θraiv] 성장하다, 잘 자라다 **inquiry** [ínkwəri] 탐구
infectious [infékʃəs] 전염성 있는 **diverse** [dáivə:rs] 다양한
standout [stǽndàut] 주목할 만한, 눈에 띄는
ingenuity [ìndʒənjú:əti] 기발함, 재주

challenging[tʃǽlindʒiŋ] 어려운, 도전적인
competition[kàmpətíʃən] 경쟁

13 Main Purpose Question
게시물의 주된 목적은 무엇인가?
ⓐ 과학 박람회에서 우승한 프로젝트를 소개하기 위해
ⓑ 과학 박람회의 성공을 설명하기 위해 ✓
ⓒ 과학 박람회 심사위원으로서의 경험을 공유하기 위해
ⓓ 과학 박람회 조직을 비판하기 위해

14 Inference Question
과학 박람회에 대해 추론할 수 있는 것은?
ⓐ Willow Creek의 학생들만 참여했다.
ⓑ 지역 행사와 동시에 개최되었다.
ⓒ 젊은 참가자들에게 열려 있었다. ✓
ⓓ 지역 교육자들이 심사했다.

어휘 accompany[əkʌ́mpəni] 동시에 일어나다, 수반하다

15 Detail Question
다음 중 과학 박람회에서 전시되지 않았던 것은?
ⓐ 역동적인 태양계 모형들
ⓑ 지속가능한 지역 농업에 대한 실험들
ⓒ 스마트 재활용 분류 장치
ⓓ 학생이 만든 로봇들 ✓

6. News Article

Example   p.185
기사를 읽으시오.

> 만추에 접어든 예술가들이 캔버스에서 새로운 목적을 찾다
>
> Amherst Mills 아트 센터에서 열리는 새 전시회 "Lifelong Studio"는 예술적 창의성을 받아들이는 데는 늦은 시기가 없다는 것을 증명하고 있다. ¹이 전시회는 은퇴 후 예술을 통해 새로운 목적을 찾은 고령자들을 집중 조명한다.
>
> 참여 작가 중에는 78세의 Beverly Kendrick이 있는데, 그녀는 노후에 처음으로 그림을 그리기 시작했다. Kendrick은 그림을 그리는 것이 새로운 활력을 찾는 데 도움이 되었다는 말을 해주었다. 그녀의 유화 ²"Twilight Reflections"는 활기찬 도시 풍경을 포착하며, 이번 전시회의 하이라이트이다.
>
> 아트 센터 대변인은 이 전시회가 고령자들이 지역 사회의 활동적이고 중요한 일원으로 남아 있으며, 지속적으로 새로운 기술을 배우고 문화에 기여한다는 점을 보여주기 위해 기획되었다고 언급했다.
>
> 전시회는 다음 달 말까지 계속된다.
>
> purpose[pə́ːrpəs] 목적 exhibition[èksəbíʃən] 전시회
> prove[pruːv] 증명하다 embrace[imbréis] 받아들이다
> retirement[ritáiərmənt] 은퇴 golden years 노후
> vitality[vaitǽləti] 활력 vibrant[váibrənt] 활기찬
> spokesperson[spóukspə̀ːrsn] 대변인
> contribute[kəntríbjuːt] 기여하다

1 Main Purpose Question
이 기사의 주된 목적은 무엇인가?
ⓐ 고령자를 위한 그림 수업을 광고하기 위해
ⓑ 고령 작가들을 특집으로 하는 미술 전시회를 알리기 위해 ✓
ⓒ 은퇴자들에게 유화를 시작하도록 장려하기 위해
ⓓ 전시회에 출품된 미술 작품을 비평하기 위해

2 Detail Question
"Twilight Reflections"는 무엇을 묘사하는가?
ⓐ 해 질 녘의 조용한 시골 풍경
ⓑ 작가의 자화상
ⓒ 활기찬 도시 풍경 ✓
ⓓ 어느 예술가의 스튜디오

HACKERS TEST   p.186

01 ⓓ	02 ⓐ	03 ⓒ	04 ⓑ	05 ⓐ
06 ⓒ	07 ⓒ	08 ⓑ	09 ⓓ	10 ⓑ
11 ⓐ	12 ⓑ	13 ⓓ	14 ⓓ	15 ⓐ

[01-02] 기사를 읽으시오.

> 시립 수영장 하루 휴장
>
> Meadville—시립 수영장이 7월 10일에 유지보수를 위해 휴장한다. ⁰¹이번 휴장은 새로운 여과 시스템 설치를 가능하게 할 것이다. ⁰²수영장은 7월 11일에 평소와 같은 오후 운영 시간으로 돌아갈 것이며, 모든 수영 강습은 예정대로 계속될 것이다.
>
> maintenance[méintənəns] 유지보수 closure[klóuʒər] 휴장
> installation[ìnstəléiʃən] 설치 filtration[filtréiʃən] 여과
> resume[rizúːm] 다시 돌아가다

01 Detail Question
수영장이 임시 휴장하는 이유는?
ⓐ 수영 강습 공간을 제공하기 위해
ⓑ 일부 시스템을 확인하기 위해
ⓒ 수영장 물을 정화하기 위해
ⓓ 새로운 장비를 설치하기 위해 ✓

어휘 accommodate[əkɑ́ːmədèit] 공간을 제공하다, 수용하다

02 Inference Question
수영장에 대해 추론할 수 있는 것은?
ⓐ 매일 아침 휴장한다. ✓
ⓑ 직원 채용 문제를 겪고 있다.
ⓒ 새로운 유지보수 직원들을 고용하고 있다.
ⓓ 강습 시간을 추가하고 있다.

어휘 staffing[stǽfiŋ] 직원 채용

[03-04] 기사를 읽으시오.

> ⁰³/⁰⁴지역 기술 기업인 Quantum Innovations사가 Harrington 고등학교에 노후화된 과학 실험실을 업그레이드하고 완전히 자금이 지원되는 새로운 방과후 로봇 동아리를 개설하도록 10,000달러를 기부했다. 이번 기부는 학생들의 관심을 고취하고 지역 교육의 전반적인 질과 미래 직업 기술을 향상시키는 것을 목표로 한다.
>
> **donate** [dóuneit] 기부하다　**outdated** [àutdéitid] 노후화된
> **laboratory** [lǽbərətɔ̀ːri] 실험실　**establish** [istǽbliʃ] 설립하다
> **contribution** [kɑ̀ntrəbjúːʃən] 기부, 기여　**aim** [eim] 목표로 하다
> **inspire** [inspáiər] 고취하다　**enhance** [inhǽns] 향상시키다

03 Main Purpose Question
기사의 주된 목적은 무엇인가?
(A) 지역 학교를 위한 추가 기부를 요청하기 위해
(B) 지역 학교의 과학 교과 과정을 자세히 설명하기 위해
✓ 지역 학교에 대한 한 기업의 재정적 기여를 보도하기 위해
(D) 지역 학교의 노후화된 시설을 비판하기 위해

어휘　**curriculum** [kəríkjuləm] 교과 과정

04 Detail Question
Quantum Innovations사의 기부금은 어떤 분야에 자금을 지원했는가?
(A) 직업 훈련 수업을 개설하는 것
✓ 과학 시설을 현대화하는 것
(C) 과학 교사를 채용하는 것
(D) 새로운 교과서를 구매하는 것

[05-06] 기사를 읽으시오.

> Eastwick 시가 새로운 브랜드 정체성을 도입한다. ⁰⁵새 로고는 여러 색으로 된 디자인을 특징으로 하는데, 이는 기존 로고와 뚜렷한 대비를 이룬다. ⁰⁶웹사이트가 업데이트되었으며, 공식 문서와 표지판이 뒤이을 예정이다. 새로운 브랜드를 내세운 공식 상품도 출시될 예정이다.
>
> **stark** [stɑːrk] 뚜렷한, 완전한　**contrast** [kɑ́ntræst] 대비

05 Inference Question
기존 로고에 대해 추론할 수 있는 것은?
✓ 여러 가지 색이 없었다.
(B) 지역 회사에서 디자인했다.
(C) 인쇄물에서의 사용만을 위한 것이었다.
(D) 주민들에게 인기가 없었다.

06 Detail Question
새 로고는 현재 어디에서 찾을 수 있는가?
(A) 공공 도로 표지판
(B) 공식 상품
✓ 공식 온라인 페이지
(D) 정부 발행 문서

[07-09] 기사를 읽으시오.

> ⁰⁷국립기상청은 주 북서부 지역 모든 지역사회에 겨울 폭풍 경보를 발령했다. 이 지역 주민들은 폭설, 빙판길, 강풍이 예상됨을 인지하고, 필수 예방조치를 취해야 한다. 날씨는 12월 2일부터 악화되기 시작할 것으로 예상되며, 폭풍은 2~3일간 지속될 것이다. ⁰⁸이 기간 동안, 주 도로 작업단은 모든 주요 도로에 눈과 얼음이 없도록 확실히 하기 위해 추가 교대근무를 할 예정이지만, 예상되는 다량의 눈으로 인해 이것이 불가능할 수도 있다는 우려가 있다. 그러므로, 주민들은 절대적으로 필요한 경우에만 운전하도록 요청받고 있다. 이러한 상황을 고려하여, ⁰⁹교육부는 이미 수많은 학교에 임시 휴교령을 내리기로 했다. 이 학교들은 교육부 웹사이트에 게재되어 있으며, 필요에 따라 업데이트될 예정이다.
>
> **aware** [əwɛ́ər] 인지하는, 알고 있는
> **necessary** [nésəsèri] 필수의, 필요한
> **precaution** [prikɔ́ːʃən] 예방조치
> **deteriorate** [ditíəriərèit] 악화되다　**shift** [ʃift] 교대근무
> **absolutely** [ǽbsəlùːtli] 절대적으로　**in light of** ~을 고려하여

07 Main Purpose Question
기사의 주된 목적은 무엇인가?
(A) 지역 사회로 방문객을 맞이하기 위해
(B) 행사의 취소를 설명하기 위해
✓ 안전하지 못한 상황에 대해 주민들에게 경고하기 위해
(D) 이전의 일기예보를 정정하기 위해

08 Detail Question
기사에 따르면 주 도로 작업단은
(A) 임시로 다른 지역으로 배치될 것이다
✓ 할당된 임무를 수행할 수 없을 것이다
(C) 다른 부서들과 협력할 준비가 되어 있을 것이다
(D) 오도 가도 못하는 운전자들을 도울 것이다

어휘　**strand** [strænd] 오도 가도 못하게 하다

09 Detail Question
온라인에서 찾을 수 있는 것은?
(A) 프로젝트 비용에 대한 업데이트
(B) 대체 경로 지도
(C) 학교 정책에 관한 보고서
✓ 폐쇄된 학교 목록

[10-12] 기사를 읽으시오.

> 도서관이 변경사항을 발표하다
>
> Franklinton—지역사회에 더 나은 서비스를 제공하기 위해, Franklinton 공립도서관은 운영시간 대폭 확대를 발표했다. ¹⁰다음 주부터, 도서관은 평일 오전 8시부터 오후 10시까지, 주말 오전 10시부터 오후 8시까지 개방된다. 도서관 직원들은 ¹⁰매일 2시간씩 더 늦게 문을 닫음으로써 학습 공간이 필요한 학생들, 연구에 종사하는 전문가들, 그리고 무료 인터넷과 영상 시청실과 같은 도서관의 다른 서비스를 이용하는 사람들의 요구에 더 잘 부응하기를 바란다.
>
> ¹²여기에 더해, 도서관은 이용자들의 요구에 응답하기 위해 다른 변화들도 시행할 것이다. 여기에는 더 많은 개인 학습 공간과 그룹

회의실 추가뿐만 아니라 [12]연구 기법, 데이터베이스 사용법, 기초 디지털 활용 능력에 관한 저녁 워크숍 제공이 포함된다. 관계자들은 이 변화들이 지역사회에 더 나은 서비스를 제공하고 평생학습을 위한 더 많은 기회를 제공하기를 바란다.

expansion[ikspǽnʃən] 확대 operation[ὰpəréiʃən] 운영
accommodate[əkά:mədèit] (요구 등에) 부응하다, 협조하다
involve[inválv] 종사시키다, 참여시키다
patron[péitrən] 이용자, 고객

10 Inference Question
변경 이전의 도서관에 대해 추론할 수 있는 것은?
Ⓐ 장소가 더 작았다.
☑ 평일 오후 8시에 문을 닫았다.
Ⓒ 직원이 더 적었다.
Ⓓ 무료 인터넷 서비스를 제공하지 않았다.

11 Vocabulary Question
첫 문단의 단어 "patrons"와 의미상 가장 유사한 것은?
☑ 방문자
Ⓑ 고용인
Ⓒ 관찰자
Ⓓ 자원봉사자

12 Detail Question
도서관이 추가로 시행할 변화는?
Ⓐ 운영 시간을 추가로 연장하는 것
☑ 디지털 및 언어 기술에 관한 교육을 제공하는 것
Ⓒ 지역 연구자를 위한 지원 프로그램을 시작하는 것
Ⓓ 새로운 멀티미디어 시설을 추가하는 것

[13-15] 기사를 읽으시오.

[13]Sedona 교통부는 도시의 통근 환경 개선을 희망하며 새로운 자전거 공유 프로그램을 테스트하고 있다.

시범 프로그램의 초기 단계에서는 도심 전역에 있는 20개의 도킹 스테이션에서 200대의 자전거를 이용할 수 있다. 자전거를 빌리려면, 사용자들은 단지 이 서비스의 모바일 애플리케이션에 로그인하면 된다. 이용이 끝나면, 자전거는 어느 스테이션에든 반납할 수 있다. 각 탑승 이용료는 시간과 이동 거리에 따라 다르지만, 프로그램 책임자는 여정당 평균 비용이 3달러 미만일 것으로 추산하며, 모든 소득 수준의 사람들에게 경제적인 선택지가 될 것이라고 밝혔다.

자동차가 보다 적게 필요하게 되므로, [14]시 공무원들은 이 프로그램이 교통 혼잡을 줄일 것으로 기대한다. 성공한다면, 그들은 이 프로그램을 도시의 다른 지역으로 확장하고 모든 시내 도로에 자전거 전용 도로를 추가할 것이라고 말한다.

improve[imprú:v] 개선하다 commute[kəmjú:t] 통근하다
phase[feiz] 단계 estimate[éstəmèit] 추산하다
economical[èkənάmikəl] 경제적인, 알뜰한
income[ínkʌm] 소득 congestion[kəndʒéstʃən] 혼잡
dedicated[dédikèitid] 전용의, 전념하는

13 Main Topic Question
이 기사는 주로 무엇에 대한 것인가?
Ⓐ 어느 도시가 교통 체증을 관리한 방법
Ⓑ 자전거 공유 프로그램의 인기 증가
Ⓒ 자전거 도로 수요의 급증
☑ 어느 도시의 신규 교통 사업

14 Inference Question
새로운 프로그램에 대해 추론할 수 있는 것은?
Ⓐ 저소득층을 주 대상으로 할 것이다.
Ⓑ 개인 기부를 필요로 할 것이다.
Ⓒ 예상보다 더 많은 금액이 들어갈 수 있다.
☑ 새로운 기반시설로 이어질 수 있다.

15 Intention Question
이 문맥에서 "pilot program"이라는 용어는 무엇을 의미할 가능성이 가장 높은가?
☑ 새로운 프로젝트의 소규모 테스트
Ⓑ 전문 사이클 선수를 위한 프로그램
Ⓒ 도시 전체의 교통 계획
Ⓓ 새로운 서비스에 대한 마케팅 캠페인

7. Form

Example
양식을 읽으시오.

수업 만족도 설문조사

Rhythm Street 댄스 학원에서 수업을 수강해 주셔서 감사합니다! 여러분의 의견은 저희가 수업을 개선하고 가능한 최고의 경험을 제공하는 데 도움이 됩니다. 잠시 시간을 내어 이 설문조사를 작성해 주십시오. [1]작성을 완료하시면, 다음 수업에 10퍼센트 할인 받으실 것입니다.

수강생 이름: Kathy Chen
코스명: 힙합 기초
강사 이름: Ethan Brooks

	나쁨	보통	좋음	우수
교육의 질				X
수업 안무				X
음악 선곡			X	
시설		X		

의견:

강사님은 정말 에너지가 넘쳤고 수업을 매우 재미있게 만들어 주셨어요! 안무는 도전적이었지만 할 만했어요. 스튜디오 공간은 깨끗하고 넓어서 연습에 딱 맞았어요. 하지만, [2]연습실의 환기는 더 개선될 수 있을 것 같아요. 활동을 많이 하고 난 후 수업 중에 약간 답답하게 느껴졌어요. 이곳에서 저의 댄스 여정을 계속할 것이 기대돼요!

improve[imprú:v] 개선하다 provide[prəváid] 제공하다
experience[ikspíəriəns] 경험 completion[kəmplí:ʃən] 완료

choreography [kɔ̀riáːgrəfi] 안무
manageable [mǽnidʒəbl] 할 만한   **ventilation** [vèntəléiʃən] 환기
stuffy [stʌ́fi] 답답한   **activity** [æktívəti] 활동

1 Detail Question
Ms. Chen이 설문조사 완료 후에 받게 될 것은?
Ⓐ 스튜디오 대여료 할인
Ⓑ 무료 수업 쿠폰
Ⓒ 친구 무료 초대권
☑ 수강료 할인

2 Detail Question
Ms. Chen의 불만은 무엇인가?
Ⓐ 강사가 불친절하다.
Ⓑ 안무가 너무 어렵다.
☑ 연습실의 환기가 잘 안된다.
Ⓓ 스튜디오 공간이 너무 작고 비좁다.

HACKERS TEST
p.194

01 Ⓑ	02 Ⓑ	03 Ⓒ	04 Ⓑ	05 Ⓓ
06 Ⓒ	07 Ⓑ	08 Ⓓ	09 Ⓑ	10 Ⓒ
11 Ⓑ	12 Ⓑ	13 Ⓒ	14 Ⓒ	15 Ⓑ

[01-02] 영수증을 읽으시오.

Brentwood 백화점
20년 가까이 시카고에서 서비스를 제공해 옴!

날짜: 8월 18일   지점: 10번가

노트북 가방		20.00달러
배터리 충전기		5.00달러
텀블러		12.00달러
자전거 자물쇠		18.00달러
⁰¹모든 전자제품 10퍼센트 할인	세금	6.00달러
	총합	61.00달러

⁰²7월과 8월에는 오후 10시까지 영업합니다. 폐점 시간은 9월에 다시 오후 9시로 되돌아갑니다.

---

01 Detail Question
어떤 상품이 할인되었는가?
Ⓐ 노트북 가방
☑ 배터리 충전기
Ⓒ 텀블러
Ⓓ 자전거 자물쇠

02 Inference Question
Brentwood 백화점에 대해 추론할 수 있는 것은?
Ⓐ 여러 도시에 지점을 열었다.
☑ 여름에 운영시간을 연장한다.
Ⓒ 9월에 판촉 행사를 열 것이다.
Ⓓ 20년 넘게 운영되어 왔다.

[03-04] 메뉴를 읽으시오.

Salsa on Wheels
샌디에이고에서 가장 인기 있는 푸드트럭!

점심 특선	
치킨 부리토	8.00달러
생선 타코	7.00달러
소고기 퀘사디아	10.00달러

⁰³저희 해산물 요리에는 무엇이든 그날 시장에서 가장 신선한 재료가 포함됩니다. ⁰⁴저희 웹사이트에 후기를 남기시고 무료 탄산음료 디지털 쿠폰을 받으세요.

complimentary [kàːmpləméntəri] 무료의

---

03 Inference Question
생선 타코에 대해 암시되는 것은?
Ⓐ 점심시간에만 제공된다.
Ⓑ 평일에는 주문 가능한 양에 제한이 있다.
☑ 재료가 정기적으로 바뀐다.
Ⓓ 가장 인기있는 메뉴이다.

04 Detail Question
고객들은 어떻게 무료 음료를 받을 수 있는가?
Ⓐ 사전 주문을 함으로써
☑ 온라인 후기를 올림으로써
Ⓒ 점심 특선을 구매함으로써
Ⓓ 애플리케이션을 다운로드함으로써

[05-06] 영수증을 읽으시오.

ElectroMarket
1741번지 Talbot가
전화: (701) 555-8000

날짜: 4월 10일
계산원: P. Blanda

· ⁰⁶USB 충전 케이블······ 25.00달러
   ⁰⁶-50% 재고 정리 할인······-12.50달러
· ePhone Max(검은색)······ 499.00달러

소계:	511.50달러
판매세(8퍼센트):	40.92달러
⁰⁵총계:	552.42달러

지불 수단: 현금

보증 또는 반품을 위해서는 이 영수증을 보관하십시오.
⁰⁶모든 세일 상품은 교환 및 환불 불가입니다.

---

clearance [klíərəns] (재고 등의) 정리, 청소
final [fáinəl] 변경 불가능한, 최종적인

05 Detail Question
현금으로 얼마가 지불되었는가?
Ⓐ 40.92달러
Ⓑ 499.00달러

ⓒ 511.50달러
✓ⓓ 552.42달러

06 Inference Question
USB 충전 케이블에 대해 추론할 수 있는 것은?
Ⓐ 한 가지 색상으로만 구매 가능했다.
Ⓑ 휴대전화 전용이다.
✓ⓒ 반품이 불가하다.
Ⓓ 이전에 사용되었다.

[07-09] 송장을 읽으시오.

```
                        Fresh Farms
                      도매 농산물 공급업체
```

날짜: 5월 13일   송장 번호: 948958
배송지: ⁰⁷Belmont 식당   청구 대상: ⁰⁷Casey Robbins
1402번지 Station가,   계좌번호: 938475
시애틀, 워싱턴주 98039   555-0394

품목	양	가격
로메인 상추	10킬로그램	40.00달러
백감자	50킬로그램	35.00달러
파	20킬로그램	25.00달러
	세금	15.00달러
	배송	해당 없음
	총합	115.00달러

참고: ⁰⁸100달러 이상 주문 시 배송비가 면제됩니다. 그렇지 않으면 15달러의 배송비가 적용됩니다. 사업자 계좌가 있는 고객께서는 상품 수령 후 21일 이내에 전액 결제하셔야 합니다. 그렇지 않으면 연체료가 부과됩니다.

상품 도착 즉시 품질을 확인해 주십시오. ⁰⁹상한 품목이 있으면, 사진을 찍어 service@freshfarms.com으로 보내주십시오. 그 뒤 상한 품목의 가격이 귀하의 계정에 입금됩니다.

account[əkáunt] 계좌 **waive**[weiv] 면제하다, 포기하다
spoil[spɔil] 상하게 하다 **credit**[krédit] 입금하다

07 Inference Question
Ms. Robbins에 대해 암시된 것은?
Ⓐ Fresh Farms의 새로운 고객이다.
✓Ⓑ 식당 주인이다.
ⓒ 연체료를 지불해야 한다.
Ⓓ 할인받을 자격이 있다.

08 Detail Question
고객들이 배송비를 피하려면 무엇을 해야 하는가?
Ⓐ 특별 프로모션에 가입한다
Ⓑ 사업자 계정을 생성한다
ⓒ 선불로 결제한다
✓Ⓓ 최소 주문 금액을 주문한다

09 Detail Question
고객은 왜 Fresh Farms에 이미지를 보낼 것 같은가?
Ⓐ 제품 선호도를 나타내기 위해
✓Ⓑ 부분 환불을 요청하기 위해
ⓒ 배송 도착을 확인하기 위해
Ⓓ 품목 교환을 요구하기 위해

어휘 **replacement**[ripléismənt] 교환

[10-12] 일정표를 읽으시오.

Bradley Institute의 인적자원 및 인재개발 콘퍼런스가 9월 3일에 개최됩니다. ¹⁰이번 콘퍼런스는 지난 몇 년보다 두 배 넘게 많은 참가자를 끌어모을 것으로 예상됩니다. 예정된 연사들은 다음과 같습니다:

시간	연사	발표 제목
오전 9시 ~ 10시	Tina Ellis	재능 있는 지원자들을 알아보는 효과적인 선별 방법
¹¹오전 10시 30분 ~ 11시 30분	Bill Cooke	경험 있는 직원들이 새로운 기술을 갖추게 하는 방법
점심시간		
오후 1시 30분 ~ 2시 30분	Sara Yang	보상: 급여와 복리후생 간의 관계
오후 3시 ~ 4시	Matt Gomez	회사 정책 형성에서 직원 의견의 역할

콘퍼런스에 등록하려면, www.bradleyinstitute.com을 방문하십시오. 25달러 등록비가 있음을 유념 부탁드립니다. ¹²그러나 15명 이상 단체에는 1인당 20달러의 특별 가격을 제공합니다. 이에 해당하신다면 저희 행사 책임자 Dale Peterson에게 555-0938로 전화하십시오.

human resources 인적자원 **attract**[ətrǽkt] 끌어모으다
screening[skríːniŋ] 선별, 검사 **applicant**[ǽplikənt] 지원자
equip[ikwíp] 갖추게 하다 **compensation**[kàmpənséiʃən] 보상
salary[sǽləri] 급여

10 Inference Question
Bradley Institute에 대해 추론할 수 있는 것은?
Ⓐ 행사를 9월 3일까지 연기했다.
Ⓑ 기업 연수 프로그램을 전문으로 다룬다.
✓ⓒ 이전에 콘퍼런스를 조직한 적이 있다.
Ⓓ 회사들에게 컨설팅 서비스를 제공한다.

11 Detail Question
교육에 관한 발표는 언제 시작되는가?
Ⓐ 오전 9시
✓Ⓑ 오전 10시 30분
ⓒ 오후 1시 30분
Ⓓ 오후 3시

12 Detail Question
참가자가 Mr. Peterson에게 연락할 이유는?
Ⓐ 등록 날짜를 확정하기 위해
✓Ⓑ 할인 요금을 요청하기 위해
ⓒ 단체 세션을 준비하기 위해
Ⓓ 행사 주제를 논의하기 위해

[13-15] 양식을 읽으시오.

Metro Sportswear – 지원서 양식

지원 직책: 판매 담당자 근무 시작 가능일: 5월 25일
¹³선호 지점: 근무시간:
Fresno의 모든 매장 전일제 □ 파트타임 ■

개인정보

이름: Neal Owen	이메일: n.owen@ymail.com
주소: 15번지 Elm가, Fresno, 캘리포니아주 93611	전화번호: 555-0093

학력

¹⁴ᴬ**Coast 고등학교**	고등학교 졸업장
¹⁴ᴮ**Cheswick 대학교**	재학 중(경영학과 3학년)

경력

Vera Office Supply	¹⁴ᴰ계산원(1년 2개월)
Core Sportswear	판매 담당자(8개월)

참고사항: 파트타임 여름 일자리를 찾고 있습니다. 하지만 ¹⁵저희 학교에서 주관하는 학술 콘퍼런스에서 자원봉사를 하는 데 동의했기 때문에, 8월 첫째 주에 휴가를 내야 한다는 점을 말씀드려야 합니다. 이것이 문제가 되지 않기를 바랍니다. 제 지원서를 검토해 주셔서 감사드리며, 질문이 있으시다면 언제든지 연락 주시기 바랍니다.

---

representative[rèprizéntətiv] 담당자, 대리인
diploma[diplóumə] 졸업장, 수료증
mention[ménʃən] 말하다, 언급하다
volunteer[vɑ̀:ləntíər] 자원봉사를 하다
take ~ off ~ 동안 휴가를 내다, 쉬다
application[æ̀pləkéiʃən] 지원서

---

13 Fact Question

Metro Sportswear에 대해 명시된 것은?
Ⓐ 파트타임 직원만 고용하고 있다.
Ⓑ 최근에 Fresno로 이전했다.
✓ Fresno에 여러 지점을 운영한다.
Ⓓ 새 매장 개점을 계획하고 있다.

14 Negative Fact Question

Mr. Owen에 대한 진술 중 사실이 아닌 것은?
Ⓐ Coast 고등학교 졸업생이다.
Ⓑ 대학교에 3년째 재학 중이다.
✓ 이전에 Metro Sportswear에서 근무한 적이 있다.
Ⓓ 1년이 넘는 계산원 경험이 있다.

15 Detail Question

Mr. Owen이 8월에 휴가를 내야 하는 이유는?
Ⓐ 해외 연수 프로그램에 참여하기 위해
✓ 대학교 행사를 돕기 위해
Ⓒ 지역 자선단체에서 자원봉사하기 위해
Ⓓ 학술 강의를 수강하기 위해

TASK 3 | Read an Academic Passage

Section I Question Types

1. Main Topic Questions

Example p.207

망각의 가치

망각은 기억에 부여되는 높은 평가에 비하여 흔히 저평가되어 왔다. **하지만, 망각은 뇌가 새로운 과제에 집중하는 것을 돕고 인지적 과부하를 방지하며,** 반면 불필요한 과거 세부 사항을 계속 유지하는 것은 사고 과정을 늦추고 의사 결정에 해를 끼칠 수 있다.

신경과학 분야는 이제 망각을 수동적인 쇠퇴가 아니라 능동적인 조절 과정으로 본다. Frankland Lab의 연구는 해마 신경 발생, 즉 새로운 뉴런이 탄생하는 과정에 집중하였다. 쥐를 대상으로 한 연구에서, 연구진은 신경 발생 속도와 기억 지속성 사이에 반비례 관계를 발견했다. 연구자들이 유전적 또는 환경적 요인으로 새로운 뉴런의 생성을 증가시켰을 때, 쥐들은 오래된 기억을 측정 가능할 정도로 잃어버린다는 점을 보였다.

이는 새로운 세포들이 기억 회로를 재구성하여 오래된 정보를 제거함으로써, 뇌가 더 새롭고 유용한 지식을 우선순위에 두고 저장할 수 있도록 함을 시사한다. 바로 이 메커니즘이 유아기 기억상실을 설명하는 주요 가설인데, 초기 발달 단계에서 높은 신경 발생률이 장기적인 기억 통합을 방해할 수 있기 때문이다.

정보의 손실은 결함이 아니며, 더 유용한 지식을 위한 공간을 마련하여 지적 효율성을 높인다. **불필요한 세부 사항을 정리함으로써, 뇌는 새로운 환경에 빠르게 적응하고 현재 시점에서 진정 중요한 것이 무엇인지 우선순위를 정할 수 있게 된다.**

regard[rigá:rd] 평가 task[tæsk] 과제
prevent[privént] 방지하다 cognitive[kágnətiv] 인지적인
overload[òuvərlóud] 과부하 retain[ritéin] 유지하다
reasoning[rí:zniŋ] 사고 과정 regulatory[régjulətò:ri] 조절의
decay[dikéi] 쇠퇴 inverse relationship 반비례 관계
persistence[pərsístəns] 지속성
genetically[dʒənétikəli] 유전적으로
demonstrate[démənstrèit] 보이다
measurable[méʒərəbl] 측정 가능한
prioritize[praió:rətàiz] 우선순위에 두다
hypothesis[haipá:θəsis] 가설 infantile[ínfəntàil] 유아기의
amnesia[æmní:ʒə] 기억상실 efficiency[ifíʃənsi] 효율성

다음 중 지문의 중심 생각을 가장 잘 나타낸 것은?
Ⓐ 뇌는 약한 기억력 때문에 뜻하지 않게 망각한다.
✓ 불필요한 정보를 잊는 것이 더 나은 결정과 적응을 가능하게 한다.
Ⓒ 효과적인 의사 결정은 기억해내는 것에 달려있다.
Ⓓ 기억을 억제하는 것은 항상 중요한 지식의 손실로 이어진다.

어휘 adaptability[ədæptəbíləti] 적응력
      hinge on ~에 달려 있다 suppression[səpréʃən] 억제

HACKERS PRACTICE p.208

01 Ⓒ   02 Ⓑ   03 Ⓑ   04 Ⓑ

01 Main Topic Question

식품 사막은 사람들이 신선하고 저렴한 식품을 이용하기 어려운 지역이다. 이러한 지역은 흔히 소수 집단 공동체에서 찾을 수 있다. **불공정한 주택 정책과 주택 담보 대출 관행은 역사적으로 저소득층을 식료품점과 같은 소매업체들을 유지하는 데 필요한 투자가 부족한 지역들로 몰아넣었다.** 이러한 지역에 건설하는 대신, 개발업자들은 확보 가능한 자본을 따라 교외에 슈퍼마켓을 열었다.

도심 지역 거주자 중 많은 이들이 자동차를 소유하고 있지 않으며, **대중교통은 느리고 여러 번의 환승을 필요로 하여, 교외로의 장보기를 지나치게 시간 소모가 크게 만든다.** 결과적으로, 사람들은 번화한 도로를 따라 밀집한 패스트푸드 체인점과 편의점으로 향하게 되는데, 이것들은 간편하지만 건강하지 않은 음식을 제공한다. 이는 신선 식품이 적은 식단과 식이 관련 질병의 더 높은 발병률을 초래한다.

affordable[əfɔ́:rdəbl] 저렴한
minority[mainɔ́:rəti] 소수 집단 policy[pá:ləsi] 정책
practice[prǽktis] 관행 district[dístrikt] 지역
investment[invéstmənt] 투자 retail[rí:teil] 소매의
grocery store 식료품점

지문은 주로 무엇에 대한 것인가?
Ⓐ 식단 형성에서 패스트푸드 체인점의 역할
Ⓑ 도시의 대중교통 개선을 위한 정책
✓ 주택 정책이 신선 식품 이용 가능성에 미치는 영향
Ⓓ 공동체 투자 프로젝트와 지역 공동체 결속

어휘 cohesion[kouhí:ʒən] 결속

02 Main Topic Question

화물 숭배는 멜라네시아에서 시작된 종교적 운동으로, 전통 사회의 붕괴 속에서 기원했다. 이 지역 사회들은 식민지화를 겪었는데, 이는 그들의 전통적 권위를 박탈했고 이전과는 매우 다른 물질적 재화를 도입했다. 이후, 제2차 세계 대전 기간에 이 섬들이 전략적인 군사 기지가 되면서, 이 지역 사회들은 외국 군인들이 막대한 양의 식량, 무기 및 기타 "화물"을 가지고 도착하는 것을 목격하였다. 사람들은 그들이 본 현상을 의식의 중요성에 관한 그 지역 고유의 신앙 체계를 통해 해석했고, 외부인들의 행동을 모방함으로써 물질적 풍요를 공유할 방법을 모색했다.

가장 흔하게 인용되는 예시는 바누아투 Tanna 섬의 John Frum 운동이다. 이 운동의 추종자들은 예상되는 물품 전달을 환영하기 위해 의식을 거행하고, 깃발을 게양하며, 때로는 상징적인 활주로나 나무로 만든 라디오를 제작한다. 오늘날, 막대한 양의 화물이 곧 문자 그대로 전달될 것이라는 원래의 믿음은 약해졌지만, 관련된 의식의 수행은 지속되고 있는데, 이는 영구적인 공동체 정체성을 나타내는 효과적인 상징의 역할을 한다.

cargo[ká:rgou] 화물 religious[rilídʒəs] 종교적인
disruption[disrʌ́pʃən] 붕괴

colonization [kɑ̀ːlənizéiʃən] 식민지화   authority [əθɔ́ːrəti] 권위
strategic [strətíːdʒik] 전략적인   military base 군사 기지
military personnel 군인   quantity [kwɑ́ːntəti] 양
framework [fréimwərk] 체계   ritual [rítʃuəl] 의식
abundance [əbʌ́ndəns] 풍요   behavior [bihéivjər] 행동
airstrip [ɛ́ərstrip] 활주로   imminent [ímənənt] 곧 닥친
literal [lítərəl] 문자 그대로의   wane [wein] 약해지다
persist [pərsíst] 지속되다   enduring [indjúəriŋ] 영구적인

지문은 주로 무엇에 대한 것인가?
Ⓐ 제2차 세계 대전 동안 군대에 물품을 보급한 물류 시스템
Ⓑ 붕괴와 불평등에 대한 대응으로 탄생한 의례적 운동 ✓
Ⓒ 선교사들에 의해 주도된 멜라네시아의 종교 개종
Ⓓ 섬 사회의 전통적인 지도 체계와 사회 질서

어휘   logistical [loudʒístikəl] 물류의
       inequality [ìnikwɑ́ːləti] 불평등   conversion [kənvə́ːrʒən] 개종

03 Main Topic Question

신체 개조는 신체에 영구적인 변화를 가하는 것을 수반한다. **세계 여러 문화에서, 사람들은 표현의 한 형태로 자신의 신체에 표시를 하고, 구멍을 뚫고, 모양을 만든다.** 예를 들어, 폴리네시아에서는 조밀한 문신 패턴이 가족 관계와 사회적 지위를 드러내며, 이와 유사하게 마오리족 사이에서는 혈통을 나타내는 얼굴 디자인을 통해 **사회적 정체성이 전달된다.** 개조는 또한 **특별한 인생 단계에 도달했음을** 의미할 수 있다. 서아프리카 일부 지역에서는 흉터 내기가 성인기 진입을 나타낸다. 이누이트 공동체 사이에서는 여성의 얼굴 문신이 역사적으로 성숙함과 결혼 준비를 알렸다. 마찬가지로, 남아시아에서는 귀와 코 피어싱이 혼인 여부와 연결되어 가족 내에서 그 사람이 맡은 역할을 공개적으로 인정한다.

modification [mɑ̀ːdəfikéiʃən] 개조
permanent [pə́ːrmənənt] 영구적인
represent [rèprizént] 나타내다
ancestry [ǽnsèstri] 혈통, 가계
scarification [skæ̀rəfikéiʃən] 흉터 내기
maturity [mətjúərəti] 성숙함   marital [mǽrətl] 혼인의

다음 중 지문의 중심 생각을 가장 잘 나타낸 것은?
Ⓐ 신체 개조는 문화 전반에 걸쳐 비판받아 온 부정적이고 위험한 관행이다.
Ⓑ 신체 개조는 정체성과 사회적 의미를 전달하는 인류 보편적 관행이다. ✓
Ⓒ 신체 개조는 역사적 의의가 거의 없는 현대 도시 유행이다.
Ⓓ 신체 개조는 개인의 외모 향상에 초점을 맞춘 세련된 미용 기법이다.

어휘   criticize [krítəsàiz] 비판하다   significance [signífikəns] 의의

04 Main Topic Question

Zeigarnik 효과는 사람들이 완료된 과업보다 미완료되거나 중단된 과업을 더 쉽게 기억한다는 것을 시사한다. 심리학자 Bluma Zeigarnik은 정산된 주문보다 미지불 주문을 더 잘 기억하는 종업원들에 대해 듣고 나서 이것을 연구하기로 결정했다. Zeigarnik이 그녀의 실험을 수행했을 때, 그녀는 사람들이 실제로 완료된 과업보다 중단된 과업을 기억할 가능성이 두 배 높다는 것을 발견했다. **이 발견은 미완료 활동이 인지적 긴장을 만들어 기억에서 더욱 두드러지게 만든다는 견해를 뒷받침했다.** 학생들은 이 효과를 활용할 수 있다. 공부 시간 중 휴식을 취함으로써, 그들은 인지적 긴장을 유지하게 되고, 이는 공부하고 있는 자료에 대한 그들의 기억력을 향상하는 데 도움이 된다.

interrupted [ìntərʌ́ptid] 중단된   settle [sétl] 정산하다
conduct [kəndʌ́kt] 수행하다
cognitive [kɑ́gnətiv] 인지적인
salient [séiliənt] 두드러진   improve [imprúːv] 향상하다

다음 중 지문의 중심 생각을 가장 잘 나타낸 것은?
Ⓐ 중단은 일반적으로 기억과 동기 부여를 방해한다.
Ⓑ 미완료 과업은 인지적이고 동기적인 효과를 가질 수 있다. ✓
Ⓒ 특정 과업의 즐거움은 기억에 영향을 미치는 주 요인이다.
Ⓓ 과업을 완수하는 것이 미완료로 두는 것보다 항상 더 유익하다.

어휘   hinder [híndər] 방해하다   factor [fǽktər] 요인
       rewarding [riwɔ́ːrdiŋ] 유익한, 수익이 나는

HACKERS TEST   p.210

01 Ⓒ	02 Ⓒ	03 Ⓒ	04 Ⓓ	05 Ⓒ
06 Ⓑ	07 Ⓒ	08 Ⓒ	09 Ⓐ	10 Ⓓ
11 Ⓓ	12 Ⓐ	13 Ⓑ	14 Ⓑ	15 Ⓒ
16 Ⓑ	17 Ⓓ	18 Ⓒ	19 Ⓐ	20 Ⓒ

[01-05]

수평적 유전자 이동

[01]수평적 유전자 이동은 유전 물질이 부모-자손 관계가 아닌 서로 다른 생물체 사이에서 이동하는 과정이다. 이 빠른 교환은 세균 내에서 세 가지 주요 방법을 통해 이루어지는데, 직접적인 물리적 접촉(접합), [03]바이러스에 의한 전달(형질도입), 그리고 환경으로부터 유전 물질 조각을 흡수하는 것(형질전환)이 그것이다. [03]이 과정은 항생제 내성을 부여하는 것과 같은 유전적 특성들이 서로 다른 종들 사이에서 빠르고 광범위하게 퍼질 수 있게 한다.

이 현상은 세균에만 국한되지 않는다. 예를 들어, 일부 식물은 인근 종으로부터 저항 유전자를 획득하여 환경적 위험에서 생존하는 데 도움을 받았다. [04]동물 중에서는 특정 진딧물(작은 곤충의 한 종류) 종들이 곰팡이로부터 관련 유전자를 얻은 후 빨간 색소를 생산하는 능력을 얻었다. 이러한 예들은 수평적 유전자 이동이 매우 다른 유형의 생물체들 사이에서도 일어날 수 있음을 보여준다.

[01/05]수평적 유전자 이동의 중요성은 상당하다. 그것은 진화와 적응을 가속해 생물체들이 여러 세대를 기다리지 않고도 유용한 특성을 얻을 수 있게 한다. 이 때문에, 과학자들은 수평적 유전자 이동을 지구상의 생명을 끊임없이 새롭게 바꾸어 가는 힘으로 여긴다.

horizontal [hɔ̀ːrəzɑ́ːntl] 수평적인
genetic [dʒənétik] 유전의   organism [ɔ́ːrgənìzm] 생물체
offspring [ɔ́ːfspriŋ] 자손   physical [fízikəl] 물리적인
absorption [æbsɔ́ːrpʃən] 흡수   fragment [frǽgmənt] 조각
trait [treit] 형질   confer [kənfə́ːr] 부여하다
phenomenon [finɑ́ːmənɑ̀n] 현상
acquire [əkwáiər] 획득하다   peril [pérəl] 위험
aphid [éifid] 진딧물   pigment [pígmənt] 색소

01 Main Topic Question
지문은 주로 무엇에 대한 것인가?
Ⓐ 진화 중 유전자 손실에 관한 생물학적 이론
Ⓑ 생물체들 사이의 흔하지 않은 유전적 돌연변이
☑ 유전 물질 전달의 중요한 방법
Ⓓ 유전적 성질의 예상치 못한 패턴

어휘 mutation[mju:téiʃən] 돌연변이 method[méθəd] 방법
inheritance[inhérətəns] 유전적 성질, 유산

02 Vocabulary Question
두 번째 단락의 단어 "peril"과 의미상 가장 유사한 것은?
Ⓐ 단점
Ⓑ 내구성
☑ 위협
Ⓓ 장애물

어휘 drawback[drɔ́:bæk] 단점 durability[djùərəbíləti] 내구성
obstacle[ábstəkl] 장애물

03 Rhetorical Purpose Question
글쓴이는 왜 바이러스를 언급하는가?
Ⓐ 일부 생물체가 새로운 특성을 획득할 수 없는 이유를 설명하기 위해
Ⓑ 바이러스가 유전적 진화에서 작은 역할만 한다는 것을 암시하기 위해
☑ 유전 물질이 공유되는 메커니즘을 구체화하기 위해
Ⓓ 수평적 유전자 이동의 한계를 강조하기 위해

어휘 limitation[lìmitéiʃən] 한계

04 Detail Question
일부 진딧물들은 어떻게 빨간 색소 생산 능력을 얻었는가?
Ⓐ 자신들 유전자의 돌연변이를 통해
Ⓑ 연구자들에 의한 선택적 번식을 통해
Ⓒ 빨간색 먹이로부터 색소를 흡수함으로써
☑ 다른 유형의 생물체로부터 유전자를 획득함으로써

05 Fact Question
수평적 유전자 이동이 진화 속도에 미치는 영향에 대해 지문이 명시하는 것은?
Ⓐ 후손에게로의 전달 속도를 높인다.
Ⓑ 대부분의 생물체에서 적응을 지연시킨다.
☑ 유익한 특성이 빠르게 퍼질 수 있게 한다.
Ⓓ 매우 작은 종들에서만 변화를 가속한다.

어휘 transmission[trænsmíʃən] 전달, 전송

[06-10]

심장 주기

⁰⁶심장 주기는 심장이 온몸으로 혈액을 펌프질하는 일련의 반복적인 과정을 의미한다. 이 과정은 심방 수축으로 시작되며, 얇은 벽을 가진 좌우 심방이 더 두꺼운 심실로 혈액을 밀어 넣는다. ⁰⁸그 다음 심실 수축이 이어지고, 좌우 심실이 혈액을 신체의 다른 부위로 이어지는 동맥으로 내보낸다. 이후, 충만기에 네 개의 모든 심장 방이 이완한다.

Ⓐ 이러한 단계들은 전기적 자극에 의해 조정되어, 심장이 정상적으로 뛰도록 한다. Ⓑ 이러한 전기적 활성화는 심장 전체에 걸쳐 균일하게 일어나지 않기 때문에, 각 심장 방은 심장 주기의 각 단계에서 몇 분의 1초 차이를 두고 수축을 시작한다. Ⓒ 이러한 지연은 과정의 정상적인 부분이지만, 다른 장애는 건강 문제를 초래할 수 있다. Ⓓ 예를 들어, 타이밍의 불규칙은 피로감이나 현기증 같은 증상을 유발할 수 있다.

⁰⁹심장 주기는 적응성이 매우 뛰어나다. 신체 활동이나 스트레스에 반응하여, 주기가 더 빨라지며, 이완기의 상대적 길이를 줄이면서도 효과적인 혈류를 유지한다. ⁰⁹반대로, 수면 중에는 주기가 느려진다. 또한 심장은 사람이 운동을 하거나 강한 감정을 경험할 때처럼, 신체의 변화하는 산소 요구에 맞추어 수축의 강도를 조절한다.

cardiac[ká:rdiæk] 심장의 contraction[kəntrǽkʃən] 수축
atrium[éitriəm] 심방(pl. atria) ventricle[véntrikl] 심실
artery[á:rtəri] 동맥 phase[feiz] 단계
coordinate[kouɔ́:rdəneit] 조정하다
impulse[ímpʌls] 자극 disruption[disrʌ́pʃən] 장애
adaptive[ədǽptiv] 적응성이 뛰어난

06 Main Topic Question
지문은 주로 무엇에 대한 것인가?
Ⓐ 비정상 심장박동의 경고 신호
☑ 각 심장박동의 복잡한 과정
Ⓒ 심장 주기를 관찰하는 방법
Ⓓ 심장 근육의 물리적 구조

어휘 abnormal[æbnɔ́:rməl] 비정상적인 physical[fízikəl] 물리적인
structure[strʌ́ktʃər] 구조

07 Vocabulary Question
지문의 단어 "sequence"와 의미상 가장 유사한 것은?
Ⓐ 회전
Ⓑ 분할
☑ 과정
Ⓓ 부분

어휘 rotation[routéiʃən] 회전 division[divíʒən] 분할
progression[prəgréʃən] 과정 segment[ségmənt] 부분

08 Detail Question
심실 수축 단계에서 무엇이 일어나는가?
Ⓐ 심장 내 혈류가 역전된다.
Ⓑ 신체의 혈압이 최저치로 떨어진다.
☑ 혈액이 신체의 다른 부위로 전달된다.
Ⓓ 심장의 왼쪽만 활발하게 수축한다.

09 Rhetorical Purpose Question
글쓴이는 왜 수면 중에 심장 주기가 느려진다는 것을 언급하는가?
☑ 심장이 변화하는 필요에 어떻게 적응하는지 보여 주기 위해
Ⓑ 과도한 수면이 심장에 부담을 줄 수 있음을 나타내기 위해
Ⓒ 휴식이 운동보다 더 중요하다고 주장하기 위해
Ⓓ 심장이 가장 취약할 때를 제시하기 위해

어휘 strain[strein] 부담을 주다 vulnerable[vʌ́lnərəbl] 취약한

10 Insertion Question

다음 문장이 삽입될 수 있는 네 곳이 지문에 표시되어 있다.

예를 들어, 타이밍의 불규칙은 피로감이나 현기증 같은 증상을 유발할 수 있다.

그 문장은 어디에 가장 적절한가? 그 문장이 삽입될 수 있는 곳을 고르시오.

[11-15]

공유지의 비극

[11]공유지의 비극은 자신의 이익에 따라 합리적으로 행동하는 개인들이 어떻게 궁극적으로 공유 자원을 고갈시키거나 파괴할 수 있는지 설명하는 경제적이고 사회적인 개념이다. [13]흔히 인용되는 예시는 공용 목초지의 사용이다. 각 목축업자는 더 많은 동물을 추가함으로써 이익을 얻지만, 모든 목축업자가 이렇게 한다면 목초지에는 동물이 과도하게 방목되어 결국 모두에게 쓸모없게 된다.

또 다른 예는 바다에서의 남획이다. 국제 수역에서는 엄격한 어획량 제한을 시행할 수 있는 단일 기관이 없으므로, 어선들은 다른 사람들이 같은 일을 하기 전에 가능한 한 많은 물고기를 잡을 동기가 부여된다. 각 행위자는 단기적으로 이익을 얻지만, 누적된 효과는 어류 개체군의 감소로 이어져 생태계 및 그와 관련된 모든 사람의 생계를 위협한다. 유사한 상황이 공유 강 유역에서의 물 사용과 규제가 없는 산림에서의 벌목에서도 발생한다.

자원 고갈을 방지하기 위해, 지역사회와 정부는 공유 자원의 사용을 제한하는 전략을 시행할 수 있으며, 이는 [15B]자원 할당량과 [15A]모니터링 시스템을 포함한다. 지속 가능한 수확으로 얻은 이익의 공유와 [15D]자원 보전 관행을 유지하는 지역사회에 혜택을 제공하는 보상 시스템 등과 같은 경제적 장려책도 있을 수 있다. 어떤 형태의 협력이나 감독 없이는 장기적 지속 가능성을 위해 중요한 자원이 소진되거나 파괴될 수 있다.

---

rationally [rǽʃənəli] 합리적으로
self-interest [sèlfíntərəst] 자신의 이익
deplete [diplí:t] 고갈시키다   pasture [pǽstʃər] 목초지
herder [hə́:rdər] 목축업자
overgraze [òuvərgréiz] 과도하게 방목하다
authority [əθɔ́:rəti] 기관   enforce [infɔ́:rs] 시행하다
unregulated [ʌnrégjulèitid] 규제가 없는
depletion [diplí:ʃən] 고갈
compensation [kàmpənséiʃən] 보상
oversight [óuvərsàit] 감독

11 Main Topic Question

다음 중 지문의 중심 생각을 가장 잘 나타낸 것은?
Ⓐ 공동 자원은 기술 발전을 통해 보존될 수 있다.
Ⓑ 공유 재산의 과도한 사용은 주로 비효율적인 분배 시스템에 의해 발생한다.
Ⓒ 경제 성장은 주로 공유 자원에 대한 경쟁에 의해 원동력이 부여된다.
✓ 공동 자산의 규제되지 않은 사용은 그것들의 궁극적 손실로 이어질 수 있다.

어휘 collective [kəléktiv] 공동의   preserve [prizə́:rv] 보존하다

12 Vocabulary Question

첫 번째 단락의 단어 "deplete"와 의미상 가장 유사한 것은?
✓ 고갈시키다
Ⓑ 감독하다
Ⓒ 보호하다
Ⓓ 전달하다

어휘 exhaust [igzɔ́:st] 고갈시키다   supervise [sú:pərvàiz] 감독하다
transfer [trǽnsfə:r] 전달하다

13 Rhetorical Purpose Question

글쓴이는 왜 공유 목초지를 언급하는가?
Ⓐ 공동 토지 소유권이 흔히 비효율적이라고 주장하기 위해
Ⓑ 공유 토지에서 농민 간의 경제적 불평등을 강조하기 위해
Ⓒ 남획의 예시가 여타 예시들과 어떻게 다른지 보여주기 위해
✓ 지문 앞부분에서 제시된 개념의 간단한 예시를 제공하기 위해

14 Rhetorical Purpose Question

2단락에서 공유 자원 손실의 원인이 되는 구체적인 상황을 규명하는 문장을 클릭하시오.
Ⓐ 또 다른 예는 바다에서의 남획이다.
✓ 국제 수역에서는 엄격한 어획량 제한을 시행할 수 있는 단일 기관이 없으므로, 어선들은 다른 사람들이 같은 일을 하기 전에 가능한 한 많은 물고기를 잡을 동기가 부여된다.
Ⓒ 각 행위자는 단기적으로 이익을 얻지만, 누적된 효과는 어류 개체군의 감소로 이어져 생태계 및 그와 관련된 모든 사람의 생계를 위협한다.
Ⓓ 유사한 상황이 공유 강 유역에서의 물 사용과 규제가 없는 산림에서의 벌목에서도 발생한다.

15 Detail Question

다음 중 지속 가능한 자원 관리를 위한 가능한 조치로 언급되지 않은 것은?
Ⓐ 모니터링 시스템
Ⓑ 자원 할당량
✓ 천연자원의 국가 소유
Ⓓ 보전에 대한 보상

[16-20]

낯선 상황 실험

[16]1970년대에 심리학자 Mary Ainsworth에 의해 실시된 낯선 상황 실험은 아기가 보호자에게 보이는 애착 행동을 규명했다. 이 실험에서, 엄마는 장난감이 있는 방으로 아기를 데려왔다. 잠시 후, 엄마는 아이를 혼자 두거나 낯선 사람과 함께 둔 채 방을 떠났고, 그 이후에 다시 돌아왔다. 연구자들은 분리와 재회 동안 아기의 반응을 면밀히 관찰했다.

이와 같은 관찰을 바탕으로, 다양한 애착 유형이 발견되었다. [18/20]어떤 아기들은 엄마가 떠날 때 눈에 띄게 불안해했지만 엄마가 돌아오자 곧 진정되었고, 이들은 안정형 애착으로 분류되었다. 다른 아기들은 불안과 회피를 보이거나 엄마가 돌아온 뒤에도 달래기 어려웠다. 소수의 아기들은 엄마가 돌아왔을 때 위로를 원하면서도 동시에 거부하는 등 혼재된 반응을 보였다.

이 실험은 각기 다른 아동-보호자 유대에 대해 구체적인 명칭을 제시했다는 점에서 획기적이었다. [19]후속 연구는 초기 애착 양식이 이후 발달에 영향을 미친다는 것을 확인했다. [20]이 실험에서 얻은 통찰은 사회 정책, 조기 교육 접근법, 그리고 부모-자녀 관계에 대한 이해를 형성하는 데 도움을 주었고, 건강한 초기 유대가 정서적 안녕을 위해 중요하다는 것을 강조했다.

conduct[kəndʌ́kt] 실시하다
psychologist[saikά:lədʒist] 심리학자
determine[ditə́:rmin] 규명하다
attachment[ətǽtʃmənt] 애착   infant[ínfənt] 아기
observe[əbzə́:rv] 관찰하다   separation[sèpəréiʃən] 분리
reunion[rijú:njən] 재회   observation[ὰbzərvéiʃən] 관찰
identify[aidéntəfài] 발견하다, 확인하다
classify[klǽsəfài] 분류하다   securely[sikjúərli] 안정적으로
console[kənsóul] 달래다
groundbreaking[gráundbrèikiŋ] 획기적인
underline[ʌ́ndərlàin] 강조하다   bond[band] 유대

16   Main Topic Question

지문은 주로 무엇에 대한 것인가?
Ⓐ 언어 발달에 관한 심리학 연구의 결과
✅ 각기 다른 유아 애착 유형을 분류한 실험
Ⓒ 분리 후 어린아이를 달래는 방법에 관한 연구
Ⓓ 양육 방식이 아동-보호자 관계에 미치는 영향

어휘   nurture[nə́:rtʃər] 양육하다

17   Vocabulary Question

지문의 단어 "console"과 의미상 가장 유사한 것은?
Ⓐ 주의를 돌리다
Ⓑ 칭찬하다
Ⓒ 지지하다
✅ 달래다

어휘   distract[distrǽkt] 주의를 돌리다, 산만하게 하다
        praise[preiz] 칭찬하다   soothe[su:ð] 달래다

18   Detail Question

다음 중 아기가 실험에서 보인 반응으로 언급되지 않은 것은?
Ⓐ 엄마가 돌아왔을 때 빠르게 진정되는 것
✅ 보호자의 부재를 알아채지 못한 채 혼자 노는 것
Ⓒ 보호자가 돌아온 뒤 불안한 행동을 보이는 것
Ⓓ 위로를 구하면서 동시에 거부하는 것

19   Inference Question

초기 애착에 대해 암시된 것은?
✅ 이후 발달에 큰 영향을 미친다.
Ⓑ 초기 교육을 통해 강화된다.
Ⓒ 성인기의 인간관계와 관련이 없다.
Ⓓ 아이가 어른이 될 때까지 변하지 않는다.

어휘   mature[mətjúər] 어른이 되다

20   Rhetorical Purpose Question

2단락과 3단락의 관계는?
Ⓐ 3단락은 2단락에서 규명된 애착 유형의 예시를 제공한다.
Ⓑ 3단락은 2단락에서 설명한 실험의 한계를 논의한다.
✅ 3단락은 2단락에서 언급된 발견의 광범위한 영향을 소개한다.
Ⓓ 3단락은 2단락에서 논의된 애착 문제에 대한 해결책을 제시한다.

2. Detail Questions

Example   p.219

인간의 이주

인간의 이주는 수천 년 동안 전 세계의 사회를 형성해 왔다. 역사를 통틀어, 전쟁, 기근, 경제적 상황, 정치적 변화와 같은 다양한 힘이 사람들의 이주를 촉발하여 모든 대륙의 문화적 지형을 형성했다. 인간 이주의 역사는 인간의 적응력과 기회 및 안정을 향한 끊임없는 탐색을 입증하는 증거이다.

초기 이주는 유목 집단이 식량과 유리한 기후를 찾아 이동하면서 발생했으며, 인간 개체군을 먼 지역까지 확산시켰다. 실크로드는 동양과 서양 사이의 이동을 용이하게 했으며, 상품뿐만 아니라 언어, 종교, 사상까지도 광대한 거리를 이동할 수 있게 했다. 19세기와 20세기에는 산업화와 도시 성장이 수백만 명의 사람들이 급속히 팽창하는 도시에서 새로운 삶을 찾도록 자극했다. 이주는 세계화와 환경 변화와 같은 요인들에 의해 주도되어 오늘날에도 계속되고 있다.

이주가 문화 교류와 다양성을 증진할 수 있지만, 이주민과 수용 공동체 모두에게 적응과 통합과 같은 어려움 또한 제시한다. 현대 사회는 인구 이동을 관리하고, 권리를 보호하며, 사회적 결속을 증진하기 위해 효과적인 정책에 의존한다. 이동의 원인과 영향을 이해하는 것은 이주 및 정체성과 관련된 현대적 문제들을 다루는 데 필수적이다.

migration[maigréiʃən] 이주   famine[fǽmin] 기근
condition[kəndíʃən] 상황   prompt[prampt] 촉발하다
relocate[ri:loukéit] 이주하다
landscape[lǽndskèip] 지형, 경관
testament[téstəmənt] 증거
adaptability[ədæptəbíləti] 적응력   security[sikjúərəti] 안정
nomadic[noumǽdik] 유목의   favorable[féivərəbl] 유리한
climate[kláimit] 기후   facilitate[fəsílətèit] 용이하게 하다
industrialization[indʌ́striəlizéiʃən] 산업화
expand[ikspǽnd] 팽창하다
environmental[invàiərənméntl] 환경의
adaptation[ædəptéiʃən] 적응   integration[ìntəgréiʃən] 통합
host community 수용 공동체   cohesion[kouhí:ʒən] 결속
contemporary[kəntémpərèri] 현대적인
displacement[displéismənt] 이주

19세기와 20세기 동안 산업화는 어떤 변화를 가져왔는가?
Ⓐ 도시 생활의 질 저하
✅ 인구의 도시 지역으로의 이동
Ⓒ 고용 기회의 증가
Ⓓ 언어와 종교의 교류

HACKERS PRACTICE   p.220

01 Ⓓ   02 Ⓒ   03 Ⓑ   04 Ⓒ

01   Detail Question

의인화는 인간 이외의 존재에게 인간의 특성을 부여하는 것이다. 이는 우리의 진화적 역사에 뿌리를 두고 있으며 우리가 세상을 이해하는 데 도움을 주지만, 다른 종에 이를 적용할 때는 신중해야 한다. 인간 이외의 동물이 하는 행동에 대해 결론을 내리는 것은 자연스럽

게 느껴지는데, 이는 우리 또한 동물이기 때문이다. 그들처럼, 우리는 먹이와 따뜻함을 추구하고 새끼를 돌본다. 그러나, 인간 이외의 동물들은 우리와 다른 조건에서 진화해 왔으며, **그들이 우리와 똑같은 감정이나 동기를 가지고 있다고 가정하는 것은 오해나 폐해까지도 초래할 수 있다.**

예를 들어, 동물원의 방문객들은 울타리 안에서 혼자 사는 호랑이가 외로우리라고 걱정할 수도 있는데, 이는 그들 자신이 그러한 상황에서 느낄 감정이기 때문이다. 실제로는, 호랑이는 영역 동물이며, 울타리 안에 다른 호랑이를 들여오는 것은 그 동물에게 스트레스를 유발할 것이다.

동물을 연구하는 학자들은 의인화를 경계해야 하는데, 이는 그들의 연구에 편향을 가져올 수 있기 때문이다. 예를 들어, 침팬지들은 고통스러울 때 흔히 미소처럼 보이는 것을 드러낸다. 이 표현이 인간의 시각을 통해 잘못 해석된다면, 행복으로 오해될 수 있다.

> **anthropomorphism**[æ̀nθrəpəmɔ́:rfìzm] 의인화
> **attribution**[æ̀trəbjúː∫ən] 부여 **entity**[éntəti] 존재
> **cautious**[kɔ́:∫əs] 신중한 **conclusion**[kənklúːʒən] 결론
> **assume**[əsúːm] 가정하다 **identical**[aidéntikəl] 똑같은
> **enclosure**[inklóuʒər] 울타리 **territorial**[tèrətɔ́:riəl] 영역의
> **bias**[báiəs] 편향을 가져오다
> **misinterpret**[mìsintə́:rprit] 잘못 해석하다

인간 이외의 동물에 대한 흔한 오해는 무엇인가?
Ⓐ 새끼를 돌본다.
Ⓑ 혼자 사는 것을 선호한다.
Ⓒ 정서적 욕구를 신체적 욕구보다 우선시한다.
Ⓓ 인간과 같은 감정을 경험한다.

어휘 **prefer**[prifə́:r] 선호하다 **solitary**[sɑ́lətèri] 혼자의
prioritize[praiɔ́:rətàiz] 우선시하다

02 Detail Question

자기공명영상(MRI)은 신체 내부의 영상을 만들기 위해 사용되는 비외과적 의료 방법이다. MRI 중에 환자는 강한 자기장 내에 놓이며, 이는 신체의 많은 수소 원자가 특정 방향으로 일시적으로 정렬되도록 한다. 수소 원자는 스캔을 위한 이상적인 표적인데, 이는 인체가 주로 물과 지방으로 구성되어 있으며 이것들에 수소가 풍부하기 때문이다.

MRI 기계는 짧은 전파 펄스를 방출한다. 이 파동들은 수소 원자 중심부의 양성자들을 교란하여, 정렬된 상태에서 벗어나게 한다. **전파가 멈추면 양성자들은 원래 위치로 돌아간다.** 이 과정에서 그것들은 희미한 신호를 방출한다. 스캐너는 이 신호들을 포착하고, 컴퓨터는 이를 자세한 횡단면 영상으로 변환한다.

> **resonance**[rézənəns] 공명
> **invasive**[invéisiv] 외과적인, 침습적인
> **hydrogen**[háidrədʒən] 수소 **atom**[ǽtəm] 원자
> **consist**[kənsíst] 구성되다 **emit**[imít] 방출하다
> **disrupt**[disrʌ́pt] 교란하다 **proton**[próutɑn] 양성자
> **cross-sectoral**[krɔ̀:sséktərəl] 횡단면의

MRI 스캔에서 전파가 멈추면 무엇이 일어나는가?
Ⓐ 양성자들이 자기장에서 사라진다.
Ⓑ 자기장이 전류를 생성하기 시작한다.
Ⓒ 양성자들이 이전의 정렬된 상태로 되돌아간다.
Ⓓ 스캐너가 횡단면 영상을 생성한다.

어휘 **current**[kə́:rənt] 전류, 흐름

03 Detail Question

선태양계 입자는 46억 년보다 더 이전, 태양이 형성되기 전에, 죽어가는 별들에 의해 방출된 작은 고체 입자들이다. 이것들은 지구상의 그 어떤 것보다도 오래되었다.

과학자들은 1960년대에 고대 운석의 구조를 연구하면서 처음으로 선태양계 입자가 존재하리라고 짐작했다. 그들은 태양계 모델과 부합하지 않는 많은 양의 원소를 발견했다. 그들의 짐작은 그 후 실험실 기술이 충분히 발전한 1980년대에 입증되었다. 연구자들은 2010년대에 인근 소행성들에서 높은 농도의 표본들을 얻으면서 추가적 진전을 얻었다. 소행성들은 우주에 떠다니기 때문에 입자 보존에 영향을 미치는 화학적 과정에 덜 노출된다.

과학자들은 이제 수천 개의 입자를 분류하여 선태양계 입자 데이터베이스로 정리했다. 이것들 대부분은 다이아몬드, 흑연 등과 같은 탄소 기반 물질들이다. 이것들은 초기 별들의 직접적인 증거를 제공할 뿐만 아니라 우리 태양계의 진화에 대한 단서도 드러낸다.

> **presolar**[pri:sóulər] 선태양계의 **grain**[grein] 입자
> **particle**[pɑ́:rtikəl] 입자 **eject**[idʒékt] 방출하다
> **suspect**[səspékt] 짐작하다
> **composition**[kɑ̀:mpəzí∫ən] 구조 **quantity**[kwɑ́:ntəti] 양
> **concentration**[kɑ̀:nsəntréi∫ən] 농도
> **asteroid**[ǽstərɔ̀id] 소행성 **preservation**[prèzərvéi∫ən] 보존
> **graphite**[grǽfait] 흑연

과학자들은 선태양계 입자에 대해 무엇을 알게 되었는가?
Ⓐ 실험실에서 인공적으로 재현할 수 있다.
Ⓑ 주로 탄소 화합물로 구성되어 있다.
Ⓒ 실용적 응용이 가능한 특성이 있다.
Ⓓ 다른 태양 입자들보다 더 흔하다.

어휘 **compound**[kɑmpáund] 화합물 **property**[prɑ́pərti] 특성
application[æ̀pləkéi∫ən] 응용

04 Detail Question

제3문화 아이들(TCK)은 인격의 형성기 중 상당 부분을 부모의 문화와는 다른 문화에서 보내는 아이들이다. 그 이유는 흔히 부모의 직업과 관련된 국제 이주 때문이다. TCK들은 부모 문화(제1문화)의 가치와 관습을 거주국(제2문화)의 것들과 균형을 맞추며 성장하여 독특한 제3문화를 만든다.

TCK로 성장하는 것은 여러 장점을 제공한다. 이런 아이들은 일반적으로 강력한 문화 간 의사소통 기술, 세계 인식, 낯선 환경에서의 적응성을 발달시킨다. 그들은 열린 마음을 갖는 경향이 있어, 다양한 공동체에 걸쳐 우정을 쌓기가 더 쉽다.

하지만 TCK로서의 경험에는 어려움도 있다. 그것은 A**사회관계망을 교란하며**, 이 아이들이 의지할 곳이 없고 B**자신의 문화적 정체성에 대해 확신이 없다고 느끼게 만들 수 있다.** 일부 TCK들은 D**영구적으로 불안정하다고 느끼고 자신이 어디 출신인지 정의하기 어려워할 수 있다.**

> **formative**[fɔ́:rmətiv] (인격 등이) 형성되는
> **relocation**[rì:loukéi∫ən] 이주 **develop**[divéləp] 발달시키다
> **flexibility**[flèksəbíləti] 적응성, 유연성
> **rootless**[rúːtlis] 의지할 곳이 없는
> **permanently**[pə́:rmənəntli] 영구적으로

다음 중 지문에서 TCK들이 직면하는 어려움으로 언급되지 않은 것은?
Ⓐ 사회적 관계를 잃는 것
Ⓑ 문화적 소속감을 확정하는 데 어려움을 겪는 것

✓ 의사소통에 어려움을 겪는 것
ⓓ 오래 가는 불안정함을 겪는 것

HACKERS TEST
p.222

01 ⓑ	02 ⓒ	03 ⓑ	04 ⓒ	05 ⓒ
06 ⓑ	07 ⓓ	08 ⓑ	09 ⓐ	10 ⓐ
11 ⓑ	12 ⓒ	13 ⓑ	14 ⓑ	15 ⓓ
16 ⓒ	17 ⓒ	18 ⓒ	19 ⓑ	20 ⓒ

[01-05]

유당불내증

유당불내증은 성인이 우유의 주된 당인 유당을 소화하기 어려워하는 상태이다. 이 문제가 생기는 이유는 대부분의 포유류에서 유년기를 지난 뒤에는 소화기관에서 유당을 분해하는 효소인 락타아제의 생산이 크게 줄어들기 때문이다. **02락타아제가 충분하지 않으면, 유당은 소화되지 않은 채 결장으로 넘어가**, 그곳에서 박테리아와 상호작용하여 복부 팽만감과 설사 같은 증상을 유발한다. **05전 세계적으로 나타나지만, 유당불내증은** 동아시아인, 아프리카인, 미주 및 호주의 원주민 집단에서 특히 두드러진다.

유당불내증이 일반적인 것이라면, 일부 사람들은 어떻게 성인이 되어서도 유당을 소화하는 능력을 갖게 되었을까? 이는 진화적 역사와 문화적 식습관의 결과이다. 수많은 세대에 걸쳐, **03특히 북유럽계 사람들을 중심으로 특정 집단에서는 유제품을 오래도록 섭취해 온 데에 대한 반응으로 락타아제 생산을 지속할 수 있게 하는 유전적 적응을 발달시켰다.** 흥미롭게도, **04몽골 목축업자들은 락타아제 지속성과 관련된 유전적 돌연변이가 없음에도 불구하고 유당불내증의 증상을 거의 보이지 않는다.** 이러한 현상은 프로바이오틱 미생물을 공급함으로써 유당 소화를 용이하게 하는 발효 유제품이 풍부한 식단을 섭취한 것에서 기인한다.

---

lactose [lǽktous] 유당　digest [daiʒést] 소화하다
mammal [mǽməl] 포유류　juvenile [dʒúːvənl] 유년기의
enzyme [énzaim] 효소　digestive [daidʒéstiv] 소화의
colon [kóulən] 결장　symptom [símptəm] 증상
bloating [bloutiŋ] 복부 팽만감　diarrhea [dàiərí:ə] 설사
indigenous [indídʒənəs] 원주민의
adaptation [ædəptéiʃən] 적응
herder [hə́ːrdər] 목축업자
mutation [mju:téiʃən] 돌연변이
persistence [pərsístəns] 지속성
attribute [ətríbju:t] 기인하다
fermented [fə́ːrmentid] 발효된　dairy [déəri] 유제품의
microbe [máikroub] 미생물

01 Vocabulary Question

지문의 단어 "adaptation"과 의미상 가장 유사한 것은?
ⓐ 질병
✓ 변화
ⓒ 구성
ⓓ 반응

어휘　disease [dizíːz] 질병　composition [kà:mpəzíʃən] 구성

02 Detail Question

락타아제가 충분하지 않으면 무엇이 일어나는가?
ⓐ 유당이 위에서 더 쉽게 흡수된다.
ⓑ 유당이 장내 박테리아에 의해 단백질로 변환된다.
✓ 유당이 소화되지 않은 채 결장으로 넘어간다.
ⓓ 유당이 위산과 서로 작용해 복부 팽만을 일으킨다.

어휘　stomach acid 위산

03 Fact Question

지문에 따르면, 북유럽계 사람들은
ⓐ 유당으로 인한 설사보다 복부 팽만을 더 겪는 경향이 있다
✓ 일반적으로 성인기에도 락타아제를 계속 생산한다
ⓒ 대개 심한 유당불내증 증상을 보인다
ⓓ 어린 시절 이후에 유당 소화 능력을 잃는 경향이 있다

04 Rhetorical Purpose Question

글쓴이는 왜 몽골 목축업자를 언급하는가?
ⓐ 중앙아시아에서 유제품 섭취의 역사적 기원을 소개하기 위해
ⓑ 유당불내증이 여러 인구 집단에 걸쳐 주로 유전적 특징에 의해 결정됨을 주장하기 위해
✓ 유전적 한계에도 불구하고 식단이 유당 소화를 가능하게 하는 예외를 강조하기 위해
ⓓ 아시아인 집단이 일반적으로 유제품을 피한다는 것을 암시하기 위해

05 Inference Question

지문은 유당불내증에 대해 무엇을 암시하는가?
ⓐ 심각한 건강상의 결과를 초래할 수 있다.
ⓑ 결장 기능의 이상이 원인이다.
✓ 지리적 분포가 광범위하다.
ⓓ 주된 원인은 발효 식품의 섭취다.

어휘　consequence [kánsəkwèns] 결과
　　　distribution [dìstrəbjúːʃən] 분포　extensive [iksténsiv] 광범위한

[06-10]

심리적 투사

심리적 투사는 개인이 자신의 바람직하지 않은 생각이나 감정을 타인에게 돌리는 보호적 반응이다. **07투사는 내적 갈등을 피하고 원치 않는 감정을 외부로 옮김으로써 개인이 자신의 이미지를 보호하도록 한다.** 심리학 이론에서, 이 과정은 의도적인 행위가 아닌 무의식적 전략으로 간주된다.

06한 직원이 자신의 업무 성과에 대해 심한 불안을 겪고 있다고 가정해 보자. 자신의 불안정을 인정하고 도움을 구하는 대신, 그 직원은 불안을 느끼는 사람이 동료들이라고 주장하며 그들을 비판적으로 판단한다. **08불안을 내적으로 인식하기보다 타인에게 떠넘기는 이러한 양상은 흔하다.** 그리고 직원이 피드백을 받거나 자신의 행동에 대해 통찰을 얻을 때까지 지속될 수 있다. 개입이 없으면, 이러한 투사는 직장 내 긴장을 증대시키고 팀의 역학 관계에 영향을 줄 수 있다.

투사는 개인의 성장을 지연시킬 수 있다. **10내적 갈등을 외면화함으로써, 사람들은 자신의 정서적 문제를 해결할 가능성이 낮아질 수 있으며**, 이는 의사소통의 어려움과 타인과의 긴장된 관계로 이어질 수 있다. **09투사에 대한 자각과 인식은 치료적 접근에서 핵심으로 여겨지며**, 개인이 더 건강한 대처 전략을 개발하고 사회적 상호작용

을 개선하도록 돕는다.

- projection [prədʒékʃən] 투사
- attribute [ətríbjuːt] 돌리다, 탓하다
- conflict [kánflikt] 갈등
- unconscious [ʌnkάnʃəs] 무의식적인
- deliberate [dilíbərət] 의도적인   intense [inténs] 심한
- acknowledge [əknάlidʒ] 인정하다
- insecurity [ìnsikjúərəti] 불안정
- insist [insíst] 주장하다   colleague [káliːg] 동료
- recognize [rékəgnàiz] 인식하다
- intervention [ìntərvénʃən] 개입
- escalate [éskəlèit] 증대시키다   tension [ténʃən] 긴장
- therapeutic [θèrəpjúːtik] 치료적인   cope [koup] 대처하다

06 Vocabulary Question

지문의 단어 "attribute"와 의미상 가장 유사한 것은?
- Ⓐ 질문하다
- ✓ 탓으로 하다
- Ⓒ 거부하다
- Ⓓ 표현하다

어휘 assign [əsáin] 탓으로 하다   reject [ridʒékt] 거부하다

07 Detail Question

사람은 왜 투사를 사용하는 것 같은가?
- Ⓐ 자신의 환경을 통제하기 위해
- Ⓑ 타인과의 대립을 막기 위해
- Ⓒ 동료들의 인정을 얻기 위해
- ✓ 내적 갈등에 직면하는 것을 피하기 위해

08 Rhetorical Purpose Question

글쓴이는 왜 동료들이 불안해한다고 주장하는 직원을 언급하는가?
- Ⓐ 명확한 의사소통이 오해를 해결할 수 있음을 보여주기 위해
- Ⓑ 현대 직장 역학을 비판하기 위해
- ✓ 투사가 일상적 상황에서 어떻게 작동하는지 설명하기 위해
- Ⓓ 직업 환경에서 불안이 흔하다는 것을 시사하기 위해

어휘 professional [prəféʃənl] 직업의

09 Fact Question

지문은 투사에 관한 치료적 접근에 대해 무엇을 제시하는가?
- ✓ 투사에 대한 인식을 높이는 데 초점을 맞춘다.
- Ⓑ 사람들이 어려운 감정만 투사하도록 권장한다.
- Ⓒ 사람들이 통제된 환경에서 감정을 투사하도록 돕는다.
- Ⓓ 자기성찰보다 타인의 감정을 분석하는 것을 우선시한다.

어휘 prioritize [praiɔ́ːrətàiz] 우선시하다
      self-reflection [sèlfriflékʃən] 자기성찰

10 Detail Question

투사를 사용함으로 인해 가능한 결과 중 하나는 무엇인가?
- ✓ 사람들이 자신의 정서적 문제를 해결하지 못하게 만들 수 있다.
- Ⓑ 사람들이 자신의 행동에 지나치게 비판적으로 되게 할 수 있다.
- Ⓒ 사람들로 하여금 타인의 인격을 맹렬하게 공격하도록 유도한다.
- Ⓓ 타인에 대한 개인의 공감 능력을 감소시킬 수 있다.

어휘 resolve [rizɔ́lv] 해결하다   empathize [émpəθàiz] 공감하다

[11-15]

방사성 탄소 연대측정

[12]방사성 탄소 연대측정은 한때 살아 있던 유기체의 일부였던 물질을 포함하는 물체의 연대를 규명하는 데 사용되는 기법이다. 이것은 나무, 뼈, 숯과 같은 유기 물질에서 발견되는 탄소-14라고 불리는 특수한 형태의 탄소의 양을 측정하는 것에 기반한다. 탄소-14는 대기에서 생성되어 생명체가 살아 있는 동안 내내 흡수된다. [13]유기체가 죽으면, 탄소-14를 흡수하는 것이 중단되고, 내부에 있던 탄소-14는 감소하기 시작한다.

[14]과학자들은 남아 있는 탄소-14의 양을 측정함으로써 그 유기체가 죽은 지 얼마나 지났는지 추정할 수 있다. 이 방법은 최대 약 5만 년 전의 물체까지 연대를 규명할 수 있다. 고고학자들은 방사성 탄소 연대측정을 사용해 인류의 역사를 연구하고 과거의 환경을 알게 된다. 이것은 선사시대 도구, 화석, 동굴벽화, 고대 건축물의 연대를 밝히는 데 도움을 주었다.

[14]결과는 과거 대기 속 탄소-14 농도의 변화에 영향받기 때문에 방사성 탄소 연대측정은 항상 정확한 것이 아니다. 이를 보완하기 위해, [15]과학자들은 장기간에 걸친 변화를 추적할 수 있도록 나이테 자료와 해양 저장소 자료를 수집한다. 이러한 정보는 그 후에 방사성 탄소 연대측정 결과를 조정하는 데 사용된다.

- substance [sʌ́bstəns] 물질   organic [ɔːrgǽnik] 유기의
- atmosphere [ǽtməsfìər] 대기   absorb [æbsɔ́ːrb] 흡수하다
- estimate [éstəmèit] 추정하다   residual [rizídʒuəl] 남아 있는
- archaeologist [ὰːrkiάːlədʒist] 고고학자   fossil [fάːsəl] 화석
- atmospheric [ætməsférik] 대기의
- concentration [kὰnsəntréiʃən] 농도
- reservoir [rézərvwὰːr] 저장소
- calibrate [kǽləbrèit] 조정하다

11 Vocabulary Question

지문의 단어 "residual"과 의미상 가장 유사한 것은?
- Ⓐ 결핍된
- ✓ 남아 있는
- Ⓒ 줄어드는
- Ⓓ 증가하는

어휘 lacking [lǽkiŋ] 결핍된

12 Fact Question

지문은 방사성 탄소 연대측정에 대해 무엇을 명시하는가?
- Ⓐ 이 방법은 자연물을 연대 측정하는 데 사용될 수 없다.
- Ⓑ 이 방법의 측정 결과는 보정이 필요하지 않다.
- ✓ 이 방법은 무기물의 연대를 측정할 수 없다.
- Ⓓ 이 방법의 정확도는 대상 물체의 연대에 따라 달라진다.

13 Detail Question

유기체가 죽으면 탄소-14는 어떻게 반응하는가?
- Ⓐ 시간이 지남에 따라 서서히 축적된다.
- Ⓑ 변화 없이 일정하게 유지된다.
- ✓ 서서히 감소한다.
- Ⓓ 산소로 변한다.

14 Rhetorical Purpose Question
2단락과 3단락의 관계는?
- Ⓐ 3단락은 2단락에서 설명한 현상에 대한 대안적 설명을 제시한다.
- ☑ 3단락은 2단락에서 상세히 설명된 기법의 결함을 제시하고 그 해결책을 제공한다.
- Ⓒ 3단락은 2단락에서 논의된 방사성 탄소 연대측정의 과학적 활용을 자세히 설명한다.
- Ⓓ 3단락은 2단락에서 제시된 설명에 추가적인 과학적 배경을 제공한다.

15 Inference Question
과학자들이 사용하는 나이테 자료와 해양 저장소 자료에 대해 추론할 수 있는 것은?
- Ⓐ 보정 기법이 개선될 필요가 있음을 암시한다.
- Ⓑ 대상의 연대를 계산하는 또 다른 방법을 가능하게 한다.
- Ⓒ 방사성 탄소 연대측정 결과와 직접적으로 모순된다.
- ☑ 과거 대기 속 탄소-14의 변화를 나타낸다.

어휘 contradict[kὰ:ntrədíkt] 모순되다

[16-20]

> **효모 발효**
>
> 효모 발효는 효모균이 당을 에너지로 전환하는 대사 과정이다. 이 반응은 일반적으로 산소가 거의 없거나 전혀 없는 환경에서 일어난다. [16]발효는 효모가 생성한 효소가 포도당이나 다른 단순 당을 분해할 때 시작된다. 당이 효모 내부에서 분해되면서 중간 산물이 배출되고, 이는 이어서 에탄올과 이산화탄소로 변한다.
>
> 이 과정은 빵, 맥주, 포도주를 만드는 데 필수적이다. [18]제빵에서, 이산화탄소가 밀가루 반죽을 부풀게 하여 가벼운 식감을 만든다. 알코올음료 생산에서, 원하는 에탄올 함유량을 얻기 위해 발효를 조절한다. [20]효모 발효는 바이오 연료와 의약품 생산에서도 핵심적인 역할을 한다.
>
> [19]발효의 속도와 효율은 효모의 균주에 따라 달라진다. 다른 효모 균주는 효모가 설탕을 에탄올과 이산화탄소로 얼마나 빠르고 완전히 전환하는지에 영향을 미치는 고유한 대사적 특성을 가진다. [19]예를 들어, 빵 효모는 당을 빠르게 발효시켜 제빵에 흔히 사용되며, 에일 효모는 당을 보다 완전하게 전환하므로, 맥주 양조에 가장 알맞다. 일부 효모 균주는 더 높은 알코올 농도를 견딜 수 있어 와인과 증류주 생산에 적합하다.

> fermentation[fə̀:rmentéiʃən] 발효
> metabolic[mètəbάlik] 대사의   enzyme[énzaim] 효소
> glucose[glú:kous] 포도당   intermediate[ìntərmí:diət] 중간의
> compound[kάmpaund] 산물   carbon dioxide 이산화탄소
> essential[isénʃəl] 필수적인   production[prədʌ́kʃən] 생산
> obtain[əbtéin] 얻다   content[kάntent] 함유량
> pharmaceutical[fὰ:rməsú:tikəl] 의약품
> efficiency[ifíʃənsi] 효율   strain[strein] 균주
> conversion[kənvə́:rʒən] 전환
> optimal[άptəməl] 가장 알맞은   tolerate[tάlərèit] 견디다

16 Detail Question
효모는 어떻게 발효 과정을 시작하는가?
- Ⓐ 에탄올과 이산화탄소로 변한다.
- Ⓑ 당액에서 영양분을 흡수한다.
- ☑ 당을 분해하는 효소를 생성한다.
- Ⓓ 이산화탄소를 알코올과 결합한다.

17 Vocabulary Question
지문의 단어 "intermediate"과 의미상 가장 유사한 것은?
- Ⓐ 정교한
- Ⓑ 순간적인
- ☑ 중간의
- Ⓓ 의무적인

어휘 elaborate[ilǽbərət] 정교한   mandatory[mǽndətɔ̀:ri] 의무적인

18 Detail Question
효모 발효 동안 빵 반죽이 부푸는 원인은 무엇인가?
- Ⓐ 에탄올의 생성
- Ⓑ 물의 흡수
- ☑ 이산화탄소의 방출
- Ⓓ 산소의 부재

어휘 absorption[æbsɔ́:rpʃən] 흡수   absence[ǽbsəns] 부재

19 Rhetorical Purpose Question
글쓴이는 왜 "빵 효모"와 "에일 효모"를 언급하는가?
- Ⓐ 다양한 문화권에서의 발효 역사를 설명하기 위해
- ☑ 다양한 목적에 사용되는 효모 균주의 예시를 제시하기 위해
- Ⓒ 빵 효모가 일반적으로 발효에 더 적합하다고 제안하기 위해
- Ⓓ 발효가 현대 기술 없이는 일어날 수 없음을 보여주기 위해

20 Detail Question
지문에서 언급된 효모 발효의 한 가지 산업적 활용은 무엇인가?
- Ⓐ 식품 방부제의 개발
- Ⓑ 이산화탄소의 추출
- ☑ 의약품의 생산
- Ⓓ 원유의 정제

어휘 preservative[prizə́:rvətiv] 방부제   crude oil 원유

3. Fact/Negative Fact Questions

Example

> **음향 위장**
>
> 음향 위장은 다양한 동물종이 포식자나 먹잇감으로부터 탐지를 피하기 위해 소리를 조작하는 적응 전략이다. 예를 들어, 어떤 나방은 특수한 날개 비늘을 가지고 있어 포식자들이 탐지를 위해 사용하는 음파를 흩뜨리거나 흡수하여 탐지되기 어렵게 한다. 올빼미는 특수한 깃털을 지니고 있어 소리 없는 비행이 가능하며, 이는 먹잇감이 올빼미의 접근을 듣지 못하도록 한다.
>
> 해부학적 적응 외에 행동적 전략이 중요한 역할을 한다. 여치와 같은 일부 곤충은 환경의 배경 소음을 활용하여 자신의 울음을 가려, 음향 환경 속에 섞여 포식당할 위험을 줄인다. 비슷하게, **개구리는 울음을 동기화하여 소리가 겹치게 함으로써 포식자가 개별 울음을 구별하기 어렵게 만든다.** 한편, 박쥐는 울음의 타이밍이나 주파수를

조절하여 간섭을 피하거나 먹잇감에 의해 탐지될 가능성을 줄인다.

연구에 따르면 많은 음향 위장 메커니즘은 포식자가 사용하는 특정 청각 기술, 예를 들어 반향정위에 대응하여 진화한 것으로 보인다. 이러한 진화적 군비 경쟁은 포식자-피식자 상호작용에서 소리의 중요성을 보여준다. 과학자들은 동물이 생존을 위해 음향적 특성을 어떻게 이용하는지를 더 잘 이해하기 위해 이 상호작용을 연구하고 있으며, 이는 감각 생태학과 긴밀히 연결된 정교한 적응을 드러낸다.

acoustic [əkúːstik] 음향의   adaptive [ədǽptiv] 적응의
detection [ditékʃən] 탐지   predator [prédətər] 포식자
prey [prei] 먹잇감   manipulation [mənìpjuléiʃən] 조작
possess [pəzés] 가지다   scatter [skǽtər] 흩뜨리다
anatomical [æ̀nətámikəl] 해부학적인
adaptation [æ̀dəptéiʃən] 적응
behavioral [bihéivjərəl] 행동적인   katydid [kéitidid] 여치
exploit [ikspl5it] 활용하다   predation [prideiʃən] 포식
modulate [mάdʒuleit] 조절하다   frequency [fríːkwənsi] 주파수
interference [ìntərfíərəns] 간섭
detectability [ditèktəbíləti] 탐지 가능성
echolocation [èkouloukéiʃən] 반향정위
property [práːpərti] 특성   intricate [íntrikət] 정교한

지문은 개구리에 대해 무엇을 명시하는가?
ⓐ 울음을 조절하여 각각의 소리를 듣기 힘들게 한다. ✓
ⓑ 배경 환경 소음을 활용해 울음을 감춘다.
ⓒ 주로 해부학적 적응을 사용한다.
ⓓ 반향정위 울음의 타이밍을 조절한다.

HACKERS PRACTICE   p.232

| 01 Ⓒ | 02 Ⓐ | 03 Ⓒ | 04 Ⓒ |

01 Fact Question

가이아 가설은 지구와 그 생명체들이 생명 거주 가능성을 유지하는 스스로 조정되는 체계로서 집합적으로 기능한다고 주장한다. 화학자 James Lovelock은 생명이 어떻게 행성 내 대기의 화학적 조성을 변화시킬 수 있는지를 연구하면서 1970년대에 이 개념을 제시했다.

이 가설에 따르면, 지구의 생물학적, 물리적 체계는 행성을 안정적으로 유지하기 위해 신체의 기관들처럼 작동한다. **예를 들어, 해양 플랑크톤은 구름 형성을 촉진하는 특정 화합물을 방출하고, 이는 행성을 거주 가능한 온도로 냉각시킨다.** 또한 식물들은 이산화탄소를 흡수하고 산소를 방출하여 생명을 부양하는 대기 구성을 조절하는 데 도움을 준다.

이 가설에는 "약한" 버전과 "강한" 버전이 있다. 약한 버전은 생물학적 및 물리적 과정들이 지구의 환경 조건에 수동적으로 영향을 미친다고 제안한다. 반면 강한 버전은 생명이 의도적으로 지구의 안정성을 유지한다고 주장한다.

hypothesis [haipάːθəsis] 가설   function [fʌ́ŋkʃən] 기능하다
sustain [səstéin] 유지하다
habitability [hæ̀bitəbíləti] 생명 거주 가능성
examine [igzǽmin] 연구하다   alter [5ːltər] 변화시키다
composition [kàːmpəzíʃən] 조성, 구성
atmosphere [ǽtməsfìər] 대기   operate [άpəreit] 작동하다
compound [kəmpáund] 화합물   absorb [æbs5ːrb] 흡수하다
carbon dioxide 이산화탄소   modulate [mάdʒuleit] 조절하다

passively [pǽsivli] 수동적으로
intentionally [inténʃənəli] 의도적으로
stability [stəbíləti] 안정성

지문이 해양 플랑크톤에 대해 명시하는 것은?
ⓐ 온실가스를 방출하여 대기를 온난화시킨다.
ⓑ 산소를 흡수하고 이산화탄소를 방출한다.
ⓒ 구름 생성을 촉진하여, 지구의 기후를 시원하게 한다. ✓
ⓓ 낮은 강수량을 상쇄하기 위해 수분 증발을 방지한다.

어휘 stimulate [stímjuleit] 촉진하다
      evaporation [ivæ̀pəréiʃən] 증발

02 Fact Question

젠트리피케이션은 소득 수준이 낮은 도시 지역으로 부유한 사람들이 이주하여 지역 환경과 공동체에 상당한 변화를 가져오는 과정이다. 이러한 유입은 일반적으로 새로운 사업체, 개조된 건물, 그리고 부동산 가격 상승을 초래한다. 이러한 변화가 기반 시설을 개선하고 새로운 편의시설을 제공할 수 있지만, 또한 생활비를 상승시키고 지역의 사회적 구조를 변화시키는 경향이 있다.

예를 들어, 뉴욕시의 Williamsburg는 젠트리피케이션의 물결을 겪었다. **이 지역은 예술가들과 젊은 전문직 종사자들이 정착하면서 유행하게 되었고,** 그 뒤를 이어 고급 상점들이 들어섰다. 그러나 오랜 거주민들은 높은 임대료와 재산세에 자주 직면하여 자신들의 집에 계속 거주하기 어려워졌다. 때로는 지역과 오랜 관계를 맺어온 사업체들이 더 새롭고 부유한 고객들의 요구에 부응하는 업소들로 대체되었다.

affluent [ǽfluənt] 부유한   neighborhood [néibərhud] 지역
influx [ínflʌks] 유입   property [práːpərti] 부동산
amenity [əménəti] 편의시설   alter [5ːltər] 변화시키다
fabric [fǽbrik] 구조   settle [sétl] 정착하다
upscale [ʌ́pskèil] 고급의
establishment [istǽbliʃmənt] 업소, 점포   cater [kéitər] 부응하다

뉴욕시의 Williamsburg에 대해 명시된 것은?
ⓐ 주민들은 전문직 젊은이들을 포함한다. ✓
ⓑ 지역 사업체들은 지역의 변화에 반대했다.
ⓒ 재개발 이전에 고급 상점이 많이 있었다.
ⓓ 새로운 사업체들과 투자자들에게 덜 매력적이게 되었다.

어휘 redevelopment [rìːdivéləpmənt] 재개발
      attractive [ətrǽktiv] 매력적인

03 Negative Fact Question

Stendhal 증후군은 사람들이 뛰어난 예술 작품이나 압도적인 아름다움에 노출될 때의 강렬한 심리적, 신체적 증상으로 특징지어지는 질환이다. 이 증후군은 피렌체에서 르네상스 걸작들을 감상하면서 그러한 증상을 경험했다고 기술한 19세기 프랑스 작가 Stendhal의 이름을 따서 명명되었다.

여러 사례가 보고되었는데, 특히 피렌체의 Uffizi 미술관과 같은 ᴮ**예술 작품이 풍부한 장소를 방문하는 관광객들 사이에서 그러했다.** ᴬ**증상으로는 강력한 예술 또는 건축 전시에 대한 반응으로 빠른 심장 박동, 어지러움, 혼란, 실신, 공황 등이 포함될 수 있다.** ᴰ**일부 방문객들은 또한 강한 실존적 불안감과 심지어 환각까지 경험했다.**

condition [kəndíʃən] 질환   intense [inténs] 강렬한

symptom [símptəm] 증상　exceptional [iksépʃənl] 뛰어난
overwhelming [òuvərwélmiŋ] 압도적인
fainting [féintiŋ] 실신　architectural [à:rkətéktʃərəl] 건축의
existential [ègzisténʃəl] 실존적인
hallucination [həlù:sənéiʃən] 환각

다음 중 Stendhal 증후군에 대해 언급되지 않은 것은?
Ⓐ 빠른 심장 박동과 어지러움을 유발할 수 있다.
Ⓑ 예술 작품이 풍부한 장소를 방문하는 관광객들에게 영향을 미친다.
✓ 전문 예술가들 사이에서 가장 빈번하게 발생한다.
Ⓓ 예술 전시에 대한 반응으로 환각을 유발할 수 있다.

04　Negative Fact Question

담석은 담낭에 형성되는 고체 침전물로, 담낭은 간 아래에 있는 작은 기관이며 담즙이라 불리는 소화액을 저장한다. ^A담석은 콜레스테롤과 같은 담즙 내 물질들이 농축되어 결정화될 때 형성된다. 담석은 미세한 입자부터 골프공 크기의 결석까지 크기가 다양할 수 있다. 담석이 담관을 막을 때, 이러한 폐색은 극심한 통증을 초래한다. 담석은 전 세계 수백만 명의 사람들에게 영향을 미치며, ^D특정 집단들이 다른 집단들보다 더 취약하다.

^B치료되지 않은 결석은 심각한 담관 감염인 담관염을 유발하거나, 이동하여 췌장을 막고 급성 췌장염을 유발할 수 있다. 담낭 염증이 조직 괴사로 진행될 때, 응급 수술은 불가피해진다. 그러나 이러한 생명을 위협하는 합병증들은 결석 형성의 근본 원인을 해결하는 생활 습관 변화를 통해 대부분 예방 가능하다.

gallstone [gɔ́:lstòun] 담석　deposit [dipázit] 침전물
gallbladder [gɔ́:lblædər] 담낭　digestive fluid 소화액
bile [bail] 담즙　substance [sʌ́bstəns] 물질
concentrate [kánsəntrèit] 농축되다　particle [pá:rtikəl] 입자
obstruction [əbstrʌ́kʃən] 폐색　susceptible [səséptəbl] 취약한
cholangitis [kòulændʒáitis] 담관염　infection [infékʃən] 감염
migrate [máigreit] 이동하다　pancreas [pǽnkriəs] 췌장
acute [əkjú:t] 급성의　pancreatitis [pæ̀nkriətáitis] 췌장염
inflammation [inflǝméiʃən] 염증　tissue [tíʃu:] 조직
complication [kàmpləkéiʃən] 합병증
modification [mà:dəfikéiʃən] 변화　address [ədrés] 해결하다

다음 중 담석에 대해 사실이 아닌 것은?
Ⓐ 담즙 물질이 농축될 때 형성된다.
Ⓑ 급성 췌장염을 유발할 수 있다.
✓ 즉시 수술을 통한 개입이 필요하다.
Ⓓ 일부 집단에서 더 흔하게 발생한다.

어휘　surgical [sə́:rdʒikəl] 수술을 통한, 수술의
　　　intervention [ìntərvénʃən] 개입
　　　prevalent [prévələnt] 흔한, 널리 퍼진

HACKERS TEST　　p.234

01 Ⓑ	02 Ⓒ	03 Ⓒ	04 Ⓒ	05 Ⓑ
06 Ⓑ	07 Ⓐ	08 Ⓒ	09 Ⓓ	10 Ⓐ
11 Ⓑ	12 Ⓓ	13 Ⓓ	14 Ⓑ	15 Ⓓ
16 Ⓓ	17 Ⓒ	18 Ⓑ	19 Ⓐ	20 Ⓓ

[01-05]

환상통

환상통은 대개 절단 후에 더 이상 존재하지 않는 신체 부위에서 사람들이 감각, 주로 통증을 느끼는 현상이다. 이 유형의 통증은 외부의 부상 때문에 생기는 것이 아니며 가벼운 따끔거림에서 강한 고통까지 다양할 수 있다. 예를 들어, ^02다리를 잃은 사람은 다리가 있던 부위에서 따끔거림, 화끈거림, 압박감을 경험할 수 있다.

가장 널리 받아들여지는 설명은 ^04D뇌와 신경계가 환상통의 원인이라는 것이다. ^01절단 이후, 결손된 사지에서 뇌로 신호를 전달하던 신경들은 여전히 활동한다. 이 신경들은 예상치 못한 신호를 보낼 수 있고, 뇌는 이를 없는 신체 부위에서 오는 것처럼 해석한다. 또한, 잃어버린 사지로부터 오는 정보를 처리하던 뇌의 영역은 여전히 활동하고 있으며 인접한 신체 부위로부터 오는 자극에 반응할 수 있다.

^04A환상통은 수술 직후 짧은 기간 동안 혹은 수개월이나 수년 동안 지속될 수도 있다. ^05치료는 통증 완화 방법, 물리치료, 그리고 ^04B시각적 피드백을 이용해 뇌의 통증 신호에 대한 반응을 재훈련하는 거울 치료를 통해 증상을 관리하는 데 초점을 맞춘다. ^04D환상통은 신경계와 뇌가 지각을 만들어내는 방식의 복잡성을 드러낸다.

phenomenon [finámənàn] 현상　sensation [senséiʃən] 감각
amputation [æ̀mpjutéiʃən] 절단　tingling [tíŋgliŋ] 따끔거림
intense [inténs] 강한　discomfort [diskʌ́mfərt] 고통
nervous system 신경계　responsible [rispánsəbl] 원인이 되는
nerve [nə:rv] 신경　limb [lim] 사지
interpret [intə́:rprit] 해석하다　absent [ǽbsənt] 없는
persist [pərsíst] 지속되다　relief [rilí:f] 완화
retrain [ri:tréin] 재훈련하다　perception [pərsépʃən] 지각

01　Detail Question

없어진 사지에서 뇌가 감각을 인지하는 이유는?
Ⓐ 절단이 전기 신호가 잘못 발화되도록 만드는 신경 결손을 일으킨다.
✓ 활동하는 신경들이 예상치 못한 신호를 뇌로 보낸다.
Ⓒ 손상된 신경 말단이 잘못 재생되어 잘못된 메시지를 보낸다.
Ⓓ 근육 수축이 잘못된 신경 신호를 유발한다.

어휘　misfire [misfáiər] (신경 신호가) 잘못 발화되다
　　　contraction [kəntrǽkʃən] 수축

02　Rhetorical Purpose Question

글쓴이는 왜 따끔거림, 화끈거림, 압박감을 언급하는가?
Ⓐ 환상통의 치료법을 설명하기 위해
Ⓑ 의사가 환상통을 어떻게 진단하는지의 예를 제시하기 위해
✓ 사람들이 환상통으로 느낄 수 있는 감각을 보여주기 위해
Ⓓ 환상통이 다른 통증 유형보다 덜 심각하다고 주장하기 위해

어휘　diagnose [dáiəgnòus] 진단하다　severe [səvíər] 심각한

03　Vocabulary Question

지문의 단어 "responsible"과 의미상 가장 유사한 것은?
Ⓐ 부주의한
Ⓑ 보조의
✓ 책임이 있는
Ⓓ 민감한

어휘　negligent [néglidʒənt] 부주의한, 태만한
　　　auxiliary [ɔ:gzíljəri] 보조의

04 Negative Fact Question

다음 중 환상통에 대해 사실이 아닌 것은?
Ⓐ 팔다리가 절단된 이후 수개월 혹은 수년까지도 지속될 수 있다.
Ⓑ 뇌의 반응을 조절하는 치료법으로 완화될 수 있다.
☑ 남아 있는 신경 조직의 외과적 제거가 필요하다.
Ⓓ 뇌와 신경계의 복합적인 활동으로 인해 발생한다.

05 Rhetorical Purpose Question

다음 중 세 번째 단락의 목적을 가장 잘 설명한 것은?
Ⓐ 3단락은 환상통을 다른 신경성 통증 유형과 비교한다.
☑ 3단락은 환상통의 가능한 치료법을 논의한다.
Ⓒ 3단락은 앞서 언급된 환상통의 원인을 요약한다.
Ⓓ 3단락은 환상통이 전적으로 심리적인 것임을 암시한다.

어휘 **neurological**[njùərəládʒikəl] 신경성의
summarize[sʌ́məràiz] 요약하다

[06-10]

단순 노출 효과

심리학자 Robert Zajonc가 처음 확인한 단순 노출 효과는 사람들이 어떤 것을 더 자주 접할수록, 상호작용이나 관심이 아주 작더라도 그것을 더 좋아하게 되는 경향이 있다는 것을 보여준다. ⁰⁸ᴮ이 과정은 무의식적으로 작용하며 사람, 제품, ⁰⁸ᴬ나아가 아이디어에 대한 태도에까지 영향을 미칠 수 있다.

예를 들어, ⁰⁷새로운 노래를 들으면 무관심하거나 심지어 반감이 생길 수 있다. 그러나, 몇 번 반복해서 듣고 나면, 대개 더 매력적으로 느껴진다. 이와 마찬가지로, 광고에서 반복적으로 노출되는 제품들은 시청자들이 그 광고 자체에 직접적으로 별 관심을 기울이지 않더라도 더 긍정적으로 인식되는 경우가 많다.

이 효과는 사회적 상황에서도 분명하게 나타난다. 사람들은 상호작용이 피상적이더라도 ⁰⁸ᴰ자주 보는 동료나 이웃을 더 선호하는 경향이 있다. 팀이나 동아리 내에서, 반복 노출은 인식되는 신뢰감과 협력 의지를 높이고, 이것은 집단의 협동을 강화하고 공유된 규범의 형성으로 이어진다.

¹⁰장점에도 불구하고, 이 효과에는 한계가 있다. ⁰⁹주로 중립적이거나 약간 긍정적인 자극에 영향을 미친다. 그리고 자극이 긍정적일 때에도, 과잉 노출은 결국 부정적 반응을 유발할 수 있다. 이 효과를 인식하는 것은 자신의 현재 관심사가 단지 익숙함에서 기인한 것인지 돌아보는 데 도움이 된다. 만약 그렇다면, 진정으로 즐기는 일을 찾으려고 선택할 수 있다.

encounter[inkáuntər] 접하다
awareness[əwéərnis] 관심, 인식 **operate**[ápərèit] 작용하다
unconsciously[ʌnkánʃəsli] 무의식적으로
indifference[indífərəns] 무관심 **perceive**[pərsíːv] 인식하다
evident[évədənt] 분명한 **superficial**[sùːpərfíʃəl] 피상적인
increase[inkríːs] 높이다
trustworthiness[trʌ́stwəːrðinis] 신뢰감
willingness[wíliŋnis] 의지 **cooperate**[kouápərèit] 협력하다
coordination[kouɔ̀ːrdənéiʃən] 협동
stimulus[stímjuləs] 자극 (pl. stimuli)
provoke[prəvóuk] 유발하다

06 Vocabulary Question

지문의 단어 "superficial"과 의미상 가장 유사한 것은?
Ⓐ 정중한
☑ 표면적인
Ⓒ 진지한
Ⓓ 영구적인

어휘 **casual**[kǽʒuəl] (관계 등이) 표면적인
permanent[pə́ːrmənənt] 영구적인

07 Rhetorical Purpose Question

글쓴이는 왜 "새로운 노래"를 언급하는가?
☑ 친숙함이 점차 호감도를 높일 수 있음을 보여주기 위해
Ⓑ 반복이 때때로 지루함을 유발할 수 있음을 강조하기 위해
Ⓒ 노래가 광고에서 효과적인 도구임을 보여주기 위해
Ⓓ 음악 선호에서 의식적 선택의 역할을 강조하기 위해

어휘 **conscious**[kánʃəs] 의식적인 **preference**[préfərəns] 선호

08 Negative Fact Question

다음 중 단순 노출 효과에 대해 사실이 아닌 것은?
Ⓐ 아이디어에도 적용될 수 있다.
Ⓑ 일반적으로 사람의 의식적인 통제 범위 밖에 있다.
☑ 청중의 관심이 높을 때 발생한다.
Ⓓ 사람들이 자주 보는 사람들을 더 선호하는 이유를 설명한다.

어휘 **engagement**[ingéidʒmənt] 관심, 참여

09 Detail Question

다음 상황 중 단순 노출 효과가 가장 명확하게 관찰되는 것은 언제인가?
Ⓐ 사람들이 처음에 혐오하는 무언가를 접할 때
Ⓑ 텔레비전 광고가 기억에 남게끔 의도적으로 설계될 때
Ⓒ 동료들이 인사 이상의 교류를 거의 하지 않을 때
☑ 자극이 강하게 매력적이지도 혐오스럽지도 않을 때

어휘 **detest**[ditést] 혐오하다, 몹시 싫어하다
repulsive[ripʌ́lsiv] 혐오스러운

10 Rhetorical Purpose Question

3단락과 4단락의 관계는?
☑ 4단락은 3단락에서 언급되지 않은 한계를 소개한다.
Ⓑ 4단락은 3단락에서 제시된 예시를 보충한다.
Ⓒ 4단락은 3단락에서 논의된 예시를 비판한다.
Ⓓ 4단락은 3단락의 정보를 반박하는 사례를 제공한다.

[11-15]

토템 숭배

¹²토템 숭배는 자연물, 동물, 또는 식물(토템)이 영적으로 중요하며 그것들이 인간 집단과 상징적으로 연결되어 있다고 보는 믿음 및 사회 조직 체계이다. 많은 사회에서, 공동체는 ¹³특정 동물을 신성시하여 사냥을 삼가고, 그 동물의 형상을 의례에 사용하기도 한다. 이러한 관습은 공동체의 공유된 가치를 강화하고 자연에 대한 존중과 사회적 책임에 관한 ¹⁴ᴬ도덕적 교훈을 제공한다.

¹⁴ᴰ토템은 씨족이나 혈통과 같은 집단 정체성을 나타내며, 구성원들 사이에 친밀감과 협력을 형성한다. 이러한 상징들은 친족 관계를 나타내는 표시로 기능하여, ¹⁴ᶜ공동체 내의 의무를 규정하고 혼인에 관한 규칙을 정하는 데 지침이 된다. 예를 들어, 같은 토템을 공유하는 구성원들은 형제자매로 간주되기 때문에 그들 사이의 결

혼이 금지될 수 있다.

A 토템 숭배는 광범위한 사회적 및 문화적 관습을 포함한다. **B** 이러한 더 넓은 틀에서, 학자들은 토템 숭배를 주로 사회 체계로 이해해야 하는지, 아니면 환경을 해석하는 방식으로 이해해야 하는지를 두고 논쟁한다. **C** 이러한 이견에도 불구하고, [12]대부분은 인간이 사회생활을 구조화하기 위해 자연계에 상징적 의미를 부여하는 방식을 보여준다는 데 동의한다. **D** 반대 이론들조차 토템이 물리적 환경을 사회 규칙으로 전환한다는 점을 인정한다. 이런 의미에서, 토템 숭배는 문화, 믿음, 생태 사이의 깊은 연결을 강조한다.

spiritually [spíritʃuəli] 영적으로　significant [signífikənt] 중요한
symbolically [simbá:likəli] 상징적으로　refrain [rifréin] 삼가다
strengthen [stréŋkθən] 강화하다
responsibility [rìspànsəbíləti] 책임
collective [kəléktiv] 집단의　clan [klæn] 씨족
lineage [líniidʒ] 혈통　belonging [bilɔ́:ŋiŋ] 친밀감
kinship [kínʃip] 친족 관계　obligation [àbləgéiʃən] 의무
prohibit [prəhíbit] 금지하다　sibling [síbliŋ] 형제자매
encompass [inkʌ́mpəs] 포함하다　illustrate [íləstrèit] 보여주다
assign [əsáin] 부여하다　ecology [ikálədʒi] 생태

11 Vocabulary Question
지문의 단어 "obligations"와 의미상 가장 유사한 것은?
Ⓐ 장식
☑ 의무
Ⓒ 입력
Ⓓ 축하 행사

12 Inference Question
토템 숭배의 역할에 대해 추론할 수 있는 것은?
Ⓐ 모든 개인이 동일한 의례적 관행을 채택하도록 보장한다.
Ⓑ 주로 인접 공동체에 영향을 미치는 수단으로 기능한다.
☑ 자연적 상징을 사회 조직 체계에 통합한다.
Ⓓ 초기 과학적 사고의 직접적 증거가 된다.

어휘 identical [aidéntikəl] 동일한　integrate [íntəgrèit] 통합하다

13 Rhetorical Purpose Question
글쓴이는 왜 신성한 동물을 언급하는가?
Ⓐ 초기 문화에서 종교적 관습이 정치 제도를 대체했음을 보여주기 위해
Ⓑ 전통 사회에서 동물이 식물보다 더 중요했음을 주장하기 위해
Ⓒ 토템 숭배가 주로 동물 숭배의 형태로 발전했음을 암시하기 위해
☑ 자연적 상징이 공동체 정체성의 기반으로 기능할 수 있음을 설명하기 위해

어휘 institution [ìnstitú:ʃən] 제도, 기관　worship [wɔ́:rʃip] 숭배

14 Negative Fact Question
다음 중 토템에 대해 사실이 아닌 것은?
Ⓐ 도덕적 교훈을 제공한다.
☑ 자연 현상을 설명한다.
Ⓒ 공동체의 규칙을 정하는 데 지침이 된다.
Ⓓ 집단적 연대감을 강화한다.

어휘 solidarity [sà:lədǽrəti] 연대감

15 Insertion Question
다음 문장이 삽입될 수 있는 네 곳이 지문에 표시되어 있다.

반대 이론들조차 토템이 물리적 환경을 사회 규칙으로 전환한다는 점을 인정한다.

그 문장은 어디에 가장 적절한가? 그 문장이 삽입될 수 있는 곳을 고르시오.

[16-20]

입면 환각

입면 환각은 잠들기 직전의 순간에 발생하는 생생한 감각 경험이다. [17A]이러한 지각 작용은 현저하게 실제처럼 느껴지는 시각적, 청각적, 또는 촉각적 감각을 포함할 수 있다. [16]일반적인 꿈과 달리, 입면 환각은 깨어 있는 환경의 요소들과 정신이 스스로 만들어낸 것들을 혼합하여 의식과 수면을 연결하는 혼합적 경험을 만든다. 이 현상은 뇌가 깨어 있는 상태에서 수면으로 전환하는 과정을 어렴풋이 엿보는 흥미로운 기회를 제공한다. [18]입면 환각은 기면증과 같은 수면 장애가 있는 사람들에게 특히 흔하다.

연구자들은 입면 환각의 여러 역할을 확인했다. [17D]그것들은 뇌가 외부 현실로부터 분리되며 휴식을 준비하는 과정과 연결된 것으로 여겨진다. [17B]일부 과학자들은 이러한 환각이 뇌가 하루 동안 축적된 인상들을 정리하거나 통합하는 데 도움을 준다고 제안한다.

[20]연구에 따르면 입면 환각은 각성을 조절하는 신경계와 수면을 시작하는 신경계 사이의 불안정한 상호작용에서 비롯될 수 있다. 뇌 영상 연구는 이러한 전환 상태 동안 특정 뇌 영역이 부분적으로 활성 상태를 유지하는 반면, 다른 영역들은 수면이 시작되면서 활동을 감소시키기 시작한다는 것을 나타낸다. 그러나 입면 환각을 유발하는 정확한 신경 화학적 과정은 여전히 완전히 이해되지 않았으며 지속적인 연구 영역으로 남아 있다.

hallucination [həlù:sənéiʃən] 환각
perception [pərsépʃən] 지각, 지각 작용
auditory [ɔ́:ditɔ̀:ri] 청각적인　tactile [tǽktil] 촉각적인
glimpse [glimps] 엿보기, 짧은 경험
narcolepsy [ná:rkəlèpsi] 기면증
disengage [dìsengéidʒ] 분리되다
integrate [íntəgrèit] 통합하다　impression [impréʃən] 인상
accumulate [əkjú:mjulèit] 축적하다
initiate [iníʃièit] 시작하다　investigation [invèstəgéiʃən] 연구

16 Detail Question
입면 환각은 일반적인 꿈과 어떻게 다른가?
Ⓐ 주로 수면의 가장 깊은 단계에서 발생한다.
Ⓑ 수면 마비를 일으킬 가능성이 더 높다.
Ⓒ 깨어난 후 기억될 가능성이 더 높다.
☑ 정신이 여전히 현실 세계를 부분적으로 인식하고 있는 동안에 일어난다.

어휘 paralysis [pərǽləsis] 마비

17 Negative Fact Question
다음 중 입면 환각에 대해 사실이 아닌 것은?
Ⓐ 시각, 소리, 또는 신체적 느낌의 형태를 띨 수 있다.
Ⓑ 하루의 경험을 정리하려는 뇌의 활동에 기여한다.

ⓒ 내적 사고로부터의 분리를 반영한다.
ⓓ 뇌의 일부 영역이 활동 정도를 낮추는 것을 수반한다.

18 Rhetorical Purpose Question
글쓴이는 왜 기면증을 언급하는가?
ⓐ 기면증이 입면 환각의 주요 원인임을 시사하기 위해
☒ 입면 환각과 수면 장애 사이의 연관성을 지적하기 위해
ⓒ 기면증 환자들이 외부 자극에 대해 고조된 반응을 보인다는 것을 보여주기 위해
ⓓ 입면 환각이 대부분 무해한 경험이라고 주장하기 위해

어휘 heightened[háitnd] 고조된

19 Vocabulary Question
두 번째 단락의 단어 "integrate"와 의미상 가장 유사한 것은?
☒ 결합하다
ⓑ 고립시키다
ⓒ 지우다
ⓓ 확인하다

20 Fact Question
신경계에 대해 지문이 명시하는 것은?
ⓐ 사람들이 창의적이 되도록 한다.
ⓑ 신경 화학 물질의 배출을 활발하게 한다.
ⓒ 수면 전환 동안 완전히 활성 상태를 유지한다.
☒ 신체의 휴식과 각성의 주기를 좌우한다.

어휘 govern[gʌ́vərn] 좌우하다, 지배하다

4. Vocabulary Questions

Example   p.243

인쇄기

인쇄기의 발명은 현대 문명을 형성하는 데 중대한 역할을 하였다. 인쇄기 발명 이전에는 책을 손으로 베껴 써야 했는데, 이는 힘든 과정이었고 지식의 전파를 소수의 특권 계층으로 제한했다. 15세기 중반, Johannes Gutenberg는 유럽에 가동 활자 인쇄를 도입하여 정보 접근을 혁신적으로 변화시켰다. 이 기술은 책을 빠르고 효율적으로, 대량으로 제작할 수 있게 하였다.

기술이 발전하면서, 유럽 전역에 초기 인쇄소가 생겨났고, 새로운 책 제작 방식이 확산되었다. 장인과 상인들은 종교 서적, 과학 논문, 문학 작품을 빠르게 복제할 기회를 맞이했다. 인쇄물에 대한 수요는 빠르게 증가하였고, 베네치아, 파리, 런던과 같은 도시들에 인쇄 중심지가 설립되었다. 이러한 확산은 인쇄업자와 출판업자의 네트워크를 형성하여 유럽 대륙 전역의 정보 흐름을 가속하였다.

인쇄기의 확산은 중요한 사회적 및 문화적 변화를 가져왔다. 책의 광범위한 보급은 더 넓은 계층의 문해력을 촉진하였다. 사상과 과학적 발견은 빠르게 보급되어 르네상스와 종교 개혁과 같은 주요 운동을 촉발하였다. 또한 인쇄기는 언어와 텍스트의 표준화를 가능하게 하여 수작업 필사에서 생기는 불일치를 줄였다. 신문과 팜플릿은 흔해졌고, 이는 여론 형성과 정치적 참여를 촉진하였다.

pivotal[pívətl] 중대한 civilization[sìvəlaizéiʃən] 문명

privileged[prívəlidʒd] 특권을 가진
artisan[ɑ́:rtəzən] 장인 duplication[djù:plikéiʃən] 복제
treatise[trí:tis] 논문 establishment[istǽbliʃmənt] 설립
dissemination[disèmənéiʃən] 확산
literacy[lítərəsi] 문해력 segment[ségmənt] 계층
circulate[sə́:rkjəleit] 보급되다, 퍼지다
facilitate[fəsílətèit] 가능하게 하다

지문의 단어 "initiating"과 의미상 가장 유사한 것은?
☒ 유발하다
ⓑ 지속시키다
ⓒ 강조하다
ⓓ 방해하다

어휘 sustain[səstéin] 지속시키다 hinder[híndər] 방해하다

HACKERS PRACTICE   p.244

01 ⓑ   02 ⓒ   03 ⓒ   04 ⓒ

01 Vocabulary Question

1965년에 시작된 암스테르담의 White Bicycle Plan은 유럽 최초의 공공 자전거 공유 시스템이었다. 이 프로젝트는 여러 대의 흰색 자전거를 대중이 무료로 사용할 수 있도록 제공했다. 이 계획은 도난과 기물 파손으로 인해 단명했지만, 유사한 프로젝트들에 영감을 주었다.

코펜하겐과 파리 같은 도시들은 자체적인 자전거 공유 시스템을 도입했다. 코펜하겐의 Bycyklen은 개선된 자전거 설계와 픽업 및 반납을 위한 지정된 대여소를 도입했다. 파리는 도시 전역에 자동화된 대여소를 사용하는 대규모 Vélib' 시스템을 시작했다. 각 도시는 도난과 기물 파손을 방지하기 위한 조치를 취했다. 코펜하겐은 부품이 도난당하지 않도록 하기 위해 다른 자전거와 호환되지 않는 맞춤형 부품을 사용했고, 파리는 자전거를 추적하기 위해 GPS를 사용했다.

scheme[ski:m] 계획 vandalism[vǽndəlìzm] 기물 파손
implement[ímpləmènt] 도입하다
designated[dézignèitid] 지정된
incompatible[ìnkəmpǽtəbl] 호환되지 않는
component[kəmpóunənt] 부품

첫 번째 단락의 단어 "inspired"와 의미상 가장 유사한 것은?
ⓐ 개발했다
☒ 영향을 주었다
ⓒ 버렸다
ⓓ 방해했다

어휘 abandon[əbǽndən] 버리다, 버리고 떠나다

02 Vocabulary Question

연구자들은 다양한 유형의 유머의 심리적 근거를 설명하기 위한 이론들을 제시해 왔다. 그중 하나는 부조화 이론으로, 사람들이 기대와 현실 사이에 차이가 있을 때 재미를 느낀다고 제시한다. 예를 들어, 친숙한 이야기 구조를 예상치 못하게 파괴하는 핵심 구절은 청자를 놀라게 하기 때문에 웃음을 유발한다.

또 다른 이론은 해소 이론이다. 이 이론은 유머가 심리적 긴장의 해소를 가능하게 한다고 설명한다. 직장이나 시험과 같이 스트레스가

많은 상황에 대한 농담은 흔히 청자들 사이의 불안을 줄이는 역할을 한다. 웃음은 감정적 해소 역할을 하여, 개인과 집단에게 어려운 사건들을 더 감당하기 쉽게 만든다.

우월성 이론은 다른 설명을 제공한다. 이 이론에 따르면, 사람들은 다른 사람들에 대해 우월감을 느낄 때 유머를 경험한다. 예를 들어, 한 등장인물이 반복적으로 실패하거나 실수를 하는 슬랩스틱 코미디는 웃음을 불러일으키는데, 관객이 무대나 스크린 속의 인물보다 우월하다고 느끼기 때문이다.

theory[θíːəri] 이론 incongruity[ìnkəŋgrúːəti] 부조화
disparity[dispǽrəti] 차이
expectation[èkspektéiʃən] 기대
punch line (농담에서) 핵심 구절 disrupt[disrʌ́pt] 파괴하다
relief[rilíːf] 해소 release[rilíːs] 해소
manageable[mǽnidʒəbl] 감당하기 쉬운
superiority[səpìəriɔ́ːrəti] 우월성 evoke[ivóuk] 불러일으키다

지문의 단어 "disparity"와 의미상 가장 유사한 것은?
Ⓐ 어려움
Ⓑ 비교
Ⓥ 차이
Ⓓ 이유

어휘 comparison[kəmpǽrəsn] 비교 reason[ríːzən] 이유

03 Vocabulary Question

일본의 목판화는 "덧없는 세상의 그림"이라는 ukiyo-e라는 이름으로 알려져 있다. 용어 ukiyo("덧없는 세상"이라는 뜻)는 원래 삶의 덧없음을 표현하는 불교의 개념을 설명하는 데 처음 사용되었으나, 이후 17세기부터 19세기까지 일본 도시의 쾌락 중심적인 생활 방식을 나타내게 되었다. ukiyo-e 판화에는 일상생활, 자연, 그리고 오락과 관련된 장면들이 담겨 있다.

이 판화의 제작에는 협업이 필요했다. 화가는 이미지를 디자인하고, 조각가는 목판을 준비했으며, 인쇄공은 정밀한 층을 이루도록 종이에 잉크를 발랐다. 선명한 색상, 강한 윤곽선, 그리고 미세한 종이 질감의 차이와 같은 섬세한 세부 사항이 이 판화를 돋보이게 했다. 이것들은 대량으로 제작되어 저렴했기 때문에, 새롭게 부상하는 중산층에게 예술을 접할 기회를 제공했다.

transient[trǽnʃənt] 덧없는 represent[rèprizént] 나타내다
pleasure[pléʒər] 쾌락 collaboration[kəlæ̀bəréiʃən] 협업
carver[káːrvər] 조각가 nuanced[njúːɑːnst] 섬세한
texture[tékstʃər] 질감 distinguish[distíŋgwiʃ] 돋보이게 하다
affordable[əfɔ́ːrdəbl] 저렴한
emerging[imə́ːrdʒiŋ] 부상하는

지문의 단어 "nuanced"와 의미상 가장 유사한 것은?
Ⓐ 분명한
Ⓑ 반복적인
Ⓥ 미묘한
Ⓓ 정교한

어휘 apparent[əpǽrənt] 분명한 subtle[sʌ́tl] 미묘한
    intricate[íntrikət] 정교한

04 Vocabulary Question

종양바이러스는 인간이나 동물에게 암을 유발할 수 있는 바이러스이다. 이러한 바이러스 중 많은 것들이 숙주 세포에 자신의 유전 물질을 삽입하는 방식으로 작용하며, 이는 정상적인 세포 조절을 방해하고 통제되지 않는 세포 성장과 종양 형성을 초래할 가능성이 있다. 종양바이러스의 흔한 예로는 자궁경부암 및 다른 유형의 암과 연관된 인유두종 바이러스(HPV)와 간암과 연관된 B형 및 C형 간염 바이러스가 있다.

종양바이러스에 감염된 모든 사람이 암에 걸리는 것은 아니다. 암 위험은 개인의 유전적 배경, 면역 체계 상태, 환경적 영향과 같은 추가적인 요인들에 달려 있다. 예를 들어, HPV에 감염된 젊고 건강한 사람의 약 90퍼센트는 어떤 증상도 나타내지 않고 2년 이내에 면역 체계를 통해 자연스럽게 바이러스를 제거한다. HPV 예방 접종과 같은 발전도 감염률을 줄이고 암 위험을 낮추는 데 성공적임이 입증되었다.

oncovirus[ɑ́ːŋkɑvàiərəs] 종양바이러스 genetic[dʒənétik] 유전의
regulation[règjuléiʃən] 조절
unhampered[ʌ̀nhǽmpərd] 통제되지 않는 tumor[tjúːmər] 종양
cervical[sə́ːrvikəl] 자궁경부의 hepatitis[hèpətáitis] 간염

지문의 단어 "unhampered"와 의미상 가장 유사한 것은?
Ⓐ 완성되지 않은
Ⓑ 일관되지 않은
Ⓥ 억제되지 않는
Ⓓ 보이지 않는

어휘 inconsistent[ìnkənsístənt] 일관되지 않은
    unrestrained[ʌ̀nristréind] 억제되지 않는

HACKERS TEST   p.246

01 Ⓐ	02 Ⓑ	03 Ⓑ	04 Ⓐ	05 Ⓓ
06 Ⓐ	07 Ⓒ	08 Ⓒ	09 Ⓑ	10 Ⓓ
11 Ⓑ	12 Ⓓ	13 Ⓓ	14 Ⓑ	15 Ⓒ
16 Ⓐ	17 Ⓒ	18 Ⓐ	19 Ⓐ	20 Ⓓ

[01-05]

효율적 시장 가설

효율적 시장 가설(EMH)은 금융 시장의 자산 가격이 이용 가능한 정보를 매우 효율적으로 반영하기 때문에, 02평균 시장 수익률을 능가하는 수익(초과 수익)을 얻는 것이 불가능하다고 단정한다. 이는 미국 경제학자 Eugene Fama에 의해 개발되었으며, 03A그는 자신의 연구로 2013년 노벨 경제학상을 수상하였다.

04전통적으로 투자자들은 주로 차익 거래를 통해 수익을 얻는다고 생각되었는데, 차익 거래는 동일한 자산에 대한 시장 간의 일시적인 가격 차이나 사람들의 정보 격차를 이용한다. 03D그러나 Fama는 시장이 관련 가격 정보를 매우 빠르게 통합하여 차익 거래 기회를 없애는 것을 관찰하였다. 그는 또한 03C단기 자산 가격은 예측하는 것이 불가능하며, 본질적으로 "아무렇게나 걷는 걸음"을 따른다는 것을 발견하였는데, 이는 일련의 데이터가 시간이 지남에 따라 취하는 자의적 변동을 가리키는 통계 용어이다.

EMH는 어떤 투자자도 시장 타이밍과 같은 적극적 투자 전략(미래 시장 가격 움직임을 예측하려고 시도하는 전략)을 이용해서 시장보다 더 나은 결과를 낼 수 없음을 시사하였다. 05EMH는 오히려 인덱스 펀드를 통해 전반적인 시장 성과를 좇음으로써 더 나은 결과를 얻을 수 있음을 제안하였는데, 인덱스 펀드는 S&P 500과 같은 특

정 시장 지수 상의 모든 주식을 보유함으로써 시장 지수의 성과와 일치하도록 설계된 펀드이다.

hypothesis[haipάːθəsis] 가설   posit[pάzit] 단정하다
asset[ǽset] 자산   receive[risíːv] 수상하다
investor[invéstər] 투자자   arbitrage[άːrbətrὰːʒ] 차익 거래
exploit[ikspló it] 이용하다   observe[əbzə́ːrv] 관찰하다
incorporate[inkɔ́ːrpərèit] 통합하다
statistical[stətístikəl] 통계의   fluctuation[flʌ̀ktʃuéiʃən] 변동
imply[implái] 시사하다   consistently[kənsístəntli] 지속적으로
obtain[əbtéin] 얻다   index[índeks] 지수
hold[hould] 보유하다   stock[stak] 주식

01 Vocabulary Question

첫 번째 단락의 단어 "reflect"와 의미상 가장 유사한 것은?
- Ⓐ 반영하다 ✓
- Ⓑ 보여주다
- Ⓒ 영향을 주다
- Ⓓ 포함하다

02 Main Topic Question

다음 중 지문의 중심 생각을 가장 잘 나타낸 것은?
- Ⓐ 충분한 정보를 가진 투자자만이 초과 수익을 달성할 수 있다.
- Ⓑ 정보에 기반하여 꾸준히 초과 수익을 얻는 것은 불가능하다. ✓
- Ⓒ 주식 데이터에 대한 통계적 분석은 긍정적인 결과를 산출한다.
- Ⓓ 어떤 시장도 Fama의 효율성 정의를 충족시키지 못한다.

어휘 definition[dèfəníʃən] 정의

03 Negative Fact Question

다음 중 Eugene Fama에 대해 사실이 아닌 것은?
- Ⓐ 자신의 연구로 2013년에 노벨 경제학상을 수상하였다.
- Ⓑ 인덱스 펀드라고 알려진 대중적 투자 수단을 개발하였다. ✓
- Ⓒ 단기 가격 변동은 예측 불가능하다는 것을 발견하였다.
- Ⓓ 빠른 정보 처리가 차익 거래 기회를 제거한다는 것을 입증하였다.

04 Rhetorical Purpose Question

글쓴이는 왜 차익 거래를 언급하는가?
- Ⓐ 효율적 시장 가설 이전에 수익이 어떻게 이해되었는지를 보여주기 위해 ✓
- Ⓑ 효율적인 시장이 작동하는 메커니즘을 설명하기 위해
- Ⓒ 적극적 투자자가 성공할 수 있는 유일한 방법이 차익 거래라고 주장하기 위해
- Ⓓ 초과 수익을 달성하기 위해 정보 격차를 이용하는 방법을 설명하기 위해

05 Detail Question

효율적 시장 가설에 의해 지지되는 투자 전략은?
- Ⓐ 단기 가격 변동을 연구하는 것
- Ⓑ 일시적인 가격 차이를 이용하는 것
- Ⓒ 미래 가격 움직임을 예측하려고 시도하는 것
- Ⓓ 특정 시장 지수의 성과를 추적하는 것 ✓

[06-10]

점박이하이에나 무리

점박이하이에나 무리는 암컷이 수컷보다 상위에 있는 모계 중심의 사회 구조를 전형적으로 보여준다. 이런 집단에서, 지배적인 암컷, 즉 암컷 우두머리는 무리의 이동을 결정하고 먹이에 대한 우선 접근권을 가진다.

점박이하이에나 사회의 핵심 특징은 서열의 세습이다. [07]암컷 새끼들은 어미의 사회적 지위를 점차 물려받고 지배력에서 성체 수컷을 능가한다. 예를 들어, [06]높은 사회적 지위를 지닌 어린 암컷들이 먹이가 있는 자리를 장악하는 모습이 자주 관찰되며, 성체 수컷들은 무리의 화합을 유지하기 위해 마지막에 먹고 암컷에게 도전하는 것을 피하면서 그들에게 양보한다.

[10]하이에나 무리의 모계 서열은 무리의 역학 관계와 생존 전략에 크게 영향을 미친다. 연구자들은 혈연관계의 암컷들이 무리 내에서 강력한 동맹을 형성하여, 갈등 상황이나 외부로부터 영역을 방어할 때 서로를 지원한다는 점을 지적해 왔다. 이들의 리더십은 또한 먹이의 효율적 분배를 보장해, 경쟁을 줄이고 모든 구성원의 생존을 돕는다. 동시에, 높은 서열의 암컷과 그 새끼들은 사체와 사냥감에 대한 우선 접근권을 얻는다. [09]이러한 먹이 확보 가능성은 더 높은 번식 성공, 더 짧은 출산 간격, 더 높은 새끼 생존율로 이어지며, 이는 혈통의 우위를 강화하며 무리의 사회적 안정성을 지탱한다.

clan[klæn] 무리   exemplify[igzémpləfài] 전형적으로 보여주다
matriarchal[mèitriάːrkl] 모계 중심의
dominant[dάmənənt] 지배적인
matriarch[méitriὰːrk] 암컷 우두머리
priority[praiɔ́ːrəti] 우선권   inheritance[inhérətəns] 세습
cub[kʌb] 새끼   inherit[inhérit] 물려받다
dominance[dάːmənəns] 지배력   defer[difə́ːr] 양보하다
distribute[distríbjuːt] 분배하다   carcass[kάːrkəs] 사체
availability[əvèiləbíləti] (확보) 가능성
reproductive[rìːprədʌ́ktiv] 번식의
juvenile[dʒúːvənl] 새끼의, 청소년의

06 Inference Question

하이에나 무리에서 높은 사회적 지위를 가진 암컷 새끼들에 대해 추론할 수 있는 것은?
- Ⓐ 성체 수컷에 대해 권위를 행사한다. ✓
- Ⓑ 무리 내 동맹에 거의 참여하지 않는다.
- Ⓒ 보통 수컷보다 낮은 지위를 가진다.
- Ⓓ 자라면 무리를 떠난다.

어휘 authority[əθɔ́ːrəti] 권위

07 Detail Question

점박이하이에나 무리에서는 서열이 어떻게 결정되는가?
- Ⓐ 나이가 많은 하이에나는 자동으로 더 높은 서열을 얻는다.
- Ⓑ 수컷은 아비로부터 사회적 지위를 물려받는다.
- Ⓒ 암컷 새끼는 어미의 지위를 물려받는다. ✓
- Ⓓ 각 구성원은 신체적 힘에 따라 서열이 매겨진다.

08 Vocabulary Question

두 번째 단락의 단어 "deferring"과 의미상 가장 유사한 것은?
- Ⓐ 매달리는
- Ⓑ 반대하는
- Ⓒ 양보하는 ✓

ⓓ 조언하는

어휘 cling[klíŋ] 매달리다   yield[jiːld] 양보하다

09 Rhetorical Purpose Question
글쓴이는 왜 높은 서열의 암컷들이 더 높은 번식 성공을 보이는 경향이 있다는 것을 언급하는가?
ⓐ 번식 양상이 생태적 적응 메커니즘을 어떻게 반영하는지 보여 주기 위해
☑ⓑ 서열 사회 구조가 무리의 생존에 어떤 이점을 주는지 설명하기 위해
ⓒ 줄어든 경쟁이 모계적 리더십과 상관관계가 있음을 입증하기 위해
ⓓ 성별이 하이에나의 사회적 서열에 영향을 주지 않음을 강조하기 위해

10 Rhetorical Purpose Question
2단락과 3단락의 관계는?
ⓐ 3단락은 2단락에서 언급된 사회적 지위로 인해 발생하는 문제들을 제시한다.
ⓑ 3단락은 2단락에서 언급된 무리 협력에 관한 정보를 확장한다.
ⓒ 3단락은 2단락에서 설명된 사회적 역학 관계의 예외들을 제시한다.
☑ⓓ 3단락은 2단락에서 설명된 사회 구조의 보다 광범위한 영향을 소개한다.

[11-15]

대기천

대기천은 대기 속을 이동하는 길고 좁은 형태의 응축된 수증기 띠로, 길이가 수백에서 수천 킬로미터에 이르는 경우가 많다. 이러한 흐름이 육지에 도달하면, 주로 해안 지역을 따라 막대한 양의 비를 쏟아낼 수 있다. ¹¹대기천과 관련된 집중호우는 캘리포니아와 같은 지역에서 연간 강수량의 상당한 부분을 차지한다.

대기천은 그 극심함과 지역 여건에 따라, 필수적인 수자원 공급원이자 파괴적인 힘으로 기능한다. 수분이 풍부한 이 시스템은 농업 지역에 꼭 필요한 강수를 제공하고 건기 동안 저수지를 다시 채우는 데 도움을 준다. 그러나, 대기천이 더 강해지면, 그것들은 기반 시설에 손해를 입히고, 주민들을 이주시키며, ¹³수십억 달러 규모의 경제적 손실을 초래하는 파괴적인 홍수를 일으킨다. 생명을 유지하는 물을 제공하는 바로 그 현상이 생명을 위협하는 재난으로 바뀔 수 있다.

¹⁴/¹⁵기후 변화는 대기와 해양의 온도를 높이고, 이것은 대기천이 훨씬 더 많은 수분을 운반할 수 있게 함으로써 그 형성을 강화하여 이러한 위험을 증폭시킨다. 과학자들은 강화된 시스템이 육지에 도달함에 따라 더 극단적인 강수 현상이 발생할 것으로 예측한다. 대기천이 점점 더 예측 불가능하고 파괴적으로 변하고 있기 때문에, 물 안보와 홍수 방어의 균형을 맞추기 위해 종합적인 관찰과 적응적 관리 전략이 필수적이다.

atmospheric [ætməsférik] 대기의
concentrated [kɑ́ːnsəntrèitid] 응축된
span [spæn] ~에 이르다, 걸쳐 이어지다
precipitation [prisìpətéiʃən] 강수량   supplier [səpláiər] 공급원
severity [səvérəti] 극심함   laden [léidn] 풍부한, 가득한
replenish [riplénɪʃ] 다시 채우다   reservoir [rézərvwɑːr] 저수지
unleash [ʌnlíːʃ] 일으키다   devastating [dévəstèitiŋ] 파괴적인
displace [displéis] 이주시키다, 쫓아내다
amplify [æmpləfài] 증폭시키다

11 Rhetorical Purpose Question
글쓴이는 왜 캘리포니아를 언급하는가?
ⓐ 전 세계 기후의 최근 변화로 영향받은 지역의 예를 제시하기 위해
☑ⓑ 대기천으로부터 많은 강수를 받는 지역을 강조하기 위해
ⓒ 대기천이 홍수와 재산 피해를 일으킨 장소를 보여 주기 위해
ⓓ 수자원 관리가 특히 중요한 지역을 설명하기 위해

12 Vocabulary Question
지문의 단어 "adaptive"와 의미상 가장 유사한 것은?
☑ⓐ 적응성 있는
ⓑ 엄격한
ⓒ 방어의
ⓓ 관습적인

어휘 rigid [rídʒid] 엄격한, 뻣뻣한
     conventional [kənvénʃənl] 관습적인, 전통적인

13 Detail Question
대기천은 어떻게 위험을 초래할 수 있는가?
ⓐ 오염물질을 장거리로 운반함으로써
ⓑ 더 따뜻한 기온이 기압을 낮추게 함으로써
ⓒ 해양 온도 균형을 교란하는 수분을 운반함으로써
☑ⓓ 해안 지역에 극심한 홍수를 유발함으로써

어휘 pollutant [pəlúːtnt] 오염물질   disrupt [disrʌ́pt] 교란하다

14 Detail Question
대기천이 미래에 더 강해질 것으로 예측되는 이유는?
ⓐ 해양을 가로질러 더 먼 거리를 이동할 것이다.
☑ⓑ 상승하는 해양 온도에 의해 강화될 것이다.
ⓒ 기압 변화로 인해 더 강한 바람 패턴을 만들어 낼 것이다.
ⓓ 현재의 관찰 시스템으로 탐지가 더 어려워질 것이다.

어휘 detectable [ditéktəbl] 탐지가 가능한

15 Rhetorical Purpose Question
다음 중 세 번째 단락의 목적을 가장 잘 설명한 것은?
ⓐ 3단락은 관찰 시스템이 대기천 형성을 어떻게 예측할 수 있는지 분석한다.
ⓑ 3단락은 대기천의 부정적 영향을 완화하기 위한 해결책을 소개한다.
☑ⓒ 3단락은 기후 변화가 대기천의 위험을 증대시키는 메커니즘을 설명한다.
ⓓ 3단락은 대기천의 이로운 측면과 해로운 측면을 대조한다.

어휘 enhance [inhǽns] 증대시키다

[16-20]

Hotelling의 법칙

Hotelling의 법칙은 1929년 경제학자 Harold Hotelling이 제안한 경쟁 이론이다. 이 원리는 장소가 다른 것을 제외하면 동일한 제품을 비슷한 가격에 제공하는 경쟁 기업들이 서로 다른 위치로 분산되기보다는 함께 무리를 이루는 경향이 있는 이유를 설명한다. ¹⁷소비자 수요의 중심 근처에 위치함으로써, 그들은 가능한 한 가장 높은 시장 점유율을 확보하려고 한다.

¹⁸도시에서 커피숍들의 밀집을 생각해 보자. Hotelling의 법칙에

따르면, 각 경쟁자는 지역의 다른 부분에서 접근하는 고객들을 끌어들이기에 최적의 자리를 잡는 것을 목표로 한다. 한 커피숍이 도보로 왕래하는 사람들의 중심에 더 가까이 이동하면, 경쟁업체는 시장 점유율을 잃지 않기 위해 따라서 이동할 것이며, [18]이는 대형 체인점과 지역 커피숍들이 서로 몇 블록 내에 위치하는 도시 상업 지구에서 우리가 관찰하는 군집 현상을 초래한다.

[19]Hotelling의 법칙은 개별적 이익 극대화의 부정적 효과를 보여준다. [20]사회적으로 최적의 해결책은 기업들이 지리적으로 분산되어 소비자 이동 비용을 최소화하고 서비스 위치 선택권을 확대하는 것이지만, [19]경쟁 역학은 기업들이 한 지점으로 모이게끔 만들어, 궁극적으로 전체적인 사회 복지를 감소시킨다.

competition[kàmpətíʃən] 경쟁　theory[θíːəri] 이론
comparable[kámpərəbl] 비슷한　cluster[klʌ́stər] 무리를 이루다
capture[kǽptʃər] 확보하다　market share 시장 점유율
concentration[kàːnsəntréiʃən] 밀집, 집중
optimally[ɑ́ːptəməli] 최적으로　follow suit 따라하다
phenomenon[finɑ́mənən] 현상(pl. phenomena)
adverse effect 부정적 효과
geographically[dʒìːəgrǽfikəli] 지리적으로
convergence[kənvə́ːrdʒəns] 한 지점으로 모임, 수렴

16 Vocabulary Question
지문의 단어 "adverse"와 의미상 가장 유사한 것은?
☑ 해로운
Ⓑ 도움이 되는
Ⓒ 정기적인
Ⓓ 주된

17 Detail Question
기업들이 경쟁업체 근처에 군집하도록 만드는 한 가지 요인은?
Ⓐ 운영 비용을 줄이고자 하는 욕구
Ⓑ 소비자 이동 거리를 최소화해야 하는 필요성
☑ 최대 시장 점유율을 확보하려는 노력
Ⓓ 서비스를 차별화해야 하는 필요조건

어휘　revenue[révənjùː] 수익　distribution[dìstrəbjúːʃən] 분배

18 Rhetorical Purpose Question
두 번째 단락의 목적은?
☑ 군집화의 구체적 사례를 들어 이론적 원리를 설명한다.
Ⓑ 경쟁하는 커피숍들이 사용하는 다양한 사업 모델을 비교한다.
Ⓒ 도시 전체의 커피숍 위치에 대한 통계적 증거를 제시한다.
Ⓓ 상점들이 함께 군집하는 것은 고객들이 접근하기 더 쉽게 만든다는 점을 증명한다.

19 Inference Question
개별적 이익 극대화에 대해 추론할 수 있는 것은?
☑ 소비자에게 가장 유익한 것과 상충할 수 있다.
Ⓑ 모든 경쟁업체의 총 결합 수익을 극대화한다.
Ⓒ 경쟁업체들 간 고객의 균등한 분배를 보장한다.
Ⓓ 최적의 사회적 결과로 이어지는 경향이 있다.

어휘　conflict[kənflíkt] 상충하다　distribution[dìstrəbjúːʃən] 분배

20 Detail Question
기업들이 한 지점으로 모이는 것은 소비자들의 쇼핑 경험에 어떻게 영향을 미치는가?
Ⓐ 소비자들이 필요로 하는 상품을 찾는 것을 더 어렵게 만든다.
Ⓑ 여러 장소에서 이용 가능한 상품의 다양성을 줄인다.
Ⓒ 소비자들이 한 번의 방문으로 다수의 경쟁적인 기업들을 방문할 수 있도록 한다.
☑ 여러 지역에서 서비스를 이용하는 편의성을 제한한다.

5. Rhetorical Purpose Questions

Example　　　　　　　　　　　　　　p.255

장-뇌 상호작용

신경과학의 신흥 분야 중 하나는 장-뇌 상호작용에 초점을 맞추어, 장 신경계가 중추 신경계와 어떻게 소통하는지를 연구한다. 이러한 쌍방향 소통은 신경, 호르몬, 면역 경로를 통해 이루어지며, 기분, 인지, 스트레스 반응에 영향을 미치는 것으로 나타났다. 최근 연구는 장내 미생물군이 혈류로 들어가 뇌 기능에 영향을 줄 수 있는 대사 물질 및 신경전달물질과 비슷한 분자를 생성함으로써, 신경 활동을 형성하는 데 중요한 역할을 할 수 있음을 시사한다.

특히 흥미로운 발견은 장 건강과 정신 건강 상태 간의 관계이다. 미생물 조성의 변화는 우울증과 불안과 같은 질병과 연관되어 있으며, 식단, 프로바이오틱스, 표적 치료를 통해 미생물군을 조절하면 뇌 활동을 변화시킬 수 있음을 시사한다. 동물 연구는 스트레스 받거나 불안한 개체로부터 장내 세균을 옮기면 그것을 받은 개체에서 유사한 행동 패턴이 나타날 수 있음을 보여주며, 이는 인과 관계의 가능성을 제기한다.

향후 연구는 장이 특정 뇌 회로와 행동에 영향을 미치는 메커니즘을 보여주는 것을 목표로 한다. 신경 영상 기술과 분자 분석의 발전은 영양학, 미생물학, 신경과학을 통합한 새로운 치료 전략을 밝힐 것으로 기대된다. 이러한 통합적 관점은 신체와 깊게 연결된 시스템으로서의 뇌에 대한 우리의 이해를 재정의할 수 있다.

emerging[imə́ːrdʒiŋ] 신흥의
neuroscience[njùərousáiəns] 신경과학　gut[gʌt] 장
nervous system 신경계　cognition[kɑːgníʃən] 인지
microbiota[màikroubaiòutə] 미생물군
metabolite[mətǽbəlàit] 대사물질
neurotransmitter[njùəroutrǽnsmítər] 신경전달물질
molecule[mɑ́ːləkjùːl] 분자　alteration[ɔ̀ːltəréiʃən] 변화
disorder[disɔ́ːrdər] 질병　depression[dipréʃən] 우울증
manipulate[mənípjulèit] 조절하다
modulate[mɑ́dʒulèit] 변화시키다　causal[kɔ́ːzəl] 인과적인
circuit[sə́ːrkit] 회로　integrative[íntəgrèitiv] 통합적인

글쓴이는 왜 우울증과 불안을 언급하는가?
Ⓐ 스트레스로 인한 호르몬 변화를 설명하기 위해
Ⓑ 면역 경로와 뇌의 연관성을 제안하기 위해
☑ 장내 미생물군의 변화와 관련된 질환의 예시를 제시하기 위해
Ⓓ 프로바이오틱스의 정신 건강 질환 치료 효과를 강조하기 위해

HACKERS **PRACTICE** p.256

01 ⓒ 02 Ⓐ 03 Ⓐ 04 Ⓓ

01 Rhetorical Purpose Question

디아스포라 공동체는 출신국에서 이주해 새로운 지역에 정착하여, 해외에서 뚜렷한 문화 집단을 형성한 사람들의 집단을 지칭한다. 이러한 공동체는 일반적으로 그들의 본국에서의 경제적 필요와 환경적 압박에 대응하여 만들어진다. 교통 및 통신망은 그 후 이주민들이 해외 공동체와 연결을 형성하고 초국가적 네트워크를 구축할 수 있게 함으로써 지속적인 성장을 촉진한다.

디아스포라 공동체는 새로운 환경에 있는 구성원들을 지원하기 위한 경제적 및 직업적 네트워크를 형성할 수 있다. 예를 들어, 유대인 디아스포라 공동체는 International Association of Jewish Free Loans를 유지한다. 이 네트워크 산하 조직들은 전 세계 유대인들에게 무이자 대출을 제공하여, 기존 이민자들과 새로운 이민자들이 소규모 사업체를 설립하고 주택을 구입하는 것을 돕는다.

migrate[máigreit] 이주하다 necessity[nəsésəti] 필요
facilitate[fəsílətèit] 촉진하다 professional[prəféʃənl] 직업의
organization[ɔ̀ːrgənizéiʃən] 조직 interest[íntərəst] 이자
immigrant[ímigrənt] 이민자

글쓴이는 왜 International Association of Jewish Free Loans를 언급하는가?
Ⓐ 디아스포라 공동체가 적응을 위해 재정 지원에 의존한다는 것을 시사하기 위해
Ⓑ 유대인들이 디아스포라 집단에게 재정 지원을 제공한 최초의 사람들이었다는 것을 보여주기 위해
✓ⓒ 디아스포라 공동체가 구성원들을 위해 지원 네트워크를 어떻게 만드는지를 설명하기 위해
Ⓓ 디아스포라 네트워크가 주택과 소규모 사업체 지원으로 한정된다는 것을 나타내기 위해

02 Rhetorical Purpose Question

1951년, 사회심리학자 Solomon Asch는 동조와 집단 심리에 관한 일련의 실험을 수행했으며, 한 사람이 집단에 동조하라는 압력에 어떤 식으로 영향을 받을 수 있는지를 보여주었다.

실험을 위해, Asch는 일치하는 길이의 두 선을 식별하는 것으로 구성된 단순한 시지각 검사를 위해 학생들을 모집했다. 그러나 각 집단에서 오직 한 명의 참가자만이 진짜 실험 대상이었다. 나머지는 Asch가 때때로 의도적으로 틀린 답을 고르도록 지시한 배우들이었으며, 따라서 **대상들로 하여금 명백히 정확한 답과 틀림에도 불구하고 집단의 의견과 일치하는 답 사이에서 선택하도록 강요했다.**

동조하라는 압력 없이는, 대상들이 1퍼센트 미만의 경우에만 틀리게 선택했다. 그러나 실험 조건에서는, 그 수치가 36퍼센트로 상승했다. **그들의 결정을 설명해달라는 요청을 받았을 때, 대부분은 집단의 반감을 피하고 싶다고 말했고, 보다 소수는 집단의 영향이 그들로 하여금 진정으로 자신들의 믿음을 의심하게 했다고 말했다.**

conduct[kəndʌ́kt] 수행하다 conformity[kənfɔ́ːrməti] 동조
recruit[rikrúːt] 모집하다 perception[pərsépʃən] 지각
subject[sʌ́bdʒikt] 대상 instruct[instrʌ́kt] 지시하다
evidently[évədəntli] 명백히 disapproval[dìsəprúːvəl] 반감
genuinely[dʒénjuinli] 진정으로

2단락과 3단락의 관계는?
✓Ⓐ 3단락은 2단락에서 서술한 실험의 결과를 제시한다.
Ⓑ 3단락은 2단락에서 설명한 실험의 타당성에 의문을 제기한다.
ⓒ 3단락은 2단락에서 논의한 행동에 대한 대안적 설명을 제공한다.
Ⓓ 3단락은 2단락에서 언급한 실험과 관련 없는 새로운 실험을 소개한다.

03 Rhetorical Purpose Question

심해 염수호는 매우 깊은 바다의 고립된 해저 구역에 있는 독특한 환경이다. 이러한 호수들은 염분 농도가 극도로 높은 물을 포함하는데, 이는 그것들이 주변 해수보다 훨씬 밀도가 높게 만든다. 이러한 밀도 차이는 뚜렷한 경계를 만들어내며, 일부가 수중 호수라고 묘사하는 환경을 낳는다. 그것들은 산소 농도가 극도로 낮거나 존재하지 않는 수준이며 많은 형태의 해양 생물에게 매우 유독하다.

이처럼 거주하기 어려운 조건에도 불구하고, 호염성 세균과 고세균과 같은 특정 미생물들은 염수호에서 번성할 수 있다. 이 생물들은 높은 염분과 낮은 산소 수준의 물에서 생존하도록 적응했으며, **그들의 대사 과정은 생명의 한계에 대한 중요한 정보를 드러낼 수 있다. 과학자들은 극한 환경에서 생명이 어떻게 존재할 수 있는지 더 잘 이해하기 위해 이러한 미생물들을 연구한다.**

brine[brain] 염수(소금물) locate[lóukeit] ~에 위치시키다
concentration[kὰːnsəntréiʃən] 농도
dense[dens] 밀도가 높은, 밀집한 boundary[báundəri] 경계
inhospitable[inháspitəbl] 거주하기 어려운
halophilic bacteria 호염성 세균 archaea[ɑːrkíːə] 고세균
thrive[θraiv] 번성하다 metabolic[mètəbálik] 대사의

2단락에 대해 결론지을 수 있는 것은?
✓Ⓐ 특이한 환경의 미생물들이 연구되는 이유를 설명한다.
Ⓑ 해양 연구에서 생명공학 응용의 예를 제시한다.
ⓒ 염수호가 전 지구적 생물지구화학 순환에 기여하는 방식을 묘사한다.
Ⓓ 해양 온도 조절에서 심해 염수호의 역할을 강조한다.

어휘 application[æ̀pləkéiʃən] 응용
biogeochemical[bàioudʒìːoukéməkəl] 생물지구화학적인

04 Rhetorical Purpose Question

호주 동부의 토착종인 오리너구리는 세계에서 가장 특이한 동물 중 하나이다. 젖을 생산하는 능력이 있고 신체에 털이 있기 때문에 포유류로 분류된다. 그러나 오리 같은 부리와 물갈퀴가 있는 발도 가지고 있다. 포유류 중에서 특히 드물게, 알을 낳고 수중에서 먹이의 움직임을 감지하기 위해 전기수용을 사용한다. 수컷 오리너구리는 심지어 뒷다리의 가시에서 독을 생산하며, 이 독을 사용해서 포식자를 막는다.

오리너구리의 존재는 동물 분류와 진화에 대한 우리의 이해 방식에 도전이 되었다. 18세기 말 최초의 오리너구리 표본이 호주에서 영국으로 보내졌을 때, 과학자들은 그것이 조작이라고 생각했다. 그들은 누군가 서로 다른 동물들의 신체 부위를 꿰매어 놓았다고 믿었다. 더 많은 표본이 연구되고 해부되어 오리너구리의 진위가 확인될 때까지 수십 년간 이 회의론이 지속되었다.

platypus[plǽtipəs] 오리너구리 mammal[mǽməl] 포유류
bill[bil] 부리 webbed[webd] 물갈퀴가 있는
electroreception[ilèktrourisépʃən] 전기수용
spur[spəːr] 가시 deter[ditə́ːr] 막다
specimen[spésəmən] 표본 hoax[houks] 조작

sew[sou] 꿰매다   skepticism[sképtəsìzm] 회의론
dissect[daisékt] 해부하다   authenticity[ɔ̀ːθentísəti] 진위

2단락에서 오리너구리 발견의 입증이 얼마나 어려웠는지를 보여주는 문장을 선택하시오.
Ⓐ 오리너구리의 존재는 동물 분류와 진화에 대한 우리의 이해 방식에 도전이 되었다.
Ⓑ 18세기 말 최초의 오리너구리 표본이 호주에서 영국으로 보내졌을 때, 과학자들은 그것이 조작이라고 생각했다.
Ⓒ 그들은 누군가 서로 다른 동물들의 신체 부위를 꿰매어 놓았다고 믿었다.
☑ 더 많은 표본이 연구되고 해부되어 오리너구리의 진위가 확인될 때까지 수십 년 이 회의론이 지속되었다.

HACKERS TEST   p.258

01 Ⓐ	02 Ⓒ	03 Ⓑ	04 Ⓓ	05 Ⓑ
06 Ⓑ	07 Ⓑ	08 Ⓒ	09 Ⓑ	10 Ⓐ
11 Ⓒ	12 Ⓑ	13 Ⓑ	14 Ⓑ	15 Ⓐ
16 Ⓐ	17 Ⓑ	18 Ⓒ	19 Ⓒ	20 Ⓑ

[01-05]

센트럴 파크

맨해튼 중심부에 800에이커가 넘는 면적을 차지하는 뉴욕시의 센트럴 파크는 미국에서 가장 상징적인 도시공원 중 하나이다. 19세기 중반에 구상되어, ⁰¹이 공원은 급격한 도시화와 산업 성장으로 도시 거주자들이 자연 지역에 거의 접근하지 못하게 된 상황에 대한 대응으로 조성되었다. ⁰³Calvert Vaux와 함께 공원을 공동 설계한 Frederick Law Olmsted는 공원이 더 건강하고 더 평등한 도시를 만드는 데 필수적이라고 보았다.

⁰⁴Olmsted와 Vaux는 자연주의적 양식을 채택하여, 목초지, 삼림지, 수역을 포함함으로써 도시 안에서 시골 풍경을 떠올리게 했다. 그들은 또한 구불구불한 산책로, 경관을 조망할 수 있는 지점, 아름다움과 기능을 모두 갖춘 다양한 식재를 계획했다. 이러한 실용과 미학의 균형은 미국 조경 건축의 중요한 발전을 나타냈다.

다양한 배경을 지닌 도시 거주자들에게, 이 공원은 산업화된 도시 생활의 압박으로부터 안도감을 주었다. 그곳의 녹지 공간은 신중한 계획이 공중 보건을 개선하고 지역사회의 복지를 향상할 수 있음을 입증했다. 오늘날, ⁰⁵센트럴 파크는 도시공원 설계자들에게 사례 연구의 대상으로 남아 있으며 조경 설계가 미학과 사회적 혜택을 통해 도시 생활을 어떻게 형성할 수 있는지를 보여주는 지속적인 상징으로 남아 있다.

iconic[aiká:nik] 상징적인   conceive[kənsíːv] 구상하다
urbanization[ə̀ːrbənizéiʃən] 도시화
industrial[indʌ́striəl] 산업의   integral[íntigrəl] 필수적인
democratic[dèməkrǽtik] 평등한   employ[implɔ́i] 채택하다
incorporate[inkɔ́ːrpərèit] 포함하다
meadow[médou] 목초지   evoke[ivóuk] 떠올리게 하다
scenic[síːnik] 경관의   aesthetics[esθétiks] 미학
dweller[dwélər] 거주자   demonstrate[démənstrèit] 입증하다
thoughtful[θɔ́ːtfəl] 신중한

01 Detail Question
센트럴 파크가 건설된 역사적 배경은 무엇이었는가?
☑ 산업 발전과 도시 성장이 가속화되던 시기
Ⓑ 자연 지역 접근이 풍부한 교외 확장 시대
Ⓒ 뉴욕시가 인구가 감소하고 농지가 풍부하던 시기
Ⓓ 전후 재건과 현대 도시 계획이 지배적이던 시기

어휘   context[ká:ntekst] 배경, 전후 사정
       abundant[əbʌ́ndənt] 풍부한

02 Vocabulary Question
첫 번째 단락의 단어 "integral"과 의미상 가장 유사한 것은?
Ⓐ 충분한
Ⓑ 전형적인
☑ 필수적인
Ⓓ 기능적인

어휘   adequate[ǽdikwət] 충분한   typical[típikəl] 전형적인

03 Rhetorical Purpose Question
글쓴이는 왜 Frederick Law Olmsted의 공원에 대한 견해를 언급하는가?
Ⓐ Olmstead가 자연주의적 조경 양식의 창시자였음을 보여주기 위해
☑ 공원 설계의 기초가 된 철학적 이유를 제시하기 위해
Ⓒ Olmsted가 미적 아름다움에만 집중했음을 강조하기 위해
Ⓓ 도시 계획에서 민주적 절차의 중요성을 보여주기 위해

어휘   underlying[ʌ̀ndərlàiiŋ] 기초가 되는

04 Rhetorical Purpose Question
다음 중 2단락의 목적을 가장 잘 설명한 것은?
Ⓐ 2단락은 센트럴 파크에서 파생된 사회적 이점을 상세히 다룬다.
Ⓑ 2단락은 센트럴 파크를 다른 도시 공원들과 비교한다.
Ⓒ 2단락은 센트럴 파크 설립의 목표를 개괄한다.
☑ 2단락은 센트럴 파크의 구체적인 설계 특징을 설명한다.

05 Inference Question
현대의 도시공원에 대해 추론할 수 있는 것은?
Ⓐ 토지 가용성을 극대화하기 위해 도시 외곽에 자주 위치한다.
☑ 센트럴 파크에서 얻은 교훈을 반영하여 설계되는 일이 많다.
Ⓒ 설계와 목적에서 센트럴 파크를 복제하려는 의도로 주로 만들어진다.
Ⓓ 주로 사회적 혜택보다 미적 매력 때문에 가치가 인정된다.

어휘   outskirt[áutskə̀ːrt] 외곽   land availability 토지 가용성
       replicate[réplikèit] 복제하다

[06-10]

침입성 식물

침입성 식물은 원래의 토착 분포 지역 밖으로 퍼지는 식물이다. 이러한 식물이 공격적 성장, 높은 번식률, 지역 해충에 대한 저항성과 같은 특성을 지닐 때, 햇빛, 물, 영양분을 두고 토착 식생을 앞설 수 있다. 침입종은 습지와 숲에서 도시 지역에 이르기까지 다양한 생태계에서 발견될 수 있다. 이들의 존재는 생물의 다양성을 감소시키고, 토양 성분을 변화시키며, 물 순환을 교란할 수 있다.

이러한 식물은 자연 생태계와 인위적으로 관리되는 생태계 모두에 영향을 미친다. 자연 지역에서는 토착 식물 개체군이 줄어들 수 있으며, 이는 그것들에 의존하는 곤충과 동물에도 부정적 영향을 준다. [07]농지에서는 침입성 식물이 통제하기 어려워 곡물 수확량 감소가 자주 발생한다. 일부 종은 홍수 위험을 높이기도 한다. [08]예를 들어, 호장근은 하천 둑을 뒤덮어 물이 쉽게 넘치게 만들고, 털부처꽃은 습지에서 밀집 군락을 형성한다.

[10]침입성 식물은 화물에 실린 씨앗이 무심결에 옮겨지는 것과 같이 [09A]인간 활동의 결과로 확산되는 일이 잦다. 정원의 관상식물이 인근 지역에 새로운 개체군을 형성하는 일도 있다. [09C]동물과 바람은 씨앗을 먼 거리로 흩뜨려 침입성 식물의 확산을 더 돕는다. 게다가, [09D]삼림 벌채와 같은 토지 이용 변화는 침입종에 유리한 환경을 만들 수 있다.

invasive[invéisiv] 침입성의　trait[treit] 특성
reproductive[rìprádʌktiv] 번식의
resistance[rizístəns] 저항성　pest[pest] 해충
outcompete[àutkəmpíːt] (경쟁자를) 앞서다
indigenous[indídʒənəs] 토착의　vegetation[vèdʒətéiʃən] 식생
nutrient[njúːtriənt] 영양분　presence[prézns] 존재
biodiversity[bàioudivə́ːrsəti] 생물 다양성　alter[ɔ́ːltər] 변화시키다
composition[kàːmpəzíʃən] 성분, 구성　disrupt[disrʌ́pt] 교란하다
rely on ~에 의존하다　diminished[dimíniʃt] 감소된
yield[jiːld] 수확량　cargo[káːrgou] 화물
ornamental[ɔ́ːrnəməntl] 관상용의, 장식용의
disperse[dispə́ːrs] 흩뜨리다
deforestation[diːfɔ̀ːristéiʃən] 삼림 벌채

06 Vocabulary Question
지문의 단어 "unintentional"과 의미상 가장 유사한 것은?
Ⓐ 고의의
☑ 우연한
Ⓒ 필요한
Ⓓ 자주 일어나는

어휘　deliberate[dilíbərət] 고의의

07 Detail Question
침입성 식물이 농지에 미치는 영향은 무엇인가?
Ⓐ 더 빠른 토양 침식
☑ 줄어든 곡물 수확량
Ⓒ 수분의 방해
Ⓓ 식물 병해의 전파

어휘　erosion[iróuʒən] 침식　pollination[pàːlənéiʃən] 수분
　　　transmission[trænsmíʃən] 전파

08 Rhetorical Purpose Question
글쓴이는 왜 호장근과 털부처꽃을 언급하는가?
Ⓐ 침입종이 지역 야생동물 개체수를 감소시킨다는 점을 강조하기 위해
Ⓑ 경제적 가치가 있는 특이한 침입성 식물을 소개하기 위해
☑ 특정 침입종이 물에 관련된 위험 요소를 증가시킨다는 것을 보여주기 위해
Ⓓ 일부 침입성 식물이 실제로 농부들에게 이로울 수 있음을 암시하기 위해

09 Detail Question
다음 중 지문에서 침입성 식물 확산의 원인으로 언급되지 않은 것은?
Ⓐ 인간 활동
☑ 계절성 홍수
Ⓒ 동물에 의한 확산
Ⓓ 경관의 변형

어휘　dispersal[dispə́ːrsəl] 확산　modification[màːdəfikéiʃən] 변형

10 Rhetorical Purpose Question
2단락과 3단락의 관계는?
☑ 3단락은 2단락에서 논의된 문제들의 가능한 원인을 설명한다.
Ⓑ 3단락은 2단락에서 묘사된 문제로 인해 영향받는 토착 식물의 예시를 제시한다.
Ⓒ 3단락은 2단락에 언급되지 않은 침입성 식물의 또 다른 부정적 영향을 소개한다.
Ⓓ 3단락은 2단락과 대비되는 침입성 식물의 경제적 이점을 제시한다.

[11-15]

아비투스

아비투스는 프랑스 사회학자 Pierre Bourdieu가 발전시킨 개념이다. 이는 개인이 문화적 및 사회적 경험을 통해 형성하는 깊이 새겨진 습관, 기술, 세상을 인식하는 방식을 가리킨다. [13]아비투스는 일상에서의 무의식적 행동, 사고의 패턴, 선호를 형성하며 비슷한 배경을 가진 사람들이 유사한 행동을 자주 보이는 이유를 설명한다.

아비투스의 친숙한 예는 교실 예절에서 볼 수 있다. 시간 엄수, 조용한 경청, 권위에 대한 존중을 강조하는 가정에서 자란 아이들은 이런 성향을 졸업할 때까지 유지하는 경우가 많다. 이러한 학생들은 교실의 기대를 본능적으로 이해하고 그에 맞춰 적응한다. 반면, 이런 규범에 일찍 노출되지 못한 아이들은 그에 맞추고자 하는 마음이 있더라도 적응에 어려움을 겪을 수 있는데, 이는 아비투스가 의식적인 자각 아래에서 작동한다는 점을 보여준다.

[15]아비투스는 성인기에도 여전히 행동에 영향을 미친다. 예를 들어, 기업 환경에서 일하는 가족에서 성장한 오늘날의 전문직 종사자들은 격식을 차린 비즈니스 환경에서 더 편안함을 느끼고, 네트워킹의 암묵적인 규칙을 이해하며, 상황에 맞는 비즈니스 복장을 선택할 가능성이 높다. [12]아비투스가 만들어내는 이 눈에 보이지 않는 틀은 삶 전반에 걸쳐 선택과 반응을 이끌며, 사회적 지위와 삶의 경험이 개인의 정체성과 집단의 문화적 관습을 어떻게 형성하는지를 반영한다.

sociologist[sòusiáːlədʒist] 사회학자
embed[imbéd] 마음에 새기다
unconscious[ʌ̀nkáːnʃəs] 무의식적인
comparable[kámpərəbl] 유사한
punctuality[pʌ̀ŋktʃuǽləti] 시간 엄수　authority[əθɔ́ːrəti] 권위
retain[ritéin] 유지하다　disposition[dìspəzíʃən] 성향
graduate[grǽdʒuèit] 졸업하다
instinctively[instíŋktivli] 본능적으로
conscious[káːnʃəs] 의식적인　corporate[kɔ́ːrpərət] 기업의
attire[ətáiər] 복장　framework[fréimwə̀rk] 틀, 체계

11 Vocabulary Question
지문의 단어 "dispositions"와 의미상 가장 유사한 것은?
Ⓐ 지시사항
Ⓑ 겉모습

✓ 성향
Ⓓ 자원

어휘 instruction[instrʌ́kʃən] 지시사항
tendency[téndənsi] 성향 resource[risɔ́ːrs] 자원

12 Main Topic Question
지문은 주로 무엇에 대한 것인가?
Ⓐ 아비투스 형성에서 고용 이력의 중요성
✓ 아비투스가 개인과 집단의 행동에 미치는 영향
Ⓒ 아비투스가 학생들의 교실 예절에 미치는 영향
Ⓓ 아비투스 형성에서 정규 공교육의 역할

어휘 public education 공교육

13 Inference Question
유사한 아비투스를 가진 사람들에 대해 추론할 수 있는 것은?
Ⓐ 거의 동일한 개인적 관심사를 발전시킬 수 있다.
Ⓑ 같은 수준의 학업 성취를 이룰 것이다.
✓ 같은 상황에서 유사한 행동을 보이는 경향이 있다.
Ⓓ 결국 공동체에서 동등한 지위에 도달할 수 있다.

14 Rhetorical Purpose Question
2단락에서 아비투스가 개인의 의도적인 행위와는 관계없이 행동을 형성한다는 것을 보여주는 문장을 클릭하시오.
Ⓐ 아비투스의 친숙한 예는 교실 예절에서 볼 수 있다.
Ⓑ 시간 엄수, 조용한 경청, 권위에 대한 존중을 강조하는 가정에서 자란 아이들은 이런 성향을 졸업할 때까지 유지하는 경우가 많다.
Ⓒ 이러한 학생들은 교실의 기대를 본능적으로 이해하고 그에 맞춰 적응한다.
✓ 반면, 이런 규범에 일찍 노출되지 못한 아이들은 그에 맞추고자 하는 마음이 있더라도 적응에 어려움을 겪을 수 있는데, 이는 아비투스가 의식적인 자각 아래에서 작동한다는 점을 보여준다.

15 Rhetorical Purpose Question
3단락에 대해 결론지을 수 있는 것은?
✓ 아비투스의 영향이 청소년기 이후까지 포괄한다는 것을 보여준다.
Ⓑ 성인은 아동보다 아비투스의 영향을 덜 받는다는 것을 보여준다.
Ⓒ 현대 직장 환경을 기반으로 Bourdieu의 이론에 대한 비판을 제시한다.
Ⓓ 전문직 가정이 자녀에게 야망을 심어주는 방식을 설명한다.

어휘 adolescence[ædəlésns] 청소년기 ambition[æmbíʃən] 야망

[16-20]

인류의 조상 Lucy

1974년, 한 인류학자 팀이 에티오피아에서 한 인류 조상(초기 인류)의 화석화된 유해를 발견하였다. 이후 "Lucy"라고 명명된 이 골격은 47개의 뼛조각(전체의 약 40%)으로 이루어져 있었다. 작은 성인 여성으로 추정되는 Lucy는 키가 1미터를 조금 넘었고 무게는 약 29킬로그램이었다. 그녀의 해부학적 구조, 즉 긴 팔과 굽어진 손가락 및 발가락뼈는 그녀가 나무를 오르는 데 적합한 적응력을 유지했음을 시사했다.

Lucy가 발견되기 전, 과학자들은 이족보행(두 발로 곧게 걷기)과 뇌 발달 중 어느 것이 먼저 진화했는지에 대해 논쟁하였다. ¹⁶초기 화석들은 두개골 아래의 뼈가 거의 없는 상태로 발견되는 경우가 많았기 때문에 직립 보행의 시간 순서를 확립하기 어려웠다. ¹⁷Lucy의 골격에서 나온 골반과 다리 조각은 초기 인류 조상이 직립 보행을 했지만 뇌는 작았다는 명확한 증거를 제공함으로써, 이족보행이 큰 뇌 발달보다 먼저 진화했음을 확인시켜 주었다.

¹⁸ᴰ/²⁰Lucy의 발견은 또한 이족보행을 하는 인류 조상이 동아프리카에 320만 년 전 존재했음을 연대 측정함으로써 ¹⁸ᴮ인류 분산 패턴에 대한 인류학적 이해에 핵심적인 증거를 제공하였다. 인류 조상들의 초기 진화의 결정적인 단계를 아프리카 대륙에 둠으로써, ¹⁸ᴬLucy의 발견은 "인류의 요람"으로서 아프리카의 역할을 공고히 하였으며, 인류의 근본 특성의 기원으로서 동아프리카가 갖는 중요성을 강화하였다.

anthropologist[ænθrəpάlədʒist] 인류학자
fossilize[fάːsəlàiz] 화석화하다
hominid[hάːmənid] 인류 조상, 인류(사람과 그 조상을 포함함)
comprise[kəmpráiz] ~으로 이루어지다
estimate[éstəmèit] 추정하다 anatomy[ənǽtəmi] 해부학적 구조
retain[ritéin] 유지하다 adaptation[ædəptéiʃən] 적응
bipedalism[baipédlìzm] 이족보행 pelvis[pélvis] 골반
dispersal[dispə́ːrsəl] 분산 solidify[səlídəfài] 공고히 하다
cradle[kréidl] 요람 reinforce[rìːinfɔ́ːrs] 강화하다

16 Inference Question
Lucy에 관해 추론할 수 있는 것은?
✓ 골격은 이전에 발견된 인류 조상의 골격보다 더 온전했다.
Ⓑ 뇌는 이후의 인류 조상과 비교하여 작았다.
Ⓒ 화석화되었을 때 완전히 성장하지 않은 상태였다.
Ⓓ 나무를 오를 수 없었다.

17 Rhetorical Purpose Question
글쓴이는 왜 골반과 다리 조각을 언급하는가?
Ⓐ Lucy의 골격이 조각난 상태로 발견된 이유를 설명하기 위해서
✓ 인류 조상의 진화 순서를 밝혀낸 증거를 강조하기 위해서
Ⓒ Lucy의 뼛조각들의 크기를 비교하기 위해서
Ⓓ 골반과 다리가 초기 인류에게 중요한 해부학적 구조였음을 보여주기 위해서

18 Detail Question
다음 중 Lucy 발견의 영향으로 언급되지 않은 것은?
Ⓐ 아프리카를 인류의 진화적 발상지로 뒷받침한 것
Ⓑ 인류 조상들의 진화에 대한 인류학적 견해를 재정립한 것
✓ 큰 뇌가 직립 보행보다 먼저 생겨났음을 증명한 것
Ⓓ 이족보행의 연대 측정을 확립한 것

19 Vocabulary Question
지문의 단어 "instrumental"과 의미상 가장 유사한 것은?
Ⓐ 이론적인
Ⓑ 복잡한
✓ 중대한
Ⓓ 설득력 있는

20 Rhetorical Purpose Question
2단락과 3단락의 관계는?
Ⓐ 3단락은 2단락에서 언급된 다른 화석 발견과 Lucy의 발견을 대조한다.

ⓑ 3단락은 2단락에서 제시된 인류 진화에 대한 증거가 추가로 시사하는 바를 설명한다.
ⓒ 3단락은 2단락에서 다루지 않은 대안 이론을 소개한다.
ⓓ 3단락은 2단락에서 시작된 발굴 과정의 연대순 설명을 제시한다.

6. Inference Questions

Example
p.267

유전적 다양성

유전적 다양성은 한 종의 유전적 구성 내에 존재하는 변이의 전체 개수이다. 이러한 다양성은 개체군이 새로운 질병이나 기후 변화와 같은 환경 변화에 대응할 수 있도록 한다. 예를 들어, 한 종 내에서 일부 개체는 특정 질병에 저항력을 갖게 하는 유전자를 지닐 수 있고, 다른 개체는 민감할 수 있다. **이는 어떤 질병이 개체군에 영향을 미칠 때 모든 개체가 똑같은 방식으로 영향받지 않아, 일부 개체가 생존하고 번식할 수 있도록 한다는 의미이다.**

유전적 다양성은 농업에 매우 중요하다. 식물 육종가들은 선택적 육종을 이용하여 높은 수확량과 같이 원하는 형질을 가진 작물을 개발한다. 이는 흔히 유전적 균일성을 초래하는데, 유전적 균일성은 전체 작물을 새로운 질병에 매우 취약하게 만든다. 일례로, 1970년 미국에서 발생한 남부 옥수수 잎마름병은 옥수수 수확량의 절반 이상을 파괴했는데 대부분의 상업용 옥수수가 취약한 유전적 기반을 공유했기 때문이다.

이러한 손실을 막기 위해, 과학자들은 유전자은행에 보관된 광범위한 유전적 다양성을 적극적으로 활용한다. 이 시설들은 야생종을 포함하여 수천 가지 식물 품종의 씨앗을 보관하고 있다. 연구자들은 이 다양성을 연구하여 저항성이 있는 유전자를 식별하고, 육종을 통해 이를 상업용 작물에 도입함으로써 미래의 위협에 대비하는 중요한 유전적 방어 체계를 구축하고 있다.

genetic[dʒənétik] 유전적인 diversity[daivə́ːrsəti] 다양성
sensitive[sénsətiv] 민감한 reproduce[rìːprədjúːs] 번식하다
agriculture[ǽgrəkʌ̀ltʃər] 농업
desirable[dizáiərəbl] 원하는, 바람직한 yield[jiːld] 수확량
uniformity[jùːnəfɔ́ːrməti] 균일성
vulnerable[vʌ́lnərəbl] 취약한 blight[blait] 잎마름병, 병충해
maize[meiz] 옥수수 susceptible[səséptəbl] 취약한
foundation[faundéiʃən] 기반 utilize[júːtəlàiz] 활용하다

유전적 다양성이 높은 종에 대해 추론할 수 있는 것은?
Ⓐ 자연적으로 더 높은 수확량을 낸다.
Ⓑ 질병이 그 종의 일부만을 공격하기 때문에 살아남는다. ✓
Ⓒ 다양한 번식 및 교배 패턴을 보인다.
Ⓓ 환경 변화에 더 취약하다.

HACKERS PRACTICE
p.268

01 Ⓓ   02 Ⓓ   03 Ⓐ   04 Ⓓ

01 Inference Question

약 300만 년 전까지, 최상위 해양 포식자는 *Carcharocles megalodon*이라고 불리는 18미터 길이의 상어였다. 이 종의 종말은 여러 요인에 기인한다. 최초 촉발 요인은 지구 바다의 냉각이었는데, 메갈로돈은 연안 열대 해역에 적응해 있었기 때문이다. 이 종이 존재했던 대부분의 기간 동안, 지구에는 다양한 해양 생물을 부양하는 따뜻하고 얕은 바다의 면적이 광대했는데, 이는 메갈로돈에게 완벽한 사냥터였다. 그러나 지구 대륙의 움직임이 바다를 변화시키기 시작했고, 전반적인 냉각 경향과 그것에 동반하는 메갈로돈에게 적합한 서식지의 감소를 초래했다.

메갈로돈이 끝내 새로운 조건에 적응했을 수도 있지만, 그 동물은 다른 어려움들에도 직면했다. 무엇보다 중요하게, **주요 먹이인 수염고래와 다른 중간 크기의 고래들도 지구 냉각으로 인해 개체수가 감소하기 시작했다.** 존재했다고 알려진 20종 중에서, 14종이 이 기간 사라졌다. 동시에 현대 범고래의 조상과 같은 새로운 포식자들이 나타났으며, 이들은 메갈로돈이 식량으로 의존했던 해양 종들을 공격적으로 사냥했다.

apex[éipeks] 최상위, 정점 demise[dimáiz] 종말
attribute[ətríbjuːt] ~에 기인한다고 본다 factor[fǽktər] 요인
catalyst[kǽtəlist] 촉발 요인, 촉매 swath[swɑθ] 면적
shallow[ʃǽlou] 얕은 landmass[lǽndmæs] 대륙
corresponding[kɔ̀ːrəspɑ́ndiŋ] 상응하는, 대응하는
reduction[ridʌ́kʃən] 감소 suitable[súːtəbl] 적합한
habitat[hǽbitæt] 서식지 prey[prei] 먹이
baleen whale 수염고래 predator[prédətər] 포식자
orca[ɔ́ːrkə] 범고래 nourishment[nə́ːriʃmənt] 식량

수염고래에 대해 추론할 수 있는 것은?
Ⓐ 새로운 먹이를 찾아 이주했다.
Ⓑ 다른 종류의 고래들을 경쟁에서 이겼다.
Ⓒ 여러 독특한 종들로 분화했다.
Ⓓ 기후 변화에 적응하지 못했다. ✓

02 Inference Question

영지식 증명(ZKP)은 암호학의 개념으로, 특정한 사실을 알고 있음을 그 사실에 관한 어떠한 정보도 드러내지 않고 증명할 수 있게 해준다. **이 발상은 전자 투표에서 암호화폐에 이르기까지, 디지털 시스템에서 개인 데이터가 관리되고 보호되는 방식을 탈바꿈시켰다.**

영지식이란 검증자가 오직 그 명제가 참이라는 사실만 알 뿐, 다른 어떤 정보도 배우지 않는 것을 의미한다. Alice와 Bob이 있는 상황을 생각해 보자. Alice는 금고의 비밀번호를 알고 있다고 주장하지만, Bob은 그 비밀번호를 모른다. Alice의 주장을 증명하기 위해, Bob은 Alice에게 비밀번호를 공개하지 않고 금고를 열어 보라고 요청한다. Alice는 금고를 열고, Bob에게 금고가 열렸음을 보여준 뒤, 다시 닫는다. Bob은 그 자신이 비밀번호가 무엇인지는 모른 채, 그녀가 실제로 비밀번호를 알고 있다는 사실을 확신하게 된다.

proof[pruːf] 증명 cryptography[kriptɑ́grəfi] 암호학
verifier[vérəfàiər] 검증자
combination[kɑ̀mbənéiʃən] 비밀번호, 자물쇠의 숫자 배합
safe[seif] 금고 convince[kənvíns] 확신시키다

영지식 증명에 대해 추론할 수 있는 것은?
Ⓐ 원래 전자 투표를 위해 개발되었다.
Ⓑ 작동하기 위해 부분적 정보 공개를 필요로 한다.
Ⓒ 특정 유형의 사실 진술로 한정된다.
Ⓓ 그저 지식을 증명하는 것 이상의 활용처들이 있다. ✓

어휘 partial[pɑ́ːrʃəl] 부분적인

03 Inference Question

텔로미어는 보호 역할을 하는 DNA-단백질 구조로서 염색체 끝에 있으며 세포 노화를 가리키는 분자 시계 역할을 한다. 이 구조들은 세포가 분열할 때마다 짧아지며, 세포가 복제할 수 있는 횟수를 제한한다. 텔로미어가 너무 짧아지면, 세포들은 손상 신호를 켜고 휴지 상태에 들어가거나 자멸한다. 최근 연구는 텔로미어 길이가 외부 요인들에 강한 영향을 받는다는 것을 보여준다. **만성 스트레스, 나쁜 식단, 그리고 많이 움직이지 않는 생활 방식은 단축을 상당히 가속화한다.**

텔로머라제 효소는 DNA를 추가함으로써 텔로미어의 길이를 유지한다. 텔로머라제는 줄기세포의 증식 능력을 유지하기 때문에, 조직 퇴행으로 인한 연령 관련 질병들을 표적으로 하는 치료법이 될 잠재력을 가지고 있다. 동시에, 암세포들은 자신들의 한계 없는 복제를 지원하기 위해 텔로머라제를 악용할 수 있으며, 이는 종양 형성으로 이어진다. 따라서 건강한 노화와 장수를 위한 개입에 대해 장래성 있는 통찰을 제공하는 텔로머라제 활성제에 대한 현재 임상시험들은 암 위험이 면밀히 모니터링되고 평가되어야 한다.

- chromosome[króuməsòum] 염색체
- molecular[məlékjulər] 분자의   cellular[séljulər] 세포의
- replicate[répləkèit] 복제하다
- self-destruct[sèlfdistrʌ́kt] 자멸하다   chronic[kránik] 만성의
- sedentary[sédntèri] 많이 움직이지 않는
- maintain[meintéin] 유지하다   proliferative[prəlífərèitiv] 증식의
- capacity[kəpǽsəti] 능력   potential[pəténʃəl] (~이 될) 잠재력
- exploit[iksplɔ́it] 악용하다   indefinite[indéfənit] 한계가 없는
- activator[ǽktəvèitər] 활성제   longevity[lɑːndʒévəti] 장수
- intervention[ìntərvénʃən] 개입   evaluate[ivǽljuèit] 평가하다

텔로미어에 대해 추론할 수 있는 것은?
- ✓ⓐ 길이는 생활습관 요인에 따라 달라진다.
- ⓑ 가능한 분열 횟수는 세포 종류에 따라 달라진다.
- ⓒ 스트레스 상황에서 세포가 계속 분열하도록 신호를 보낼 수 있다.
- ⓓ 자연적인 노화 과정을 늦추는 데 도움을 준다.

04 Inference Question

준사회적 관계는 사람들이 허구의 인물을 포함한 미디어 속 인물들과 형성하는 일방적인 감정적 유대이다. 이러한 관계는 사람들이 반복적으로 어떤 인물을 보거나, 듣거나, 또는 그에 대해 읽을 때 시작되는 경우가 많다. 시간이 지나면서, 그들은 연결되어 있다는 뚜렷한 느낌이 생겨나고, 직접적인 상호작용이 없음에도 불구하고 그 인물과 잘 아는 사이라고 믿기까지 한다.

이러한 관계에는 몇 가지 문제점이 있을 수 있다. 그것은 고립 또는 현실 세계의 연결에 대한 비현실적인 기대로 이어질 수 있다. 극단적인 경우, 사람들은 자신이 동경하는 인물들에 대한 이야기에 지나치게 몰두하여 현실의 사회적 관계를 소홀히 할 수 있다.

그러나 긍정적인 효과도 있을 수 있다. 준사회적 유대는 위안을 제공하고, 외로움을 줄이며, 자존감을 높일 수 있다. 이는 특히 가까운 친구나 가족 구성원들로부터 도움을 받지 못하는 사람들에게 해당된다. 또한, 사람들은 자신이 좋아하는 인물들을 역할 모델로 여기거나, 그들의 이야기에서 영감을 얻거나, 또는 사회적 상황들을 탐구하는 안전한 방법으로 그들을 이용할 수 있다.

- fictional[fíkʃənl] 허구의   drawback[drɔ́ːbæ̀k] 문제점
- isolation[àisəléiʃən] 고립   expectation[èkspektéiʃən] 기대
- absorbed[æbsɔ́ːbd] 몰두한, 열중한
- neglect[niglékt] 소홀히 하다   inspiration[ìnspəréiʃən] 영감

친구나 가족 구성원들의 도움을 받지 못하는 사람들에 대해 추론할 수 있는 것은?
- ⓐ 준사회적 관계를 형성할 가능성이 낮다.
- ⓑ 준사회적 관계를 위험하다고 여길 수 있다.
- ⓒ 일방적인 관계를 피하는 경향이 있다.
- ✓ⓓ 준사회적 유대의 긍정적인 효과를 경험할 수 있다.

HACKERS TEST p.270

01 ⓑ	02 ⓑ	03 ⓒ	04 ⓑ	05 ⓓ
06 ⓑ	07 ⓓ	08 ⓐ	09 ⓒ	10 ⓑ
11 ⓒ	12 ⓑ	13 ⓓ	14 ⓒ	15 ⓒ
16 ⓒ	17 ⓑ	18 ⓑ	19 ⓓ	20 ⓑ

[01-05]

파레이돌리아

01**파레이돌리아는 뇌가 무작위 패턴이나 사물 속에서, 특히 얼굴과 같이 알아볼 수 있는 형태를 빠르게 인지하는 현상이다.** 연구에 따르면 01**파레이돌리아는 뇌의 패턴 인식 체계가 과민해져, 모호한 시각적 자극을 의미 있는 대상으로 잘못 해석하도록 신경 경로가 작동할 때 발생한다.** 이러한 02**인지적 지름길은 저장된 기억과 기대를 바탕으로 누락된 정보를 뇌가 "채워 넣도록" 만든다.**

파레이돌리아의 유명한 사례로, 1976년 NASA의 바이킹 우주 탐사선이 화성 표면 사진을 전송했을 때 발생한 "화성의 얼굴"이라 불리는 사건이 있다. 그 이미지에는 거대한 사람 얼굴처럼 보이는 형상이 나타나, 화성 생명체 존재에 대한 대중의 광범위한 추측을 불러일으켰다. 이후, 다른 조명 조건에서 촬영된 더 높은 화질의 사진들은 04**그것이 지구에서도 흔한 일종의 암석 지형인 메사임을 밝혀냈다.** 그럼에도 불구하고, 이 사건은 전 세계적 관심을 끌었고 외계 지적 생명체의 존재 가능성에 대한 논의를 부추겼다.

진화론적 관점에서, 05**파레이돌리아는 생존 상의 이점 때문에 발달했을 가능성이 크다.** 얼굴을 감지하는 데 매우 민감했던 우리 조상들은 사회적 동맹자와 잠재적 포식자를 더 잘 식별할 수 있었다. 이 과민한 얼굴 탐지 체계는 유익한 "거짓 양성"을 만들었는데, 존재하지 않는 얼굴을 가끔 보는 것이 실제 얼굴을 놓치는 것보다는 나았다.

- phenomenon[finámənàn] 현상(pl. phenomena)
- perceive[pərsíːv] 인지하다, 지각하다
- recognizable[rékəgnàizəbl] 알아볼 수 있는
- recognition[rèkəgníʃən] 인식   ambiguous[æmbígjuəs] 모호한
- stimulus[stímjuləs] 자극(pl. stimuli)
- cognitive[kágnətiv] 인지적인   shortcut[ʃɔ́rtkʌ̀t] 지름길
- probe[proub] 우주 탐사선   Martian[máːrʃən] 화성의
- speculation[spèkjuléiʃən] 추측
- high-definition[háidèfəníʃən] 높은 화질의
- incident[ínsidənt] 사건   fuel[fjuəl] 부추기다
- extraterrestrial[èkstrətəréstriəl] 외계의
- intelligence[intélədʒəns] 지적 생명체
- perspective[pərspéktiv] 관점   sensitive[sénsətiv] 민감한
- ally[əlái] 동맹자   potential[pəténʃəl] 잠재적인
- predator[prédətər] 포식자

01 Detail Question
파레이돌리아는 왜 발생하는가?
- Ⓐ 사람들은 환경에서 적극적으로 패턴을 찾는다.
- ✅ 뇌는 익숙한 형태를 빠르게 인식하는 경향이 있다.
- Ⓒ 과도하게 저장된 기억이 모호한 시각 정보를 왜곡한다.
- Ⓓ 뇌는 무작위 패턴을 처리할 수 없다.

어휘 distort[distɔ́ːrt] 왜곡하다

02 Rhetorical Purpose Question
글쓴이는 왜 "지름길"을 언급하는가?
- Ⓐ 파레이돌리아가 특정한 사람들에게만 발생하는 이유를 설명하기 위해
- ✅ 파레이돌리아의 이면에 있는 정신적 메커니즘을 설명하기 위해
- Ⓒ 파레이돌리아가 학습된 반응임을 암시하기 위해
- Ⓓ 기대와 기억 사이의 연관성을 보여주기 위해

어휘 learned[lɔ́ːrnid] 학습된 expectation[èkspektéiʃən] 기대

03 Vocabulary Question
지문의 단어 "ambiguous"와 의미상 가장 유사한 것은?
- Ⓐ 구체적인
- Ⓑ 잘못된
- ✅ 불분명한
- Ⓓ 진품인

어휘 specific[spisífik] 구체적인 incorrect[ìnkərékt] 잘못된

04 Detail Question
더 높은 화질의 사진들은 "화성의 얼굴"에 대해 무엇을 밝혀냈는가?
- Ⓐ 대기 조건으로 인한 그림자였다.
- ✅ 지구에서도 발견되는 지질학적 지형이었다.
- Ⓒ 바람에 의해 형성된 모래 지형이었다.
- Ⓓ 화산의 용암류로 인해 만들어진 무늬였다.

05 Inference Question
파레이돌리아에 대해 추론할 수 있는 것은?
- Ⓐ 인간이 첨단 기술을 개발하면서 덜 중요해졌다.
- Ⓑ 증가한 뇌 크기의 부산물로 나타났다.
- Ⓒ 주로 예술적 및 창의적 목적에 유용했다.
- ✅ 위협과 동맹자를 감지하는 데 도움을 주었다.

어휘 byproduct[báiprɑ̀ːdəkt] 부산물

[06-10]

> **중국어 방**
>
> 철학자 John Searle이 고안한 중국어 방 사고 실험은 컴퓨터가 진정으로 언어를 이해하는지, 아니면 단지 기계적으로 기호를 처리하는 것뿐인지 의문을 제기하도록 설계되었다. 이 시나리오에서는, 중국어를 하지 못하는 한 사람이 방 안에 앉아 있다. [06]이 사람은 중국어로 쓰인 질문을 받고 지침서를 사용해 올바른 중국어 기호를 답으로 선택한다. 외부인에게, 그 답변은 유창해 보이지만, 이 사람은 그 언어를 이해하지 못한다. [09]Searle은 이 사람이 의미가 아니라 규칙에 따라 기호를 조작할 뿐이라고 주장한다.
>
> 이 주장은 여러 반응을 낳았다. [07A]어떤 철학자들은 개인이 중국어를 이해하지 못하더라도 방, 사람, 지침서로 이루어진 전체 체계가 언어를 이해하는 정신을 구성한다고 주장한다. [07B]다른 이들은 진정한 이해를 발전시키려면 그 전체 체계가 외부 세계와 상호작용을 할 수 있어야 한다고 제안한다. [07C]또 다른 반응은 그 체계가 인간 뇌의 정확한 생물학적 과정을 복제한다면 중국어에 대한 진정한 이해가 나타날 것이라고 제안한다.
>
> [10]중국어 방 사고 실험은 인공지능(AI)의 핵심 논쟁을 강조하는데, 계산 과정만으로 진정한 이해나 의식을 만들 수 있는지다. 인공지능 시스템은 의식적 자각 없이도 유창한 응답을 만들어낸다. 기술이 발전함에 따라, 진정한 이해와 정교한 기호 조작을 구분하는 일이 중요해진다.

mechanically[məkǽnikəli] 기계적으로 fluent[flúːənt] 유창한
manipulate[mənípjuleit] 조작하다
instruction[instrʌ́kʃən] 지침서 constitute[kánstətjùːt] 구성하다
genuine[dʒénjuin] 진정한 replicate[réplikèit] 복제하다
biological[bàiəláːdʒikəl] 생물학적인 emerge[imɔ́ːrdʒ] 나타나다
computational[kàːmpjutéiʃənl] 계산의
conscious[kánʃəs] 의식적인 distinguish[distíŋgwiʃ] 구분하다
sophisticated[səfístəkèitid] 정교한

06 Detail Question
중국어 방 사고 실험에서 지침서는 무슨 역할을 하는가?
- Ⓐ 사람이 중국어를 유창하게 말하도록 가르친다.
- ✅ 기호를 답으로 선택하는 규칙을 제공한다.
- Ⓒ 사람이 질문을 중국어로 번역하는 데 도움을 준다.
- Ⓓ 사람의 답변에서 오류를 수정한다.

07 Detail Question
다음 중 지문에서 Searle의 주장에 대한 반응으로 언급된 것이 아닌 것은?
- Ⓐ 이해는 단일 구성 요소가 아니라 전체 시스템에서 발생한다.
- Ⓑ 현실 세계와의 상호작용이 이해로 이어질 수 있다.
- Ⓒ 뇌의 생물학적 과정을 복제하면 이해에 도달할 수 있다.
- ✅ 여러 시스템의 협력으로 이해가 발생할 수 있다.

어휘 collaboration[kəlæ̀bəréiʃən] 협력

08 Vocabulary Question
두 번째 단락의 단어 "constitutes"와 의미상 가장 유사한 것은?
- ✅ 구성하다
- Ⓑ 대표하다
- Ⓒ 간주하다
- Ⓓ 설명하다

어휘 represent[rèprizént] 대표하다

09 Inference Question
컴퓨터와 이해에 관한 Searle의 견해에 대해 추론할 수 있는 것은?
- Ⓐ 계산적 과정만으로도 진정한 이해에 충분하다고 믿는다.
- Ⓑ 모든 계산 시스템이 깊은 이해를 할 수 있다고 주장한다.
- ✅ 컴퓨터가 기계적인 규칙을 넘어 진정으로 이해한다고 보지 않는다.
- Ⓓ 인공지능에서 단순한 규칙 기반 시스템의 사용을 거부한다.

10 Rhetorical Purpose Question
글쓴이는 왜 인공지능을 언급하는가?
- Ⓐ 컴퓨터를 사용한 이해에 대한 폭넓은 관심을 보여주기 위해

ⓑ 진행 중인 논의에서 중국어 방 사고 실험의 중요성을 강조하기 위해
ⓒ 중국어 방 사고 실험이 현대 인공지능에 미친 영향을 강조하기 위해
ⓓ 언어 처리를 위해 사용되는 현대 기술을 소개하기 위해

어휘 relevance[réləvəns] 중요성, 관련성
contemporary[kəntémpərèri] 현대의, 동시대의

[11-15]

여객 제트기의 역사

여객 제트기의 역사는 진보와 발전의 서사를 반영한다. 제트 시대 이전에, 상업적 항공 여행은 느린 프로펠러 항공기에 의존했다. 1952년에, De Havilland Comet이 최초의 상업용 제트기로서 운항을 시작했으며, 더 짧은 비행시간과 더 큰 편안함을 제공할 것으로 기대되었다.

그러나 Comet을 둘러싼 초기의 열광은 곧 심각한 안전 우려로 바뀌었다. 불과 몇 년 사이에, Comet은 여러 건의 비극적인 사고를 겪었다. ¹¹**반복적인 객실 가압과 결함 있는 창문 설계는 금속 피로를 야기했고**, 그 결과 비행 중 파열로 이어졌다. 이러한 사건들은 여객 제트기에 대한 대중의 신뢰를 심각하게 약화시켰다.

🅐 Comet으로부터의 교훈은 보다 신뢰할 수 있는 제트기의 등장을 위한 길을 열어주었다. 🅑 그중 하나인 Boeing 707은 1958년에 운항을 시작했으며, 현대의 제트기에 비해 규모는 작았지만, 항공사들에 의해 널리 채택되었다. 🅒 이 성공은 제트기 여행의 안전성과 수익성을 확고히 정립하여, 이후 세대의 대형 상업용 항공기들이 등장할 수 있는 발판을 마련했다. 1970년대에, ¹³**최초의 광동체 여객기인 Boeing 747이 운항을 시작했다.** 🅓 광동체 제트기의 등장은 항공 산업뿐만 아니라 세계적 연결성까지 변화시켜, 국제 관광과 무역을 훨씬 더 수월하게 만들었다.

오늘날, 여객 제트기는 계속 진화하고 있다. ¹⁴**탄소섬유 복합체와 같은 새로운 소재는 기체 구조를 더 가볍고 더 강하게 만들었고**, 더 조용하면서도 더 강력한 엔진은 승객의 편안함을 개선했다. 이러한 혁신은 앞으로 세계 운송의 미래를 빚어갈 것이다.

passenger[pǽsəndʒər] 여객   commercial[kəmə́:rʃəl] 상업적인
rely on ~에 의존하다   initial[iníʃəl] 초기의
excitement[iksáitmənt] 열광   catastrophic[kæ̀təstráfik] 비극적인
pressurization[prèʃərəzéiʃən] 가압   flawed[flɔːd] 결함 있는
fatigue[fətíːg] 피로   rupture[rʌ́ptʃər] 파열
undermine[ʌ̀ndərmáin] 약화시키다   pave the way 길을 열다
reliable[riláiəbl] 신뢰할 수 있는   adopt[ədʌ́pt] 채택하다
connectivity[kɑ̀ːnektívəti] 연결성   fiber[fáibər] 섬유
composite[kəmpázit] 복합체
transportation[træ̀nspərtéiʃən] 운송

11 Detail Question

De Havilland Comet 제트기에 영향을 미친 한 가지 중대한 문제는 무엇이었는가?
ⓐ 결함 있는 설계로 인한 엔진 고장
ⓑ 항공기 날개의 구조적 약점
✅ 반복적인 가압으로 인한 금속 피로
ⓓ 전자 항법 장치의 오작동

12 Vocabulary Question

지문의 단어 "undermined"와 의미상 가장 유사한 것은?
ⓐ 지연시켰다
✅ 약화시켰다
ⓒ 간과했다
ⓓ 정당화했다

어휘 justify[dʒʌ́stəfài] 정당화하다

13 Inference Question

Boeing 747에 대해 추론할 수 있는 것은?
ⓐ 주로 국내선에 집중했다.
ⓑ 이전의 제트기보다 더 먼 거리를 비행할 수 있었다.
ⓒ 이전 모델들만큼의 좋은 평가를 받지 못했다.
✅ 이전 기종들보다 더 컸다.

어휘 domestic[dəméstik] 국내의

14 Rhetorical Purpose Question

글쓴이는 왜 탄소 섬유 복합체를 언급하는가?
ⓐ 소재 혁신이 승객의 편안함을 향상한다는 것을 제시하기 위해
ⓑ 현대 제트기가 구형 모델보다 더 비싼 이유를 설명하기 위해
✅ 항공기를 더 가볍고 강하게 만든 혁신을 구체적으로 명시하기 위해
ⓓ 항공기 제작의 환경적 지속 가능성을 강조하기 위해

어휘 environmental[invàiərənméntl] 환경의
sustainability[səstèinəbíləti] 지속 가능성

15 Insertion Question

다음 문장이 삽입될 수 있는 네 곳이 지문에 표시되어 있다.

이 성공은 제트기 여행의 안전성과 수익성을 확고히 정립하여, 이후 세대의 대형 상업용 항공기들이 등장할 수 있는 발판을 마련했다.

그 문장은 어디에 가장 적절한가? 그 문장이 삽입될 수 있는 곳을 고르시오.

[16-20]

피구세

피구세는 기업 활동이 사회의 다른 구성원들에게 의도하지 않은 비용을 발생시킬 때 실질적인 해결책을 제공한다. ¹⁶예를 들어, 공장들은 상품 제조 비용은 고려하지만 유해한 오염물질 배출을 통해 대중에게 가하는 건강 및 환경적 부담에 대해 책임질 의무는 없다. 이러한 간접적 영향들은 외부효과라고 불리며, ¹⁸생산 비용에 반영되지 않고 대신 대중이 감당한다.

¹⁶/²⁰**피구세는 기업이나 개인이 그들이 발생시키는 더 광범위한 비용에 대해 재정적 책임을 지도록 함으로써 이러한 문제를 해결한다.** 추산되는 피해와 동일하게 세금을 설정하는 것은 시장 효율성을 유지하게끔 보장하는 동시에 생산자와 소비자가 더 큰 공익을 위해 해로운 관행을 포기하도록 장려한다. 이 메커니즘은 탄소 배출을 발생시키는 제조업체, 또는 상점에서 비닐봉지를 선택하는 개인에게 세금을 부과하기 위해 정부에 의해 널리 사용된다.

¹⁹/²⁰**외부효과는 예방접종과 같은 긍정적인 경우에서도 나타날 수 있는데, 이는 질병 확산을 줄이고 개인의 의료 필요성을 낮춤으로써 지역사회의 모든 사람에게 간접적으로 이익을 준다.** 백신과 같은 사회적으로 유익한 제품의 경우, 이러한 상품을 보다 저렴하고 따라서 이용하기 쉽게 만드는 피구 보조금은 사적 이익을 사회 복지와 일치시킨다.

practical[prǽktikəl] 실질적인   burden[bə́ːrdn] 부담
pollutant[pəlúːtnt] 오염물질

externality[èkstəːrnǽləti] 외부효과 bear[bɛər] 감당하다
financially[finǽnʃəli] 재정적으로
responsible[rispánsəbl] 책임지는 abandon[əbǽndən] 포기하다
emission[imíʃən] 배출 opt for 선택하다
emerge[imə́ːrdʒ] 나타나다 vaccination[væksənéiʃən] 예방접종
subsidy[sʌ́bsədi] 보조금 affordable[əfɔ́ːrdəbl] 저렴한
accessible[æksésəbl] 이용(접근)하기 쉬운

16 Detail Question

피구세의 주 기능은 무엇인가?
Ⓐ 생산 비용의 불확실성을 줄여 시장을 안정화하기
Ⓑ 예방접종과 같은 긍정적 외부효과를 위한 정부 예산을 늘리기
✓ 사회적 비용을 발생시키는 자들이 그들의 영향에 대해 책임지도록 하기
Ⓓ 기업이 운영을 확장하도록 재정적 인센티브를 제공하기

어휘 uncertainty[ənsə́ːrtənti] 불확실성

17 Vocabulary Question

지문의 단어 "practical"과 의미상 가장 유사한 것은?
Ⓐ 이상적인
✓ 현실적인
Ⓒ 공정한
Ⓓ 비판적인

18 Inference Question

생산 비용에 대해 추론할 수 있는 것은?
Ⓐ 흔히 환경 비용을 포함한다.
✓ 사회에 대한 실제 비용을 완전히 반영하지는 않는다.
Ⓒ 정부 결정에 의해 설정된다.
Ⓓ 소비자에게 필요한 것보다 높다.

19 Detail Question

예방접종이 외부효과를 가진다고 여겨지는 이유는?
Ⓐ 정부가 공공 의료에 투자할 필요를 없애기 때문이다
Ⓑ 백신 생산자가 시장에서 충분한 이익을 받도록 보장하기 때문이다
Ⓒ 예방접종을 선택한 사람들의 의료비를 낮추기 때문이다
✓ 예방접종을 받은 개인을 넘어서 전체 지역사회에 이익을 주기 때문이다

20 Rhetorical Purpose Question

2단락과 3단락의 관계는?
Ⓐ 3단락은 공중보건 위험에 초점을 맞추는 반면 2단락은 환경 비용을 강조한다.
✓ 3단락은 긍정적 외부효과를 설명하는 반면 2단락은 부정적 외부효과에 초점을 맞춘다.
Ⓒ 3단락은 피구 정책의 결함을 지적하는 반면 2단락은 그 적용을 설명한다.
Ⓓ 3단락은 더 광범위한 사회적 이익을 소개하는 반면 2단락은 개인을 다룬다.

7. Insertion Questions

Example
p.279

문학이 개인에게 미치는 영향

문학은 개인에게 깊은 영향력을 행사하며, 그들의 생각, 감정, 세계관을 오래가는 방식으로 형성한다. 사람들이 소설, 시, 수필을 읽을 때, 그들은 자신의 경험을 반영하는 등장인물과 상황을 만나거나 완전히 새로운 관점을 접하게 된다. 복잡한 이야기에 몰입함으로써 독자들은 다른 사람들, 심지어는 자신과 매우 다른 사람들의 동기와 감정까지 이해하며 공감을 발전시킨다. 규칙적인 독서는 정서적 지능을 향상시켜 사람들이 일상에서 타인과 더 효과적으로 연결되도록 한다.

문학은 개인적 성찰의 강력한 도구 역할 또한 한다. 독자들은 읽는 이야기 속에서 자신의 고통을 발견할 수 있으며, 이는 어려운 시기에 위로와 통찰을 제공할 수 있다. 문학적 요소를 해석하는 과정은 비판적 사고를 촉진하여 독자들이 자신의 신념과 관점을 재고하게 만든다. **A** 많은 사람이 문학이 슬픔을 극복하고, 편견을 없애거나, 새로운 포부를 찾도록 도와주었다고 말한다. **B** **이러한 경험은 문학이 실질적인 차원에서 성장을 가능하게 하는 힘을 지녔음을 보여준다.**

더 나아가, 문학은 독자들이 사회와 집단적 책임에 관해 성찰하도록 이끈다. **C** 예를 들어, Albert Camus의 *The Plague*에서 파괴적인 전염병에 맞서려는 시민들의 노력은 협력과 연대를 보여준다. **D** 이는 개인이 공동체에 어떻게 기여하는지, 그리고 사회적 결속과 윤리적 행동을 증진하는 데 있어 자신의 역할을 독자들이 성찰하도록 격려한다.

exert[igzə́ːrt] 행사하다 profound[prəfáund] 깊은
perspective[pərspéktiv] 관점 intricate[íntrikət] 복잡한
empathy[émpəθi] 공감 struggle[strʌ́gl] 고통
confront[kənfrʌ́nt] 극복하다 prejudice[prédʒudis] 편견
prompt[prɑmpt] 이끌다 responsibility[rispɑ̀nsəbíləti] 책임
cope with ~에 맞서다 devastating[dévəstèitiŋ] 파괴적인
epidemic[èpədémik] 전염병 solidarity[sɑ̀ːlədǽrəti] 연대
foster[fɔ́ːstər] 증진하다 cohesion[kouhíːʒən] 결속

다음 문장이 삽입될 수 있는 네 곳이 지문에 표시되어 있다.

이러한 경험은 문학이 실질적인 차원에서 성장을 가능하게 하는 힘을 지녔음을 보여준다.

그 문장은 어디에 가장 적절한가? 그 문장이 삽입될 수 있는 곳을 고르시오.

HACKERS PRACTICE
p.280

01 Ⓒ   02 Ⓑ   03 Ⓓ   04 Ⓑ

01 Insertion Question

20세기 초 이후 이산화탄소(CO2) 배출량의 증가는 지구 온난화의 주된 요인이다. 이러한 추세를 뒤집기 위해 동원할 수 있는 가장 효과적인 도구 중 하나는 지구의 숲으로, 모두 합쳐 매년 대기로부터 거의 160억 톤의 CO2를 포집한다.

이 놀라운 성과는 광합성, 즉 나무가 생존에 필요한 물질을 생산하는 과정을 통해 달성된다. **A** 나무들은 대기로부터 CO2를 흡수한 다음 햇빛과 물을 사용하여 그것을 포도당으로 전환하는데, 이는 에너지를 제공하는 당의 일종이다. **B** 즉시 활용되지 않는 포도당은

나무 몸통에 목질로서 저장된다. **C** 이는 나무의 생애 거의 전체 동안 그곳에 남아 있을 것이며, 일부 종의 경우 수백 년이 될 수 있다. 비록 나무가 포도당을 합성할 때 약간의 CO2가 방출되지만, 그 양은 축적되는 것보다 현저히 적다. **D**

---

carbon dioxide 이산화탄소 emission[imíʃən] 배출량
atmosphere[ǽtməsfiər] 대기 feat[fiːt] 성과, 위업
photosynthesis[fòutəsínθəsis] 광합성
substance[sʌ́bstəns] 물질 absorb[æbsɔ́ːrb] 흡수하다
glucose[glúːkous] 포도당 trunk[trʌŋk] (나무의) 몸통
synthesize[sínθəsàiz] 합성하다
accumulate[əkjúːmjuleìt] 축적하다

다음 문장이 삽입될 수 있는 네 곳이 지문에 표시되어 있다.

이는 나무의 생애 거의 전체 동안 그곳에 남아 있을 것이며, 일부 종의 경우 수백 년이 될 수 있다.

그 문장은 어디에 가장 적절한가? 그 문장이 삽입될 수 있는 곳을 고르시오.

02 Insertion Question

고대 로마인들은 뛰어난 건축가로, 수도교, 경기장, 군사 요새 등을 건설했다. 그들의 가장 중요한 건축 자재 중 하나는 현대의 콘크리트보다 훨씬 더 손상에 강한 것으로 입증된 종류의 콘크리트였다. 그 이유는 오랫동안 미스터리였다.

로마 콘크리트의 단단함 뒤에 숨겨진 비밀은 거의 2,000년 후에 마침내 발견되었다. **A** 연구팀은 그 핵심이 작은 석회 조각에 있음을 확인했다. **B** 이전에 대부분의 전문가는 이러한 조각이 우연히 포함된 것이라고 생각했지만, 그 조각은 사실 모든 로마 콘크리트에서 발견된다. 물이 균열 사이로 로마 콘크리트 조각에 들어갈 때, 그것은 석회와 닿게 된다. **C** 이것은 화학 반응을 일으켜 탄산칼슘이라는 물질을 생산한다. **D** 그것은 빠르게 팽창한 뒤 굳어서, 균열을 메우고 추가 손상을 방지한다. 사실상 로마 콘크리트는 스스로 수리되는 것이며, 이것이 로마 콘크리트가 오래 가는 이유를 설명한다.

---

aqueduct[ǽkwədʌkt] 수도교 fortification[fɔ̀ːrtəfikéiʃən] 요새
counterpart[káuntərpàːrt] 대응하는(해당하는) 것
determine[ditɔ́ːrmin] 확인하다 lime[laim] 석회
calcium carbonate 탄산칼슘 prevent[privént] 방지하다
account for ~을 설명하다 longevity[lɑːndʒévəti] 오래감, 장수

다음 문장이 삽입될 수 있는 네 곳이 지문에 표시되어 있다.

이전에 대부분의 전문가는 이러한 조각이 우연히 포함된 것이라고 생각했지만, 그 조각은 사실 모든 로마 콘크리트에서 발견된다.

그 문장은 어디에 가장 적절한가? 그 문장이 삽입될 수 있는 곳을 고르시오.

03 Insertion Question

위험에 처한 사람은 주변에 많은 사람들이 있을 때 도움받을 가능성이 더 높다는 것이 일반적인 추측이다. 그러나 방관자 효과로 인해, 그것이 항상 사실인 것은 아니다. 이 현상은 긴급 상황에 목격자가 둘 이상 있음이 피해자에게 도움이 제공될 가능성을 감소시킬 때 발생한다. 이는 심리학자 Bibb Latané와 John Darley에 의해 처음 연구되었다.

Latané와 Darley는 이러한 행동의 두 가지 주요 원인을 규명했다. 첫째, 방관자의 수가 많을수록, 각 개인이 개입해야 한다고 느끼는 개인적 책임감이 줄어든다. **A** 모두 다른 누군가가 도울 것이라고 생각한다. **B** 다른 요인은 낯선 상황에 처한 사람은 적절한 반응을 결정하기 위해 다른 사람들을 관찰한다는 것이다. **C** 따라서, 긴급 상황에서 아무도 즉각적인 행동을 취하지 않을 때, 방관자들은 개입하지 않는 것을 올바른 반응으로 해석한다. **D** 즉, 각 개인이 아무 행동도 하지 않는 것이 다른 사람들에게 사회적 신호로 작용한다. Latané와 Darley가 규명한 것은 방관자 효과가 무정함의 결과가 아니라 집단 역학의 불행한 산물이라는 것이다.

---

assumption[əsʌ́mpʃən] 추측 peril[pérəl] 위험
aid[eid] 도움 bystander[báistændər] 방관자
presence[prézns] 존재 witness[wítnis] 목격자
likelihood[láiklihùd] 가능성
responsibility[rispɑ̀nsəbíləti] 책임감
intervene[ìntərvíːn] 개입하다 assume[əsúːm] 생각하다
observe[əbzɔ́ːrv] 관찰하다 determine[ditɔ́ːrmin] 결정하다
appropriate[əpróupriət] 적절한
callousness[kǽləsnəs] 무정함
unfortunate[ʌnfɔ́ːrtʃənət] 불행한

다음 문장이 삽입될 수 있는 네 곳이 지문에 표시되어 있다.

즉, 각 개인이 아무 행동도 하지 않는 것이 다른 사람들에게 사회적 신호로 작용한다.

그 문장은 어디에 가장 적절한가? 그 문장이 삽입될 수 있는 곳을 고르시오.

04 Insertion Question

공감각은 한 감각이나 인지 경로의 자극이 또 하나의 관련 없는 경로에서 무의식적인 경험을 일으키는 신경학적 상태이다. 그 결과, 감각의 경계가 혼합되어 특정 유형의 자극이 다른 감각에서 느낌을 유발한다. **A** 공감각의 정확한 원인은 아직 완전히 밝혀진 것은 아니나, 일반적으로 유전적 요소가 있으며 서로 다른 감각을 처리하는 뇌 영역 간의 연결성 증가와 연관될 수 있다고 여겨진다. **B** 공감각자를 대상으로 한 신경 영상 연구들은 평상시 분리된 상태를 유지하는 뇌 영역 간의 더 강력한 기능적, 구조적 연결을 보여주었다. 하지만 이러한 연구 결과들은 연구와 공감각 유형에 따라 차이를 보인다. **C** 연구자들은 인간의 뇌에서 감각 처리가 어떻게 발생하는지에 대한 더욱 수준 높은 이해를 얻기 위해 관련된 특정 신경 메커니즘을 지속적으로 조사하고 있다. **D**

---

synesthesia[sìnəsθíːʒə] 공감각
neurological[njùərəlɑ́dʒikəl] 신경학적인
cognitive[kɑ́gnətiv] 인지의
automatic[ɔ̀ːtəmǽtik] 무의식적인, 자동적인
genetic[dʒənétik] 유전적인 component[kəmpóunənt] 구성 요소
investigate[invéstəgèit] 조사하다
sophisticated[səfístəkèitid] 수준 높은, 정교한

다음 문장이 삽입될 수 있는 네 곳이 지문에 표시되어 있다.

공감각자를 대상으로 한 신경 영상 연구들은 평상시 분리된 상태를 유지하는 뇌 영역 간의 더 강력한 기능적, 구조적 연결을 보여주었다.

그 문장은 어디에 가장 적절한가? 그 문장이 삽입될 수 있는 곳을 고르시오.

HACKERS TEST

p.282

01 Ⓒ	02 Ⓑ	03 Ⓑ	04 Ⓐ	05 Ⓒ
06 Ⓐ	07 Ⓒ	08 Ⓐ	09 Ⓐ	10 Ⓒ
11 Ⓐ	12 Ⓓ	13 Ⓒ	14 Ⓑ	15 Ⓑ
16 Ⓒ	17 Ⓑ	18 Ⓒ	19 Ⓐ	20 Ⓒ

[01-05]

청자고둥

청자고둥은 주로 ⁰⁴열대 바다의 암초와 모래 해안 지역에서 발견된다. ⁰²이들의 껍질은 생생한 색깔과 독특한 무늬를 보여주어 수집가들에게 매우 인기가 높다. 청자고둥은 천천히 움직이며 사이펀이라 불리는 관 모양 기관을 사용하여 ⁰⁴해저에서 작은 물고기, 바다 벌레, 그리고 다른 연체동물과 같은 먹이를 탐지한다.

청자고둥의 가장 주목할 만한 특징 중 하나는 그들의 독이다. ⁰³먹이를 잡기 위해 그들은 특수한 작살 같은 이빨을 사용하며, 이것은 코노톡신이라 알려진 강력한 독소 혼합물을 주입한다. 이 독소는 공격당한 생물의 신경 신호에 지장을 줌으로써 먹잇감을 빠르게 무력화시킨다. 인간의 경우, 특정 종에게 찔리면 생명이 위협당할 수 있으며, 특별한 해독제가 없다. 사람이 청자고둥 쏘임으로 죽지 않더라도, 독은 극심하고 심각한 증상을 일으킬 수 있다.

A 그럼에도 불구하고, 이 달팽이들은 유익하다. **B** 그들은 작은 해양 동물들이 생태계가 지탱할 수 있는 수준보다 너무 많아지기 전에 그들을 잡아먹는다. **C** <u>이것은 특정 무척추동물들의 과잉 번식을 방지하여 산호초의 생태적 균형을 유지하는 데 도움을 준다.</u> 과학자들은 또한 새로운 진통제와 신경계 질환 치료법을 개발하기 위해 코노톡신을 연구하는데, 이는 이러한 물질들이 표적 신경 채널을 차단하는 능력 덕분이다. **D**

reef [ri:f] 암초 mollusk [mά:ləsk] 연체동물
feature [fí:tʃər] 특징 deploy [diplɔ́i] 사용하다
harpoon [ha:rpú:n] 작살 inject [indʒékt] 주입하다
potent [poutnt] 강력한 toxin [tά:ksin] 독소
immobilize [imóubəlàiz] 무력화시키다, 움직이지 못하게 하다
sting [stiŋ] 쏨, 찌름 antivenom [æntivénəm] 해독제
painkiller [péinkìlər] 진통제 treatment [trí:tmənt] 치료법
disorder [disɔ́:rdər] 질환

01 Vocabulary Question

두 번째 단락의 단어 "potent"와 의미상 가장 유사한 것은?
Ⓐ 활성의
Ⓑ 자연적인
☑ 강력한
Ⓓ 일상적인

02 Rhetorical Purpose Question

글쓴이는 왜 청자고둥 껍질의 색깔과 무늬를 언급하는가?
Ⓐ 야생에서 여러 종들을 식별하는 것의 어려움을 보여주기 위해
☑ 청자고둥이 수집가들 사이에서 인기가 있는 이유를 설명하기 위해
Ⓒ 먹이를 유인하는 시각적 특징의 예를 제공하기 위해
Ⓓ 독이 있는 동물의 일반적인 특징을 제시하기 위해

어휘 identify [aidéntəfài] 식별하다 attract [ətrǽkt] 유인하다
venomous [vénəməs] 독이 있는

03 Detail Question

청자고둥은 작살 같은 이빨을 무엇을 위해 사용하는가?
Ⓐ 포식자로부터 숨으려 모래 속으로 파고드는 것
☑ 독소를 주입하여 먹이를 잡는 것
Ⓒ 다른 연체동물의 껍질을 부수는 것
Ⓓ 암석과 산호에 자신을 부착시키는 것

04 Inference Question

바다 벌레에 대해 추론할 수 있는 것은?
☑ 열대의 해저에서 생존할 수 있다.
Ⓑ 신경 신호를 가지고 있지 않다.
Ⓒ 코노톡신에 면역이 있다.
Ⓓ 작은 물고기에 의해 잡아먹힌다.

05 Insertion Question

다음 문장이 삽입될 수 있는 네 곳이 지문에 표시되어 있다.

이것은 특정 무척추동물들의 과잉 번식을 방지하여 산호초의 생태적 균형을 유지하는 데 도움을 준다.

그 문장은 어디에 가장 적절한가? 그 문장이 삽입될 수 있는 곳을 고르시오.

[06-10]

잠복 기억

잠복 기억은 자신이 독창적인 아이디어, 기억, 또는 창작물을 만들어냈다고 믿지만, 실제로는 이전에 접했던 것을 무의식적으로 기억해내는 것인 심리적 현상이다. 이 용어는 스위스 심리학자 ⁰⁷Theodore Flournoy가 자동 기술, 즉 의식적 사고 없이 글을 써내는 것에 관한 연구 중에 피험자들이 실제로는 잊힌 원천에서 유래한 것을 "새로운" 내용인 양 만들어내는 것을 관찰한 것에서 만들어졌다.

⁰⁸연구자들은 잠복 기억이 흔히 원천 모니터링의 실패에서 비롯된다고 제시한다. 원천 모니터링은 사람들이 기억된 아이디어와 새로 형성된 아이디어를 구분할 수 있게 해주는 정신적 과정을 말한다. ⁰⁸이 체계가 붕괴되면, 과거의 자료가 마치 독창적인 것인 양 다시 떠오를 수 있다. 이러한 실수는 기억의 불안정과, 개인이 사고하고 창작하며 자신의 아이디어의 독창성을 판단하는 방식에 미치는 폭넓은 영향을 분명히 보여준다.

⁰⁹잠복 기억은 확신을 가지고 판별할 수 없는데, 무의식적 재사용과 의도적 표절을 신뢰성 있게 구분할 수 있는 단일한 방법은 없기 때문이다. **A** 행동적 원천 모니터링 연구, 초안과 날짜 기록, 또는 컴퓨터 기반 유사성 도구는 각각 부분적인 통찰을 제공한다. **B** 그러나, 연구자들은 여러 단서를 교차 점검하는 것의 중요성을 강조한다. **C** <u>개별 단서 하나만으로는 의도를 입증할 수 없지만, 여러 단서가 모인 것은 판단에 합리적 근거를 제공할 수 있다.</u> 이런 방식으로, 그것들은 잠재적 표절에 대한 정당한 의심을 제기하는 데 도움을 준다. **D**

unconsciously [ʌnkάnʃəsli] 무의식적으로
subject [sʌ́bdʒikt] 피험자 derive [diráiv] 유래하다
distinguish [distíŋgwiʃ] 구분하다
lapse [læps] 실수 underscore [ʌ̀ndərskɔ̀:r] 분명히 보여주다
instability [ìnstəbíləti] 불안정 deliberate [dilíbərət] 의도적인
justified [dʒʌ́stəfàid] 정당한 suspicion [səspíʃən] 의심

06 Vocabulary Question
지문의 단어 "coined"와 의미상 가장 유사한 것은?
- Ⓐ 고안되었다 ✓
- Ⓑ 채택되었다
- Ⓒ 대중화되었다
- Ⓓ 번역되었다

어휘 invent[invént] 고안하다, 발명하다　adopt[ədápt] 채택하다
　　 translate[trænsléit] 번역하다

07 Inference Question
Theodore Flournoy의 연구에 대해 추론할 수 있는 것은?
- Ⓐ 피험자들이 이전에 접한 내용에서 아이디어를 의도적으로 베꼈다는 것을 시사했다.
- Ⓑ 자동 기술이 항상 완전히 새로운 내용을 산출한다고 제시했다.
- Ⓒ 피실험자들이 이전 자료를 독창적인 것으로 생각하며 제시했음을 보여주었다. ✓
- Ⓓ 무의식적 기억 과정이 모든 개인에게 동일하게 작동한다는 결론을 내렸다.

어휘 identically[aidéntikəli] 동일하게

08 Rhetorical Purpose Question
두 번째 단락의 목적은 무엇인가?
- Ⓐ 독창적인 아이디어와 이전에 접했던 기억을 구분하는 정신 과정의 실패와 잠복 기억을 연결 짓는다. ✓
- Ⓑ 잠복 기억을 설명하기 위해 사람들이 이 현상을 겪은 역사적 사례와 일화를 제시한다.
- Ⓒ 모든 창작물이 궁극적으로 이전 기억과 과거 경험의 영향을 받는다고 주장한다.
- Ⓓ 연구자들이 실제 환경에서 무의식적 표절 사례를 탐지하는 데 사용하는 방법과 전략을 논의한다.

09 Detail Question
잠복 기억을 판별하기 어려운 이유는 무엇인가?
- Ⓐ 순수한 기억 착오와 고의적인 모방 행위를 구별하기가 어렵다. ✓
- Ⓑ 잊어버린 기억의 원천을 추적하는 것이 거의 불가능하다.
- Ⓒ 독창성에 대한 판단은 본질적으로 주관적이며 객관적인 단서로 정보를 얻을 수 없다.
- Ⓓ 이 현상이 최근에야 발견되었기 때문에 충분한 학술 연구가 부족하다.

어휘 inherently[inhérəntli] 본질적으로

10 Insertion Question
다음 문장이 삽입될 수 있는 네 곳이 지문에 표시되어 있다.

단서 하나만으로는 의도를 입증할 수 없지만, 여러 단서가 모인 것은 판단에 합리적 근거를 제공할 수 있다.

그 문장은 어디에 가장 적절한가? 그 문장이 삽입될 수 있는 곳을 고르시오.

[11-15]

수면 방추

수면 방추는 수면 중에 발생하는 짧은 뇌 활동의 폭발로, 0.5초에서 2초 동안 지속된다. 그것은 일반적으로 비렘 수면(NREM) 동안 3초

에서 6초마다 나타난다. [11]수면 방추의 생성은 감각 신호를 전달하는 시상과 고등 인지 기능을 담당하는 뇌의 바깥층인 대뇌 피질 사이의 상호작용을 수반한다.

[12]연구는 뇌가 새로운 기억을 공고히 하는 것을 돕는 데 수면 방추가 필수적이라는 것을 검증했다. 아동과 성인 모두를 포함한 연구에서, [12]방추 빈도와 수면 후 새로운 사실이나 절차를 기억하는 능력 사이에 직접적인 관계가 발견되었다. 어쩌면 이와 동등하게 중요한 것은, 방추가 수면자가 소음이나 방해에 의해 깨지 않게끔 보호하는 것으로 보인다는 점이다.

[13]추가 연구들은 수면 방추가 그 밖의 정신적, 신체적 상태와도 관련이 있을 수 있음을 나타낸다. **Ⓐ** 연구 분야 중 하나는 감정 조절에 대한 수면 방추의 중요성이다. **Ⓑ** 연구들은 방추율이 불안에 반응하여 증가함을 보여주었는데, 이는 수면 방추가 부정적 감정을 처리하는 데 도움을 준다는 것을 암시한다. 이 외에도, 수면 패턴의 변화, 더 구체적으로는 빈도와 진폭의 감소가 특정 질병을 나타낼 가능성이 점점 더 커지는 것으로 보인다. **Ⓒ** 방추 활동 장애는 인지 저하와 알츠하이머병뿐만 아니라 파킨슨병과 같은 신경학적 질환의 생체 지표라는 점이 확인되기까지 했다. **Ⓓ**

spindle[spíndl] 방추, 기계의 축　thalamus[θǽləməs] 시상
relay[ríːlei] 전달하다　cerebral cortex 대뇌 피질
responsible[rispάnsəbl] 담당하는, 책임이 있는
consolidate[kənsάːlədèit] 공고히 하다, 통합하다
frequency[fríːkwənsi] 빈도, 진동수　rouse[rauz] 깨우다
disruption[disrΛ́pʃən] 방해, 붕괴　regulation[règjuléiʃən] 조절
amplitude[ǽmplətjùːd] 진폭　indicative[indíkətiv] 나타내는
biomarker[báioumàːrkər] 생체 지표

11 Inference Question
수면 방추에 대해 추론할 수 있는 것은?
- Ⓐ 여러 뇌 영역 간의 협응을 필요로 한다. ✓
- Ⓑ 생활 방식이나 생리적 상태에 의해 영향을 받을 수 있다.
- Ⓒ 주로 외부 환경 요인에 따라 달라진다.
- Ⓓ 뉴런 간의 상호작용을 반영할 수도 있다.

12 Detail Question
수면 방추의 규명된 기능 중 하나는 무엇인가?
- Ⓐ 신경 질환을 치료하는 데 도움을 준다.
- Ⓑ 성장 호르몬의 방출을 조절한다.
- Ⓒ 여러 유형의 수면 장애를 완화한다.
- Ⓓ 새로운 기억을 처리하는 데 도움을 준다. ✓

13 Rhetorical Purpose Question
세 번째 단락의 기능은?
- Ⓐ 수면 방추가 어떻게 뇌 기능과 수면의 질에 도움이 되는지 설명한다.
- Ⓑ 수면 방추를 다른 유형의 뇌파 패턴과 비교한다.
- Ⓒ 수면 방추의 임상적 중요성을 소개한다. ✓
- Ⓓ 수면 방추 빈도를 측정하는 데 사용되는 방법을 설명한다.

14 Vocabulary Question
두 번째 단락의 단어 "roused"와 의미상 가장 유사한 것은?
- Ⓐ 바뀐
- Ⓑ 깨어난 ✓
- Ⓒ 혼란스러운
- Ⓓ 방해받는

15 Insertion Question

다음 문장이 삽입될 수 있는 네 곳이 지문에 표시되어 있다.

연구들은 방추율이 불안에 반응하여 증가함을 보여주었는데, 이는 수면 방추가 부정적 감정을 처리하는 데 도움을 준다는 것을 암시한다.

그 문장은 어디에 가장 적절한가? 그 문장이 삽입될 수 있는 곳을 고르시오.

[16-20]

굴광성

굴광성은 빛에 반응한 식물의 움직임 또는 성장이다. 이 현상은 식물이 태양 쪽으로 구부러져, 광합성을 위한 [17C]햇빛 흡수 능력을 극대화할 때 가장 뚜렷하게 관찰된다. 예컨대, 어린 콩 식물은 잎을 빛을 향하여 굽힌다. 근본적인 메커니즘은 [17D]옥신과 같은 식물 호르몬으로, 식물 내에서 재분배되면서, 그늘진 쪽 세포가 길게 늘어나 식물이 빛 쪽으로 자라게 한다.

[A] 굴광성은 식물의 생존에 필수적인 역할을 한다. [B] 잎과 줄기를 태양 쪽으로 향하게 함으로써, 식물은 광합성 효율을 높이고, 그 결과 [17A]에너지 생산과 성장이 증가한다. [C] 이러한 적응은 또한 경쟁이 심하거나 밀집된 환경에서 묘목이 더 빨리 빛을 확보할 수 있도록 해준다. 어떤 경우에는, 뿌리가 음성적인 굴광성을 보여, 직사광선을 피하고 더 깊은 토양 속으로 자란다. [D] 이러한 방향으로의 성장은 뿌리가 생존에 필요한 물과 영양분을 찾도록 해 준다.

현재 진행 중인 연구는 다양한 조건에서 서로 다른 식물종이 굴광성을 어떻게 조절하는지를 이해하고자 한다. [18]이 연구에서 얻은 통찰은 작물 배치 최적화와 빛 이용 효율이 향상된 신품종 개발과 같은 농업 기술의 발전으로 이어질 수 있다. [19]옥신 재분배에 대해 더 많이 이해하는 것은 햇빛 노출이 제한된 지역에서도 광합성 잠재력을 최대화하는 식물을 개발할 수 있게 할 수도 있다.

phototropism [foutá:trəpìzm] 굴광성
phenomenon [fináməˌnàn] 현상 (pl. phenomena)
photosynthesis [fòutəsínθəsis] 광합성
underlying [ʌ́ndərlàiiŋ] 근본적인
orient [ɔ́:riənt] (특정 방향을) 향하게 하다 stem [stem] 줄기
efficiency [ifíʃənsi] 효율 nutrient [njú:triənt] 영양분
regulate [régjulèit] 조절하다 optimize [áptəmàiz] 최적화하다

16 Vocabulary Question

지문의 단어 "elongate"와 의미상 가장 유사한 것은?
Ⓐ 증식하다
Ⓑ 분열하다
✓Ⓒ 늘어나다
Ⓓ 강화되다

17 Detail Question

지문에 따르면, 다음 중 굴광성과 관련된 것이 아닌 것은?
Ⓐ 증가된 에너지 생산
✓Ⓑ 최적화된 작물 배치
Ⓒ 극대화된 햇빛 흡수
Ⓓ 식물 호르몬의 재분배

18 Rhetorical Purpose Question

글쓴이는 왜 "신품종"을 언급하는가?
Ⓐ 전통 농업에서 작물 심기 과정이 어떻게 계획되는지를 설명하기 위해
Ⓑ 작물 배치가 뿌리의 굴광성에 영향을 미친다는 것을 암시하기 위해
✓Ⓒ 연구 분야에서 잠재적 결과의 예를 제시하기 위해
Ⓓ 환경 보전에서 굴광성의 역할을 언급하기 위해

19 Inference Question

굴광성 연구의 농업적 응용에 관해 추론할 수 있는 것은?
✓Ⓐ 빛이 적은 지역에서 성공적으로 경작하게 할 수도 있다.
Ⓑ 잠재적으로 토양 침식의 속도를 줄일 수 있다.
Ⓒ 작물에서 질병 저항성이 향상되는 결과를 낳을 수 있다.
Ⓓ 농부들이 햇빛 없이 작물을 재배할 수 있도록 해줄 수도 있다.

20 Insertion Question

다음 문장이 삽입될 수 있는 네 곳이 지문에 표시되어 있다.

이러한 적응은 또한 경쟁이 심하거나 밀집된 환경에서 묘목이 더 빨리 빛을 확보할 수 있도록 해준다.

그 문장은 어디에 가장 적절한가? 그 문장이 삽입될 수 있는 곳을 고르시오.

Section II Passage Types

1. Humanities

HACKERS TEST   p.296

01 Ⓑ	02 Ⓓ	03 Ⓐ	04 Ⓓ	05 Ⓒ
06 Ⓒ	07 Ⓑ	08 Ⓑ	09 Ⓓ	10 Ⓒ
11 Ⓓ	12 Ⓐ	13 Ⓓ	14 Ⓒ	15 Ⓐ
16 Ⓑ	17 Ⓑ	18 Ⓐ	19 Ⓒ	20 Ⓓ

[01-05]

도시 위생 개혁

도시 위생은 수천 년 전으로 거슬러 올라간다. 로마인들은 신선한 물을 공급하기 위한 수도교와 폐수를 제거하기 위한 배수시설을 건설했다. [02]그러나 중세 시대에 이르러, 많은 유럽 도시는 구덩이와 노출된 배수로에 의존해서 오물을 저장했다. 19세기 산업화로 인해 유럽 도시들이 과밀해지면서, 폐기물이 강으로 흘러들어 수원을 더럽히고 유행병을 촉발했다.

전환점이 찾아온 것은 1854년 런던이었다. [01]의사 John Snow는 콜레라 사례를 지도에 표시하고 발병의 원인이 어느 펌프에 있음을 추적하여 밝혀냈다. 그는 오염이 해결될 때까지 물 접근을 제한하기 위해 펌프 손잡이를 제거하도록 공무원들을 설득했다. 이 조치는 추가 노출을 줄였다. 오염원을 식별한 Snow의 증거 기반 방법은 신중한 관찰과 결정적인 증거를 활용했으며, 이는 공중 보건 담론을 변화시켰다.

[A] 거의 같은 시기에, 엔지니어 Joseph Bazalgette는 현대적 하수도를 설계했지만 아직 그의 계획을 실행하지는 않았다. [B] [04]1858년

의 대약취 동안, 따뜻한 날씨가 템즈강이 악취를 풍기게 만들었다. **C** 심지어 의회 의원들도 악취를 감추려 커튼을 표백제에 적셔 걸었고, 증가하는 언론 비판과 대중 청원이 입법부가 행동하도록 압박했다. 04이것이 Bazalgette의 하수도 시스템의 자금 조달과 건설을 가속했다. **D** 이 시스템은 질병 위협을 줄이고, 보다 깨끗한 도시 공기에 기여했으며, 다른 도시들에서 유사한 개혁을 촉발했다. 현대 위생은 이러한 개혁들에 기초해 과학, 정책, 그리고 공학을 연결하고 있다.

---

sanitation [sæ̀nitéiʃən] 위생   aqueduct [ǽkwədʌkt] 수도교
drain [drein] 배수시설   rely on ~에 의존하다   pit [pit] 구덩이
gutter [gʌ́tər] 배수로   overcrowded [òuvərkráudid] 과밀한
industrialization [indʌ̀striəlizéiʃən] 산업화   foul [faul] 더러운
epidemic [èpədémik] 유행병   outbreak [áutbrèik] 발병
persuade [pərswéid] 설득하다   restrict [ristríkt] 제한하다
contamination [kəntæ̀mənéiʃən] 오염   discourse [dískɔːrs] 담론
sewer [súːər] 하수도   implement [ímpləmènt] 실행하다
reek [riːk] 악취를 풍기다

01 Fact Question
지문에서 John Snow에 대해 제시된 것은?
Ⓐ 폐기물을 하류로 운반하기 위해 런던의 현대적 하수도를 건설했다.
☑ 공무원들을 설득하여 펌프 손잡이를 제거함으로써 발병 사례를 줄였다.
Ⓒ 가정에서 일상적 사용 전에 물을 끓이도록 요구하는 도시 전체 정책을 도입했다.
Ⓓ 점차적으로 콜레라 발병을 중단시킨 백신을 개발했다.

02 Rhetorical Purpose Question
글쓴이는 왜 구덩이와 노출된 배수로를 언급하는가?
Ⓐ 로마 수도교가 중세 유럽 도시에 미친 영향을 보여주기 위해
Ⓑ 현대의 폐기물 저장 방식과 초기 처분 방식을 대조하기 위해
Ⓒ 중세 유럽 도시를 발굴하는 데 사용된 고고학적 방법을 언급하기 위해
☑ 19세기 유럽 도시의 위생 문제를 야기한 역사적 배경을 암시하기 위해

03 Vocabulary Question
지문의 단어 "conclusive"와 의미상 가장 유사한 것은?
☑ 결정적인
Ⓑ 잠정적인
Ⓒ 모호한
Ⓓ 통계적인

어휘 tentative [téntətiv] 잠정적인
   statistical [stətístikəl] 통계적인

04 Detail Question
어떤 사건이 Bazalgette의 하수도 시스템 자금 조달과 건설을 가속화했는가?
Ⓐ 몇 주간 템즈강 물이 마르게 한 가뭄
Ⓑ 거리로 광범위한 하수 범람을 야기한 홍수
Ⓒ 오염된 물과 연결된 질병의 발병
☑ 템즈강의 악취와 관련된 위기

05 Insertion Question
다음 문장이 삽입될 수 있는 네 곳이 지문에 표시되어 있다.

심지어 의회 의원들도 악취를 감추려 커튼을 표백제에 적셔 걸었고, 증가하는 언론 비판과 대중 청원이 입법부가 행동하도록 압박했다.

그 문장은 어디에 가장 적절한가? 그 문장이 삽입될 수 있는 곳을 고르시오.

[06-10]

광란의 20년대

광란의 20년대는 미국에서의 제1차 세계대전 이후 10년간, 즉 1920년부터 1929년까지를 가리킨다. 이 시기는 급속한 경제 확장, 도시 소득 증가, 그리고 소비재의 광범위한 보급으로 특징지어졌다.

이 10년은 대량 생산, 광고, 그리고 신용 거래를 기반으로 하는 소비 경제를 형성하는 데 중심적인 역할을 했다. 공장들이 생산량을 늘려서, 자동차, 가전제품, 라디오가 널리 보급될 수 있게 했다. 할부 신용 거래의 증가는 대량 소비를 촉진했고, 낮은 금리는 건설, 주택 구매, 그리고 투자를 부추겼다. 저렴한 자동차와 할부 제도의 광범위한 보급은 교외 지역의 성장을 직접적으로 용이하게 만들었는데, 노동자들이 이제 도심 밖으로 쉽게 통근하고 집을 마련할 수 있었기 때문이다.

그러나 이는 또한 10A증가하는 가계 및 기업 부채, 불충분한 금융 보호장치, 그리고 광범위한 투기 행위라는 주요한 취약점들을 초래했다. 많은 상품의 소비자 가격은 하락했지만, 08농민들은 떨어지는 농작물 가격과 늘어나는 부채에 직면하여 많은 농촌 가정이 뒤처졌다. 이민 제한과 10C약화된 노동조합은 노동 인구를 재편하였다. 09주류 금지는 세수에 영향을 미쳤고, 10D제한적인 정부 감독은 은행과 금융시장에서 취약점을 만들어냈다. 더구나, 10B소득과 지역 불평등이 확대되고 인종 폭력이 심화되면서 사회적 분열도 심해졌다.

---

roaring [rɔ́ːriŋ] 광란의, 떠들썩한   decade [dékeid] 10년
income [ínkʌm] 소득   diffusion [difjúːʒən] 보급
mass production 대량 생산   credit [krédit] 신용 거래
appliance [əpláiəns] 가전제품   affordable [əfɔ́ːrdəbl] 저렴한
facilitate [fəsílətèit] 용이하게 하다   suburb [sʌ́bəːrb] 교외
commute [kəmjúːt] 통근하다
vulnerability [vʌ̀lnərəbíləti] 취약점
speculation [spèkjuléiʃən] 투기
immigration [ìməgréiʃən] 이민   tax revenue 세수
racial [réiʃəl] 인종의   intensify [inténsəfài] 심화되다

06 Vocabulary Question
첫 번째 단락의 단어 "diffusion"과 의미상 가장 유사한 것은?
Ⓐ 집중
Ⓑ 분리
☑ 유통
Ⓓ 형성

어휘 segregation [sègrigéiʃən] 분리
   distribution [dìstrəbjúːʃən] 유통

07 Rhetorical Purpose Question
2단락에서 소비자 상품의 광범위한 보급을 초래한 구체적인 환경을 밝히는 문장을 클릭하시오.
Ⓐ 이 10년은 대량 생산, 광고, 그리고 신용 거래를 기반으로 하는 소비 경제를 형성하는 데 중심적인 역할을 했다.

ⓑ 공장들이 생산량을 늘려서, 자동차, 가전제품, 라디오가 널리 보급될 수 있게 했다.
ⓒ 할부 신용 거래의 증가는 대량 소비를 촉진했고, 낮은 금리는 건설, 주택 구매, 그리고 투자를 부추겼다.
ⓓ 저렴한 자동차와 할부 제도의 광범위한 보급은 교외 지역의 성장을 직접적으로 용이하게 만들었는데, 노동자들이 이제 도심 밖으로 쉽게 통근하고 집을 마련할 수 있었기 때문이다.

08 Inference Question

1920년대 미국 농촌의 농민들에 대해 추론할 수 있는 것은?
ⓐ 소비자 가격 하락을 통해 가장 많은 혜택을 받았다.
ⓑ 도시 사람들과 같은 수준의 번영을 경험하지 못했다.
ⓒ 용품과 장비 비용을 댈 신용 거래를 이용할 수 없었다.
ⓓ 노동조합 활동을 통해 스스로를 보호할 수 있었다.

어휘 **prosperity**[prɑspérəti] 번영 **equipment**[ikwípmənt] 장비 **labor union** 노동조합

09 Rhetorical Purpose Question

글쓴이는 왜 주류 금지를 언급하는가?
ⓐ 그것이 어떻게 산업 생산성과 효율성을 증진했는지 강조하기 위해
ⓑ 과도한 주류 소비의 위험성을 강조하기 위해
ⓒ 도덕적 개혁 운동이 어떻게 미국의 가치관을 형성했는지 보여주기 위해
ⓓ 정책들이 어떻게 경제 상황에 영향을 미쳤는지 설명하기 위해

어휘 **productivity**[pràdəktívəti] 생산성 **efficiency**[ifíʃənsi] 효율성

10 Detail Question

1920년대 미국 경제의 약점으로 지문에 언급되지 않은 것은?
ⓐ 과도한 기업 및 가계 부채 수준
ⓑ 소득 불평등 심화
ⓒ 강력한 노동조합의 빈번한 파업
ⓓ 불충분한 시장 감독

[11-15]

> **미국 의회 도서관**
>
> 의회 도서관은 세계에서 가장 큰 도서관이자 **¹²미국의 비공식적인 국립 도서관**이다. 몇 가지 핵심적인 순간들이 그 도서관의 설립에 기여했다.
>
> **¹³미국의 초기 지도자들은 고전 교육을 받은 독서가였으며, 민주주의를 유지하는 데 책과 지식이 매우 중요하다고 믿었다.** 그래서 1790년 워싱턴 D.C.가 미국의 수도가 되었을 때, 도서관 설립을 위한 기반이 마련되었다. 의회 도서관은 1800년에 공식적으로 설립되었다. 초기 소장 자료는 새로 지어진 국회의사당 내부의 한 방에 보관되었다.
>
> 불행히도, 국회의사당은 미국과 영국 간의 1812년 전쟁 중에 공격받았다. **¹⁴초기 지도자 중 한 명인 Thomas Jefferson은 그 후 그의 개인 소장 도서 6,000여 권을 정부에 매각하겠다고 제안했다.** 이 결정은 의회도서관이 책의 완전한 보고가 되겠다는 고유 임무를 채택하도록 영감을 주었다. 나아가, 1870년에는 의회도서관이 미국 저작권청의 본거지가 되었는데, 이는 도서관이 출판된 자료의 소장품을 지속적으로 늘릴 수 있게 해주었다.
>
> **¹⁵20세기가 시작될 무렵, 의회 도서관은 모든 미국인을 위한 국가 기관으로 자리 잡았으며, 그 자료를 모든 시민이 이용할 수 있게 되었다.**

어휘 **unofficial**[ʌ̀nəfíʃəl] 비공식적인 **contribute**[kəntríbjuːt] 기여하다
crucial[krúːʃəl] 매우 중요한 **maintain**[meintéin] 유지하다
democracy[dimáːkrəsi] 민주주의
groundwork[gráundwə̀ːrk] 기반
establishment[istǽbliʃmənt] 설립
subsequently[sʌ́bsikwəntli] 그 후에
collection[kəlékʃən] 소장품
inspire[inspáiər] 영감을 주다 **mission**[míʃən] 임무
repository[ripɑ́ːzətɔ́ːri] 보고

11 Vocabulary Question

지문의 단어 "subsequently"와 의미상 가장 유사한 것은?
ⓐ 이전에
ⓑ 즉시
ⓒ 그동안에
ⓓ 그 후에

12 Fact Question

의회 도서관에 대해 명시된 것은?
ⓐ 국립 도서관의 역할을 하고 있으나 정식 국립 도서관으로 인정되지는 않는다.
ⓑ 미국인의 읽고 쓰는 능력을 향상하는 데 핵심적인 역할을 했다.
ⓒ 미국의 문화적 정체성을 만드는 데 큰 기여를 했다.
ⓓ 미국의 새로운 책들이 출판되는 곳이다.

어휘 **recognize**[rékəgnàiz] 인정하다 **literacy**[lítərəsi] 읽고 쓰는 능력

13 Detail Question

미국의 초기 지도자들이 도서관을 설립하고자 했던 이유는?
ⓐ 자신들의 도서 소장품을 보관할 장소가 없었다.
ⓑ 민주주의 정신을 장려하고자 했다.
ⓒ 미국 대중을 교육하기를 희망했다.
ⓓ 국가의 역사 기록을 보존해야 했다.

어휘 **promote**[prəmóut] 장려하다 **preserve**[prizə́ːrv] 보존하다

14 Rhetorical Purpose Question

글쓴이는 왜 1812년 전쟁을 언급하는가?
ⓐ 미국 초기 역사의 주요 사건을 묘사하기 위해
ⓑ 영국이 어떻게 정보를 억압했는지를 보여주기 위해
ⓒ 도서관 발전의 전환점을 강조하기 위해
ⓓ 미국 건국에 대한 도서관의 중요성을 설명하기 위해

어휘 **suppress**[səprés] 억압하다

15 Inference Question

20세기의 의회 도서관에 대해 암시되는 것은?
ⓐ 일반 대중에게 개방되었다.
ⓑ 현재 위치로 이전되었다.
ⓒ 또 다른 전쟁으로 다시 파괴되었다.
ⓓ 외국 국가 원수들이 방문하였다.

어휘 **head of state** 국가 원수

[16-20]

저자의 죽음

문학 이론가 Roland Barthes는 "독자의 탄생은 저자의 죽음을 대가로 이루어져야 한다"라고 저술했다. 이를 통해, [16/19]그는 의미가 독자의 해석 활동으로부터 발생하며, 단일하고 올바른 해석을 확립하기 위해 저자의 의도에 호소하는 것은 잘못이라고 주장했다. 이 "저자의 죽음" 개념은 의미에 대한 권위를 저자로부터 독자에게로 옮겨 놓았다.

예를 들어, 작가가 정치적 메시지를 전달하려고 의도했다는 전기적 설명이 그 글을 그 하나의 의미로 한정 짓는 것은 아니다. [18]혹은 화자가 작가처럼 들리는 소설을 상상해 보라. 둘 사이에 공통점이 있을지라도, 중요한 과제는 글이 의견과 관점을 어떻게 구성하는지를 분석하여 의미를 형성하는 것이지, 화자가 곧 저자라고 가정하고 해석을 전기적 정보의 흡수로 축소시키는 것이 아니다.

A 이 견해는 저자가 선언한 목적을 신봉하기보다는 다양한 분석적 해석을 수용함으로써 비평을 민주화한다. **B** 하지만, 이는 결코 완벽한 이론은 아니다. **C** 비평가들은 저자를 무시하는 것이 소외된 의견을 지우거나 권력관계를 파악하기 어렵게 할 수 있다고 주장한다. **D** 학자들은 또한 고정된 의미의 부재가 일종의 해석적 혼란을 초래하여, 객관적인 문학 연구의 가능성을 약화시킬 수 있다고 지적한다. 그럼에도 불구하고, 의미는 글과 독자 사이의 만남에서 만들어진다는 주장은 해석의 자유를 위한 중요한 주장으로 남아있다.

theorist[θíːərist] 이론가 **at the cost of** ~을 대가로
interpretive[intə́ːrpritiv] 해석의 **intent**[intént] 의도
authority[əθɔ́ːrəti] 권위 **biographical**[bàiəgrǽfikəl] 전기의
overlap[òuvərlǽp] 겹치다 **construct**[kənstrʌ́kt] 구성하다
perspective[pərspéktiv] 관점 **assume**[əsúːm] 가정하다
intake[íntèik] 흡수 **marginalize**[máːrdʒinəlàiz] 소외시키다
obscure[əbskjúər] 모호하게 하다

16 Main Topic Question
다음 중 지문의 중심 생각을 가장 잘 나타낸 것은?
Ⓐ 독자가 문학 작품을 인식하는 방식에 대해 비평가는 통제권이 거의 없다.
Ⓑ ✓ 글의 의미는 의도보다는 해석에서 비롯된다.
Ⓒ 저자는 항상 자신의 텍스트가 의도하는 의미를 명확히 해야 한다.
Ⓓ 이야기에서 화자는 의미의 주요 원천이다.

17 Vocabulary Question
지문의 단어 "adhering"과 의미상 가장 유사한 것은?
Ⓐ 유도하기
Ⓑ ✓ 따르기
Ⓒ 제시하기
Ⓓ 의문 제기하기

18 Rhetorical Purpose Question
글쓴이는 왜 화자가 저자인 것처럼 들리는 소설을 언급하는가?
Ⓐ ✓ 독자들이 글의 의미를 독립적으로 분석해야 함을 강조하기 위해
Ⓑ 화자가 저자를 반영할 때 소설을 신뢰할 수 없음을 시사하기 위해
Ⓒ 글의 분석보다 전기적 맥락이 우선해야 함을 보여주기 위해
Ⓓ 글을 해석하는 데 작가의 삶 이야기를 아는 것이 필요하다고 주장하기 위해

어휘 **mirror**[mírər] 반영하다 **precedence**[présədəns] 우선

19 Inference Question
Roland Barthes에 대해 추론할 수 있는 것은?
Ⓐ 문학 작품 저술에 있어 저자보다 독자가 더 중요하다고 생각했다.
Ⓑ 문학이 정치적 논평을 위한 수단이 되어서는 안 된다고 주장했다.
Ⓒ ✓ 글에 대한 다양한 해석의 중요성을 강조했다.
Ⓓ 독립적인 글 기반 분석의 한계를 규명했다.

어휘 **vehicle**[víːikl] 수단 **commentary**[káməntèri] 논평

20 Insertion Question
다음 문장이 삽입될 수 있는 네 곳이 지문에 표시되어 있다.

학자들은 또한 고정된 의미의 부재가 일종의 해석적 혼란을 초래하여, 객관적인 문학 연구의 가능성을 약화시킬 수 있다고 지적한다.

그 문장은 어디에 가장 적절한가? 그 문장이 삽입될 수 있는 곳을 고르시오.

2. Arts

HACKERS TEST p.308

01 Ⓑ	02 Ⓑ	03 Ⓐ	04 Ⓑ	05 Ⓐ
06 Ⓒ	07 Ⓐ	08 Ⓓ	09 Ⓐ	10 Ⓐ
11 Ⓑ	12 Ⓑ	13 Ⓑ	14 Ⓑ	15 Ⓒ
16 Ⓒ	17 Ⓑ	18 Ⓐ	19 Ⓒ	20 Ⓓ

[01-05]

한시적 예술

한시적 예술은 짧은 시간 동안만 지속되도록 의도된 예술 작품을 의미한다. 갤러리에 보존되고 가치가 매겨져 판매되는 작품들과 달리, 한시적 작품들은 풍화되거나, 녹거나, 퇴색되거나, 해체되도록 설계된다. 한시적 예술은 매체, 메시지, 그리고 파괴 방법이 다양하다.

유명한 예는 모래 만다라이다. [02]티베트 불교 승려들이 수 시간에 걸쳐 힘들여 모아 만든 만다라는 화려하고 복잡한 디자인을 형성하지만, 결국 마치 존재하지 않았던 것처럼 빗자루로 쓸린다. 이 관행은 삶의 무상함을 나타내며 완성된 산물보다는 창조하는 의식에 가치를 둔다. 한시적 예술은 자연환경에서도 자주 전시된다. [04]하루 종일에 걸쳐 녹는 얼음 조각은 기후와 열을 눈에 보이는 힘으로 만든다. [03]낙엽의 배치나 강의 돌탑은 자연이 허용하는 한에서만 존재한다.

행위예술은 본질적으로 한시적 예술의 한 유형이다. 반복되더라도, 예술가가 결코 같은 마음가짐을 갖고 있지 않기 때문에 공연은 결코 동일하지 않다. [05]야외나 색다른 공간에서 공연할 때, 행위 예술은 지나가는 사람들의 일상을 방해하고 그들이 갤러리나 박물관 밖에서 예술적 표현을 감상하도록 조장한다. 이것은 관람자들에게 예술이 어디서든 나타나고 또 사라질 수 있음을 상기시킨다.

ephemeral[ifémərəl] 한시적인 **preserve**[prizə́ːrv] 보존하다
weather[wéðər] 풍화되다 **dismantle**[dismǽntl] 해체하다
painstakingly[péinstèikiŋli] 힘들여
assemble[əsémbl] 모으다, 조립하다 **intricate**[íntrikət] 복잡한

sweep away 쓸어버리다, 완전히 없애다
impermanence[impə́:rmənəns] 무상함
arrangement[əréindʒmənt] 배치
unconventional[ʌ̀nkənvénʃənəl] 색다른
passerby[pǽsərbài] 지나가는 사람(pl. passersby)

01 Vocabulary Question
지문의 단어 "dismantled"와 의미상 가장 유사한 것은?
Ⓐ 건설되다
Ⓑ 분리되다
Ⓒ 기억되다
Ⓓ 전시되다

어휘 construct[kənstrʌ́kt] 건설하다 separate[sépərèit] 분리하다

02 Detail Question
지문에 따르면, 티베트 승려들이 모래 만다라를 파괴하는 이유는?
Ⓐ 완벽함은 결코 달성될 수 없음을 보여주기 위해
Ⓑ 삶의 일시적인 본질을 나타내기 위해
Ⓒ 자연의 중요성을 인식하기 위해
Ⓓ 의식적 관행의 가치를 무시하기 위해

어휘 temporary[témpərèri] 일시적인
downplay[dàunpléi] 무시하다, 경시하다

03 Fact Question
자연 속의 한시적 예술에 대해 제시된 것은?
Ⓐ 환경이 허용하는 한에서만 지속된다.
Ⓑ 관람자들의 마음에 오래 지속되는 인상을 남길 수 있는 능력이 있다.
Ⓒ 일반적으로 완성되자마자 파괴된다.
Ⓓ 자연의 반복되는 패턴을 반영한다.

어휘 recurring[rikə́:riŋ] 반복되는, 순환하는

04 Rhetorical Purpose Question
글쓴이는 왜 얼음 조각을 언급하는가?
Ⓐ 얼음 조각가들이 고도로 숙련된 예술가임을 시사하기 위해
Ⓑ 예술이 자연의 힘을 눈에 보이는 현상으로 바꿀 수 있는 방법을 보여주기 위해
Ⓒ 한시적 예술의 본질적 무작위성을 강조하기 위해
Ⓓ 한시적 예술 작품이 어떻게 보존될 수 있는지 설명하기 위해

어휘 inherent[inhérənt] 본질적인

05 Detail Question
야외 행위 예술의 한 가지 효과는?
Ⓐ 관람자들이 색다른 방식으로 예술을 감상하도록 격려한다.
Ⓑ 현실 맥락에서 예술가의 마음가짐을 드러낸다.
Ⓒ 예술이 감상되는 동시에 가치가 매겨져 판매될 수 있음을 증명한다.
Ⓓ 예술의 사회 참여 역할에 주목하게 한다.

[06-10]

제4의 벽

06제4의 벽은 무대 위의 공연자와 관객을 분리하는 상상 속의 보이지 않는 장벽이다. 일반적인 극장 구조에서는 세 개의 물리적 벽이 공연의 경계를 정하고, 관객을 마주 보는 네 번째 면은 열려 있다. 이 관습은 관객이 독립적인 현실 속의 사건들을 관찰하고 있을 뿐이며, 등장인물들은 자신들이 관찰당하고 있다는 사실을 알지 못한다는 점을 확고히 한다. 07제4의 벽을 받아들이는 것은 연극이라는 환상을 유지하는 데 필수적인데, 이는 관객이 일시적으로 현실적인 의심을 접어두고 이야기에 몰입할 것을 요하기 때문이다. 이를 통해 관객은 이야기에 정서적으로 몰두하게 된다.

제4의 벽 깨기는 이 장벽을 의도적으로 무너뜨리는 것이다. 이는 등장인물이 관객의 존재를 직접 인정하거나, 그들에게 말을 걸거나, 작품이 만들어진 것이라는 본질을 언급할 때 발생한다. 08고대 연극에도 독백과 같은 유사한 기법이 포함되었지만, 이 장치는 현대 연극, 특히 Bertolt Brecht의 서사극에서 새로운 중요성을 얻었다. Brecht는 이를 이야기 속에 수동적으로 흡수되는 것을 막기 위한 소외 효과로 사용했다. 09대신, 그는 관객이 연극의 사회적 또는 정치적 주제에 대해 비판적으로 성찰하도록 촉구했다. 따라서 이 기법은 관객들에게 그들이 공연을 목격하고 있음을 명시적으로 상기시키는 역할을 한다.

spectator[spékteitər] 관객 theatrical[θiǽtrikəl] 연극의
set aside 접어두다 immerse[imə́:rs] 몰두하다
invest[invést] 몰두하게 하다, (시간 등을) 들이다
deliberate[dilíbərət] 의도적인 disruption[disrʌ́pʃən] 파괴
acknowledge[əknɑ́lidʒ] 인정하다 presence[prézns] 존재
soliloquy[səlíləkwi] 독백 prominence[prɑ́mənəns] 중요성
alienation[èiljənéiʃən] 소외 absorption[æbsɔ́:rpʃən] 흡수
reflect[riflékt] 성찰하다, 숙고하다

06 Main Topic Question
이 지문은 주로 무엇에 관한 것인가?
Ⓐ 연극과 무대 디자인의 진화
Ⓑ 제4의 벽이 어떻게 창의성을 제한하는지
Ⓒ 연극에서의 개념적 경계
Ⓓ 관객이 제4의 벽 때문에 왜 방해받는지

어휘 evolution[èvəlú:ʃən] 진화, 발전 creativity[krì:eitívəti] 창의성
conceptual[kənséptʃuəl] 개념적인

07 Detail Question
제4의 벽을 확고히 함으로써 얻는 한 가지 이점은?
Ⓐ 공연을 더 진정성 있고 믿을 수 있게 만든다.
Ⓑ 관객이 그들의 일상생활과 주변 환경을 잊게 한다.
Ⓒ 배우들이 그들 자신의 연기에 집중하도록 돕는다.
Ⓓ 관객이 지나치게 몰입하는 것을 막는다.

어휘 authentic[ə:θéntik] 진정성 있는

08 Rhetorical Purpose Question
글쓴이는 왜 독백을 언급하는가?
Ⓐ 현대극에서 사용되는 기법을 언급하기 위해
Ⓑ 고대 기법이 어떻게 부활했는지 보여주기 위해
Ⓒ 제4의 벽보다 더 나은 기법이라고 주장하기 위해
Ⓓ 현대 기법과 역사적으로 유사한 것을 제시하기 위해

어휘 parallel[pǽrəlèl] 유사한 것, 대등한 것

09 Detail Question

Brecht는 제4의 벽을 깨뜨림으로써 무엇을 성취할 수 있었는가?
- Ⓐ 사회정치적 주제에 대한 비판적인 고찰 ✓
- Ⓑ 연극 속 이야기의 수동적 흡수
- Ⓒ 연극의 주요 등장인물에 대한 완전한 집중
- Ⓓ 연극 역사에 대한 더 깊은 이해

어휘 sociopolitical[sòusiəpəlítikəl] 사회정치적인

10 Vocabulary Question

지문의 단어 "explicitly"와 의미상 가장 유사한 것은?
- Ⓐ 명확히 ✓
- Ⓑ 조심스럽게
- Ⓒ 부분적으로
- Ⓓ 막연하게

어휘 vaguely[véigli] 막연하게

[11-15]

할렘 르네상스

할렘 르네상스는 1920년대에 뉴욕 할렘을 중심으로 번성했던 문화적 각성 운동이다. ¹¹아프리카계 미국인들이 남부 시골에서 북부 도시로 대량 이동한 것에 힘입어, 이 시기에는 인종적 고정관념에 도전하며 대담하고 새로운 흑인 정체성을 표현하는 예술, 문학, 음악의 현저한 분출이 있었다.

이 창작 운동은 다양한 분야의 선구적인 인물들에 의해 형성되었다. ¹²ᶜ문학에서는 Langston Hughes와 같은 시인들이 재즈와 블루스의 리듬을 그들의 운문에 불어넣어, 일상적인 아프리카계 미국인들의 진정한 목소리를 포착하였으며, ¹³Zora Neale Hurston은 그녀의 소설에서 흑인 민속 전통과 여성의 자율성을 찬양하였다. ¹²ᴬ음악적으로 이 시대를 정의하는 사운드트랙은 재즈였으며, Duke Ellington과 Louis Armstrong 같은 예술가들의 탁월한 즉흥 연주가 이를 이끌었다. ¹²ᴰ시각 예술에서는 Aaron Douglas와 같은 화가들이 투쟁, 회복력, 그리고 자부심에 대한 서사를 묘사하며 뚜렷하게 아프리카 중심적인 모더니즘을 발전시켰다.

강력한 집단 정체성을 구축하고 흑인의 인간성을 긍정함으로써, 할렘 르네상스는 흑인 공동체 내에 깊은 문화적 자부심과 자존감을 고취했다. ¹⁵그것은 또한 활동가들이 제도적 불의에 도전하고 미국 문화를 영구적으로 재편할 수 있도록 힘을 실어준 지적, 정신적 기반, 즉 회복력과 창조적 천재성에 대한 서사를 제공하였다.

awakening[əwéikəniŋ] 각성　flourish[flə́:ri∫] 번성하다
migration[maigréi∫ən] 이동　witness[wítnis] 벌어지다, 목격하다
outpouring[àutpɔ́:riŋ] 분출　racial[réi∫əl] 인종적인
assert[əsə́:rt] 표명하다　bold[bould] 대담한
infuse[infjú:z] 불어넣다　verse[və:rs] 운문
authentic[ɔ:θéntik] 진정한　autonomy[ɔ:tánəmi] 자율성
improvisational[imprὰ:vəzéi∫ənəl] 즉흥적인
brilliance[bríljəns] 탁월함　resilience[rizíljəns] 회복력
forge[fɔ:rdʒ] 구축하다　affirm[əfə́:rm] 긍정하다
empower[impáuər] 힘을 실어주다, 권한을 주다
systemic[sistémik] 제도적인, 체계의

11 Detail Question

할렘 르네상스에 기여한 한 가지 요인은?
- Ⓐ 대중의 문화적 취향의 변화
- Ⓑ 북부 도시 중심부로의 인구 이동 ✓
- Ⓒ 출판사와 후원자들의 지원
- Ⓓ 새로운 예술 형식의 부상

어휘 demographic[dèməgrǽfik] 인구의, 인구 통계학의

12 Detail Question

할렘 르네상스의 영향을 받은 것으로 언급된 장르가 아닌 것은?
- Ⓐ 음악
- Ⓑ 연극 ✓
- Ⓒ 문학
- Ⓓ 회화

13 Rhetorical Purpose Question

작가는 왜 Zora Neale Hurston을 언급하는가?
- Ⓐ 할렘이 흑인 공동체에 어떻게 영향을 미쳤는지 보여주기 위해
- Ⓑ 문학이 사회 현실을 어떻게 반영했는지 강조하기 위해 ✓
- Ⓒ 문학이 음악이나 시각 예술보다 덜 영향력이 있었다는 것을 시사하기 위해
- Ⓓ 할렘 르네상스가 오락에 국한되었다는 것을 강조하기 위해

어휘 influential[influén∫əl] 영향력이 있는

14 Vocabulary Question

지문의 단어 "forging"과 의미상 가장 유사한 것은?
- Ⓐ 창조하는 ✓
- Ⓑ 적응시키는
- Ⓒ 변화시키는
- Ⓓ 저항하는

어휘 adapt[ədǽpt] 적응시키다　resist[rizíst] 저항하다

15 Inference Question

할렘 르네상스에 대해 추론할 수 있는 것은?
- Ⓐ 주로 즉흥적인 예술에 기반을 두었다.
- Ⓑ 할렘을 아프리카계 미국인 문화의 중심지로 확립하였다.
- Ⓒ 활동가들이 인종 불평등에 맞서도록 도왔다. ✓
- Ⓓ 평등권을 위한 조직적인 운동을 촉발하였다.

어휘 confront[kənfrʌ́nt] 맞서다

[16-20]

Seikilos 비문

기원후 1세기 또는 2세기로 거슬러 올라가는 Seikilos 비문은 현존하는 역사상 가장 오래된 완전한 음악 작품 중 하나이다. 이 음악 작품은 1883년 한 고대 그리스 도시에서 대리석 기둥에서 발견되었으며, 그것에 새겨진 글은 그 기원과 목적에 대한 단서를 제공한다. 학자들은 이 비문이 사랑하는 사람의 죽음을 기리기 위해 만들어졌다고 생각한다. Ⓐ ¹⁸비문의 가사는 삶의 본질에 대한 더 광범위한 철학적 메시지를 전달한다. Ⓑ ¹⁷그 글은 상실을 애도하기보다는 청취자가 기쁘게 살고 시간을 염두에 두도록 격려한다. Ⓒ ¹⁸그것은 개인적인 추모이자 인간 존재에 대한 보편적인 고찰의 역할을 한다. Ⓓ 이 이중적 기능은 이것이 오늘날 사람들에게 지속적인 공감을 불러일으키는 점을 설명한다.

Seikilos 비문은 오늘날 들을 수 있다. ¹⁹현대 연구자들은 작품의 고대

그리스 기보법 체계를 해독함으로써 선율을 재구성할 수 있었는데, 이는 텍스트 위에 배치된 글자를 사용하여 음높이를 나타낸다. 학자들은 또한 텍스트의 시적 운율을 분석함으로써 작품의 리듬을 추론했다. 음악과 가사가 결합하자 나타난 노래는 복잡하지 않고, 노래와 간단한 악기 반주에 잘 맞는 명확하고 반복되는 리듬 패턴을 지녔다.

epitaph [épitæf] 비문   composition [kɑ̀:mpəzíʃən] 작품
column [káləm] 기둥   inscription [inskrípʃən] 새겨진(적힌) 글
mourn [mɔ:rn] 애도하다   meditation [mèditéiʃən] 고찰, 명상
reconstruct [rìkənstrʌ́kt] 재구성하다
decipher [disáifər] 해독하다
notation [noutéiʃən] 기보법, 표기법   infer [infə́:r] 추론하다
poetic [pouétik] 시적인   meter [mí:tər] 운율
straightforward [strèitfɔ́:wərd] 복잡하지 않은, 직관적인
instrumental [ìnstrəméntl] 악기의
accompaniment [əkʌ́mpənimənt] 반주

16 Vocabulary Question
지문의 단어 "inscription"과 의미상 가장 유사한 것은?
Ⓐ 장식품
Ⓑ 예언
✓ⓒ 글
Ⓓ 상징

어휘 ornament [ɔ́:rnəmənt] 장식품   prediction [pridíkʃən] 예언
symbol [símbəl] 상징

17 Detail Question
Seikilos 비문의 가사는 어떤 철학적 메시지를 전달하는가?
Ⓐ 애도는 치유와 고통 극복에 필요하다.
✓Ⓑ 삶은 즐겨야 하고 시간은 소중히 여겨야 한다.
Ⓒ 학문과 명상을 통해 지혜를 추구하라.
Ⓓ 세속적 쾌락을 포기하여 내세를 준비하라.

어휘 contemplation [kɑ̀:ntəmpléiʃən] 명상   earthly [ə́:rθli] 세속적인
afterlife [ǽftərlàif] 내세, 사후 세계

18 Rhetorical Purpose Question
다음 중 두 번째 단락의 목적을 가장 잘 설명하는 것은?
✓Ⓐ 작품의 주제와 관련이 있는 정서적 메시지를 고찰한다.
Ⓑ 고대 음악 연구에 사용된 방법론적 접근법을 간추려 설명한다.
Ⓒ 고대 그리스 시와 현대 문학 형식을 비교한다.
Ⓓ 비문의 원래 기능에 대한 대안 이론들을 소개한다.

어휘 examine [igzǽmin] 고찰하다, 검토하다
methodological [mèθədəlɑ́:dʒikəl] 방법론적인

19 Inference Question
고대 그리스 음악 기보법에 대해 추론할 수 있는 것은?
Ⓐ 주로 상세한 기악곡을 기록하는 데 사용되었다.
Ⓑ 각 음악 구절에 대한 정확한 리듬 패턴을 전달한다.
✓Ⓒ 현대 학자들이 해석할 수 있는 기호들을 사용한다.
Ⓓ 시 작품들의 특징이 되기도 했다.

어휘 instrumental [ìnstrəméntl] 기악의, 악기에 의한

20 Insertion Question
다음 문장이 삽입될 수 있는 네 곳이 지문에 표시되어 있다.

이 이중적 기능은 이것이 오늘날 사람들에게 지속적인 공감을 불러일으키는 점을 설명한다.

그 문장은 어디에 가장 적절한가? 그 문장이 삽입될 수 있는 곳을 고르시오.

3. Social Science

HACKERS TEST   p.320

01 Ⓑ	02 Ⓓ	03 Ⓑ	04 Ⓒ	05 Ⓑ
06 Ⓑ	07 Ⓒ	08 Ⓐ	09 Ⓑ	10 Ⓑ
11 Ⓒ	12 Ⓒ	13 Ⓑ	14 Ⓑ	15 Ⓒ
16 Ⓑ	17 Ⓑ	18 Ⓐ	19 Ⓒ	20 Ⓓ

[01-05]

상상된 공동체

Benedict Anderson은 1983년에 상상된 공동체 개념을 제시하여, 국가가 이전부터 있었던 실체가 아니라 공유된 믿음이 만들어낸 인위적인 창조물이라고 주장했다. ⁰¹그는 국가를 상상되었지만 자주적인 정치 공동체로 정의했다. 그것이 상상된 것인 이유는 구성원들이 대부분의 동료 시민을 만난 적이 없음에도 불구하고 자신들을 하나의 "민족"으로 결속시키는 깊은 동료애를 그려내기 때문이다.

Anderson에 따르면, 상상된 공동체의 확산은 미디어와 기관들에 의존했다. ⁰³신문은 자국의 활자어를 표준화했고, ⁰³독자들이 매일 아침 같은 보도를 접하게 하면서 시간을 공유한다는 감각을 만들어냈다. 학교, 철도, 전신, 그리고 나중에는 라디오와 영화가 이와 비슷하게 삶을 동시에 움직이게 만들었다. 그는 또한 국가 주도의 세 가지 기법을 강조했는데, 인구 조사는 인구를 분류하고 셀 수 있게 만들었고, 지도는 국경을 고정하고 영토의 통일성을 투영했으며, 박물관은 유물들을 선별해 연속적인 국가적 과거로 만들어냈다. 이러한 관행들이 모여 국가를 상상 가능하고 통치 가능한 것으로 만들었다.

⁰⁴/⁰⁵현대의 맥락에서, 상상된 공동체는 디지털 수단을 통해 계속해서 국가 정체성을 형성한다. 텔레비전 방송, 소셜 미디어 플랫폼, 온라인 뉴스는 지리적으로 분산된 인구에 걸친 공유된 경험과 서사를 만들어낸다. ⁰⁴한편으로, 디지털 미디어와 인터넷은 또한 전통적인 국경과 주권 개념에 도전하여, 국가가 상상되는 방식을 점진적으로 변화시키고 있다.

artificial [ɑ̀:rtəfíʃəl] 인위적인   entity [éntəti] 실체
sovereign [sávərən] 자주적인   institution [ìnstitú:ʃən] 기관
vernacular [vərnǽkjulər] 자국의, 자국어에 의한
telegraph [téləgræf] 전신
triad [tráiæd] 세 가지로 이루어진 것   census [sénsəs] 인구 조사
render [réndər] ~하게 만들다   project [prədʒékt] 투영하다
territorial [tèrətɔ́:riəl] 영토의   curate [kjuəréit] 선별하다
artifact [ɑ́:rtəfæ̀kt] 유물   conceivable [kənsí:vəbl] 상상 가능한
governable [gʌ́vərnəbl] 통치 가능한

01 Detail Question
Anderson이 국가를 "상상된" 것이라 묘사하는 이유는?
Ⓐ 국가에는 진정한 제도적 기반이 없음을 시사하기 위해
✓Ⓑ 구성원들이 서로를 개인적으로 알지 못함에도 불구하고 통합감을 느낀다는 것을 강조하기 위해
Ⓒ 국가 정체성이 공통의 조상과 민족성에서 비롯된다고 주장하기 위해
Ⓓ 정부의 기법들이 단지 기존 공동체를 발견할 뿐임을 보여주기 위해

어휘 ancestry[ǽnsèstri] 조상   ethnicity[eθnísiti] 민족성

02 Vocabulary Question
지문의 단어 "sovereign"과 의미상 가장 유사한 것은?
Ⓐ 구체적인
Ⓑ 강력한
Ⓒ 전통적인
✓Ⓓ 독립적인

어휘 concrete[kánkri:t] 구체적인   traditional[trədíʃənl] 전통적인

03 Detail Question
신문은 상상된 공동체의 창조에서 어떤 역할을 했는가?
Ⓐ 전신을 대신하는 주요 정보 수단이 되었다.
✓Ⓑ 사람들에게 통일된 시간적 경험을 확립했다.
Ⓒ 지역 간 말하는 억양을 표준화했다.
Ⓓ 지역 라디오 보도의 필요성을 없앴다.

어휘 establish[istǽbliʃ] 확립하다   uniform[júːnəfɔ̀ːrm] 통일된
temporal[témpərəl] 시간적인

04 Fact Question
디지털 미디어와 국가 정체성의 관계에 대해 제시된 것은?
Ⓐ 19세기 신문과 정확히 같은 방식으로 기능한다.
Ⓑ 주로 문화적 소속감보다 시민 참여를 장려한다.
✓Ⓒ 전통적인 국가 개념을 강화하면서 동시에 도전한다.
Ⓓ 국가가 인구 조사, 지도, 박물관을 효과적으로 사용하는 것을 막는다.

어휘 reinforce[rìːinfɔ́ːrs] 강화하다

05 Rhetorical Purpose Question
2단락과 3단락의 관계는?
Ⓐ 3단락은 2단락에서 논의된 미디어 기법들의 한계를 고찰한다.
✓Ⓑ 3단락은 2단락의 Anderson 이론 체계를 현대 디지털 맥락에 적용한다.
Ⓒ 3단락은 2단락에서 소개된 Anderson 이론의 배경 정보를 제공한다.
Ⓓ 3단락은 온라인 플랫폼으로 인해 2단락의 기법들이 이제 시대에 뒤떨어졌음을 시사한다.

어휘 framework[fréimwə̀ːrk] (이론 등의) 체계, 뼈대
irrelevant[irélavənt] 시대에 뒤떨어진, 무관한

[06-10]

소프트 파워
소프트 파워는 군사력이나 경제력이 아닌 문화, 가치관, 외교를 통해 다른 국가에 영향을 미치는 한 국가의 능력을 의미한다. 정치학자 Joseph Nye에 의해 대중화된 이 개념은 매력이 강압보다 더 효과적일 수 있음을 부각한다. [07]직접적인 압력 행사에 의존하는 하드 파워와 달리, 소프트 파워는 세계인의 인식을 감지하기 힘든 방식으로 형성한다.

문화는 소프트 파워에서 중심적 역할을 한다. [08]일본은 대중문화, 요리, 기술을 통해 세계적 존재감을 확장해 왔으며, 이 모든 것들이 각국의 청중을 매혹시키고 해외에서 일본의 이미지를 향상한다. 마찬가지로, 프랑스는 패션, 음식, 예술을 통해 소프트 파워를 행사하며, 우아함과 창의성이라는 정체성을 표현한다. 이러한 문화 수출은 관광과 무역을 증진하는 동시에 우호를 구축하고 여론을 형성하여, [08]두 국가 모두 영향력을 확장할 수 있게 한다.

[09]그러나 소프트 파워에는 한계가 있다. 문화적 계획들이 선전이나 지역 전통에 대한 위협으로 여겨질 경우 저항에 직면할 수 있다. [10]또한 소프트 파워를 유지하려면 교육, 문화 교류, 외교에 대한 투자가 필요하며, 이는 자원을 많이 요구할 수 있다. 이러한 어려움에도 불구하고, 소프트 파워는 갈등보다는 상호 존중과 자발적 협력을 장려하기 때문에 지속적인 영향력을 추구하는 국가들에게 필수적 도구로 남아 있다.

---

diplomacy[diplóuməsi] 외교   attraction[ətrǽkʃən] 매력
coercion[kouə́ːrʒən] 강압   perception[pərsépʃən] 인식
subtly[sʌ́tli] 감지하기 힘들게, 미묘하게
presence[prézns] 존재감   cuisine[kwizíːn] 요리
exert[igzə́ːrt] 행사하다   project[prədʒékt] 표현하다
limitation[lìmitéiʃən] 한계   initiative[iníʃiətiv] 계획
propaganda[prὰːpəgǽndə] 선전   investment[invéstmənt] 투자
mutual[mjúːtʃuəl] 상호의   voluntary[vάːləntèri] 자발적인
cooperation[kouὰːpəréiʃən] 협력   conflict[kάnflikt] 갈등

06 Vocabulary Question
첫 단락의 단어 "coercion"과 의미상 가장 유사한 것은?
Ⓐ 양보
✓Ⓑ 강제
Ⓒ 협상
Ⓓ 설득

어휘 concession[kənséʃən] 양보   compulsion[kəmpʌ́lʃən] 강제
negotiation[nigòuʃiéiʃən] 협상

07 Inference Question
소프트 파워의 효과에 대해 추론할 수 있는 것은?
Ⓐ 모든 국가가 한 국가의 문화적 가치관을 차용할 것을 보장한다.
Ⓑ 전통적인 외교와 협상을 불필요하게 만든다.
✓Ⓒ 한 국가에 대한 국제적 관점을 간접적인 방식으로 재정의한다.
Ⓓ 국가들이 선전을 통해 다른 국가들의 여론을 형성할 수 있게 한다.

어휘 guarantee[gæ̀rəntíː] 보장하다
conventional[kənvénʃənl] 전통적인

08 Rhetorical Purpose Question
글쓴이는 왜 일본과 프랑스를 언급하는가?
✓Ⓐ 문화 수출이 영향력의 도구 역할을 할 수 있음을 보여주기 위해
Ⓑ 특정 국가들이 세계 문화 시장을 지배하는 방식을 설명하기 위해
Ⓒ 기술적으로 발전한 국가들만이 소프트 파워를 개발한다고 주장하기 위해
Ⓓ 문화적 매력이 경제력보다 더 중요하다는 것을 보여주기 위해

어휘 dominate[dάmənèit] 지배하다

09 Rhetorical Purpose Question
3단락에 대해 결론지을 수 있는 것은?
Ⓐ 이전에 간략히 언급된 외교 전략에 대해 부연한다.
Ⓑ 소프트 파워와 관련된 어려움과 한계를 강조한다. ✓
Ⓒ 지문 앞부분에서 설명된 문화 수출을 자세히 서술한다.
Ⓓ 소프트 파워의 가치를 지지하는 새로운 관점을 소개한다.

10 Detail Question
일부 국가들에게 소프트 파워 유지가 어려울 수 있는 이유는?
Ⓐ 수많은 지역 관습과 충돌한다.
Ⓑ 상당한 수준의 투자가 필요하다. ✓
Ⓒ 단기적 유행에 너무 크게 의존한다.
Ⓓ 군사력으로 뒷받침되었을 때만 성공할 수 있다.

어휘 clash[klæʃ] 충돌하다

[11-15]

Jevons 역설

Jevons 역설은 직관에 반하는 경제학적 현상으로, 기술적 효율성의 개선이 실제로는 전체 자원 소비를 줄이는 대신 증가시킬 수 있다는 것이다. 영국 경제학자 William Stanley Jevons의 이름을 따서 명명된 ¹²이 역설은 19세기 영국의 석탄 사용에서 처음 관찰되었다. 증기기관이 더욱 효율적으로 변하면서, ¹²증기기관 운영 비용의 감소가 더 많은 사용을 장려했기 때문에 석탄 수요가 증가했다.

이 역설은 현대 자원 관리와 환경 정책에 영향을 미친다. **A** 예를 들어, ¹⁴자동차의 연료 효율 향상은 사람들로 하여금 더 많이 운전하게 하여 총 연료 소비를 증가시킬 수 있다. **B** 이러한 효과는 에너지 자원에만 국한되지 않는다. ¹⁴농업에서, 더 효율적인 관개 시스템은 더 많은 작물 생산을 가능하게 하여 궁극적으로 물 사용을 증가시킬 수 있다. **C** 이러한 반응들은 효율성만으로는 자원 보존을 보장하지 못할 수 있음을 보여준다. **D** 대신, 그것은 초기 절약을 상쇄하는 방식으로 우리의 행동을 변화시킬 수 있다.

Jevons 역설을 해결하려면 기술 개선보다 더 많은 것이 필요하다. ¹⁴/¹⁵효과적인 정책은 효율성 증대, 그리고 소비를 관리하는 규제나 장려책을 결합해야 한다. 이러한 조치 없이는, 기술적 진보가 자원 고갈을 늦추기는커녕 가속할 수 있다. 성공적인 환경 정책은 ¹⁵기술적 진보만으로는 자원의 지속가능성을 보장할 수 없음을 인식하는 것을 요구한다.

counterintuitive[kàuntərintjúːitiv] 직관에 반하는
consumption[kənsʌ́mpʃən] 소비 steam engine 증기기관
operate[ápərèit] 운영하다 irrigation[ìrəgéiʃən] 관개
conservation[kàːnsərvéiʃən] 보존 depletion[diplíːʃən] 고갈
sustainability[səstèinəbíləti] 지속가능성

11 Vocabulary Question
지문의 단어 "offset"과 의미상 가장 유사한 것은?
Ⓐ 높이다
Ⓑ 대체하다
Ⓒ 상쇄하다 ✓
Ⓓ 통제하다

어휘 heighten[haitn] 높이다 substitute[sʌ́bstətjùːt] 대체하다
counteract[kàuntərǽkt] 상쇄하다

12 Rhetorical Purpose Question
글쓴이는 왜 증기기관을 언급하는가?
Ⓐ 최근의 연료와 물 소비 사례들과 대조되는 예를 제공하기 위해
Ⓑ 산업화가 제한된 자원 문제 해결에 도움이 되었음을 시사하기 위해
Ⓒ 효율성이 때때로 자원 사용을 증가시킬 수 있다는 개념의 기원을 소개하기 위해 ✓
Ⓓ 과거의 기술이 더 환경적으로 지속 가능했음을 보여주기 위해

어휘 sustainable[səstéinəbl] 지속 가능한

13 Insertion Question
다음 문장이 삽입될 수 있는 네 곳이 지문에 표시되어 있다.

이러한 효과는 에너지 자원에만 국한되지 않는다.

그 문장은 어디에 가장 적절한가? 그 문장이 삽입될 수 있는 곳을 고르시오.

14 Rhetorical Purpose Question
2단락과 3단락의 관계는?
Ⓐ 3단락은 효율성이 역효과를 낳는 추가 사례를 제공하여 2단락의 예시들을 강화한다.
Ⓑ 3단락은 2단락에서 설명된 문제에 대응하는 효과적인 정책의 특징을 서술한다. ✓
Ⓒ 3단락은 기술적 효율성이 자원 소비를 줄인다고 주장하여 2단락의 주장에 반박한다.
Ⓓ 3단락은 기술적 진보를 해결책으로 강조하여 2단락에서 제기된 우려를 일축한다.

어휘 backfire[bǽkfàir] 역효과를 낳다

15 Fact Question
Jevons 역설 해결에서 기술적 진보의 역할에 대해 지문이 제시하는 것은?
Ⓐ 정부 개입 없이도 보통 전체 소비를 줄인다.
Ⓑ 자원 고갈을 방지하기 그 자체로 충분하다.
Ⓒ 자원 지속가능성을 달성하기 위해 다른 조치들과 결합되어야 한다. ✓
Ⓓ 효과적이기 위해서는 엄격한 규제 접근법으로 대체되어야 한다.

어휘 involvement[invɑ́ːlvmənt] 개입 strict[strikt] 엄격한

[16-20]

거석 기념물

¹⁷세계 많은 지역에서, 거대한 돌들이 수천 년 전 초기 사회들에 의해 세워지고 배치되었으며, 이는 초기 사회들의 공학 능력과 협력 노력의 증거로 남아있는 기념물들을 남겼다. ¹⁸거석 기념물로 알려진 이러한 거대 구조물들은 크기, 모양, 형태가 다양하다. 예를 들어, 몇몇 구조물은 Stonehenge처럼 원형 배치를 특징으로 하는 데 비해, 다른 구조물은 몰타의 신전처럼 사각형이다.

연구자들은 거석 기념물의 여러 목적을 제시해 왔다. ¹⁹ᴬ일부 이론은 그것들이 매장 의식에 사용되었다고 제안한다. ¹⁹ᴰ다른 이론은 이러한 기념물들이 종교 의식에서 역할을 했다고 믿는다. 또한 그들의 위치와 배치에 근거한 이론도 있는데, 특정 기념물들이 태양이나 달의 주기에 맞춰 신중하게 정렬되었다는 것이다. ¹⁹ᴮ그것들은 계절 변화와 천체 현상을 추적하는 초기 천문 관측소 역할을 했을 수 있다.

현대적 기계와 도구의 부재를 보완하기 위해, 이러한 기념물을 건설하는 것은 진보된 지질학, 물리학, 수학 지식을 필요로 했다. [20]스페인의 Dolmen de Menga에 대한 연구는 850미터 떨어진 채석장에서 최대 150톤에 달하는 돌들을 운반하기 위해 썰매와 평형추 시스템을 설계하는 데 사용된 정교한 공학 기술을 드러낸다. 이러한 거대한 돌들은 그 뒤 매우 정밀하게 배치되어 구조물이 거의 6천 년 동안 서 있을 수 있었다.

Ⓑ 천체의 주기에 맞춰 세심하게 배치되었다.
Ⓒ 연구는 남아있는 잔해에 근거하는데, 구조물이 온전하지 않기 때문이다.
✓ 건설에는 거대한 돌을 운반하고 균형을 맞추기 위한 발전된 도구가 사용되었다.

어휘 **facilitate**[fəsílətèit] 용이하게 하다 **intact**[intǽkt] 온전한
haul[hɔːl] 운반하다

colossal[kəlásəl] 거대한 **position**[pəzíʃən] 배치하다
megalithic[mègəlíθik] 거석의, 거석 문화 시대의
burial[bériəl] 매장의 **ritual**[rítʃuəl] 의식
religious[rilídʒəs] 종교적인 **align**[əláin] 정렬하다
astronomical[æstrənámikəl] 천문학적인
observatory[əbzá:rvətɔ̀ri] 관측소, 천문대
celestial[səléstʃəl] 천체의 **compensate**[kámpənsèit] 보완하다
geology[dʒiá:lədʒi] 지질학 **physics**[fíziks] 물리학
sophisticated[səfístəkèitid] 정교한 **sledge**[sledʒ] 썰매
quarry[kwɔ́:ri] 채석장 **precision**[prisíʒən] 정밀함

16 Vocabulary Question
지문의 단어 "celestial"과 의미상 가장 유사한 것은?
Ⓐ 고대의
✓ 천체의
Ⓒ 문화적인
Ⓓ 보이는

17 Inference Question
거석 기념물을 건설한 사회들에 대해 추론할 수 있는 것은?
Ⓐ 노동력과 자원을 할당하는 공식적인 행정 시스템을 운영했다.
✓ 대규모 협력을 위한 확립된 체계를 가지고 있었다.
Ⓒ 유사한 목적을 위한 구조물을 만들도록 영향을 받았다.
Ⓓ 먼 지역에서 돌을 확보하기 위해 무역 동맹을 설립했다.

어휘 **administrative**[ædmínəstrèitiv] 행정의
alliance[əláiəns] 동맹

18 Rhetorical Purpose Question
글쓴이는 왜 Stonehenge와 몰타의 신전을 언급하는가?
✓ 거석 기념물의 구조적 다양성을 설명하기 위해
Ⓑ 정교한 공학 기술을 보여주는 사례를 제공하기 위해
Ⓒ 많은 기념물에서 의식적 목적이 공학적 필요보다 더 중요했음을 주장하기 위해
Ⓓ 그것들의 형태 차이가 각각 다른 목적을 암시한다는 것을 제안하기 위해

19 Detail Question
다음 중 거석 기념물의 목적이었을 가능성이 있는 것으로 지문에서 언급되지 않은 것은?
Ⓐ 매장 의식을 위한 장소
Ⓑ 천문 관측을 위한 장소
✓ 토지 소유권의 상징
Ⓓ 종교 의식을 위한 장소

20 Fact Question
지문은 Dolmen de Menga에 대해 무엇을 명시하는가?
Ⓐ 돌의 운반을 용이하게 하기 위해 채석장 근처에 지어졌다.

4. Physical Science

HACKERS TEST
p.332

01 Ⓓ	02 Ⓑ	03 Ⓒ	04 Ⓑ	05 Ⓒ
06 Ⓒ	07 Ⓐ	08 Ⓒ	09 Ⓑ	10 Ⓒ
11 Ⓑ	12 Ⓑ	13 Ⓒ	14 Ⓐ	15 Ⓓ
16 Ⓒ	17 Ⓓ	18 Ⓑ	19 Ⓓ	20 Ⓒ

[01-05]

지진학의 역사

[01]19세기가 되어서야 비로소 지진을 과학적으로 이해하고 예측하려는 체계적인 노력이 이루어졌다. 연구자들은 영향받은 지역의 지진 활동과 패턴을 기록하기 시작했다. [05]진동은 추와 같은 기초적인 장비를 사용해 측정되었다.

[01/04]1800년대 후반에 이르러, 정식 과학 분야로서의 지진학이 나타나기 시작했다. [03D]John Milne과 같은 초기 선구자들은 진동과 그 전파에 대한 연구를 수행했다. [05]흔히 현대 지진학의 창시자로 평가받는 Milne은 1880년대에 수평 추 지진계를 개발하는 데 기여했으며, [03A]이 장치는 지동을 지속적으로 기록할 수 있게 해주었다. 이것은 과학자들이 더 높은 정확도로 지진을 관측할 수 있게 했다. [03B]지진 활동의 지속적 기록은 추세의 식별을 용이하게 했고, 이후 수십 년간 예측 모델 개발의 토대를 마련했다.

[04]20세기와 21세기의 발전은 이 분야에 혁신을 일으켰다. 과학자들은 고밀도 지진 관측망, 인공위성, 정교한 컴퓨터 모델에서 얻은 데이터를 통합하여 단층 응력과 지반 변형을 분석했다. 실시간 데이터 공유 시스템과 AI 기반 알고리즘과 같은 최근의 기술은 지진학자들의 역량을 더욱 향상시키고 있다. 이러한 도구들은 지역적 위험을 평가하고 주민들에게 적시에 경보를 발령하는 것을 가능하게 한다. 그럼에도 불구하고, 지진의 정확한 시점과 위치를 정밀하게 예측하는 것은 여전히 불가능하다.

systematic[sìstəmǽtik] 체계적인 **predict**[pridíkt] 예측하다
earthquake[ə́:rθkwèik] 지진 **seismic**[sáizmik] 지진의
rudimentary[rù:dəméntəri] 기초적인
pendulum[péndʒuləm] 추 **seismology**[saizmáládʒi] 지진학
scientific[sàiəntífik] 과학적인 **discipline**[dísəplin] 분야
conduct[kəndʌ́kt] 수행하다 **propagation**[prὰpəgéiʃən] 전파
seismograph[sáizməgræ̀f] 지진계 **accuracy**[ǽkjurəsi] 정확도
facilitate[fəsílətèit] 용이하게 하다 **fault**[fɔ:lt] 단층
deformation[dì:fɔːrméiʃən] 변형 **regional**[rí:dʒənl] 지역적인

01 Inference Question

19세기 이전의 지진 연구에 대해 추론할 수 있는 것은?
Ⓐ 서로 다른 지역에 걸친 지진의 영향을 비교하는 데 초점을 맞추었다.
Ⓑ 현대 지진학 분야의 토대 역할을 했다.
Ⓒ 사람들이 지진을 정확히 예측할 수 있도록 했다.
☑ 정식 과학 분야에 기반하지 않았다.

02 Vocabulary Question

첫 단락의 단어 "systematic"과 의미상 가장 유사한 것은?
Ⓐ 논쟁적인
☑ 체계적인
Ⓒ 학문적인
Ⓓ 일시적인

어휘 controversial[kàntrəvə́ːrʃəl] 논쟁적인
organized[ɔ́ːrɡənàizd] 체계적인
academic[ӕkədémik] 학문적인

03 Detail Question

다음 중 초기 지진학의 발전으로 지문에서 언급되지 않은 것은?
Ⓐ 지진 활동의 지속적인 기록
Ⓑ 지진 추세의 식별
☑ 지진 이후 단층대의 지도화
Ⓓ 진동 전파의 체계적인 연구

04 Rhetorical Purpose Question

2단락과 3단락의 관계는?
Ⓐ 3단락은 2단락에서 언급된 기법의 예시를 제공한다.
☑ 3단락은 2단락에서 소개된 분야의 더 고도화된 발전을 서술한다.
Ⓒ 3단락은 2단락에서 설명된 방법의 효과에 이의를 제기한다.
Ⓓ 3단락은 2단락에서 논의된 지진학적 발전의 한계를 설명한다.

05 Inference Question

수평 추 지진계에 대해 추론할 수 있는 것은?
Ⓐ 19세기 이전에 지진학자들에 의해 사용되었다.
Ⓑ 잦은 지진 발생 시기에 발명되었다.
☑ 이전의 지진 기록 기술에 의해 영향받았다.
Ⓓ 주로 실험실 환경에서 사용하기 위해 개발되었다.

어휘 invent[invént] 발명하다 laboratory[lǽbərətɔ̀ːri] 실험실의

[06-10]

해양 쓰레기 지대

해양 쓰레기 지대는 떠다니는 쓰레기들이 해류로 인해 축적되는 전 세계 바다의 광대한 지역이다. 08A이러한 지대는 주로 폐기된 어업 장비로 이루어지지만, 병, 봉지, 그리고 다른 작은 플라스틱 제품들도 포함한다. 가장 거대한 것은 하와이와 캘리포니아 사이에 있는 태평양 거대 쓰레기 지대이다.

10이러한 오염된 지역은 해양 서식지를 교란하고 많은 생물체에 해를 끼친다. 07이러한 지역의 플라스틱 쓰레기는 어류와 해양 포유류에 의해 섭취된다. 07/08B이는 부상, 굶주림, 그리고 독성 화학 물질 축적을 야기할 수 있다. 09일부 과학자들은 또한 쓰레기 지대가 침입종을 퍼뜨릴 수도 있다고 지적하는데, 떠다니는 물체들이 바다를 가로질러 생물체를 운반하기 때문이다.

10/08D이 문제를 해결하는 것은 쓰레기 지대의 증가를 촉진하는 플라스틱 생산을 줄이는 것부터 시작되어야 한다. 정부들은 일회용 플라스틱의 사용을 제한하는 정책을 시행해야 한다. 정화와 예방을 위해서는, 물에 뜨는 장벽과 같은 기술이 기존 잔해물을 수집하는 데 도움이 될 수 있으며, 개선된 재활용 시스템은 플라스틱이 바다에 도달하는 것을 방지할 수 있다. 10궁극적으로, 이러한 전 지구적 규모의 문제를 해결하는 것은 국제 협력과 모든 사람의 집단적 행동을 필요로 한다.

debris[dəbríː] 쓰레기, 잔해 accumulate[əkjúːmjulèit] 축적되다
discard[diskáːrd] 폐기하다
contaminate[kəntǽmənèit] 오염시키다
disrupt[disrʌ́pt] 교란하다 habitat[hǽbitæt] 서식지
ingest[indʒést] 섭취하다 starvation[stɑːrvéiʃən] 굶주림
implement[ímpləmènt] 시행하다 prevention[privénʃən] 예방
cooperation[kouàːpəréiʃən] 협력

06 Vocabulary Question

지문의 단어 "accumulate"와 의미상 가장 유사한 것은?
Ⓐ 흐르다
Ⓑ 운반하다
☑ 모이다
Ⓓ 나누다

어휘 transport[trænspɔ́ːrt] 운반하다 gather[gǽðər] 모이다

07 Detail Question

플라스틱 쓰레기가 해양 동물들에게 영향을 미치는 한 가지 방식은 무엇인가?
☑ 생존에 필수적인 영양소를 섭취하는 동물들의 능력을 저해한다.
Ⓑ 동물들이 새로운 먹이를 찾아 오염된 지역으로 이동하도록 만든다.
Ⓒ 포식자를 감지하는 동물들의 능력을 시각적 방해로 인해 감소시킨다.
Ⓓ 질병에 대한 동물들의 취약성을 지속적인 스트레스로 인해 증가시킨다.

08 Negative Fact Question

해양 쓰레기 지대에 관해 사실이 아닌 것은?
Ⓐ 주로 상업용 어구로 구성되어 있다.
Ⓑ 해양 생물의 체내에 축적될 수 있는 독소를 포함하고 있다.
☑ 해수의 자연적인 순환 패턴을 방해한다.
Ⓓ 억제되지 않은 플라스틱 생산으로 인해 면적이 확대되고 있다.

어휘 obstruct[əbstrʌ́kt] 방해하다 circulation[sə̀ːrkjuléiʃən] 순환

09 Inference Question

침입종에 대해 추론할 수 있는 것은?
Ⓐ 해양 플라스틱 쓰레기의 주요 피해자이다.
☑ 쓰레기 지대를 이용하여 다양한 지역으로 퍼질 수 있다.
Ⓒ 식단은 바다에서 유래한 식량원으로 구성된다.
Ⓓ 활동은 하와이 근처 바다에서 가장 두드러진다.

10 Rhetorical Purpose Question

2단락과 3단락 사이의 관계는?
Ⓐ 3단락은 2단락의 위험과 비교하여 해양 플라스틱의 근원을 논의한다.
Ⓑ 3단락은 2단락에서 언급된 환경적 영향의 예를 제공한다.
☑ 3단락은 2단락에서 강조된 문제들에 대한 가능한 해결책을 설명한다.
Ⓓ 3단락은 2단락의 문제들과 관련된 기후 예측을 개략적으로 설명한다.

[11-15]

북극 툰드라

북극 툰드라는 북미와 유라시아의 극권 근처에 위치한 광활하고 나무가 없는 지대이다. 이 지역은 지속적으로 매우 추운 기온, 강한 바람, 그리고 영구 동토층이라는 표면층을 가지고 있는데, 영구 동토층은 일 년 내내 얼어 있는 토양층이다. 이 얼어붙은 땅은 대부분의 식물이 자라기 어렵게 만들며, 그 결과 이끼, 지의류, 작은 관목과 같은 단순한 식생이 대부분의 식물 생명체를 차지하게 된다.

혹독한 조건에도 불구하고, [15]툰드라 생태계는 다양한 동물 생명체를 부양한다. 이 생물들은 생존을 가능하게 하는 여러 물리적, 행동적 적응 형태가 있다. [12]예를 들어, 사향소는 추위에 맞서 몸을 단열시키는 빽빽한 털과 두꺼운 지방층이 있다. 순록과 거위 같은 다른 동물들은 매년 가을 기후가 더 온화한 지역에서 겨울을 보내기 위해 남쪽으로 이주한다.

[15]툰드라 생태계는 심각한 환경 문제에 직면해 있다. [13B]자원 추출과 [13D]화석 연료 연소를 포함한 인간의 활동은 이 지역의 취약한 생물학적 균형을 직접적으로 위협한다. 게다가, [13A]기후 변화는 영구 동토층을 녹게 하고 있다. [14]이러한 해빙은 동식물의 서식지를 변화시킬 뿐만 아니라, 온실가스를 방출하고 어쩌면 고대 병원균을 되살림으로써 전 세계 인류 건강을 위태롭게 한다.

Arctic [á:rktik] 북극의 vast [væst] 광활한 polar circle 극권
persistently [pərsístəntli] 지속적으로 frigid [frídʒid] 매우 추운
permafrost [pá:rməfrɔ:st] 영구 동토층
vegetation [vèdʒətéiʃən] 식생 moss [mɔ:s] 이끼
lichen [láikən] 지의류 shrub [ʃrʌb] 관목
behavioral [bihéivjərəl] 행동적인, 행동의
adaptation [ædəptéiʃən] 적응 musk ox 사향소
insulate [ínsəlèit] 단열시키다 caribou [kǽrəbù:] 순록
migrate [máigreit] 이주하다 extraction [ikstrǽkʃən] 추출
fossil fuel 화석 연료 fragile [frǽdʒəl] 취약한
equilibrium [ì:kwəlíbriəm] 균형, 평형 thaw [θɔ:] 녹다, 해빙하다
jeopardize [dʒépərdàiz] 위태롭게 하다
pathogen [pǽθədʒən] 병원균

11 Vocabulary Question

지문의 단어 "equilibrium"과 의미상 가장 유사한 것은?
Ⓐ 대칭
☑ Ⓑ 균형
Ⓒ 갈등
Ⓓ 평등

12 Detail Question

지문에서 언급된 툰드라 동물의 적응 형태 중 하나는?
Ⓐ 매년 털갈이를 하는 것
☑ Ⓑ 대량의 지방을 저장하는 것
Ⓒ 해안 지역으로 이주하는 것
Ⓓ 겨울 동안 움직임을 제한하는 것

어휘 shed [ʃed] 털갈이를 하다

13 Negative Fact Question

다음 중 툰드라에 대한 환경적 위협으로 언급되지 않은 것은?
Ⓐ 기후 변화
Ⓑ 자원 추출
☑ Ⓒ 해안 침식
Ⓓ 에너지 생산

14 Rhetorical Purpose Question

글쓴이는 왜 고대 병원균을 언급하는가?
☑ Ⓐ 기후 변화와 관련하여 발생할 수 있는 국제적 위험 한 가지를 보여주기 위해
Ⓑ 병원균이 어떻게 툰드라의 혹독한 기후에 적응했는지 설명하기 위해
Ⓒ 기후 변화가 질병 발생의 주요 원인임을 시사하기 위해
Ⓓ 병원균이 고대 인류에게 주요 위협이었음을 강조하기 위해

15 Rhetorical Purpose Question

2단락과 3단락의 관계는?
Ⓐ 3단락은 2단락에서 논의된 식생의 유형을 자세히 설명한다.
Ⓑ 3단락은 2단락에서 설명된 적응 전략에 이의를 제기한다.
Ⓒ 3단락은 2단락에서 언급된 이주 패턴의 예를 제공한다.
☑ Ⓓ 3단락은 2단락에서 서술된 생태계가 직면한 위험을 제시한다.

[16-20]

Tunguska 사건

1908년 6월 30일, 러시아 동부의 Tunguska 강 근처에서 약 2,000제곱킬로미터에 달하는 면적의 나무들을 쓰러뜨린 대재앙적 폭발이 발생하였다. [17]목격자들은 최대 800킬로미터 떨어진 곳에서도 화구를 관측하였으며, 지진파는 멀리 유럽까지 감지되었다. Tunguska 사건의 정확한 원인은 여전히 알려지지 않았다.

[18]과학자들은 처음에 소행성이 지구와 충돌했을 것이라고 가정하였으나, 이 이론에는 큰 결함이 하나 존재하였는데, 바로 충돌 분화구가 전혀 발견되지 않았다는 점이다. 이러한 불일치는 경쟁하는 여러 가설을 낳았는데, [19]러시아 지질학자 Vladimir Epifanov는 이 폭발이 메테인과 같은 가스에 의해 발생했다고 제안하였는데, 메테인이 지하의 원천으로부터 공기 중으로 누출되었을 때 점화되었다.

그러나, 가장 가능성이 높은 설명은 Tunguska 사건이 지구와 충돌하기 전에 폭발한 소행성 또는 혜성과 관련이 있다는 것이다. [20]이 이론에 따르면, 물체가 대기권을 통과하면서 공기 분자와 접촉하여 발생하는 마찰이 강렬한 열을 생성하였다. 지상에서 불과 수 킬로미터 상공에 있을 때, 축적된 열에너지가 폭발을 유발하였고, 그 주변의 전원 지역을 완전히 파괴한 거대한 충격파를 방출했다.

cataclysmic [kætəklízmik] 대재앙적인
flatten [flǽtn] 쓰러뜨리다 eyewitness [aiwítnis] 목격자
seismic [sáizmik] 지진의 asteroid [ǽstərɔ̀id] 소행성
collide [kəláid] 충돌하다 crater [kréitər] 분화구
discrepancy [diskrépənsi] 불일치 friction [fríkʃən] 마찰
molecule [má:ləkjù:l] 분자 thermal [θə́:rməl] 열의
detonation [dètənéiʃən] 폭발 devastate [dévəstèit] 파괴하다

16 Vocabulary Question

첫 번째 단락의 단어 "cataclysmic"과 의미상 가장 유사한 것은?
Ⓐ 주목할 만한
Ⓑ 갑작스러운
☑ Ⓒ 격렬한
Ⓓ 다양한

어휘 notable [nóutəbl] 주목할 만한 diverse [dáivə:rs] 다양한

17 Rhetorical Purpose Question

글쓴이는 왜 유럽을 언급하는가?
Ⓐ 지역의 외진 정도를 강조하기 위해서
Ⓑ 현상의 발견자를 규명하기 위해서
Ⓒ 화구의 엄청난 크기를 설명하기 위해서
☑ 사건의 중대함을 보여주기 위해서

어휘 occurrence[əkɔ́:rəns] 사건, 발생하는 것

18 Detail Question

소행성 충돌을 수반하는 설명에 의문이 제기된 이유는?
Ⓐ 현지 목격자의 진술이 허위였다.
☑ 물질적 증거가 부재했다.
Ⓒ 과학적 실험이 결론에 도달하지 못했다.
Ⓓ 다른 이론이 설득력이 있었다.

어휘 inconclusive[ìnkənklú:siv] 결론에 도달하지 못하는
persuasive[pərswéisiv] 설득력 있는

19 Detail Question

Vladimir Epifanov는 Tunguska 사건의 원인을 무엇이라고 보았는가?
Ⓐ 지질학적 과정의 가속
Ⓑ 대기 이상 현상의 발생
Ⓒ 지하 구조물의 붕괴
☑ 가연성 물질의 방출

어휘 anomaly[ənáməli] 이상 현상 collapse[kəlǽps] 붕괴
emission[imíʃən] 방출, 배출 flammable[flǽməbl] 가연성의
substance[sʌ́bstəns] 물질

20 Detail Question

세 번째 단락에 따르면, 폭발의 원인이 된 요인은?
Ⓐ 외부 에너지원
Ⓑ 속도 감소
☑ 온도 변화
Ⓓ 화학 반응

어휘 reduction[ridʌ́kʃən] 감소 temperature[témpərətʃər] 온도

5. Life Science

HACKERS TEST   p.346

01 Ⓑ	02 Ⓑ	03 Ⓓ	04 Ⓒ	05 Ⓑ
06 Ⓒ	07 Ⓐ	08 Ⓒ	09 Ⓓ	10 Ⓒ
11 Ⓒ	12 Ⓑ	13 Ⓐ	14 Ⓑ	15 Ⓓ
16 Ⓑ	17 Ⓒ	18 Ⓓ	19 Ⓐ	20 Ⓓ

[01-05]

핵심종

핵심종은 그 수가 시사하는 바보다 훨씬 더 큰 영향을 생태계에 미치는 생물이다. 생태학자 Robert Paine은 조수 웅덩이가 생태계의 최상위 포식자인 불가사리를 연구하면서 이 개념을 발전시켰다. ⁰²그는 불가사리 외에 14종의 생물이 있던 생태계에서 불가사리를 없앴다. 3년 후, 그는 그 종들의 절반이 사라진 것을 관찰했다. 10년 후, 일반적으로 불가사리에게 잡아먹히는 홍합이 그 환경을 완전히 장악했다.

핵심종은 포식자 역할 외에도 생태계에서 다른 역할을 수행할 수 있다. 예를 들어, 비버는 서식지를 조성하는 건축가이다. 비버가 만든 댐은 ⁰³ᴬ홍수를 억제하고, ⁰³ᴮ가뭄으로부터 보호하며, ⁰³ᶜ높은 수질을 유지함으로써 생명이 가득한 건강한 습지의 성장을 돕는다. 꿀벌을 비롯하여 ⁰⁴꽃가루를 매개하는 곤충 및 조류 또한 환경에서 중요한 역할을 하는데, 이는 전 세계 식물의 80%가 번식하는 것을 도우며 그 식물들이 수많은 초식 동물 종의 핵심 식량원이 되기 때문이다.

핵심종을 보호하는 것은 그들의 큰 환경적 영향 때문에 우선순위가 높다. ⁰⁵아르헨티나의 노력은 핵심종이 어떻게 성공적으로 보존될 수 있는지 보여준다. 재규어는 만약 통제되지 않으면 식물을 과도하게 섭취하게 될 먹이 개체군을 통제하며, 대형 국립 공원에서 보호되어 왔다. 번식 프로그램은 재규어의 개체수를 안정시켰고, 이는 생태학적 균형을 회복하는 데 도움이 될 것이다.

keystone[kí:stòun] 핵심 organism[ɔ́:rɡənìzm] 생물
predator[prédətər] 포식자 tide pool 조수 웅덩이
ecosystem[í:kousìstəm] 생태계 observe[əbzə́:rv] 관찰하다
mussel[mʌ́səl] 홍합 consume[kənsú:m] 먹다, 섭취하다
dominate[dámənèit] 장악하다 habitat[hǽbitæt] 서식지
teem with ~으로 가득하다 flooding[flʌ́diŋ] 홍수
drought[draut] 가뭄
pollinate[pɑ́:lənèit] 꽃가루를 매개하다, 수분하다
reproduce[rì:prədjú:s] 번식하다
herbivore[ə́:rbəvɔ̀:r] 초식 동물 priority[praiɔ́:rəti] 우선순위
demonstrate[démənstrèit] 보여주다
vegetation[vèdʒetéiʃən] 식물 stabilize[stéibəlàiz] 안정시키다
restore[ristɔ́:r] 회복하다 ecological[ìkəlá:dʒikəl] 생태학적인

01 Vocabulary Question

지문의 단어 "stabilized"와 의미상 가장 유사한 것은?
Ⓐ 영향을 미쳤다
☑ 보호했다
Ⓒ 분석했다
Ⓓ 무시했다

02 Inference Question

불가사리에 대해 추론할 수 있는 것은?
Ⓐ 개체 수가 결국 3년 후에 감소했다.
☑ 없어지자 다른 종들의 생존 가능성을 감소시켰다.
Ⓒ 같은 먹이원을 두고 홍합과 경쟁했다.
Ⓓ 그 환경의 최상위 포식자에 의해 죽임을 당했다.

어휘 absence[ǽbsəns] 없음, 부재

03 Detail Question
다음 중 비버가 습지 생태계를 지탱하는 방식으로 언급되지 않은 것은?
Ⓐ 홍수 억제
Ⓑ 가뭄 방지
Ⓒ 높은 수질 유지
✓ 초식 동물의 서식지 제공

04 Detail Question
두 번째 단락에 따르면, 일부 조류는 환경에서 어떤 중요한 역할을 하는가?
Ⓐ 해충을 섭취한다.
Ⓑ 둥지는 다른 종을 보호한다.
✓ 식물 번식을 돕는다.
Ⓓ 존재함으로써 식량원이 있음을 나타낸다.

05 Rhetorical Purpose Question
세 번째 단락의 목적은?
Ⓐ 특정 먹이 개체군의 중요성을 설명하기 위해
✓ 핵심종 보호의 성공적인 사례를 보여주기 위해
Ⓒ 아르헨티나 전역에서 발견되는 생태학적 문제를 설명하기 위해
Ⓓ 국립 공원에서 핵심 식물의 성장을 축하하기 위해

[06-10]

> **성별 결정에 온도가 미치는 영향**
>
> 많은 파충류에서 성별은 유전적 특징이 아닌 부화 온도에 의해 결정되며, 이러한 과정을 온도 의존적 성 결정이라고 한다. 이 기제는 성 호르몬의 균형을 조절하는 핵심 효소인 아로마타제를 포함한다. **07이 효소의 기능은 온도에 매우 민감하여, 결정적 발달 시기의 특정 온도가 효소를 활성화하거나 억제할 수 있다.** 이는 배아의 발달을 수컷 또는 암컷 경로로 유도하여 궁극적으로 개체군 내의 성비에 영향을 미친다. **08예를 들어, 일부 거북 개체군에서는 둥지의 온도가 높을수록 더 많은 암컷 새끼가 부화한다.**
>
> 최근의 기후 변화 연구는 이것이 온도 민감종에 영향을 미칠 수 있음을 보여준다. **09상승된 온도는 암컷 또는 수컷의 불균형적인 증가를 초래할 수 있다.** 많은 개체군 집단이 번식 활동의 감소를 겪을 수 있다. 연구자들은 이러한 문제들을 해결하기 위한 개입 방법을 시험하고 있다. 둥지 위에 **10A햇빛 가리개를 설치하거나 10B알을 더 시원한 지역으로 옮기는** 등의 기법이 극심한 성 불균형을 예방하기 위해 현재 탐색 되고 있다. 연구자들은 또한 **10D야생 알의 온도를 면밀히 추적하고 있다.** 성 결정에 미치는 온도의 영향을 관리하는 것은 영향받는 종들의 장기적인 생존에 필수적일 것이다.
>
> ---
> genetics[dʒənétiks] 유전적 특징
> incubation[ìŋkjubéiʃən] 부화, 알을 품음 involve[inválv] 포함하다
> enzyme[énzaim] 효소 developmental[divèləpméntl] 발달의
> activate[ǽktəvèit] 활성화하다 suppress[səprés] 억제하다
> embryo[émbriòu] 배아 hatchling[hǽtʃliŋ] (갓 부화한) 새끼
> elevate[éləvèit] 상승시키다
> disproportionate[dìsprəpɔ́ːrʃənət] 불균형적인
> intervention[ìntərvénʃən] 개입 relocate[rìːloukéit] 옮기다

06 Vocabulary Question
지문의 단어 "ultimately"와 의미상 가장 유사한 것은?
Ⓐ 즉시
Ⓑ 처음에
✓ 결국
Ⓓ 직접적으로

07 Fact Question
아로마타제에 대해 명시된 것은?
✓ 기능은 발달의 주요 단계 동안 열 노출에 의해 조절된다.
Ⓑ 온도가 감소함에 따라 발달을 수컷 경로로 유도한다.
Ⓒ 활동은 부화 온도가 낮아질 때 억제된다.
Ⓓ 파충류의 성 결정에서 부차적인 요인이다.

어휘 modulate[mɑ́dʒuleit] 조절하다 thermal[θə́ːrməl] 열의
steer[stiər] 유도하다 secondary[sékəndèri] 부차적인

08 Detail Question
일부 거북 개체군에서 온도 상승의 결과로 나타나는 것은?
Ⓐ 발달 기간의 연장
Ⓑ 부화 성공률의 감소
✓ 암컷 새끼의 증가
Ⓓ 신생 거북의 더 긴 수명

어휘 hatch[hætʃ] 부화하다

09 Inference Question
기후 변화에 대해 추론할 수 있는 것은?
Ⓐ 수컷 새끼에게만 유리하게 작용할 것이다.
Ⓑ 아로마타제의 생성을 감소시킨다.
Ⓒ 파충류 개체군의 번식 활동을 중단시킨다.
✓ 파충류의 성비를 왜곡할 가능성이 있다.

어휘 halt[hɔːlt] 중단시키다 skew[skjuː] 왜곡하다

10 Detail Question
온도 민감종을 돕기 위한 방법으로 언급되지 않은 것은?
Ⓐ 햇빛을 차단하기 위한 가리개 설치
Ⓑ 열을 덜 받는 환경으로 알 재배치
✓ 알 서식지 주변에 조명 설치
Ⓓ 알의 온도 조건 추적

[11-15]

> **호르몬 조절**
>
> 호르몬 조절은 인체에서 많은 필수 작용을 조절하는 데 도움을 주는 기본 메커니즘이다. 호르몬은 특수한 샘에서 생성되어 혈류로 분비되는 화학적 전달 물질이다. 그것들은 다양한 장기와 조직으로 이동해, 특정 활동을 시작하거나 멈추는 신호를 전달한다. 예를 들어, 신장에서 분비되는 **12에리트로포이에틴은 적혈구 생성을 활성화한다.**
>
> 호르몬 조절은 세포 간 신호 전달을 통해 이루어진다. **13모든 호르몬은 상호 보완적 수용체를 가진 표적 세포를 찾는다.** 호르몬이 수용체에 결합하면 발달 촉진, 에너지 생성, 체액 농도 조절 등 특정 반응이 개시된다. **14이 모든 메커니즘은 조절 피드백에 크게 의존한다.** 신체가 특정 물질의 과잉이나 부족을 감지하면, 항상성을 재확립하기 위해 호르몬 분비가 변화한다. **15예를 들어, 갑상샘 호르몬은 신체의 대사율을 관리한다.** 이 수치가 너무 높아지면, 추가 분비를

억제하는 신호가 발생하며, 수치가 떨어지면 분비량이 증가한다.

호르몬 조절은 몸이 환경 변화에 적응하고 안정된 내부 상태를 유지하도록 한다. 이 체계는 성장, 에너지 사용, 스트레스 반응, 회복과 같은 활동을 신체가 조정할 수 있게 한다. 호르몬의 정밀한 작용은 신체의 모든 시스템을 조화롭게 유지하고 질환이 발생하는 것을 예방하는 데 매우 중요하다.

regulate[régjuleit] 조절하다　chemical[kémikəl] 화학적인
gland[glænd] (인체의) 샘, 분비선　initiate[iníʃièit] 시작하다
suspend[səspénd] 멈추다　release[rilí:s] 분비하다
stimulate[stímjulèit] 활성화되다, 자극하다
production[prədʌ́kʃən] 생성　intercellular[ìntərséljulər] 세포간의
complementary[kà:mpləméntəri] 상호 보완적인
receptor[riséptər] 수용체　concentration[kà:nsəntréiʃən] 농도
body fluid 체액　rely on ~에 의존하다
regulatory[régjulətɔ:ri] 조절의　deficiency[difíʃənsi] 부족
secretion[sikrí:ʃən] 분비　homeostasis[hòumiəstéisis] 항상성
inhibit[inhíbit] 억제하다　coordinate[kouɔ́:rdənèit] 조정하다

11　Vocabulary Question
첫 번째 단락의 단어 "suspend"와 의미상 가장 유사한 것은?
Ⓐ 관찰하다
Ⓑ 피하다
✓Ⓒ 멈추다
Ⓓ 보존하다

어휘　monitor[mɑ́nətər] 관찰하다　preserve[prizə́:rv] 보존하다

12　Detail Question
에리트로포이에틴의 주요 기능은 무엇인가?
Ⓐ 신체 활동 중 근육 성장을 자극한다.
Ⓑ 체액 균형을 위한 피드백 고리를 조절한다.
✓Ⓒ 적혈구 생성을 유발한다.
Ⓓ 장기에서 죽은 혈구를 제거한다.

13　Inference Question
표적 세포에 대해 추론할 수 있는 것은?
✓Ⓐ 짝이 맞는 호르몬과 결합하여 특정 활동을 시작한다.
Ⓑ 신체에 필요한 모든 호르몬을 생산할 수 있다.
Ⓒ 호르몬에 노출되면 비활성화된다.
Ⓓ 물질의 양이 너무 많은지 또는 너무 적은지를 감지한다.

14　Fact Question
지문에서 조절 피드백에 대해 명시된 것은?
Ⓐ 특수한 호르몬 샘의 필요성을 없앤다.
✓Ⓑ 균형을 회복하기 위해 호르몬 생성을 조절한다.
Ⓒ 호르몬이 일시적으로만 작동하도록 한다.
Ⓓ 호르몬이 혈류로 들어가는 것을 막는다.

어휘　adjust[ədʒʌ́st] 조절하다

15　Rhetorical Purpose Question
글쓴이는 왜 갑상샘을 언급하는가?
Ⓐ 뼈와 근육 성장에 관여하는 샘을 소개하기 위해
Ⓑ 호르몬이 신진대사에 의해 선택적으로 표적화되는 방식을 보여주기 위해

Ⓒ 호르몬 불균형으로 인해 발생하는 질환을 설명하기 위해
✓Ⓓ 피드백 메커니즘이 작동하는 방식의 예를 들기 위해

어휘　selectively[siléktivli] 선택적으로

[16-20]

새 영역

새들은 먹이와 둥지 영역 같은 필수적인 자원을 보호하기 위해 영역을 설정한다. 이러한 영역은 선택되어, 특히 번식기에는 적극적으로 방어된다. 새들은 흔히 노래를 부르거나 시각적 신호를 보여 영역 경계를 설정한다. 예를 들어, [17]개똥지빠귀는 경쟁자를 쫓아내기 위해 노래를 부르고, 붉은날개검은새는 화려한 날개 부분을 보여 소유권을 알린다.

영역의 크기는 새의 종류에 따라 다르다. [18]매는 넓은 사냥 범위 때문에 넓은 영역을 방어하는 반면, 굴뚝새와 참새는 둥지 주변의 작은 구역만 지킨다. 일부 열대 벌새는 꽃식물을 개별적으로 방어한다. [19]갈매기처럼 군체를 이루는 새들은 밀집된 둥지 영역에서 아주 작은 구역만 보호할 수도 있다.

새들은 때때로 영역 경계를 유지하기 위해 신체적 충돌을 벌인다. 제비갈매기는 군집에서 둥지 구역을 맹렬히 보호하며, 침입자를 쫓아내기 위해 조직적인 공중 공격을 수행한다. 마찬가지로, 북방흉내지빠귀도 자신의 영역을 지키기 위해 공중 공격을 감행한다.

일부 새들은 자원 가용성의 변화에 맞춰 영역 전략을 달리하기도 한다. 해안 지역에서, 검은머리물떼새는 썰물 때 먹이 먹는 곳에서 침입자를 공격적으로 쫓아낸다. [20]그러나, 조수가 오르면, 먹이 먹는 곳이 잠기고 먹이가 사라지면서 이러한 충돌이 빠르게 줄어든다.

indispensable[ìndispénsəbl] 필수적인
robin[rɑ́:bin] 개똥지빠귀
patch[pætʃ] (주변과는 다른) 부분, (덧대는) 조각
wren[ren] 굴뚝새　sparrow[spǽrou] 참새
hummingbird[hʌ́miŋbə̀:rd] 벌새　conflict[kɑ́nflikt] 충돌
colony[kɑ́:ləni] 군집　aerial[ɛ́əriəl] 공중의
repel[ripél] 쫓아내다　intruder[intrú:dər] 침입자
mockingbird[mɑ́:kiŋbə:rd] 흉내지빠귀
oystercatcher[ɔ́istərkætʃər] 검은머리물떼새
aggressively[əgrésivli] 공격적으로
submerge[səbmə́:rdʒ] 잠기다

16　Vocabulary Question
첫 문장의 단어 "indispensable"과 의미상 가장 유사한 것은?
Ⓐ 접근 가능한
✓Ⓑ 중요한
Ⓒ 특이한
Ⓓ 풍부한

어휘　abundant[əbʌ́ndənt] 풍부한

17　Detail Question
개똥지빠귀는 보통 어떻게 자신의 영역 경계를 표시하는가?
Ⓐ 더 큰 둥지를 지음으로써
Ⓑ 다른 개똥지빠귀를 쫓아냄으로써
✓Ⓒ 노래를 부름으로써
Ⓓ 큰 무리를 지어 모임으로써

어휘　chase away 쫓아내다　flock[flɑ:k] 무리, 떼

18 Rhetorical Purpose Question

글쓴이는 왜 굴뚝새와 참새를 언급하는가?
Ⓐ 두 종류의 새가 같은 둥지 구역을 공유한다는 것을 암시하기 위해
Ⓑ 일부 새들이 영역 경계를 설정하지 않는 이유를 설명하기 위해
☑ 넓은 영역을 지키는 새와 대비를 보여주기 위해
Ⓓ 서로 다른 종류의 새들이 영역을 어떻게 방어하는지 보여주기 위해

19 Fact Question

지문에서 갈매기에 대해 명시된 것은?
☑ 둥지 근처의 작은 영역만 보호한다.
Ⓑ 번식을 위해 외딴 지역을 선택한다.
Ⓒ 영역을 방어하기 위해 공중 공격을 벌인다.
Ⓓ 경쟁을 막기 위해 단독으로 둥지 트는 것에 의존한다.

어휘 isolated [áisəlèitid] 외딴, 고립된
        solitary [sálətèri] 단독으로 하는
        competition [kàmpətíʃən] 경쟁

20 Detail Question

조수가 오르면 검은머리물떼새의 행동은 어떻게 변하는가?
Ⓐ 다른 조류와 협력한다.
Ⓑ 주로 먹이를 찾는 데 집중한다.
Ⓒ 둥지 영역을 방어할 가능성이 높아진다.
☑ 갈등에 개입할 가능성이 낮아진다.

어휘 prone [proun] ~할 가능성이 높은, ~하기 일쑤인

ACTUAL TEST 1

p.356

Module 1

01 plague	02 responsible	03 only
04 the	05 nearly	06 entire
07 but	08 for	09 acute
10 shortages	11 ⓓ	12 ⓐ
13 ⓑ	14 ⓓ	15 ⓒ
16 ⓐ	17 ⓒ	18 ⓒ
19 ⓓ	20 ⓑ	

Module 2

01 are	02 for	03 tentacles
04 give	05 precise	06 control
07 distinguishes	08 from	09 other
10 can	11 ⓒ	12 ⓐ
13 ⓑ	14 ⓑ	15 ⓓ

Module 1

[01-10]

14세기에 유럽을 휩쓴 흑사병은 유럽 문명의 궤도를 바꾼 대재앙적 범유행병이었다. 이 역병은 전체 인구의 거의 절반 가까이를 사망에 이르게 했을 뿐만 아니라 극심한 노동력 부족을 유발하고 광범위한 사회 불안을 촉발하는 원인이 되었다. 그 결과, 살아남은 노동자들은 더 높은 임금을 협상할 수 있는 위치에 놓였고, 많은 이들이 더 나은 경제적 전망을 추구하며 봉건제의 의무를 버렸다. 이 변화들은 대륙 전역에 걸쳐 더 큰 사회적 유동성을 향한 기반을 닦았다.

---

sweep[swi:p] 휩쓸다
cataclysmic[kætəklízmik] 대재앙적인, 대변동의
trajectory[trədʒéktəri] 궤도 **civilization**[sìvəlaizéiʃən] 문명
plague[pleig] 역병 **responsible**[rispánsəbl] 원인이 되는
demise[dimáiz] 사망 **shortage**[ʃɔ́:rtidʒ] 부족
unrest[ʌnrést] (사회적인) 불안 **abandon**[əbǽndən] 버리다
feudal[fjú:dl] 봉건제의 **obligation**[àbləgéiʃən] 의무
pursuit[pərsú:t] 추구 **prospect**[práspekt] 전망

[11-12] 이메일을 읽으시오.

날짜: 5월 11일
제목: 면접 일정 확정

Mr. Brandt께,

면접을 ¹¹5월 15일에서 그 다음 날로 변경해 달라고 5월 9일에 보내신 메시지를 받았습니다. 요청하신 대로, 귀하의 면접은 그날 오후 2시로 일정이 변경되었습니다. ¹²면접에 접속할 수 있는 링크를 이메일로 받으실 것입니다. 시작 시간 10분 전에 링크를 열어 주세요.

Olivia Sweeney 드림

---

confirmation[kὰnfərméiʃən] 확정

11 Detail Question

면접일은 언제인가?
Ⓐ 5월 9일
Ⓑ 5월 11일
Ⓒ 5월 15일
✓ 5월 16일

12 Inference Question

Mr. Brandt의 면접에 대해 추론할 수 있는 것은?
✓ 온라인 회의 플랫폼을 통해 진행될 것이다.
Ⓑ 이전에 진행된 면접의 후속 미팅이다.
Ⓒ 회사 내부 문제로 인해 일정이 변경되어야 했다.
Ⓓ 고위 경영진 직위를 위한 면접이다.

[13-15] 메시지 대화문을 읽으시오.

Elena Patel (오전 9:15)
팀원 여러분, 다음 주 화요일 회의에 필요한 발표 자료를 마무리해야 해요. 자료가 완벽하게 준비되고 체계적으로 구성되었는지 확인해요.

Sarah Kim (오전 9:20)
알겠어요! 저는 지금 슬라이드 작업을 하고 있어요. 저희 제품 라인업 중 상위 세 가지 전기 자전거에 중점을 두고 있어요.

Thomas Rivera (오전 9:25)
¹³나머지는 제가 만들고 있는 인쇄물 자료에 포함할게요. 그런데 제품 사양에서 몇 가지 불일치하는 점을 발견했어요. 누군가 이 수치들을 재확인해 주시겠어요?

Shawn Gibbs (오전 9:30)
물론이죠. ¹⁴제가 예산 보고서 검토를 마무리한 후, 오늘 오전에 기술 문서와 대조하여 그 수치들을 검증할 수 있어요. 거의 다 끝냈어요.

Elena Patel (오전 9:35)
잘 발견했어요, Thomas. ¹⁵모두들 자신의 담당 섹션을 주의 깊게 검토하고 모든 내용이 정확한지 확인해 주세요. CEO가 이 프레젠테이션에 참석할 예정이에요.

---

inconsistency[ìnkənsístənsi] 불일치
specification[spèsəfikéiʃən] 사양 **verify**[vérəfài] 검증하다
documentation[dὰkjumentéiʃən] 문서
budget[bʌ́dʒit] 예산 **accurate**[ǽkjurət] 정확한

13 Detail Question

Thomas Rivera의 책임은 무엇인가?
Ⓐ 슬라이드를 만드는 것
✓ 인쇄물을 준비하는 것
Ⓒ 제품 사양을 재확인하는 것
Ⓓ 전기 자전거를 조사하는 것

14 Inference Question

Shawn Gibbs에 대해 추론할 수 있는 것은?
Ⓐ 마감일까지 슬라이드 준비 작업을 마쳐야 한다.
Ⓑ 예산 보고서 검토를 연기할 것이다.
Ⓒ 잔업을 할 만큼 한가하지 않을 것이다.
☑ 추가적인 업무를 맡을 시간이 있을 것이다.

어휘 **postpone**[poustpóun] 연기하다

15 Intention Question

오전 9시 35분에, Elena Patel이 "The CEO will be sitting in on this presentation"이라고 썼을 때, 그녀가 의미한 것은?
Ⓐ CEO가 팀의 능력에 대해 우려하고 있다고 생각한다.
Ⓑ 직접 회의를 주도하지는 않을 것이다.
☑ 팀의 작업물이 높은 기준을 충족하기를 바란다.
Ⓓ CEO가 이 프레젠테이션에만 참석할 것임을 언급하고 있다.

[16-20]

화학 합성 생태계

대부분의 사람은 광합성, 즉 식물이 햇빛을 이용해 에너지를 생산하는 과정에 대해 익히 알고 있다. 하지만, 햇빛이 침투할 수 없는 가장 깊은 바다 속에서는, 햇빛 대신 화학 물질을 이용해 먹이와 영양분을 생산하는 화학 합성을 통해 생태계가 번성한다. 그렇다면 화학 합성은 어떻게 작용하는 것일까?

이 생태계의 기반에는 황화수소와 같은 화학 물질을 에너지로 전환하는 박테리아가 있는데, 이는 식물이 햇빛을 전환하는 방식과 유사하다. 이 화학 합성 박테리아는 다수의 기이한 생물들을 지탱하는 복잡한 먹이 사슬의 기초를 형성한다. ¹⁷거대 관벌레 중에는 길이가 8피트에 달하는 것도 있는데, 특수한 신체 기관을 이 박테리아에게 보금자리로 제공하고 그 대가로 영양분을 얻는다. ¹⁸ᴰ특정 종의 조개와 홍합은 화학 합성 박테리아와의 공생 관계를 진화시켰는데, 이는 그 종들이 초고온의 물이 ¹⁸ᴬ해저에서 분출되는 ¹⁸ᴮ열수 분출구와 같은 혹독한 환경에서도 번성할 수 있게 만들었다.

²⁰이 화학 합성 군집을 대단히 흥미롭게 만드는 것은 태양 에너지로부터의 독립성이며, 이는 우리가 서식 가능한 환경이라고 여기는 것의 정의를 확장한다. 이러한 군집에 대한 연구는 ¹⁹햇빛이 없는 곳에서 생명체가 어떻게 존재할 수 있을지에 대한 이해를 제공할 수 있다. 예를 들어, Europa나 Enceladus와 같은 얼음 위성들도 이러한 화학 반응에 기반하여 생명체를 지탱할 수도 있다.

photosynthesis[fòutəsínθəsis] 광합성
penetrate[pénətrèit] 침투하다, 뚫다   **thrive**[θraiv] 번성하다
chemosynthesis[kèmousínθəsis] 화학 합성
chemical[kémikəl] 화학 물질   **nutrient**[njú:triənt] 영양분
convert[kənvə́:rt] 전환하다   **hydrogen sulfide** 황화수소
array[əréi] 다수   **bizarre**[bizá:r] 기이한
house[haus] 보금자리(집)를 제공하다   **mussel**[mʌ́səl] 홍합
symbiotic[sìmbiátik] 공생의   **flourish**[flə́:riʃ] 번성하다
hydrothermal vent 열수 분출구   **erupt**[irʌ́pt] 분출하다
habitable[hǽbitəbl] 서식 가능한   **reaction**[riǽkʃən] 반응

16 Vocabulary Question

지문의 단어 "penetrate"와 의미상 가장 유사한 것은?
☑ 꿰뚫다
Ⓑ 용해하다
Ⓒ 반사하다
Ⓓ 탈출하다

어휘 **dissolve**[dizɑ́:lv] 용해하다   **reflect**[riflékt] 반사하다

17 Detail Question

거대 관벌레가 특수한 신체 기관을 화학합성 박테리아에게 보금자리로 제공하는 이유는 무엇인가?
Ⓐ 박테리아를 이용해서 물의 독소를 여과한다.
Ⓑ 박테리아가 더 효과적으로 번식하도록 돕는다.
☑ 박테리아가 생산한 영양분을 얻는다.
Ⓓ 박테리아가 화학 물질을 흡수할 수 있도록 만든다.

어휘 **reproduce**[rì:prədjú:s] 번식하다

18 Negative Fact Question

다음 중 특정 종의 조개에 대해 사실이 아닌 것은?
Ⓐ 햇빛이 닿을 수 없는 지역에 존재한다.
Ⓑ 열수 분출구 주변에서 발견될 수 있다.
☑ 초고온의 물로부터 화학 에너지를 생성한다.
Ⓓ 일부 박테리아와 협력 관계를 발전시켰다.

19 Rhetorical Purpose Question

글쓴이는 왜 얼음 위성을 언급하는가?
Ⓐ 화학 합성 박테리아가 우주에서 유래했을 수 있음을 시사하기 위해
Ⓑ 지구 해저의 환경을 천체 환경과 비교하기 위해
Ⓒ 화학 합성이 불가능한 환경의 예를 제공하기 위해
☑ 화학 합성 생태계가 외계 생명체에 대한 단서를 제공할 수 있음을 나타내기 위해

어휘 **extraterrestrial**[èkstrətəréstriəl] 외계의

20 Rhetorical Purpose Question

세번째 단락의 기능은?
Ⓐ 2단락에서 언급된 박테리아의 구체적인 예를 제공한다.
☑ 화학 합성 군집의 더 광범위한 의의와 시사점을 설명한다.
Ⓒ 1단락에서 제시된 광합성에 대한 정보를 반박한다.
Ⓓ 화학 합성 군집 연구의 어려움을 언급하며 지문을 마무리한다.

Module 2

[01-10]

문어는 비상한 신체적, 인지적 능력을 가진 두족류 연체동물이다. 문어는 촉수로 잘 알려져 있는데, 촉수는 문어에게 정교한 운동 통제력을 부여한다. 이 점이 문어를 다른 대부분의 무척추동물로부터 돋보이게 한다. 문어는 또한 몸의 형태, 색깔, 질감을 바꿀 수 있어서 그들이 포식자들에게 거의 보이지 않게 만든다. 관찰자들은 문어가 매우 튼튼하게 울타리를 두른 공간에서 탈출하는 것과 같이 정교한 행동을 하는 것을 기록했으며, 문어는 사람 개개인의 얼굴을 인식하는 능력이 있다. 그 결과, 문어는 척추동물 이외의 동물에 복합적 지능이 존재함을 진화가 가장 눈에 띄게 증명하는 사례라고 여겨진다.

cephalopod[séfələpàd] 두족류   **mollusk**[máləsk] 연체동물
cognitive[kágnətiv] 인지적인   **capability**[kèipəbíləti] 능력
tentacle[téntəkl] 촉수   **invertebrate**[invə́:rtəbrət] 무척추동물
predator[prédətər] 포식자
enclosure[inklóuʒər] 울타리를 두른 공간
demonstration[dèmənstréiʃən] 증명, 입증
vertebrate[və́:rtəbrət] 척추동물

[11-15]

심리적 거리

심리적 거리는 우리의 정신이 사건들을 설명하는 방식이 우리가 인식하는 거리에 따라 어떻게 변화하는지 설명한다. 이 거리는 시간적 거리(언제), 공간적 거리(어디서), 사회적 거리(누가), 또는 가설적 거리(가능성)일 수 있다. 사건이 심리적으로 멀게 느껴질 때, 사람들은 추상적으로 생각하는 경향이 있으며, 핵심적인 특징과 광범위한 양상에 초점을 맞춘다. 반대로, [11]사건이 심리적으로 가깝게 느껴질 때, 사고는 더 구체적이 되며, 세부 사항과 상황 정보에 더 큰 중점을 둔다.

연구는 이 이론이 현실 세계에서 갖는 의의를 입증한다. [12]심리학자 Yaacov Trope와 Nira Liberman이 수행한 연구에서, 참가자들은 시간의 범위에 따라 다른 선택을 했다. "내년에" 발생할 사건에 대해 질문받았을 때, 그들은 바람직함(왜 행동해야 하는가)을 우선시한 반면, "내일" 발생할 사건에 대해서는 실현 가능성(어떻게 행동할 것인가)이 우세했다. 이러한 양상은 소비자 행동으로 확장된다. 멀리 떨어진 구매는 품질과 이점에 초점을 맞추는 반면, 즉각적인 구매는 가격과 편리성을 강조한다. 이러한 정신적 변화는 사람들이 자신의 관점을 조정함으로써 현명한 결정을 내리도록 돕는다.

[15]심리적 거리가 시사하는 바는 조직 전략 및 공공 정책에도 적용된다. 미래 제품을 출시하는 기업은 이상적인 특징을 강조하는 것이 이득인 반면, 즉각적인 홍보는 실용성을 강조해야 한다. 마찬가지로, [14]정책 입안자들은 기후 변화의 즉각적이고 구체적인 측면을 강조함으로써 시민들의 더 큰 참여와 행동을 장려할 수 있다.

representation[rèprizentéiʃən] 설명, 표상
perceive[pərsíːv] 인식하다   temporal[témpərəl] 시간적
spatial[spéiʃəl] 공간적   hypothetical[hàipəθétikəl] 가설적
psychologically[sàikəládʒikəli] 심리적으로
abstractly[æbstræktli] 추상적으로
concrete[káːnkriːt] 구체적인   emphasis[émfəsis] 강조
contextual[kəntékstʃuəl] 상황과 관련된
demonstrate[démənstrèit] 입증하다   relevance[réləvəns] 의의
conduct[kəndʌ́kt] 수행하다   prioritize[praiɔ́ːrətàiz] 우선시하다
desirability[dizàiərəbíləti] 바람직함
feasibility[fìːzəbíləti] 실현 가능성
dominate[dámənèit] 우세하다
judicious[dʒuːdíʃəs] 현명한   perspective[pərspéktiv] 관점
implication[ìmplikéiʃən] 시사점
aspirational[æspəréiʃənl] 이상적인
practicality[præktikǽləti] 실용성
engagement[ingéidʒmənt] 참여

11 Detail Question

지문에서 사건을 심리적으로 가깝다고 인지하는 것의 한 가지 결과로 언급된 것은?
Ⓐ 사람들이 사건 발생 가능성에 초점을 맞춘다.
Ⓑ 사람들이 시간을 얼마나 쓸 수 있는지에 대해 걱정하게 된다.
☑ 사람들이 구체적인 세부 사항과 상황에 주의를 기울인다.
Ⓓ 사람들이 시간적 정보와 공간적 정보를 비교한다.

12 Rhetorical Purpose Question

글쓴이는 왜 지문에서 Yaacov Trope와 Nira Liberman의 연구를 언급하는가?
☑ 심리적 거리가 의사 결정의 우선순위에 어떻게 영향을 미치는지 보여주기 위해

Ⓑ 연구에 사용된 특정 연구 방법론을 비판하기 위해
Ⓒ 소비자가 가격보다 품질을 선호하는 이유를 설명하기 위해
Ⓓ 장기 계획이 단기 계획보다 더 효과적이라고 주장하기 위해

어휘   methodology[mèθədálədʒi] 방법론

13 Vocabulary Question

지문의 단어 "judicious"와 의미상 가장 유사한 것은?
Ⓐ 자신감 있는
☑ 현명한
Ⓒ 전략적인
Ⓓ 충동적인

어휘   sensible[sénsəbəl] 현명한   strategic[strətíːdʒik] 전략적인
impulsive[impʌ́lsiv] 충동적인

14 Detail Question

지문에 따르면, 정책 입안자들은 어떻게 시민 참여를 장려할 수 있는가?
Ⓐ 구체적이고 물질적인 혜택을 강조함으로써
☑ 즉각적인 결과를 중점적으로 다룸으로써
Ⓒ 장기적인 영향과 단기적인 실현 가능성을 병치함으로써
Ⓓ 삶의 여러 측면에 나타나는 영향을 비교함으로써

어휘   material[mətíəriəl] 물질적인
consequence[kánsəkwèns] 결과
juxtapose[dʒʌ̀kstəpóuz] 병치하다, 나란히 놓다

15 Rhetorical Purpose Question

2단락과 3단락의 관계는?
Ⓐ 3단락은 2단락에서 제시된 연구 결과와 모순되는 정보를 제공한다.
Ⓑ 3단락은 2단락에서 설명된 연구와 관련된 대안 이론을 소개한다.
Ⓒ 3단락은 2단락에서 언급된 연구에 대해 상세한 설명을 제공한다.
☑ 3단락은 2단락에서 논의한 사고 양상이 활용되는 경우를 추가로 덧붙인다.

ACTUAL TEST 2

p.366

Module 1

01 This	02 which	03 organized
04 components	05 as	06 heart
07 vessels	08 into	09 both
10 critical	11 When	12 is
13 not	14 engage	15 particular
16 can	17 resistance	18 intensify
19 inclination	20 their	21 Ⓓ
22 Ⓐ	23 Ⓑ	24 Ⓓ
25 Ⓐ	26 Ⓑ	27 Ⓒ
28 Ⓒ	29 Ⓑ	30 Ⓐ
31 Ⓓ	32 Ⓒ	33 Ⓑ

Module 2

01 demonstrates	02 our	03 diet
04 levels	05 even	06 can
07 influence	08 individual	09 expressed
10 mutating	11 Ⓐ	12 Ⓑ
13 Ⓒ	14 Ⓑ	15 Ⓓ

Module 1

[01-10]

순환계는 인체 내에 꼭 필요한 생리학적 연결망이다. 심장과 혈관 같은 구성 요소들로 조직된 이 계통은 두 개의 회로로 나뉘며, 두 회로 다 중요하고 전문적인 기능을 수행한다. 하나는 폐순환으로, 산소가 제거된 혈액을 가스 교환을 위해 폐로 운반하고 산소가 공급된 혈액을 심장으로 되돌려 보낸다. 다른 하나는 체순환으로, 심장에서 말초 조직으로 산소가 풍부한 혈액을 분배하고 산소가 고갈된 혈액을 심장의 심실로 다시 보낸다.

circulatory [sə̀:rkjulətɔ́:ri] 순환계의
physiological [fìziəlɑ́dʒikəl] 생리학적인
component [kəmpóunənt] 구성 요소 blood vessel 혈관
circuit [sə́:rkit] 회로 function [fʌ́ŋkʃən] 기능
pulmonary [pʌ́lmənèri] 폐의
deoxygenated [di:ɑ́ksidʒənèitid] 산소가 제거된 lung [lʌŋ] 폐
oxygenated [ɑ́ksidʒənèitid] 산소가 공급된
distribute [distríbju:t] 분배하다
peripheral [pərífərəl] 말초의, 주변부의 channel [tʃǽnl] 보내다
deplete [diplí:t] 고갈시키다 cardiac chamber (심장의) 심실

[11-20]

반대 심리는 다른 사람의 행동에 영향을 미치기 위해 그와 반대되는 행동 방침을 옹호하는 설득력 있는 전략이다. 누군가로부터 특정한 행동에 관여하지 말라는 말을 들을 때, 이는 저항감을 유발하고 자신의 자율성을 주장하려는 그들의 성향을 강화할 수 있다. 비록 반대 심리가 감지하기 힘든 형태의 조종이라고 여겨지기는 하지만, 이해관계가 크지 않은 행동 계획에 사용될 경우 일반적으로 해가 없는 것으로 여겨지는데, 예를 들어 부모가 아이들에게 채소를 먹을 필요는 없다고 말하는 경우가 있다.

persuasive [pərswéisiv] 설득력 있는
advocate [ǽdvəkət] 옹호하다, 지지하다
contrary [kɑ́ntreri] 반대되는 elicit [ilísit] 유발하다
intensify [inténsəfài] 강화하다 inclination [ìnklənéiʃən] 성향
autonomy [ɔ:tɑ́nəmi] 자율성
constitute [kɑ́nstətjù:t] ~이라고 여겨지다, 구성하다
subtle [sʌ́tl] 감지하기 힘든, 미묘한
manipulation [mənìpjuléiʃən] 조종, 조작
innocuous [inɑ́kjuəs] 해가 없는, 악의 없는

[21-22] 이메일을 읽으시오.

날짜: 8월 10일
제목: 단수

입주민께,

8월 15일 오전 9시부터 오후 2시까지 ²¹수도 사용이 불가능할 것임을 알려드리게 되어 유감입니다. 기본 생활에 필요한 물을 미리 비축해두시는 것을 권장합니다. ²¹/²²이번 중단은 건물 수도관의 정기적인 유지보수 작업을 수행하는 데 필수적입니다. 이로 인해 발생할 수 있는 불편에 대해 사과드립니다.

건물 관리소 드림

interruption [ìntərʌ́pʃən] 중단
inconvenience [ìnkənví:njəns] 불편

21 Main Purpose Question

이메일의 주된 목적은 무엇인가?
Ⓐ 건물 수도관에 대한 입주민 회의 일정을 잡기 위해
Ⓑ 입주민들에게 물 절약을 위해 노력해달라고 요청하기 위해
Ⓒ 입주민들에게 건물에 대한 새로운 수도 요금 청구 절차를 알리기 위해
☑ 예정된 유지보수 작업에 대해 입주민들에게 통지하기 위해

어휘 conserve [kənsə́:rv] 절약하다

22 Detail Question

수도가 중단되어야만 하는 이유는 무엇인가?
☑ 배관 시스템의 정기 유지 관리를 수행하기 위해
Ⓑ 각 세대에 새로운 수도 계량기를 설치하기 위해
Ⓒ 주 수도관에 있을 수도 있는 누수를 점검하기 위해
Ⓓ 건물의 수압 장비를 업그레이드하기 위해

어휘 upkeep [ʌ́pki:p] 유지 (관리) plumbing [plʌ́miŋ] 배관
leak [li:k] 누수, 새는 곳 equipment [ikwípmənt] 장비

[23-25] 이메일을 읽으시오.

날짜: 7월 20일
제목: 기숙사 입주

학생 여러분께,

²³가을 학기 기숙사 입주는 8월 28-30일에 예정되어 있습니다. 새 학년을 준비하면서 아래 세부 사항을 꼼꼼히 확인하시기 바랍니다.

학생들은 건물과 층에 따라 배정된 시간대에 입주할 것입니다. 자신의 구체적인 입주 시간은 주거 포털에서 확인할 수 있습니다. ²⁴모든 학생은 먼저 학생회관에 있는 환영 센터에서 체크인을 해야 합니다. 그곳에서 물건을 옮기기 위한 카트를 빌리거나 주차 허가증을 구매할 수도 있습니다.

알림: 공간이 제한된 관계로, 차량은 짐을 내리는 동안 최대 30분까지만 주차할 수 있습니다. ²⁵한시적으로, 입주 시기에 유효한 학생 주차 허가증이 있는 경우 C 주차장에 장기 주차가 가능합니다.

구체적인 숙소 요구 사항이나 질문이 있는 경우, 주거 사무실에 문의하시기 바랍니다. 캠퍼스 지도 등 추가 자료는 웹사이트에서 확인할 수 있습니다.

James Wilson 드림

dormitory [dɔ́ːrmətɔ̀ːri] 기숙사 **semester** [siméstər] 학기
prepare [pripɛ́ər] 준비하다 **assign** [əsáin] 배정하다
belonging [bilɔ́ːŋiŋ] 소지품, 소유물 **permit** [pə́ːrmit] 허가증, 허가
valid [vǽlid] 유효한 **specific** [spisífik] 구체적인, 특정한
accommodation [əkɑ̀mədéiʃən] 숙소

23 Detail Question
이 이메일은 누구에게 발송되었을 가능성이 가장 높은가?
Ⓐ 복귀하는 교수진
✅ 캠퍼스 기숙사 입주 예정자
Ⓒ 캠퍼스 시설 관리 직원
Ⓓ 주차 허가증을 신청한 학생

어휘 **faculty** [fǽkəlti] 교수진

24 Detail Question
입주 시 사람들이 먼저 해야 할 일은 무엇인가?
Ⓐ 주거 보증금을 제출한다
Ⓑ 주차 허가증을 수령한다
Ⓒ 환영 세미나에 참석한다
✅ 등록을 마친다

어휘 **deposit** [dipázit] 보증금 **registration** [rèdʒistréiʃən] 등록

25 Inference Question
C 주차장에 대해 추론할 수 있는 것은?
✅ 보통 학생 장기 주차용으로는 사용되지 않는다.
Ⓑ 캠퍼스 지도가 없으면 찾기 어렵다.
Ⓒ 대학 주거 사무실에서 관리한다.
Ⓓ 짐을 내리고 올리는 용도로만 지정되어 있다.

어휘 **designate** [dézignèit] 지정하다

[26-28] 소셜 미디어 게시물을 읽으시오.

William Harris

기술 역량을 향상시키고 싶으신가요? ²⁶Tech Hub Academy에서는 이제 매주 화요일과 목요일 저녁에 온라인 코딩 워크숍을 제공합니다! 우리의 쌍방향 수업은 프로그래밍의 기초를 마스터하고자 하는 초급 및 중급 학습자에게 완벽하게 적합합니다.

²⁷각 수업 전반에 걸쳐 개인 맞춤형 피드백과 지도를 제공하는, 일류 기술 기업 출신의 경험 많은 강사들에게 배워보세요. 소규모 수업으로 운영되기 때문에 모든 학생이 필요한 관심과 지원을 받을 수 있습니다. 저희의 프로그램을 수료한 이후, 많은 졸업생들이 기술 분야의 커리어로 성공적으로 전환했습니다.

조기 등록 시 50달러 상당의 독점 학습 자료와 코딩 리소스를 이용할 수 있습니다. ²⁸또한, 온라인 커뮤니티에 가입하시면 동료 학습자 및 업계 전문가들과 교류하며 인적 네트워크 형성 기회를 가질 수 있습니다. 소셜 미디어에서 저희를 팔로우하고 저희 프로그램을 공유하시면 15퍼센트 할인 비밀 코드를 받을 수 있습니다! techhubacademy.com을 방문해 자세한 내용을 확인하고 오늘 자리를 확보하세요.

interactive [ìntərǽktiv] 쌍방향의 **session** [séʃən] 수업
intermediate [ìntərmíːdiət] 중급의
fundamental [fʌ̀ndəméntl] 기초 **instructor** [instrʌ́ktər] 강사
personalize [pə́ːrsənəlàiz] 개인 맞춤화하다
guidance [gáidns] 지도 **attention** [əténʃən] 관심
transition [trænzíʃən] 전환하다 **exclusive** [iksklúːsiv] 독점의
secure [sikjúər] 확보하다

26 Main Purpose Question
게시물의 주된 목적은 무엇인가?
Ⓐ 코딩 기술이 프로그래밍 작업을 어떻게 지원하는지 설명하기 위해
✅ 기술 교육 프로그램에서 제공하는 코딩 워크숍을 홍보하기 위해
Ⓒ 다양한 수준의 온라인 학습 코스를 비교하기 위해
Ⓓ 기술 업계의 채용 공고를 알리기 위해

어휘 **job opening** 채용 공고, 구인

27 Detail Question
강사들은 학생들을 어떻게 지원하는가?
Ⓐ 보충 학습 자료를 제공함으로써
Ⓑ 일대일 커리어 상담을 제공함으로써
✅ 개인별 피드백과 지도를 제공함으로써
Ⓓ 다양한 취업 기회를 소개함으로써

어휘 **supplementary** [sʌ̀pləméntəri] 보충의, 추가의

28 Detail Question
학생들은 온라인 커뮤니티에서 누구를 만나게 되는가?
Ⓐ Tech Hub Academy 강사
Ⓑ 이전 프로그램 졸업생
✅ 다른 학생과 기술 전문가
Ⓓ 채용 담당자와 인사 담당자

[29-33]

중세 길드

11세기부터 16세기까지, 길드는 유럽 전역에서 번성했다. 이 직업 협회들은 특정 지역 내에서 같은 일을 업으로 삼는 사람들을 하나로 모았다.

길드는 위계질서 속에서 운영되었으며, 구성원들은 경험에 따라 상위 단계로 올라갈 수 있었다. 젊은이들은 수년 동안 견습생으로 훈련을 받았고, ³⁰이후 임금을 받고 일할 수 있는 직인이 되었으며, 충분한 재능이 있는 사람들은 장인으로 승급할 수도 있었다. 그러나, 이러한 지위를 얻기 위해서는 길드의 기준에 부합하는 '걸작'을 제출하는 것뿐 아니라, 작업장, 도구, 축하 연회에 융통할 자금도 필요했다. 이것은 길드가 가진 많은 규칙 중 하나에 불과했다. ³¹임금은 억제되었고, 노동자들은 자신들만의 협회를 결성하는 것이 금지되었는데, 이 제한은 플랑드르와 피렌체에서의 봉기로 이어졌다.

시간이 흐르면서 기존 구성원들이 가입비를 인상함에 따라 길드에 들어가는 일은 점점 더 어려워졌다. 이 비용은 행정 경비를 마련하는 데 도움이 되었고, 회원들에게 의료 서비스나 장례 비용과 같은 복지 혜택을 제공하는 데 쓰였다. 길드 제도는 경쟁을 제한하고 길드 내부의 높은 품질 기준을 유지했지만, 동시에 불평등을 강화했다. ³²이 제도는 책임자들의 경제적 및 사회적 지위를 보호하는 역할을 하였으며, 자신의 사업체를 운영할 자원이나 기술이 부족한 노동자들과의 격차를 더욱 벌려 놓았다.

medieval [míːdiːvəl] 중세의 flourish [fləː́riʃ] 번성하다
professional [prəféʃənl] 직업의 practice [prǽktis] 업으로 삼다
trade [treid] 일, 사업 operate [ápərèit] 운영하다
hierarchy [háiərà:rki] 위계질서 apprentice [əpréntis] 견습생
journeyman [dʒə́ːrnimən] 직인 status [stéitəs] 지위
presentation [prìːzentéiʃən] 제출
masterpiece [mǽstərpìs] 걸작
finance [fáinæns] (돈을) 융통하다 banquet [bǽŋkwit] 연회
wage [weidʒ] 임금 prohibit [prəhíbit] 금지하다
restriction [ristríkʃən] 제한 administrative [ædmínəstrèitiv] 행정의
funeral [fjúːnərəl] 장례의 competition [kàmpətíʃən] 경쟁
reinforce [rìːinfɔ́ːrs] 강화하다 standing [stǽndiŋ] 지위

29 Vocabulary Question
지문의 단어 "hierarchy"와 의미상 가장 유사한 것은?
ⓐ 전통
☑ 서열
ⓒ 환경
ⓓ 일상

어휘 tradition [trədíʃən] 전통 setting [sétiŋ] 환경

30 Fact Question
지문에서 직인에 대해 명시된 것은?
☑ 노동의 대가로 임금을 받았다.
ⓑ 일의 일환으로 견습생을 훈련시켰다.
ⓒ 길드에서 제공한 도구를 사용했다.
ⓓ 자신의 작업장을 보유해야 했다.

31 Rhetorical Purpose Question
글쓴이는 왜 플랑드르와 피렌체에서의 봉기를 언급하는가?
ⓐ 길드의 쇠퇴로 이어진 사건들을 강조하기 위해
ⓑ 노동자들이 자신들만의 협회를 만든 결과를 보여주기 위해
ⓒ 서로 다른 지역의 길드 구성원들이 서로 교류했음을 제시하기 위해
☑ 길드 규정이 억압적이라고 길드 구성원들이 생각했음을 보여주기 위해

어휘 oppressive [əprésiv] 억압적인

32 Detail Question
길드 제도는 책임자들에게 어떻게 이익이 되었는가?
ⓐ 행정 업무를 통해 수입을 제공함으로써
ⓑ 길드의 품질 기준을 세울 수 있게 함으로써
☑ 경쟁으로부터 그들의 경제적·사회적 지위를 보호함으로써
ⓓ 회원비 납부를 면제함으로써

33 Rhetorical Purpose Question
3단락에서 길드 입회비 인상으로 인한 구체적 혜택을 언급하는 문장을 클릭하시오.
ⓐ 시간이 흐르면서 기존 구성원들이 가입비를 인상함에 따라 길드에 들어가는 일은 점점 더 어려워졌다.
☑ 이 비용은 행정 경비를 마련하는 데 도움이 되었고, 회원들에게 의료 서비스나 장례 비용과 같은 복지 혜택을 제공하는 데 쓰였다.
ⓒ 길드 제도는 경쟁을 제한하고 길드 내부의 높은 품질 기준을 유지했지만, 동시에 불평등을 강화했다.
ⓓ 이 제도는 책임자들의 경제적·사회적 지위를 보호하는 역할을 하였으며, 자신의 사업체를 운영할 자원이나 기술이 부족한 노동자들과의 격차를 더욱 벌려 놓았다.

Module 2

[01-10]

후성유전학은 생활방식과 유전자 사이의 설득력 있는 연결고리를 제공한다. 이는 DNA 서열 그 자체를 변형하지 않고도 우리의 환경, 식단, 스트레스 수준, 그리고 심지어 나이가 개별 유전자의 발현 방식에 극적인 영향을 미칠 수 있음을 보여준다. 후성유전적 표지가 유전체 위의 기억 체계이며 그것이 우리의 경험을 기록한다고 생각하라. 이는 일란성 쌍둥이처럼 유전적 구성이 동일한 사람들이 시간이 지나면서 각자의 몸이 유전자에 가하는 조정에 따라 서로 다른 건강 결과가 생길 수 있음을 의미한다.

epigenetics [èpidʒənétiks] 후성유전학
demonstrate [démənstrèit] 보여주다
environment [inváiərənmənt] 환경
express [iksprés] 발현시키다 mutate [mjúːteit] 변형하다
sequence [síːkwəns] 서열, 순서 genetic [dʒənétik] 유전적인
identical twin 일란성 쌍둥이 adjustment [ədʒʌ́stmənt] 조정

[11-15]

팝아트와 소비지상주의

¹¹팝아트는 제2차 세계대전 이후 사회를 지배하던 소비자 문화에 대한 반응으로 1950년대 중반 영국에서 등장했다. 이 운동의 예술가들은 일상적인 제품, 유명인, 광고 등에서 그들의 작품에 대한 영감을 얻었다.

팝아트는 1960년대에 최고조에 달했으며 이 시기에 Andy Warhol과 Roy Lichtenstein 등의 미국 예술가들이 ¹³ᴬ대량생산 기법을 수용하고 ¹³ᴰ만화의 이미지를 대형 회화 작품으로 변환시킨 것으로 유명한데, ¹²그 후 1970년대에 미니멀리즘이 예술계를 장악하면서 그 영향력은 감소했다. ¹³ᴮ일상적인 사물을 순수미술의 가치 있는

주제로 다룸으로써, 팝아트 예술가들은 보통 미술관에서 접하는 "고급" 예술과 광고와 연관되는 "저급" 예술의 경계를 흐리게 하며, 예술적 관습에 도전하고 관람객들에게 익숙한 이미지의 가치를 다시 생각해보도록 유도했다.

A ¹⁴자신들의 작품을 사고팔고 소비할 수 있는 상품으로 바꾸는 것은 그들이 소비주의에 대해 취한 입장의 연장선이었다. **B** 1964년, The American Supermarket이라는 전시회에서, 벨벳으로 덮인 과일과 채소, 그리고 Campbell 수프 깡통 같은 가짜 상품들이 뉴욕 Bianchini Gallery에서 판매용으로 전시되었다. **C** 그러나 이 공간은 전통적인 미술관처럼 보이지 않았고, 오히려 진짜 슈퍼마켓처럼 보였다. **D** 저명한 예술가들이 만든 비전통적 작품들의 이와 같은 도발적 전시는 대중이 "예술이란 무엇인가?"라는 영원한 질문을 마주하게 했다.

emerge[imə́:rdʒ] 등장하다　dominate[dɑ́mənèit] 지배하다
inspiration[ìnspəréiʃən] 영감　celebrity[səlébrəti] 유명인
peak[piːk] 최고조　decline[dikláin] 감소하다　take over 장악하다
mundane[mʌndéin] 일상적인　worthy[wə́:rði] 가치 있는
blur[bləːr] 경계를 흐리다　convention[kənvénʃən] 관습
commodity[kəmɑ́dəti] 상품　extension[iksténʃən] 연장선
exhibition[èksəbíʃən] 전시회　velour[vəlúər] 벨벳
resemble[rizémbəl] ~처럼 보이다

11　Detail Question
지문에 따르면, 팝아트는 영국에서 어떤 것에 대한 반응으로 발전했는가?
- Ⓐ 소비지상주의의 발생 ✓
- Ⓑ 예술계의 엘리트주의
- Ⓒ 새로운 재료의 보급
- Ⓓ 제2차 세계대전의 희생자들

어휘　casualty[kǽʒuəlti] 희생자, 사상자

12　Inference Question
미니멀리즘에 대해 암시된 것은?
- Ⓐ 대량생산 기법의 사용을 거부했다.
- Ⓑ 팝아트 이후 예술계의 주류가 되었다. ✓
- Ⓒ 광고와 소비자 문화에서 영감을 받았다.
- Ⓓ 익숙한 이미지의 가치를 재고하도록 예술가들에게 자극을 주었다.

어휘　reject[ridʒékt] 거부하다

13　Detail Question
다음 중 팝아트 예술가들이 사용한 접근 방식으로 언급된 것이 아닌 것은?
- Ⓐ 제조업 방식의 절차를 도입하기
- Ⓑ 평범한 사물을 순수미술의 수준으로 격상시키기
- Ⓒ 유명인과 상업 이미지를 풍자하기 ✓
- Ⓓ 만화의 삽화를 대형 예술 작품의 소재로 사용하기

어휘　adopt[ədɑ́pt] 도입하다　elevate[éləvèit] 격상시키다
　　satirize[sǽtəràiz] 풍자하다

14　Rhetorical Purpose Question
글쓴이는 왜 The American Supermarket을 언급하는가?
- Ⓐ 1960년대 예술가들이 예술의 상업화에 비판적이었음을 보여주기 위해
- Ⓑ 팝아트 예술가들이 소비중심주의에 대한 시각을 예술에 어떻게 적용했는지를 보여주기 위해 ✓
- Ⓒ 팝아트 운동이 1960년대에 최고조에 달했음을 입증하기 위해
- Ⓓ 뉴욕 팝아트 계에서 이 전시회의 중요성을 강조하기 위해

15　Insertion Question
다음 문장이 삽입될 수 있는 네 곳이 지문에 표시되어 있다.

저명한 예술가들이 만든 비전통적 작품들의 이와 같은 도발적 전시는 대중이 "예술이란 무엇인가?"라는 영원한 질문을 마주하게 했다.

그 문장은 어디에 가장 적절한가? 그 문장이 삽입될 수 있는 곳을 고르시오.

MEMO

MEMO

해커스인강 HackersIngang.com
본 교재 인강 · 단어암기 MP3 · iBT 리딩 실전모의고사

고우해커스 goHackers.com
토플 보카 외우기 · 토플 스피킹/라이팅 첨삭 게시판 · 토플 공부전략 강의 · 토플 자료 및 유학 정보

고우해커스

토플 시험부터
학부·석박사, 교환학생,
중·고등 유학정보까지

고우해커스에 다 있다!

유학전문포털 235만개 정보 보유
고우해커스 내 유학 관련 컨텐츠 누적게시물 수 기준(~2022.04.06.)

200여 개의 유학시험/생활 정보 게시판

17,200여 건의 해외 대학 합격 스펙 게시글
고우해커스 사이트 어드미션포스팅 게시판 게시글 수 기준(~2022.10.14.)

goHackers.com

1위 해커스어학원
260만이 선택한 해커스 토플

단기간 고득점 잡는 해커스만의 체계화된 관리 시스템

01 토플 무료 배치고사
현재 실력과 목표 점수에 딱 맞는 학습을 위한 무료 반배치고사 진행!

토플 Trial Test
월 2회 실전처럼 모의테스트 가능한 TRIAL test 응시기회 제공!

02

1:1 개별 첨삭시스템
채점표를 기반으로 약점파악 및 피드백, 1:1 개인별 맞춤 첨삭 진행!

03

[260만] 해커스어학원 누적 수강생 수, 해커스인강 토플 강의 누적 수강신청건수 합산 기준 (2003.01~2018.09.05. 환불자/중복신청 포함)
[1위] 한경비즈니스 2024 한국브랜드만족지수 교육(온·오프라인 어학원) 1위

해커스어학원 단기 졸업 시스템으로
빠르게 토플 졸업 go ▶